DIRECT JURISDICTION

The second thematic volume in the series Studies in Private International Law – Asia looks into direct jurisdiction, that is, the situations in which the courts of 15 key Asian states (Mainland China, Hong Kong, Taiwan, Japan, South Korea, Malaysia, Singapore, Thailand, Vietnam, Cambodia, Myanmar, the Philippines, Indonesia, Sri Lanka, and India) are prepared to hear a case involving cross-border elements. For instance, where parties are habitually resident abroad and a dispute has only some, little or no connection with an Asian state, will the courts of that state accept jurisdiction and hear the case, and if so, on what conditions? More specifically, the book's chapters explore the circumstances in which different Asian states assume or decline jurisdiction not just in commercial matters, but also in other types of action, such as family, consumer and employment disputes.

The introduction defines terminology and identifies similarities in the approaches to direct jurisdiction taken by the 15 Asian states in civil and commercial litigation. Taking its cue from this, the conclusion assesses whether there should be a multilateral convention or soft law instrument articulating principles of direct jurisdiction for Asia. The conclusion also discusses possible trajectories that Asian states may be taking in respect of direct jurisdiction in light of the COVID-19 pandemic and the political tensions currently besetting the world. The book suggests that enacting suitable rules of direct jurisdiction requires an Asian state to strike a delicate balance between affording certainty and protecting its nationals. At heart, direct jurisdiction involves sometimes difficult policy considerations and is not just about drawing up lists of jurisdictional grounds and exceptions to them.

Volume 4 in the series Studies in Private International Law – Asia

Studies in Private International Law – Asia

Editor: Anselmo Reyes
Advisory Editor: Paul Beaumont

Much has been written about private international law in the EU and the US. Less is known about the conflict of laws in Asia. Thus, little attention has been paid so far to the modernisation of private international law codes and rules that has been taking place over the last decade all over Asia. That trend continues. Now is the time to take stock of those reforms that have already taken place and suggest further improvements for the future.

Published under the celebrated series *Studies in Private International Law*, this monograph sub-series provides a forum for discussion and analysis of private international law in Asia. The series is not solely a survey of jurisdictions for practitioners. Comprising in-depth thematic and country-specific studies, each volume considers the private international law of Asian countries from a variety of perspectives. An underlying assumption is that private international law in different jurisdictions follow broad discernible patterns. Each volume in this sub-series highlights those patterns and discusses how rules in different Asian jurisdictions are either converging with, or diverging from, the patterns identified. Such an analytical framework will assist academics, judges, lawyers and legislators to envisage ways in which laws affecting cross-border relationships can be harmonised across jurisdictions and be made more responsive to the needs of citizens in Asia and elsewhere.

Volume 1: Recognition and Enforcement of Judgments in Civil and Commercial Matters
Edited by Anselmo Reyes

Volume 2: Indonesian Private International Law
Afifah Kusumadara

Volume 3: Chinese Private International Law
Edited by Xiaohong Liu and Zhengyi Zhang

Volume 4: Direct Jurisdiction: Asian Perspectives
Edited by Anselmo Reyes and Wilson Lui

Direct Jurisdiction

Asian Perspectives

Edited by
Anselmo Reyes
and
Wilson Lui

·HART·
OXFORD · LONDON · NEW YORK · NEW DELHI · SYDNEY

HART PUBLISHING

Bloomsbury Publishing Plc

Kemp House, Chawley Park, Cumnor Hill, Oxford, OX2 9PH, UK

1385 Broadway, New York, NY 10018, USA

29 Earlsfort Terrace, Dublin 2, Ireland

HART PUBLISHING, the Hart/Stag logo, BLOOMSBURY and the Diana logo are trademarks of Bloomsbury Publishing Plc

First published in Great Britain 2021

A catalogue record for this book is available from the British Library.

Library of Congress Cataloging-in-Publication data

Names: Reyes, Anselmo, editor. | Lui, Wilson, editor.

Title: Direct jurisdiction : Asian perspectives / edited by Anselmo Reyes and Wilson Lui.

Description: Oxford ; New York : Hart, 2021. | Series: Studies in private international law – Asia; volume 4 | Includes bibliographical references and index.

Identifiers: LCCN 2021021429 (print) | LCCN 2021021430 (ebook) | ISBN 9781509936427 (hardback) | ISBN 9781509936434 (pdf) | ISBN 9781509936441 (Epub)

Subjects: LCSH: Conflict of laws—Asia.

Classification: LCC KNC126 .D57 2021 (print) | LCC KNC126 (ebook) | DDC 340.9/095—dc23

LC record available at https://lccn.loc.gov/2021021429

LC ebook record available at https://lccn.loc.gov/2021021430

ISBN: HB: 978-1-50993-642-7
ePDF: 978-1-50993-643-4
ePub: 978-1-50993-644-1

Typeset by Compuscript Ltd, Shannon
Printed and bound in Great Britain

To find out more about our authors and books visit www.hartpublishing.co.uk. Here you will find extracts, author information, details of forthcoming events and the option to sign up for our newsletters.

SERIES EDITOR'S PREFACE

ANSELMO REYES

This is the fourth volume of Hart's *Studies in Private International Law – Asia*. It is the second book in the Thematic Series of those volumes, the first book having focused on the recognition of judgments in civil and commercial matters within Asia. The other two books that have appeared so far are in the Country Series. They covered Indonesian and Chinese private international law respectively. Future books in the Country Series will systematically analyse the conflict of laws in specific Asian jurisdictions. Currently, in the pipeline are separate volumes on Japanese, Indian, Thai, Philippine, Cambodian, Taiwanese, and Vietnamese private international law. By contrast, the Thematic Series considers specific topics, examining how particular issues within those topics are dealt with across a number of representative Asian states. The next book in the Thematic Series will look into Asian practices in selected cross-border family law questions, especially in relation to the well-being of the child. Thereafter, volumes will explore cross-border insolvency, proof of foreign law, intellectual property, and data protection in Asia. The intention is that, over time, the Country and Thematic Series will together convey, to practitioners, academics, students and general readers, some idea of the ever-evolving state of the conflict of laws in Asia as a whole. To provide greater depth, there will eventually be a third series comprising scholarly monographs on aspects of Asian private international law.

The format of this book mirrors that of the first book in the Thematic Series. The first book focused among other matters on indirect jurisdiction. This book on direct jurisdiction therefore complements it. The core of this book consists of fifteen chapters, each setting out how the courts of a given state have grappled (and continue to grapple) with the question of when to hear a case having foreign elements and when to decline to do so. The Introduction presents a conceptual framework for the reader who wishes to know more but is not a specialist in the subject. The Conclusion pulls together key themes across chapters and envisages the future of direct jurisdiction in Asia. Throughout, the book eschews academic jargon in favour of being plain and direct. The aspiration is that over its run the Thematic and Country Series (including this book) will be accessible to all and concentrate on the practical issues underlying current questions of private international law, proffering realistic (as opposed to fanciful or overly theoretical) ways of resolving ongoing controversies.

I end this Preface with an observation that, while self-evident from the first two books in the Thematic Series, should be explicitly acknowledged. That is how much the development of the conflict of laws in Asia owes to the work of the Hague Conference on Private International Law (HCCH). The HCCH's instruments and *travaux préparatoires* have served as catalysts for the reform of private international law in Asia, not least in the areas of indirect and direct jurisdiction. HCCH established a Regional Office for Asia and the Pacific (ROAP) in Hong Kong in December 2012. Looking back over the near decade which has ensued, that bold initiative has proven to be prescient and cathartic.

Anselmo Reyes
Kyoto
5 May 2021

ACKNOWLEDGEMENTS

The chapters in this book were written during the height of the COVID-19 pandemic when much of Asia was under one form or other of lockdown. Consequently, it could not have been an easy task for individual contributors to write about direct jurisdiction in their assigned state. We are therefore deeply appreciative of their efforts at providing comprehensive accounts of their designated state in circumstances of unprecedented difficulty. We would further single out and express our gratitude to Professor Joongi Kim for his readiness to help during a moment of crisis in the course of putting together this book. Having worked in the background during the production of the first book in the *Studies in Private International Law – Asia* series, Wilson Lui officially joins the editorial team for the thematic volumes. He would like to thank his parents for their unfailing and unstinting support.

Anselmo Reyes
Wilson Lui
Kyoto and Hong Kong
1 March 2021

CONTENTS

LIST OF CONTRIBUTORS

Rong-Chwan Chen is University Distinguished Professor of Law at the National Taipei University and an Associate Member of the International Academy of Comparative Law.

Sungjae Chun is a Senior Associate of the Maritime and Aviation Team at Jipyong LLC in Korea.

Jocelyn P Cruz is an Associate Professor in the Department of Commercial Law of the Ramon V del Rosario College of Business at De La Salle University in the Philippines.

Ramesh Fernando holds a Master of Law (Commercial) from the University of Cambridge. Since 2019, he has been practising as a Counsel in the Chambers of Mr Geoffrey Alagaratnam, President's Counsel, in Sri Lanka. As of January 2021, he is Research Assistant for the Commercial Law Reforms Sub-Committee under the Ministry of Justice.

Sai Ramani Garimella is an Assistant Professor at the Faculty of Legal Studies of South Asian University in India and Visiting Senior Research Associate at the Research Centre for Private International Law in Emerging Countries of University of Johannesburg in South Africa.

Ho Minh Thanh is an LLM (Bournemouth) Lecturer at University of Law, Hue University, Vietnam.

Hoang Thao Anh is an LLM (Toulouse) Lecturer at University of Law, Hue University, Vietnam.

Afifah Kusumadara is a Lecturer at the Law Faculty of Brawijaya University in Indonesia.

Akawat Laowonsiri is a Lecturer at the Law Faculty of Thammasat University in Thailand.

Fuldien Li is Professor of Law at the Chinese Culture University and Chairman of the Chinese Arbitration Association, Taipei.

Wilson Lui is an independent researcher in law and former Chief Editor of the *Hong Kong Journal of Legal Studies*. He is a Chartered Linguist, a Member of the Chartered Institute of Linguists and an Associate of the Chartered Institute of Arbitrators. He is pursuing an MPhil at the University of Oxford and holds an LLM from the University of Cambridge.

Nitin V Nadkarni is an arbitrator and counsel in Malaysia with over 35 years of experience. He read law at the London School of Economics.

Kazuaki Nishioka is a Visiting Research Fellow at the Law Faculty of University of Zurich.

Nguyen Thi Hong Trinh is a PhD (Hamburg) Lecturer at University of Law, Hue University, Vietnam.

Arvin Kristopher A Razon is a Lecturer in the Department of Commercial Law of the Ramon V del Rosario College of Business at De La Salle University in the Philippines.

Anselmo Reyes is Guest Professor at the Law Faculty of Doshisha University in Kyoto and an International Judge of the Singapore International Commercial Court.

Jianping Shi is an Associate Professor at Shanghai University of Political Science and Law.

Justin De Jesus Sucgang is an Associate Professor in the College of Law at De La Salle University in the Philippines.

Wai Fung Teh practises as a lawyer in Malaysia. He read law at Durham University and has also been called to the Bar of England and Wales.

Nobumichi Teramura is an Assistant Professor at the Institute of Asian Studies, University of Brunei Darussalam (UBD) and an Associate at the University of Sydney Law School Centre for Asian and Pacific Law (CAPLUS), specialising in business law, with a particular interest in arbitration, private international law, contract law and Asian law.

Zaw Thura is a Deputy District Judge at the Western Yangon District Court, the Republic of the Union of Myanmar.

James Y P Wong is a dispute resolution lawyer at Dentons Hong Kong LLP. He has a broad civil and commercial practice.

Zhengyi Zhang is an Associate Professor at Shanghai University of Political Science and Law.

LIST OF CASES

Japan

South Korea

India

Indonesia

International Court of Justice

Italy

Malaysia

Myanmar

Philippines

Singapore

Sri Lanka

Taiwan

Thailand

Vietnam

United Kingdom

United States

Arbitral Awards

LIST OF STATUTES AND INSTRUMENTS

International Instruments

Bilateral Instruments

National Statutes, Rules and Other Instruments

Cambodia

European Union

Hong Kong

India

Taiwan

United States

1

Introduction

WILSON LUI AND ANSELMO REYES

I. Purpose

Private international law traditionally answers three questions.[1] First, there is the question of jurisdiction: when can parties seise a national court in connection with matters involving foreign elements or (conversely) what are the conditions under which national courts will accept jurisdiction to deal with such matters? Second, there is the question of applicable law: what system or systems of law will be applied to resolve a dispute involving foreign elements? Third, there is the question of recognition and enforcement of foreign judgments: in what circumstances will they be recognised and enforced? This book considers the first question. It will do so by looking at the issue of direct jurisdiction across 15 Asian states. It comes after the first book in the *Studies in Private International Law – Asia* series ('Volume One') which dealt with the recognition and enforcement of judgments in civil and commercial matters in the same 15 Asian states. Volume One thus concerned the third question and, in so doing, touched on what is sometimes referred to as 'indirect jurisdiction'. By way of contrast, this book can be said to concern 'direct jurisdiction'.[2]

The modern discipline of private international law adds a fourth question to the three traditional considerations just mentioned. That fourth question centres on the harmonisation of private international law rules. To what extent is it possible, desirable, or worthwhile to harmonise the various rules of different states on cross-border matters? At a global level, the objective of the Hague Conference on Private International Law is to 'work for the progressive unification of the rules of private international law', that is, to achieve the harmonisation of private international law.[3] Some of the Hague Conference's recent efforts in this respect include the 2005 Hague Convention on Choice of Court Agreements and the 2019 Hague Convention on the Recognition and Enforcement of Foreign Judgments in Civil or Commercial Matters, both of which have a bearing on the question of direct jurisdiction. On a regional level, there have been efforts at harmonisation within the EU, culminating insofar as direct jurisdiction is concerned

[1] See eg Lord Collins of Mapesbury (ed), *Dicey, Morris and Collins on Conflict of Laws* 15th edn, vol 1 (London, Sweet and Maxwell, 2012) para 1–003; David Hill, *Private International Law* (Edinburgh, Edinburgh University Press, 2014) 1; Peter Hay, *Advanced Introduction to Private International Law and Procedure* (Cheltenham, Edward Elgar, 2018) 3.

[2] See Section II below on 'direct jurisdiction' and 'indirect jurisdiction'.

[3] Statute of the Hague Conference on Private International Law, Art 1. Among the 15 Asian states surveyed in this book, China, Hong Kong (through China), Japan, South Korea, Singapore, Malaysia, Vietnam, Philippines, Thailand, Sri Lanka and India are member states of the Hague Conference on Private International Law, while Cambodia, Myanmar and Indonesia are not. Taiwan is unable to join due to its political status.

in (among others) the Brussels I Regulation, the Lugano Convention and the Brussels I (recast) Regulation.[4] Accordingly, in the spirit of the fourth question, a focus of this book will be whether it is necessary to have a convention or soft law instrument setting out general principles of direct jurisdiction for Asia. This chapter will provide the backdrop for that inquiry and the question will be revisited in the Conclusion, Chapter 17.

In actuality, the four questions of modern private international law are intertwined. The question of what judgments should states enforce depends in part on the grounds upon which the courts whose judgments are sought to be enforced accepted direct jurisdiction in the underlying dispute. Thus, internationally accepted grounds of indirect jurisdiction will inevitably influence the bases upon which rendering courts exercise direct jurisdiction. In the absence of good reason to the contrary, the way in which a state answers the first and third questions might be expected to mirror each other.[5] On the other hand, the law applicable to a particular case or an aspect of a case involving foreign elements will often hinge on a connecting factor. For instance, capacity to contract a marriage will typically depend on whether a person had capacity to marry under the law of his or her domicile. The connecting factor of 'domicile' accordingly indicates that, if a person is domiciled in a given state, the laws of that state should in the absence of compelling reason allow the person to bring a dispute on the validity of his or her foreign marriage before the court of that state. In the normal course of events, the way in which a state answers the second question in a specific situation should be suggestive of how the state answers the first question in an analogous situation. In fact, a quick glance through the next 15 chapters will show that the jurisdictional rules of many states have been predicated on their choice of law rules, with the result that in their discussions of direct jurisdiction a number of contributors have also dealt with choice of law.

The heart of this book then are the 15 chapters that follow this Introduction. Each will describe when and how a given Asian state decides whether to accept or decline jurisdiction in various situations. The respective Asian states are China, Hong Kong, Taiwan, Japan, South Korea, Singapore, Malaysia, Vietnam, Cambodia, Myanmar, Philippines, Indonesia, Thailand, Sri Lanka and India. The chapters, however, are not intended to be mere national reports. Contributors were invited to comment on the jurisdictional rules of their assigned state. They were encouraged to identify recent developments and potential avenues of reform. How can and should the jurisdictional regime being described be reformed to fit with the current trend of increasing cross-border interactions in commercial and non-commercial matters and to make justice in such matters more accessible to ordinary citizens in Asia?

II. Scope

This section provides simple working definitions of concepts and terms that will repeatedly feature in the next 15 chapters of this book.

'Jurisdiction' has multiple meanings. Depending on context, it can simply be a synonym for 'courts', 'states', or 'legal systems'.[6] In this book, it will usually refer to the power or ability

[4] Council Regulation (EC) No 44/2001 of 22 December 2000 on jurisdiction and the recognition and enforcement of judgments in civil and commercial matters [2001] OJ L12/1; Lugano Convention on jurisdiction and the recognition and enforcement of judgments in civil and commercial matters [2007] OJ L339/3; Regulation (EU) No 1215/2012 of the European Parliament and of the Council of 12 December 2012 on jurisdiction and the recognition and enforcement of judgments in civil and commercial matters [2012] OJ L351/1.

[5] See Section II below.

[6] Hay (n 1) 5. See also István Szásky, *International Civil Procedure: A Comparative Study* (Leyden, AW Sijthoff, 1967) 290–426.

of courts to hear and determine matters before it and render judgments, orders, decisions, etc, in those matters with binding effect on parties. The general principles for assuming jurisdiction will be discussed in Section III and general principles for declining jurisdiction will be canvassed in Section IV.

Most jurisdictions distinguish between *in personam* and *in rem* jurisdiction, an exception being South Korea. A court exercises *in personam* jurisdiction when it adjudicates on a dispute concerning the personal obligations that one litigant owes to another. To establish *in personam* jurisdiction, the court must be satisfied that it has the power to make a ruling that will be binding on the parties personally. A court exercises *in rem* jurisdiction when it adjudicates on rights in movable or immovable property (the *res*). To establish *in rem* jurisdiction, the court has to be satisfied that it has a power to make a ruling on the relevant property that will be binding on all the world. There is further a commonly made distinction between 'personal jurisdiction' and 'subject-matter jurisdiction'. 'Subject-matter jurisdiction' concerns the authority of a court to adjudicate on substantive matters of a certain type, while 'personal jurisdiction' describes the power of a court to affect the rights and duties of the parties before it.[7]

It is convenient to distinguish between 'direct jurisdiction' (*compétence directe*) and 'indirect jurisdiction' (*compétence indirecte*). The former is the power or ability of a court to hear a case and render a decision on that matter (the jurisdiction to decide). The latter concerns the power or ability of a requested court to recognise and enforce a judgment by the rendering court (the jurisdiction to recognise).[8] One might ask: are direct and indirect jurisdiction the same? In Section I, it was suggested that they might be expected to mirror each other. The Hague Conference has prepared a comparative table setting out direct and indirect grounds of jurisdiction in various jurisdictions.[9] On a theoretical level, three theories have been advanced in answer to the query just posed. The first answer is the mirror theory, which essentially posits that the two types of jurisdiction should be reflections of each other.[10] This approach is widely adopted in practice. For instance, the 1999 Preliminary Draft Hague Convention dealing with both jurisdiction and the recognition and enforcement of judgments was 'based on the premise that the rules of jurisdiction used to review indirect jurisdiction are those defined by the first part of the [Convention], [that is,] the rules of direct jurisdiction'.[11] A second response is the derivative theory. Professor von Mehren summarised this theory as follows:[12]

> Derivative theories take the position that the content of jurisdictional tests for recognition purposes must, in principle and as a matter of logic, stem from the basis on which jurisdiction to adjudicate

[7] ibid.

[8] See Ralf Michaels, 'Some Fundamental Jurisdictional Concepts as Applied in Judgment Conventions' in Eckart Gottschalk and others (eds), *Conflict of Laws in a Globalized World* (Cambridge, Cambridge University Press, 2007) 35–36. See also eg Arthur Nussbaum, 'Jurisdiction and Foreign Judgments' (1941) 41(2) *Columbia Law Review* 221.

[9] 'Comparative Table on Grounds of Jurisdiction' (*Hague Conference on Private International Law*, January 2015), available online: https://assets.hcch.net/docs/03c39e9f-878b-400d-a359-e70b7937edde.pdf. Regrettably, the table only covers around 20 jurisdictions. This book, together with Volume One, seeks to provide a comprehensive overview of the direct and indirect grounds of jurisdiction in 15 Asian states.

[10] See also Professor Brand's argument regarding the 2018 Hague Draft Convention on the Recognition and Enforcement of Judgments in Civil and Commercial Matters: Ronald A Brand, 'The Circulation of Judgments under the Draft Hague Convention' University of Pittsburgh School of Law Legal Studies Research Paper Series Working Paper No 2019-02 (February 2019), available online: https://papers.ssrn.com/sol3/papers.cfm?abstract_id=3334647.

[11] Catherine Kessedjian, 'Synthesis of the Work of the Special Commission of March 1998 on International Jurisdiction and the Effects of Foreign Judgments in Civil and Commercial Matters' (*Hague Conference on Private International Law*, July 1998) para 21, available online: https://assets.hcch.net/docs/3385edb5-6f63-4624-934c-4d4245fdcef6.pdf.

[12] Arthur Taylor von Mehren, *Recognition and Enforcement of Foreign Judgments – General Theory and the Role of Jurisdictional Requirements* (Alphen aan den Rijn, Sijthoff and Noordhoff, 1981) 56.

> is asserted. The jurisdictional bases from which the recognition test is derived can be those of the State of origin, of the State addressed, or of both States.

In substance, this theory suggests that direct jurisdiction may or may not be precisely the same as the grounds of indirect jurisdiction of an enforcing state, since the latter's grounds for recognising a judgment may be derived from the jurisdictional tests of the rendering state, the enforcing state or both. The third explanation is a non-derivative or policy-driven theory. Under this theory, 'jurisdictional tests rest on, and give expression to, the policies and purposes that are, in the view of the State addressed, implicated when recognition or enforcement of a foreign judgment is sought'.[13] Thus, the adjudicatory jurisdiction and jurisdictional tests for recognition need not correspond or even overlap with each other. Professor Michaels argues that direct and indirect jurisdiction are logically unconnected, the former being a privilege (if state X decides to exercise direct jurisdiction in a matter, state Y has no right to restrain state X from so doing) and the latter a power (insofar as state X has exercised jurisdiction on a basis accepted by state Y as a legitimate ground of indirect jurisdiction, the judgment of state X can be recognised).[14] According to Professor Michaels, the asymmetry is important because

> states may find it important to secure access to their courts and therefore provide certain bases of direct jurisdiction, but accept that other states do not recognize ensuing decisions, and perhaps even reject foreign judgments rendered on such bases. Tag jurisdiction for human rights violation could be an example. On the other hand, states may be ready to accept certain bases of indirect jurisdiction, even though they do not use the same bases of direct jurisdiction – perhaps because they have other, functionally equivalent, bases.[15]

Professor Michaels thus proposes the employment of a conceptual matrix of required/permitted/excluded, direct/indirect 3x3 nine-way jurisdictional bases in any convention or soft law instrument dealing with direct jurisdiction. This (it is suggested) would allow for a richer and more precise approach to grounds of jurisdiction in conventions or soft law instruments.[16]

In contrast to the complications involved in harmonising direct jurisdiction especially under the third theory, the standardisation of procedures to 'make … improvements in the international administration of justice' among states is more readily attainable.[17] To this end, the use of various Hague Conventions has been proving attractive to the Asian states surveyed here.[18] The relevant instruments are the 1961 Hague Convention Abolishing the Requirement of Legalisation for Foreign Public Documents, the 1965 Hague Convention on the Service Abroad of Judicial and Extrajudicial Documents in Civil or Commercial Matters, and the 1970 Hague Convention on the Taking of Evidence Abroad in Civil or Commercial Matters. The 1961 Hague Apostille Convention abolished the need for diplomatic or consular legalisation of foreign public documents. The 1965 Hague Service Convention provides a simplified process for the service of process in other countries. The 1970 Hague Evidence Convention ensures that evidence can be taken in foreign countries. For family matters, there is the 1980 Hague Convention on the Civil

[13] ibid 57.
[14] Michaels (n 8) 38.
[15] ibid 39.
[16] ibid 52–62. See also Eva Jueptner, 'The Hague Jurisdiction Project – What Options for the Hague Conference?' (2020) 16(2) *Journal of Private International Law* 247–74.
[17] Peter North, *Essays in Private International Law* (Oxford, Oxford University Press, 1993) 245–46, 255.
[18] China, Hong Kong (through China), India, Japan, South Korea, Philippines, and Singapore are now signatories to the 1961 Hague Apostille Convention. China, Hong Kong (through China), Japan, South Korea, Vietnam, Sri Lanka, India, and the Philippines are now signatories to the 1965 Hague Service Convention. China, Hong Kong (through China), India, South Korea, Singapore, Sri Lanka, and Vietnam are now signatories to the 1970 Hague Evidence Convention.

Aspects of International Child Abduction.[19] The applications of these Conventions are discussed to varying extents in the succeeding chapters. It is submitted that there will be great utility for other Asian states to consider joining these Conventions to facilitate the efficient and effective resolution of cross-border disputes. It is also submitted that a shift to electronic service to facilitate the initiation of lawsuits in cross-border disputes can be readily accommodated within the existing framework of the 1965 Hague Service Convention.[20]

III. Assuming Jurisdiction

In general terms, the common law approach on assuming jurisdiction may be regarded as broader than the civil law approach. A claimant can usually commence an action in a common law court subject only to modest limitations, such as the existence of a choice of court or arbitration agreement.[21] As long as proper service is effected or deemed to have been effected, there is jurisdiction to hear a dispute. The common law then relies on the doctrine of *forum non conveniens* to control situations where the plaintiff initiates an action before a court which has little or no connection to the dispute. On the other hand, civil law jurisdictions have comparatively more detailed codes of civil procedure specifying whether a given court can assume jurisdiction in a case. For example, in many civil law jurisdictions (such as China and Indonesia), a plaintiff is supposed to accommodate the defendant by bringing an action before the court in the place where the defendant is resident or domiciled.[22]

There are two principal bases upon which courts can assume jurisdiction.

First, courts often assume jurisdiction on the basis of a defendant's domicile.[23] There is no specific definition of the word 'domicile' in private international law. At common law, a natural person's domicile would typically be the latter's 'permanent home'.[24] The common law attributes a domicile of origin to each person at birth. That will normally be based on the domicile of an individual's parents. Upon attaining full age and capacity, a person can acquire a domicile of choice in some state if one resides there and forms an intention to reside there permanently or indefinitely.[25] A natural person can have one and only one domicile at any point in time. This is because of the practical necessity to connect a person with one system of law so that the individual's legal relationships with the world at large can be regulated with certainty and predictability.[26] The domicile of a legal person is usually determined through its place of registration, incorporation, formation, or central administration, or its principal place of business.

Second, a court can take jurisdiction where the parties have agreed to confer jurisdiction on it. Parties can have a jurisdiction clause (also referred to as a choice of court agreement, especially in a contracting state to the 2005 Hague Convention)[27] in their agreement. Jurisdiction

[19] Hong Kong (through the UK, and extended by China's declaration to continue to apply), Japan, South Korea, the Philippines, Singapore, Sri Lanka, and Thailand are now signatories to the Convention.

[20] See the Conclusion chapter to this book: Section III of ch 17.

[21] *Tomolugen Holdings Ltd v Silica Investors Ltd* [2016] 1 SLR 373 [187].

[22] See eg Section III.A.i of ch 2, Section I.A.i of ch 13.

[23] Sometimes, this might be 'habitual residence', 'residence', or 'nationality'. See also the discussion in Adrian Briggs, *The Conflict of Laws* 4th edn (Oxford, Oxford University Press, 2019) 24–30.

[24] *Wicker v Hume* (1858) 7 HLC 124, 160.

[25] *Udny v Udny* (1868) LR 1 Sc & Div 441.

[26] *Dicey, Morris and Collins* (n 1) para 6–012. See also *Re Craignish* [1892] 3 Ch 180, 192. To achieve certainty and predictability, the common law rules of domicile are codified in some jurisdictions: see eg Domicile Ordinance (Cap 596) (Hong Kong).

[27] See eg Choice of Court Agreements Act 2016 (Singapore). See also Section II.A.iv of ch 7.

clauses may be exclusive (in the sense of requiring disputes to be determined by a specific court) or non-exclusive (in the sense of allowing disputes to be brought before any one of a number of courts). Jurisdiction clauses may also be asymmetric, requiring one party to the contract, but not the other party, to bring a relevant dispute before a specified court. In a number of states, the parties' ability to designate a court for the determination of their dispute may be subject to constraint.[28] For example, most courts will decline jurisdiction where the main issue in a case is title to real property situated in another state, with Japan being a potential exception.[29] The absence of jurisdiction in such situations is a consequence of what is known as the *Moçambique* rule in common law systems.[30] In addition, most states regulate jurisdiction clauses in consumer, labour and insurance contracts, as those agreements are likely to have been concluded between parties in unequal bargaining positions. There will usually be a policy of protecting the weaker party (the consumer, the employee, the insured) in such transactions. For instance, under the Brussels I (recast) Regulation, protection is afforded by enabling courts in various locations to assume jurisdiction where the weaker party sues the stronger and restricting the venues where the stronger party can sue the weaker.[31] Often the stronger will only be permitted to sue the weaker before the court of the latter's domicile. Any choice of court agreement to the contrary will usually be ineffective, unless entered into after a dispute has arisen between the parties.[32] An example would be Articles 27 and 28 of the Act on Private International Law in South Korea.[33] By contrast, in purely commercial cases, where parties deal with each other at arm's length, choice of court agreements will normally be enforced. For instance, the jurisdiction of the Singapore International Commercial Court (SICC) over a dispute mainly arises as a result of the parties' agreement to bring disputes arising in connection with their commercial contract to the SICC. It has been suggested that the assumption of jurisdiction on this basis by the SICC 'should be governed by a unique test that leans strongly towards the exercise of jurisdiction but has flexibility to decline to exercise jurisdiction in exceptional circumstances in order to take into account the competing policy considerations it has to balance'.[34] It appears that the China International Commercial Court (CICC) adopts a similar liberal approach to the assumption of jurisdiction in commercial cases, with recent CICC decisions holding that the CICC has jurisdiction to rule on the validity of arbitration agreements.[35]

An important restriction on a court's ability to assume jurisdiction over a matter is immunity.[36] Most states studied in this book respect state immunity, at least insofar as a state engages in

[28] This subject has been extensively discussed by the Indian courts: Section II.A.ii of ch 16. See also generally Adrian Briggs, *Agreements on Jurisdiction and Choice of Law* (Oxford, Oxford University Press, 2008); Zheng Sophia Tang, *Jurisdiction and Arbitration Agreements in International Commercial Law* (Oxon, Routledge, 2014).

[29] See Section IV.B.ii.a of ch 5.

[30] From *British South Africa Co v Companhia de Moçambique* [1893] AC 602. However, this tends to be relaxed in some states such as Hong Kong: Section III.B.i of ch 3.

[31] See Brussels I (recast) Regulation, Arts 18, 21.

[32] ibid, Arts 19, 23.

[33] See Sections III.H and III.I of ch 6.

[34] Wei Yao Kenny Chng, 'Exploring a New Frontier in Singapore's Private International Law: *IM Skaugen SE v MAN Diesel & Turbo SE* [2016] SGHCR 6' (2016) 28 *Singapore Academy of Law Journal* 649, 651. See also Section II.A.i of ch 7.

[35] (2019) Zui Gao Fa Min Te Nos 1–3. English translations are available online: http://cicc.court.gov.cn/html/1/219/211/376/index.html.

[36] See generally Hazel Fox and Philippa Webb, *The Law of State Immunity* revised and updated 3rd edn (Oxford, Oxford University Press, 2015). See also Malcolm N Shaw, *International Law* 8th edn (Cambridge, Cambridge University Press, 2018) ch 12; Malcolm D Evans (ed), *International Law* 5th edn (Oxford, Oxford University Press, 2018) chs 11–12; James Crawford, *Brownlie's Principles of Public International Law* (Oxford, Oxford University Press, 2019) chs 20–22.

sovereign acts, as opposed to purely commercial activities.[37] Most states also have rules regulating diplomatic and consular immunity and whether state-owned enterprises may be sued. It has been argued that immunity is not a restriction as such on a court's jurisdiction by choice, but relates instead to the exercise of sovereignty.[38] 'Sovereign immunity is a concept of international law, developed out of the principle *par in parem non habet imperium* ['equals have no authority over each other'], by virtue of which one State shall not be subject to the jurisdiction of another State.'[39]

IV. Declining Jurisdiction

There is a subtle difference between declining a jurisdiction that one might otherwise have and completely lacking jurisdiction, although in the end the two situations may lead in practical terms to the same outcome – namely, a court refusing to hear a case. Almost all courts retain a discretion in appropriate circumstances to decline jurisdiction that a plaintiff has properly invoked.[40] However, the basis and extent to which this discretion is exercised varies among different states. A court may decline to exercise a jurisdiction that it would otherwise have in the following situations: (1) *forum non conveniens* (when the forum in which a party has commenced an action is clearly inappropriate, or another forum is clearly more appropriate to try the parties' dispute); (2) *lis alibi pendens* (when there are parallel or concurrent proceedings between the same parties concerning the same subject matter in different jurisdictions at the same time); (3) *res judicata* (when there have been decided cases on the same facts or issues as those sought to be raised before a court); (4) where there is an exclusive jurisdiction agreement between the parties designating another court as the forum for the resolution of their disputes; and (5) where the exercise of jurisdiction would be contrary to public policy (for example, national sovereignty, national security, the aims and spirit of national laws, and national conceptions of morality).[41] These grounds for declining jurisdiction are extensively discussed in the succeeding chapters of this book, insofar as they are applied in the respective Asian jurisdictions canvassed.[42]

It has been suggested that the need to regulate the circumstances in which national courts decline jurisdiction at an international level, is highly desirable in order to promote certainty and

[37] There are two approaches to state immunity: a restrictive and an absolute approach. Under the former approach, a foreign country may be sued before a state's court in relation to transactions of a purely commercial nature. In contrast, where a state follows the latter approach, a foreign country cannot be sued at all before the courts of that state. Among the jurisdictions surveyed here, many have adopted the restrictive immunity approach. However, notably, China (including Hong Kong) maintains an absolute immunity approach: *Democratic Republic of the Congo v FG Hemisphere Associates LLC (No 1)* (2011) 14 HKCFAR 95; *Democratic Republic of the Congo v FG Hemisphere Associates LLC (No 2)* (2011) 14 HKCFAR 395. See also Section VI.A of ch 2 and Section V.A of ch 3.

[38] *Holland v Lampen-Wolfe* [2000] 1 WLR 1573, 1588D (Lord Millett). See also Hazel Fox, 'Approaches of Domestic Courts to the Assertion of International Jurisdiction' in Patrick Capps, Malcolm Evans and Stratos Konstadinidis (eds), *Asserting Jurisdiction: International and European Legal Perspectives* (Portland, Hart Publishing, 2003) 181–86.

[39] See eg *Al-Adsani v UK* (2002) 34 EHRR 11 [54].

[40] JJ Fawcett, 'General Report' in JJ Fawcett (ed), *Declining Jurisdiction in Private International Law* (New York, Oxford University Press, 1995) 2.

[41] See also eg Alex Mills, 'The Dimensions of Public Policy in Private International Law' (2008) 4(2) *Journal of Private International Law* 201–36; *Dicey, Morris and Collins* (n 1) paras 5R-001–5-018; Kenny Chng, 'A Theoretical Perspective of the Public Policy Doctrine in the Conflict of Laws' (2018) 14(1) *Journal of Private International Law* 130–59.

[42] See also eg *Dicey, Morris and Collins* (n 1); Richard Fentiman, *International Commercial Litigation* (Oxford, Oxford University Press, 2015); Alejandro Carballo Leyda (ed), *Asian Conflict of Laws: East and South East Asia* (Alphen aan den Rijn, Kluwer Law International, 2015); Paul Torremans and others (eds), *Cheshire, North & Fawcett Private International Law* 15th edn (Oxford, Oxford University Press, 2017); Adrian Briggs, *Civil Jurisdiction and Judgments* 7th edn (London, Informa Law, 2021).

predictability; ensure proper allocation of jurisdiction between courts and discourage improper forum shopping; and reduce the unnecessary incidence of concurrent jurisdiction and the risk of irreconcilable judgments.[43] More specifically, it has been argued that there should be a principled approach to the treatment of public policy; that such treatment is possible despite the diversity of social, moral, cultural, political, economic, and historical circumstances in different jurisdictions, and that such approach is essential to ensure judicial legitimacy.[44] Moreover, races to the courthouse or judgments, parallel proceedings, and anti-suit injunctions should be avoided whenever possible.[45] However, there is unlikely to be traction for such international regulation in Asia, where each state will likely wish to retain a high degree of autonomy in determining whether its courts should assume jurisdiction in specific situations.

It may instead be sufficient for the purposes of modest harmonisation to have a soft law instrument setting out a few general guidelines for the grant of anti-suit injunctions.[46] Those basic principles might be along the following lines:

(1) Where a creditor initiates parallel actions against a debtor in states X and Y, the creditor should be made to choose whether to pursue its claim in state X or state Y. The creditor should not be allowed to pursue both actions at the same time.
(2) Where a creditor initiates an action against a debtor in state X in accordance with a choice of court agreement and the debtor commences a parallel action against the creditor in state Y, party autonomy should prevail in the absence of good reason to the contrary. The debtor can be enjoined by the court of state X from pursuing its parallel action and breaching the parties' choice of court agreement.
(3) Where a creditor initiates an action against a debtor in state X and the debtor initiates a parallel action in state Y for a negative declaration (that is, a declaration that the debtor does not owe money or is not liable to the creditor), the court of state Y should refuse to entertain the debtor's claim. Alternatively, the court of state X may issue an injunction prohibiting the debtor from pursuing its claim for a negative declaration. The tactic of seeking a negative declaration is an artificial means of turning a debtor into a plaintiff when it should be more natural for the creditor to sue the debtor.[47]

It should be stressed that anti-suit injunctions are orders directed at a party to court proceedings. They are not orders directed at a foreign court, questioning the jurisdiction of a foreign court, or telling a foreign court to cease and desist from hearing a case. Given the principle of

[43] Peter Nygh, 'Declining Jurisdiction under the Brussels I Regulation and the Preliminary Draft Hague Judgments Convention: A Comparison' in James Fawcett (ed), *Reform and Development of Private International Law: Essays in Honour of Sir Peter North* (Oxford, Oxford University Press, 2002) 304–07. But see Franco Ferrari, *Forum Shopping Despite Unification of Law* (Leiden, Brill, 2021).

[44] Sundaresh Menon, 'Taming the Unruly Horse: The Treatment of Public Policy Arguments in the Courts' (*Supreme Court of Singapore*, 19 February 2019), available online: www.supremecourt.gov.sg/Data/Editor/Documents/Public%20Policy%20Lecture%20-%2019Feb2019.pdf.

[45] Fawcett (n 40) 67, Nygh (n 43) 332.

[46] Some Asian states (particularly those belonging to the civil law family), such as Vietnam and Cambodia, do not have the concept of anti-suit injunction: Section II.D.iii of ch 9 and Section II.A.ii of ch 10. However, as observed in the Sri Lanka chapter, the courts 'are not prevented from creatively and innovatively adopting such private international law principles': Section II.D of ch 15. A potentially similar 'soft law instrument' is the Institut de Droit International's resolution in 2003, albeit it will give the court first seised the carriage of a case: Institut de Droit International, 'The Principles for Determining When the Use of the Doctrine of Forum Non Conveniens and Anti-suit Injunctions is Appropriate' (*Institut de Droit International*, 2 September 2003), available online: www.idi-iil.org/app/uploads/2017/06/2003_bru_01_en.pdf.

[47] See eg *Messier Dowty Ltd v Sabena SA* [2000] 1 WLR 2040 [34]–[43]; *Mizuho Corporate Bank Ltd v Cho Hung Bank* [2004] 4 SLR 67 [13].

international comity, it should not be for the court of one country to dictate how the court of another country should approach a matter before it. Consequently, an anti-suit injunction being solely an order directed at a party to proceedings before the court rendering the injunction, the order will only be effective if the target party has a presence or assets within the territory of the rendering court. In such case, if the injunction is disobeyed, the party may either be jailed or its assets seised for acting in contempt of a court order. If the targeted party has no person or assets amenable to the jurisdiction of the rendering court, then an anti-suit injunction will be of little or no practical utility.[48]

V. Grounds of Direct Jurisdiction in Asia

Focusing on civil and commercial matters, Volume One put forward a rudimentary system for the recognition and enforcement of judgments. That rudimentary system posited a minimum list of grounds of indirect jurisdiction that Volume One suggested should be acceptable to all Asian jurisdictions.[49] Applying a similar approach here, a minimum list of grounds of direct jurisdiction for Asian countries would be as follows:

(1) The court of a given state may assume jurisdiction if, at the start of the relevant proceedings, the defendant is habitually resident in that state.
(2) The court of a given state may assume jurisdiction if, at the start of the relevant proceedings the defendant has a principal place of business or an establishment, branch or agency in that state, provided that such place of business, establishment, branch or agency is closely connected to the plaintiff's claim.
(3) The court of a given state may assume jurisdiction if a defendant has submitted to that court's jurisdiction:
    (a) by express agreement (for example, a choice of court agreement before the dispute arose or a bespoke agreement after a dispute has arisen);
    (b) by appearing before that court without challenging jurisdiction, or
    (c) by bringing a counterclaim related to the plaintiff's claim.
(4) When a claim concerns title to immovable property located a given state, that state may assume jurisdiction.
(5) When a claim concerns a non-contractual obligation and the act that gave rise to the relevant damage occurred in a given state, that state may assume jurisdiction.
(6) When a claim involves a contractual obligation which was agreed, performed or breached in a state, that state may assume jurisdiction.

Situations (1) to (5) mirror the general grounds of indirect jurisdiction espoused in Volume One. There is an additional situation (6) on contractual obligations. This appears from the accounts in this book to be a common ground for establishing direct jurisdiction among the 15 Asian states examined. Table I below summarises the extent to which the six general grounds of

[48] On anti-suit injunctions generally, see Thomas Raphael, *The Anti-Suit Injunction* 2nd edn (Oxford, Oxford University Press, 2019); Steven Gee, *Commercial Injunctions* 7th edn (London, Sweet and Maxwell, 2021) ch 14.

[49] Anselmo Reyes, 'Introduction: Towards a System for the Recognition and Enforcement of Judgments' in Anselmo Reyes (ed), *Recognition and Enforcement of Judgments in Civil and Commercial Matters* (Oxford, Hart Publishing, 2019) 29–30. See also the Conclusion chapter to that book: Anselmo Reyes, 'Conclusion: Towards an Asia of Judgments without Borders' in Reyes (n 49) 309–26.

direct jurisdiction in (1) to (6) have been adopted by the 15 Asian states studied here in civil and commercial matters. For completeness, the position in Macao SAR in China has also been included in Table I.[50]

The succeeding chapters also look into direct jurisdiction in other areas of law – intellectual property law, family law, company law, insolvency law, bankruptcy law, and competition law – to varying degrees. The contributors were given the liberty to focus on the areas that are pertinent to their respective state's circumstances and legal development. The wide divergences in how the different Asian states assume or refuse jurisdiction in these other areas do not allow for any easy or useful identification of common grounds similar to those just discussed in relation to general civil and commercial matters. The difficulty is that harmonisation 'implies a concern to reconcile the preoccupations and the interests of … various systems'.[51] That will inevitably be difficult to achieve where there are differing political, economic, social, and cultural factors involved. For instance, in family law, it would seem that there is generally a reluctance to assume jurisdiction among the 15 Asian jurisdictions in cases with foreign elements. None of the 15 Asian states surveyed have entered into the 1996 Hague Convention on Jurisdiction, Applicable Law, Recognition, Enforcement and Co-operation in Respect of Parental Responsibility and Measures for the Protection of Children. This might be contrasted with the harmonisation achieved within the EU through (most notably) the Brussels IIa Regulation and the Maintenance Regulation on various aspects of family law.[52]

Table I Grounds of Direct Jurisdiction among Asian states

	(1) Place of Habitual Residence	**(2) Principal Place of Business**	**(3) Submission by (a) Express Agreement, (b) Appearance without Challenging Jurisdiction, (c) Bringing Counterclaim**	**(4) Place of Immovable Property**	**(5) Place of Act Which Caused Damage**	**(6) Place Where Contractual Obligation Agreed, Performed, or Breached**
China	Yes (CPL Article 21)	Yes (CPL Article 265)	Yes (CPL Article 34)	Yes (CPL Article 33)	Yes (Section V.B of chapter 2)	Yes (CPL Article 265, CPL Interpretation Articles 18–21)
Hong Kong	Yes (RHC Order 11 rule 1(1)(a))	Yes (Companies Ordinance section 803)	Yes (Section II.D of chapter 3)	Yes (RHC Order 11 rules 1(1)(g)–(i))	Yes (RHC Order 11 rule 1(1)(f))	Yes (RHC Order 11 rule 1(1)(d))

(continued)

[50] Sources from Macao come from 'Comparative Table on Grounds of Jurisdiction' (n 9) 13–14. 'CPC' in Macau refers to the *Código de Processo Civil* [Code of Civil Procedure], available online (in Portuguese): https://bo.io.gov.mo/bo/i/99/40/codprocivpt/codprociv0001.asp. Macao is also a member state of the Hague Conference on Private International Law (through China).

[51] Ferrari (n 43) 34, fns 48, 50.

[52] Council Regulation (EC) No 2201/2003 of 27 November 2003 concerning jurisdiction and the recognition and enforcement of judgments in matrimonial matters and the matters of parental responsibility, repealing Regulation (EC) No 1347/2000; Council Regulation (EC) No 4/2009 of 18 December 2008 on jurisdiction, applicable law, recognition and enforcement of decisions and cooperation in matters relating to maintenance obligations.

Table I ***(Continued)***

	(1) Place of Habitual Residence	(2) Principal Place of Business	(3) Submission by (a) Express Agreement, (b) Appearance without Challenging Jurisdiction, (c) Bringing Counterclaim	(4) Place of Immovable Property	(5) Place of Act Which Caused Damage	(6) Place Where Contractual Obligation Agreed, Performed, or Breached
Macao	Yes (CPC Article 17(a))	Yes (CPC Article 17(c))	Yes (CPC Article 29)	Yes (CPC Article 20(a))	Yes (CPC Article 15(a))	Yes (CPC Article 16(a))
Taiwan	Yes (TCCP Article 1)	Yes (TCCP Article 2)	Yes (TCCP Article 24)	Yes (TCCP Article 10(1))	Yes (TCCP Article 15(1))	Yes (TCCP Article 12)
Japan	Yes (CCP Article 3-2) ('residence')	Yes (CCP Article 3-2(3))	Yes (CCP Articles 3-7 and 3-8)	Yes (CCP Article 3-3(xi))	Yes (CCP Article 3-3(viii))	Yes (CCP Article 3-3(i))
South Korea	Yes (CPA Articles 2 and 3)	Yes (CPA Articles 5 and 12)	Yes (CPA Articles 29 and 30)	Yes (CPA Articles 11 and 20)	Yes (CPA Article 18(1))	Yes (CPA Article 8)
Singapore	Yes (ROC Order 11 rule 1(1)(a))	Yes (Companies Act section 365)	Yes (CCAA section 11)	Yes (ROC Order 11 rules 1(1)(g) and (i))	Yes (ROC Order 11 rule 1(1)(f))	Yes (ROC Order 11 rules 1(1)(d) and (e))
Malaysia	Yes (CJA 1964 section 23(1)(b), ROC 2012 Order 11 rule 1(1)(C))	Yes (CJA 1964 section 23(1)(b), ROC 2012 Order 11 rule 1(1)(C))	Yes (ROC 2012 Order 11 rule 2, Order 12 rule 10(6))	Yes (CJA 1964 section 23(1)(d), ROC 2012 Order 11 rules 1(1)(A)–(B))	Yes (CJA 1964 sections 23(1)(a) and (c), ROC 2012 Order 11 rule 1(1)(H))	Yes (CJA 1964 sections 23(1)(a) and (c), ROC 2012 Order 11 rules 1(1)(F)–(G))
Vietnam	Yes (CPC Article 469(1)(a), national law on residence)	Yes (CPC Article 469(1)(b))	Yes (CPC Article 470(1)(c), subject to Draft Resolution 2019 Articles 3(2)(a)–(c))	Yes (CPC Article 470(1)(a))	Yes (CPC Article 469(1)(dd))	Yes (CPC Article 469(1)(dd))
Cambodia	Yes (CCP Article 8(a))	Yes (CCP Articles 8(b)–(c))	Yes (CCP Articles 13(1), 14)	Yes (CCP Article 9(g), Joint Prakas)	Yes (CCP Article 9(f))	Yes (CCP Articles 8 and 9)
Myanmar	Yes (Orders IV and V)	Yes (Order I Rules 1 and 3, CPC section 20, Explanation II to CPC section 20)	Yes (case law)	Yes (CPC section 16)	Yes (CPC section 19)	Yes (CPC section 20)

(continued)

Table I ***(Continued)***

	(1) Place of Habitual Residence	**(2) Principal Place of Business**	**(3) Submission by (a) Express Agreement, (b) Appearance without Challenging Jurisdiction, (c) Bringing Counterclaim**	**(4) Place of Immovable Property**	**(5) Place of Act Which Caused Damage**	**(6) Place Where Contractual Obligation Agreed, Performed, or Breached**
Philippines	Yes (Rules of Civil Procedure Rule 14 sections 5, 6(a))	Yes (Rules of Civil Procedure Rule 14 sections 5, 6(b))	Yes (Rules of Civil Procedure Rule 14 section 23)	Yes (Civil Code Article 16)	Yes (Section II.B.ii of chapter 12)	Yes (Section II.B.i of chapter 12)
Indonesia	Yes (HIR Article 118(1), Rv Article 99(2))	Yes (prevailing judicial practice, Act on Foundations Article 56(1))	Yes (HIR Article 118(4), Rv Article 99(16))	Yes (HIR Article 118(3), Rv Articles 99(8), (10))	Likely yes. Rv Article 100 provides that a foreign national with a legal obligation arising in Indonesia can be sued.	Yes (HIR Article 118 and Rv Article 99)
Thailand	Yes (CPC section 4(1))	Yes (CPC section 4 *quinque*)	Yes (case law)	Yes (CPC section 4 *bis*)	Yes (CPC section 4(1))	Yes (CPC section 4(1))
Sri Lanka	Yes (CPC section 9)	Yes (case law)	Yes (case law)	Yes (CPC section 9)	Likely yes. Case law suggests that a defendant not domiciled in Sri Lanka can be sued if there is a clear connection with Sri Lanka.	Yes (CPC section 9)
India	Yes (Section II.A.i of Chapter 16)	Yes (CPC section 20)	Yes (case law, Section II.A.i of Chapter 16)	Yes (CPC sections 15–20)	Yes (CPC section 9)	Yes (CPC section 20)

2

China

ZHENGYI ZHANG AND JIANPING SHI

I. Introduction

Direct jurisdiction in China refers to whether a Chinese court can directly decide civil and commercial cases in accordance with its domestic procedure laws. Unlike indirect jurisdiction which decides whether foreign courts have jurisdiction, direct jurisdiction focuses on whether domestic courts would have jurisdiction over cases.[1] This chapter explores both the legislation and judicial practice for direct jurisdiction in Chinese private international law.

As the first issue the courts will encounter when adjudicating international civil cases, establishing jurisdiction is the starting point of international civil procedure. Jurisdiction is the pre-condition for courts to accept and try a case. It is also a pre-condition which influences the recognition and enforcement of judgments by other states. It is thus directly related to the vindication of the parties' rights and the exercise of a nation's sovereignty. Jurisdiction in international civil procedure refers to the authority of the courts or other organs of a state having judicial power to accept and try cases with international factors. It is the legal basis for a state's court to accept and try cases with foreign-related factors.

II. Background

The sources of law on direct jurisdiction in China can be categorised into the following two types: (1) domestic legislation such as the Civil Procedure Law of the People's Republic of China (CPL), the Special Maritime Procedure Law of the People's Republic of China (SMPL) and related judicial interpretations; and (2) international treaties in which China has acceded to.

China has no specific legislation on jurisdiction as a matter of international civil procedure. However, a special chapter in the CPL contains provisions relating to the issue. Since its enactment, the CPL has adopted the model of separate legislation on international and domestic jurisdiction of civil procedure. The first version of the CPL was in 1982, and amendments followed in 1991, 2007, 2012 and 2017. Part IV of the CPL was entitled 'Special Provisions on Foreign-Related Civil Procedures', in which Chapter 24 provides the rules on jurisdiction in detail. The SMPL stipulates the jurisdiction in maritime cases. It was implemented from 2000 with Chapter 2 entitled 'Jurisdiction'.

[1] Yitong Liu, *International Civil Proceeding Jurisdiction and Establishment of Harmonised International Society* (Beijing, Chinese People's University of Public Security Press, 2017) 254.

The Supreme People's Court (SPC) also issued an Interpretation on the Application of the Civil Procedure Law of the PRC ('CPL Interpretation') in 2015 with observations on jurisdiction which are also applicable to foreign-related matters.[2]

As for international treaties, to date, China has become party to only a few treaties on jurisdiction, including the 1951 Agreement on International Goods Transport by Rail, the 1992 International Convention on Civil Liability for Oil Pollution Damage, and the 1999 Convention for the Unification of Certain Rules for International Carriage by Air (the Montreal Convention). In addition, China signed (but has yet to ratify) the 2005 Hague Convention on Choice of Court Agreements in September 2017. China also sent a strong government delegation, including judges from the SPC, experts from the Department of Treaty and Law within the Ministry of Foreign Affairs, and law professors to participate in the negotiations for the 2019 Hague Convention on the Recognition and Enforcement of Foreign Judgments in Civil or Commercial Matters.[3] With the 2005 and 2019 Conventions, there is little, if any, need for a convention on direct jurisdiction.[4] This means that the jurisdiction of most other international civil and commercial cases other than those mentioned above shall be determined in accordance with the relevant provisions in the CPL.

In addition, China has concluded 37 bilateral judicial assistance treaties in the civil and commercial fields. Some of those, including bilateral treaties between China and Peru, Egypt, Cyprus, Tunisia, and Bosnia and Herzegovina,[5] contain a provision on jurisdiction to presume the court that made the judgment is deemed to enjoy the power of jurisdiction.

III. Jurisdiction under CPL

The determination of jurisdiction of international civil litigation in China involves at least two issues: (1) whether Chinese courts have jurisdiction; and (2) if so, which Chinese court will specifically exercise jurisdiction.[6]

The preliminary Articles in Part IV of the CPL provided the overall framework on jurisdiction for foreign-related civil actions. Article 259 stipulates that: 'The provisions of this Part shall apply to foreign-related civil actions within the territory of the People's Republic of China. Where this Part is silent, other relevant provisions of this Law shall apply.' Article 260 stipulates that: 'Where there is any discrepancy between an international treaty concluded or acceded to

[2] Opinions of the Supreme People's Court on Some Issues Concerning the Application of the Civil Procedure Law of the People's Republic of China (Supreme People's Court, Fa Fa [1992] No 22, 14 July 1992, effective 14 July 1992). This was replaced by Interpretations of the Supreme People's Court on Applicability of the Civil Procedure Law of the People's Republic of China (Supreme People's Court, Zhu Shi [2015] No 5, 18 December 2014, effective 4 February 2015) ('CPL Interpretation').

[3] Guojian Xu, 'To Establish an International Legal System for Global Circulation of Court Judgments' [2017] 5 *Wuhan University International Law Review* 100.

[4] Ronald A Brand, 'Comparative Method and International Litigation' [2020] 2 *Journal of Dispute Resolution* 292.

[5] Treaty between the People's Republic of China and the Republic of Peru Judicial Assistance in Civil and Commercial Matters, Art 25; Agreement between the People's Republic of China and the Arab Republic of Egypt on Judicial Assistance in Civil, Commercial and Criminal Matters, Art 22; Treaty between the People's Republic of China and the Republic of Cyprus on Judicial Assistance in Civil, Commercial and Criminal Matters, Art 26; Treaty between the People's Republic of China and the Republic of Tunisia on Judicial Assistance in Civil and Commercial Matters, Art 23; Treaty between the People's Republic of China and Bosnia and Herzegovina on Judicial Assistance in Civil and Commercial Matters, Art 24.

[6] Wang Li, 'The Analysis on Jurisdiction of Transnational Civil Litigation: Evaluating the Provisions on Jurisdiction of Transnational Civil Litigation in Civil Procedure Law of PR China (Amended in 2012)' [2014] 1 *Chinese Review of International Law* 89.

by the People's Republic of China and this Law, the provisions of the international treaty shall prevail, except clauses to which the People's Republic of China has declared reservations.'

Articles 265 and 266 in Chapter 24 contain the provisions on jurisdiction. Article 265 provides for contractual disputes or other property rights disputes, and Article 266 provides for exclusive jurisdiction in some circumstances. Otherwise, the general provisions on jurisdiction in Chapter 2 of CPL (Articles 17–38) will apply to matters on foreign-related procedures. As mentioned above, the SPC has also issued an CPL Interpretation in 2015.[7]

From the perspective of both legislation and judicial practice, China's jurisdiction over foreign-related civil cases can be divided into four types: general territorial jurisdiction, special territorial jurisdiction, exclusive jurisdiction, and agreed jurisdiction.

A. Territorial Jurisdiction

The principle of territorial jurisdiction is based on the fact that the facts giving rise to international civil and commercial cases have a certain relationship with that country's legal system; more precisely, the exercise of jurisdiction comes about due to the presence of legal facts based on the legal relationship in civil procedure,[8] or the fact that the relevant subject matter regarding which the parties have engaged in civil procedures is within the territory of the country, such as tort, contract, and disputes of property rights. This principle of jurisdiction is a manifestation of the national territorial principle in international civil and commercial procedure and is commonly and broadly adopted by countries around world. China has always followed the principle of 'plaintiff accommodating the defendant' in determining the jurisdiction, which essentially determines the criterion of jurisdiction by the defendant's domicile (for example, if the defendant resides in China, the jurisdiction would be China's). Therefore, China is a typical country that adopts the principle of territorial jurisdiction.

i. General Territorial Jurisdiction

As noted, China's approach to jurisdiction in international cases (as with many countries) follows the principle that 'the plaintiff should accommodate the defendant'. CPL Article 21 accordingly provides:

> A civil action instituted against a citizen shall be under the jurisdiction of the people's court at the place of domicile of the defendant; or if the defendant's place of domicile is different from his or her place of habitual residence, the civil action shall be under the jurisdiction of the people's court at the place of habitual residence of the defendant. A civil action instituted against a legal person or any other organization shall be under the jurisdiction of the people's court at the place of domicile of the defendant. Where the places of domicile or places of habitual residence of several defendants in the same action are located within the jurisdictions of two or more people's courts, both or all of such people's courts shall have jurisdiction over the action.

While the CPL in general prioritises the principle that 'the plaintiff should accommodate the defendant', the court may also consider the plaintiff's domicile and habitual residence. CPL Article 22 stipulates that a personal action instituted against a person not residing within the

[7] CPL Interpretation (n 2).
[8] Civil Procedure Law of the People's Republic of China (9 April 1991, effective 9 April 1991), Art 2.

territory of PRC whose whereabouts is unknown or who has been declared missing shall be under the jurisdiction of the people's court at the place of plaintiff's domicile or habitual residence.[9]

ii. Special Territorial Jurisdiction

Special territorial jurisdiction rules are based on the fact that certain types of international civil litigation are connected with particular countries. CPL Article 265 stipulates:

> Where an action is instituted against a defendant which has no domicile within the territory of the People's Republic of China for a contract dispute or any other property right or interest dispute, if the contract is signed or performed within the territory of the People's Republic of China, the subject matter of action is located within the territory of the People's Republic of China, if the defendant has any impoundable property within the territory of the People's Republic of China, or the defendant has any representative office within the territory of the People's Republic of China, the people's court at the place where the contract is signed or performed, where the subject matter of action is located, where the impoundable property is located, where the tort occurs, or where the domicile of the representative office is located may have jurisdiction over the action.

In addition, CPL Articles 23 to 32 contain provisions for special jurisdiction, which enable Chinese courts to assert jurisdiction over international civil and commercial cases. The specific provisions will be discussed in detail.

iii. Exclusive Jurisdiction

Exclusive jurisdiction means that a country's courts will have jurisdiction over specified types of foreign-related civil cases, to the exclusion of the courts in all other countries, in accordance with domestic legislation or international treaties. Exclusive jurisdiction prevents parties from going to some other court or asserting the jurisdiction of other courts in relation to their case.[10] Exclusive jurisdiction is a reflection of a country's national judicial sovereignty. It emphasises that a designated domestic court is to have unconditional jurisdiction over civil cases that are closely concerned with the fundamental interests of the country and people. Typically, national public policy or important political and economic issues will be involved. If one party does not abide by a country's rules on exclusive jurisdiction and submits the case to another country's court, the judgment of the latter court will not normally be recognised and enforced in the country exerting exclusive jurisdiction. However, this doctrine may cause conflicts in the adjudication of international civil cases since the scope of exclusive jurisdiction is not consistent in different countries.

Article 266 in Part IV of CPL provides for foreign-related exclusive jurisdiction:

> Actions instituted for disputes arising from the performance of contracts for Chinese-foreign equity joint ventures, Chinese-foreign contractual joint ventures, or Chinese-foreign cooperative exploration and exploitation of natural resources in the People's Republic of China shall be under the jurisdiction of the people's courts of the People's Republic of China.

Some scholars take the view that not all of the three categories of foreign-related contracts mentioned in Article 266 are intended to be subject to exclusive jurisdiction, particularly the

[9] See also CPL Interpretation, Art 15.
[10] Shuang-yuan Li, *Private International Law* 3rd edn (Beijing, Beijing University Publishing House, 2012) 315.

first two classes of contract, which are not substantially different from general foreign-related contracts and have no obvious connection with the public interest of the PRC.[11]

In addition, by CPL Article 33, the following cases fall under the exclusive jurisdiction of the people's courts: (1) an action instituted in a real estate dispute involving land in China; (2) an action instituted in a dispute relating to harbour operations in China; and (3) an action instituted in an inheritance dispute, where the deceased passed away while domiciled in China or the bulk of the deceased's estate is located in China. Disputes relating to harbour operations are divided into two categories: the first comprises cargo handling and storage disputes associated with the harbour, while the second covers damage compensation disputes due to torts committed in the course of harbour operations. Inheritance disputes involve conflicts over private rights. Notably, there is no inevitable connection between these disputes and China's political and economic interests. Focusing narrowly on jurisdiction does not ensure the recognition or enforcement of judgments abroad. In this light, it is arguably unnecessary that cases relating to harbour operations and inheritance should be treated as matters falling within the exclusive jurisdiction of the Chinese court.

iv. Agreed Jurisdiction

Agreed jurisdiction (also known as consensual jurisdiction) occurs where parties are allowed to select the court which will exercise jurisdiction over an international civil dispute. An increasing number of countries no longer insist on exercising jurisdiction over cases that have little connection with that country or society. Thus, countries have gradually recognised and established a system of agreed jurisdiction in their legislative and judicial practice.[12] In theory, actual connection is believed to consist of two assertions: one is factual connection, the other is legal connection.[13]

CPL Article 34 also clearly stipulates the existence of agreed jurisdiction:

> Parties to a dispute over a contract or any other right or interest in property may, by a written agreement, choose the people's court at the place of domicile of the defendant, at the place where the contract is performed or signed, at the place of domicile of the plaintiff, at the place where the subject matter is located, or at any other place actually connected to the dispute to have jurisdiction over the dispute, but the provisions of this Law regarding hierarchical jurisdiction and exclusive jurisdiction shall not be violated.

The provision, in addition to acknowledging the existence of agreed jurisdiction in Chinese law, imposes limits on what can be agreed:

(1) where matters such as civil status, personal relations, legal capacity, and domestic relations are concerned, the parties may not choose the court to hear their dispute;
(2) an agreement on jurisdiction must be written and the court selected by the agreement must have an actual connection with the dispute;
(3) the jurisdictional agreement can only change general and special jurisdiction and cannot be contrary to exclusive jurisdiction provisions;

[11] Lifeng Tao and Yongfu Gao, 'Reconstruction of the Exclusive Jurisdiction Clause over the Three Types of Contract Disputes Involving Foreign Element in China' [2013] 4 *International Business Research* 80.

[12] Xiaohong Liu and Qi Zhou, 'The Principle of Actual Connection in the System of Agreement Jurisdiction and the Principle of Inconvenient Court' (2014) 12 *Law Science* 43.

[13] Li Liu (ed), *The Study on Legislation of International Civil Procedure Jurisdiction and Judicial Assistance* (Beijing, China University of Political Science and Law Press, 2016) 113.

(4) the parties can only choose the court of first instance by agreement and should not contravene provisions of hierarchical jurisdiction;
(5) the jurisdictional agreement must be the result of equal consultation between the parties so that, if one party obtains agreement by deception, coercion, etc, the court will treat the ostensible choice as invalid.

There is a common point of view from legal practice that agreed jurisdiction should be based on explicit agreement. If the parties have not explicitly defined non-exclusive jurisdiction, exclusive agreement would be presumed.[14] This viewpoint is also in conformity with the 2005 Hague Convention on Choice of Court Agreements which include exclusive choice of court agreements in Article 3.

Although there is a general trend to recognise the legitimacy of jurisdiction agreements between the parties, due to the influence of national sovereignty and the procedural law to maintain legal order, the scope of the agreement jurisdiction system has also been subject to many restrictions. As a result, the issue of legitimacy and rationality of agreement jurisdiction is transformed into a consideration of how national sovereignty restricts the jurisdiction agreements.[15]

B. Hierarchical Jurisdiction

Hierarchical jurisdiction identifies which court will have jurisdiction to hear a case from first instance onwards, and is determined according to the nature, complexity, effect and controversiality of a case. CPL Articles 17 to 20[16] deal with hierarchical jurisdiction. The court of first instance for a foreign-related civil case will typically be a basic people's court in typical cases, and only a 'major' foreign-related civil case may fall within the jurisdiction of an intermediate or higher people's court. Article 1 of the CPL Interpretation defines a 'major' foreign-related case as one in which a large number of issues are in dispute, complex cases, or cases involving many parties who live abroad.

Following China's accession to the WTO and the need to adapt for international civil and commercial cases, the SPC passed the 'Provisions of the Supreme People's Court on Some Issues Concerning the Jurisdiction of Civil and Commercial Cases Involving Foreign Elements' on 25 December 2001 to implement a system for centralised jurisdiction over specific civil and commercial cases.[17] Under these new regulations, foreign civil and commercial cases of the first

[14] Yizhou Deng, *The Practice Essence of PRC Cross-Border Civil and Commercial Litigation* (Beijing, China Legal Publishing House, 2018) 56.

[15] Qi Zhou and Jun Zhao, 'The Origin and Development of International Civil and Commercial Agreement Jurisdiction System Theory' [2014] 6 *Nanjing Social Science* 108.

[16] These articles state:

> Article 17. The basic people's courts shall have jurisdiction over civil cases as a court of first instance, except as otherwise provided for in this Law.
>
> Article 18. The intermediate people's courts shall have jurisdiction over the following civil cases as a court of first instance: (1) major foreign-related cases; (2) cases which have a major impact within their respective jurisdictions; (3) cases which are under the jurisdiction of the intermediate people's courts as determined by the Supreme People's Court.
>
> Article 19. The higher people's courts shall have jurisdiction over civil cases which have a major impact within their respective jurisdictions as a court of first instance.
>
> Article 20. The Supreme People's Court shall have jurisdiction over the following civil cases as a court of first instance: (1) cases which have a major impact nationwide; (2) cases which the Supreme People's Court deems shall be tried by itself.

[17] Provisions of the Supreme People's Court on Some Issues Concerning the Jurisdiction of Civil and Commercial Cases Involving Foreign Elements (Supreme People's Court, Fa Shi [2002] No 5, 25 December 2001, effective 1 March 2002).

instance will come within the jurisdiction of the following people's courts: (1) people's courts within the economic and technological development zones approved by the State Council; (2) intermediate people's courts in the provincial capital, an autonomous region's capital, or a municipality under the Central Government; (3) intermediate people's courts in special economic zones and municipalities with independent planning status; (4) other intermediate people's courts designated by the SPC; and (5) higher people's courts.

The Regulations apply to: (1) foreign-related contracts and cases of tort; (2) letters of credit disputes; (3) applications for the revocation, recognition or enforcement of international arbitral awards; (4) applications for the review of foreign-related arbitration agreements; and (5) applications for the recognition and enforcement of civil and commercial judgments of foreign courts.

For foreign-related cases not mentioned above, hierarchical jurisdiction is followed pursuant to the previous rules.

C. *Forum non conveniens*

The principle of *forum non conveniens* refers to instances where a court has jurisdiction to hear an international civil case but declines to exercise such jurisdiction, because it would be inconvenient or unfair to do so and would be more convenient and appropriate for the parties to litigate their dispute before a court in another country.[18] Article 532 of the CPL Interpretation states:

> Where a foreign-related civil case falls under all the following circumstances, the people's court may render a ruling to dismiss the plaintiff's action, and instruct the plaintiff to institute an action in a more convenient foreign court:
>
> (1) The defendant raises a claim that the case shall be subject to the jurisdiction of a more convenient foreign court, or raises an objection to jurisdiction;
> (2) The parties do not have an agreement specifying the jurisdiction of a court of the People's Republic of China;
> (3) The case does not fall under the exclusive jurisdiction of a court of the People's Republic of China;
> (4) The case does not involve the national interest, or the interest of any citizen, legal person or any other organization of the People's Republic of China;
> (5) The people's court has great difficulties in the determination of facts and the application of laws since major facts of disputes in a case did not occur within the territory of the People's Republic of China, and the laws of the People's Republic of China do not apply to the case; and
> (6) The foreign court has jurisdiction over the case and it is more convenient for it to try the case.

The establishment of the *forum non conveniens* principle could avoid parallel proceedings by reducing the possibility of their occurrence.[19] The rationale for applying a doctrine of *forum non conveniens* is as follows: (1) it is helpful in resolving conflicts of international civil jurisdiction, especially for disputes that are not strongly connected with China or are inconvenient to resolve in China; (2) it is beneficial to optimise the allocation of judicial resources, so as to reduce unnecessary burdens on the Chinese courts and better balance the interests of the parties; (3) insofar as Hong Kong, Macao, and Taiwan are concerned, their legal systems differ from that of Mainland China so that the application of *forum non conveniens* may resolve inter-regional jurisdictional conflicts, avoid conflicting judgments rendered by different regions within China, and aid in the maintenance of consistency within the PRC legal system. The search for the

[18] Xianglin Zhao, *Private International Law* (Beijing, China University of Political Science and Law Press, 2000) 366.
[19] Liu (n 1) 204.

'proper forum', at least where there is one, is a welcome effort to replace judicial chauvisim with judicial comity.[20]

D. *Lis alibi pendens*

Lis alibi pendens is a Latin term meaning that an action on the same cause of action is pending elsewhere. When two courts hear the same dispute, they can reach inconsistent decisions. The doctrine of *res judicata* provides that, once a case has been determined, it is final subject only to appeal. No party to the case can commence another case on the same dispute in another court. When a case is pending, no other case on the same issue should be commenced in another court. *Lis alibi pendens* is based on international comity. It permits a court to refuse to exercise jurisdiction when there is parallel litigation pending in another jurisdiction. However, when the other litigation is about materially different issues, documents, and parties, the doctrine of *lis alibi pendens* will not apply. In most common law jurisdictions (for example, England, Singapore, Hong Kong, Malaysia), *lis alibi pendens* is not a distinct doctrine on its own, but merely one of several factors for a court to take into account when applying the doctrine of *forum non conveniens*.[21] In the US, however, *lis alibi pendens* and *forum non conveniens* are distinct doctrines. In China, there are only two provisions in the CPL Interpretation dealing with *lis alibi pendens*.[22] In Chinese practice, if the courts of two countries have jurisdiction over a certain case, they may exercise their respective jurisdictions concurrently. The people's court may accept a party's claim, without checking whether the defendant has filed a lawsuit in the court of another state or whether the court of another state is trying the same matter. Some scholars believe that, even if a foreign court has rendered final judgment in a case, it will not preclude the Chinese court from hearing the case at the suit of one of the parties. After China's court has rendered judgment, the foreign court's judgment will not be recognised or enforced in China.[23]

E. Interim Measures

Interim measures in civil procedure are temporary protective measures against the person or property of a party issued before or during the process of accepting and hearing civil cases.

[20] Wendy Collins Perdue (ed), *Procedure and Private International Law* (Cheltenham, Edward Elgar Publishing, 2017) 78.

[21] JJ Fawcett, 'General Report' in JJ Fawcett (ed), *Declining Jurisdiction in Private International Law* (New York, Oxford University Press, 1995) 29.

[22] See CPL Interpretation, Arts 15 and 533:

> Article 15. Where both spouses are Chinese citizens but one lives abroad and the other lives in China, the people's court at the place of domicile of the spouse who lives in China shall have jurisdiction over a divorce action between them, regardless of which spouse institutes a divorce action in a people's court. Where the spouse who lives abroad institutes an action in a court of the country of residence of the spouse, and the spouse who lives in China institutes an action in a people's court, the people's court in which the action is instituted shall have jurisdiction over the divorce case.
>
> Article 533. For a case over which both a people's court of the People's Republic of China and a foreign court have jurisdiction, if one party institutes an action in the foreign court whereas the other party institutes an action in the people's court of the People's Republic of China, the people's court may accept the case. If, after a judgment is rendered, the foreign court or a party requests the people's court's recognition and enforcement of the judgment or ruling rendered by the foreign court concerning this case, the people's court shall not consent to the request, unless it is otherwise prescribed by an international treaty concluded or acceded to by both countries.

[23] See Yuan Ma (ed), *Explanation of 'Opinions on the Application of the Civil Procedure Law'* (Beijing, China Procuratorate Publishing House, 1994) 217ff.

Interim measures typically ensure that when final judgment is rendered in favour of a party, it will not be an empty judgment because the successful party is unable to enforce the judgment against assets of the losing party. Often interim measures are sought at an early stage of litigation, in order to prevent a defendant from hiding away its assets. They are temporary in the sense that they are only valid from the time when they are made until the time of final judgment. They may also be subject to review from time to time depending upon the circumstances. Such temporary protection enforcement measures are accordingly designed to guarantee the smooth conduct of a trial and the effective enforcement of future judgments.[24] As a matter of international civil procedure, the jurisdiction to grant interim measures is exercised pursuant to international treaties and domestic laws.

The CPL provides for two types of foreign-related property preservation measures: pre-litigation preservation of property and preservation of property in litigation. Article 31 of the CPL Interpretation stipulates:

> For the preservation of property before the institution of an action, the party concerned shall file an application with the people's court at the place where the property is located. If an applicant files a lawsuit after a people's court took measures for preservation of property before the institution of an action, the lawsuit may be filed with the people's court that took the measures for preservation of property before the institution of an action or any other competent people's court.

However, Article 32 states:

> If the party concerned fails to file a lawsuit within the statutory term after applying for preservation of property before the institution of an action, and a lawsuit has resulted from the loss of property to the party against whom the application is filed, the lawsuit shall be under the jurisdiction of the people's court that took the measure for preservation of property before the institution of an action.

It appears from the two Articles above that both the court that has jurisdiction over the substance of the case and the court where the property is located have jurisdiction to issue property preservation measures.

F. Jurisdiction of Service Abroad

Service abroad refers to the situation where judicial authorities of one country deliver judicial and extrajudicial documents to parties or litigants living in another country in accordance with the domestic legislation of the latter country or the provisions of an international treaty.[25] China's position regarding service abroad is shaped by international treaties, bilateral treaties, and domestic laws. As a party to the 1965 Hague Service Convention, China has signed mutual legal assistance agreements with more than 30 countries. The procedures for serving judicial documents to parties outside China follow those set out in the 1965 Hague Service Convention and notices issued by the SPC, the Ministry of Foreign Affairs and the Ministry of Justice.[26] The procedure can be cumbersome and inefficient. The success rate of service abroad has been relatively low. By way of improvement, in September 2003 the SPC issued the 'Notice on the Designation of the High Courts of Beijing, Shanghai, Guangdong, Zhejiang, and Jiangsu Provinces',

[24] Ping Liu, 'Study on Jurisdiction of Temporary Protection Measures in International Civil Litigation' [2004] 9 *Journal of Litigation Law* 489.

[25] Jin Huang (ed), *Private International Law* (Beijing, Legal Publishing House, 1999) 918.

[26] Qisheng He, *Studies on Service of Process Abroad* (Beijing, Peking University Press, 2006) 199.

pursuant to the 1965 Hague Service and 1970 Hague Evidence Conventions, as the PRC's Central Authorities for transmitting mutual legal assistance requests and related materials to foreign Central Authorities. The Notice further provides that the courts at all levels in the foregoing five provinces and municipalities may transmit judicial documents to the Central Authorities of the 1965 Hague Service Convention's member states through the High Court of their respective provinces, without the need to report to the SPC and the Ministry of Justice. This has had the effect of simplifying procedures and shortening the time needed for service. If a state that has signed a legal assistance agreement with China wishes to request the people's court to facilitate service from abroad, the Central Authority of the requesting state shall submit a form to that effect. The relevant materials should thereafter be forwarded by the Ministry of Justice, reviewed by the SPC, and submitted to the relevant High Court. The intermediate people's court designated by the High Court will then be responsible for the service.

IV. Jurisdiction under the Special Maritime Procedure Law (SMPL)[27]

The SMPL stipulates that:

> Whoever engages in maritime litigation within the territory of the People's Republic of China shall apply the Civil Procedure Law of the People's Republic of China and this Law. Where otherwise provided for by this Law, such provisions shall prevail.

Therefore, the SMPL, as a special piece of legislation on litigation procedures, is applied in preference to the CPL in maritime matters. According to the SMPL, maritime disputes include maritime tortious disputes, maritime contract disputes, and other maritime disputes brought by the parties as provided for by law.

A. Exclusive Jurisdiction

Article 7 of the SMPL stipulates that:

> The following maritime litigation shall be under the exclusive jurisdiction of the Maritime Courts specified in this Article,
>
> (1) A lawsuit brought over a dispute regarding harbour operations shall be under the jurisdiction of the maritime court of the place where the harbour is located;
>
> (2) A lawsuit brought over a dispute regarding pollution damage from a ship's discharge, omission or dumping of oil or other harmful substances, or maritime production, operations, ship scrapping, or repairing operations shall be under the jurisdiction of the maritime court of the place where the oil pollution occurred, where the result of the injury occurred, or where preventive measures were taken;
>
> (3) A lawsuit brought over a dispute regarding the performance of a maritime exploration and development contract within the territory of the People's Republic of China and the waters under its jurisdiction shall be under the jurisdiction of the maritime court of the place where the contract is performed.

[27] This section is largely derived from Jianping Shi and Zijun Zhai, 'Jurisdiction in Shipping Claims' in Xiaohong Liu and Zhengyi Zhang (eds), *Chinese Private International Law* (Oxford, Hart Publishing, 2021).

In fact, among the three categories of 'exclusive jurisdiction' listed in Article 7, only the third truly falls within the internationally exclusive jurisdiction of the Chinese Maritime Court to the exclusion of other courts.

B. Prescribed Jurisdiction

Article 8 of the SMPL stipulates that:

> Where the parties to a maritime dispute are foreign nationals, stateless persons, or foreign enterprises or organisations, and the parties, through written agreement, choose the maritime court of the People's Republic of China to exercise jurisdiction, the maritime court of the People's Republic of China shall also have jurisdiction over the dispute even if the place which has practical connections with the dispute is not within the territory of the People's Republic of China.

Compared with the CPL, the conditions for establishing jurisdiction by agreement in foreign-related maritime cases may vary from case to case. When the parties are foreign nationals, their jurisdiction agreement may designate the Chinese Maritime Court, even if the latter has no actual connection with their case. However, when one or more of the parties is a Chinese national, their jurisdiction agreement is subject to the provisions of the CPL. This means that 'actual connection' is an important condition for the validity of the jurisdiction agreement.

C. Jurisdiction Over Maritime Tort Cases

Maritime tort disputes refer to claims due to ship collisions or other accidents due to ships and their navigation. Claims will typically include compensation for damage from ship collisions, collisions with offshore facilities, oil pollution from spillages, and so on.[28] The Maritime Court's jurisdiction over maritime torts is different from that of the ordinary courts in relation to general tort disputes. With maritime torts, it is often difficult to determine the precise time and place when the wrong occurred, so other places that have actual connection with the case must be taken as the basis for determining whether the Maritime Court has jurisdiction. An example of such a connecting factor would be the first port where a vessel arrives following a collision. In addition to complying with the jurisdictional conditions in CPL Articles 29 to 31, the basis of determining jurisdiction has to comply with SMPL Article 6. The latter would include consideration of one or more places where a defendant is domiciled, the place where the vessel first arrived, the place where a collision occurred, the place where a vessel first arrived following a collision, the place where the vessel at fault is detained, the place where a salvaged vessel first arrives, the place of salvage, and the place of port registry. In short, the jurisdictional provisions of maritime tort cases are flexible and similar to the 'minimum links' in US maritime jurisdiction.

D. Jurisdiction Over Maritime Contract Disputes

Maritime contract disputes include litigation in relation to contracts for the carriage of goods by sea, ship mortgages, charterparties, marine insurance policies, crewing contracts, maritime

[28] Provisions of the Supreme People's Court on the Scope of Cases to be Accepted by Maritime Courts (Supreme People's Court, 24 February 2016, effective 1 March 2016).

guarantees, and so on.[29] These disputes may be under the jurisdiction of the people's court of the place where a voyage originated, the destination of a voyage, or the defendant's domicile in accordance with the provisions of CPL Article 27. At the same time, according to SMPL, several types of maritime contracts may also fall under the jurisdiction of the Maritime Courts:

(1) A lawsuit brought over a maritime transportation contract may also be under the jurisdiction of the Maritime Court of the place for its port of re-transportation.
(2) A lawsuit brought over maritime charter parties may be under the jurisdiction of the Maritime Court for its port of ship delivery, port of ship return, port of ship registry, or port where the defendant is domiciled.
(3) A lawsuit brought on a maritime protection and indemnity contract may be under the jurisdiction of the Maritime Court of the place where the object of the action is located, the place where the accident occurred, or the place where the defendant is domiciled.

E. Preservation Measures in Support of Maritime Claims

In maritime claims, Maritime Courts may issue compulsory preservation measures against defendants' properties in order to ensure the successful exercise of certain rights when applied for by maritime claimants. This includes interlocutory applications for the arrest of ships (except those engaged in military or government duties) and the sequestration of a ship's cargo fuel and supplies. Parties may also apply for the freezing of funds or the sealing of property pending litigation. A claimant may apply to a Maritime Court for preservation measures regardless of any jurisdictional agreements or arbitration agreements between the relevant parties relating to the said maritime claims. Before bringing a lawsuit, a claimant must file an application with the Maritime Court of the place where the property to be arrested, sequestered or preserved is located. This typically refers to the place where the ship or cargo is located. Where a party applies for the preservation of cargo that has already been unloaded but remains under the control of the carrier, if the location of the cargo is not within the jurisdictional area of a Maritime Court, the party may file its claim with the Maritime Court of the place of discharge or with the local people's court of the place where the cargo is located.[30]

V. Special Rules for Different Types of Claims[31]

A. Jurisdiction in Foreign-Related Contractual Claims

According to the provisions of the 1991 CPL and its judicial interpretations, there are two types of judicial jurisdiction over foreign-related contract litigation: agreed jurisdiction and legal jurisdiction. The parties have the right to choose the court to deal with their dispute by agreement. Chinese courts will apply CPL Article 34 to determine the validity of the parties' jurisdictional agreement. Additionally, there must be compliance with CPL Article 266.

[29] ibid.
[30] CPL, Art 30.
[31] For a detailed account of the private international law rules involved in these claims, see Xiaohong Liu and Zhengyi Zhang (eds), *Chinese Private International Law* (Oxford, Hart Publishing, 2021), in particular chs 14 to 19.

Where the parties have not designated a court in their agreement, jurisdiction will depend on whether the defendant is domiciled in the PRC. If so, the plaintiff may file a suit in the people's court where the defendant is domiciled or where the contract is to be performed. The place of contractual performance can be determined by reference to Articles 18 to 21 of the CPL Interpretation.[32] If the defendant is not domiciled in the PRC and either: (1) the contract was signed or is to be performed in China; (2) the subject matter of the action is situated in the PRC; (3) the defendant has property available for seizure in the PRC; or (4) the defendant has a representative office in the PRC, then the people's court having jurisdiction is the one located: (1) where the contract was signed; (2) where the contract is to be performed; (3) where the subject matter of the action is situated; or (4) where the defendant's property is available for seizure.

It may be difficult in some cases to determine where a contract is to be performed. In Chinese civil procedure law, the concept of the place of performance is narrowly defined. To a large extent, it is only a procedural concept designed to facilitate the easy determination of the court of jurisdiction, while substantive law regarding the place of performance simply guides parties in paying their debts at the correct place, encourages performance in accordance with the terms of a contract, and helps to reduce disputes over the performance of a contract. For the litigation process, the 'place of performance' will be regarded as ambiguous if the contract merely provides for the jurisdiction of the court in the place of performance in the event of a dispute. According to Article 1 of the Beijing Higher People's Court Provisions on Several Issues concerning the Jurisdiction in Civil Procedures and Article 18(1) of the CPL Interpretation, 'if the place of performance has been agreed upon in the contract, the agreed place of performance shall be the place of performance of the contract'. But there will only be an 'agreed place of performance' where the 'place of performance of the contract' is expressly identified in the parties' contract. Contractual terms on the place of delivery, place of payment, and alternative places of performance of a contractual obligation cannot be the basis for determining the place of performance for the purpose of establishing jurisdiction. Therefore, an agreement that 'the court in the place of performance is to have jurisdiction' would be an unclear agreement and would not

[32] The CPL Interpretation provides as follows:

Article 18. If the contract stipulates the place of performance, the agreed place of performance shall be the place of performance. If the place of performance is not specified in the contract or the agreement is not clear and the subject of the dispute is the payment currency, the place of performance of the contract shall be the place where the party receiving the currency is located. If the real estate is delivered, the place where the real estate is located is the place where the contract is performed; For other subjects, the place where the party performing the obligation is located is the place where the contract is performed. For contracts that are settled immediately, the place of transaction is the place where the contract is performed. If the contract is not actually performed and both parties' domiciles are not in the place agreed upon in the contract, the jurisdiction of the people's court in the place where the defendant is domiciled shall be exercised.

Article 19. Property lease contracts and finance lease contracts shall be performed in the place where the leased property is used. If the contract has an agreement on the place of performance, the agreement shall prevail.

Article 20. If the subject matter of a sales contract concluded through an information network is delivered through the information network, the place of performance shall be the place of domicile of the buyer; If the subject matter is delivered by other means, the place of receipt is the place of performance of the contract. If the contract has an agreement on the place of performance, the agreement shall prevail.

Article 21. A lawsuit brought over a dispute over a property insurance contract may be under the jurisdiction of the people's court of the place where the transportation vehicle is registered, the transportation destination and the place where the insurance accident occurred if the subject matter of the insurance is the transportation vehicle or the goods in transit. A lawsuit brought over a dispute over a personal insurance contract may be under the jurisdiction of the people's court in the place where the insured is domiciled.

be sufficient to establish jurisdiction. By Article 30 of the CPL Interpretation, in the absence of a valid jurisdictional agreement, the provisions of the 1991 CPL would be applicable and suit should be commenced in the people's court where the defendant is domiciled.

Suppose now that the parties' agreement provides that 'either party may directly bring an action to the people's court in the place where the plaintiff is located'. It might be suggested that the clause is unclear, because it would not be possible at the time of contracting to know which party (if either) will be the plaintiff. If both parties sue at the same time, there would then be two courts having jurisdiction under the agreement. However, the agreement would be valid. Although the parties have potentially agreed on two or more courts having jurisdiction in the event of a dispute, according to the second paragraph of Article 30 of the CPL Interpretation, 'where two or more people's courts substantively related to a dispute are stipulated in a jurisdiction agreement, the plaintiff may file a lawsuit at any of such people's courts'.

B. Jurisdiction in Foreign-Related Tort Claims

With the development of science and technology and the deepening of international interactions, new types of rights infringement are constantly emerging. In addition to the traditional types of infringement, there are now maritime infringements, aviation infringements, product liability infringements, transnational network infringements, etc. In cases of foreign-related tortious disputes, the first step is to determine whether the infringement is a wrong relating to property rights. If so, CPL Article 265 on 'Special Territorial Jurisdiction' will apply. As for the other types of tortious infringement, the general rule (which applies to actions for damages from all torts and accidents) is that suit should be brought before the court in the place where the infringement occurred or where the defendant is domiciled. The place of infringement can either be the place where the act of infringement is committed or the place where the result of the infringement occurred.

Two specific cases worth further elaboration. For disputes over product quality (for example, a defective product that causes property or personal injury), the people's court in the place where the product is manufactured, sold, used, or where the defendant is domiciled has jurisdiction over a lawsuit brought. For reputation cases, the court in the place where the infringement occurred or where the defendant is domiciled has jurisdiction.

C. Jurisdiction in Intellectual Property Infringement Claims

For copyright infringement cases, the people's courts of the following places have jurisdiction: (1) the place where the infringement was committed; (2) the place where the infringing copies were stored (that is, the place where a large number of infringing copies are stored or hidden for business purposes); (3) the place where the seizure or detention took place (that is, the place where the customs, copyright, industry and commerce, and other administrative organs seize or detain infringing copies according to law); or (4) the place where the defendant is domiciled. The plaintiff may choose the court in the place where the infringement by one of the defendants is committed to have jurisdiction over the joint lawsuit brought against multiple defendants engaged in different places where the infringement is committed. The people's court of the place where the defendant's infringement was committed has jurisdiction only over the lawsuit against any one of the defendants.

For patent infringement cases, the people's court of the place where the infringement occurred or where the defendant is domiciled has jurisdiction. If the plaintiff only brings a lawsuit against the manufacturer of the infringing product instead of the seller, and the manufacturing site of the infringing product is inconsistent with the place of sale, the people's court for the manufacturing site shall have jurisdiction. If the manufacturer and the seller are co-defendants, the people's court at the place of sale shall have jurisdiction. If the seller is a manufacturing branch, the people's court at the place of sale has jurisdiction if the plaintiff sues the manufacturer of infringing products for manufacturing or selling.

For registered trademark infringement cases, the people's court of the place where the infringement was committed, the place where the infringing goods are stored, the place where the seizure was made, or the place where the defendant is domiciled has jurisdiction.

D. Jurisdiction in Foreign-Related Family Litigation

China's regulations on jurisdiction over foreign-related divorces are messy. There are two principal sources. The first comes from the CPL and the CPL Interpretation. The second is the Responses of the Supreme People's Court, that is, the Supreme Court's opinion on a particular case in response to questions raised by the lower courts. The CPL has no special provisions on jurisdiction over foreign-related divorces, but stipulates in Article 22:

> The people's court in the place where the plaintiff is domiciled shall have jurisdiction over lawsuits concerning identity relations brought against persons who do not reside within the territory of the People's Republic of China. If the domicile of the plaintiff is inconsistent with his habitual residence, the people's court of the plaintiff's habitual residence shall exercise jurisdiction.

Articles 13 to 17 of the CPL Interpretation regulates arrangements for jurisdiction over foreign-related divorces. However, those five Articles mainly cover parties with or without Chinese nationality. Their scope of application is narrow, and it cannot completely resolve the question of jurisdiction in foreign-related divorce cases where the parties have different nationalities. There is no uniform standard of jurisdiction. This situation therefore allows for the occurrence of parallel litigation. Further, China's divorce jurisdiction does not distinguish between divorce and the annulment of a nuptial relationship. The rules of jurisdiction apply to all issues of property distribution and child support in foreign-related divorce proceedings.

E. Jurisdiction in Cross-Border Corporate Bankruptcy Claims

Jurisdiction over cross-border corporate bankruptcy is a prerequisite for the commencement of cross-border corporate insolvency proceedings and an important guarantee for their smooth development.[33] The Enterprise Bankruptcy Law of the PRC, which came into effect on 1 June 2007, regulates the bankruptcy of enterprise legal persons in China. The previous provisions in this area of law and the corresponding judicial interpretations have been nullified by the CPL. Thus, the Enterprise Bankruptcy Law now provides a complete code on matters of corporate

[33] Minmin Liu, 'Reconstruction of China's Cross-border Bankruptcy Jurisdiction Distribution System' [2016] 2 *Daqing Social Science* 39.

insolvency. Article 3 of that statute covers jurisdiction in domestic and cross-border insolvency cases. According to the Article, domestic and cross-border bankruptcy cases are under the jurisdiction of the people's court of the debtor's domicile. The debtor's domicile is the place where its main office is located according to the CPL Interpretation. If that cannot be determined, the court in the place where the legal person is registered will have jurisdiction. It can be seen that cross-border bankruptcy jurisdiction in China applies the single standard of 'debtor's domicile'. Once established, a court's jurisdiction in bankruptcy will cover all of a debtor's asset, wherever in the world they may be situated.

In the future, China will likely join cross-border insolvency treaties and cooperate with other countries on cross-border bankruptcy jurisdiction.

F. Jurisdiction in Competition Law Claims

For anti-monopoly civil litigation cases, China currently applies the ordinary rules of jurisdiction. The specific jurisdiction provisions are mainly reflected in the Judicial Interpretation of the Supreme People's Court on the Application of Law in the Trial of Civil Disputes Caused by Monopolistic Acts, which was formally implemented on 1 June 2012. According to Article 1 of this Judicial Interpretation:

> The civil disputes caused by monopoly (hereinafter referred to as monopoly civil disputes) mentioned in these provisions refer to civil litigation cases brought to the people's court by natural persons, legal persons, or other organisations who have suffered losses from monopoly and who are engaged in disputes arising from the violation of anti-monopoly laws. …

Article 3 of the Judicial Interpretation sets out jurisdictional rules at different levels. In first instance civil disputes, jurisdiction is to be exercised by the intermediate people's court in: (1) the city where the government of a province, autonomous region, or municipality is located; or (2) a city specifically designated in an operative State Plan. Cases may also be brought before an intermediate people's court designated by the SPC. With the approval of the SPC, the basic people's court may have first instance jurisdiction in civil disputes relating to monopolies. Article 4 of the Judicial Interpretation contains provisions on regional jurisdiction. That is typically determined according to the specific circumstances of a case, civil procedure law, and judicial interpretations of jurisdiction in tort, contract and analogous disputes. As to the jurisdiction of the Chinese courts over conduct overseas that has the effect of restricting competition, there is currently no legal provision.

VI. Immunities from Jurisdiction[34]

Jurisdictional immunity reflects the principle of state sovereignty in international civil procedure. It refers to the principle that the state cannot be a defendant in a foreign court or that state-owned property cannot be the object of actions in a foreign court.[35] China lacks explicit legislation to

[34] This section is largely derived from Jianping Shi and Zijun Zhai, 'Immunities from Jurisdiction' in Xiaohong Liu and Zhengyi Zhang (eds), *Chinese Private International Law* (Oxford, Hart Publishing, 2021).

[35] Depei Han and Yongping Xiao, *Private International Law* 1st edn (Beijing, People's Court Press and China Social Science Press, 2004) 34.

determine the civil status of foreign states before China's courts, that is, whether and to what extent foreign states enjoy immunity from jurisdiction. CPL Article 261 only provides that:

> Civil actions instituted against foreign nationals, foreign organisations, or international organisations which enjoy diplomatic privileges or immunities shall be governed by the relevant laws of the People's Republic of China and the international treaties concluded or acceded to by the People's Republic of China.

A. Sovereign Immunity

China is one of the countries that insists on absolute sovereign immunity. This position has been repeatedly affirmed by its Central Government on various occasions.[36] On 16 December 2004, the UN General Assembly adopted the Convention on Jurisdictional Immunities of States and Their Property (the Immunity Convention). Its preamble states that the principle of jurisdictional immunity of states and their property is 'a generally accepted principle of customary international law'. Article 6 of the Immunity Convention additionally makes it clear that 'a state shall refrain from exercising jurisdiction in its courts over proceedings brought by another state'. However, Article 5 of the Immunity Convention provides that a state and its property enjoy immunity from jurisdiction in the courts of another state in accordance with the provisions of the Immunity Convention. Part III of the Immunity Convention qualifies that a state and its property shall not enjoy immunity in eight situations, including commercial transactions.[37] On 14 September 2005 the then Chinese Foreign Minister Li Zhaoxing signed the Immunity Convention on behalf of the Chinese Government. This has been taken by some observers as signalling that China is switching to a restrictive approach in relation to the application of the principle of state immunity. However, in *FG Hemisphere Associates v Democratic Republic of Congo*,[38] the Hong Kong Court of Final Appeal (CFA), before deciding on the issue of state immunity, ruled that a reference had to be made to the Standing Committee of the National People's Congress (NPC) pursuant to Article 158 of the Basic Law of Hong Kong. As the Standing Committee of the NPC is China's national legislature, its legislative decisions have the legal status of national law. The Standing Committee of the NPC gave its answer by issuing a legislative interpretation on 26 August 2011, clarifying that 'state immunity concerns whether the courts of a state have jurisdiction over foreign states and their properties', and 'directly relates to the state's foreign relations and international rights and obligations'. Thus, as the issue of sovereign immunity falls within the realm of foreign affairs, the Chinese Central Government has the power to decide on this issue and Hong Kong courts are bound to follow the PRC's practice in adopting the absolute approach. Consequently, the CFA formally disposed of the case by allowing the appeal by the Congo on 8 September 2011. Some scholars believe that this position of the Chinese Government is not only inconsistent with international trends, but also inconsistent with its own practice.[39] Some scholars believe that the *FG Hemisphere* has firmly situated the application of state immunity

[36] *Russell Jackson v People's Republic of China* 794 F 2d 1490 (11th Cir 1986) 1494. See also the Memorandum sent by the Chinese Embassy in Washington DC in *Morris v People's Republic of China* 478 F Supp 2d 561 (SDNY 2007).

[37] The eight situations are: Commercial transactions, Contracts of employment, Personal injuries and damages to property; Ownership possession and use of property; Intellectual and industrial property; Participation in companies or other collective bodies; Ships owned or operated by a State; Effect of an arbitration agreement.

[38] *Democratic Republic of the Congo v FG Hemisphere Associates LLC (No 1)* (2011) 14 HKCFAR 95. See also *Democratic Republic of the Congo v FG Hemisphere Associates LLC (No 2)* (2011) 14 HKCFAR 395.

[39] Yilin Ding, 'Absolute, Restrictive, or Something More: Did Beijing Choose the Right Type of Sovereign Immunity for Hong Kong?' (2012) 26 *Emory International Law Review* 997.

rules within the 'one country, two systems' context and thereby ensured that China as a whole speaks with one voice on the matter. However, considering that it is not necessarily disadvantageous for China to adopt restrictive immunity, China may consider changing its position in the future.[40] Therefore, it is still too early to conclude that China has abandoned the doctrine of absolute immunity and instead chosen to embrace a restrictive approach along the lines of the Immunity Convention. It should be noted in this connection that the Standing Committee of the NPC has yet to ratify the Immunity Convention and there is nothing to suggest that it will be doing so in the foreseeable future.

B. Jurisdictional Immunity of State-Owned Enterprises

China has always adhered to the international law principle that a state and its property enjoy immunity. Therefore, Chinese law distinguishes between actions of a state from those of state-owned enterprises. It holds that state-owned enterprises are economic entities with independent legal status and do not enjoy immunity. However, there are still many cases in which Chinese state-owned enterprises claim that they are 'part of state institutions' and so enjoy jurisdictional immunity. For instance, in *Animal Science Products Inc v China Minmetals Corp*,[41] sovereign immunity was a defence raised by Chinese state-owned Minmetals. The US court recognised Minmetals as China's 'agency or media'. But the court ruled out the application of sovereign immunity on the basis that Minmetals was engaged in commercial transactions. The Immunity Convention adopts the principle of restrictive immunity. With regard to sovereign immunity, a 'state' in Article 2 of the Convention includes:

(1) various organs of the state and its government;
(2) constituent units or political branches of the state that have the right to exercise sovereign power and act in that capacity;
(3) agencies or media or other entities of the state, which have the right to exercise and are actually exercising the sovereign rights of the state; and,
(4) representatives acting in the capacity of state representatives.

According to the principle of *par in parem imperium non habet*, the most important feature of persons who enjoy sovereign immunity is the exercise of state power. Therefore, it is only when state-owned enterprises exercise sovereign power that they can be protected by sovereign immunity. Only at that point are the sovereign immunity exceptions taken into consideration. In the future, China should further define the jurisdictional immunity of state-owned enterprises and highlight they are normally independent from the state. However, when state-owned enterprises are authorised to engage in governmental or managerial activities on behalf of the state, their sovereign immunity should be recognised.

VII. Future

The 20th Diplomatic Conference of the Hague Conference on Private International Law adopted the 2005 Hague Convention on Choice of Court Agreements (the 2005 Hague Convention) on

[40] Yujun Guo and Yuanyuan Liu, 'On the case of *FG Hemisphere Associates LLC v Democratic Republic of the Congo and Others*' [2012] 2 *Law of the Times* 10.
[41] *Animal Science Products Inc v China Minmetals Corp* 654 F 3d 462 (3rd Cir 2011).

30 June 2005. The instrument came into force on 1 October 2015. It gives detailed provisions on the recognition and enforcement of: (1) choice of court agreements designating a specific court to decide disputes arising under an international commercial contract; and (2) the judgments of the court so designated. The adoption of the Convention marks a great step forward by the international community in the process of the unification of international private law.[42]

On 12 September 2017, China signed the 2005 Hague Convention. China actively participated in the negotiation and drafting of the 2005 Hague Convention. It is anticipated that China will soon ratify the Convention,[43] to which there are currently 32 contracting states (including the EU as a Regional Economic Integration Organisation (REIO). Acceding to the 2005 Hague Convention should improve China's consensual jurisdiction system.[44] It also demonstrates that China is moving closer to the center of the world stage and becoming a pivotal force in the international community, evolving from an adapting and integrating role to an influencing and shaping role.

From the perspective of China's long-term interests, the ratification of the 2005 Hague Convention helps promote the transnational execution of Chinese court judgments, the perfection of the agreement jurisdiction system, and the recognition and implementation of the judgments system, which also in turn enhances China's competitiveness in international civil and commercial dispute settlement market (including the international commercial arbitration system), promotes the realisation of the 'Belt and Road' initiative and builds a 'community with a shared future for mankind'.[45]

VIII. Conclusion

China has established a system on direct jurisdiction by stipulations on CPL and SMPL, together with related judicial interpretations. Discussions still exist in legal practice especially on the connecting factors of agreed jurisdiction, requirements for *forum non conveniens* etc. China has also been participating in the negotiations of the Hague Conventions and signed the 2005 Hague Convention on Choice of Court Agreements. In the context of economic globalization, direct jurisdiction in China in the field of civil and commercial filed will be further developed and improved along with the judicial practice.

[42] Guojian Xu, 'Establishing a Uniform International System of Jurisdiction and Recognition and Enforcement of Foreign Judgments – Comments on the Hague Convention on Choice of Court Agreements' [2005] 5 *Present Day Law Science* 16.

[43] Jianli Song, 'Choice of Court Convention and its Influence to China' [2019] 4 *People's Judiciary* 107.

[44] For a detailed analysis of the positive and negative impacts of the 2005 Hague Convention on China, see Jianping Shi and Zijun Zhai, 'Jurisdiction *in Personam*' in Xiaohong Liu and Zhengyi Zhang (eds), *Chinese Private International Law* (Oxford, Hart Publishing, 2021).

[45] See also Yongping Xiao, 'The Pros and Cons of Ratifying the Convention on Choice of Court Agreements and China's Countermeasures' [2017] 5 *Wuhan University International Law Review* 16.

3

Hong Kong

JAMES Y P WONG

I. Overview

Hong Kong is a unique jurisdiction. It practices the common law system under the Chinese sovereign which has a civil law system, under the 'one country, two systems' principle. The laws of Hong Kong, which derived from English law, continue to evolve. Its jurisdictional rules are established by the Basic Law (Hong Kong's constitutional document), ordinances, common law and rules of court.[1] This chapter will outline the rules and principles by which the Hong Kong court determines its jurisdiction, with a focus on international or cross-border cases.

A. Foundation of the Hong Kong Courts' Jurisdiction

The jurisdiction of Hong Kong courts is founded on the Basic Law,[2] which came into effect on 1 July 1997, when the United Kingdom (UK) returned the sovereignty of Hong Kong to the People's Republic of China (PRC).

Article 19 of the Basic Law provides that:

> … The courts of the Hong Kong Special Administrative Region shall have jurisdiction over all cases in the Region, except that the restrictions of their jurisdiction imposed by the legal system and principles previously in force in Hong Kong shall be maintained. The courts of the Hong Kong Special Administrative Region shall have no jurisdiction over acts of state such as defence and foreign affairs. …

The 'legal system and principles previously in force' mean, respectively, the English common law system, and 'the common law, rules of equity, ordinances, subordinate legislation and customary law' which were in force during the colonial times. These shall be maintained unless it contravenes the Basic Law and are subject to amendments by the legislature.[3]

[1] In this chapter, references to the Orders of the Rules of Court ('Ord') refer to the Rules of the High Court (Cap 4A). The High Court is the major Court in Hong Kong which adjudicates on cross-border or international cases.

[2] Basic Law, Arts 2, 19, 85.

[3] Basic Law, Art 8.

B. Subject Matter Jurisdiction and Personal Jurisdiction

In common law, there are two components of jurisdiction. The first is 'subject matter jurisdiction' over the matter in dispute. The second is 'personal jurisdiction' over the parties.[4] The court requires both components in order to assume jurisdiction over a particular case.

As the law confers jurisdiction on the court, it also sets limits to its judicial power. Subject matter jurisdiction refers to the boundary of judicial competence and judicial power,[5] which is also described as the outer limits of the competence of a court.[6] Such limits are prescribed by the constitutional documents, ordinances, rules of court and common law. For instance, Article 19 of the Basic Law expressly excludes the Hong Kong court's jurisdiction over 'acts of state' such as defence and foreign affairs. An example is the law on state immunity. As the Court of Final Appeal (Hong Kong's highest appellate court) confirmed in the *Congo* case, state immunity is a matter of foreign affairs for the PRC Central People's Government to decide.[7] Second, ordinances and court rules delineate the court's judicial power. The High Court Ordinance (Cap 4) and the Rules of the High Court (Cap 4A) are the general source of the High Court's statutory jurisdiction, among other specific ordinances and subsidiary legislation. Third, the common law regulates the court's power over certain subject matters. There are traditional rules which restrict the court from determining the title to foreign land, the validity of foreign intellectual property rights, or the enforcement of foreign penal, revenue or other public laws.[8] Some of those rules have been modified or cast into doubt, which are discussed below. These restrictions in common law reflect the self-imposed restraints by judges when, for example, asked to wind up a foreign company[9] or bankrupt a foreign individual.[10]

Apart from the court's power over the subject matter, the court requires personal jurisdiction over the parties in a particular case. Personal jurisdiction lies in the heart of most jurisdictional disputes. Common law bases personal jurisdiction on service.[11] Service refers to the giving of notice of the court process to the parties according to the court rules. If there is valid service, the court will assert jurisdiction. This reflects the court's judicial power over all those who are present in the territory. It has been observed that the rules relating to the court's jurisdiction are 'purely procedural' in character.[12] Service within the jurisdiction is 'as of right', which generally does not require prior permission (called 'leave' in Hong Kong) from the court.[13] If the defendant cannot be served in Hong Kong, the law generally requires the plaintiff to apply for prior leave from the court before making service abroad. The plaintiff needs to satisfy several requirements and convince the court to exercise its long-arm jurisdiction. Furthermore, some defendants enjoy immunities from the court's jurisdiction. Those include sovereignty immunity, crown immunity, and diplomatic immunity (see Section IV below).

[4] Adrian Briggs, *The Conflict of Laws* 4th edn (London, Oxford University Press, 2019) 44.

[5] Albert HY Chen, 'The Concept of Justiciability and the Jurisdiction of the Hong Kong Courts' (1997) 27 *Hong Kong Law Journal* 387.

[6] Adrian Briggs and Peter Rees, *Civil Jurisdiction and Judgments* 5th edn (London, Informa Law, 2009) para 4.05.

[7] *Democratic Republic of the Congo v FG Hemisphere Associates LLC (No 1)* (2011) 14 HKCFAR 95 [321]–[331]. See Section IV.A below.

[8] Briggs and Rees (n 6) paras 4.06–4.08.

[9] *Kam Leung Sui Kwan v Kam Kwan Lai* (2015) 18 HKCFAR 501.

[10] *Re Dai Guoliang* [2019] 2 HKLRD 332, [2019] HKCFI 597.

[11] Briggs (n 4) 46.

[12] *Hong Kong Civil Procedure 2021* (Hong Kong, Sweet and Maxwell, 2020) ('White Book') para 10/0/2.

[13] There are exceptions, for example, that leave of the court is required for service of process on Sunday in case of urgency: Ord 65, r 10.

In comparison, as subject matter jurisdiction is provided by law, the parties cannot confer it on the court, unless the law empowers the parties to do so.[14] If the court lacks subject matter jurisdiction for any reason, the court will have no judicial power in any event. By contrast, parties can confer personal jurisdictional on the court, as the law enables them to. For example, where service is invalid, the parties can submit to the court's jurisdiction. Submission can cure defective service and establish the court's personal jurisdiction over the parties. Similarly, a party who is entitled to immunity can waive his immunity before the court and submit to its jurisdiction.

II. General Principles on Jurisdiction

This section will look at the basic rules and principles on jurisdiction. We will start with how a plaintiff invokes the court's jurisdiction by applying for pre-action reliefs. We will then explain how he can commence a court proceeding, by service in Hong Kong or abroad. After that, we will shift our focus to the defendant. He may submit to the court's jurisdiction, challenge it, or admit the court's jurisdiction but ask the court to stay the proceedings. We will examine two major grounds for an application for stay, which are the existence of a foreign jurisdictional agreement and *forum non conveniens*. We will also explore the court's power to make an anti-suit injunction, which restrains a party from pursuing foreign proceedings. Finally, service of foreign proceedings in Hong Kong will be discussed.

A. Applying for Pre-action Reliefs

The first opportunity for a plaintiff (or an intended one) to invoke the court's jurisdiction is to apply for a pre-action relief. The court's jurisdiction is conferred by statute, which empowers the court to grant interlocutory or interim reliefs including pre-action reliefs.[15] Common examples are interlocutory injunction, disclosure order, appointment of a receiver, etc. An application can be made before[16] or after commencement of proceedings, with or without notice to the defendant,[17] depending on the circumstances in each case.

In the cross-border context, two points should be noted. First, an intended plaintiff can apply for the relief against a foreign defendant. When he makes his application, he should also seek leave to serve on the defendant out of jurisdiction, pursuant to Order 11, rule 1(1)(b).[18] Failure to apply for and obtain leave to serve out (in addition to applying for the relief itself) may risk the interlocutory injunction being set aside in future.[19]

[14] As in *Champion Concord Ltd v Lau Koon Foo (No 2)* (2011) 14 HKCFAR 837 [3]–[4].

[15] High Court Ordinance (Cap 4), ss 21L, 21M, 21N; and others, eg Evidence Ordinance (Cap 8), s 21 for a third party disclosure order. See also Ord 29 and various Practice Directions of the High Court.

[16] Ord 29, r 1. An action before action is usually confined to a 'case of urgency': Ord 29, r 1(2).

[17] The applicant should carefully consider the timing of his application and whether to notify the respondent. If he inappropriately invokes an urgent procedure, or unreasonably fails to notify the other party, he may be criticised by the court (*Re New China Hong Kong Highway Ltd* HCCW 550/2009 (29 September 2009) [9] (Kwan JA)) or find his application refused (eg *Goliath Far East Ltd v Teng Fei Run Trade Ltd* [2019] 4 HKLRD 282, [2019] HKCFI 1959, in which a disclosure order application was initially refused when notice was not given to the respondent bank).

[18] See Section II.C below on an application for service out.

[19] *China Shanshui Cement Group Ltd v Mi Jingtian* [2018] HKCFI 1553 [182]–[191].

Second, the court may make the relief to assist foreign proceedings, even before they are commenced.[20] This is known as a 'free-standing' interim relief, which does not require a substantive cause of action in Hong Kong. For example, an intended plaintiff may apply for a *Mareva* injunction[21] to support existing or prospective foreign proceedings. The court exercises control[22] by requiring the applicant to show that: (1) if he succeeds in the foreign proceedings, the resultant judgment is one that the Hong Kong court will enforce;[23] (2) a good arguable case before the foreign court, and a real risk that the defendant will dissipate his assets if the *Mareva* injunction is not granted (which are the two requirements for a 'usual' *Mareva*); and (3) even if the court has no jurisdiction apart from section 21M, this does not make it unjust or inconvenient for the court to grant the *Mareva* injunction. Where the defendant cannot be served in Hong Kong, the plaintiff should additionally apply for leave of service out under Order 11, rule 1(1)(oc).

B. Commencing a Proceeding by Service within Hong Kong

Court proceedings are commenced when a party serves the originating process on the other party or parties. Typically, in an action *in personam*, the plaintiff needs to serve a Writ of Summons on the defendant. He can make service in Hong Kong 'as of right'. Service is the key to unlocking the court's jurisdiction. The court can assert judicial power over anyone validly served within the territory.[24]

Therefore, a foreigner who happens to be in Hong Kong and is properly served with a writ will become amenable to the court's jurisdiction,[25] however brief his presence may be.[26] Service can be valid even if the defendant refuses to accept the court document. It is sufficient if the process server 'leaves' the document with him and tells him that it is a legal document which requires his attention.[27] There is an exception if the defendant was induced by fraud to enter into the jurisdiction, for the concealed purpose of making service on him.[28]

If a defendant has an address in Hong Kong, service can be effected by sending the originating process to his usual or last known address,[29] or by insertion through the letterbox of that address in a sealed envelope addressed to the defendant.[30] For service to be effective, the actual knowledge of the defendant is necessary. The defendant need not be physically present within the jurisdiction at the precise moment when the originating process was sent

[20] Cap 4, s 21M.

[21] A *Mareva* injunction is a freezing order which prohibits a defendant within or outside Hong Kong from disposing of his assets, with the object of facilitating the enforcement of a potential future judgment against him.

[22] See *Compania Sud Americana de Vapores SA v Hin-Pro International Logistics Ltd* (2016) 19 HKCFAR 586 [53]–[54] (Lord Phillips NPJ), applied in *Gatecoin Ltd v BD Multimedia HK Ltd* [2019] HKCFI 2025; *Jiang Xi An Fa Da Wine Co Ltd v Zhan King* [2019] HKCFI 2411.

[23] On enforcement of foreign judgments in Hong Kong, see James YP Wong, 'Hong Kong' in Anselmo Reyes (ed), *Recognition and Enforcement of Judgments in Civil and Commercial Matters* (Oxford, Hart Publishing, 2019) 51–84.

[24] *John Russell and Co Ltd v Cayzer, Irvine and Co Ltd* [1916] 2 AC 298 (HL) 302 (Viscount Haldane).

[25] *Colt Industries Inc v Sarlie* [1966] 1 WLR 440.

[26] The English court described the founding of jurisdiction by service on an individual during his brief visit to the country as 'extravagant'. If the defendant later challenges jurisdiction, the court may not be prepared to assist the plaintiff by refusing a stay application: *Connelly v RTZ Corp plc* [1998] AC 854 (HL) 873 (Lord Goff).

[27] *Dynasty Line Ltd v Sukamto Sia* [2009] 4 HKLRD 454 [20]–[26] (Cheung JA).

[28] Michael Wilkinson, Eric TM Cheung and Gary Meggitt, *Civil Procedure in Hong Kong* 6th edn (Hong Kong, LexisNexis, 2017) para 5–11, citing *Watkins v North American Land and Timber Co Ltd* (1904) 20 TLR 534.

[29] Ord 10, r 1(2)(a).

[30] ibid, r 1(2)(b).

or placed through the letterbox. Service will take effect when the defendant's presence and actual knowledge coincide.[31]

Other common methods of service include service by an agreed method, for example on a process agent.[32] Service can also be made on the defendant's solicitor who accepts service,[33] which is effective even if the defendant is outside the jurisdiction.[34] If ordinary service methods are 'impracticable for any reason',[35] a plaintiff can apply for a court order for substituted service, such as by advertisement.

For partnerships, service on a foreign firm depends on whether it has partners or a place of business in Hong Kong. Service can be effected: (1) on any one or more of the partners; (2) at the principal place of business of the partnership in Hong Kong, on any person having at the time of service the control or management of the partnership business there; or (3) by sending a copy of originating process by registered post to the firm at the principal place of business of the partnership in Hong Kong.[36] Thus, a plaintiff was able to serve on a New York-registered defendant firm by serving on its 'resident partners' in Hong Kong, as the New York firm had carried on business in Hong Kong for years by performing engagements here.[37] If a foreign firm cannot be served in Hong Kong, the plaintiff will need to apply for leave to serve out of the jurisdiction.[38]

Service on companies and in specific actions will be discussed in Section III below.

C. Applying for Leave to Serve Out of Hong Kong

If a defendant cannot be served in Hong Kong, the plaintiff needs to serve him out of the jurisdiction. This generally requires prior leave from the court under Order 11.[39] The application is usually made without notice to the defendant. A Court Master will determine the application on paper without a hearing, but he may make written requisitions to the plaintiff. If he decides to grant leave, the plaintiff can serve on the defendant in accordance with the court order.

It was said that the court's power to allow service out was an 'exorbitant jurisdiction' which should not be 'exercised lightly',[40] and that service abroad was an 'interference with the sovereignty' of the foreign state.[41] In *Kayden Ltd v Securities and Futures Commission*,[42] the Court of Final Appeal advocated a strict approach towards Order 11 applications, in view of their 'extraordinary nature'. Recent cases tend to adopt a milder tone. The court recognises that the decision is generally a pragmatic one in the interests of the efficient conduct of litigation in an appropriate

[31] *Barclays Bank of Swaziland v Hahn* [1989] 1 WLR 506.
[32] Ord 10, r 3.
[33] ibid, r 1(4).
[34] Wilkinson, Cheung and Meggitt (n 28) para 5–42, citing *Manta Line Inc v Seraphim Sofianites* [1984] 1 Lloyd's Rep 14.
[35] Ord 65, r 4.
[36] Ord 81, r 3(1).
[37] *China Medical Technologies Inc (in liq) v Paul, Weiss, Rifkind, Wharton & Garrison LLP (a firm)* [2019] HKCFI 2631 [33]–[36], [103]–[106].
[38] See *Excelsior Capital Asia (HK) Ltd v Zhang Hengshun* [2018] HKCFI 181 [2]–[3].
[39] For exceptions, see Wilkinson, Cheung and Meggitt (n 28) para 5–169; *Hong Kong Civil Procedure 2021* (n 12) para 11/1/1.
[40] *Tay Choo Wah v The Singapore-Johore Express (Pte) Ltd* [1992] 1 HKLR 19, 32.
[41] *Cecil v Bayat* [2011] EWCA Civ 135, [2011] 1 WLR 3086 [65].
[42] *Kayden Ltd v Securities and Futures Commission* (2010) 13 HKCFAR 696 [36]–[37] (Ribeiro PJ).

forum.[43] That said, it would be safe for parties to make any service out application with great care, and anticipate that the court will look at it strictly.[44]

The plaintiff will need to show three things.[45] First, there is a good arguable case that his case comes within at least one of the heads under Order 11, rule 1(1), which are also known as 'gateways' to jurisdiction. The requirement is to show a 'strong case for argument', though not necessarily that he is 'probably right'.[46] But he needs to demonstrate more than a prima facie case.[47] Second, there is a serious issue to be tried on the merits of the case. This means the threshold on merits is lower than that on jurisdiction under the first requirement.[48] Third, Hong Kong is the appropriate forum under the *forum non conveniens* principle for the trial of the action.[49] Crucially, since the application is made in the defendant's absence, the plaintiff has a duty to make 'full and frank disclosure' to the court, pointing to any facts, evidence and arguments which the defendant would make. Material non-disclosure can cause the leave to be set aside.

A defendant served outside the jurisdiction may apply to the court for an order setting aside the prior leave for service, under Order 12, rule 8. The burden will remain on the plaintiff to show the above three matters.

There are 19 gateways to jurisdiction under Order 11, rule 1(1). References to a particular 'Head (*x*)' below are to Order 11, rule 1(1)(*x*). We will further investigate some of these Heads in Section III below. They define the claims for which the court may grant leave. Order 11 forms an entire code on service out, such that any gaps cannot be filled by the court's inherent powers.[50]

The methods of effecting service out of jurisdiction are set out in Order 11, rules 5–7A. These methods include personal service,[51] service on the defendant's solicitors,[52] by acknowledgment of service,[53] substituted service, service in accordance with contractual terms upon prior leave from the court,[54] service in accordance with the laws of the country in which the defendant is to be served,[55] service pursuant to the Hague Service Convention[56] or other 'Civil Procedure Convention' relating to service under Order 11, rule 6(2), or in accordance with any agreement between the Hong Kong Government and other jurisdictions.[57] There are special rules for service on a foreign state, or in certain actions under the Carriage by Air Ordinance (Cap 500), which are provided in Order 11, rules 7 and 7A.

[43] *Abela v Baadarani* [2013] UKSC 44, [2013] 1 WLR 2043 [53] (Lord Sumption JSC), cited with approval in *Deutsche Bank AG, Hong Kong Branch v Zhang Hong Li* [2016] 3 HKLRD 303 [74] (Kwan JA).

[44] *Chen Hongqing v Persons Whose Names Are Set Out in the Second Column of the Schedule to the Re-Amended Writ of Summons Filed on 26 March 2018* [2019] HKCFI 2121 [58]–[60].

[45] *Seaconsar Far East Ltd v Bank Markazi Jomhouri Islami Iran* [1994] 1 AC 438 (HL); *Dynasty Line* (n 27); *Chen Hongqing* (n 44).

[46] Graeme Johnston and Paul Harris, *The Conflict of Laws in Hong Kong* 3rd edn (Hong Kong, Sweet and Maxwell, 2017) para 3.057.

[47] Wilkinson, Cheung and Meggitt (n 28) para 5–112.

[48] ibid, para 5–153.

[49] See Section II.D.ii below.

[50] *Re Sunni International Ltd* [2014] 5 HKLRD 558 [63]–[64] (G Lam J).

[51] Ord 11, r 5(1), applying Ord 10, r 1(1).

[52] ibid, applying Ord 10, r 1(4).

[53] ibid, applying Ord 10, r 1(5).

[54] Ord 10, rr 3(1)(b), 3(2).

[55] Ord 11, r 5(3)(a).

[56] The 1965 Hague Convention on the Service Abroad of Judicial and Extrajudicial Documents in Civil or Commercial Matters.

[57] See eg the memorandum of agreement on the mutual service of judicial documents signed between the PRC Government and the Hong Kong Government, which is given effect by Ord 11, rr 5A, 8A, and Ord 69.

D. Disputing the Court's Jurisdiction

Now, we turn to consider the defendant. When served with a writ, he has three major options. The first is to acknowledge service and contest the claim. Alternatively, if he thinks the court lacks jurisdiction or should not exercise it, he can dispute the court's jurisdiction. The court rules require him to acknowledge service and lodge his jurisdictional challenge under Order 12, rule 8. Third, he can take no action at all. The obvious risk is that a judgment will be made against him at some point, which the plaintiff may enforce against him. But the more immediate problem can be interim reliefs which the Hong Kong court may grant against him. Thus, a properly advised defendant (especially with assets in Hong Kong liable for enforcement) will usually choose one of the first two options.

There are two different types of jurisdictional disputes. The first is to challenge the court's jurisdiction, which means the court does not have judicial competence. For example, the service was invalid, or the prior leave for service out should be set aside, or the court lacks subject matter jurisdiction. If the court so finds, the proceedings will terminate and cannot revive (unless the court's decision is overturned on appeal). The second type of dispute is to admit that the court has jurisdiction, but to ask the court not to exercise it. For example, there is an alternative and more appropriate forum which the court should defer to. If the court agrees, it will stay the proceedings, which is temporary in nature and may be granted upon terms.[58] The stay may be lifted by the court in future, and proceedings will resume.

There are several major grounds for a stay application: (1) the existence of a foreign jurisdiction agreement; (2) the existence of a more appropriate forum (*forum non conveniens*); (3) the existence of parallel foreign court proceedings (*lis alibi pendens*) – this used to be an independent ground of stay, but is now treated as one of the factors to be considered in the *forum non conveniens* exercise;[59] and (4) the existence of an arbitration agreement,[60] which is out of the scope of this chapter. We will focus on the first two grounds.

Notably, a defendant who has decided to dispute jurisdiction must be careful and refrain from any action which may constitute 'submission' to the jurisdiction. Submission will preclude him from disputing the court's jurisdiction in future, thereby confirming the court's jurisdiction. The court will adopt a common sense approach to assess whether there is submission. The test is 'whether a party's conduct is so inconsistent with maintaining an option to challenge forum that the party should be assumed to have waived such option'.[61] In order to constitute submission, the defendant's acts must be 'wholly unequivocal'.[62] If there is any doubt, the party proposing to challenge the forum will be given the benefit of the doubt. Typical examples of submission include filing or serving a defence, making an interlocutory application (except a jurisdictional dispute),[63] or taking other positive interlocutory activities.[64] It is therefore

[58] As in *China Construction Bank (Asia) Corp Ltd v Shanghai Pudong Development Bank Co Ltd* CACV 14/2016 (3 February 2017) [9.2] (Cheung JA).

[59] ibid [5.2] (Cheung JA), affirmed by the Court of Final Appeal in *Changhong Group (HK) Ltd v Bright Shipping Ltd* [2020] HKCFA 24 [10] (Fok PJ).

[60] Arbitration Ordinance (Cap 609), s 20(1), which gives effect to Art 8 of the 2006 UNCITRAL Model Law on International Commercial Arbitration, provides for the general principle that the court before which an action is brought in a matter subject to arbitration shall, if a party so requests, stay the proceedings and refer the parties to arbitration.

[61] *Hwoo Huang Linda v Fu Being San* [2013] 1 HKLRD 259 [26] (DHCJ Reyes).

[62] *Chan Hon v Bayer Healthcare Ltd* [2020] HKCA 1090 [4.3], [4.45] (Cheung JA).

[63] Ord 12, r 8(6).

[64] Johnston and Harris (n 46) paras 3.009–3.026.

good practice for the defendant, or his legal representatives, to expressly reserve the right to dispute jurisdiction.[65]

i. *Seeking a Stay Based on a Foreign Jurisdiction Clause*

If the parties have agreed on a jurisdiction clause, the court tends to hold them to their contractual bargain.[66] The court will start with construing the clause to determine its validity, scope and effect. It will apply the proper law of the agreement which contains the clause.[67] If it is governed by a foreign law, the court may require foreign legal expert opinion.[68] There are two common types of jurisdiction clauses: exclusive and non-exclusive. Both would provide that the parties agree to submit to the exclusive or non-exclusive jurisdiction of the chosen jurisdiction. The court applies the same principle to both types of clauses, for the purpose of a stay application.[69] If they have agreed to submit to a foreign forum, the court requires the plaintiff to demonstrate 'strong or overwhelming reasons', 'strong causes' or 'exceptional circumstances' for not granting a stay.[70] It will not be a matter of weighing up the connecting factors to determine whether there exists another forum which is more appropriate. The court described the approach as akin to the situation where a plaintiff has instituted proceedings 'as of right' (by service within jurisdiction), which means the court will not 'lightly disturb' the parties' agreed choice of jurisdiction.[71]

An example of 'strong reason' is the existence of factors not contemplated by the parties when they made the jurisdiction agreement,[72] although this is not an absolute requirement.[73] Another possible reason is the existence of multiple jurisdiction clauses in related contracts pointing to different jurisdictions. The court may decline to enforce one (or some) of the jurisdiction clauses to 'canalise' the dispute in one jurisdiction.[74] More recently, the court accepted the lack of credible defence as the reason for refusing a stay application based on an exclusive jurisdiction clause.[75]

ii. *Stay of Proceedings Due to* forum non conveniens

A typical ground for a stay application is to contend that there is another, more appropriate forum for determining the case than the Hong Kong court. The doctrine of *forum non conveniens* was

[65] As the Defendants' solicitors did in *Lehmanbrown Ltd v Union Trade Holdings* HCMP 775/2012 (18 February 2015).

[66] *Unterweser Reederei GmbH v Zapata Off-shore Co (The Chaparral)* [1968] 2 Lloyd's Rep 158.

[67] If the agreement does not have an express governing law clause, the court will ascertain if the parties have made any implied choice of law; if not, it will apply the 'closest and most real' connection test to ascertain the proper law of the agreement.

[68] *Hong Ziyun v Chan Kwan Ming* [2019] HKLRD 405, [2019] HKCFI 2125.

[69] *Noble Power Investments Ltd v Nissei Stomach Tokyo Co Ltd* [2008] 5 HKLRD 631 [29] (Ma CJHC), followed in *Chinachem Financial Services Ltd v Century Venture Holdings Ltd* HCA 410/2013 (8 January 2015) [84]–[85] (DHCJ Marlene Ng).

[70] *Madison Communications Private Ltd v Le Ecosystem Technology India Private Ltd* [2017] 5 HKLRD 284; *Deltatre SPA v Hong Kong Sports Industrial Development Ltd* [2018] 4 HKLRD 478, [2018] HKCFI 1942 [41]–[46] (Master Benny Lo); *天津市裕豐隆資產管理有限公司 v Ho Kin Wa* [2019] HKCFI 556 [26] (DHCJ Paul Lam SC); *Li Lian International Ltd v Herport Hong Kong Ltd* [2019] HKCFI 826 [31] (Ng J); *Hong Ziyun* (n 68) [39] (Mimmie Chan J).

[71] *Hong Kong Civil Procedure 2021* (n 12) para 11/1/62.

[72] *Noble Power* (n 69) [36] (Ma CJHC).

[73] *Chinachem* (n 69) [90] (DHCJ Marlene Ng).

[74] *Hong Kong Civil Procedure 2021* (n 12) para 11/1/165, citing *Donohue v Armco Inc* [2001] UKHL 64, [2002] 1 All ER 749 and others.

[75] *Madison Communications* (n 70) [49]–[66] (DHCJ William Wong SC); cf *Deltatre* (n 70) [41]–[90] (Master Benny Lo).

first developed in English law, from the seminal case of *Spiliada Maritime Corp v Cansulex Ltd*.[76] Lord Goff described it as 'one of the most civilised of legal principles',[77] which celebrates the English court's self-restraint of judicial power and deference to a foreign court. The principle has been adopted by the Hong Kong Court of Appeal in *Adhiguna Meranti*,[78] and is recently restated by the Court of Final Appeal in *SPH v SA*.[79]

The doctrine has three major limbs. The first concerns whether there is some other available forum, having competent jurisdiction, which is the appropriate forum for the trial of the action – that is, where the action may be tried more suitably for the interests of all the parties and the ends of justice. In order to answer this question, the applicant for the stay has to establish that first, Hong Kong is not the natural or appropriate forum ('appropriate' in this context means the forum has the most real and substantial connection with the action) and second, there is another available forum which is *clearly* or *distinctly* more appropriate than Hong Kong. Failure by the applicant to establish these two matters at this stage is fatal.

These two limbs are distinct although, practically speaking, the court will assess all relevant factors to decide which is the more appropriate forum. The usual factors include governing law, language, domicile or place of incorporation of parties, convenience of witnesses, and any existing or pending foreign proceedings, etc. Parallel proceedings elsewhere, or *lis alibi pendens*, is one of the factors to be considered at this stage.[80]

If the applicant can establish both of these two matters, then the respondent (plaintiff in the Hong Kong proceedings) has to show that he will be deprived of a legitimate personal or juridical advantage if the action is tried in a forum other than Hong Kong. These tend to involve 'extreme circumstances',[81] for example, when it will be unjust, or when a fair hearing cannot be obtained in the foreign court. The court will be 'extremely cautious', and requires objective and sufficiently cogent evidence for a real risk that the plaintiff cannot obtain substantial justice.[82]

If the plaintiff can establish this, the court will have to balance the advantages of the alternative forum with the disadvantages that the plaintiff may suffer. Deprivation of one or more personal advantages will not necessarily be fatal to the applicant for the stay if he is able to establish to the court's satisfaction that substantial justice will be done in the available appropriate forum.

E. Applying for an Anti-suit Injunction

Where the court assumes jurisdiction, a plaintiff may go further and apply for an anti-suit injunction. The injunction will restrict the defendant personally from commencing or continuing proceedings in a foreign court.[83]

A person has no right not to be sued in a particular forum, domestic or foreign, unless there is some specific factor.[84] For example, the court may make an injunction where the conduct of

[76] *Spiliada Maritime Corp v Cansulex Ltd* [1987] AC 460 (HL).
[77] *Airbus Industrie GIE v Patel* [1999] 1 AC 119 (HL) 141.
[78] *The Adhiguna Meranti* [1987] HKLR 904.
[79] *SPH v SA* (2014) 17 HKCFAR 364 [51].
[80] *Changhong Group* (n 59) [10] (Fok PJ).
[81] Johnston and Harris (n 46) para 3.091.
[82] *DP World Djibouti Fzco v China Merchants Port Holdings Co Ltd* [2019] HKCFI 3104 [107], [112] (Mimmie Chan J). Application for leave to appeal was granted: [2020] HKCFI 639.
[83] *Plain Sail Holdings Ltd v Lau Wing Yan* [2020] HKCFI 653 [39] (Recorder Yvonne Cheng SC).
[84] *Turner v Grovit* [2001] UKHL 65, [2002] 1 WLR 107, 118 (Lord Hobhouse).

the party to be restrained is unconscionable, vexatious or oppressive.[85] The court will exercise its power with action, having regard to comity between nations.[86]

The applicant for an injunction must establish more than an arguable case,[87] to a 'high degree of probability',[88] or to demonstrate a strong or convincing prima facie case.[89] The fact that Hong Kong is the natural forum does not automatically entitle him to an injunction.[90] The court will consider both the injustice to the applicant if the respondent is permitted to pursue foreign proceedings, and also the injustice to the respondent if, by granting the injunction, he is deprived of any advantage in the foreign forum.[91]

There is a difference between cases where the application is founded on a contractual right and others in which the foreign proceedings were commenced in bad faith for frustrating the Hong Kong proceedings.[92] If the applicant is relying upon a contractual right not to be sued in the foreign country (for example, an exclusive jurisdiction clause or an arbitration clause), then he has a legitimate interest to enforce that.[93] The court will require a 'good reason' for not making an injunction if foreign proceedings were commenced in breach of an arbitration agreement.[94] In contrast, if the applicant is not relying on a contractual right, the court requires the applicant to show a legitimate interest such as some unconscionable conduct of the other party.[95]

The case law suggests that the Hong Kong court would make an anti-suit injunction in the following circumstances: (1) the applicant is a party to existing proceedings in Hong Kong; (2) the respondent has in bad faith commenced and propose to prosecute proceedings against the applicant in another jurisdiction for the purpose of frustrating or obstructing the proceedings in Hong Kong; or (3) the court considers that it is necessary to protect the legitimate interest of the applicant in the Hong Kong proceedings to grant the applicant restraining order against the respondent.[96]

F. Service of Foreign Proceedings in Hong Kong

There are two major modes for serving foreign proceedings in Hong Kong. The first is private service. The foreign party intending to serve a document will engage a Hong Kong process server to effect service, according to requirements under the laws of the foreign country and any specific terms in the foreign court order.

The second is service through the court, in accordance with Order 69.[97] The Order covers service of judicial documents from Convention countries,[98] mainland China, and other

[85] ibid.

[86] *Suen Kwai Kam v Central China Dragon Select Growth Fund* [2020] HKCFI 69 [25(2)] (DHCJ William Wong SC), applied in *Capital Wealth Holdings Ltd v 南通嘉禾科技投资开发有限公司* [2021] HKCFI 272.

[87] ibid [25(3)].

[88] *Liaoyang Shunfeng Iron and Steel Co Ltd v Yeung Tsz Wang* CACV 234/2011 (14 June 2012) [145] (Bharwaney J).

[89] ibid [110] (Hartmann JA).

[90] *First Laser Ltd v Fujian Enterprises (Holdings) Co Ltd* HCA 4414/2001 (12 December 2002) [70] (DHCJ Lam).

[91] *Liaoyang Shunfeng* (n 88) [87] (Hartmann JA).

[92] ibid [88].

[93] *Suen Kwai Kam* (n 86) [25(7)], citing *Turner v Grovit* (n 84) 119C–D.

[94] *The Angelic Grace* [1995] 1 Lloyd's Rep 87, applied in *Dickson Valora Group (Holdings) Co Ltd v Fan Ji Qian* [2019] 2 HKLRD 173, [2019] HKCFI 482; *Giorgio Armani SpA v Elan Clothes Co Ltd* [2019] 2 HKLRD 313, [2019] HKCFI 530 and *Giorgio Armani SpA v Elan Clothes Co Ltd (No 2)* [2020] 1 HKLRD 354, [2019] HKCFI 2983; *GM1 v KC* [2020] 1 HKLRD 132, [2019] HKCFI 2793.

[95] *Suen Kwai Kam* (n 86) [25(8)], citing *Turner v Grovit* (n 84) 119D.

[96] *Turner v Grovit* (n 84) [29], cited in *Suen Kwai Kam* (n 86) [25(11)] and *Plain Sail Holdings* (n 83) [89].

[97] See generally *Hong Kong Civil Procedure 2021* (n 12) paras 69/4/1–69/4/2.

[98] Those include a foreign country in relation to which there subsists a civil procedure convention providing for service in that country of process of the Court of First Instance of the High Court, which includes a country that is a party to the Hague Service Convention: Ord 69, r 1.

countries. A request should be made to the Registrar of the High Court by: (1) the Chief Secretary for Administration, with a recommendation by him that service should be effected; (2) the court or tribunal in a convention country, or from a consular or other authority of that country; or (3) the judicial authorities of the mainland China.[99] Upon such request, the Registrar will arrange service, by the Chief Bailiff of the High Court.[100] The foreign process may be served by personal service or insertion through a letter box,[101] substituted service,[102] or in accordance with other enactments. If the documents are in a language other than English or Chinese, they shall be accompanied by a translation into either of these two languages, unless the court or tribunal of the foreign country certifies that the person to be served understands the language of the process.[103]

III. Establishing Jurisdiction in Specific Claims

This section will outline the rules on jurisdiction in several major types of claim. The general principles described in the previous section apply, with the exceptions and modifications as specified below.

A. Law of Obligations

i. Contractual Claims

If the defendant can be served in Hong Kong, the court will take jurisdiction over a contractual claim. There is no restriction on the court's subject matter jurisdiction.[104] This means that the court can determine a case even if the 'connecting factors' of the contract (governing law, parties, place of performance, etc) point to other jurisdictions. The court exercises its control by allowing a party's stay application, for example based on *forum non conveniens*, which involves the court's assessment of all factors related to forum. As explained above, if the parties have contractually agreed to submit to a foreign forum (eg under a jurisdiction clause), the plaintiff will need to demonstrate a 'strong reason' to resist any stay application.[105]

But if the defendant is outside Hong Kong, the connecting factors will take the centre stage at the beginning. When the plaintiff applies for leave to serve out, the first hurdle is to show a good arguable case that the case falls under any one of the gateways. The specific heads for contractual claims are Order 11, rules 1(1)(d)(i)–(iv), (e), (h), and (i), but other gateways can also be relied on. The contractual gateways prescribe the necessary situations in which a plaintiff may invoke the court's long-arm jurisdiction.

The first situation is where the contract was made in Hong Kong (Head (d)(i)). Under Hong Kong law, the place where the contract was made is governed by the common law rules. Sometimes those rules lead to unsatisfactory results. For instance, if the contractual acceptance

[99] Ord 69, r 2.
[100] ibid, r 4.
[101] ibid, rr 3(2), 3(3).
[102] ibid, r 3(5).
[103] ibid, r 3(1).
[104] Johnston and Harris (n 46) para 5.003.
[105] See Section II.D above.

is posted, the postal rule operates and the contract is made where the acceptance is posted; but if the acceptance is sent by instantaneous communications[106] (eg faxes and emails), the contract is made where the acceptance is received.[107] Thus, if the acceptance is sent by post, fax and email, these rules point to different places. One will also get a confusing result if a party receives an acceptance when travelling or crossing the border. In the digital age, ordinary people communicate by electronic means, and conclude contracts by emails or instantaneous communications (such as WhatsApp or WeChat). It is artificial to apply the old common law rule to decide where a contract is made, and restrict the nature of a service out claim accordingly.

Second, the contract was made by or through an agent trading or residing within Hong Kong for a principal trading or residing out of Hong Kong (Head (d)(ii)). The 'principal' here refers to the defendant.[108]

Third, the contract is governed expressly or impliedly by Hong Kong law (Head (d)(iii)). If the contract does not contain an express or implied choice of law, the court will apply the 'closest and most real connection' test by weighing the connecting factors to the contract, to determine its governing law.[109] That will require the court to consider all the circumstances related to the contract.

Fourth, the contract contains a term to the effect that the Hong Kong Court of First Instance shall have jurisdiction to hear and determine any action in respect of the contract (Head (d)(iv)). This covers both an express or implied, exclusive or non-exclusive, Hong Kong jurisdiction clause.[110]

Fifth, the breach of contract was committed within Hong Kong (Head (e)). The plaintiff has to establish all three elements of contract, breach and place of breach. If a plaintiff relies on this Head, he will effectively need to prove a good arguable case on the merits.[111]

Finally, the claim is to construe, rectify, set aside or enforce a deed or contract affecting Hong Kong land (Head (h)), or the claim is for a debt secured on land or other property in Hong Kong (Head (i)). These Heads establish and confirm the Hong Kong court's jurisdiction to determine contractual claims relating to land in Hong Kong.

ii. Tortious Claims

The primary factor which affects the court's jurisdiction is the place of commission of the tort, which is the starting point of consideration. It is important for various reasons.

First, if a plaintiff's claim is based on a tort committed outside Hong Kong, he will have to satisfy the 'double actionability rule'[112] in order to found an action in Hong Kong. The rule requires the alleged tort to be actionable (as a tort) under both Hong Kong law (*lex fori*) and the law of the place of commission (*lex loci delicti*). Exceptionally, the court may allow the plaintiff to rely exclusively on the *lex loci delicti*, for example, if that law has the most significant relationship

[106] See the provisions in Electronic Transactions Ordinance (Cap 553), Pt VI, on the time and place of sending and receiving 'electronic records', such as contractual acceptance.

[107] Wilkinson, Cheung and Meggitt (n 28) para 5–126.

[108] *Transamerica Occidental Life Insurance Co (Hong Kong Branch) v King Sound Industry Co Ltd* [2005] 1 HKLRD 125 [30] (Stone J), citing *Union International Insurance Co Ltd v Jubilee Insurance Co Ltd* [1991] 1 WLR 415.

[109] Johnston and Harris (n 46) para 5.031; Wilkinson, Cheung and Meggitt (n 28) para 5–129.

[110] Johnston and Harris (n 46) para 5.032; *Hong Kong Civil Procedure 2021* (n 12) para 11/1/327.

[111] *Seaconsar* (n 45) 454A–G (Lord Goff).

[112] Also known as the rule in *Boys v Chaplin* [1971] AC 356 (HL) which founded the rule.

with the occurrence and with the parties.[113] This rule applies to both service-in and service out cases.[114] It is a choice of law rule, not a jurisdiction test. Yet, practically speaking, the plaintiff has to overcome this hurdle in order to establish jurisdiction.

Second, if the defendant cannot be served in Hong Kong, the tort gateway to jurisdiction under Order 11 contains a requirement on the place of tort. Head (f) applies if *either*: (1) the damage was sustained in Hong Kong; *or* (2) if it resulted from an act committed in Hong Kong. Cases suggest that the first requirement refers to 'some significant damage' (though not necessarily 'the damage') being suffered here,[115] and the second requirement refers to a 'substantial and efficacious act' being committed here, even if other substantial acts were done abroad.[116] In brief, either a significant damage was suffered in Hong Kong, or the major blow must be inflicted within the jurisdiction.

Third, if the defendant disputes jurisdiction based on *forum non conveniens*, the starting point of consideration is the place of tort. The court applies the *Albaforth* principle, which says that the place of commission is prima facie the natural forum.[117] Robert Goff LJ in the *Albaforth* case stated that 'if the substance of an alleged tort is committed within a certain jurisdiction, it is not easy imagine what other facts could displace the conclusion that the Courts of that jurisdiction are the natural forum.'[118] Hong Kong judges recognise this principle,[119] but have repeatedly emphasised that this is only a starting point and not the end. The court will examine how close a connection there really exists with any given forum, based on the overall circumstances of the case. Ma CJHC commented in *The Peng Yan* that the place of commission may be 'decisive' in some cases, or 'perhaps not weighty at all' in others.[120] The basic principle in *forum non conveniens* applications remains the *Spiliada* test, as recently restated in *SPH v SA*.

In cross-border cases, the place of tort is not always easy to determine. The court has tackled this knotty problem in numerous cases, which related to 'global conspiracy',[121] negligent advice by a foreign law firm,[122] and international or worldwide defamation,[123] to name but a few. Legal tests which various labels like 'substance' and 'centre of gravity' were used. In essence, the court has to examine the chain of events to decide where the tort was in substance committed, and where the claim arose.[124] The court will undergo a factual investigation to determine the place of tort, and its connection with Hong Kong.

[113] *Galsworthy Ltd v Liu Por* [2019] HKCFI 2397 [254] (Marlene Ng J), citing *Shanghai Reeferco Container Co Ltd v Waggonbau Elze GmbH & Co Besitz KG* [2005] 2 HKLRD 711 [47] (DHCJ Poon).

[114] *Hong Kong Civil Procedure 2021* (n 12) para 11/1/338.

[115] *Dynasty Line* (n 27) [33] (Cheung JA), applied in various cases including recently in *Zhang Caikui v Zhao Yongkui* [2020] HKCFI 1170 [56] (K Yeung J).

[116] *Metall und Rohstoff AG v Donaldson Lufkin & Jenrette Inc* [1990] 1 QB 391, 437 (Slade LJ), adopted in Hong Kong in eg *Clark Quantum Kent v Hai Tin Ltd* [2019] HKCFI 2758 [44] (DHCJ Le Pichon).

[117] *Cordoba Shipping Co v National State Bank, Elizabeth, New Jersey (The Albaforth)* [1984] 2 Lloyd's Rep 91.

[118] ibid, 96(2).

[119] See eg *Esquel Enterprises Ltd v TAL Apparel Ltd* [2006] 2 HKLRD 363 [13]; *The Peng Yan* [2009] 1 HKLRD 144 [24]–[25].

[120] *The Peng Yan* (n 119) [28].

[121] *Galsworthy Ltd* (n 113). The Court was invited to apply a 'center of gravity' test to assess the natural forum: [249].

[122] *China Medical* (n 37). The Court applied the 'substance' test from *Metall und Rohstoff* (n 116) to decide whether a tort has been committed within Hong Kong: [127].

[123] *Esquel Enterprises* (n 119); *Investasia Ltd v Kodansha Co Ltd* HCA 12519/1997 (18 May 1999); *Dr Yeung Sau Shing Albert v Google Inc* [2014] 4 HKLRD 493; *Earn Crown Investment Ltd v China Free Press Inc* HCA 2250/2015 (4 September 2017).

[124] Wilkinson, Cheung and Meggitt (n 28) para 5–135.

iii. Unjust Enrichment or Restitution

Order 11 does not have a specific gateway to jurisdiction for unjust enrichment or restitution claims. If leave for service out is required, the plaintiff needs to rely on an existing Head, such as those for contract (Heads (d) and (e)), tort (Head (f)), land (Heads (g) and (h)), trusts (Head (j)) or money had and received, account or constructive trust (Head (p)), etc.

That is not a satisfactory position. Under English law (from which Order 11 was derived), there is now a specific Head for restitution under the Practice Direction for service out.[125] It enables a claimant to apply to the English court for permission to serve a writ out of the jurisdiction, where the defendant's alleged liability arises out of acts committed within the jurisdiction, or the enrichment is obtained within the jurisdiction, or the claim is governed by the law of England and Wales. It will be desirable if Order 11, rule 1(1) is likewise modernised, for instance by updating the current Head (p) or by inserting a new Head which specifically caters for claims for unjust enrichment or restitution.

iv. Trusts

The plaintiff may rely on Heads (j) and/or (p).[126] Head (j) applies to claims brought to execute the trusts of a written instrument, being trusts that ought to be executed according to Hong Kong law and of which the defendant is a trustee, or for any relief or remedy which might be obtained in any such action. The applicable law of the trusts should be determined in accordance with the Recognition of Trusts Ordinance (Cap 76), which applies the Hague Trust Convention[127] to Hong Kong.[128] The trust property does not need to be within the jurisdiction,[129] which means the trustee cannot avoid a claim by removing trust assets from Hong Kong. Head (p) applies to claims against constructive trustee as the defendant (or for money had and received, or for an account), and the defendant's alleged liability arises out of acts committed, whether by him or otherwise, within the jurisdiction.

B. Law of Property

In Hong Kong law, property is divided into movables and immovables. Immovable property essentially refers to land;[130] and everything else are movable property.[131] Movable property is sub-divided into tangibles and intangibles. In this section, we will discuss the rules on immovables, movables and the succession of property.

[125] Practice Direction 6B (Service out of the jurisdiction), which supplements Section IV of the Civil Procedure Rules Pt 6, para 3.1(16).

[126] Johnston and Harris (n 46) suggested that Head (f) (tort) also apply, for filling gaps if needed, given that the notion of tort in principle applies to breaches of trust: para 8.140.

[127] The 1985 Hague Convention on the Law Applicable to Trusts and on Their Recognition.

[128] See Johnston and Harris (n 46) para 8.140.

[129] *Winter v Winter* [1894] 1 Ch 421.

[130] Interpretation and General Clauses Ordinance (Cap 1) s 3 defines immovable property as: '(a) land, whether covered by water or not; (b) any estate, right, interest or easement in or over any land; and (c) things attached to land or permanently fastened to anything attached to land'.

[131] Cap 1, s 3 defines movable property as 'property of every description except immovable property'.

i. Immovable Property

In common law, the court has no jurisdiction to hear disputes concerning title to or interests in foreign land, under the *Moçambique* rule which originated from a nineteenth century English case.[132] Subsequently, in the *Hesperides* case, the Plaintiff commenced an action in England for conspiracy to procure trespass to land and chattels in a Cypriot hotel. Applying the *Moçambique* rule, the House of Lords held that the English court could not entertain an action for trespass or conspiracy to trespass to the Cypriot hotel, but it could hear the related claim for trespass to chattels.[133] This demonstrated that the *Moçambique* rule only applies to foreign land but not movable property. Since the Cypriot hotel case, English law has been modified by statute, which allows the court to hear tort claims affecting foreign land unless they are principally concerned with a question of the title to or right to possession of that foreign land.[134]

No similar legislative change has taken place in Hong Kong. This leaves the law in a rather uncertain state. Johnston and Harris suggested approaching the matter by applying the *forum conveniens* doctrine, and discourage a blanket exclusionary rule based on subject matter.[135] This view has been echoed and adopted by the Hong Kong courts.

In *DX v LN*,[136] the Judge surveyed the law and said (at [68]):

> ... [In] view of the many criticisms which have been levelled at a rule clearly based on historical procedural development of a decision made more than a century ago which has since been wholly or partially abrogated in other common law jurisdictions, and given the lack of direct authority of its application in Hong Kong and its questionable relevancy to our present-day law, I am inclined to echo Johnston's observation that it would indeed be more attractive that there be no exclusionary rule at all, and thus leaving our courts the discretion as to whether jurisdiction should be exercised on the doctrine of *forum conveniens*.

The above approach was adopted in two subsequent cases.[137] Accordingly, the prevailing view is against an automatic exclusionary rule which would oblige the court to strike out a claim in respect of title to foreign land subject to exceptions. Instead, the trend is for the court to approach those claims based on *forum non conveniens* principles. Under this approach, the court retains the discretion to rule on jurisdiction based on the facts of each case. The existence of issues relating to foreign land, either as the main or ancillary issue, will militate against the assumption of jurisdiction.

On the other hand, if a claim relates to land in Hong Kong, the court will assume jurisdiction in the ordinary way, based on service of claim in Hong Kong. There are specific gateways for service out under Order 11. These include Head (g), which applies if the whole subject matter of the action is land situated in Hong Kong (with or without rents or profits) or the perpetuation of testimony relating to such land, Head (h), regarding claims brought to construe, rectify, set aside or enforce an act, deed, will, contract, obligation or liability affecting land situated in Hong Kong, and Head (i), regarding claims made for a debt secured on immovable property or its made to assert, declare or determine proprietary or possessory rights, or rights of security, in or over movable property, or to obtain authority to dispose of movable property situated in Hong Kong.

[132] *British South Africa Co v Companhia de Moçambique* [1893] AC 602 (HL).
[133] *Hesperides Hotels Ltd v Muftizade* [1979] AC 508 (HL) 544 (Lord Fraser).
[134] Civil Jurisdiction and Judgments Act 1982, s 30(1), which is subject to s 30(2) relating to European Conventions.
[135] Johnston and Harris (n 46) para 4.043.
[136] *DX v LN* FCMC 7870/2014 (30 November 2015).
[137] *James Chor Cheung Wong v Hark Chung Wong* HCA 469/2013 (4 July 2017); *Chan Pui Sze v Wang Jue* [2019] HKCFI 2515.

ii. Movable Property (Tangible or Intangible)

There are no specific jurisdictional rules directed at movable property, which is a vast category comprising all property (tangible or intangible) other than land. A claim relating to movables would usually fall under some other category (the law of obligations, company, intellectual property, family, etc). It is noted that Head (i) covers claims relating to rights over movable property, as mentioned above.

iii. Succession to Property

Succession refers to the devolution of property after the death of a natural person. There are two types of succession: testamentary or intestate (that is, with or without a will). If the deceased had made a will, the executor should prove the will and apply for a grant of probate from the court. If there is no will, the personal representative(s) of the deceased (as administrator) should apply to the court for a grant of administration of the estate. Upon the court's grant of probate or administration, the personal representative (the executor or administrator) will administer the estate. He will collect the deceased's estate, pay any proven debts in order of priority, and distribute the balance of the estate. If there is a will and its distribution is valid, the balance will be distributed accordingly. Where there is no will or there is no valid provision on certain property, the distribution will be in accordance with the intestate rules. If no one can acquire the property under the will or by operation of law, the property will be vested in the Hong Kong Government as *bona vacantia* (that is, empty goods).

There are two major stages in succession: 'probate' and 'administration'. The court has statutory jurisdiction in all matters relating to both 'probate and administration'.[138] Yet the court's probate jurisdiction and administration jurisdiction are separate.[139] The function of a probate court is to ascertain and determine what testamentary papers constitute the testator's will, who should be entitled to be his personal representative, and other matters relating to the grant of probate. The court of administration is concerned with the supervision over the administration of the testator's estate, including questions such as the collection of assets belonging to the estate, the itemisation and valuation of the property in the estate, the extent of validity of the intended dispositions, etc. Parties should bear in mind this distinction. Before the grant of probate, a party cannot invoke the court's probate jurisdiction to seek directions on administration issues.[140] Administration matters are dealt with after the grant of probate by way of administration proceedings under Order 85.

At the probate stage, the court may grant probates of wills and letters of administration, and it can also alter or revoke such grants.[141] Previously, the court's common law jurisdiction was 'strictly territorial':[142] it could only make a grant if the deceased has property within the jurisdiction.[143] The Probate and Administration Ordinance (Cap 10) now empowers the court to make a grant in the absence of property in Hong Kong,[144] though such a grant remains exceptional.[145] If the deceased died domiciled in a foreign country, the court will generally make

[138] The Probate and Administration Ordinance (Cap 10), Pt I, and relevant court rules.
[139] See the discussion in *Re Estate of Cheung Hung* [2011] 1 HKLRD 455 [10]–[12] (Johnson Lam J); *Fok Po Nam v HSBC Trustee (Hong Kong) Ltd* [2018] 1 HKC 567, [2018] HKCFI 1 [41]–[42] (Anderson Chow J).
[140] ibid.
[141] Cap 10, s 3(1).
[142] *Li Chok Hung v Li Pui Choi* (1911) 6 HKLR 12.
[143] *In the Goods of Tucker* (1863) 3 Swabey & Tristram 585.
[144] Cap 10, s 3(2).
[145] See Johnston and Harris (n 46) para 8.026.

a grant to his personal representative under the law of that foreign country (*lex domicilii*).[146] The object is to facilitate the administration of the entire estate (with property in various jurisdictions) by the same person(s), with the *lex domicilii* having the best claim to decide who those persons should be.[147] If the estate includes assets outside Hong Kong, the personal representative should send the grant by the Hong Kong court to the relevant overseas jurisdiction(s) for resealing. In most cases, overseas jurisdictions will require a new grant in accordance with local law and procedure.[148] A foreign grant from a 'designated country or place'[149] can be resealed in Hong Kong under Cap 10, sections 3(3) and 49. Grants from other jurisdictions will require a new grant from the Hong Kong court.

Turning to the administration stage, a party may commence an action for the administration of the estate. The general principles on jurisdiction apply, subject to any modification in the relevant statutory provisions such as Order 85. If service out is required, Head (k) enables the court to grant leave if the claim is made for the administration of the estate of a person who died domiciled within the jurisdiction, or for any relief or remedy which might be obtained in any such action. Head (l) allows leave to be granted if the claim is brought in a probate action.[150]

C. Intellectual Property

It used to be said, with some case law authority, that a common law court had no jurisdiction to adjudicate on the validity of foreign intellectual property rights.[151] This rule has been modified and curtailed under English law. Yet the status in Hong Kong law is less certain.

Johnston and Harris traced the origin of this restriction to an Australian decision relating to infringement of foreign patent rights.[152] The High Court of Australia justified an exclusionary rule based on analogies to acts of state exclusion, the *Moçambique* rule and the double actionability rule. It is said that this restriction was not supported by significant English authorities.[153] There were English precedents where the courts did enforce goodwill and reputation in foreign countries,[154] or refused to apply the exclusionary rule to copyright cases.[155] In 2011, the UK Supreme Court concluded that there was no exclusionary rule for copyright.[156] Lord Walker

[146] Non-Contentious Probate Rules (Cap 10A), r 29.

[147] Johnston and Harris (n 46) para 8.027.

[148] Christopher H Sherrin, *Probate Practice in Hong Kong* 3rd edn (Hong Kong, Sweet and Maxwell, 2012) para 3.031.

[149] The list of designated countries and places is set out in Cap 10, Sch 2, which includes the Australian States of Tasmania, Victoria and South Australia and the Northern Territory of Australia, New Zealand, Singapore, Sri Lanka and the United Kingdom.

[150] See Ord 76 (Contentious Probate Proceedings).

[151] Briggs and Rees (n 6) paras 4.06–4.08.

[152] ibid, para 4.044, referring to *Potter v Broken Hill Pty Co Ltd* (1906) 3 CLR 479. This case was discussed at length in the UK Supreme Court: *Lucasfilm Ltd v Ainsworth* [2011] UKSC 39, [2012] 1 AC 208. See discussion below.

[153] Briggs (n 4) 291; *Tyburn Productions Ltd v Conan Doyle* [1991] Ch 75, which held that the English court had no jurisdiction in a foreign copyright case. The English Court of Appeal in *Pearce v Ove Arup Partnership Ltd* [2000] Ch 403 rejected the exclusionary rule. These conflicting authorities were referred to by the Hong Kong Court of Appeal in *Guangzhou Green-enhan Bio-engineering Co Ltd v Green Power Health Products International Co Ltd* HCA 4651/2002, HCA 2802/2003, HCMP 74/2004 (8 April 2005) [307] (Lam J). The Court did not express its view: [308]. Subsequently, in 2011, *Tyburn* was overruled by the UK Supreme Court in *Lucasfilm Ltd* (n 152).

[154] Hon Wah Ng, 'Hong Kong Courts' Jurisdiction to Enforce Intellectual Property Rights Infringed by Internet Contents' (2005) 35(2) *Hong Kong Law Journal* 367, 372, citing *John Walker v Ost* [1970] RPC 489 and *Alfred Dunhill v Sunpotic* [1979] FSR 337.

[155] *Pearce v Ove Arup* (n 153) and *R Griggs Group Ltd v Evans* [2004] EWHC 1088 (Ch), [2005] Ch 153.

[156] *Lucasfilm Ltd* (n 152).

and Lord Collins observed that it is possible to see how the rationale of the *Moçambique* rule can be applied to patents and their validity, particularly in sensitive areas such as armaments.[157] That said, they considered that there were no issues of policy which militated against the enforcement of foreign copyrights. On the contrary, states had an interest in the international recognition and enforcement of their copyrights.[158]

There is no direct Hong Kong authority for a blanket exclusion to the effect that the court lacks subject matter jurisdiction over foreign intellectual property. Instead, the court has approached these cases in the context of personal jurisdiction assessment, that is, the *forum non conveniens* exercise. For example, in *Esquel Enterprises Ltd v TAL Apparel Ltd*,[159] the first Plaintiff complained that the Defendants told their customers in Japan and the US that the first Plaintiff had infringed their Japanese and US patents. It claimed for damages for defamation, interference with economic relations and malicious falsehood. The issue of whether there was any patent infringement was a core issue in the litigation. Upon the Defendants' *forum non conveniens* application, the Court of Appeal considered that, in determining forum, it was clearly a 'weighty factor' that the case involved foreign patent infringement. It agreed that the case should be stayed. Crucially, however, the Court referred to the modern English view expressed in cases such as *Pearce* and *R Griggs* that the *Moçambique* rule does not require the English court to refuse to entertain a claim of foreign copyright.[160] On that basis, the Court did not consider that it lacked subject matter jurisdiction or that the matter was non-justiciable. The stay was based on the exercise of discretion under the *forum non conveniens* principle.

The above suggests that, similar to cases relating to foreign land, Hong Kong does not recognise an automatic exclusionary rule for foreign intellectual property disputes.[161] The court will apply the general principles by assuming jurisdiction upon service, subject to any party's right to dispute jurisdiction or seek a stay based on *forum non conveniens*, or the existence of foreign jurisdiction agreement. If the case involves foreign intellectual property rights, this will be considered as a 'weighty factor' in favour of a stay of proceedings.

D. Family Law

There are ordinances and subsidiary legislation which govern the court's jurisdiction in family law cases. They either replace or supplement the general principles, as provided in the applicable statutory provisions.

i. Marriage

The court is prepared to recognise a marriage under foreign law.[162] In order for a marriage to be considered valid, it must satisfy both the requirements of essential validity and formal validity.[163] Essential validity involves the parties' capacity under the place of their ante-nuptial

[157] ibid [106].
[158] ibid [109].
[159] *Esquel Enterprises* (n 119).
[160] ibid [38].
[161] See also Johnston and Harris (n 46) 4.048–4.050.
[162] *Wong Zhong Lan-Xiang v Frank Wong* [2003] 4 HKC 609.
[163] *Suen Toi Lee v Yau Yee Ping* (2001) 4 HKCFAR 474.

domicile (the *lex domicilii*). Formal validity involves the formalities required by the law of the place where the union was entered into (the *lex loci celebrationis*).[164]

The court has jurisdiction to grant a declaration that a marriage is valid, with the jurisdictional basis on common law. The alternative basis is the ancillary jurisdiction to the court's statutory jurisdiction to hear divorce petitions.[165]

ii. Divorce, Nullity of Marriage, Judicial Separation, etc

The Matrimonial Causes Ordinance (Cap 179) establishes the court's jurisdiction in proceedings for divorce,[166] nullity of marriage,[167] judicial separation,[168] and the presumption of death.[169] There are various jurisdictional bases and requirements, which include domicile, habitual residence, residency of the parties, substantial connection to Hong Kong, and the place where the marriage was celebrated, etc. The requirement for each type of proceedings differs from one another. Section 9 restricts the court's power to make orders under the Ordinance to 'a customary marriage celebrated in accordance with section 7 of the Marriage Reform Ordinance (Cap 178) and registered in accordance with Part IV of that Ordinance or was a monogamous marriage'. The Ordinance also enables the court to recognise overseas divorces and legal separations.[170]

There are specific rules on service of process, as provided in the Matrimonial Causes Rules (Cap 179A). Service in Hong Kong can be effected by post or personal service,[171] but the parties cannot make personal service by themselves.[172] The court may order substituted service.[173] As an exception to the general principles, no prior leave from the court is required for service out of Hong Kong.[174] As in other cases, a party may apply to stay the court proceedings based on the general principles of *forum non conveniens*.[175]

iii. Children

The court has jurisdiction to grant declarations of parentage, legitimacy or legitimation, pursuant to the Parent and Child Ordinance (Cap 429).[176] An application can be made by the child in question, if he: (1) is domiciled in Hong Kong; (2) has been habitually resident in Hong Kong throughout one year before the application; or (3) has a substantial connection with Hong Kong.[177] The court can also make a parental order in favour of gamete donors. Upon the joint application of husband and wife, the court may make an order providing for a child to be regarded as the child of their marriage.[178] The requirements are that: (1) the child's home must be with the husband and the wife or either of them; and (2) the husband and/or the wife (a) is

[164] ibid [40] (Bokhary PJ).
[165] Johnston and Harris (n 46) 7.111.
[166] Cap 179, s 3.
[167] ibid, s 4.
[168] ibid, s 5.
[169] ibid, s 6.
[170] ibid, Pt IX.
[171] Cap 179A, rr 14, 110, 111, 119.
[172] ibid, rr 14, 111.
[173] ibid, r 14.
[174] ibid, r 109.
[175] *SPH v SA* (n 79).
[176] Cap 429, ss 6, 7.
[177] ibid, ss 6(1), 6(2).
[178] ibid, s 12.

domiciled in Hong Kong, (b) has been habitually resident in Hong Kong throughout one year before the application, or (c) has a substantial connection with Hong Kong.[179] Further, the court can make an adoption order, which authorises a sole applicant or two spouses (as joint applicants) to adopt an infant, under the Adoption Ordinance (Cap 290).[180] The requirement is that both the applicant(s) and the infant reside in Hong Kong.[181] Questions of legitimacy and adoption often arise in succession proceedings.

The court can make orders regarding the custody of and right of access to a child, and his maintenance and guardianship, under the Guardianship of Minors Ordinance (Cap 13).[182] This jurisdiction can be exercised even if any party to the proceedings is not domiciled in Hong Kong.[183] Under common law, the court has wardship jurisdiction to make orders permitting the custodial parent to take the child to live abroad despite the objection by the other parent who lives in Hong Kong.[184] In exercising its discretion, the paramount consideration is the welfare of the child.[185]

Hong Kong has adopted the 1980 Hague Convention on the Civil Aspects of International Child Abduction, which is implemented by the Child Abduction and Custody Ordinance (Cap 512). It empowers the court to make an order prohibiting the removal of a child from Hong Kong except to habitual residence,[186] a recovery order relating to a child's return,[187] an order prohibiting removal of a child out of Hong Kong without consent,[188] etc.

E. Law of Company and Insolvency

Companies, whether incorporated in Hong Kong or elsewhere, can be sued in Hong Kong. In this section, we will discuss the general principles on service on a company, and the specific question of when the court will wind up a foreign company.

i. Service on Companies

Service on companies is governed by the Companies Ordinance (Cap 622), in addition to the rules of court described above. The Ordinance facilitates the service of documents on companies.

Service on a Hong Kong company can be made by leaving a document (judicial or other document) at its registered office, or by posting it to that address.[189]

A non-Hong Kong company which is registered in Hong Kong[190] can be served by making service on its authorised representative and leaving the document at or posting it to the representative's last known address in Hong Kong.[191] If no details of the authorised representative are shown on the Companies Register, or every one of the company's authorised representatives

[179] ibid, s 12(3).
[180] Cap 290, s 4.
[181] ibid, s 5(6).
[182] Cap 13, ss 10, 11.
[183] ibid, s 26.
[184] Johnston and Harris (n 46) 7.130, citing *Naziya Aslam v Rafaqat Ali* CACV 144/2003 (9 March 2004).
[185] ibid [16], [35] (Rogers VP).
[186] Cap 512, s 16.
[187] ibid, s 17.
[188] ibid, s 21.
[189] Cap 622, s 827.
[190] Under Cap 622, Pt 16.
[191] Cap 622, s 803(1).

refuses to accept service, service can be made by leaving the document at or posting it to any place of business of the company in Hong Kong.[192] If the company no longer has a place of business in Hong Kong, the document can be served by registered post to the company's registered office and principal place of business in the company's place of incorporation as shown on the Companies Register, or (where no such addresses are shown on the Companies Register) by leaving at or posting it to any place in Hong Kong at which the company has had a place of business within the previous 12 months.[193]

As for an unregistered foreign company, it can be served by leaving the document at, or sending it by post to, the company's place of business in Hong Kong. If it has established but no longer has a place of business in Hong Kong, service can be made by registered post to the company's registered office and principal place of business in the company's place of incorporation. If the address of such registered office, or principal place of business, cannot be ascertained but the company has had a place of business in Hong Kong within the previous 12 months, it can be served by leaving the document at, or sending it by post to, the place of business in Hong Kong.[194]

The above methods constitute service within the territory as of right. 'Service out' on foreign companies follows the general principles discussed above.

ii. Winding Up of Companies

The court has jurisdiction to wind up both Hong Kong and non-Hong Kong companies, including those unregistered in Hong Kong, pursuant to the Companies (Winding Up and Miscellaneous Provisions) Ordinance (Cap 32).[195] The circumstances in which the court may wind up a Hong Kong company[196] or unregistered company (which includes a registered non-Hong Kong company)[197] are specified in the Ordinance.

The court recognises that the place of incorporation is the most appropriate jurisdiction in which to wind up a company. It therefore adopts some 'self-imposed constraints' on its jurisdiction to wind up a foreign company (whether registered in Hong Kong). The principles have been considered by the court in various cases in recent years, which culminated in the decision of the Court of Final Appeal in *Kam Leung Sui Kwan v Kam Kwan Lai*.[198]

The Court summarised the position on the court's jurisdiction to wind up foreign companies, and identified the following requirements: (1) there had to be a sufficient connection with Hong Kong, but this did not necessarily have to consist of the presence of assets within the jurisdiction; (2) there must be a reasonable possibility that the winding-up order would benefit those applying for it; and (3) the court must be able to exercise jurisdiction over one or more persons in the distribution of the company's assets.[199]

In that case, the Court found that the company has significant assets in Hong Kong, which might be made available to the liquidator for distribution among creditors. The petitioner would derive significant benefit from a winding up order. In a shareholder's petition, the presence of other shareholders within the jurisdiction was an 'extremely weighty factor' in establishing the sufficiency of connection to Hong Kong.

[192] ibid, ss 803(2), 803(3).
[193] ibid, s 803(4).
[194] ibid, s 803(5).
[195] Cap 32, ss 176, 327.
[196] ibid, s 177.
[197] ibid, ss 326(2), 327.
[198] *Kam Leung Sui Kwan* (n 9).
[199] ibid [19]–[20] (Ma CJ and Lord Millett NPJ).

These principles have subsequently been widely applied by the Hong Kong courts to winding-up petitions against foreign companies.[200]

F. Personal Bankruptcy

The court can make a bankruptcy order against an individual in accordance with the Bankruptcy Ordinance (Cap 6). At least one of the jurisdictional requirements in section 4 must be satisfied: the debtor: (1) is domiciled in Hong Kong; (2) is personally present in Hong Kong on the day on which the petition is presented; or (3) at any time in the period of three years before the bankruptcy petition, (a) has been ordinarily resident, or has had a place of residence, in Hong Kong, or (b) has carried on business in Hong Kong. 'Carrying on business' includes the carrying on of business by a firm or partnership of which the debtor is a member, or by an agent or manager for the debtor or for such a firm or partnership.

If jurisdiction is established, the court may still exercise its discretion on whether to make a bankruptcy order. Such discretionary power was featured in the recent case of *Re Dai Guoliang*,[201] which involved a bankruptcy petition against a mainland Chinese individual. Mr Dai was a resident in Fujian, China, who held a Hong Kong identity card. He was a substantial indirect shareholder of a company listed in Hong Kong, and was its previous chairman and executive director. By reason of his office, he would come to Hong Kong for brief stays from time to time. But he spent most of his time in Fujian, where the operations of the company are located. The debt in question arose from a personal guarantee, which had a Hong Kong governing law clause and exclusive jurisdiction clause in favour of Hong Kong courts. It also contained a notice provision which directed notices to be given through the company's office in Hong Kong to Mr Dai. There was no dispute that Mr Dai was present in Hong Kong when the bankruptcy petition was presented to the court, which satisfied one of the jurisdictional requirements under Cap 6, section 6.

Mr Dai invited the Court to approach the exercise of discretion to bankrupt a foreigner by applying the three-stage test in the Yung Kee case for winding-up of foreign companies. DHCJ Maurellet SC declined and emphasised the difference between the winding up and bankruptcy regimes.[202] The judge considered that Mr Dai held a Hong Kong identity card, ran a business in Hong Kong and had made a guarantee here. The judge did not agree that he had a limited connection with Hong Kong or that his connection was tenuous.[203] He therefore decided to accept jurisdiction and made the usual bankruptcy order with costs.

G. Competition Law

Competition law in Hong Kong is relatively new. While the competition rules cover extra-territorial activities by foreign parties which harm competition in Hong Kong, it remains

[200] See eg *Perfect Direct Ltd v Dejin Resources Group Co Ltd* HCCW 76/2014 (19 June 2015); *Re Hong Kong Investments Group Ltd* [2018] HKCFI 984; *Champ Prestige International Ltd v China City Construction (International) Co Ltd* [2020] HKCFI 355; *Re ACE International (BVI) Ltd* [2020] 2 HKLRD 508. See also *Re China Huiyuan Juice Group Ltd* [2020] HKCFI 2940, which sets out the guiding principles on the winding-up of an offshore incorporated company listed in Hong Kong that has all of its operating assets in mainland China.

[201] *Re Dai Guoliang* (n 10).

[202] ibid [26]–[32].

[203] ibid [35]–[38].

to be seen whether the Competition Tribunal will adopt any specific rules and principles in handling cross-border cases.

IV. Action *in rem* and Shipping Claims

The distinctive feature of maritime cases is that an action can be *in rem* and/or *in personam*. As we see above, an action *in personam* is against a legal person (that is, individuals or companies). In contrast, an action *in rem* is against a property (known as the *res*) in connection with the claim. The *res* is usually a ship, but can also be the cargo, freight,[204] an aircraft or hovercraft.[205] The proceedings and any judgment would be against the *res*, without a single person being named throughout the proceedings.[206]

The plaintiff enjoys several advantages with action *in rem*. First, he can commence proceedings as of right by serving on the property in Hong Kong, even if its owner is out of jurisdiction. Unlike a writ *in personam*, a writ *in rem* is served on the property itself.[207] Second, an action *in rem* may allow him to 'arrest' the property,[208] which will operate as a security for his claim.[209] The right to arrest is a statutory right under section 12B of the High Court Ordinance (Cap 4). It remains available even if the proceedings are stayed in favour of arbitration,[210] and after an arbitral award is made (which remains unsatisfied).[211] The plaintiff will become a preferential creditor of the property owner, even though it has gone into liquidation.[212] Third, the arrest may prompt the property owner to appear in the forum and contest the claim. In order to release the property under arrest, the owner may even provide bail by bond,[213] pay into court,[214] or make other private arrangements with the plaintiff (such as undertaking, indemnity or guarantee).[215]

A. The Court's Admiralty Jurisdiction

A plaintiff needs to decide whether to commence his action *in rem*, *in personam*, or in both. To proceed in both, separate writs are required.[216]

There are restrictions in the court's jurisdiction over actions *in personam* in collision and other similar cases. These are provided in Cap 4, section 12C, as reflected in Order 75, rule 4. The plaintiff needs to satisfy at least one of these conditions: (1) the defendant has his habitual

[204] See Ord 75, r 8(1)(a).
[205] *Hong Kong Civil Procedure 2021* (n 12) para 75/1/5.
[206] See *The City of Mecca* (1881) 6 PD 106 [112] (Sir George Jessel MR).
[207] Ord 75, r 8.
[208] The plaintiff needs to satisfy the jurisdictional requirements in Cap 4, s 12B(4). See discussion below.
[209] *The Peng Yan* (n 119) [23]; *The Convenience Container* [2007] 3 HKLRD 575 [164]–[165] (Ma CJHC).
[210] Provided that the arrest is to provide security in the action *in rem*, rather than the arbitral award: *Dalmor Shipping Co Ltd v Kan's Maritime Corporation (The Britannia)* HCAJ 343/1997 (9 December 1997) [11], citing *The Rena K* [1979] QB 377.
[211] *The Alas* [2014] 4 HKLRD 160 [15], [23], [26] (Ng J), citing *The Rena K* (n 210) and *The Britannia* (n 210).
[212] *The Convenience Container* (n 209) [31]–[54], [110]–[122], [167]–[170] (Reyes J, Stone J, and Ma CJHC respectively).
[213] Ord 75, r 16.
[214] The amount of security can be assessed by the court, possibly on a 'broad brush' basis: *Hua Tian Long (No 1)* [2008] 4 HKLRD 719 [53] (Stone J).
[215] See the discussion in *Dongnama Shipping Co Ltd v Owners of the Ship or Vessel 'Alacrity'* [1994] Folio No AJ-232 (29 July 1994).
[216] *Hong Kong Civil Procedure 2021* (n 12) para 75/1/7, citing *Stolt Kestrel BV v Sener Petrol Denizcilik Ticaret AS CDE SA v Sure Wind Marine Ltd* [2015] EWCA Civ 1035, [2016] 1 Lloyd's Rep 125 [12].

residence or a place of business in Hong Kong; (2) the cause of action arose within the waters of Hong Kong; or (3) any action arising out of the same incident or series of incidents have been heard and determined, discontinued or otherwise come to an end, unless the defendant submits or has agreed to submit to the court's jurisdiction.[217] The general procedural rules apply with modifications as provided in Order 75.[218]

As to action *in rem*, the plaintiff needs to satisfy two requirements.[219] The first is that the person who would be liable on the claim in an action *in personam* was, when the cause of action arose, the owner or charterer of, or in possession or in control of, the relevant ship. Second, when the action is brought, the person who would be liable *in personam* is either the beneficial owner of the relevant ship (or a sister ship) as respects all the shares in it or the charterer of it under a charter by demise.[220] Upon meeting these requirements, the plaintiff needs to serve the writ *in rem* on the property.[221]

Similar to other actions, a party may apply to stay admiralty proceedings, for example based on *forum non conveniens*.[222] The existence of parallel foreign court proceedings (*lis alibi pendens*), which is common in maritime cases, is one of the relevant factors when the court assess if there is another forum which is clearly or distinctly more appropriate than Hong Kong.[223]

B. The Process of Ship Arrest in Hong Kong

After a writ *in rem* has been issued, a party can request the High Court Registry to issue a warrant of arrest of a ship (or other property) in Hong Kong waters. It needs to file a supporting affidavit, and procure a search by a court bailiff in the caveat book of the court. Leave of the court is necessary in certain situations, for example in an action for possession of a foreign ship belonging to a port of a state having a consulate in Hong Kong, or if the claim arose out of bottomry until the bottomry bond, with notarial translation, is produced to the court.[224] If there is no caveat in force, the bailiff will present the documentation to the Registrar of the High Court, who will issue the warrant if he is satisfied that the requirements are met.

A person who wishes to prevent the arrest of any property can file a 'praecipe' with the court, which will enter the caveat book. He or his solicitor must undertake to acknowledge issue or service of any writ that may be begun against the property, and, within three days after receiving notice that the action has begun, to give bail in the action. The existence of a caveat against arrest will not prevent the issue of a warrant of arrest. But a person who arrests a property despite a caveat without a good and sufficient reason may be ordered to pay damages.[225]

A warrant of arrest is valid for 12 months since its issue. It may be executed only by the court bailiff or his substitute, whose fees and expenses on the arrest and custody after arrest shall be covered by the party's undertaking executed before the arrest. The warrant must be served and filed.[226] The court mays give directions in relation to any property (including its release) which is under arrest.

[217] Cap 4, ss 12C(1)–(8); Ord 75, rr 4(1)–(4).
[218] See eg Ord 75, r 18 (Preliminary Acts). See also Practice Direction 1.1.
[219] Cap 4, s 12B(4).
[220] *The Convenience Container* (n 209) [166] (Ma CJHC).
[221] As provided in Ord 75, rr 8, 11.
[222] *The Peng Yan* (n 119) [21]–[23]; *The Kappa Sea* HCAJ 101/2015 (25 August 2017).
[223] *Changhong Group* (n 59) [10] (Fok PJ).
[224] Ord 75, r 5; *Hong Kong Civil Procedure 2021* (n 12) paras 75/5/2, 75/5/10.
[225] Ord 75, rr 6, 7.
[226] Ord 75, r 10.

V. Immunities from Jurisdiction

Hong Kong has a unique set of rules on immunity, which reflect its special standing as a common law jurisdiction under Chinese sovereignty. The rules have been developed on the basis of common law principles, and are adapted to Hong Kong according to PRC state policy.

The major categories of defendants who enjoy personal immunity from the Hong Kong court include foreign states (state or sovereign immunity), the PRC Government (crown immunity), foreign diplomats and consulates (diplomatic and consular immunity) and other specific persons and institutions.[227] Crown immunity extends to PRC state-owned enterprises if they are 'controlled' by the PRC Central People's Government.[228] This section will discuss state immunity and crown immunity in further detail, which demonstrate Hong Kong's special status.

A. State Immunity

In *Democratic Republic of the Congo v FG Hemisphere Associates LLC (Nos 1 and 2)*,[229] the Court of Final Appeal examined and stated the law on state immunity. The Court laid down the following principles:

1. Hong Kong follows the practice of the PRC on the doctrine and policy of state immunity. Foreign states enjoy 'absolute immunity' before the Hong Kong courts. There is no exception to commercial transactions.
2. Any waiver of immunity by a foreign state must be made unequivocally or explicitly before the Hong Kong court, after the court's jurisdiction is invoked. A state's previous entry into an arbitration agreement does not of itself constitute a waiver of its immunity before the court, whether with regard to suit (that is, immunity at the adjudication stage) or enforcement (that is, immunity at the execution stage).

The above principles have been followed in subsequent cases, including two cases where the court struck out claims against two foreign states.[230]

B. Crown Immunity and State-Owned Enterprises

Crown immunity originated from English law, based on the concept of inequality between the ruling and the ruled, and the maxim that 'the king can do no wrong'.[231] The Crown was not

[227] There are specific legislation and regulations which afford immunity to specific persons and institutions. These include eg the Regulations of the People's Republic of China Concerning Diplomatic Privileges and Immunities (5 September 1986), the International Organizations and Diplomatic Privileges Ordinance (Cap 190), the Privileges and Immunities (International Committee of the Red Cross) Ordinance (Cap 402), the Consular Relations Ordinance (Cap 557), the International Organizations (Privileges and Immunities) Ordinance (Cap 558). In the recently enacted Law of the People's Republic of China on Safeguarding National Security in the Hong Kong Special Administrative Region, Art 60 provides that the acts performed by the Office for Safeguarding National Security or its staff in accordance with the Law shall not be subject to the jurisdiction of the Hong Kong Special Administrative Region. The Office and its staff enjoy rights and immunities under Hong Kong law.

[228] *TNB Fuel Services Sdn Bhd v China National Coal Group Corp* [2017] 3 HKC 588 [9] (Mimmie Chan J).

[229] *Democratic Republic of the Congo (No 1)* (n 7); *Democratic Republic of the Congo v FG Hemisphere Associates LLC (No 2)* (2011) 14 HKCFAR 395.

[230] *陳鈺麟 對 日本* HCMP 2000/2012 (6 December 2012); *Lee Mei Chun v Republic of Philippines* HCPI 723–725/2013 (29 August 2013).

[231] This maxim has an ancient origin. It has been cited in old English cases, such as *Attorney-General v Bushopp* (1600) 1 Coke's Rep 45a, 76 ER 103, and also modern case law.

bound by statute unless expressly named or by necessary implication, and at common law the Crown enjoyed immunity from being sued in its own courts. The meaning of 'crown' extended from the person of the King/sovereign to a body corporate established by the executive arm of the Crown.

The status of crown immunity and the extent of its application were discussed in two recent cases. The first one is *Hua Tian Long (No 2)*,[232] which confirmed that crown immunity subsists under Hong Kong law since the handover in 1997.[233] The current 'crown' is the Central People's Government (CPG) of the PRC. The CPG, together with state-owned enterprises controlled by it, enjoy crown immunity before the Hong Kong court.[234] Commercial activities make no exception to crown immunity.[235] In that case, the Guangzhou Salvage Bureau (GZS) was treated as a state-owned enterprise which was immune to the court's jurisdiction.

The claim for crown immunity was rejected in a subsequent case,[236] which treated 'control' as the touchstone to immunity. Mimmie Chan J accepted that the court should assess, on a case-by-case basis, the 'nature and degree of control' by the CPG over the entity in question.[237] The tendency of the court is to require a 'high degree of control'; and 'any substantial measure of independent discretion will suffice to deny the status of Crown agent to a public body that is subject to some degree of direct control'.[238] The various factors include independent discretion enjoyed by the entity, control exercised by the Crown as investor, the separate legal personality of the entity, the power of the Crown to appoint and remove senior officers of the entity, and the financial autonomy of the entity.

In that case, the entity in question was a state-owned enterprise. The judge concluded from the evidence that it was not part of the CPG. It had a separate corporate entity and enjoyed the rights to possess, use, profit from and dispose of its property, had operation autonomy, and was able to exercise independent powers of its own which were safeguarded by law. These rights were expressly protected by the laws and regulations under PRC law.[239] It was able to exercise independent powers of its own and that its business and operational autonomy, which were enshrined in and guaranteed under PRC law. Applying the control test, even though the shares in the enterprise are state-owned assets, it was not entitled to invoke crown immunity.[240]

In summary, the CPG enjoys crown immunity before the Hong Kong courts. Such immunity extends to state-owned enterprises which are controlled by the CPG under PRC law. The law does not recognise a commercial exception per se. For state-owned enterprises, the benchmark of immunity is 'control' by the CPG. It is insufficient that an enterprise is owned by the CPG. The court will look at the various facets to corporate personality, such as independent powers, business and operational autonomy, right to own, use, profit from and dispose of property. If a state-owned enterprise possesses these attributes of an independent commercial entity, it is less likely to satisfy the control test in order to invoke crown immunity.

[232] *Hua Tian Long (No 2)* [2010] 3 HKLRD 611.
[233] ibid [82]–[90] (Stone J).
[234] ibid [98]–[126]; *TNB Fuel Services* (n 228) [9], [25]–[29] (Mimmie Chan J).
[235] *Hua Tian Long (No 2)* (n 232) [119]–[125] (Stone J).
[236] *TNB Fuel Services* (n 228).
[237] ibid [28], [86].
[238] ibid [28].
[239] ibid [70]–[80].
[240] ibid [81]–[86], [90]–[91].

VI. Conclusion

We will conclude with two observations. First, jurisdictional rules and principles are essential to the proper administration of justice. As a basic jurisdictional requirement, service of court process ensures that all parties will receive proper notice. An aggrieved party will be given the opportunity to raise his jurisdictional objection. In hearing jurisdictional disputes, the court usually has to balance the competing rights of parties to resolve their dispute in different forums. In this balancing exercise, the Hong Kong court will apply the constitutional provisions, statutes and common law, in order to achieve a fair and just result with proper regard to international comity.

Second, this jurisdictional exercise is also a meaningful one. In regard to a foreign defendant, the initial hurdle for service out requires the plaintiff to demonstrate the connection of his case to the forum and its substantive merits. This prompts him to put his cards on the table at the outset, at least to a certain extent, in line with the spirit of modern litigation. Any defendant who wishes to dispute jurisdiction can no longer keep his powder dry, but also needs to show his cards. A similar outcome can be achieved by the jurisdictional threshold in specific areas, such as *in rem* admiralty action, winding-up of foreign companies and bankruptcy of foreign individuals. The jurisdictional stage provides an early platform for the parties to assess each other's case, which allows and sometimes facilitates an early settlement. It also eliminates claims which ought not to be heard and tried in Hong Kong. The practical results of jurisdictional exercises are often encouraging to the parties and practitioners.

4

Taiwan

FULDIEN LI AND RONG-CHWAN CHEN*

I. Introduction

In civil law, the concept 'Gerichtsbarkeit' (Kompetenz) in Germany or 'compétence' in France is different from the concept 'Zuständigkeit' in Germany or 'jurisdiction' in France. In common law, jurisdiction to adjudicate means that an agency of a state (that is, the court) responds to a dispute between individuals or other legally-recognised entities for the purpose of making a determination regarding the dispute that is binding within the realm of the state.[1] On the basis of sovereignty, a nation state may, on any terms it deems appropriate, authorise its agencies to adjudicate and make decisions that are binding within that state.[2] '*Compétence nationale*' in the civil law system was translated into 'domestic jurisdiction' in common law countries. In the late Qing dynasty, China adopted the continental or modern Roman law system. The Republic of China (ROC) followed this tradition of differentiating the concept of competence from jurisdiction in procedural laws. In most civil law systems, generally the courts distinguish competence from jurisdiction. Competence means the power of the court to adjudicate. Jurisdiction means the realm of a court of which cases may be heard. Competence was described in some old textbooks on civil procedural law as judicial power or '*fa quan*' (法權) in Chinese. Without competence, courts cannot be empowered to exert jurisdiction. The court is empowered to dismiss the case without a trial on the ground of lack of '*fa quan*' (competence) by a ruling.[3]

Article 28 of Taiwan's Code of Civil Procedure (TCCP) provides: 'A court, upon determining a lack of jurisdiction over the action in whole or in part, will transfer the action to a court with jurisdiction either by ruling on the plaintiff's motion or its own initiative.' Where the civil court does not have jurisdiction over the case, and cannot transfer the case pursuant to Article 31(2), the court shall dismiss the plaintiff's action by a ruling (TCCP Article 249(1)).

However, the term 'international jurisdiction' has been used in the sense of competence since the Taiwan High Court's Civil Decision Shang-tzu No 12 of 1998. The Supreme Court ruled in its Civil Decision Tai-kang-tzu No 2 of 2006 that although the Act Governing the Choice of Law in Civil Matters Involving Foreign Elements (Choice of Law Act) does not

* The Chinese names of the case citations are as follows: Jia-shang-tzu 家上字; Kang-tzu 抗字; Min-shang-shang-keng-(1)-tzu 民商上更（一）字; Shang-tzu 上字; Shang-i-tzu 上易字; Shen-chung-su-tzu 審重訴字; Tai-kang-tzu 台抗字; Tai-shang-tzu 台上字.

[1] See Restatement (Second) of Conflict of Laws (1971), Ch 3, 100, Introductory Note.

[2] Russell J Weintraub, *Commentary on the Conflict of Laws* 4th edn (New York, Foundation Press, 2000) 114.

[3] Taiwan High Court Civil Decision Shang-tzu No 12 of 1998.

contain express provisions on jurisdictional issues, the court is required to apply by way of analogy the relevant national (domestic) laws to the facts and circumstances of the case. In its Civil Decision Tai-kang-tzu No 304 of 2012, the Supreme Court reiterated that provisions of the TCCP shall be applied by way of analogy to matters pertaining to jurisdictional issues, since there are no express provisions governing international jurisdiction in the ROC (Taiwan) and the courts do not distinguish between national (domestic) and international jurisdictions in allocating cases.[4]

II. Jurisdiction *in personam*

The TCCP adopts the traditional jurisdictional rules in civil law. Jurisdiction *in personam* and jurisdiction *in rem* are not differentiated and deployed in the legislation to decide on the court's jurisdiction. Jurisdiction *in personam* refers to jurisdiction over actions against particular persons who are subject to the court's jurisdiction because of his/her physical presence or individual relationship with that location. A ROC court may invoke jurisdiction *in personam* over an action for damages for breach of contract, an action for an injunction in a tort case, an action for possession of tangible property, or an action for family law, etc.

A. General Principles

In accordance with the Latin maxim '*potior est conditio defendentis*', a defendant may be sued in the court where the defendant is located. In its Civil Judgment Shang-tzu No 1160 of 2017, the Taiwan High Court states:

> In the event when the question of which court has international jurisdiction over a case arises, and in the absence of express provision within the Choice of Law Act, the decision relies on consideration of the following factors: interests of the parties, connection with a specific jurisdiction, domestic and international rules on civil procedure, fairness, and just and quick solutions. Unless there is a clear breach of procedural fairness or a violation of the above factors, in principle the courts of ROC will have jurisdiction in such event.

A similar statement can be found in the Intellectual Property Court's Civil Judgment Min-shang-shang-keng-(1)-tzu No 2 of 2018, which states:

> Where a civil matter involves foreign elements such as foreign persons, events occurred or properties located in a foreign state, the courts of ROC must first confirm that it has international jurisdiction over the case. The court must then look to the laws or principles to decide on the governing law applicable to the dispute through characterisation process. On deciding the applicable law, the court will look to ROC's Choice of Law Act. On deciding whether the courts of ROC have jurisdiction over a matter, in the absence of an express code, the court must look to the TCCP, rules and international law to consider the issue of procedural fairness, and to seek just and quick solutions under international principles.

[4] For a general and brief discussion on Taiwan's rules and principle on international jurisdiction, see Rong-Chwan Chen, 'Taiwan (National Report)' in Jürgen Basedow and others (eds), *Encyclopedia of Private International Law* vol 3 (Cheltenham, Edward Elgar Publishing, 2017) 2561–62.

i. Jurisdiction of Courts within the Territory

a. The Court of Defendant's Domicile

There is a distinction between 'domicile' and 'residence' under (Civil Code Articles 20–24). A defendant may be sued in the court of the defendant's domicile. Where the defendant has no place of residence in the ROC or where the defendant's place of residence is unknown, then the defendant's last place of domicile in the ROC shall be deemed the defendant's place of domicile (TCCP Articles 1(1) and 1(2)). Further, the court of a co-defendant's domicile has jurisdiction over all other co-defendants. In matters that become effective upon the death of a natural person, an action may be initiated in the court at the location of the decedent's domicile at the time of death (TCCP Article 18).

b. The Court of Defendant's Residence

When a court cannot exercise jurisdiction based on defendant's domicile, the court of the defendant's residence will have jurisdiction. Where a defendant has no place of domicile in the ROC, or where the defendant's place of domicile is unknown, then the defendant's place of residence in the ROC shall be deemed the defendant's place of domicile. A defendant may also be sued in the court at the defendant's residence when the cause of action involves transactions or occurrences taking place within the jurisdiction of that court (TCCP Article 1(1)). However, according to Article 47 of Consumer Protection Act, consumer litigation may be subject to the jurisdiction of the court where the consumer relationship happens.

c. Legal Person as a Defendant

Under the provisions of TCCP, a public juridical person may be sued in the court where its principal office is located; a central or local government agency may be sued in the court where such office is located; a private juridical person or unincorporated association that has the capacity to be a party to an action may be sued in the court in its principal office or principal place of business (TCCP Article 2). For matters relating to the business of a person's office or place of business, an action may be initiated against such person in the court where its office is located or its place of business (TCCP Article 6). Under the Enforcement Act of the Part of General Principles of the Civil Code ('Enforcement Act'), a foreign legal person recognised by the ROC has the same legal capacity as a ROC legal person of the same kind, and are equally subject to the ROC laws (Article 12). The individual who made a juridical act in the name of an unrecognised foreign legal person with the other persons shall be held jointly liable for such act with the unrecognised foreign legal person (Enforcement Act Article 15). According to Article 40(3) of the TCCP, an unincorporated association with a representative or an administrator has the capacity to be a party in civil proceedings.

For example, in its Civil Judgment Tai-shang-tzu No 267 of 2018, the Supreme Court affirmed the lower court's ruling that although the companies are registered in the US, Bermuda, and France, and have not been approved as registered foreign companies in Taiwan, they may be sued in Taiwan's courts since they are unincorporated associations with their own legal representatives and has standing as a party to a civil proceeding.[5] The case also affirmed that Taiwan's courts

[5] Article 13 of the Choice of Law Act 2010 adopted the principle of incorporation theory and stated that a foreign legal person's national law is the law under which it was established without mentioning its recognition by the ROC Government. Taiwan's Company Act replaced the system of recognising foreign companies with a new system of

have international jurisdiction over the case against a foreign company as a party to the tort claim because it conducted business in Taipei and the alleged tortious acts and the default in debt occurred in Taiwan.

ii. Forum non conveniens, lis alibi pendens, *Anti-suit Injunctions, Interim Measures, and Choice of Court Agreements*

a. *Forum non conveniens*

Under the doctrine of national competence, the court may dismiss the case on the ground of lack of '*fa quan*' (competence). However, in recent years, there has been a rise in the concept of international jurisdiction and it has replaced the traditional concept of national competence. The principle of *forum non conveniens* had a significant role throughout this change.

When exercising jurisdiction, the courts will look at the connecting factors between the facts of the case and the nation state in which the court is located. When multiple states have connections with the case and a conflict of jurisdictions arises in practice, the principle of *forum non conveniens* theoretically may apply to determine whether, in light of fairness to and interests of the parties and other circumstances, the court is the appropriate forum to exercise jurisdiction.[6]

Forum non conveniens is not stipulated in either the TCCP or the Choice of Law Act 2010. However, in some cases, this doctrine was applied by the courts. In its Civil Decision Tai-kang-tzu No 185 of 2008, the Supreme Court ruled:

> For cases where the foreigners' presence raise the question of whether the courts in ROC has international jurisdiction over a tort claim, although the Choice of Law Act does not expressly provide for such, the courts would still have international jurisdiction, as TCCP Articles 1(1), 15(1), and 22 shall be applicable by way of analogy in determining the ROC court's jurisdiction on the basis of the respondent's place of residence and the place where the tort was committed. … As none of the place of the tort, the place of the respondent's residence and the place of conducting business are in the ROC under any applicable standards, the courts of ROC will not have international jurisdiction. Even if such standards exist, the principle of *forum non conveniens* would render the court not to exercise jurisdiction in this case.

The Taiwan High Court followed in its Civil Decision Kang-tzu No 850 of 2012 by ruling that:

> Further, the courts of ROC will have no international jurisdiction since both the act and the consequence followed by the event took place in the United States, on the basis of *forum non conveniens* and *actor sequitur forum rei*. This court is therefore entitled to dismiss the current case pursuant to Article 249(1) Items 2 and 6 of the TCCP.

b. *Lis alibi pendens*

According to Article 182 of the TCCP, when the decision, in whole or in part, is premised upon certain legal relations to be determined in another action, the court may stay the proceeding until that other action is concluded. Although the rule does not clarify whether 'that other action' can be proceeded in a foreign jurisdiction, the interpretation of Article 182 should include the action brought before a Taiwan court as well as before a foreign state.

establishing and registering a branch in Taiwan in 2018. It is likely that the basis for an unrecognised foreign legal person's standing to be a party will shift from an 'unincorporated association' to a 'legal person'.

[6] Taiwan Hsinchu District Court Civil Decision Shen-chung-su-tzu No 85 of 2010.

In its Civil Decision Kang-tzu No 1293 of 2000, the Taiwan High Court was faced with a situation where it had to determine whether the guarantor liability at issue was premised upon the decision pending from the High Court of Malaysia on the parties' primary liability under Malaysian law. To prevent any contradictory decisions, the Taiwan High Court ruled that such domestic proceedings shall stay until the High Court of Malaysia concludes its case on the primary liability issue.

c. Anti-suit Injunctions

Article 22 of the TCCP states that when several courts have jurisdiction over an action, a plaintiff may choose to initiate the action in any one of those courts. When the court with jurisdiction cannot exercise jurisdiction due to legal or actual impediments, or when special circumstances suggest that the exercise of jurisdiction of the court may affect the public order or the fairness of the proceeding, or a court with jurisdiction cannot be determined because the jurisdictional boundaries are unascertainable, the immediate court above shall, on motion or at the request of the court in which the action is pending, designate a court to exercise jurisdiction.

According to Article 4 of ROC's Arbitration Law, the court may, in the event that one of the parties to an arbitration agreement commences a legal action contrary to the arbitration agreement, suspend the legal action and order the plaintiff to submit to arbitration within a specified time upon application by the adverse party, unless the defendant proceeds to respond to the legal action. Choice of court is addressed in Article 24 of the TCCP. Parties may, by written agreement, designate a court of first instance to exercise jurisdiction. A court obtains jurisdiction over an action where the defendant proceeds oral argument on the merits without contesting lack of jurisdiction.[7]

iii. Service of Process Outside of the Territory

Unlike the jurisdictional requirements in some common law jurisdictions, the jurisdiction of the Taiwanese court cannot be assumed by personal service in Taiwan. It is not surprising that service of process within and outside of Taiwan is comprehensively stipulated in the TCCP, in addition to other relevant provisions on jurisdiction. Personal service by parties is not acceptable under TCCP. Service of process is administered by the court clerk on his/her own authority (TCCP Article 123). Service of process shall be effectuated by an execution officer or post office delegated by the court clerk (Article 124). Service is deemed effectuated when the court clerk delivers the paper to be served to the person in the courthouse (Article 126). In an action regarding a business, service may be effectuated upon the manager (Article 131). However, in case the manager is a prisoner, service upon the manager shall be effectuated by the chief officer in charge of the prison, who is to serve the documents as requested by the court (Article 130).

For service of process to be conducted in a foreign country, the TCCP does not provide a separate sub-chapter for such purpose but provides special rules on service of process on foreign nationals for the Taiwanese courts. Where service is to be effectuated in the domicile, residence, or office of a person who enjoys immunity, the Ministry of Foreign Affairs may be requested to effect service (Article 144). Where service is to be made in a foreign country, it shall

[7] For further discussion, see Tieh-cheng Liu and Rong-chwan Chen, *Liu and Chen on Private International Law* 6th edn (Taipei, San Min, 2018) 639; Rong-chwan Chen, 'Legislation and Practice on Choice of Court Agreements in Taiwan' in Mary Keyes (ed), *Optional Choice of Court Agreements in Private International Law* (Switzerland, Springer, 2020) 387–407.

be effectuated by the competent authorities of such country, or the relevant ROC ambassador, minister envoy, or consul, or other authorised institutes or organisations in that country. Where service cannot be effectuated in accordance with the provisions of the preceding paragraph, it may be effectuated by dispatching the documents to be served by registered and receipt-requested mail (Article 145). However, if the foreign legal person or unincorporated association has set up an office or a place of business in the ROC, service upon that place shall be effectuated on its representative or administrator in the ROC (Article 128). Service upon a ROC ambassador, minister envoy, or consul, or any other staff stationed in a foreign country shall be effectuated by the Ministry of Foreign Affairs, upon being requested to do so (Article 146).

It is noteworthy that the exceptional constructive notice (public notice) can be applied to service of process outside Taiwan under some circumstances. The court in which the action is pending may, on motion, permit service upon a party to be effectuated by constructive notice under the following circumstances: (1) where the place of service shall be made is unknown; (2) where service effectuated in the domicile or residence or office of a person who enjoys immunity is ineffective; and (3) where service in a foreign country cannot be effectuated in accordance with Article 145, or it is foreseeable to be futile even if it has been so effectuated. When no person moves for such service by constructive notice in the cases prescribed above, the court in which the action is pending may on its own initiative order service to be effectuated by constructive notice, if it considers it necessary to avoid delay. Where the plaintiff or the defendant who has been served previously fails to notify the court in which the action is pending of the change of place where he/she can be served, and such failure results in the above situation, the court may, on its own initiative, order service to be effectuated by constructive notice (Article 149).

In the case of service by constructive notice, the paper to be served shall be kept in the court clerk's custody and a notice shall be posted on the court's bulletin board, indicating that the person to be served shall collect the paper from the court clerk at any time. Notwithstanding, where the paper to be served is a summons, the summons shall be posted on the bulletin board. In addition, the court shall order a written copy, photocopy, or excerpted copy of the paper to be posted on the court's website. Where the court considers it necessary, the court may order a written copy, photocopy, or excerpted copy of the paper to be published in official gazettes or newspapers. (Article 151). Service by constructive notice shall take effect 20 days after the date of posting the notice or summons on the court's bulletin board or the court's website, and in case of publication in an official gazette or newspaper, from the last day of such publication. Where service is effectuated in a foreign country by constructive notice, such service shall take effect 60 days after the posting or publication date (Article 152). When service by constructive notice is effectuated, the court clerk shall make a report, indicating the purpose of service and the date of service, and include it in the record (Article 153). Any litigation paper may be transmitted by telefax or by any other technological device, and such transmission shall render service effectuated when: (1) the person to be served notifies the court that he/she has received the documents served by telefax or by other technological device; or (2) an interested party moves for the transmission of a specific litigation paper (Article 153-1).

iv. Service of Foreign Proceedings within the Territory

Documents of foreign proceedings are basically served under the relevant laws of the foreign country. Unless required by the effective bilateral treaties or multilateral conventions to which Taiwan and the foreign country are signatory parties, and the parties to the legal proceedings are nationals of those signatories, Taiwanese courts will rarely have a role to play in the procedure. By now, the sole international instrument found to be for such purpose is the Agreement between the Taipei Economic and Cultural Office in Vietnam and the Vietnam Economic and Cultural Office in Taipei on Judicial Assistance in Civil Matters signed in 2010.

The Act on Supporting Foreign Courts on Consigned Cases was announced in 1963 to pave the way for potential support for the service of foreign proceedings. It mainly provides rules for Taiwanese courts when they are consigned by a foreign court to assist with foreign civil or criminal cases (Article 1). A court, when consigned by a foreign court to assist with foreign civil or criminal cases, shall not act in conflict with the laws of the ROC (Article 2). The consigned cases shall be conveyed in writing through foreign affairs authorities (Article 3). The country of the consigning foreign court shall declare reciprocal support to the ROC courts when similar situations arise (Article 4). The documents of civil or criminal cases for which a court is consigned by a foreign court to for assistance shall be duly served in accordance with the document service provisions under the ROC's Code of Civil Procedure or the Code of Criminal Procedure. The service document shall expressly state the name, nationality, domicile, address or office of the party to be served (Article 5).

A Taiwanese court shall follow the provisions of the TCCP to support a foreign court in the service of process. Again, personal service by parties is not acceptable under the TCCP. The rules are in TCCP Articles 123, 124, 126, 128, 130, and 131 as in the first paragraph of Section II.A.iii above.

B. Special Rules for Establishing Jurisdiction

Although not stated explicitly, the general rule is that a Taiwanese court has competence to decide whether it is competent to determine cases involving foreign elements. The principle embodied in Article 31-2 of the TCCP can be interpreted as the basis of such competence: if the party of a case disputes on whether the civil court has jurisdiction over the case, the civil court should adjudicate on such dispute as its first priority (Article 31-2(3)). Likewise, if a defendant disputes not only on a specific court's competence but generally the Taiwanese courts' competence to hear the case or the international jurisdiction of Taiwanese courts, such disputed court or the higher court is competent to decide whether Taiwanese courts have jurisdiction over the case and whether it is the court which is attributed with special jurisdiction.[8] Once a Taiwanese court determines that the Taiwanese courts have jurisdiction over a case, and delivers a final and binding judgment, all other Taiwanese courts are bound by such ruling (Article 31-2(1)), though such judgment could still be potentially disregarded by foreign courts where recognition or enforcement of the judgment is sought. In practice, some Taiwanese courts ruled *ex officio* that Taiwanese courts have general jurisdiction over the case before the court, and it has special jurisdiction over it.

As a general principle, the Taiwanese courts' jurisdiction over a case with foreign elements is based on the defendant's general connection with Taiwan and special factors legitimising the exercise of a Taiwanese court's jurisdiction. The special factors are framed and categorised in the TCCP. Not only do the provisions enable the specific Taiwanese court to hear the case, but they also provide the reason why Taiwanese courts have jurisdiction.[9]

[8] See TCCP, Art 23(2); Act on Labour Matters 2018, Art 22(2).

[9] Rong-chwan Chen, 'Jurisdiction, Choice of Law and the Recognition of Foreign Judgments in Taiwan' in Jürgen Basedow and Knut B Pissler (eds), *Private International Law in Mainland China, Taiwan and Europe* (Tübingen, Mohr Siebeck, 2014) 25.

i. Law of Obligations

An obligation is the legal relationship by which a claimant can exercise the right against the debtor to perform an act or fulfil obligations arising from an omission. The sources of obligations are divided into four categories under Taiwan's Civil Code: contracts (Article 153), management of affairs without mandate (Article 174), unjust enrichment (Article 179), and torts (Article 184). Special factors are respectively provided for a court to exercise jurisdiction over a case brought before it.

a. Specific Contracts

A contract creates a particular legal relation between the parties. Parties under contractual relations may 'by agreement, designate a court of first instance to exercise jurisdiction, provided that such agreement relates to a particular legal relation' and is evidenced in writing (TCCP Article 24). In the absence of such agreement, an action may be initiated in the court at the agreed place of performance of the contract (TCCP Article 12). If the parties agreed to perform their obligation in Taiwan, this connection forms a legal ground for the Taiwanese court to exercise jurisdiction. It has domestic jurisdiction as well as international jurisdiction over the case. The Taiwanese court at such place is appropriate to decide on the disputes concerning the validity, effect, performance, and damages or remedies for default or non-performance. This jurisdiction is in parallel with the *in personam* jurisdiction based on the defendant's domicile or residence.

It is noteworthy that the TCCP is in favour of the weaker party in a standard contract to disregard the choice of court clause. TCCP Article 28(2) provides that before proceeding debates on the merits of the case, notwithstanding Article 24, a party may move the court to transfer the action to another court with jurisdiction, provided that such choice of court agreement is part of a standard contract prepared by the opposing party who is either a legal person or a merchant, and that the contract is manifestly unfair under the circumstances. However, Article 28 does not apply when both parties are legal persons or merchants. Consumers and employees are often referred to as the legally weaker parties. Apart from the inequality of the bargaining power during contract negotiation, for the choice of court clause to be invalidated, the formation of the clause has to be 'manifestly unfair under the circumstances'. The court of the place of performance of the contract can thus exercise its jurisdiction over the relevant disputes. The test of 'manifest unfairness' in Article 28 is an exception to validity of a jurisdictional agreement and strictly construed in practice.

In the Supreme Court's Civil Decision Tai-kang-tzu No 445 of 2017, the parties disputed on the effect of a clause they agreed to in their Sales Representative Agreement. It states: 'All disputes arising from or in connection with this Agreement shall be submitted to the jurisdiction of Kunshan People's Court.' The Supreme Court affirmed that under the principles of freedom of contract and procedural disposition, it is exceptional to invalidate the clause by applying such a test. It also ruled that when the parties dispute on the contents of their real intention and whether they resulted in unfairness, the court shall look into the relevant factual background, the economic purposes, the common knowledge in society, usage of trade, the objective circumstances and the legal effects desired by the parties, and decide the issue in light of the principle of good faith. Since the parties are equal in their contracting position and bargaining power, and the clause in question was agreed upon under the full consideration of reducing the uncertainty, costs, risks and expenses in potential litigation, the result of such clause is not manifestly unfair to any party of it.

Obligations can also arise from other juridical acts. The fundamental principle on which the courts' jurisdiction arises is similar to contracts. Article 13 of the TCCP provides: 'In matters relating to negotiable instruments, an action may be initiated in the court at the location where the instruments are to be honored.' If the negotiable instrument at issue is to be honoured in Taiwan, Taiwanese courts have jurisdiction to decide on the disputes regarding its validity and effects.

b. Specific Torts

According to TCCP Article 15(1), the Taiwanese court for the location where the tortious act occurred has jurisdiction over the relevant disputes. The key factor – 'location where the tortious act occurred' – was interpreted by the Supreme Court in 1967 to include locations where any part of the tortious act was committed and where any part of consequence resulted from such act took place (Supreme Court's Civil Decision Tai-kang-tzu No 369 of 1967). The courts' special jurisdiction over maritime torts and aeronautic torts matters are addressed in TCCP Articles 15(2) and 15(3). Claims for damages arising from a collision of ships or other accidents at sea may be subject to jurisdiction of the court at the location where the damaged ship first arrived or where the ship inflicting damages is seized or registered, while claims for damages arising from a crash of aircraft or other aviation accidents may be subject to jurisdiction of the court at the location where the damaged aircraft first arrived, or where the aircraft inflicting damages is seized.

The above rules apply to all cases involving foreign elements. The Supreme Court clearly ruled in 2008 that the Taiwanese courts' international jurisdiction over a foreigner's claim for damages of torts was not stipulated in the Choice of Law Act. Therefore, TCCP Articles 1(1), 15(1), 15(2) and 22 of the TCCP shall apply by way of analogy, which provide both the Taiwanese courts of domicile and where the tortious act occurred with jurisdiction over the case (Supreme Court's Civil Decision Tai-kang-tzu No 185 of 2008).

In cases where there is concurrent liability in tort and in contract under a licensing agreement between the plaintiff and the defendant, jurisdictional issues arise so the plaintiff then claims under both causes of action. The Supreme Court ruled in 2005 that a claim of tort is separate from a claim of contract, and they are subject to different courts' jurisdictions under respective rules. On the basis of tort, the jurisdiction of a Taiwanese court will not be bound by the choice of court clause in the licensing contract. Rather, the Taiwanese court of the defendant's domicile or where the tortious act occurred will have jurisdiction over the case. The decision accords with the principle that the defendant shall be better protected (*potior est condtio defendentis*). The court's jurisdiction is not excluded by the choice of Japanese law and a Japanese court in the licensing contract under a tort claim (Supreme Court's Civil Decision Tai-kang-tzu No 164 of 2005).

c. Unjust Enrichment

Unjust enrichment is an independent cause of action under the law of obligations along with tort, contract and *negotiorum gestio*. A person who acquires interests without any legal grounds thus prejudicing the other is unjustly enriched and is obliged to make restitution. Unjust enrichment stands even if there existed a legal relationship but was subsequently extinguished (Article 179 of the Civil Code). An action of unjust enrichment or management of affairs without mandate is not characterised as an equitable remedy under Taiwanese law. Instead, it is categorised as a restitutionary claim under the law of obligations in civil law. With regard to the issue of jurisdiction, the general rules of jurisdiction in *personam* are applicable. Since an action of marine salvage is subject to the jurisdiction of the court at the location where the salvage took place (TCCP

Article 16) and the court at the location where the property is to be managed (TCCP Article 14), the court at the location where the enrichment occurred or where the affairs are managed shall likewise have jurisdiction over the action of unjust enrichment or management of affairs without mandate.

d. Trusts and Charitable Foundations

Charitable foundations are legal persons established and regulated by the provisions of the Civil Code and the Foundation Act. According to Article 2 of the TCCP, the Taiwanese courts have jurisdiction over the case if the defendant foundation's principal office or principal place of business is located in Taiwan.

A trust is legislatively defined under Article 1 of the ROC's Trust Law as 'the legal relationship in which the settlor transfers or disposes of a right of property and the trustee agreed to administer or dispose of the trust property according to the stated purposes of the trust for the benefit of a beneficiary or for a specified purpose'. Such juridical act does not create a legal entity. Depending on the nature of legal relation at issue, the special jurisdiction of Taiwanese courts can be based on special provisions of the TCCP. For example, Article 14 stipulates that: 'In matters relating to claims arising from the management of property, an action may be initiated in the court at the location where the property is to be managed.' If the legal relation at issue is the trust registration which is required to have been duly completed to be valid against third parties (Trust Act Article 4), the Taiwanese court at the location where the registration is administered will have jurisdiction (TCCP Article 17).

ii. Law of Property

A right relating to property might be obligatory or proprietary. The TCCP states that if the legal relation at issue is an obligatory right concerning properties where the defendant's attachable property or the subject matter of a claim is a creditor's right, then either the place of the debtor's domicile or the location of the subject matter of the security shall be deemed to be the location of the defendant's attachable property or the subject matter of the claim (TCCP Article 3). The court at the location of the defendant's attachable property or the subject matter of the claim will have jurisdiction, in the event that a defendant does not have a place of domicile in the ROC or whose domicile is unknown (TCCP Article 3). It also provides special rules concerning jurisdiction *in personam* for property matters. For instance, if the defendant is an apprentice, an employee, or any other sojourners, the court for the sojourning place of such person will have jurisdiction (TCCP Article 4). If the defendant is a soldier or seaman, the court at the location of the principal office or where the warship or ship is registered will have jurisdiction (TCCP Article 5).

a. Immovable Property

Rights *in rem* or proprietary rights over things are regulated by the law of property. They are subject to mandatory norms and the principle of *numerus clausus* which is contrary to the basic rule of freedom of contract within the law of obligations. This is particularly the case concerning immovable properties which are universally subject to strict registration rules, which are prima facie evidence to bring an *in rem* action to determine ownership of a property. In line with the universal rule on a court's jurisdiction over *in rem* actions concerning immovable properties, TCCP Article 10(1) provides: 'In matters relating to rights *in rem*, partition, or demarcation of real property, exclusive jurisdiction resides in court for the place where the real property is located.'

It is unquestionable that matters involving foreign elements shall be subject to the exclusive jurisdiction of the courts of the country where the immovable or real property is located. Therefore, courts of other countries will have no jurisdiction over such case. Likewise, the Taiwanese courts will not have jurisdiction over disputes *in rem* actions on immovable properties located outside its territory.

The rule of exclusive jurisdiction applies solely to rights in accordance with TCCP Article 10(2). Further: 'In other matters relating to real property, an action may be initiated in the court at the place where the real property is located.' In practice, the characterisation problem may arise when the right at issue is characterised as proprietary in one legal system while as obligatory in another. For the Taiwanese courts to exercise jurisdiction, the standards in Taiwanese law or *lex fori* might naturally be followed, while the laws of the recognising country might be applied when the resulting judgment is sought for recognition and enforcement in a foreign country.

An exception to such exclusive jurisdiction is when rights *in rem* are subordinated to an obligation of surety. The legislative policy is rather to loosen jurisdiction over the right *in rem* than to confine the obligation under such jurisdiction. TCCP Article 11 provides that: 'In matters relating to debts or rights *in rem* of any real property provided as a security for such debt, an action may be initiated against the same defendant in the court for the place where the real property is located.' In other words, if a right *in rem* over an immovable property at issue is also an *in rem* security for a debt, and the defendant is sued for both the debt and the security right *in rem*, then the court at the place where the real property is located will have jurisdiction over the case.

b. Intangible Property

Besides intellectual property which will be discussed in Section II.B.iii, intangible property also covers obligatory claims and other rights of economic values. Although there are no specific rules on jurisdiction over cases of intangible property under Taiwanese law, in general the above rules on *in rem* rights apply.

c. Succession to Property

A case before a Taiwanese court on succession to property might be a litigation (contentious matter) or a non-litigation matter (non-contentious matter). A litigation is an action initiated by the plaintiff against the defendant over any disputes between them. A non-litigation matter is petitioned by the applicant to ask the court to decide on matters as required by the law in order to fulfill the provisions of the law. The causes of non-litigation matters are those stipulated expressly in the Civil Code or other legislations, and their procedures are governed by the Act on Non-Litigation Matters 1964 (last revised 2018). The TCCP basically addresses the procedures for litigation.

For litigations on succession, the TCCP states generally that: 'In matters that become effective upon the death of a natural person, an action may be initiated in the court of jurisdiction at the location where the decedent resided at the time of death.' (TCCP Article 18(1)). In the event where jurisdiction cannot be exercised by the court prescribed in Article 18(1), or where the incident giving rise to such matter occurred at the decedent's place of residence, or where the decedent as a ROC citizen either did not have a place of domicile in the ROC or whose place of domicile is unknown at the time of death, then the provision of TCCP Article 1 shall apply *mutatis mutandis* in determining jurisdiction (TCCP Article 18(2)). If the legal relation at issue relates to an encumbrance upon the decedent's estate, jurisdiction may be exercised by the Taiwanese court at the place where the estate in whole or in part is located (TCCP Article 19).

Therefore, if the decedent had personal connection in terms of citizenship, domicile, or residence in Taiwan, or any part of the decedent's estate is located within the territory of Taiwan, Taiwanese courts will have jurisdiction over the relevant disputes.

In 2012, the Act on Family Matters (also known as the Family Act, *Jiashi Shijian Fa*) was promulgated to comprehensively govern all the procedural issues (covering both litigation and non-litigation issues) concerning family law matters. Matters on inheritance or succession to property are included in this Act and are divided into litigation matters and non-litigation matters. Litigation matters include claims for restitution of inheritance, partition of estate, forced shares, bequeath, probate of will, and other claims on succession among inheritors. According to Article 70 of the Act on Family Matters, the following courts will have jurisdiction over the above matters: (1) the Taiwanese court at the place of the domicile of the successor at the opening of the succession; and (2) the Taiwanese court at the place of the primary property of the decedent.

Non-litigation matters on succession to property include matters concerning: (1) submission of a list of the decedent's estate to the court; (2) a creditor's petition for ordering the inheritors to submit a list of the decedent's estate to the court; (3) waiver of inheritance; (4) unacknowledged succession; (5) preservation of the decedent's estate; (6) designation or re-designation of an executor of a will; and (7) other matters concerning succession. These matters, according to Article 127 of the Act on Family Matters, are subject to the exclusive jurisdiction of the Taiwanese court at the domicile of the decedent when the succession commenced. On matters pertaining to preservation of the decedent's estate, the Taiwanese court at the place where any part of the estate is located could also exercise jurisdiction. In addition, as Article 52(4) of this Act shall apply *mutatis mutandis* to such matters, the Taiwanese court at the place where the defendant has domicile or residence can exercise its jurisdiction as well.

The legal relation of inheritance results in some non-ligation matters on family council as well. The court's jurisdiction over the constitution of a family council for a matter is also addressed in Article 181 of the Act on Family Matters. According to Article 181(2), a petition for designating members of the family council for the estate is subject to exclusive jurisdiction of the successor's court of domicile at the opening of the succession. Article 181(5) stipulates that a petition to court for the following matters that are required to be dealt with by the family council is subject exclusively to the jurisdiction at the place of the domicile or residence of the heir: (1) matters concerning giving a portion of the estate to a person; (2) matters concerning supervising the manager of the estate; (3) matters concerning determining the remuneration of a manager of the estate; (4) matters concerning determining the authenticity of an oral will; (5) matters concerning tendering of a will; (6) matters concerning opening and viewing a sealed will; and (7) other matters that shall be dealt with by the family council.

iii. Intellectual Property

There are several enactments on intellectual property in Taiwan, including the Copyright Act 1928 (last revised 2019), Trademark Act 1930 (last revised 2016), Patent Act 1944 (last revised 2019), Integrated Circuit Layout Protection Act 1995 (last revised 2002), and Trade Secrets Act 1996 (last revised 2020). To adjudicate disputes of such nature systematically, the Intellectual Property Court enjoys exclusive jurisdiction to adjudicate all cases concerning intellectual property rights in Taiwan, pursuant to Articles 2 and 3 of the Intellectual Property Court Organisation Act 2007 and Article 7 of the Intellectual Property Case Adjudication Act 2007. Such exclusivity is based on subject matter jurisdiction rather than territorial jurisdiction and is applicable neither directly nor by way of analogy to the issue of international jurisdiction. Hence, if an international case involving intellectual property rights is within the exclusive jurisdiction of the Intellectual

Property Court in Taiwan, it is not necessarily the situation that the Taiwanese courts' jurisdiction can exclude courts of other countries from exercising their jurisdiction over the same case. It is noteworthy that the Intellectual Property Court is set to be merged into the Intellectual Property and Commercial Court when the Commercial Case Adjudication Act 2020 and the Intellectual Property and Commercial Court Organization Act 2020 come into effect on 1 July 2021.

Since there are no special provisions for international jurisdiction on any issue concerning intellectual property, Taiwanese courts' jurisdiction over actions against infringement of intellectual property rights is to be decided by way of analogy using the rules on other actions on property matters mentioned above. Unlike the disputes on rights *in rem* over an immovable property, all issues concerning intellectual property are not subject to the exclusive jurisdiction of any single court of another country, even though the validity of a registered intellectual property is subject to such exclusive jurisdiction in some foreign legal systems such as Article 24(4) of EU's Brussels I Regulation (Recast).[10]

In practice, most cases on intellectual property rights are international in nature and relate to infringement of such rights. It is quite common that a foreign company files a lawsuit against a Taiwanese company or an individual for infringing its patent in a Taiwanese court. The Taiwanese courts' jurisdiction is normally established based on connecting factors such as Taiwanese nationality, domicile and residence of the parties.[11]

In the Supreme Court's Civil Decision Tai-kang-tzu No 1004 of 2015, a dispute over a domain name (tvbs.com) registered in the US registry was decided by the Asian Domain Name Dispute Resolution Center (ADNDRC) in Hong Kong against its Taiwanese owner. The owner initiated an action in Taiwan to seek for judicial declaration that the domain name registration did not infringe the right on the trademark of TVBS combination. The court of first instance ruled that Taiwanese courts had no jurisdiction. The court of second instance reversed it and claimed that Taiwanese courts did have jurisdiction. The second-instance decision was upheld by the Supreme Court. According to the Supreme Court's decision, the ground to support the Taiwanese courts' jurisdiction is the link that the trademark at issue is registered and protected under the Taiwan Trademark Act. The problem is that the dispute had been decided by the ADNDRC in accordance with Uniform Domain Name Dispute Resolution Policy (UDRP) established by the Internet Corporation for Assigned Names and Numbers (ICANN). This dispute relates to the conflict of legal systems of the cyber world and the real world. A deeper and thorough re-consideration has been called for in future development.

In addition to traditional transactions, e-commerce also resulted in some novel problems. In the Supreme Court's Civil Decision Tai-kang-tzu No 256 of 2019, the Taiwanese plaintiff sued the Japanese defendant company in a Taiwanese court asserting that some counterfeit items (made in China) were sold in the defendant's store in Japan and on the defendant's website which could be accessed from Taiwan via the Internet, while announcing overseas purchase orders will not be processed. The court of first instance ruled that Taiwanese courts have no jurisdiction over such a foreign defendant and such an e-commerce transaction. The court of second instance reversed it and ruled that Taiwanese courts have jurisdiction. The Supreme Court upheld the second-instance decision and stated that the Taiwanese courts' jurisdiction is fundamentally based on the fact that the consequence of such infringement occurred in Taiwan. It is quite clear that the

[10] Regulation (EU) No 1215/2012 of the European Parliament and of the Council of 12 December 2012 on jurisdiction and the recognition and enforcement of judgments in civil and commercial matters (recast) [2012] OJ L351/1.

[11] Rong-chwan Chen, 'International Civil Litigations on Patent Infringements: Focusing on the Supreme Court Decisions and the Application of the Latest Legislation' (2013) 215 *Taiwan Law Journal* 1–10 (Part 1); (2013) 216 *Taiwan Law Journal* 1–17 (Part 2).

provisions of TCCP Article 15(1) were applied by way of analogy to this case. In light of the ubiquity of the internet and the fact that the website was established for online purchasing within Japan, it is suggested that the principle of intellectual property rights' territoriality could serve as a legal basis for the Taiwanese court's jurisdiction. Taiwan is the appropriate forum for the case, as it concerns an infringement of the trademark right, which was characterised as a Taiwanese intellectual property right.

iv. Family Law

The Act on Family Matters 2012 revised the rules on the allocation of cases to specific courts in Taiwan that have domestic jurisdiction. The rules replace the previous relevant provisions under the TCCP which used to be applicable to family law matters. It also prescribes the basic rule for Taiwanese courts in determining whether or not to exercise their international jurisdiction.

a. Marriage

The Civil Code defines marriage as a legal relation between a man and a woman and establishes its relevant rules (Articles 980, 1000 to 1003-1). In 2019, a special enactment (Act for Implementation of Judicial Yuan Interpretation No 748) stipulated that two persons of the same sex may form a permanent union of intimate and exclusive nature for the purpose of living a common life (Article 2), and that disputes arising within such a union are considered as family matters, which is subject to the provisions of the Act on Family Matters. The following discussion on marriages in this chapter is hence applicable to unions mentioned in the special enactment.

The drafters of the Act on Family Matters put validity, nullification, revocation of a marriage and a divorce together into a single group called 'marriage matters'. Article 52 deals with allocations of such cases to specific Taiwanese courts. It stipulates that a matter seeking the nullification or revocation of a marriage or a divorce, or seeking a declaratory judgment confirming the existence or non-existence of a marriage, is subject to the exclusive jurisdiction of: (1) the court of the husband's and wife's common domicile; (2) the court of the husband's and wife's common habitual residence; or (3) the court at the place where the husband or the wife resides and the grounds or occurrences giving rise to the action took place (Article 52(1)). However, notwithstanding Article 52(1), the parties may agree on the competent court in writing (Article 52(2)). If the husband or wife who is a party to such matter has died, the proceedings are subject exclusively to the jurisdiction of the court of the husband's or wife's domicile at the time of death; if no court can be found to be competent in this way, the court of the defendant's domicile or residence has jurisdiction; if the defendant's domicile or residence cannot be established, the matter is then subject to the court at the location of the central government (Article 52(3)).

The Act on Family Matters sets particular rules to deal with the Taiwanese courts' exercise of international jurisdiction over marriage matters involving foreign elements. Article 53 states that ROC courts are competent to exercise jurisdiction over and to rule on marriage matters where any of the following four conditions exists: (1) the husband or the wife is a ROC citizen; (2) neither the husband nor the wife is a ROC citizen, but they are domiciled or have had common residence within the ROC for over one year; (3) the husband or the wife is stateless and has habitual residence within the ROC; or (4) the husband or the wife has had habitual residence within the ROC for over one year, unless the ROC court judgments or decisions are manifestly unlikely to be recognised by the state of the husband's or wife's nationality (Article 53(1)). It is notable that the *forum non conveniens* principle is embodied in this enactment. In circumstances where it is manifest that the defendant will have difficulties in appearing before the ROC courts, the above provisions shall not apply, that is, the ROC courts shall not exercise international jurisdiction (Article 53(2)). There is no legislative definition of 'habitual residence'. Whether a residence is habitual is to be decided by the court on a case-to-case basis.

b. Divorce, Nullity and Separation

Under Taiwan's Civil Code, the spouses may divorce by mutual consent (Article 1049) or by a court's decree of divorce (Article 1052). Legal separation is not adopted in the Civil Code as a legal process for a married couple. In addition to the situation that the supposed marriage is null and void, the Civil Code also stipulates some conditions under which a spouse may apply to the court for revocation or annulment of a marriage. As mentioned above, the Taiwanese courts' international jurisdiction over the relevant matters is contained in Article 53 of the Act on Family Matters.

Among all the marriage matters, divorce is the most typical one. It has been established that the ROC courts have to address whether they have international and domestic jurisdiction before dealing with the merits of the divorce. For example, in the Taiwan High Court Civil Judgment Jia-shang-tzu No 130 of 2007, a particular part entitled 'Choice of Applicable Law in Civil Matters Involving Foreign Elements' was included and the following four problems on private international law were discussed in detail:

(1) Is there any foreign element involved in this case?
(2) Do Taiwanese courts have international jurisdiction?
(3) Is the specific Taiwanese court in which the plaintiff initiated the action has domestic jurisdiction?
(4) What is the law applicable to this case?

These discussions have been a standard formality of judgments involving foreign elements.[12]

Articles 52 and 53 of the Act on Family Matters apply directly to litigation in marriage matters. Article 98 of the Act provides that the same provisions apply *mutatis mutandis* to the court's jurisdiction over non-litigation marriage matters. Among these non-litigation marriage matters are matters concerning mutual obligation of cohabitation between spouses, designation of domicile for a spouse by a court, mutual obligation between the spouses to inform each other of the condition of his or her property acquired in marriage, payment for living expenses of the household, expenses of maintenance, or alimony, or a court order of the application of the separation of property regime for matrimonial property. The Supreme Court ruled in its Civil Decision Tai-kang-tzu No 1020 of 2014 that such rules of jurisdiction apply to a Taiwanese court's provisional measures to preserve for a future judgment in a US court.

c. Matters Relating to the Well-being of the Child

Besides marriage matters, parent-child matters are also a major issue within family matters. These jurisdictional issues are dealt with by Article 61 of the Act on Family Matters. The jurisdiction to hear the proceedings exclusively belongs to the following courts: (1) the court at the place of the domicile of the child or the adopted child; and (2) the court at the place of the father, the mother, the adoptive father, or the adoptive mother (Article 61(1)). However, where a minor child or

[12] For details, see Chen (n 9) 26–27.

an adopted child is listed among the defendants in any matter mentioned above, the court at the place of the domicile of such child shall have exclusive jurisdiction to hear the proceedings (Article 61(2)). The rules of domestic jurisdiction and international jurisdiction over marriage matters apply *mutatis mutandis* to parent-child matters (Article 69).

Article 104 of the Act on Family Matters formulates some domestic jurisdictional rules on parent-child non-litigation matters. Article 104(1) stipulates that the following matters are subject to the exclusive jurisdiction of the court at the place of the domicile or habitual residence of the child: (1) matters concerning the minor child's claim of maintenance, the petition for determination, change, or modification of parental rights and obligations, or the petition for determination of exercising rights with regard to important matters of the minor child; (2) matters concerning the change of surname of the minor child; (3) matters concerning the cessation of parental power; (4) matters concerning the designation of a special agent for the minor child; (5) matters concerning the handing over of a child; (6) other matters concerning parent-child relations. If the said child does not have a domicile or residence, the court shall determine an appropriate place where its court shall have jurisdiction. Moreover, 'where there are more than one minor child and their domiciles or habitual residences do not locate in the jurisdiction *ratione loci* of one single court, the courts that have jurisdiction *ratione loci* may exercise concurrent jurisdictions' (Article 104(2)). With no further provisions on international jurisdiction, by analogy to the above rules, if the minor child has a domicile or residence within Taiwan, then the Taiwanese courts will have jurisdiction over the parent-child non-litigation matter.

According to Taiwan's Civil Code, agreement of adoption shall be in writing and petitioned to the court for approval (Article 1079(1)). The relationship between an adopted child and his/her adoptive parents may be terminated by mutual agreement in writing. Where the adopted child is a minor, the termination shall be petitioned to the court (Article 1080(2)). The court proceedings to approve or to terminate adoption is a non-litigation matter. The decision must be based on the best interest of the minor. Further, the principle of the best interest of the child will also have to be considered when determining the court's jurisdiction. Article 114 of the Act on Family Matters deals with matters on adoption and on termination of adoption separately. Article 114(1) stipulates that the matter on approving the adoption of a child is subject exclusively to the jurisdiction of the court at the place of domicile of the adopter or the adoptee; or, if the adoptee has no domicile within Taiwan, of the court at the place of the domicile of the adopter. Article 114(2) stipulates that matters on acknowledgement, approval, or declaration of the termination of adoption is subject exclusively to the jurisdiction at the place of the domicile of the adoptee. It is apparent that Taiwanese courts have international jurisdiction over matters involving foreign elements where the said domicile of the adopter or adoptee is located within Taiwan.

Other non-litigation matters are also provided for in the Act on Family Matters. Article 120(1) stipulates that the following matters concerning guardianship of minors are subject exclusively to the jurisdiction for the place of the domicile or residence of the minor concerned; where the said minor does not have a domicile or residence, the court shall determine an appropriate place where its court shall have jurisdiction: (1) matters concerning the designation, re-designation, or change of a guardian for a minor; (2) matters concerning reports or submissions by the guardian; (3) matters concerning the resignation of a guardian; (4) matters concerning the determination of the rights exercised by a guardian; (5) matters concerning the determination of the remuneration of a guardian; (6) matters concerning the designation of a special agent for the ward; (7) matters concerning the authorisation of an action taken by the guardian; (8) matters concerning the handing over of a child; (9) matters concerning damages out of guardianship;

and (10) other matters concerning guardianship of minors. Article 125(1) stipulates that the following matters concerning maintenance are subject exclusively to the jurisdiction for the place of the domicile or residence of the person who is entitled to maintenance: (1) matters concerning claims for maintenance; (2) matters concerning claims for reduction or waive of maintenance obligation; (3) matters concerning claims for modifying the extent or manner of furnishing maintenance on grounds or change of circumstances; and (4) other matters concerning maintenance. The rule on concurrent jurisdiction for multiple minor children in Article 104(2) of the Act on Family Matters (see above) applies *mutatis mutandis* to the above two groups of matters.

v. Law of Corporations and Insolvency

Corporations are entities with legal personality established under corporate law. The jurisdictional issue that may arise before the court dealing with a corporation is which court has jurisdiction, either over a litigation matter or a non-litigation matter pursuant to the Company Act 1929 (last revised 2018).

Article 2 of the TCCP addresses the jurisdictional problem over litigations of which the defendant is a corporation. Article 2(2) states: 'A private juridical person or unincorporated association that has the capacity to be a party to an action may be sued in the court for the location of its principal office or principal place of business.' Taiwanese courts can exercise international jurisdiction over the defendant corporation, whatever its nationality may be, as long as its principal office or principal place of business is located in Taiwan. For foreign corporations, Article 2(3) stipulates that a foreign juridical person or unincorporated association may be sued in the court of the principal office or principal place of business of such entity in Taiwan. In other words, a foreign corporation with offices or businesses in Taiwan is subject to the jurisdiction of where its Taiwanese principal office or principal place of business is located, despite having other principal offices and principal places of business abroad.

Article 9 of the TCCP also addresses jurisdiction over disputes between a corporation and its shareholders. In matters relating to claims arising from its membership, an action may be initiated by a corporation or any association, or its creditor or member, against a member in the court at the location of the corporation's or association's principal office or principal place of business. Such provision shall apply *mutatis mutandis* to an action initiated by an association or its creditor or member against such association's staff or former member.

Corporation insolvency and its reorganisation is specifically addressed in Article 282 of the Company Act. Article 282 provides that:

> (1) Where a company which publicly issues shares or corporate bonds suspends its business due to financial difficulty or where there is an apprehension of suspension of business thereof, but there is a possibility for the company to be constructed or rehabilitated, the company or any of the following interested parties may apply to the court for reorganisation: (1) Shareholders who have been continuously holding shares representing ten per cent or more of the total number of issued shares for a period of six months or longer; (2) Creditors of the company who have claims equivalent to ten per cent or more of the capital from the total number of issued shares; (3) Labor unions; or (4) Two-thirds or more of the employees of a company.
>
> (2) For filing the reorganisation application by a company under the preceding paragraph, the Board of Directors of the company shall adopt a resolution by a majority vote of the directors present at a meeting of the Board of Directors attended by over two-thirds of all directors.

The filing of an application for reorganisation is categorised as a non-contentious matter, which will become subject to the provisions under the Act on Non-Litigation Matters 1964 (last revised 2018). According to Article 82 of the Act, matters concerning registration of a legal person is subject to the jurisdiction at the place where the office is located. Article 171 stipulates that matters to be dealt with under the Company Act is subject to the jurisdiction of where the company is present. Consequently, corporations governed by Taiwanese law will render the courts in Taiwan with subject matter jurisdiction over non-litigation matters. According to Articles 13 and 14 of the Choice of Law Act 2010, legal persons are subject to the laws of Taiwan, as Taiwan was where they were incorporated. Their internal affairs will be governed under Taiwanese laws, as stated in Article 14. The specific court at the place where the principal office of the corporation is located can exercise its domestic jurisdiction over the relevant matters.

vi. Law of Bankruptcy

Bankruptcy is a legal process that applies to a debtor who cannot repay debts to its creditors. Bankruptcy can only be declared by a court order. The standard and procedure are provided for in the Bankruptcy Act 1935 (last revised 2018). Article 2 stipulates that the bankruptcy matter is subject exclusively to the jurisdiction of the district court at the place where the debtor or the bankrupt is domiciled; if the debtor or the bankrupt has a place of business, then jurisdiction is invoked at the district court in the place of business. If the principal place of business of the debtor or the bankrupt is located in a foreign country, the bankruptcy matter is subject exclusively to the jurisdiction of the district court in their Taiwanese principal place of business. If the court of jurisdiction cannot be determined by the above rules, the district court at the place where the principal property of the debtor or the bankrupt is located can exercise its jurisdiction. In simple terms, the Taiwanese courts have jurisdiction over a bankruptcy matter if the debtor or the bankrupt has a domicile or an office of business within Taiwan, or that the principal property of the debtor or the bankrupt is located within Taiwan. The Supreme Court ruled in its Civil Decision Tai-kang-tzu No 1195 of 2005 that the determination of whether the debtor is capable of repaying the debts or shall be declared bankrupt is within the exclusive jurisdiction of the aforementioned court.

The Act on Liquidation of Consumer Debts 2007 (last revised 2018) follows and adopts similar jurisdictional rules. Article 5 provides that matters of regeneration or liquidation are subject to the exclusive jurisdiction of the court at the place of the debtor's domicile or residence; if jurisdiction cannot be determined by the above rules, the district court at the place where the principal property of the debtor is located can exercise jurisdiction. With regard to the international effects of bankruptcy settlements or court orders, Article 4 of the Bankruptcy Act provides that a bankruptcy settlement concluded abroad, or a bankruptcy order rendered by a foreign court has no binding force over the properties of the debtor or the bankrupt located in Taiwan. This protective policy may raise problems in recognising foreign court judgments and create a disharmonious phenomenon that a bankrupt is unexpectedly protected from the effects of a foreign bankruptcy order.[13] Likewise, the question of whether a bankruptcy order rendered by a Taiwanese court is binding or has legal effect in a foreign country is subject to the laws of such foreign country.

vii. Competition Law

The Fair Trade Act was promulgated as Taiwan's antitrust law or competition law in 1991. The enactment's main objective is to establish a responsible administrative authority and to grant such authority the power to investigate and impose administrative sanctions on

[13] Rong-Chwan Chen, 'The Domestic Effects of an Insolvency Decree of Foreign Court' (2015) 154 *Taiwan Jurist* 30–32.

anti-competitive conducts. The Fair Trade Commission under the Executive Yuan has established some guidelines on extraterritorial mergers concerning the problems surrounding the exterritorial effects of the domestic legislation. They basically follow the principles developed in US antitrust law, applicable to an exterritorial anti-competitive conduct if it results in some prescriptive effects in the domestic market. The EU courts interpreted the concept of an anti-competitive conduct to include its conclusion and implementation, so that EU competition law also applies to a conduct concluded outside its territory but implemented within the EU. It is recommended that Taiwan should refer to Article 6 of the Administrative Penalty Act and Article 4 of the ROC's Criminal Code and adopt the principles developed in the EU for effective enforcement.[14]

Private international law does not concern itself with the imposition of administrative and criminal sanctions. Compensatory claims could be addressed by resorting to the Fair Trade Act which provides civil remedies. Claims for removal or prevention of an infringement (Article 29), compensatory damages (Article 30), and treble damages (Article 31) are all available. For issues relating to jurisdiction, Article 27 of the Choice of Law Act 2010 stipulates that:

> where an obligation arises from a disruption of the order of a market by an act of unfair competition or of restriction of competition, the obligation is governed by the law of the place where the market is located. However, where the unfair competition or restriction of competition is produced by a juridical act, and where the law governing the juridical act is more beneficial to the injured person, that law is applied.

The antitrust law or competition law of a foreign country shall not be excluded simply because of its public law nature. Since no provision on jurisdiction over civil matters on anti-competitive conducts is provided, they shall be categorised as a relevant legal relation (for example, tort) and the provisions of the TCCP shall be applied by way of analogy in determining jurisdiction.

III. Jurisdiction *in rem* with Special Focus on Shipping Claims

A. Jurisdiction *in rem* of the Courts within the Territory

The distinction between suits *in personam* and suits *in rem* is not adopted and stated in the TCCP. Maritime cases will be brought against the owner of the ship, even if a case was brought before the court based on maritime lien. In its Civil Judgment Tai-kang-tzu No 2197 of 2015, the Supreme Court ruled that the ROC does not adopt the common law system of *in rem* jurisdiction, however, if the plaintiff exercises a maritime lien against a non-debtor who holds ownership of the vessel, he/she can seek for a declaratory judgment in order to confirm priority rights over the maritime property, shipping charges or other auxiliary equipment. When a declaratory judgment is rendered in the plaintiff's favour, he/she can apply to the court for enforcement of the judgment, in which the court will apply the Taiwanese laws and regulations on mortgage by way of analogy.

B. The Process of Ship Arrest in the Territory

According to the Maritime Act 1929 (*Hai Shang Fa*, last revised 2009), the claims secured by maritime liens are entitled to a preferential right of compensation (Article 24). In the event

[14] Rong-Chwan Chen, 'Jurisdiction and the Law Applicable to Anti-Competitive Conduct Involving Foreign Elements' (2014) 22(2) *Fair Trade Quarterly* 93–162.

that the right of retention is granted in respect of a ship in possession of a creditor for securing claims for shipbuilding or repair of the ship, such right of retention shall be postponed to all maritime liens, but shall have priority over ship mortgages (Article 25).

In the Supreme Court's Civil Judgment Tai-shang-tzu No 4299 of 1971, a creditor who has maritime lien over the ship seized the property for satisfaction of claims. The appellant argued that when the pilotage and port charges had been paid by him, and was entitled to receive reimbursement later on, he as the creditor should be granted with a preferential right of compensation. The Supreme Court granted such preferential right to the creditor under common practice in maritime commerce, and such preferential right is an *erga omnes* entitlement. His right is an absolute right in nature of a property interest over the ship to entitle him, as a creditor, to seize the ship for satisfaction of claims. The creation and enjoyment of such a right against the ship is one of the extraordinary outcomes of the 'personification' of the ship. The ship was conferred a legal personality to enable the creditor to seize the ship and secure the satisfaction of his claims in case the ship owner refused to honour payment. Both the security of transactions on seas and the safety of navigation are thus protected. The provisions of Articles 24 and 25 of the Maritime Act concerning maritime liens are consistent with such common practice.

IV. Immunities from Jurisdiction

Taiwanese courts' jurisdiction over a civil matter involving foreign elements is based on the express language of legislation or, in the absence of such, the underlying legislative spirit of the provisions for allocating domestic jurisdiction to courts. It is noteworthy that some entities enjoy immunity under international law. The TCCP recognises such reality and stipulates a supplement to the principle '*actor sequitur forum rei*'. Where a Taiwanese citizen is located in a foreign nation and enjoys immunity from the jurisdiction of such foreign nation, he/she cannot be sued in the courts of that nation. To ensure that justice prevails, TCCP Article 1(3) stipulates that if no Taiwanese court can exercise jurisdiction on the basis of his/her domicile or residence, then the place where the central government is located shall be deemed to be the place of domicile of that citizen.

A. Sovereign and Diplomatic Immunity

Under the principle '*par in parem non habet imperium*', a country that exercises jurisdiction to adjudicate on the conduct of a foreign country would violate the basic principle of sovereign equality under international law as well as the principle of comity. Such principles lie at the very heart of international practice, and it is widely accepted that each country's sovereignty and dignity should be equally respected. Immunity is based on the classical concept of sovereignty in the sense that all sovereign states are equal and shall not be subject to the jurisdiction of another sovereign state without its consent. The courts would therefore not have jurisdiction to hear a plea against another sovereign state.[15]

Taiwan promulgated its Statute Governing the Privileges and Immunities of Foreign Offices and their Personnel in the Republic of China in 1982 to deal with the problems of diplomatic immunity. Yet, there is no such comprehensive legislation on sovereign immunity in Taiwan

[15] Taiwan High Court Civil Decision Shang-tzu No 1224 of 1998.

similar to the US Foreign Sovereign Immunity Act 1976. The immunity of foreign heads of states and foreign states are to be decided by the 2004 United Nations Convention on Jurisdictional Immunities of States and Their Property and the relevant principles under international law.

Many countries are moving away from the doctrine of absolute immunity, which grants foreign sovereign states absolute immunity from the jurisdiction of local courts for all transactions in which the foreign sovereign state is involved, to the doctrine of restrictive immunity, which only grants a foreign sovereign state immunity for its official act or act *jure imperii*. A foreign sovereign state is not immune to the jurisdiction of local courts if the action is resulted from a private act or act *jure gestionis*. Taiwanese courts have adopted this restrictive immunity approach in several cases.

In its Civil Judgment Tai-shang-tzu No 46 of 2017, the Supreme Court was faced with the permissibility of a suit brought against the Japanese Prime Minister and the Coast Guard of Japan, and ruled as follows:

> In accordance with the principle of sovereignty equality, with the exception that a sovereign voluntarily involves itself in a civil litigation, or where the subject matter involves private legal relations such as real property, commercial transactions or other non-governmental business activities within the territory of ROC, the courts of ROC will not be the competent court for adjudicating matters where foreign governments and its representative bodies are parties to a claim. The Japanese government's act to expel Taiwanese fishing vessels was not an act conducted in its private capacity (*acta iure gestionis*). Japan did declare its refusal to be subjected to the Taiwanese courts' competence to adjudicate on such matter. The action brought before this court is impermissible and shall be duly dismissed.

In its Civil Decision Kang-tzu No 850 of 2012, the Taiwan High Court ruled that the US and other foreign governmental bodies can assert their immunity from any suit initiated in the Taiwanese court. It mentioned that pursuant to international customary law, unless there is voluntary submission to the case or a treaty to the same effect is present, immunity is not waived. As a result, it ruled that the Taiwanese courts have no competence over the criminal case against them (Taiwan High Court Criminal Judgment Shang-tzu No 1591 of 2001). The civil case before this court as supplementary action to the criminal trial is therefore not permissible. It also ruled as *obiter dicta* that the Taiwanese courts will have no international jurisdiction due to the fact that both the act and its consequences took place in the US. The Taiwanese courts are thus entitled to reject exercising jurisdiction over this civil case on the basis of *forum non conveniens* and *actor sequitur forum rei*. The case was therefore duly dismissed under TCCP Article 249(1).

In the Taiwan High Court's Civil Decision Shang-tzu No 12 of 1998, the US International Trade Commission and the US Department of Commerce were the appellees that were sued for asserted wrongful acts in the US. The Taiwan High Court ruled that such a case was beyond the reach of Taiwanese courts' competence and jurisdiction and the case was dismissed. The Taiwan High Court quoted the maxim '*par in parem non habet imperium*' and provided the following reasoning. Under international law, the right of equality is one of the fundamental powers of each state. The fundamental rights under international law of a state will be infringed if it is subject to adjudication by the courts of another state. The exercise of adjudicatory jurisdiction is one of the supreme functions of a sovereign state. So, unless it has consented, a sovereign state should in no way be subject to the jurisdiction of the courts of another state. This is required by the principle of comity in international law. Such principle is necessary for the maintenance of peaceful international relations and has received worldwide acceptance among scholars and courts around the world. Hence, all states should respect the independence, equality and dignity of each sovereign state. If a foreign sovereign state enjoys immunity in the domestic court for the official acts or acts *jure imperii* from which the action was initiated, the case should be dismissed for the court's lack of competence or jurisdiction over it.

The Statute Governing the Privileges and Immunities of Foreign Offices and their Personnel in the Republic of China stipulates in Articles 5(4) and 6(1) that a foreign office itself and its personnel shall be immune from civil, criminal and administrative jurisdictions to the extent that the acts concerned are within the scope of their authorised functions. Notably, the following four exceptions are also explicitly provided in Article 5(4): (1) waiver of immunity by the foreign office; (2) a counterclaim with respect to any action brought by the foreign office; (3) an action arising from a commercial activity carried on by the foreign office; and (4) an action arising from disputed immovable property situated in the Republic of China. Item (3) enunciates the policy of restrictive immunity.

Under such provision, a distinction between acts of a foreign sovereign state nature (acts *jure imperii*) and acts of a commercial nature (acts *jure gestionis*) must be drawn.[16] The Taiwan High Court's Civil Judgment Shang-i-tzu No 875 of 2003 illustrates such judicial practice. In this case, the Taiwanese plaintiff sued the Panama Embassy for unjust enrichment resulting from receiving proceeds from selling a luxurious limousine that belonged to the plaintiff but was registered under the defendant's name. The Taiwan High Court ruled that Panama's Embassy was not immune from the jurisdiction of Taiwanese courts, along the following lines of reasoning:

1. The Panama's Embassy carries out sovereign functions of the Republic of Panama, and the ambassador is its diplomatic agent to Taiwan.
2. According to Article 31(1) of the 1961 Vienna Convention on Diplomatic Relations, the embassy and the ambassador may enjoy immunity from civil jurisdiction of the receiving state.
3. In light of the fact that the defendant is the embassy rather than the ambassador, although the ambassador is the representative of the embassy, the issue is about whether the embassy, not the ambassador, is immune from jurisdiction of Taiwanese courts.
4. The principle of absolute sovereign immunity used to prevail in the early ages, yet the contemporary international practice and customary international law seem to prefer the restrictive sovereign immunity approach.
5. Along with the US Foreign Sovereign Immunities Act 1976 and the UK State Immunity Act 1978, the foreign sovereign acts are to be distinguished between non-commercial acts (acts *jure imperii*) and commercial acts (acts *jure gestionis*).
6. The nature of a foreign sovereign act shall be decided by the court where the issue is brought up.
7. In this case, the plaintiff alleged that the defendant had no power to dispose of the limousine that had been sold to him, the receiving of proceeds from the second sale conferred interest to the embassy at the cost of his damage and constituted an unjust enrichment. The nature of reselling the limousine to get the proceeds is commercial. It is far from the defendant's exercise of sovereign power. Therefore, the defendant is not immune from the civil jurisdiction of this litigation. The Taiwanese courts have jurisdiction over this litigation.

B. State-Owned Enterprises (SOEs)

State-owned enterprises (SOEs) are legal, private entities which could either be formed by private persons, or by the government. Such entities could allow the government to take effective control and take part in commercial activities through full, majority or significant minor ownership.

[16] Rong-Chwan Chen, 'The Immunity of Diplomatic Personnel from Foreign Countries' (2005) 24 *Taiwan Jurist* 24–25.

They operate in commercial affairs and activities and have specific public policy objectives. Thus, SOEs should be differentiated from government agencies or state entities established to pursue purely governmental objectives and from business enterprises established mainly to obtain profits for the owners. The Act on Administration of State-owned Enterprises 1949 (last revised 2011) provides the basic rules on their finance, operation and personnel. Under the current Taiwanese legal system, SOEs are separate legal entities rather than part of the government.

For the purpose of foreign sovereign state immunity, foreign SOEs are separated from their owners in a certain form. No Taiwanese enactment grants foreign SOEs sovereign immunity. Yet, it is in the authors' opinion that since the restrictive sovereign state immunity approach was adopted by domestic legislation, attention shall be paid on the nature of activity concerning the litigation rather than the legal formalities of SOEs. Therefore, the courts can interpret the concept of a sovereign state broadly to include SOEs, looking into the nature of the act in issue and characterising such an act as either as a commercial or non-commercial act. It is suggested that a foreign SOE, if treated as an instrumentality of a foreign government, is immune from jurisdiction of the Taiwanese courts only over a matter concerning non-commercial acts (acts *jure imperii*), while is subject to its jurisdiction under its relevant provisions over matters concerning commercial acts.

C. Other Immunities

Just two years after the United Nations was founded, the ROC promulgated its Regulation Governing the Privileges and Immunities of the United Nations Missions and Their Personnel in the Republic of China in 1947 to grant the UN employees privileges and immunities when performing official functions in the ROC territory. Article 2 of the Regulation provides that UN employees are immune from all litigations arising out of their exercise of official functions. By limiting the scope of immunity only to the acts performed within 'their exercise of official functions', the regulation implicitly adopted a restrictive immunity approach. However, ever since the ROC was ousted from the UN in 1971 by the General Assembly Resolution No 2758, these provisions hardly apply. Nonetheless, as the World Trade Organisation (WTO) remains to be one of the few international organisations Taiwan can accede to as a member, such regulation remains applicable to the WTO's office and personnel, which is to be granted with privileges and immunities in accordance with the regulation. Thus, an Article was inserted in the aforementioned Statute for this purpose. The inserted Article 7-1 stipulates that the provisions on privileges and immunities of foreign offices and their personnel may apply *mutatis mutandis* to its offices stationed in the ROC and its personnel, and to the officials and representatives of its members for their exercise of official functions. It is thus apparent that the restrictive immunity approach is also applicable under such circumstances.

5

Japan

KAZUAKI NISHIOKA*

I. Introduction

In 2011, Japan for the first time introduced in the Code of Civil Procedure (CCP)[1] black-letter rules for jurisdiction in civil and commercial matters.[2] These new rules entered into force on 1 April 2012. In respect of cases relating to family matters, the statutory rules were recently introduced into the Personal Status Litigation Act (PSLA)[3] and the Domestic Relations Case Procedure Act (DRCPA),[4] which came into force on 1 April 2019.[5] Although they cover family matters, the PSLA and DRCPA offer different dispute resolution methods. The PSLA covers contentious matters such as divorce and dissolution and offers open-court proceedings, namely, litigation. On the other, the DRCPA mainly covers non-contentious matters such as administration of absentee's property and annulment of disappearance adjudication and offers closed proceedings, more particularly, adjudication by court. It further offers, as an alternative dispute resolution method, conciliation by court in both contentious and non-contentious matters, providing several grounds for this purpose.

As to international (direct) jurisdiction, Japan has concluded some international conventions in specific legal areas,[6] but it has not ratified any Hague Conventions in this respect. Therefore, international jurisdiction of the Japanese courts is mainly subject to domestic laws. The main legal sources are the CCP, PSLA, and DRCPA.

* This chapter is largely based on the relevant chapters in Kazuaki Nishioka and Yuko Nishitani, *Japanese Private International Law* (Oxford, Hart Publishing, 2021). Abbreviations: 'JAIL': Japanese Annual of International Law; 'JYIL': Japanese Yearbook of International Law.

[1] Act No 109 of 26 June 1996, as amended.

[2] For Japanese rules on jurisdiction in civil and commercial matters from a comparative perspective see eg Koji Takahashi, 'The Jurisdiction of Japanese Courts in A Comparative Context' (2015) 11(1) *Journal of Private International Law* 103–27; Yuko Nishitani, 'International Jurisdiction of Japanese Courts in A Comparative Perspective' (2013) 60 *Netherlands International Law Review* 251–73.

[3] Act No 109 of 16 July 2003, as amended on 18 April 2018.

[4] Act No 52 of 25 May 2011, as amended on 18 April 2018.

[5] For the new rules in family matters, see Yuko Nishitani, 'New International Civil Procedure Law of Japan in Status and Family Matters' (2019) 62 *JYIL* 119–50.

[6] For instance, the 1929 Convention for the Unification of Certain Rules Relating to International Carriage by Air; the 1976 Convention on Limitation of Liability for Maritime Claims; the 1992 International Convention on Civil Liability for Oil Pollution Damage; the 1992 International Convention on the Establishment of an International Fund for Compensation for Oil Pollution Damage; the 1997 Convention on Supplementary Compensation for Nuclear Damage; and the 1999 Convention for the Unification of Certain Rules for International Carriage by Air (the Montreal Convention). This chapter does not deal with the jurisdictional rules in these treaties.

II. General Principles and Framework for Jurisdiction

A. General Principles

The aforementioned statutes, in particular the CCP, provide various jurisdictional grounds based on the ideas of 'fairness between the parties' and 'the sound and prompt administration of justice' (justice at the procedural law level), which Japanese courts had adopted even prior to the 2011 CCP amendment.[7] Besides, there are some other principles at work, for instance, national sovereignty. Aiming to pursue its national interest or protect its national sovereignty, Japan has had certain matters subject to the exclusive jurisdiction of the Japanese courts. In the area of family law, the PSLA and DRCPA are also based on the principles discussed. In certain matters of family law, more importance is attached to justice at the substantive law level, such as the best interest of a child or minor.

B. General Framework

The CCP, PSLA and DRCPA adopt a two-pronged approach. First, Japanese courts must examine whether a jurisdictional ground set out in relevant provisions lies in Japan; second, it must examine whether to take jurisdiction, by taking into consideration the circumstances in individual cases (CCP Article 3-9; PSLA Article 3-5; DRCPA Article 3-14). In other words, there is always a 'safety valve' under these statutes.

The CCP, PSLA and DRPCA adopt different structures for jurisdictional grounds. The CCP contains two heads of jurisdiction, namely, general jurisdiction and specific jurisdiction. The former applies to all the cases irrespective of whether the claim has arisen out of the defendant's particular contact with the forum state which supports the jurisdiction, and thereby it is referred to all-purpose jurisdiction. To the contrary, the latter applies only in specific cases which each head refers to (see Sections III.B and D). The PSLA sets out extensively the general grounds applicable in family matters governed by it (see Section V.A.i), while the DRPCA only provides specific grounds applicable in particular cases (see Section V).

III. Service of Process

For service of process, international conventions or arrangements are most important means, in particular, the 1954 Hague Convention on Civil Procedure (the Hague Civil Procedure Convention) and the 1965 Hague Convention on the Service Abroad of Judicial and Extrajudicial Documents in Civil or Commercial Matters (the Hague Service Convention). To implement certain provisions of these conventions, Japan has enacted a statute, the Act on Special Provisions Concerning Civil Procedure Attendant upon Implementation of the Convention on Civil Procedure and Another Convention (ASPCP),[8] and the relevant procedural Rules.[9] Furthermore, there are two

[7] See eg Judgment of the Supreme Court, 16 October 1981, *Minshu* 35(7), 1224 ((1983) 26 *JAIL* 122); Judgment of the Supreme Court, 11 November 1997, *Minshu* 51(10), 4055 ((1988) 41 *JAIL* 117). See also Masato Dogauchi, 'New Japanese Rules on International Jurisdiction: General Observation' (2011) 54 *JYIL* 265.

[8] Act No 115 of 5 June 1970; Amendment of Act No 53 of 2011.

[9] Rules of the Supreme Court (No 6 of 7 July 1970, as amended).

bilateral consular conventions with the US[10] and the UK[11] and some judicial arrangements with other states.[12] In the absence of any international conventions or arrangements, service of process may be conducted in accordance with relevant national laws. Service of process outside Japan (that is, from Japan to abroad) is subject to the CCP, while service of process in Japan (namely, from abroad to Japan) is governed by the Act on Assistance Based on Commission by Foreign Courts (AABC).[13]

A. Service of Process Outside Japan

As to service of process outside Japan, there are basically five ways, though the available methods varied from one instrument to another:

(1) service through diplomatic or consular agents stationed in the state addressed of the requesting state;
(2) service through a designated authority in the state addressed;
(3) service through a central authority in the state addressed;
(4) service through diplomatic channels, and
(5) service through a competent court of the state addressed.[14]

In a case where 'it is impossible to effect service through the means under CCP Article 108 or it is found to be impossible to effect service even through such means', or where 'even after six months have elapsed since the competent government agency of a foreign country is issued a commission pursuant to the provision of Article 108, no paper document that certifies that the agency has effected service is sent' (CCP Articles 110(1)(i), 110(1)(iii) and 110(1)(iv)), the court clerk may effect service by publication on a bulletin board of a relevant court. Where service of process is to be made in foreign states which Japan does not have a diplomatic relationship with, process may not be forwarded to the relevant authorities of the foreign states or an ambassador, minister, or consul of Japan there. In such a case, service by publication must be made.[15]

B. Service of Foreign Proceedings in Japan

For service of process from foreign states to Japan, the five methods discussed are also available.[16] Both the designated authority under the Hague Civil Procedure Convention and the central authority under the Hague Service Convention are the Minister of Foreign Affairs (ASPCP Articles 2 and 24). Accordingly, service of foreign proceedings will be forwarded from a designated or central authority of the foreign requesting state to the Minister. In this regard, it should

[10] Consular Convention between Japan and the United States of America (entered into force on 1 August 1959).

[11] Consular Convention between Japan and the United Kingdom of Great Britain and Northern Ireland (entered into force on 10 October 1965).

[12] For instance, Switzerland, Denmark, Italy, Sri Lanka, Brazil, Thailand, Germany, the UK, Norway, Australia, Iran, Austria, Kuwait, Iraq, and Israel. In addition, some states have served process upon individual agreements (without any arrangements), for instance, Singapore and Peru. See Saiko Saibansho Jimu Sokyoku Minjikyoku (ed), *Kokusai Minji Jiken Tetsuzuki Handbook* [*Handbook on International Civil Procedure Cases*] (Tokyo, Hosokai, 2013) ('Handbook') 223–25, 431–33.

[13] Act No 63 of 1905.

[14] See Handbook (n 12) 30–42.

[15] ibid 42.

[16] ibid 52.

be noted that in December 2018, Japan objected to Articles 8 and 10(a) of the Hague Service Convention and thereby service directly through its diplomatic or consular agents and service by post are not available. The exception for service directly through its diplomatic or consular agents is 'where the documents for foreign proceedings is to be served upon a national of the State in which the documents originate'.

Where the Hague Conventions and consular conventions have no application, service of foreign proceedings in Japan may be effected through a competent court in accordance with bilateral arrangements or the relevant national law, namely the Act on Assistance Based on Commission by Foreign Courts (AABC).[17] AABC Article 1-2 requires documents to be forwarded through diplomatic channels and sets out the requirements such as attaching a Japanese translation of the document, and the relevant foreign state guarantees that the seeking state bears the necessary costs for service of process, and provides the same or similar assistance based on commission by Japanese courts. Where a Japanese translation is not attached, service will not be effected.[18]

IV. Civil and Commercial Matters

A. General Rules

i. Defendant's Domicile

CCP Article 3-2 sets out the general rule for the jurisdiction of the Japanese courts in civil and commercial matters. Insofar as a natural person is concerned, general jurisdiction is first found at the defendant's domicile, second at his/her residence (in the absence of his/her domicile in Japan or abroad), third at his/her last domicile in Japan (if he/she does not have domicile abroad). These rules are to secure that at least one state on earth has general jurisdiction over the defendant.[19] The rules adopt domicile as the indicator pointing to the centre of life of a natural person. As to a legal person or any other association or foundation, general jurisdiction is found at the place of its principal office (Article 3-2(3)). If the registered principal office and the factual principal office (or place of central administration) are located in different states, both can ground general jurisdiction.[20] If the entity does not have any office in Japan or its location is unknown, the general jurisdiction of the Japanese courts is grounded on the domicile of its representative or any other person in charge of leading its business in Japan. With regard to an ambassador, minister, or any other Japanese national in a foreign country who enjoys immunity from the jurisdiction of that country, Japanese courts may take jurisdiction over them (Article 3-2(2)). This rule is to ensure that at least one state on earth has general jurisdiction over a Japanese national, whether or not he/she is domiciled in Japan.[21]

[17] See n 13.

[18] Handbook (n 12) 57.

[19] Japan Institute of Business Law, 'Kokusai Saibankankatsu ni kansuru Chosa Kenkyu Hokokusho' ['Research Report on International Jurisdiction'] (*Ministry of Justice*, April 2008) 7, available online: www.moj.go.jp/content/000012193.pdf ('Hokokusho (CCP)').

[20] ibid 11.

[21] Tatsufumi Sato and Yasuhiko Kobayashi, *Ichimon Itto Heisei 23 Nen Minji Soshoho to Kaisei: Kokusai Saiban Kankatsu Hosei no Seibi* [*Explanatory Note on the 2011 Reform of the Code of Civil Procedure and Others: Improvement of the Institution on International Jurisdiction*] (Tokyo, Shojihomu, 2012) 25.

ii. Forum non conveniens

CCP Article 3-9 sets out a corrective rule, which is the 'special circumstances' test that originates from a previous case law.[22] Pursuant to this rule:

> [e]ven where the Japanese courts have jurisdiction over an action (except where the action has been brought on the basis of an exclusive jurisdiction agreement in favor of the Japanese courts), the court may dismiss the whole or part of the proceedings if, taking into account the nature of the case, the burden of the defendant to answer the claim, the location of evidence and any other factors, the court finds that there are special circumstances in which hearing and determining the case in Japan would impair fairness between the parties or hinder the proper and efficient conduct of the hearing.[23]

To decide whether there exist special circumstances, a court seised is supposed to consider the circumstances of individual cases. The application of Article 3-9 is only excluded when Japanese courts have exclusive jurisdiction on the basis of the choice of court agreements between the parties (Article 3-9) or by statute (Article 3-10). There has been one example of case law in which the Supreme Court declined jurisdiction, applying the special circumstances test under CCP Article 3-9.[24] In this case involving a dispute between a Japanese corporation, its chairperson, and a Nevada corporation, the Court held that hearing and determining the case in Japan would impair fairness between the parties or hinder the proper and efficient conduct of the hearing, considering factors such as the progress of the proceedings in the US, the close connection with the proceedings in the US, the location of the relevant evidence, and the previous communications between the parties in terms of dispute resolution.

iii. International Parallel Litigations: Lis alibi pendens

There is no explicit rule on *lis alibi pendens*, even though whether to regulate these parallel litigations by adopting a specific rule was extensively deliberated in the proceedings of the 2011 CCP amendment.[25] When seeking a solution, it is expedient to refer to a previous court decision in the *Masaki Bussan* case (1991)[26] involving a Japanese company's claim seeking a negative declaration of liability to hamper the enforcement of a future US judgment. In this case, although Japanese courts were competent as the *locus delicti commissi* of the alleged liability, the court declined international jurisdiction by applying the 'exceptional circumstances' test. In light of this case, international parallel litigations could be regulated by Japanese courts restricting international jurisdiction under the 'special circumstances' test.

iv. Anti-suit Injunctions

There is no rule for jurisdiction over anti-suit injunctions that prohibit a party from bringing or maintaining actions before a foreign court. Although some commentators opined that

[22] Judgment of the Supreme Court, 11 November 1997 (n 7). See also Dogauchi (n 7) 265–68.

[23] Cited from Koji Takahashi, 'Japan's Newly Enacted Rules on International Jurisdiction: with a Reflection on Some Issues of Interpretation' (2011) 13 *Japanese Yearbook of Private International Law* 156.

[24] Judgment of the Supreme Court, 10 March 2016, *Minshu* 70(3), 846 ((2017) 60 *JYIL* 488).

[25] Counsellor's Office of the Civil Affairs Bureau of the Ministry of Justice, 'Kokusai Saibankankatsu Hosei ni kansuru Chukan Shian Hosoku Setsumei' [*Supplemental Explanatory Note on the Interim Draft on the Institution on International Jurisdiction*] (*Doshisha University*, July 2009) 55–60, available online: www1.doshisha.ac.jp/~tradelaw/UnpublishedWorks/ExplanatoryNoteOnBillOfJurisdictionAct.pdf ('Explanatory Note (CCP)').

[26] Judgment of the Tokyo District Court, 29 January 1991, 1390 *Hanrei Jiho* 98.

anti-suit injunctions may be issued as interim measures,[27] it is generally understood that anti-suit injunctions are not permissible under Japanese law on the ground that it is highly unlikely that the requirements for interim measures are satisfied.[28]

v. Interim Measures

In 2011, the first black-letter rule on international jurisdiction over interim measures such as freezing orders or injunctions was introduced in the Civil Provisional Remedies Act (CPRA),[29] which is applicable to both personal and family litigations. According to CPRA Article 11, a party may file a petition for interim measures: (1) where an action on the merits may be brought before the Japanese courts; or (2) where the property to be temporally seised or the object in dispute is found in Japan. But, where parties agree on the exclusive jurisdiction of a foreign court or arbitration abroad, Japan will refuse potential jurisdiction over the main proceeding, resulting in the jurisdiction of Japanese courts based on the first head being denied as well.[30] In such cases, a party seeking interim measures in Japan needs to rely on the second head.

vi. Choice of Court Agreements

A choice of court agreement is largely governed by CCP Article 3-7.[31] Parties may agree to the exclusive or non-exclusive jurisdiction of a court or courts, in Japan or elsewhere, unless the special rules on exclusive jurisdiction in Article 3-5 or on consumer contracts and employment relations in Articles 3-7(5) and (6) apply. To be valid, a choice of court agreement must be in writing and 'concerned with an action arising from a particular legal relationship' (Article 3-7(2)). An agreement conferring exclusive jurisdiction on a foreign court may not be invoked if the designated court is legally or factually unable to exercise jurisdiction, for instance, due to a lack of jurisdiction (based on the invalidity of the agreement) or war (Article 3-7(4)). Notably, the 'special circumstances' test under Article 3-9 does not apply when the parties agree to confer exclusive jurisdiction on the Japanese court.

The prevailing view[32] is that an exclusive choice of court agreement must further satisfy an unwritten requirement, namely, the 'public policy' requirement introduced by the Supreme Court of Japan in the *Chisadane* case (1975). According to this, an agreement will be unenforceable 'if it is excessively unreasonable and is against public policy rules'.[33] Lower courts have applied the public policy requirement on a case-by-case basis, checking whether an agreement is unreasonable in all the circumstances. In determining unreasonableness, courts have taken into account factual elements such as: (1) connection with Japan; (2) connection with the *situs* of the designated court;

[27] Masato Dogauchi, 'Concurrent Litigations in Japan and the United States' (1994) 37 *JAIL* 72.

[28] Nishitani (n 2) 273; Yoshimasa Furuta, 'Sosho Sashitome Meirei' in Akira Takakuwa and Masato Dogauchi (eds), *Shin Saiban Jitsumu Taikei (3) Kokusai Minji Sosho-ho (Zaisan-ho Kankei)* [*International Civil Litigation Law (Proprietary Matters)*] (Tokyo, Seirinshoin, 2002) 157–60.

[29] Act No 91 of 22 December 1989, as amended.

[30] Decision of the Tokyo District Court, 28 August 2007, 1991 *Hanrei Jiho* 89; Yasunori Honma, Shun'ichiro Nakano and Hajime Sakai, *Kokusai Minji Tetsuzuki Ho* [*International Civil Procedure Law*] 2nd edn (Tokyo, Yuhikaku, 2012) 205.

[31] See eg Shun'ichiro Nakano, 'Agreement on Jurisdiction' (2011) 54 *JYIL* 278; Shiho Kato, 'Recent Developments in Rules on Choice of Court Agreements in Japan: New Codification and Remaining Problems' in Alexander Bruns and Masabumi Suzuki (eds), *Preventive Instruments of Social Governance* (Tübingen, Mohr Siebeck, 2017) 173.

[32] See eg Sato and Kobayashi (n 21) 140.

[33] Judgment of the Supreme Court, 28 November 1975, *Minshu* 29(4), 572 ((1976) 20 *JYIL* 106). See also Nakano (n 31) 280–83.

(3) any difficulties in accessing the designated court; (4) the location of evidence; (5) the process whereby the agreement was concluded; and (6) the necessity of protecting consumers.[34]

It is disputed in Japan how best to determine the substantive validity of a choice of court agreement, which is severable from the main contract. Recent authors have increasingly pointed to the law chosen by the parties to govern the choice of court agreement. In its absence, the law with the closest connection applies, which usually coincides with the law governing the main contract (Act on General Rules of Application of Laws (AGRAL), Articles 7 and 8).[35]

vii. Submission

Pursuant to CCP Article 3-8, Japanese courts may take jurisdiction 'when the defendant, without objecting to the jurisdiction, made an oral argument on the merits or made a statement in preparatory proceedings'. It is not regarded as submission to the court if the defendant appears before the court for the sole purpose of objecting to jurisdiction of that court. Accordingly, jurisdiction of the Japanese courts is only grounded if the defendant replies to the merits of the case, without making any opposing argument to the jurisdiction.[36] Pursuant to Article 3-10, Article 3-8 'shall have no application where, with respect to the action in question, the exclusive jurisdiction of the Japanese courts is prescribed by legislation'. Therefore, Japanese courts are obliged to dismiss a claim when it has no jurisdiction in accordance with the rule on exclusive jurisdiction under Article 3-5, even where a defendant submits himself/herself to the court.[37]

viii. Exclusive Jurisdiction

For the national interest of Japan, Japan has had certain types of matters subject to exclusive jurisdiction of the Japanese courts. CCP Article 3-5 covers three items. Article 3-5(1) covers corporation matters such as disputes over the validity of the constitution or dissolution of a company (or other entity), the nullity of the decisions of its organs, and liability and discharge of officers of a company, aiming at uniform decisions and procedural convenience for companies and shareholders.[38] Article 3-5(2) deals with matters relating to registration. Japanese courts have exclusive jurisdiction for disputes over a registration to be made in Japan. This provision specifically covers the entries in public registers about immovable property situated in Japan and the registration of intellectual property (IP) rights (including patent rights, trademarks, design rights, and utility model rights).[39] Further, insofar as the action relates to the registration, all categories of IP rights – including copyright that come into existence without formalities but can be registered in order to oppose third parties – are subject to the exclusive jurisdiction of the country of protection or registration.[40] Article 3-5(3) covers the existence and validity of intellectual property rights registered in Japan. The term 'intellectual property rights' in this item covers intellectual property rights that are established by registration (Intellectual Property Basic Act Article 2(2)),[41] such as a patent right, a trademark right, a design right, and a utility

[34] See eg Kato (n 31) 182–91.
[35] Act No 78 of 21 June 2006; Nakano (n 31) 287–88.
[36] Sato and Kobayashi (n 21) 155.
[37] ibid 155–56.
[38] Explanatory Note (CCP) (n 25) 17–20; Sato and Kobayashi (n 21) 102–03.
[39] Sato and Kobayashi (n 21) 109.
[40] ibid.
[41] Act No 122 of 4 December 2002.

model right. This jurisdictional ground whereby the country of registration was considered the most adequate forum was justified because patents, trademarks and other comparable IP rights are granted by an administrative act and are subject to specific proceedings for their invalidation or revocation with *erga omnes* effect.[42] Insofar as those rights which need to be registered in Japan are concerned, a dispute over their existence and validity is subject to exclusive jurisdiction of the Japanese courts.

Although their wording is restricted to Japan's jurisdiction, CCP Articles 3-5(1) to 3-5(3) are understood to have reflexive effect on foreign courts. Accordingly, when the place where a registration to be made lies in Japan, Japanese courts have exclusive jurisdiction thereof, while if such place is located abroad, Japanese courts are obliged to decline jurisdiction, even where there is any alternative jurisdictional ground such as the defendant's domicile under Article 3-2.[43]

ix. Plurality of Parties or Claims

Once Japanese courts are competent to decide a claim, other claims between the same parties that are closely related to the principal claim can be joined in accordance with CCP Article 3-6 ('objective joinder of claims'). A close connection between the claims is required, aiming at the protection of the defendant and procedural economy.[44]

By CCP Article 146(3), Japan's jurisdiction can be extended to a counterclaim that is closely related to the subject matter of the principal claim or the allegations and evidence for the defence.[45] The requirement of a 'close connection' aims to prevent proceedings from being protracted due to a counterclaim without that connection. Further, plaintiffs or defendants can be joined with the principal parties insofar as the rights or obligations constituting the subject matter of the claim are common between them or arise out of the same factual or legal grounds in accordance with Article 3-6 and the first sentence in Article 38 ('subjective joinder of claims').[46]

B. Special Rules

The CCP provides various specific grounds in Articles 3-3 to 3-8 that are available in particular cases. Japanese courts may take jurisdiction when any of the general or specific grounds lie in Japan, subject to Article 3-9.

i. Law of Obligations

a. Contracts

Applicable grounds depend on the type of contractual disputes, in particular, the status of parties. For instance, pursuant to CCP Article 3-4(3), Article 3-3 'shall have no application to an action brought by a business operator against a consumer with respect to a consumer contract or to an action brought by an employer against its employee with respect to a civil dispute over individual

[42] Explanatory Note (CCP) (n 25) 36–37; Sato and Kobayashi (n 21) 111.
[43] Sato and Kobayashi (n 21) 108.
[44] Explanatory Note (CCP) (n 25) 47–48; Sato and Kobayashi (n 21) 118.
[45] Sato and Kobayashi (n 21) 125–26.
[46] It is not required, though, that the parties be joined *ex lege* as under CCP Art 40: Explanatory Note (CCP) (n 25) 50.

employment relations'. The following passages will first describe relevant specific grounds in contractual disputes, and then deal with special rules in consumer contracts and individual labour relations.

Article 3-3(i) provides the place of performance as an alternative and specific jurisdiction in contractual disputes such as an action for the enforcement of a contractual obligation, an action arising from *negotiorum gestio* performed in connection with a contractual obligation, an action relating to unjust enrichment arising in connection with a contractual obligation, and an action seeking damages for the breach of a contractual obligation. Pursuant to this provision, Japanese courts may take jurisdiction 'when the place of performance of the obligation as specified in the contract is located in Japan[,] or when the place of performance of the obligation is located in Japan according to the governing law chosen in the contract'. The place of performance is determined in relation to the contractual obligation in question. This jurisdiction not only covers validity and primary claims of the contract, but also claims pertaining to accessory duties and remedies for non-performance, including restitution and damages. Even in the event of non-performance, jurisdiction lies at the place of performance of the underlying contractual obligation. In a sales contract, for instance, the seller's claim for restitution of the delivered goods in default of the buyer's payment is subject to Japan's jurisdiction insofar as the buyer's payment was to be performed in Japan, independent of the place of performance of the restitution itself.[47]

In order to guarantee the parties' foreseeability, Article 3-3(i) restricts the relevant place of performance to the one designated in the contract or as determined by the applicable law that has been explicitly or implicitly chosen by the parties. Accordingly, the place of performance designated under the applicable law determined by an objective connecting factor in the absence of a choice of law does not ground jurisdiction.[48]

CCP Article 3-3(iii) sets out the situs of property as an alternative ground. Pursuant to this Article, insofar as an action relating to a property right is concerned, Japanese courts may take jurisdiction 'when the object of the claim is located in Japan; or if the action is for the payment of money, when the defendant's asset capable of being seized is located in Japan (except where the value of the asset is extremely low)'. Although jurisdiction based on the situs of the defendant's seizable property in general is questionable, the legislature justified it, in view of guaranteeing the enforcement of claims against the defendant's assets.[49] This jurisdiction may well have an impact on cross border litigations, since the party who has tangible or intangible seizable property, including claims or intellectual property rights in Japan, is in principle subject to Japan's jurisdiction.[50] To restrict the scope of the situs jurisdiction, the relevant subject matter of the claim is limited to the payment of money. Further, the situs jurisdiction is precluded when the value of property is extremely low. The value is not assessed in relation to the amount in dispute, but according to the absolute criteria that at least allow minor assets such as samples of goods or utensils to be disregarded.[51]

The CCP provides grounds on the defendant's office and business activity. Pursuant to Article 3-3(iv), insofar as action against a person having an office and relating to his/her

[47] Explanatory Note (CCP) (n 25) 9–11; Akira Saito, 'International Civil Jurisdiction Based on the Place of Performance of Obligation Relating to a Contract' (2011) 54 *JYIL* 304–08. See also Judgment of the Osaka District Court, 25 March 1991, 1408 *Hanrei Jiho* 100; cf Judgment of the Nagoya High Court, 12 November 1979, 402 *Hanrei Taimuzu* 102.

[48] Jun Yokoyama, *Private International Law in Japan* 2nd edn (Alphen aan den Rijn, Kluwer Law International, 2020) 135.

[49] Hokokusho (CCP) (n 19) 20; Sato and Kobayashi (n 21) 45.

[50] Kazuhiko Yamamoto, 'International Jurisdiction Based on the Location of Property' (2011) 54 *JYIL* 319–20.

[51] Sato and Kobayashi (n 21) 45–46; cf Takao Sawaki and Masato Dogauchi, *Kokusai Shiho Nyumon* 8th edn (Tokyo, Yuhikaku, 2018) 276.

business conducted at that office is concerned, Japanese courts may take jurisdiction 'when the office is located in Japan'. This jurisdiction is understood as only addressing the business directly conducted at the relevant office, not the business in abstract terms that could have been undertaken by that office.[52] Further, pursuant to Article 3-3(v), insofar as an action against a person engaged in business in Japan (including a foreign company which continuously carries out transactions in Japan) is concerned, Japanese courts may take jurisdiction 'when the action relates to the business in Japan'. This ground primarily targets foreign companies that are continuously doing business in Japan. Since 2002 these foreign companies are no longer required to establish an office in Japan, but only to designate a principal representative (Company Act Article 817(1)(2)),[53] so CCP Article 3-3(iv) would not suffice to consistently subject them to Japan's jurisdiction. This jurisdiction is comparable to the US 'doing business' jurisdiction. It is to be noted, however, that the US activity-based jurisdiction principally comprises all kinds of disputes as a general jurisdiction and is often deemed exorbitant, whereas Article 3-3(v) provides only for special jurisdiction and is limited to disputes arising out of the defendant's business activities in Japan.[54]

Notably, consumer contracts and individual labour relationships are subject to the special rules in CCP Articles 3-4, 3-7(5), and 3-7(6) for the purpose of the protection of weaker parties. Pursuant to Article 3-4(3), where the business operator or employer brings a suit against the consumer or employee, the available forum is restricted to that of the consumer's or employee's domicile. Exceptions are where the parties enter into a choice of court agreement (Articles 3-7(5) and 3-7(6)) or where a defendant submits himself/herself to Japanese courts (Article 3-8).[55] Conversely, the consumer can file an action against the business operator before the courts of the state in which the consumer was domiciled at the time of the filing of the action or at the conclusion of the contract (Article 3-4(1)), besides the competent courts pursuant to Articles 3-2 and 3-3. The employee can sue the employer at the place of the performance of labour under the contract,[56] or, if that is not ascertainable, at the place of the office through which the employee was employed (Article 3-4(2)), in addition to the venues provided by Articles 3-2 and 3-3.[57]

After a dispute has arisen out of a consumer or employment contract, the parties are free to designate a competent court (Articles 3-7(5) and 3-7(6)). Prior to that date, a choice of court agreement is valid if: (1) the parties confer non-exclusive jurisdiction on the courts of a state where the consumer was domiciled at the time of the conclusion of the consumer contract; or (2) the employee carried out his/her labour at the time of the termination of the employment contract (Article 3-7(5)(i) or 3-7(6)(i)). This is also the case if the consumer or employee institutes proceedings at the designated forum or invokes the choice of court agreement when sued in a different forum (Article 3-7(5)(ii) or 3-7(6)(ii)).

[52] Sato and Kobayashi (n 21) 52.

[53] Law No 86 of 26 July 2005. See Yoshiaki Nomura, 'Activity-Based Jurisdiction of Japanese Courts – A Bold but Unnecessary Departure –' (2012) 55 *JYIL* 269–72.

[54] Dogauchi (n 7) 273–74; Nomura (n 53) 277–86.

[55] It is still debatable whether CCP Article 3-6 on the joinder of claims should be applicable as well. See Tadashi Kanzaki, 'Jurisdiction over Consumer Contracts and Individual Labour-Related Civil Disputes' (2012) 55 *JYIL* 312–13, 315–16.

[56] When the employee performs his/her labour at several ascertainable places, all of them constitute jurisdiction: Kanzaki (n 55) 311–12; Minutes of the 8th meeting (CCP). Minutes of CCP meetings are available online: www.moj.go.jp/shingi1/shingi_kokusaihousei_index.html.

[57] Kanzaki (n 55) 310–12.

b. Tort

When it comes to tortious disputes, the CCP contains only one specific ground in Article 3-3(viii). Pursuant to this Article, Japanese courts may take jurisdiction 'when the tort occurred in Japan (except where the result of a harmful act committed abroad has occurred in Japan and the occurrence of that result in Japan would have been normally unforeseeable)'. The scope of Article 3-3(viii) extends to all tortious cases such as product liability and defamation[58] and covers all tortious remedies including damages and injunctions.[59] It also extends to a negative declaration of liability.[60] The notion of 'the place of tort' comprises both 'the place where the harmful act was committed (*locus delicti commissi*)' and 'the place where the injury occurred, or is likely to occur (*locus damni*)'. Accordingly, as long as either of these grounds is found in Japan, Japanese courts may hear and determine the tortious claim in question. However, it should be noted that the place where the injury occurred, or is likely to occur, may be precluded when the occurrence of the injury at that place could not be predicted. Moreover, it is understood that the place where the indirect or secondary injury occurred or is likely to occur does not constitute a jurisdictional ground.[61] The predictability requirement for the place of injury aims to balance the parties' interests and to live up to their risk calculation.[62] Moreover, it duly restricts indirect jurisdiction of foreign courts in recognising their judgments in Japan, especially in product liability cases.[63] The 'predictability' concerns only the normative one that the injury could occur under normal circumstances, and does not concern an abstract possibility that the injury could occur by releasing a product into the 'stream of commerce'. To decide whether the occurrence of the injury is predictable, only objective factors are considered, and such subjective factors as the tortfeasor's intent are not considered.[64] Whereas the court *ex officio* examines international jurisdiction (Article 3-11), the plaintiff victim has the burden of proving the objective factual relationships underlying the wrongful act and the violation of the legally protected right to establish jurisdiction of the court at the place of tort.[65] On the other hand, the facts for determining the predictability of the occurrence of the injury at *locus damni* are to be proven by the defendant tortfeasor.[66]

Both the place of a harmful act and the place of injury are general concepts. It must be interpreted and materialised in individual cases in light of the characteristics of a tort in question. It should also be noted that when locating the place of tort, the focus of Article 3-3(viii) is on where a harmful act occurs and where the injury occurs, no matter whether the liability is based on negligence, nuisance or others.

In addition to Article 3-3(viii), other grounds may ground jurisdiction of the Japanese courts. In particular, Articles 3-3(iii), 3-3(iv) and 3-3(v) will often come into play (see Section IV.B.i.a).

[58] Sawaki and Dogauchi (n 51) 280.

[59] Judgment of the Supreme Court, 24 April 2014, *Minshu* 68(4), 329; Sato and Kobayashi (n 21) 69.

[60] Yuko Nishitani, 'Internationales Privat- und Zivilverfahrensrecht' ['International Private and Civil Procedure Law'] in Harald Baum and Moritz Bälz (eds), *Handbuch Japanisches Handels- und Wirtschaftsrecht* [*Handbook on Japanese Commercial and Business Law*] (Köln, Carl Heymanns Verlag, 2011) para 132; Sawaki and Dogauchi (n 51) 282; Nozomi Tada, 'International Civil Jurisdiction Based on the Place of the Tort' (2012) 55 *JYIL* 296–97. See also Judgment of the Tokyo District Court, 27 November 1998, 1037 *Hanrei Taimuzu* 235.

[61] Sato and Kobayashi (n 21) 69; Judgment of the Tokyo District Court, 15 February 1984, 1135 *Hanrei Jiho* 70; Judgment of the Tokyo District Court, 31 October 2006, 1241 *Hanrei Taimuzu* 338.

[62] Sato and Kobayashi (n 21) 70–71.

[63] Explanatory Note (CCP) (n 25) 21–22.

[64] Sato and Kobayashi (n 21) 71.

[65] ibid 72. See also Judgment of the Supreme Court, 8 June 2001, *Minshu* 55(4), 727; cf Sawaki and Dogauchi (n 51) 282–83.

[66] Minutes of the 2nd meeting (CCP).

c. Unjust Enrichment

CCP Article 3-3(i) provides a special ground for unjust enrichment disputes, according to which, a party may file an action relating to 'unjust enrichment arising in connection with a contractual obligation' with Japanese courts, when: (1) the place of performance of the obligation as specified in the contract is located in Japan; or (2) the place of performance of the obligation is located in Japan according to the governing law chosen in the contract. Accordingly, for instance, where a seller to a sales contract seeks the restitution of the delivered good after he/she terminates the contract upon the buyer's failure to make a payment, Japanese courts may take jurisdiction if the payment was to be made in Japan.[67] This head of jurisdiction does not cover an action relating to unjust enrichment 'not' arising in connection with a contractual obligation. For this type of action, a party will need to rely on other grounds.

d. Trusts and Charitable Foundations

There are no special rules for trusts and charitable foundations, and when Japanese courts may take jurisdiction over these matters is open to interpretation. Various disputes may arise out of trusts. They occur either in: (1) internal relationship (between trustee, trustor and beneficiary); or (2) external relationship (between a trustee and a third party). In the latter relationship, a trustee simply appears as the owner of a set of assets and the dispute has nothing to do with the administration of the trust itself. Therefore, disputes arising out of external relationships are simply regarded as ordinary disputes and thereby should be subject to the ordinary rules of the CCP. With regard to the former relationship, the ordinary rules of the CCP are to be applied, in view of the absence of explicit jurisdictional rules. Accordingly, Japanese courts would be able to take jurisdiction when any of relevant grounds lie in Japan. When a trust agreement is regarded as a consumer contract, the special rule for consumer contracts in Article 3-4 applies.

ii. Law of Property

a. Immovable Property

As to disputes over immovable property, CCP Article 3-3(xi) provides the situs jurisdiction. It is conceived as a non-exclusive jurisdiction for all kinds of litigation, including rights *in rem*. The reasoning was that the exclusive jurisdiction limited to disputes *in rem* would entail defining its scope, while rights or claims *in rem* cannot be defined categorically. Nor can claims for restitution anchored in contract be clearly discerned from claims for restitution *in rem*. Furthermore, it was opined that Japanese courts should always be available to parties domiciled in Japan, even for disputes concerning immovable property located abroad.[68] It is only for disputes over entries in public registers that the situs of immovable property is exclusively competent pursuant to Article 3-5(2) (see Section IV.A.viii).

b. Intangible Property

Intangible property covers a very wide range of property and matters such as contractual debts (or claims), shares in companies, securities and other financial instruments, and intellectual property (see Section IV.B.ii.c). Under Japanese law, disputes over intangible property

[67] Sato and Kobayashi (n 21) 36.
[68] Explanatory Note (CCP) (n 25) 23–24; Minutes of the 7th meeting (CCP).

(except for certain matters relating to registration of intellectual property) do not fall under the exclusive jurisdiction of the Japanese courts, resulting in them being governed by the non-exclusive and ordinary jurisdictional rules in the CCP. Most disputes relating to intangible property are contractual in nature, for instance, disputes arising out of the sales or assignment contract of intangible property such as contractual debts and securities. In such a case, the relevant jurisdictional rules in contractual cases (in particular, Articles 3-3(i), 3-3(iv) and 3-3(v)) are to be considered.

c. Intellectual Property

With regard to disputes over intellectual property rights,[69] there is a distinction to be made between disputes relating to: (1) the existence, registration or validity of such rights; and (2) other disputes relating to contractual obligations and infringements of such rights. Aiming to realise the public interest, Japan has had type (1) disputes being subject to the exclusive jurisdiction of Japanese courts (see Section IV.A.viii). On the other hand, type (2) disputes are subject to the ordinary and non-exclusive rules in the CCP. As to the latter group, Japanese courts may thus hear and determine those cases if any of the grounds in CCP Articles 3-2 to 3-8 lie in Japan. In particular, Articles 3-2[70] and 3-3(i), 3-3(iii), 3-3(iv), 3-3(v), and 3-3(viii) may come into play (see Section IV.B.i.a). With regard to Article 3-3(viii), the place of tort must be interpreted in light of the characteristics of intellectual property law. It is submitted that the place of a harmful act should be considered, as the tortfeasor acted or induced the infringement, including acts taken outside the country of registration, and the place where the injury occurs should be considered as the country of protection or registration, namely, in which intellectual property right is effective and damage is felt.[71]

iii. Law of Corporations

With a view to securing and realising the public interest, Japan has had certain types of corporation matters subject to exclusive jurisdiction of the Japanese courts (see Section IV.A.viii). Other matters relating to corporations/legal persons are governed by ordinary and non-exclusive rules in the CCP. Amongst others, specific grounds in CCP Article 3-3(vii) are noteworthy. Pursuant to this, 'if the association or foundation is a legal person, when it was incorporated under Japanese law; and if it is not a legal person, when its principal office is located in Japan', Japanese courts may have jurisdiction over actions with regard to: (1) an action by a company or other association against its present or former member, an action by a member against a present or former member, or an action by a former member against a present member, each of which is based on

[69] For international jurisdiction of Japan in intellectual property matters, see eg Toshiyuki Kono, 'Recent Judgments in Japan on Intellectual Property Rights, Conflict of Laws and International Jurisdiction' in Josef Drexl and Annette Kur (eds), *Intellectual Property and Private International Law: Heading for the Future* (Oxford, Hart Publishing, 2005) 229; Yuko Nishitani, 'Intellectual Property in Japanese Private International Law' (2005) 48 *JAIL* 87; Shigeki Chaen, Toshiyuki Kono and Dai Yokomizo, 'Jurisdiction in Intellectual Property Cases: The Transparency Proposal' in Jürgen Basedow, Toshiyuki Kono and Andreas Metzger (eds), *Intellectual Property in the Global Arena* (Tübingen, Mohr Siebeck, 2010) 77.

[70] See Judgment of the Supreme Court, 26 September 2002, *Minshu* 56(7), 1551. In the case involving alleged infringements of US patents between a Japanese national and a Japanese company, the Supreme court took jurisdiction, although it did not touch and decide on whether it had jurisdiction.

[71] Nishitani (n 2) 267; Yuko Nishitani, 'Supreme Court 26 September 2002, Fujimoto v. Neuron Co. Ltd. ('Card Reader' case)' in Moritz Bälz and others (eds), *Business Law in Japan* (Alphen aan den Rijn, Kluwer Law International, 2012) 679–89.

his/her status as a member; (2) an action by an association or foundation against its present or former officer based on his/her status as an officer; (3) an action by a company against its present or former incorporator or inspector, based on his/her status as an incorporator or inspector; or (4) an action by a creditor of a company or other association against its present or former member, based on his/her status as a member.[72]

V. Family and Personal Status Matters

A. General Part

i. Jurisdictional Rules in PSLA

The PSLA covers matters relating to personal status. Article 2 defines 'personal status litigation' as 'litigation related to … actions seeking the formation, or a declaration of the existence, of family relationships'. Specifically, 'personal status litigation' covers actions, for instance, to seek invalidation or annulment of a marriage, to seek a divorce, to seek a declaratory judgment on the existence of a marital relationship, to rebut the presumption of a child in wedlock, to seek recognition of parentage, to seek a declaratory judgment on the existence of a natural parent-child relationship, to seek invalidation or revocation of adoption, and to seek dissolution of an adoptive relationship.

Reflecting on previous case law,[73] the legislator introduced the new jurisdictional rules in 2018. PSLA Article 3-2 sets out seven grounds, according to which an action concerning personal status may be filed with the courts of Japan in cases where:

(1) an action is filed against either party to the family relationship and the party has his/her domicile in Japan (or residence in Japan, when he/she has no domicile or his/her domicile is unknown);
(2) an action is filed against both parties to the family relationship and one or both of the parties have their domicile in Japan (or residence in Japan, when one or both of the parties have no domicile, or their domicile is unknown);
(3) an action is filed by either party to the family relationship and the other party had his/her domicile in Japan at the time of his/her death;
(4) both parties to the family relationship have died and one or both of them had their domicile in Japan at the time of their death;
(5) both parties to the family relationship have the Japanese nationality (including cases where one or both of them had the Japanese nationality at the time of their death);
(6) an action is filed by either party to the family relationship who has his/her domicile in Japan and both parties had their last common domicile in Japan; or
(7) an action is filed by either party to the family relationship who has his/her domicile in Japan, and the whereabouts of the other party are unknown; a final and binding judgment concerning the same family relationship as the action at hand rendered in the state where the other party has his/her domicile does not have effects in Japan; or there are other special circumstances under which a trial and judicial decision by the courts of Japan would support equity between the parties or ensure the realisation of a proper and prompt trial'.[74]

[72] Each of these items, respectively, covers various claims. For details, see Sato and Kobayashi (n 21) 219–23.
[73] In particular, Judgment of the Supreme Court, Grand Bench, 25 March 1964, *Minshu* 18(3), 486 ((1965) 8 *JAIL* 175) and Judgment of the Supreme Court, Second Petty Bench, 24 June 1996, *Minshu* 50(7), 1451 ((1997) 40 *JAIL* 132).
[74] An English translation of the jurisdictional rules in the PSLA is available at (2019) 62 *JYIL* 486–88.

The PSLA contains in Article 3-5 a corrective rule similar to that under CCP Article 3-9. Pursuant to PSLA Article 3-5:

> [e]ven where the courts of Japan have jurisdiction over an action, the court may dismiss the whole or part of such action when it finds special circumstances under which a trial and judicial decision by the courts of Japan would undermine the equity between the parties or disturb the realisation of a proper and prompt trial, considering the nature of the case, the degree of the defendant's burden of submitting a defense, the location of evidence, the interest of a minor child of the parties to the family relationship involved in the action, and other relevant circumstances.

The PSLA does not mention the parties' choice of court agreement as a jurisdictional ground. Accordingly, Japanese courts may not take jurisdiction in personal status 'litigation' upon such agreement. In the proceedings relating to personal status, parties are allowed to agree on the jurisdiction of the Japanese courts only for conciliation, insofar as personal status matters subject to domestic relations conciliation (such as divorce and dissolution) are concerned (DRCPA Article 13-3(1)(3)).[75] Further, PSLA Article 3-5 expressly requires the interest of a minor child to the family relationship to be taken into consideration.[76] This requirement clearly shows that great value should be attached to the interest of a minor child in the cases relating to family relationship.[77]

Japanese courts may extend jurisdiction to some related matters pursuant to PSLA Articles 3-3 ('joinder of related claims') and 3-4 ('custody of the child'). Further, pursuant to Article 18(1), a plaintiff may amend a claim or statement of claims (and a defendant may file a counterclaim) until the conclusion of the oral arguments in the first or second instance.

As to family law matters, the PSLA does not contain any explicit rule on *lis alibi pendens*. In the course of legislative process, the question of whether to adopt a specific rule to regulate them was deliberated. It was suggested[78] that the judge should be authorised to stay proceedings if there is a foreign action involving the same cause of action between the same parties, and a recognisable judgment under CCP Article 118 on the merits is expected to be rendered. Eventually that suggestion was not adopted.

ii. *Jurisdictional Rules in Domestic Relations*

The DRCPA principally covers non-contentious matters relating to domestic relations. It offers two methods for dispute resolution: adjudication by court and conciliation by court. As to matters to be addressed in adjudication by court, DRCPA Articles 3-2 to 3-12 provide specific grounds in particular cases (see Sections V.B to V.D). As opposed to the CCP or PSLA, the DRCPA does not provide the general ground (that is, all-purpose jurisdiction). With regard to conciliation

[75] Ayako Ikeda (ed), *Shokai Kokusai Kaji Jiken no Saiban Kankatsu* [*Commentary on Jurisdictional Rules in International Family Cases*] (Tokyo, Nihon Kajo Syuppan, 2019) 17.

[76] Muneki Uchino (ed), *Ichimon Itto Heisei 30 Nen Jinji Soshoho Kaji Jiken Tetsuzukiho to Kaisei: Kokusai Saiban Kankatsu Hosei no Seibi* [*Explanatory Note on the 2018 Reform of the Personal Status Litigation Act, Domestic Relations Case Procedure Act: Improvement of the Institution on International Jurisdiction*] (Tokyo, Shojihomu, 2019) 63. The legislator takes a hypothetical divorce case involving a minor child as example, mentioning that it will be considered whether the child is able to appear before the Japanese court to deliver a statement, and, if not, whether there are alternative methods of understanding his/her opinion correctly.

[77] Sawaki and Dogauchi (n 51) 320.

[78] Counsellor's Office of the Civil Affairs Bureau of the Ministry of Justice, 'Jinji Sosho Jiken oyobi Kaji Jiken no Kokusai Saibankankatsu Hosei ni kansuru Chukan Shian no Hosoku Setsumei' ['Supplemental Explanatory Note on the Interim Draft on the Institution on International Jurisdiction in Personal Status Litigation and Domestic Relations Cases'] (*Ministry of Justice*, March 2015) 59–62, available online: www.moj.go.jp/content/001141607.pdf.

by court, DRCPA Article 3-13 offers three grounds. According to this, Japanese courts may take jurisdiction to hold conciliation: (1) where the courts of Japan have jurisdiction over an action or case for a particular issue that constitutes the subject-matter of the conciliation; (2) where the respondent has his/her domicile in Japan (or residence in Japan, when he/she has no domicile or his/her domicile is unknown); or (3) where the parties have agreed that a petition for conciliation should be filed with a court or courts of Japan. However, insofar as personal status matters other than divorce and dissolution are concerned, (2) and (3) are not available (Article 3-13(3)). Where parties agree on conciliation by Japanese courts in accordance with Article 3-13, to be valid, such agreement must satisfy the requirements of CCP Articles 3-7(2) and 3-7(3) (DRCPA Article 3-13(2)). It is not required that a plaintiff has his/her domicile in Japan.

The DRCPA also has a corrective rule in Article 3-14, according to which:

> [e]ven where the courts of Japan have jurisdiction over a case specified under Articles 3-2 to [3-13] (excluding a case pertaining to the division of an estate being filed on the ground of an agreement designating the courts of Japan as having exclusive jurisdiction), the court may dismiss the whole or a part of such case when it finds special circumstances under which a trial and judicial decision by the courts of Japan would disturb the realisation of a proper and prompt trial or, in contentious cases, undermine the equity between the parties, considering the nature of the case, the degree of the burden to the persons concerned other than the petitioner, the location of evidence, the interest of a minor child, and any other circumstances.[79]

This corrective rule contains a reservation of non-application to cases which are pecuniary in nature and where parties have agreed on exclusive jurisdiction of the Japanese courts. In the other cases, where parties simply agree on (non-exclusive) jurisdiction of the Japanese courts, a court seised may decline jurisdiction under Article 3-14.

B. Persons and Protection of Adults

The AGRAL and DRCPA provide various specific jurisdictional rules as to persons and protection of adults. As to a declaration of disappearance, according to AGRAL Article 6(1), Japanese courts may make an adjudication on his/her disappearance under Japanese law, 'where an absentee had domicile in Japan or had Japanese nationality, at the latest point of time when he/she was found to be alive'. Accordingly, Japanese courts may make such adjudication on an allegedly disappeared person irrespective of nationality, as long as the absentee's last domicile is in Japan. In addition, Japanese courts have always had jurisdiction over Japanese citizens who had allegedly disappeared (including those disappeared abroad). Further, pursuant to Article 6(2), even if an absentee did not have his/her last domicile in Japan or did not have Japanese nationality at the relevant time, Japanese courts may make such adjudication in two exceptional cases: (1) 'if an absentee's property is situated in Japan'; or (2) 'if an absentee's legal relationship should be governed by Japanese law or is connected with Japan in light of the nature of the legal relationship, his/her domicile or nationality and any other circumstances concerned'. As evident from its wording, it should be noted that Japan's jurisdiction pursuant to this provision may reach only the relevant property or legal relationship in Japan, respectively.

When it comes to the administration of an absentee's property, pursuant to DRCPA Article 3-2, Japanese courts may make an adjudication if an absentee's property is situated in Japan. This is because Japanese courts are in the best position to decide on the administration

[79] An English translation of the jurisdictional rules in the DRCPA is available at (2019) 62 *JYIL* 488–94.

of the absentee's relevant property.[80] Following this reasoning, Japan's jurisdiction should be limited to the property situated in Japan. The nationality of an absentee does not come into play.

With regard to the annulment of disappearance adjudication, pursuant to DRCPA Article 3-3, Japan's jurisdiction will be grounded where: (1) such adjudication has been made in Japan; or (2) the absentee is domiciled in Japan or has Japanese nationality; or (3) an absentee had domicile in Japan or had Japanese nationality at the latest point of time when he/she was found to be alive. The third ground corresponds to AGRAL Article 6(1). In addition, where Japanese courts have made an adjudication on an absentee's disappearance in either of the aforementioned two exceptional case under AGRAL Article 6(2), the first ground will be available.

Japan has some legal institutions to protect mentally incapacitated adults due to impaired intelligence or age-related illness such as Alzheimer's disease. Japanese law offers, for instance, guardianship (*kouken*), curatorship (*hosa*) or assistance (*hojo*). As regards a ruling for commencement of guardianship, curatorship or assistance, pursuant to AGRAL Article 5, Japanese courts may make such a ruling under Japanese law, 'where a person who is to become an adult ward, person under curatorship, or person under assistance has domicile or residence in Japan or has Japanese nationality'. The legislator does not adopt the location of property as an alternative ground, as such ground might be regarded as exorbitant and the legal institution of guardianship simply aims at the person concerned.[81] As regards to other matters regarding guardianship of adults, such as the annulment of a ruling for commencement of guardianship, curatorship, or the assistance of adults and relevant protective measures (including the designation or dismissal of a guardian, and the appointment of a special agent), similar jurisdictional rules were proposed in the 2018 amendment proceedings.[82] However, the proposed rules were not adopted for several reasons, for instance, it was unclear whether a decision by foreign courts for commencement of guardianship or others was recognisable in Japan, and it was deemed inappropriate on this occasion to set out jurisdictional rules presupposing recognisability of such decisions.[83] Therefore, it is still an open question as to whether Japanese courts may have jurisdiction over these matters.

C. Matrimonial Matters (Marriage, Divorce, Nullity and Separation)

i. *Marriage*

For a marriage to form validly, it must satisfy the requirements of applicable laws designated under AGRAL Article 24. Disputes relating to the formation of marriage only arise in the form of its invalidity or annulment (for these matters, see Section V.C.ii). Apart from these matters, some disputes may arise out of cross-border marriages, for instance, cooperation and mutual assistance between a couple, and the sharing of living expenses.[84] Pursuant to DRCPA Article 3-10, Japanese courts may take jurisdiction to make an adjudication on these matters,

[80] Uchino (n 76) 89.

[81] Kunio Koide (ed), *Chikujo Kaisetsu Ho no Tekiyo ni kansuru Tsusokuho* [*Commentary on the Act on General Rules for Application of Laws*] expanded edn (Tokyo, Shojihomu, 2015) 58.

[82] Counsellor's Office of the Civil Affairs Bureau of the Ministry of Justice, 'Jinji Sosho Jiken oyobi Kaji Jiken no Kokusai Saibankankatsu Hosei ni kansuru Chukan Shian' ['Interim Draft on the Institution on International Jurisdiction in Personal Status Litigation and Domestic Relation Cases'] (*Ministry of Justice*, February 2015) 16, available online: www.moj.go.jp/content/001141605.pdf. Under the proposed rules, the domicile or residence and the nationality of a guardian, curator, assistant as well as the adjudication that a Japanese court has made were also jurisdictional grounds.

[83] 'Supplementary Explanatory Note' (n 78) 32.

[84] For the new jurisdictional rules in matrimonial matters, see also Yuko Nishitani, 'International Adjudicatory Jurisdiction in Matrimonial Matters in Japan' (2019) 62 *JYIL* 151–88.

where a party who is obliged to provide support or a support obligee has domicile in Japan (or residence if his/her domicile does not exist or is unknown). Also, Japanese courts may take jurisdiction to hold conciliation on these matters, if parties have agreed to refer them to conciliation by Japanese courts in accordance with DRCPA Article 3-13(1)(iii). In this regard, it was deliberated in the course of legislative proceedings whether to require the case to have some connection with Japan (such as the petitioner should be domiciled in Japan).[85] However, the legislators eventually decided not to impose such a condition. Accordingly, it is not required that the case has any particular connection with Japan.

The DRCPA does not contain jurisdictional rules on matrimonial property matters such as change of an administrator of property (including upon the commencement of bankruptcy proceedings). Accordingly, whether Japanese courts may take jurisdiction to make adjudication on such matters will be determined based on *jori*. In this regard, it is submitted that Japanese courts should be authorised to take jurisdiction, at least, where either a petitioner, an administrator, or an insolvent is domiciled in Japan, or where, even if any of the parties are not domiciled in Japan, the parties have entered and registered their matrimonial contract in accordance with Japanese law.[86]

ii. Divorce, Nullity and Separation

Insofar as divorce (or nullity of marriage and separation) claims are concerned, Japanese courts may take jurisdiction when any of the requirements under PSLA Article 3-2 (more particularly, Article 3-2(1), (5), (6) and (7)) is fulfilled (see Section V.A.i). Needless to say, Japanese courts may dismiss the whole or part of the proceedings under Article 3-5.

For ancillary issues relating to divorce such as claims seeking damages, distribution of property, designation of a person to have parental authority or custody over their child(ren), and disposition regarding custody of the child, Japanese courts may extend jurisdiction to those matters if the relevant requirements of PSLA Article 3-4 or DRCPA Article 3-12 are fulfilled.

Pursuant to DRCPA Article 3-12, Japanese courts may take jurisdiction to hold adjudication on division of property, where: (1) the defendant has domicile in Japan; (2) the parties have Japanese nationality; (3) the parties had the last common domicile in Japan; or (4) there are special circumstances that hearing and determining the case in Japan would materialise fairness between the parties and secure the sound and prompt administration of justice. These grounds are identical to most of the grounds in PSLA Article 3-2. Therefore, where Japanese courts may take jurisdiction over claims seeking divorce or annulment of a marriage, a court may extend jurisdiction to cases relating to division of property.[87]

D. Matters Relating to the Well-being of the Child

A wide range of matters may arise in relation to children. They can be divided into two groups: (1) matters that come under the definition of 'personal status litigation' of PSLA Article 2; and (2) matters that are subject to adjudication by court under the DRCPA.[88]

[85] ibid 162–63.

[86] Ikeda (n 75) 34.

[87] Yuko Nishitani, 'Jinji Sosho Jiken oyobi Kaji Jiken no Kokusai Saibankankatsu tou ni kansuru Shin Hosei (2)' ['New Rules on International Jurisdiction in Personal Status Litigation and Domestic Relations Cases (2)'] (2019) 71(4) *Hoso Jiho* [*Lawyers Association Journal*] 744.

[88] See also Masako Murakami, 'International Jurisdiction of Child-Related Cases in Japan' (2019) 62 *JYIL* 189–208.

The first group covers, for instance: (1) rebuttal to the presumption of a child in wedlock; (2) recognition of parentage; (3) invalidation or annulment of a recognition of parentage; (4) declaration of the existence of parentage between a natural parent and a child; (5) invalidation or annulment of adoption; (6) dissolution of an adoptive relationship; (7) invalidation or revocation of the dissolution of an adoptive relationship by agreement; and (8) declaration of the existence of an adoptive parent-child relationship.

Where one party to the family relationship brings an action against the other party, the discussion in the context of divorce applies (see Section V.C.ii). Therefore, Japanese courts may take jurisdiction if any of the requirements under PSLA Articles 3-2(1), 3-2(5), 3-2(6) and 3-2(7) are fulfilled. In addition, where one party to the family relationship passed away before a party brings an action, pursuant to Article 3-2(3), Japanese courts may take jurisdiction when the defendant had domicile in Japan at the time of his/her death. Furthermore, with regard to some matters coming under the first group, a third party – a person who is not a party to the family relationship – may also bring an action seeking invalidation or annulment of the status. For instance, a child may bring an action to seek a declaratory judgment on the invalidity of his/her parent's divorce by agreement, or in the case where a man adopted a child, his wife (or their child(ren)) may bring an action to seek a declaratory judgment on the invalidity of such adoption. In such cases, pursuant to Articles 3-2(2) and 3-2(5), Japanese courts may take jurisdiction if one party, or both parties, to the family relationship has/have domicile (or residence) in Japan, or if both parties are Japanese nationals.

The second group covers, for instance: (1) permission to adopt; (2) establishment of special adoption; (3) dissolution of the parental relationships based on adoption; (4) dissolution of special adoption; (5) appointment of a special agent for a child; (6) change of a guardian; (7) loss of guardianship, suspension of guardianship, or loss of right of administration of property; (8) a disposition regarding the custody of a child; and (9) support.

Insofar as (1) and (2) are concerned, DRCPA Article 3-5 allows Japanese courts to take jurisdiction, where an adoptive parent or a child to be adopted has domicile in Japan (or residence, if his/her domicile does not exist or is unknown).

A parental relationship established through an adoption is not automatically dissolved, even where one party to the adoption passed away. Accordingly, to dissolve such a relationship, a party must file a petition. When a party makes such a petition after the death of the other party to the adoption, according to DRCPA Article 3-6, Japanese courts may take jurisdiction, if any of the following requirements is satisfied: (1) where an adoptive parent or an adopted child has domicile in Japan (residence, if his/her domicile does not exist or is unknown); (2) where an adoptive parent or an adopted child had domicile at the time of his/her death; or (3) in the case where either of an adoptive parent or an adopted child has Japanese nationality, where the other party had Japanese nationality at the time of his/her death. Dissolution of special adoption is subject to DRCPA Article 3-7. This provision mainly covers situations where the adoptive parents turned out to be abusing, abandoning or causing significant harm to the adopted child, or unable to provide reasonable care for the adopted child, so that the biological parents or the public prosecutor can petition against the adoptive parents for the dissolution of full adoption.

DRCPA Article 3-8 allows Japanese courts to take jurisdiction to make an adjudication on matters of parental authority, dispositions regarding custody of the child, and other matters, when a child has his/her domicile in Japan (or residence, if his/her domicile does not exist or is unknown).[89] It should be noted that adjudication by court of the sharing of expenses for the custody of a child is subject to DRCPA Article 3-10, not Article 3-8.

[89] Special consideration is needed, where the 1980 Hague Convention on the Civil Aspects of International Child Abduction is applied. For details, see Nishitani (n 87) 728–35.

DRCPA Article 3-9 provides a special rule in matters of appointment of a guardian of a minor child. This provision comes into play where a person concerned (for instance, an adopted child) seeks the dissolution of the parentage between the adoptive parents and the child. Pursuant to DRCPA Article 3-9, Japanese courts may take jurisdiction to make such an adjudication, where a minor child has domicile in Japan or is of Japanese national.

Matters of support arising out of parentage between parents and children are subject to DRCPA Article 3-10. It covers, for instance, the establishment of an obligation to support, the determination of the order of support, and the change or annulment of such determination.[90] According to that Article, Japanese courts may take jurisdiction when a party who is under duty to support (other than a petitioner) or a support obligee (that is, a child or his/her custodian) has domicile in Japan (or residence, if his/her domicile does not exist or is unknown). The provision aims, for jurisdiction based on the domicile of persons under duty to support, to keep the balance between persons under duty to support and the support obligees, while at the same time cater for the necessity of protecting such obligee.[91]

E. Succession

Matters arising out of succession are subject to different laws due to their nature.[92] CCP Article 3-3(xii) covers an action relating to an inheritance right or a hereditary reserve, and an action relating to a testamentary gift (or bequest) or any other act taking effect upon death. Specifically, that provision deals with, for instance, an action to seek confirmation of the existence of an inheritance right, an action to seek confirmation or to claim a hereditary reserve (legitime), and an action to seek for the performance of obligations arising out of a testamentary gift or gift *causa mortis* (that is, a gift made with the expectation that the person giving the gift will soon die).[93] Insofar as these matters are concerned, usual jurisdictional grounds under CCP Articles 3-2 and the subsequent Articles are available. Furthermore, pursuant to Article 3-3(xii), Japanese courts may take jurisdiction, when any of the following requirements is fulfilled: (1) when the deceased was domiciled in Japan at the time of the commencement of succession; (2) if the deceased's domicile does not exist or is unknown, when he/she was resident in Japan at the time of the commencement of succession; or (3) if the deceased residence does not exist or is unknown, when he/she had been domiciled in Japan prior to the commencement of succession (except where he/she was domiciled abroad after he/she was last domiciled in Japan). Article 3-3(xiii) covers matters relating to an inherited obligation or any other burden of the inherited property which does not come under Article 3-3(xii), for instance, an action to seek for the performance of a deceased's obligation that an heir is supposed to assume by reason of succession, and an action seeking for payment of expenses that occurs after the commencement of succession such as funeral expenses and expenses for executing a will.[94] As to these matters, Japanese courts may take jurisdiction if any of the requirements under Article 3-3(xii) are fulfilled.

[90] Minutes of 4th, 13th, and 16th meetings (PSLA and DRCPA), available online: www.moj.go.jp/shingi1/shingikai_kokusai.html.

[91] Uchino (n 76) 131–32.

[92] See also Takami Hayashi, 'International Jurisdiction in Case Related to Succession: New Rules in Japan' (2019) 62 *JYIL* 209–25.

[93] Sato and Kobayashi (n 21) 81.

[94] ibid.

On the other hand, DRCPA Article 3-11 provides jurisdictional rules on matters that are to be decided in adjudication by court or conciliation by court, for instance, disinheritance of presumptive heirs, renunciation of inheritance, separation of property, distribution of inherited property to persons with special connections, confirmation of a will, appointment or dismissal of an executor, renunciation of a hereditary reserve (or legitime), and division of estates. As for matters relating to succession that are subject to adjudication by court, pursuant to Article 3-11(1), Japanese courts may take jurisdiction: (1) when the deceased was domiciled in Japan at the time of the commencement of succession: (2) if the deceased's domicile does not exist or is unknown at that time, when he/she was resident in Japan at the time of the commencement of succession; or (3) if the deceased's residence does not exist or is unknown at that time, when he/she had ever been domiciled in Japan prior to the commencement of succession (except where he/she was domiciled abroad after he/she was last domiciled in Japan). Article 3-11(2) allows Japanese courts to take jurisdiction to adjudicate the elimination of presumptive heirs prior to the commencement of inheritance under more or less the same conditions as in Article 3-11(1). Although the connecting indicators are identical, it must be noted that under Article 3-11(2), the relevant time is the time of application, not the commencement of inheritance. Article 3-11(3) allows Japanese courts to take jurisdiction to make adjudication on preservation or administration of inherited property if part of that inherited property is situated in Japan.

Further, pursuant to DPCRA Article 3-11(4), parties are allowed to designate a specific court for adjudication by court on division of estates, prohibition of the division of estates, and a disposition to determine an heir's contribution portion. To be valid, such an agreement must satisfy the requirements of relevant provision of CCP Article 3-7 (DRCPA Article 3-11(5)). When parties enter into an exclusive choice of court agreement designating a Japanese court, the designated Japanese court may not decline jurisdiction under the 'special circumstances' test of DPCRA Article 3-14.

VI. Specific Issues

A. Insolvency Law

A party may file a petition for commencement of bankruptcy and civil rehabilitation proceedings in Japan, only if the debtor, who is an individual, has a business office, domicile, residence or property in Japan, or if the debtor, who is a legal person or any other association or foundation, has a business office or other office or property (Bankruptcy Act (BA) Article 4; Civil Rehabilitation Act (CivRA) Article 4).[95] In addition, pursuant to the BA and CivRA Article 4(2), 'a claim for which demand by litigation may be made pursuant to the provisions of CCP shall be deemed to exist in Japan'. Accordingly, where the claim is a subject matter of an action, Japanese courts may take jurisdiction over relevant insolvency cases.[96]

Insofar as corporate reorganisation proceedings are concerned, on the other hand, only a limited (stock) company (*kabushiki gaisha*) may file a petition, if it has a business office in Japan (Corporate Reorganisation Act, Article 4).[97] As opposed to bankruptcy and civil rehabilitation

[95] Act No 75 of 2 June 2004, as amended; Act No 225 of 22 December 1999, as amended.
[96] Makoto Ito and others, *Jokai Hasan Ho* [*Commentary on Bankruptcy Act*] 2nd edn (Tokyo, Kobundo, 2014) 51.
[97] Act No 154 of 13 December 2002, as amended.

proceedings, Japanese courts may not take jurisdiction merely due to the fact that the company has properties in Japan.

The BA provides special jurisdictional rules over certain bankruptcy cases, namely, ones relating to inherited property (Article 222) and to trust property (Article 244-2). In the former cases, a party may file a petition for the commencement of bankruptcy proceedings under the BA against inherited property, only if the decedent's domicile as of the time of commencement of inheritance or property that belongs to the inherited property exists in Japan. This rule is justified by the fact that most of the inherited property and the inheritance obligee are highly likely to be found in Japan and that, when inherited property is located in Japan, it is expected that the inheritance obligee collects claims from those properties.[98] In the latter case, a party may file a petition for the commencement of bankruptcy proceedings under the BA against the trust property, only if the property that belongs to the trust property or the trustee's domicile exists in Japan. If trust property is located in Japan, a trust creditor or beneficiary expects to collect claims from those properties; even where trust property is not located in Japan, if a trustee is domiciled in Japan, such trust creditor or beneficiary normally expects a trustee to perform of his/her obligation and it is expected that information concerning trust property can be found in Japan.[99]

B. Competition Law

Competition law deals with a broad range of legal areas and thereby various legal relationships may arise. Depending on the nature, those relationships may be broken into two groups: (1) contractual relationships; and (2) tortious relationships. Competition law matters do not fall under the exclusive jurisdiction of the Japanese courts. Nor do special rules exist for competition law matters. Therefore, competition law matters are subject to ordinary and non-exclusive rules in the CCP.

The first group covers situations, for instance, where a party to a contract sues the other party to seek a declaration of the nullity of the contract or alleged unfair contractual terms, arguing that the defendant infringed competition law. In this context, a competition law matter may arise a ground for the nullity of a contract (that is, simply as a preliminary question). Such a claim is one of the ordinary contractual claims, and therefore jurisdiction rules in contractual matters are to be considered (see Section IV.B.ii.a). The second group covers situations, for instance, where victims of a cartel sue cartel-participants for damages or an injunction based on their infringements of competition law, or where a party to a contract sues the other party to seek for damages, arguing that the defendant's conduct constitutes an abuse of a dominant position and thereby being contrary to competition law. In these cases, in particular, CCP Articles 3-3(iii), 3-3(iv), 3-3(v) and 3-3(viii) may ground Japan's jurisdiction. Both the place of a harmful act and the place of injury under Article 3-3(viii) must be materialised in light of the nature of competition law. With regard to the place of injury, in view of the fact that competition law maintains market order and promotes developments in the market by way of regulating anti-competitive activities, it is submitted that the place of injury should be interpreted as the place where the market is, or likely to be, affected by anti-competitive activities. On the other hand, the place of a harmful act should be ascertained in accordance with the type of anti-competitive activities.

[98] ibid 1479.
[99] ibid 1552.

C. Jurisdiction in Shipping and Maritime Claims

i. Jurisdiction of the Japanese Courts

It is undisputed that the jurisdictional rules under CCP Articles 3-2 to 3-9 have application in cases relating to shipping and maritime claims. Amongst others, the specific grounds in Articles 3-3(iii), 3-3(iv), 3-3(vi), 3-3(viii), 3-3(ix) and 3-3(x) will play an important role. For instance, insofar as actions relating to a property right are concerned, pursuant to Article 3-3(iii), Japanese courts may take jurisdiction where the defendant's ship is situated in Japan. Notably, where the defendant is not the owner of the ship situated in Japan, Article 3-3(iii) is not available because a seizable property grounding Japan's jurisdiction has to belong to the defendant. But, pursuant to Article 3-3(vi), a party may file an action based on a maritime-lien claim and any other claim secured by a ship when the ship is located in Japan, regardless of whether the defendant is the ship's owner or not. Accordingly, even where the defendant is simply a charterer, if the ship is situated in Japan, Japanese courts may have jurisdiction insofar as a maritime-lien claim and any other claim secured by a ship is concerned.

In the case of a collision of ships and other accidents at sea, there exist additional grounds. Where a collision of ships (or other accident) occurs within the territorial waters of Japan, the place of torts under CCP Article 3-3(viii) is available (see Section IV.B.i.b), while where a collision (or other accident) occurs on high seas, a party seeking damages arising from a collision may not rely on this ground.[100] However, pursuant to Article 3-3(ix), a party may file an action before a Japanese court to seek damages if the first place at which the damaged ship arrived is located in Japan.[101] This ground is available regardless of where the collision or the other accident occurs.

Other issues may arise from shipping activities. As to claims relating to salvage, pursuant to CCP Article 3-3(x), whether a salvage is contractual or not, a party may file an action before Japanese courts if the salvage was performed in Japan or the first place at which the salvaged ship arrived is located in Japan. Where a contractual salvage is performed and a party seeks payment of salvage remuneration, Japan's jurisdiction may be granted by Article 3-3(i) if the place of payment lies in Japan.[102]

ii. The Process of Ship Arrest

Under Japanese law, ship arrest can be made as a provisional seizure under the CPRA. A party may file a petition only if an action on the merits may be filed with a court in Japan, or if the property to be provisionally seized or the disputed subject matter is located in Japan in accordance with CPRA Article 11 (see Section IV.A.v). When a party makes an application for a provisional seizure, he/she may be required to set aside a certain amount of money (CPRA Article 4). CPRA Article 20(1) stipulates that '[a]n order for provisional seizure may be issued when it is likely that a compulsory execution regarding a claim for payment of money will not be possible, or will result in the occurrence of significant difficulties'. CPRA Article 48(1) provides that the provisional seizure of a vessel can be executed in two ways: by way of registration of the provisional

[100] Sato and Kobayashi (n 21) 74.

[101] cf Judgment of the Sendai High Court, 22 September 2011, 1367 *Hanrei Taimuzu* 240. In the case where a ship's collision occurred on high seas and the first place at which the damaged ships arrived was in Japan, the Court declined to exercise jurisdiction based on special circumstances (although this judgment was rendered before the black-letter rules are introduced).

[102] Sawaki and Dogauchi (n 51) 284.

seizure, and/or by way of the submission of 'the document proving the nationality of the vessel and any other documents necessary for the navigation of the vessel' to the court executing the provisional remedy. In the latter way, the court will order a court execution officer to confiscate those documents.[103] Pursuant to Commercial Code Article 689, seizure or provisional seizure (excluding provisional seizure by means of registration) cannot be executed against a ship which is at sea, while it can be executed against a ship which is being anchored in harbour.[104]

VII. Immunities from Jurisdiction

A. Sovereign Immunity

Japan is a party to the 2004 United Nations Convention on Jurisdictional Immunities of States and Their Property.[105] Largely based on the 2004 Convention, Japan has enacted the Act on Civil Jurisdiction of Japan with respect to a Foreign State, etc (ACJJ).[106] The ACJJ came into force in 2010 and now governs the question of sovereign immunity. The ACJJ is based on the restrictive immunity doctrine. Thus, a 'foreign state' is immune from the jurisdiction of the Japanese courts only in restrictive situations. Even prior to the enactment of the ACJJ, the Supreme Court has several times proclaimed the restrictive immunity doctrine.[107]

ACJJ Article 2 defines a 'foreign state' as entities including: (1) the state and its various organs of government; (2) constituent units of a federal state and other equivalent administrative divisions of a state, which are entitled to perform acts in the exercise of sovereign authority; (3) entities that are entitled to perform acts in the exercise of sovereign authority (limited to cases in which said authority is exercised); and (4) representatives of the previous three kinds of entities acting in that capacity. Pursuant to Article 4, a foreign state generally is immune from Japan's jurisdiction. To the contrary, Articles 5 to 16 (Section 2) list cases in which a foreign state exceptionally cannot enjoy the sovereign immunity. Articles 5 to 7 cover situations where a foreign state explicitly by words or implicitly by conduct consents to submission to the jurisdiction of Japan. Articles 8 to 16 list specific matters where a foreign state cannot enjoy the sovereign immunity. They comprise matters such as commercial transactions,[108] labour contracts, death or injury of persons, loss of tangible objects, rights and interests pertaining to real property, rights and interests pertaining to the administration or disposition of property in which the court participates, intellectual property rights, operation of ships, and arbitration agreements.

In respect of commercial transactions, pursuant to Article 8, a foreign state is in principle not immune from Japan's jurisdiction. However, a foreign state can enjoy immunity if it is engaged in commercial transactions with citizens or enterprises of that foreign state or with other foreign

[103] For the detailed process, see also Rules of Civil Provisional Remedies (Rules of the Supreme Court, No 3 of 16 May 1990).

[104] Act No 48 of 9 March 1899, as amended.

[105] Adopted by the General Assembly of the United Nations on 2 December 2004. Not yet in force. See General Assembly resolution 59/38, annex, *Official Records of the General Assembly, Fifty-ninth Session, Supplement No 49* (A/59/49).

[106] Act No 24 of 24 April 2009. For details, see Kimio Yakushiji, 'Legislation of the Act on Civil Jurisdiction Over Foreign States, Acceptance of the UN Convention on Jurisdictional Immunity of States and their Property, and their Possible Effects upon the Jurisprudence of Japanese Domestic Courts on State Immunity' (2010) 53 *JYIL* 202–42.

[107] Judgment of the Supreme Court, 21 July 2006, *Minshu* 60(6), 2542; Judgment of the Supreme Court, 16 October 2009, *Minshu* 63(8), 1799.

[108] Judgment of the Tokyo District Court, 18 September 2014, 2014WLJPCA09188002.

states, or where the parties to the commercial transactions have expressly agreed otherwise. The term 'commercial transactions' means 'contracts or transactions relating to the civil or commercial buying and selling of commodities, procurement of services, lending of money, or other matters' and excludes 'labour contracts'. Whether a contract or transaction in question falls under the 'commercial transaction' within the meaning of Article 8 is in principle determined in light of the nature of the act, rather than the subjective purpose.[109]

As regards labour contracts, the ACJJ provides a special rule in Article 9. Pursuant to Article 9(1), a foreign state is not immune from Japan's jurisdiction with respect to labour contracts between that foreign state and an individual, when all or part of the labour is, or is to be, performed in Japan. Exceptions to this are, for instance, where an individual is: (1) a person who enjoys diplomatic immunity (such as a diplomat in the meaning of Article 1(e) of the 1961 Vienna Convention on Diplomatic Relations or a consular officer in the meaning of Article 1(d) of the 1963 Vienna Convention on Consular Relations); (2) a person who has been employed to perform duties pertaining to the security, diplomatic secrets, or other important interests of the foreign state; and (3) a citizen of that foreign state who does not have permanent residence in Japan.

In addition, a foreign state may also enjoy immunity for actions or petitions regarding the existence of the contract for the employment or re-employment of the individual (ACJJ Article 9(2)(iii)), and regarding the effect of the dismissal or termination of the labour contracts that would, from a perspective of the foreign state, harm its security interests (ACJJ Article 9(2)(iv)). On the other hand, actions seeking damages based on labour relationships are always subject to Japan's jurisdiction. This is because the resulting judgment in such actions is not to compel a foreign state to employ or fire an individual. Furthermore, pursuant to ACJJ Article 9(2)(vi), where the parties to the labour contract have otherwise agreed in writing, a foreign state can be immune from Japan's jurisdiction. However, if such an agreement is found to be against public policy from the viewpoint of labour protection, a foreign state is not entitled to immunity from Japan's jurisdiction.

B. State-Owned Enterprises (SOEs)

When it comes to state-owned enterprises (SOEs), the first question is whether SOEs can be regarded as a 'foreign state' as defined in the ACJJ (in particular, Article 2(3) and (4)). Some SOEs such as a central bank may come under the definition of a foreign state.[110] However, it should be noted that, according to Article 2(3), SOEs must perform an act in the exercise of sovereign power so as to enjoy the state immunity. If SOEs engage in a simply private transaction without exercising sovereign power, they are not regarded as a foreign state and thereby subject to jurisdiction of Japan. If SOEs are regarded as a foreign state, they can be immune from Japan's jurisdiction. Having said that, SOEs exceptionally cannot enjoy the immunity insofar as certain activities listed in ACJJ Articles 5–16 (for instance, commercial transaction and labour contracts) are concerned.

[109] Tomoyuki Tobisawa, *Chikujo Kaisetsu Taigaikoku Minji Saibanken Ho – waga kuni no Syuken Menjo Hosei ni tsuite* [*Commentary on the Act on Civil Jurisdiction of Japan with respect to a Foreign State, etc*] (Tokyo, Shojihomu, 2009) 35–37.
[110] Honma, Nakano and Sakai (n 30) 20.

6

South Korea

SUNGJAE CHUN

I. Introduction

At the outset, Korea is a civil law country where statutes are considered as the fundamental source of law. This said, the Act on Private International Law (KAPIL) serves as the main source of law in matters regarding conflict of laws and direct jurisdiction. Before delving into the issue of direct jurisdiction under Korean law, the legislative history of the KAPIL should be briefly explained. The Conflict of Laws Act (CLA) enacted in 1962 marks the beginning of domestic legislation on conflict of laws in Korea. The CLA had no provision on direct jurisdiction and, as a result, it was left to individual courts to handle the question of jurisdiction on a case-by-case basis.[1] Nevertheless, there was a growing need for a clear standard to determine direct jurisdiction, due to an increase in international transactions and disputes.[2] Consequently, the CLA was fully revised into the KAPIL in 2001 (with minor amendments in 2011 and 2016).[3] It is understood that that the KAPIL has been influenced by German, Japanese and Swiss law.[4] One of the main changes introduced by the KAPIL was the inclusion of a provision setting out general criteria for determining international jurisdiction. This was fully discussed during the preparation of the KAPIL and was finally included as Article 2, which will be considered in detail below. In any event, while the doctrine of *stare decisis* does not apply under Korean law, judgments rendered by the Supreme Court are indispensable in the interpretation and application of Korean law in practice. In light of the above, relevant judgments should be taken into account in order to fully understand how direct jurisdiction is dealt with in actual cases.

II. General Principles

Jurisdiction can be defined as the power or authority of a state to adjudicate on matters arising within its territory. This said, the rules on direct jurisdiction are closely related to determining the boundaries of jurisdiction.[5] Before analysing the details on the rules of direct jurisdiction

[1] Kwang Hyun Suk, *Guk-je-min-so-bub* [*International Civil Procedure Law*] (Seoul, Pakyoungsa, 2012) 67.
[2] Kwang Hyun Suk, *Guk-je-sa-bub Hae-sol* [*Commentary on Private International Law*] (Seoul, Pakyoungsa, 2013) 59.
[3] 'Act on Private International Law' (*National Law Information Center*), available online: https://law.go.kr/LSW/eng/engLsSc.do?menuId=2&section=lawNm&query=act+on+private+international+law&x=0&y=0.
[4] Suk (n 1) 13.
[5] Suk (n 2) 76.

under Korean law, some basic concepts should be briefly explained. For this purpose, KAPIL Articles 1 and 2, which serve as the backbone of legal principles on direct jurisdiction, need to be examined.

A. KAPIL Article 1

KAPIL Article 1 (Purpose) states:

> The purpose of this Act is to determine general principles and governing laws on the international jurisdiction regarding any legal relations which contain foreign factors.

Under Korean law, it is common for the first article of a statute to stipulate the act's purpose. While the KAPIL follows this structure, it is notable that the phrase 'legal relations which contain foreign factors' is inserted. That phrase is closely related to the scope of application of the KAPIL and requires further interpretation. In this regard, the Supreme Court ruled on the basis of Article 1 that the KAPIL should be applied if: (1) the nationality of the relevant parties, their addresses, the place of the subject of dispute, and the place of occurrence of a material act are closely related to a foreign country; and (2) it would be reasonable to apply conflict of law rules rather than domestic legislation.[6] The judgment has been criticised by some scholars who argue that 'reasonableness to consider rules on conflict of laws' allows excessive discretion to the court on the scope of the KAPIL.[7]

B. KAPIL Article 2

KAPIL Article 2 (International Jurisdiction) stipulates:

> (1) In case a party or a case in dispute is substantively related to the Republic of Korea, a court shall have the international jurisdiction. In this case, the court shall obey reasonable principles, compatible to the ideology of the allocation of international jurisdiction, in judging the existence of the substantive relations.
> (2) A court shall judge whether or not it has the international jurisdiction in the light of jurisdictional provisions of domestic laws and shall take a full consideration of the unique nature of international jurisdiction in the light of the purport of the provision of paragraph (1).

Article 2 is the provision which the Korean courts refer to when adjudicating matters regarding international jurisdiction.[8] Article 2 was originally inserted in the KAPIL as a temporary provision to be applied while the international community was formulating a clear unified standard on direct jurisdiction.[9] However, the harmonisation of international direct jurisdiction is yet to be achieved and Article 2 has been acting as a crucial provision to determine direct jurisdiction issues under Korean law.

[6] Judgment of the Supreme Court, 11 December 2014, 2012Da119443.

[7] Suk (n 2) 53.

[8] Kwang Hyun Suk, *Guk-je-sa-bob-gwa Guk-je-so-song* [*International Private Law and International Litigation*] vol 5 (Seoul, Pakyoungsa, 2012) 394.

[9] Ae Ra Han, 'Guk-je-jae-pan-gwan-hal-gwa gwan-ryon-deon pan-gyul-ui choo-yi mit guk-je-sa-bub-ui gae-jong-bang-an – Guk-jejae-pan-gwan-hal-ui pan-dan-gu-jo mit bub-in-e dae-han yil-bu gwa-ying-gwan-hal jaeng-jom-gwa gwan-ryon-ha-yo –' ['Trends of Court Judgments on International Jurisdiction and Amendment Proposals to the Private International Act of Korea – Focusing on the Reasoning Structure of Judgments and on Certain Exorbitant Jurisdiction Issues Regarding a Legal Entity –'] (2013) 35 *Min-sa-pan-rye-yon-gu* [*Studies on Civil Judgments*] 1079, 1081.

KAPIL Article 2 presents two key principles in deciding direct jurisdiction issues. First, a party or a case in dispute should have a 'substantial relationship' with Korea and the court should take into account 'the ideology of the allocation of international jurisdiction' in determining the existence of such relationship (paragraph 1). Next, the jurisdictional provisions of domestic legislation should be taken into account within the context of the unique nature of international jurisdiction (paragraph 2).[10] Here, 'substantial relationship' can be explained as the existence of connecting factors between the parties and a dispute to Korea so that the jurisdiction under the Korean court can be reasonably justified.[11] Further, the 'ideology of the allocation of international jurisdiction' refers to the fairness and timeliness of trial and equity between the parties.[12] Meanwhile, the 'unique nature of international jurisdiction' means that matters relating to litigation procedure, governing law, and the recognition and enforcement of judgments can differ from jurisdiction to jurisdiction.[13]

C. Meaning of 'Substantive Relationship'

KAPIL Article 2, paragraph 1 requires a substantive relationship if the Korean court is to exercise direct jurisdiction. However, the law is silent on the meaning or scope of the 'substantive relationship', thereby drawing criticism from scholars that a more concrete and detailed standard should be stipulated in law.[14] In the circumstances, the meaning and scope of the substantive relationship can be discerned by scrutinising relevant judgments. For instance, the Supreme Court has ruled that, in determining international jurisdiction, there should be adherence to basic principles, such as fairness between the parties, appropriateness of the forum, promptness, and trial efficiency. In particular, the Court stressed that: (1) the parties' interest in fair treatment, convenience, and predictability of outcome; (2) the public interest in ensuring the appropriateness of the forum, the prompt resolution of cases, procedural efficiency, and the effectiveness of judgments; and (3) the need for judges to give reasoned decisions based on the parties' relationship, the main issues of a case, and the *lex fori*, should be carefully balanced when determining international jurisdiction.[15] The Court thus took the view that in the interest of the parties, the court and the nation should be regarded as the main criteria. Scholars have further explained that the interest of the parties refers to the need to adjudicate a case in a court that is accessibly close to the parties so as to secure convenience of litigation in terms of location, language and communication.[16] Further, the interest of the court denotes convenience in obtaining and investigating relevant evidence in order to enable a full review of a case.[17] Lastly, the interest of the nation concerns the protection of the defendant without violating the rights of the plaintiff.[18] The criteria were further expounded by the Supreme Court in a 2010 case.[19] The relatives of a flight attendant

[10] Suk (n 8) 395.
[11] ibid.
[12] ibid.
[13] Tae Ak Rho, 'Guk-je-jae-pan-gwan-hal-e gwan-han choi-gun dae-bub-won-pan-gyul-ui bun-suk – sil-jil-jeok gwan-ryun-won-chik-gwa guk-je-sa-bub je-2-jo-ui hae-seok-ron-ul joong-sim-ui-ro –' ['Analysis of Recent Supreme Court Decisions on International Jurisdiction – With the Focus on Interpretation of Article 2 of the Private International Act and the Substantial Connection Principle –'] (2012) 22(1) *Sa-bub* [*Private Law Journal*] 197, 214.
[14] Han (n 9) 1126.
[15] Judgment of the Supreme Court, 27 January 2005, 2002Da59788.
[16] Kwang Hyun Suk, *Guk-je-sa-bob-gwa Guk-je-so-song* [*International Private Law and International Litigation*] vol 4 (Seoul, Pakyoungsa, 2007) 110.
[17] ibid.
[18] ibid.
[19] Judgment of the Supreme Court, 15 July 2010, 2010Da18355.

(a Chinese national), who died in a crash in Korea while carrying out duties on board a flight from Beijing to Busan, filed a claim for compensation against the airline (a Chinese company) before the Korean court. The court upheld direct jurisdiction, stating that the parties' interests and those of the court could be fully catered for by the Korean proceedings. With regards to personal interest, the court observed that: (1) since the plaintiffs had clearly stated that they wished to proceed with the case in the Korean court; (2) the defendant could have foreseen that the possibility of a lawsuit being filed against them since it operated a branch office in Korea and was fully engaged in performing commercial activities in Korea; and (3) jurisdiction could not be denied merely because it was more convenient for the defendant in terms of geographic location, language and ease of communication. The court further held that the interests of the court could be acknowledged. This was because: (1) the investigation and collection of evidence would be in Korea where the accident had taken place; (2) it was likely that the defendant had properties in Korea; and (3) the mere facts that the defendant had acknowledged responsibility and the investigation had already been carried out in a separate case were not sufficient to deny direct jurisdiction.

D. Governing Law and Jurisdiction

As explained, 'substantive relationship' is an essential criterion in determining direct jurisdiction under Korean law. Governing law is a factor to be considered when assessing whether a substantial relationship exists or not. However, the governing law may not be so crucial in determining direct jurisdiction. For instance, in a case where the plaintiff argued that an action should be dismissed since Chinese law was the governing law, the Supreme Court ruled that the mere fact that Chinese law governed was insufficient to deny a substantial relationship between the lawsuit and the Korean court.[20] In practice, it is not uncommon for the Court to exercise jurisdiction over a case where foreign law is applicable. For example, there are numerous maritime cases in which the Supreme Court has applied English law, the latter often being designated as the governing law between the parties.[21]

E. *Forum non conveniens*

Forum non conveniens, which stands for 'inconvenient forum' in Latin, is a common law doctrine that allows a court to dismiss a civil lawsuit in a situation where another court is an appropriate and more convenient forum for the adjudication of an action.[22] During the enactment process of the KAPIL, there was an in-depth discussion as to whether the principle of *forum non conveniens* should be inserted as a provision in order to provide a clear legal basis for the court to suspend or dismiss a case if a foreign court is more suitable to adjudicate the matter.[23] Although some scholars favoured the addition of such a provision to prevent plaintiffs from forum shopping, it was excluded in the final version of the KAPIL due to disagreement among the committee members who participated in the enactment process.[24] Nevertheless, the principle of *forum non conveniens*

[20] Judgment of the Supreme Court, 13 June 2019, 2016Da33752.

[21] Judgment of the Supreme Court, 14 November 2019, 2017Da224807.

[22] 'Glossary: Forum non conveniens' (*Thomson Reuters Practical Law*), available online: https://uk.practicallaw.thomsonreuters.com/2-341-8952?transitionType=Default&contextData=(sc.Default)&firstPage=true.

[23] Bub-mu-bu [Ministry of Justice], *Gae-jong Guk-je-sa-bob hae-sol* [*Commentary on the Revised Act on International Private Law*] (Gyeonggi-do, Ministry of Justice, 2001) 25, available online: https://academic.naver.com/openUrl.naver?doc_id=18073775&linkType=doclink.

[24] Suk (n 2) 70.

is not entirely ruled out under Korean law. It is still possible for the Korean court to decline jurisdiction on the basis that other foreign courts should more properly exercise jurisdiction over a matter.[25] Thus, the Korean courts have examined the issue of *forum non conveniens* from time to time. Notably, in a case where the registration of the internet domain name of 'hpweb.com' was disputed between a web designer and Hewlett-Packard, the Supreme Court ruled that Korea was not an inappropriate forum for the case, taking into account that the jurisdictions of different courts can overlap and the background facts were substantively related to Korea.[26] In a more recent ruling, the Supreme Court referred, albeit briefly, to the issue of *forum non conveniens*. The Court decided that the mere fact that a foreign court had advantages in terms of geographic location, language and telecommunication, was not a good enough reason to deny direct jurisdiction.[27]

F. *Lis alibi pendens*

Korean law does not have an explicit provision on *lis alibi pendens*.[28] While Article 259 of the Civil Procedure Act prohibits launching a repetitive lawsuit, the provision is only applicable to domestic cases (that is, cases without any foreign elements).[29] There are only a few lower court judgments on *lis alibi pendens* and the Supreme Court has not yet delivered a decision in this regard.[30] There was a case where a Korean company filed a lawsuit before the Supreme Court of California against a US company and its majority shareholder, claiming compensation for violation of a contract. The Korean company launched another lawsuit, requesting partial compensation based on identical facts before the Seoul District Court. After reviewing the matter, the Seoul court dismissed the lawsuit, stating that: (1) both parties had actively participated in the case before the US court; (2) the judgment to be delivered by the US court was unlikely to be against the public order of Korea; (3) the US court judgment was expected to be fully recognised in Korea; and (4) the reciprocity requirement was fulfilled (that is, Korean judgments were likely to be recognised and enforced in California).[31] In summary, Korean courts can consider ongoing international parallel litigation and restrict themselves from exercising jurisdiction in a newly initiated case based on the same claim as that of the ongoing case.

III. Jurisdictional Provisions under the Civil Procedure Act

A. General Overview

By KAPIL Article 2, paragraph 2, the jurisdictional provisions of domestic law should be taken into account along with the unique nature of international jurisdiction. Korean courts usually refer to the provisions in the Civil Procedure Act (CPA) which furnish a general framework

[25] ibid.
[26] Judgment of the Supreme Court, 27 January 2005, 2002Da59788 (n 15).
[27] Judgment of the Supreme Court, 13 June 2019, 2016Da33752 (n 20).
[28] Hun Mook Lee, 'Guk-je-jeok so-song-gyong-hap-ui cho-ri-e gwan-han bi-gyo-bup-juk yeon-gu' ['A Comparative Analysis on How to Deal with Lis Pendens in International Litigation'] [2019] *Guk-je-sa-bub-yeon-gu* [*Studies on Private International Law*] 383, 384.
[29] ibid 384.
[30] ibid.
[31] Judgment of the Seoul District Court, 13 December 2002, 2000Gahap90940.

of jurisdiction in civil and commercial matters.[32] The court will determine whether to exercise direct jurisdiction or not, under a comprehensive analysis of 'substantive relationship' as provided in KAPIL Article 2, paragraph 1 and the jurisdictional rules of the CPA. Those rules play a pivotal role in the matter of direct jurisdiction. This Section explains the key provisions.

B. Obligations

CPA Article 8 (Special Forum of Place of Residence or Place of Obligation Performance) states:

> A lawsuit concerning a property right may be brought to the court having the jurisdiction over the place of residence or the place of obligation performance.

Further, Article 467 of the Civil Act stipulates that, in principle, performance of an obligation should be effected at the creditor's domicile. Consequently, if a creditor wishes to bring a lawsuit against a debtor for performance of a contractual obligation, the creditor may file the lawsuit at the court having jurisdiction over its place of residence. This principle applies to tort and unjust enrichment claims as well. CPA Article 8 thereby encompasses a broad jurisdiction. The Korean courts have been applying it in cases where direct jurisdiction is an issue. Some lower court decisions have also recognised direct jurisdiction in tort and unjust enrichment cases on the basis that the place of obligation performance is in Korea.[33] But the court has also stressed the substantive relationship requirement, rather than the place of obligation performance. In a case where the plaintiff claimed payment for a consignment of frozen fish that was to be discharged in China, the Supreme Court ruled that there was direct jurisdiction for the following reasons: (1) five years had passed since the frozen fish had been sold and denying jurisdiction might result in neglecting the parties' rights in relation to the case; (2) the defendant had raised a counterclaim and the relevant claims could all be resolved at the same time; (3) the parties had entered into their contract by exchanging documents through fax in Korea; and (4) the defendant was due to receive a settlement fee in Korea.[34] With regard to the ruling, some scholars have raised concerns that the Court had over-emphasised the substantial relationship test (as stipulated by KAPIL Article 2, paragraph 2) and overlooked the jurisdiction provision in the CPA (which should have been taken into account pursuant to KAPIL Article 2, paragraph 1).[35]

C. Persons

CPA Article 3 (General Forum of Person) states:

> General forum of a person shall be determined by his/her domicile: Provided, that where the person has no domicile in the Republic of Korea or his/her domicile is unknown, it shall be determined pursuant to his/her residence, and if the residence is unfixed or unknown, it shall be determined pursuant to his/her last domicile.

[32] 'Civil Procedure Act' (*Korea Legislation Research Institute*), available online: https://elaw.klri.re.kr/kor_service/lawView.do?hseq=45913&lang=ENG.

[33] Judgment of the Seoul Central District Court, 16 November 2011, 2007Gahap33069; Judgment of the Seoul Central District Court, 29 January 2010, 2009Gahap33582; Kyung Han Sohn, 'Guk-je-sa-bub gae-jong bang-an yon-gu choi-jong-bo-go-seo' ['Final Report on the Research on the Revision of the Private International Law Act'] (*National Library*, 30 November 2012), available online: www.nl.go.kr/app/nl/search/common/download.jsp?file_id=FILE-00008504595.

[34] Judgment of the Supreme Court, 29 May 2008, 2006Da71908, 71915.

[35] Suk (n 2) 104.

CPA Article 2 states that the court having jurisdiction over the address of the defendant has general jurisdiction over a civil lawsuit. Thus, the address of a person, especially that of a defendant, is an essential factor to be taken into account in deciding proper jurisdiction. The Supreme Court has recently applied CPA Articles 2 and 3 in a lawsuit between two Chinese nationals. The Court stated that the defendant's address was an important element to consider in regard to the exercise of direct jurisdiction. Since both defendants had substantially established their living environment in Korea, the Korean court could exercise jurisdiction in the case.[36]

D. Torts

i. Torts in General

CPA Article 18, paragraph 1 (Special Forum for *Locus Delicti*) states: 'A lawsuit concerning a tort may be brought to the court in the place of an act.' The provision is applicable in cases involving direct jurisdiction as well. In practice, Korean courts may accept jurisdiction at the place of occurrence of a tortious act or the place where the damage from a tortious act has occurred. This can lead to necessary evidence at the place of a tort or damage being readily preserved and ensure relevant predictability of jurisdiction and litigation procedure.

ii. Product Liability

Issues of direct jurisdiction often arise in product liability cases. The court will apply the substantive relationship requirement between the manufacturer and the place of occurrence of damage. A manufacturer can thereby reasonably foresee that a lawsuit may be initiated against it in such place.[37] In a case where a foreign company filed a lawsuit before a Korean court for enforcement of a New York judgment, the Supreme Court dismissed the case based on the lack of jurisdiction of the New York court. The Supreme Court was of the view that the judgment could not be enforced because: (1) the defendant did not have a branch office or agent in the US; (2) the defendant had not performed any commercial act (such as advertising or customer service) in the US; and (3) the defendant had merely sold certain products to a company in New York on an Original Equipment Manufacturer (OEM) basis.[38] Korean courts are consequently cautious in deciding to exercise jurisdiction over product liability cases on the substantive relationship test.[39]

E. Corporations

CPA Articles 5 (General Forum of Juristic Person, etc) and 12 (Special Forum of Location of Office or Business Place) stipulate:

Article 5

(1) General forum of a juristic person or any other association or foundation shall be determined pursuant to the place where its principal office or business place is located, and in cases where there

[36] Judgment of the Supreme Court, 13 June 2019, 2016Da33752 (n 20).

[37] Judgment of the Supreme Court, 12 February 2015, 2012Da21737.

[38] ibid.

[39] Sa-bub-jeong-chaek-yon-gu-won [Judicial Policy Research Institute], *Oi-guk-jae-pan-ui sung-in-gwa jip-haeng-e gwan-han yon-gu* [*Study on the Recognition and Enforcement of Foreign Judgments*] (*Judicial Policy Research Institute*, 2020) 61, available online: http://jpri.scourt.go.kr/fileDownLoad.do?seq=1307.

exists no office and business place, it shall be determined pursuant to the domicile of the person principally in charge of its duties.

(2) In cases where the provisions of paragraph (1) are applied to a foreign juristic person and any other foreign association or foundation, their general forums shall be determined pursuant to their offices, business places, or the domiciles of the persons in charge of their duties, in the Republic of Korea.

Article 12

A lawsuit concerning the affairs of an office or business place against a person who keeps such an office or business place may be brought to the court located in the place of such an office or business place.

On the basis of CPA Article 5, paragraph 2, the Korean court may recognise general jurisdiction over a foreign company that has a branch office, business place in Korea or where the person in charge is domiciled in Korea.[40] CPA Article 12, on the other hand, requires that a lawsuit 'concerning the affairs of the office or business place' be brought to the court in the place of that office or business place. The lawsuit should, however, be related to the affairs of the office in order for the jurisdiction to be established. Where the court applies CPA Article 5, paragraph 2, the requirement in CPA Article 12 that an action must be one 'concerning the affairs of the office' can be circumvented.[41] In practice, the courts actively recognise direct jurisdiction by applying Article 5, paragraph 2, regardless of whether a case is related to the affairs of an office or not.[42]

F. Property

CPA Article 11 (Special Forum of Location of Property) provides:

A lawsuit concerning a property right against a person who has no domicile in the Republic of Korea or against a person whose domicile is unknown, may be brought to the court located in the place of the objects of a claim or those of the security, or any seizable property of a defendant.

Given the provision, it is possible for the court to recognise jurisdiction where a defendant owns property in Korea. Some scholars have criticised this, arguing that recognising jurisdiction based solely on the fact that property of the defendant is located in Korea would amount to exorbitant jurisdiction.[43] A critic has suggested that, in order for the location of property to be considered as a factor in determining international jurisdiction: (1) such property should have been in Korea for a considerable time; (2) ownership of the property should be validly held under Korean law; and (3) the price of the property amounts to a major portion of the claim amount.[44] In practice, Korean courts treat the location of property as a factor to be considered when deciding direct jurisdiction.[45]

[40] Here, branch office refers to a foreign company that can perform commercial activities whereas business place refers to a liaison office which can only engage in marketing activities.
[41] Judicial Policy Research Institute (n 39) 58.
[42] Judgment of the Supreme Court, 9 June 2000, 98Da35037.
[43] Suk (n 2) 80.
[44] Han (n 9) 1151.
[45] Judgment of the Seoul High Court, 26 January 2006, 2002Na32662.

G. Jurisdiction by Agreement

CPA Article 29 (Jurisdiction by Agreement) states:

(1) Parties to a lawsuit may decide by agreement the competent court of the first instance.
(2) The agreement referred to in paragraph (1) shall be valid only when it is made in writing with respect to a lawsuit based on a specific legal relationship.

Parties may determine jurisdiction by agreement in a dispute having foreign elements.[46] There are some notable judgments of the Supreme Court on exclusive jurisdiction by agreement. The Court has ruled that, in order for an exclusive jurisdiction agreement in favour of a jurisdiction outside Korea to be effective: (1) such case should not fall under the exclusive jurisdiction of Korean court under Korean law; (2) the designated foreign court should have effective jurisdiction over the case; (3) the case should be reasonably connected or related to the designated foreign court; and (4) the agreement on jurisdiction should not be excessively unreasonable or unfair to one of the parties.[47] In the case of an exclusive jurisdiction agreement in favour of the Korean court, the Supreme Court has applied the same four requirements analogously.[48] There has been discussion on whether jurisdiction by agreement on contractual issues may be extended to tort claims between the parties. The majority of scholars and lower court decisions support the view that jurisdiction can be extended by agreement to tort claims.[49]

H. Consumer Contracts

KAPIL Article 27 (Consumer Contract) states:

...
(4) In case of the contract under the provision of paragraph (1) [that is, a consumer contract], the consumer may and file a lawsuit against the opposite party of the consumer even in the country where the habitual residence of the consumer is located.
(5) In case of the contract under the provision of paragraph (1), a lawsuit entered by the opposite party of the consumer against the consumer may be filed only in the country where the habitual residence of the consumer is located.
(6) The parties of the contract under the provision of paragraph (1) may agree on the international jurisdiction in writing: Provided, that such agreement shall be effective only in any of the following subparagraphs:
   1. In case a dispute already occurred;
   2. In case filing a lawsuit with other courts in addition to the competent court under this Article is permitted to the consumer.

This is a special provision formulated for the purpose of protecting consumers. KAPIL Article 27 overrides the general rule of international jurisdiction under KAPIL Article 2. A consumer can file a lawsuit in his or her habitual residence (paragraph 4), whereas the opposite party (usually a company manufacturer or provider of a product) may only initiate a lawsuit in the consumer's habitual residence and not that of the company (paragraph 5). Such restriction of

[46] Suk (n 2) 82.
[47] Judgment of the Supreme Court, 9 September 1997, 96Da20093.
[48] Judgment of the Supreme Court, 28 April 2011, 2009Da19093.
[49] Suk (n 2) 86.

jurisdiction is exclusive. Further, a consumer and a company may agree on the issue of international jurisdiction, but this is only possible when the dispute has already occurred, or when the consumer is permitted under such agreement to file a lawsuit in other courts in addition to the competent court under Article 27 (paragraph 6).

I. Labour Contracts

KAPIL Article 28 (Employment Contract) states:

> …
>
> (3) In case of an employment contract, an employee may file a lawsuit against an employer in a country, where he/she habitually provides his/her service or even where he/she habitually provided his/her service for the last time. In case the employee does not or did not habitually provide his/her service within one country, he/she may file a lawsuit against an employer even in a country where the business office of the employer, who hired the employee, is or was located.
>
> (4) In case of an employment contract, an employer may file a lawsuit against an employee only in the country where the habitual residence of the employee is located or where the employee habitually provides his/her service.
>
> (5) The parties of an employment contract may, in writing, make an agreement on the international jurisdiction: Provided that such agreement shall be effective only in any of the following subparagraphs:
>
> 1. In case a dispute already occurred;
> 2. In case filing a lawsuit with other courts in addition to the competent court under this Article is permitted to the employee.

Article 28 has a similar structure to Article 27. This is unsurprising as Article 28 is designed to protect employees. Article 28, paragraph 3 stipulates a wide range of grounds for an employee to establish jurisdiction as against an employer, including: (1) the country where an employee habitually provides service; (2) habitually provided service; and (3) in case an employee does not or did not habitually provide service within a single country, the employee may file a lawsuit against an employer in a country where the business office of the employer is or was located. Here, the phrase 'the country where an employee habitually provides his/her service' refers to the *loci laboris*. The Korean court has ruled that the country of the registry of a ship can be regarded as the seafarer's *loci laboris*.[50] Article 28, paragraph 4 stipulates for exclusive jurisdiction to an employer, stating that a lawsuit against an employee can only be initiated in the country where the habitual residence of the employee is located or where the employee habitually provides service. An employer and employee may agree upon international jurisdiction, only when their dispute has arisen or when such agreement allows the employee to file a lawsuit in another court in addition to the competent court under Article 28. With regards to the interpretation and application of Article 28, paragraph 5, in a notable case the plaintiff Chinese nationals initiated a lawsuit based on the Labour Standards Act against a Korean company, seeking payment of the minimum wage. The plaintiffs had entered into a training agreement with a Chinese company (the defendant's subsidiary) and had come to Korea for training under that agreement. However, during their training in Korea, the defendant had instructed them to perform certain work, without providing proper compensation at the level of the minimum wage. The training agreement specified Chinese law as its governing law and that any dispute was to be decided by arbitration in China. However, the Korean court accepted jurisdiction on the ground that the arbitration clause was

[50] Judgment of the Supreme Court, 12 July 2007, 2005Da39617.

contrary to Article 28, paragraph 5 insofar as it restricted the plaintiff employees' right to file a lawsuit in Korea, the country where the plaintiffs habitually provided their services.[51]

J. Family Law

i. Overview

Korean law does not have a clear provision on direct jurisdiction in international family law matters.[52] The Korean court refers to KAPIL Article 2 and the relevant jurisdiction provisions of the CPA and the Family Litigation Act to determine direct jurisdiction in family law cases. In any event, the determination of direct jurisdiction in family law cases is a delicate matter, since family law issues can be affected by tradition, habits and ethics that are unique to each country and culture and the result of individual lawsuits can be influenced by those factors.[53]

ii. Family Litigation Act

Korean law has a statute dedicated to regulating proceedings in family law litigation: the Family Litigation Act. In particular, Article 13 (Jurisdiction) of that Act stipulates:

> …
>
> (2) Where the jurisdiction of a family litigation is to be determined by the domicile, residence or last address of a party or interested person, if such domicile, residence or last address is not located in Korea, or it is impossible to know it, the family litigation shall be under the jurisdiction of the family court in the location of the Supreme Court.

In practice, a substantial number of international family law cases in which the domicile, residence or last address of the parties or interested persons is not in Korea are being reviewed by the Seoul Family Court.[54]

iii. Divorce

Due to an increase in the number of international marriages and disputes arising therefrom, the issue of direct jurisdiction in divorce cases has recently received some attention. Korean courts have been applying the 'substantive relationship' test as provided in KAPIL Article 2, paragraph 1. For instance, where the plaintiff (a US citizen domiciled in Missouri) filed a divorce claim against the defendant (who had been a Korean citizen, but who had acquired US citizenship following marriage), the Supreme Court held there was direct jurisdiction. In particular, the Court emphasised that the substantive relationship test has been met as: (1) both parties had their habitual residence in Korea and their domicile of choice was Korea; (2) the parties had registered their marriage in Korea and the marriage had effect in Korea; (3) the parties had spent most of their marriage in Korea.[55] In another case where a plaintiff (a Korean citizen) filed for divorce and division of property against the defendant (a Spanish citizen), the Supreme Court recognised

[51] Judgment of the Supreme Court, 13 June 2019, 2016Da33752 (n 20).

[52] Sook Hee Han, 'Guk-je-ga-sa-sa-geon-ui guk-je-jae-pan-gwan-hal-gwa oi-guk-pan-gyul-ui sung-in mit jip-haeng – yi-hon-uil jung-sim-ui-ro –' ('Jurisdiction in an International Family Case and Execution of Foreign Judicial Decision – Focus on Divorce –') (2006) 12 *Guk-je-sa-bup-yon-gu* (*Studies on Private International Law*) 3, 9.

[53] ibid 7.

[54] ibid 10.

[55] Judgment of the Supreme Court, 26 May 2006, 2005Mu884.

direct jurisdiction for the following reasons: (1) the plaintiff has clearly indicated that she wished trial before a Korean court; (2) the plaintiff and the parties' child were living in Korea; (3) the parties had lived in Korea for a considerable period of time during their marriage; (4) the governing law of their marriage was Korean law; and (5) the defendant had properties in Korea.[56] In summary, in determining jurisdiction in divorce cases, the Korean courts examine multiple factors, such as nationality and addresses of the parties, the place of registration of their marriage, and the place where the parties have spent a considerable period of their marriage.[57]

iv. Parental Authority

Under Korean law, parents have authority over their minor child and such authority is jointly exercised by both parents during their marriage (Civil Act Article 909, paragraphs 1 and 2). In the case of divorce, the parents should come to an agreement on who is to exercise parental authority over the child. If the parents cannot reach an agreement, the court will designate the person having parental authority over the child (Civil Act Article 909, paragraphs 4 and 5). It is possible that both parents have parental authority over the child even after divorce, if such is deemed appropriate for the welfare of the child.[58] On the issue of direct jurisdiction, Korean law is silent on the standard to determine international jurisdiction over parental authority issues.[59] Scholars have put forward varying opinions, from an argument that the child's address should be the main standard to the argument that general jurisdiction based on the address of the opposing party to a divorce claim should be the criterion.[60]

IV. Jurisdiction *in rem* and the Process of Ship Arrest

A. Jurisdiction *in rem*

In common law jurisdictions, an action *in rem* is an action which a plaintiff initiates against an individual's property, instead of against the individually personally. Under US law, a person having a maritime lien may exercise rights *in rem* and bring a lawsuit against a vessel.[61] Nevertheless, under Korean law, while Article 777 of the Commercial Code provides for maritime lien, jurisdiction *in rem* is not recognised.[62] A claimant cannot initiate a lawsuit against a vessel, since the latter cannot be treated as the party to a lawsuit.

B. Process of Ship Arrest

Under Civil Execution Act Article 276, a creditor who has a pecuniary claim against a debtor may request a pre-judgment attachment from the court of an asset owned by the debtor. Similarly, a

[56] Judgment of the Supreme Court, 16 May 2014, 2013Mu1196.

[57] Han (n 51) 21.

[58] Judgment of the Supreme Court, 13 April 2012, 2011Mu4719.

[59] Kwang Hyun Suk, 'Guk-je-chin-gwon hoo-gyun-bup-ui dong-hyang-gwa woo-ri-yip-bup-gwa-je' ('Trends of International Parental Authority and Guardianship Law and Korea's Future Legislation') (2014) 55(4) *Seoul-dae-hak-kyo-bup-hak* [*Seoul Law Journal*] 473, 479.

[60] ibid 479–80.

[61] Jong Ho Kim, 'Mi-guk-bub-sang Dae-mul-so-song Je-do-e Gwan-han so-go' ('A Legal Consideration for the Action in Rem in the American Judicial System') (2012) 40 *Han-yang-bup-hak* [*Hanyang Law Review*] 259, 263.

[62] Jong Hyun Choi, *Hae-sang-bub-sang-ron* [*Notes on Maritime Law*] 2nd edn (Seoul, Pakyoungsa, 2014) 41.

party who has a pecuniary claim against the shipowner may apply for the pre-judgment attachment of a vessel when there is a need to secure the claim. It is not required that the creditor's claim be related to the vessel subjected to a pre-judgment attachment.[63] A general overview of the process of ship arrest is as follows: A creditor submits an application to the court, explaining that the creditor has a pecuniary claim against the shipowner and there exists a need to secure the claim. The court will review the case *ex parte*. If the court finds that the requirements for pre-judgment attachment have prima facie been established, the court will order the creditor to provide counter-security. This counter-security will generally be in the region of 10 per cent of the claim amount. It can be paid in cash or in the form of a surety bond issued by Seoul Guarantee Insurance. The type of counter-security that can be submitted is up to the court's discretion. Once the creditor has posted counter-security, the court will issue the pre-judgment attachment.[64] Under Korean practice, an application for the maintenance and preservation of a ship is submitted along with the application for arrest of the same. The maintenance and preservation order is granted along with the ship arrest order. This allows the creditor to confine the vessel to the port area where it has been arrested. The court can exercise jurisdiction only when the vessel is within the port area within the territorial limits of the court's jurisdiction. A vessel cannot be arrested under Korean law if it is not within the area of a Korean port.[65]

V. Service

Korean courts determine the legality of service based on the *lex fori*, the place where the litigation is ongoing.[66] Even when service has not been strictly effected as provided under a relevant provision, if the defendant receives the relevant materials and engaged in the litigation by submitting a brief, the defective service will be treated as having been cured.[67] Korea is a party to the 1965 Hague Convention on the Service Abroad of Judicial and Extrajudicial Documents in Civil or Commercial Matters, which has been in force in Korea since 1 August 2000.[68] The Korean Government made certain reservations when acceding to the 1965 Hague Service Convention, notably under Articles 8 and 10 thereof in respect of direct service through diplomatic or consular agents to persons other than Korean citizens.[69] Korea has entered into a number of bilateral treaties with countries, such as China, Australia, Thailand, and Uzbekistan, on the promotion of international cooperation in civil matters. With regards to the service process to and from countries under such bilateral treaties, the terms of the latter will prevail over the 1965 Hague Service Convention.[70] In the situation where a country is neither a contracting state to the 1965 Hague Service Convention nor a party to a bilateral treaty with Korea, the Act on International Judicial Mutual Assistance in Civil Matters will apply. According to that Act, service from Korea to a foreign country will be as follows: The Korean court will send the relevant documents to the Court Administration Office. From there, the documents will be forwarded to the Ministry of Foreign Affairs and thereafter to the Korean ambassador or consular office in the relevant foreign country. The documents will be passed to the Ministry of Affairs of the foreign country and then

[63] ibid 675.
[64] Choon-Won Lee and Dahee Kim, 'Korea' in Andrew Bicknell (ed), *The International Comparative Guide to: Shipping Law 2019* (London, Global Legal Group, 2019) 160.
[65] Choi (n 61) 676.
[66] Judgment of the Supreme Court, 22 July 2010, 2008Da31089.
[67] Judgment of the Supreme Court, 28 January 2016, 2015Da207747.
[68] Suk (n 1) 221.
[69] ibid 240.
[70] ibid 251.

finally sent to the opposing party in accordance with domestic regulations on service. Service from a foreign country to Korea will be as follows. The foreign court will send the documents to the Ministry of Foreign Affairs in that country in accordance with the domestic regulation on service. Then, the Ministry will pass the documents to the Korean embassy or consular office in the foreign country which will forward the papers to the Korean Ministry of Foreign Affairs. Upon receiving the documents, the latter will forward the document to the Court Administration Office. From there, the papers will go to the Korean court having jurisdiction over the matter. Finally, the document will be served on the opposing party.[71]

VI. Immunities

A. Sovereign Immunity

Korean law does not have a clear provision which stipulates the scope of sovereign immunity. The doctrine of sovereign immunity generally applies to an international organisation or foreign state or the head of a foreign state and the latter's family and entourage.[72] The Korean court previously acknowledged absolute state immunity.[73] Then, the Korean court altered its position so as to apply state immunity according to the type of act under adjudication. The courts maintained that, while state immunity applied to sovereign acts, there were exceptions in relation to a state's private acts, such as the act of entering into a purely commercial transaction or contract.[74]

On 8 January 2021, the Seoul Central District Court (34th Civil Division) has delivered a judgment in which sexual slavery victims for the Japanese imperial army (also known as 'comfort women') requested partial compensation for emotional damage in the amount of KRW100,000,000 against Japan. The Japanese Government did not submit any brief and did not respond at all during the lawsuit.[75] Nearly five years after the submission of the statement of claim, the Seoul Central District Court ruled in favour of the plaintiffs by accepting the request for compensation of KRW100,000,000 per plaintiff. The judgment was finalised without appeal.[76] In its judgment, the court ruled that the act of constant violence, torture and sexual abuse against the plaintiffs constituted a crime against humanity which is a *jus cogens* crime and that, if state immunity applied in such a case, it would be impossible to restrict a state which commits crime against humanity and the constitutional right to request a trial would be wrongfully denied. The court stressed that the principle of state immunity was intended as a matter of respect for a sovereign nation. The doctrine of sovereign immunity did not provide a ground by which a state could avoid the payment of compensation for damage arising from a crime committed by the state.

Thereafter, on 21 April 2021, the Seoul Central District Court (15th Civil Division) dismissed the claim from another group of 16 women (and their descendants, if the victims had passed away) who were forced into sexual slavery for the Japanese imperial army during the colonial period.[77] In this case, the court ruled that claim for compensation against foreign government's

[71] ibid 220.
[72] ibid 42.
[73] Decision of the Supreme Court, 23 May 1975, 74Ma281.
[74] Judgment of the Supreme Court, 17 December 1998, 97Da39216.
[75] Yong Kyong Lee, 'Il-bon-un we-wan-bu pi-hae-ja-e-ge- 1-oek-sik bae-sang-ha-ra' ['Japanese Government Ordered to Compensate KRW 100 Million to Victims of Comfort Women'] (*Bup-ryul-sin-mun* [*Legal Times*], 8 January 2021), available online: www.lawtimes.co.kr/Case-Curation/view?serial=167147.
[76] Judgment of the Seoul Central District Court, 8 January 2021, 2016Gahap505092.
[77] Judgment of the Seoul Central District Court, 21 April 2021, 2016Gahap580239. As of the time of writing, the full text of the judgment has not been released in public yet.

sovereign acts cannot be accepted based on the principle of state immunity. The court pointed out that, based on the case law in Korea and in the international community, such as the International Court of Justice,[78] sovereign acts by foreign governments enjoy state immunity. In this regard, the court ruled that an act of forcing the claimants into sexual slavery can be deemed as a sovereign act, rather than a private act.[79] Further, the court reasoned that, based on a comprehensive review of the legislation in various countries and the number of signatories of various conventions, such as the 2004 United Nations Convention on Jurisdictional Immunities of States and Their Property and the European Convention on State Immunity, it cannot be said that the customary international law has been altered so as to deny state immunity even if such sovereign acts amount to tortious acts under the laws of the forum state. The court also reviewed the Korea–Japan agreement of 28 December 2015, where the Japanese government agreed to contribute 1 billion yen for final and irreversible resolution of the issue. In this regard, the court mentioned that although the said agreement has some flaws in terms of contents and procedure, the said agreement can be deemed as the government's exercise of diplomatic protection which enjoys a wide scope of discretion and that the agreement can be regarded as an alternative remedy to protect the rights of the victims. It was reported that at least one of the claimants is planning to file an appeal.[80]

To sum up, the said two recent judgments have raised controversy in Korea due to the sensitivity of the case in political and diplomatic terms. From a legal point of view, however, it can be said that the position from the case law in Korea remains unchanged for now (that is, state immunity will apply to sovereign acts state immunity will apply to sovereign acts but not necessarily to private acts), unless the Supreme Court changes this view in the future.

B. Diplomatic and Consular Immunity

The 1961 Vienna Convention on Diplomatic Relations came into force in Korea on 27 January 1971.[81] The 1963 Vienna Convention on Consular Relations came into force in Korea on 6 April 1977.[82] Accordingly, diplomatic and consular immunity are both fully recognised in Korea.

VII. Anti-suit and Anti-arbitration Injunctions

A. Anti-suit Injunction

Korean law is silent on whether the court can effectively render an anti-suit injunction. The Supreme Court has not yet delivered a judgment on whether an anti-suit injunction can be

[78] *Jurisdictional Immunities of the State (Germany v Italy: Greece intervening)*, Judgment, ICJ Reports 2012 (3 February 2012) 99.

[79] Seoul-joong-ang-ji-bang-bup-won Je-15-Min-sa-bu [15th Civil Division of the Seoul Central District Court], 'Seoul-joong-ang-ji-bang-bup-won 2016-ga-hap-580239 pan-gyul seon-go ja-ryo' ['Press Release Materials for the Judgment of the Seoul Central District Court Case Number 2016Gahap580239'] (21 April 2021) 10, available online: https://womenandwar.net/kr/wp-content/uploads/2021/04/2016%EA%B0%80%ED%95%A9580239_%EC%84%A0%EA%B3%A0%EB%AC%B8_%EC%86%A1%EB%B6%80%EC%9A%A9.pdf.

[80] Hye Jung Jung, 'Yi-yong-soo hal-mo-ni "We-an-bu son-bae-so gak-ha" hang-so "jung-ui in-gwon yi-gil gut"' ['Yi Yong Soo Grandmother to File an Appeal to "Dismissal of Claim for Compensation for Comfort Women" "Justice and Human Rights will Prevail"'] (*Joong-ang-il-bo* [Joongang Daily], 5 May 2021), available online: https://news.joins.com/article/24050690?cloc=joongang-section-moredigitalfirst.

[81] 'Jo-yak-jung-bo' ['Information on International Convention'] (*Ministry of Foreign Affairs*), available online: www.mofa.go.kr/www/wpge/m_3835/contents.do.

[82] ibid.

rendered by Korean courts.[83] There is a decision delivered by the Seoul High Court in which the Court dismissed a request for an anti-suit injunction in respect of US legal proceedings.[84] A debtor, having partially won against a creditor in arbitration proceedings, initiated a lawsuit in the US District Court of Eastern Michigan for confirmation and recognition of the arbitral award.[85] The creditor filed an application before the Korean court for an anti-suit injunction, arguing that the US court would inevitably review the substantive matters of the dispute between the debtor and creditor which would be contrary to the arbitration agreement between the parties. The Seoul High Court ruled that the US proceedings were merely a process to confirm and recognise the arbitral award and had nothing to do with reviewing substantive issues. Therefore, the US proceedings did not violate the parties' arbitration agreement. Nor was there an urgent need to stay the US court proceedings.[86] Thus, the Korean court has not entirely ruled out the possibility of an anti-suit injunction. Nevertheless, taking into account the fact that Korean law is silent on the possibility of issuing anti-suit injunctions and that a person has a right to initiate a lawsuit in a foreign court, it is reasonable to conclude that anti-suit injunctions are not allowed under Korean law at this point in time.

B. Anti-arbitration Injunction

Korean law does not have a clear provision on whether anti-arbitration injunctions can be granted. The Supreme Court has ruled that the Korean court may not render an anti-arbitration injunction. The Court held that Article 10 of the Arbitration Act, which allows for the grant of interim measures by the court, cannot serve as a basis for an anti-arbitration injunction, since the purpose of the provision was to permit parties to preserve property and avoid significant damage before the rendering of an arbitral award.[87]

[83] Chang Hyun Lee, 'Guk-je-juk-bun-jaeng-hae-gyul-e it-oh-so so-song-gum-ji-myung-ryung-ui hwal-yong-e gwan-han yon-gu han-kuk-e-so-ui jeok-yong-ga-nung-sung-ul jung-sim-ui-ro' ('The Use of Anti-suit Injunction in Transnational Dispute Resolutions: Focusing on the Applicability in Korea') (SJD dissertation, Seoul National University 2020) 118, available online: http://dcollection.snu.ac.kr/common/orgView/000000162277.

[84] Judgment of the Seoul High Court, 8 September 2016, 2016Ra20160.

[85] Lee (n 83) 119.

[86] ibid 120.

[87] Decision of the Supreme Court, 2 February 2018, 2017Ma6087.

7

Singapore

WILSON LUI

I. Introduction

Singapore is determined to maintain and further upgrade itself as an international dispute resolution hub, in view of the increasingly fierce competition for such a position within the Asia-Pacific market. Among Singapore's many recent, notable and ground-breaking initiatives towards this objective are the establishment of the Singapore International Commercial Court (SICC) in 2015 and accessions to various international conventions facilitating legal cooperation in cross-border matters. Implicit in these developments is the question of striking a balance on issues of direct jurisdiction. This chapter will examine when and how Singapore courts assume or decline jurisdiction in cases across various areas of law, with a view to highlighting how Singapore has sought to strike an appropriate balance.

Singapore has been citing and relying on English common law cases, which have continued to be part of the law of Singapore.[1] Although the relationship between Singapore and English law has been described as 'umbilical',[2] legislative and judicial developments in Singapore demonstrate its confidence and ability in developing its own jurisprudence on a range of issues, including direct jurisdiction. The Singapore court distinguishes between jurisdiction *in personam* and *in rem*. A decision made in the exercise of *in personam* jurisdiction is binding on the parties before the court. *In personam* jurisdiction thus 'latches onto the defendant personally'. In contrast, a decision made in the exercise of *in rem* jurisdiction 'latches onto the *res*', that is, the property which is the subject matter of the parties' dispute and is 'essentially a claim against property'.[3] There is a difference in subject matter. This chapter will discuss each of these two bases of jurisdiction in turn, covering both the general principles and the specific rules for establishing jurisdiction in: (1) the law of obligations; (2) the law of property; (3) intellectual property law; (4) family law; (5) the law of corporations, insolvency and bankruptcy; (6) competition law; and (7) Admiralty law. It will also discuss immunities from jurisdiction.

[1] Application of English Law Act (Cap 7A, 1994 rev ed).
[2] Sundaresh Menon, 'The Somewhat Uncommon Law of Commerce' (2014) 26 *Singapore Academy of Law Journal* 23, 25.
[3] *The Global 1* [2006] SGHC 30 [16], [17]. See also Sections II.A.i and III.A below.

II. Jurisdiction *in personam*

A. General Principles

i. Jurisdiction of Courts within the Territory

Judicial power is vested by the Singapore Constitution in the Supreme Court and such subordinate courts as may be established by law.[4] The Supreme Court consists of the Court of Appeal and the High Court (which in turn consists of the Appellate Division and the General Division).[5] The High Court has such jurisdiction and powers as are vested in it by law, including the powers set out in the First Schedule to the Supreme Court of Judicature Act (Cap 322, 2014 rev ed) (SCJA).[6] The SCJA conferred and circumscribed the High Court's jurisdiction. The High Court has jurisdiction over defendants who have voluntarily submitted to its jurisdiction.[7] It has *in personam* jurisdiction over all cases where a defendant has been served with a writ of summons or other originating process in Singapore 'in the manner prescribed by Rules of Court or Family Justice Rules'. Outside Singapore, it has *in personam* jurisdiction 'in the circumstances authorised by and in the manner prescribed by Rules of Court or Family Justice Rules'.[8] The words 'in the circumstances authorised' denote a need for authorisation ('leave') from the court to serve defendants (and thereby establish *in personam* jurisdiction over them) outside Singapore. This long-arm jurisdiction is conferred by statute and valid service of process on a foreign defendant is a 'statutory condition precedent to the exercise of jurisdiction'.[9] In short, 'jurisdiction exists as of right over a defendant who is within Singapore, but jurisdiction over a foreign defendant is discretionary'.[10]

The subordinate courts include the District Courts, the Magistrates' Courts, the Coroners' Courts, the Small Claims Tribunals, and the Employment Claims Tribunals. The jurisdiction of these courts is governed by the State Courts Act (Cap 321, 2007 rev ed).[11] The District Court has *in personam* jurisdiction over cases in a manner similar to the High Court.[12] The Magistrates' Court has jurisdiction over civil claims not exceeding S$60,000 and criminal cases which are punishable by the imposition of a fine or no more than five years' imprisonment.[13] There are also the Family Justice Courts, consisting of the Family Division of the High Court and two subordinate courts, the Family Court and the Youth Court.[14]

[4] Constitution of the Republic of Singapore, Art 93.

[5] ibid, Art 94. The Appellate Division of the High Court was established in 2021 in response to the increasing number and complexity of cases. For the division of jurisdiction and powers between the Court of Appeal, the Appellate Division and the General Division, see the Supreme Court of Judicature (Amendment) Act 2019 (No 40 of 2019). See also the Constitution of the Republic of Singapore (Amendment) Act 2019 (No 38 of 2019); 'Second Reading Speech by Senior Minister of State for Law, Mr Edwin Tong, on The Supreme Court of Judicature (Amendment) Bill' (*Ministry of Law*, 6 November 2019), available online: <www.mlaw.gov.sg/news/parliamentary-speeches/second-reading-speech-by-senior-minister-of-state-for-law-mr-edwin-tong-on-scj-amendment-bill>.

[6] Supreme Court of Judicature Act (Cap 322, 2014 rev ed), ss 16(2), 18.

[7] ibid, s 16(1)(b).

[8] ibid, s 16(1)(a). The High Court has generally unlimited subject-matter jurisdiction under SCJA, s 16: *Allenger v Pelletier* [2020] SGHC 279 [51]–[59].

[9] *Lee Hsien Loong v Review Publishing Co Ltd* [2007] 2 SLR(R) 453 [20]–[21]; *Humpuss Sea Transport Pte Ltd (in compulsory liq) v PT Humpuss Intermoda Transportasi TBK* [2016] 5 SLR 1322 [100].

[10] *Zoom Communications Ltd v Broadcast Solutions Pte Ltd* [2014] 4 SLR 500 [26].

[11] State Courts Act (Cap 321, 2007 rev ed), s 3.

[12] ibid, s 19, which is similar to SCJA, s 16.

[13] ibid, s 52.

[14] Family Justice Act (No 27 of 2014), ss 3–5.

The Singapore International Commercial Court (SICC) was established on 5 January 2015,[15] as an initiative to 'expand the scope for the internationalisation and export of Singapore law' and 'enhance [Singapore's] status as a leading forum for legal services and commercial dispute resolution'.[16] The SICC is a division of the Singapore High Court under the SCJA.[17] It is therefore a part of the Supreme Court of Singapore and functions as a superior court of law, thereby 'maximis[ing] the international enforceability of its decisions'.[18] The SICC's jurisdiction is set out in SCJA section 18D and Order 110, rule 7 of the Rules of Court (ROC). A new section 18D(2) was added to the SCJA in 2018 to clarify the SICC's jurisdiction by expressly empowering it to hear matters relating to international commercial arbitration,[19] including challenges to an arbitral tribunal's jurisdiction and the setting aside or enforcement of arbitral awards. Consequently, the SICC has jurisdiction to hear an action that satisfies the following conditions:

(1) the action is international and commercial in nature;
(2) the action is one that the General Division of the High Court may hear and try in its original civil jurisdiction;
(3) the parties to the action have submitted to the SICC's jurisdiction under a written jurisdiction agreement;
(4) the parties do not seek relief in the form of, or connected with, a prerogative order.

On condition (1), what is 'international' and 'commercial' is defined in ROC Order 110, rules 1(2) and 1(3). A claim is 'international' if there were different places of business among the parties or between any party and the subject-matter. A claim is 'commercial' if it 'arises from a relationship of a commercial nature'; 'relates to an *in personam* intellectual property dispute'; or if the subject-matter is agreed to be commercial in nature. These definitions mirror Article 1(1) of the UNCITRAL Model Law on International Commercial Arbitration 2006. On condition (3), the jurisdictional agreement can be exclusive or non-exclusive and recorded in any form.[20] An agreement to submit to the jurisdiction of the Singapore High Court on or after 1 October 2016 is construed to include the SICC unless a contrary intention appears.[21] But an agreement to submit to the jurisdiction of the SICC does not constitute submission to other Divisions of the Singapore High Court. Cases can be transferred from the General Division of the High Court to the SICC under ROC Order 110, rule 12. When deciding whether to transfer a case to the SICC, the High Court should consider: (1) whether it has 'international jurisdiction'; and (2) whether the transfer requirements under Order 110, rule 12 are met, the latter question being purely

[15] For a review of the SICC at an early stage, see Andrew Godwin, Ian Ramsay and Miranda Webster, 'International Commercial Courts: The Singapore Experience' (2017) 18(2) *Melbourne Journal of International Law* 219–59. See also Man Yip, 'The Singapore International Commercial Court: The Future of Litigation?' (2019) 12(1) *Erasmus Law Review* 82–97.

[16] 'Report of the Singapore International Commercial Court Committee' (November 2013) [4], [55], available online: www.sicc.gov.sg/docs/default-source/about-sicc/annex-a-sicc-committee-report.pdf.

[17] SCJA, s 18D.

[18] See eg Administration of Justice Act 1920 (UK), s 9. The UK's Foreign Judgments (Reciprocal Enforcement) Act 1933 (as amended by the Civil Jurisdiction and Judgments Act 1982) does not have this restriction but does not apply to Singapore judgments in England. For an assessment of the enforcement of money judgments by the SICC in various Asian states, see Anselmo Reyes, 'Conclusion: Towards an Asia of Judgments without Borders' in Anselmo Reyes (ed), *Recognition and Enforcement of Judgments in Civil and Commercial Matters* (Oxford, Hart Publishing, 2019) 309–26. For the various regimes in Singapore on the recognition and enforcement of foreign judgments, see Kenny Chng, 'Singapore' in Reyes (n 18).

[19] See also SCJA, s 80(2A)(c).

[20] Rules of Court (Cap 322, R 5, 2014 rev ed), Ord 110, rr 1(1), 1(2)(e).

[21] ROC, Ord 110, rr 1(2)(c), 1(2)(ca), 1(2)(cb).

a matter of internal allocation of jurisdiction.[22] It should potentially also 'balance the benefits of a transfer against the inconvenience and possible expense it may cause to the litigants'.[23] The SICC can on its own motion or upon a party's application consider whether or not to exercise jurisdiction in a given case (ROC Order 110, rule 10). The test is whether it is appropriate for the SICC to hear a case. Such a threshold requirement is lower than that applied under the doctrine of *forum conveniens* and will be exercised generously.[24] The SICC can dismiss or stay proceedings or transfer the same to the High Court where suitable or with the parties' consent. When a case is transferred from the High Court to the SICC or vice versa, 'the court to which the case is transferred must not reconsider whether it has jurisdiction' (ROC Order 110, rule 12(5)). Moreover, the SICC may join persons as third parties to an action under ROC Order 110, rule 9 when it is appropriate to do so.[25] The SICC *must* have regard to its international and commercial character (rule 9(3)) when exercising such discretion. The foregoing does not, however, apply to a state or state sovereign, unless the latter has submitted to the SICC under a written jurisdiction agreement (rule 9(2)).[26]

ii. Forum non conveniens *and* Lis alibi pendens

The court's jurisdiction is invoked upon service (not necessarily personal service unless expressly required by the ROC (for example, Order 10, rule 1(1)) or ordered by the court).[27] To prevent actions being tried in an inappropriate venue, the court has the power to stay actions on the ground of *forum non conveniens*. The test in *Spiliada Maritime Corp v Cansulex Ltd*[28] remains applicable in deciding whether Singapore is a *forum non conveniens* and proceedings should be stayed in favour of some other jurisdiction.[29] In short:

> the court will first determine whether, *prima facie*, there is some other available forum that is 'clearly or distinctly more appropriate' for the case to be tried. If the court concludes that there is *prima facie* a more appropriate alternative forum, the court will ordinarily grant a stay unless there are circumstances by reason of which justice requires that a stay should nonetheless not be granted.[30]

The burden of proof in the first stage of the *Spiliada* test to demonstrate a 'clearly or distinctly more appropriate' alternative available forum is on the party seeking the stay. Showing that Singapore is not the natural or appropriate forum is not enough.[31] In doing so, the court can consider various connecting factors, such as the personal connections of the parties and witnesses, connections to relevant events and transactions, the applicable law, *lis alibi pendens*, and the shape of the litigation.

[22] ROC, Ord 110, r 12; *Rappo v Accent Delight International Ltd* [2017] 2 SLR 265 [118]–[119].

[23] Wei Yao Kenny Chng, 'Exploring a New Frontier in Singapore's Private International Law: *IM Skaugen SE v MAN Diesel & Turbo SE* [2016] SGHCR 6' (2016) 28 *Singapore Academy of Law Journal* 649, 651.

[24] Anselmo Reyes, 'Recognition and Enforcement of Interlocutory and Final Judgments of the Singapore International Commercial Court' (2015) 2 *Journal of International and Comparative Law* 337, 355. Another view is that 'the exercise of the SICC's international jurisdiction should be governed by a unique test that leans strongly towards the exercise of jurisdiction but has flexibility to decline to exercise jurisdiction in exceptional circumstances in order to take into account the competing policy considerations it has to balance': Chng (n 23) 651.

[25] The 'appropriateness' test 'permits considerations of connections of the relevant claims to Singapore': Man Yip, 'The Resolution of Disputes Before the Singapore International Commercial Court' (2016) 65 *International and Comparative Law Quarterly* 439, 441.

[26] See Section IV below on sovereign immunity.

[27] See generally ROC, Ord 62.

[28] *Spiliada Maritime Corp v Cansulex Ltd* [1987] AC 460 (HL).

[29] See eg *JIO Minerals FZC v Mineral Enterprises Ltd* [2011] 1 SLR 391 [38]–[54]; *Rappo* (n 22) [68].

[30] *Best Soar Ltd v Praxis Energy Agents Pte Ltd* [2018] 3 SLR 423, applying *Rickshaw Investments Ltd v Nicolai Baron von Uexkull* [2007] 1 SLR 377 [14].

[31] See eg *CIMB Bank Bhd v Dresdner Kleinwort Ltd* [2008] 4 SLR(R) 543 [26].

However, there is no exhaustive list of factors and, even though they may be potentially relevant, they should not be applied mechanically. It is the quality rather than the quantity of the connecting factors (those with the 'most relevant and substantial associations with the dispute') that is crucial, so that the case may be 'tried more suitably for the interests of all the parties and for the ends of justice'.[32] The burden in the second stage of the *Spiliada* test is for the party resisting a stay to demonstrate that the interests of justice nonetheless require that a stay be refused. The court's concern is whether substantial justice can be obtained in the foreign forum, balancing among factors such as comity and fairness to the parties.[33]

The fact that there can be a transfer of the case to the SICC (the 'SICC factor') is potentially relevant in the *forum non conveniens* analysis, although it is neither determinative nor does it supersede the other connecting factors. In other words, the 'SICC factor' is not a 'free pass to elude all jurisdictional objections'. The SICC's existence should not result in an 'unprincipled jurisdictional grab resulting in the Singapore courts' refusal to grant a stay in all cross-border commercial cases'. Reliance on the 'SICC factor' as a pointer to the exercise of jurisdiction by the Singapore court 'must be grounded in specificity of argument and proof by evidence'. Thus, a party 'must articulate the particular quality or feature of the SICC that would make it more appropriate for the dispute to be heard in Singapore by the SICC, as well as prove that the dispute is of a nature that lends itself to the SICC's capabilities'.[34] The fact that a law other than Singapore law applies to the dispute should carry less weight in the *forum non conveniens* analysis, as the SICC's International Judges would be familiar with and adept at applying foreign law, and foreign counsel can appear before the SICC to argue foreign law.[35] However, where there is a clause agreeing to the SICC's jurisdiction, the SICC should not decline jurisdiction solely because SICC is the *fourm non conveniens*.[36]

Singapore distinguishes between disputing the existence of jurisdiction and persuading a court to decline the exercise of an existing jurisdiction as a matter of discretion.[37] The former is governed by ROC Order 12, rule 7(1) while the latter is governed by ROC Order 12, rule 7(2).[38] If one wishes to dispute the existence of jurisdiction (whether *in personam* or *in rem*), one must enter an appearance and apply to the court for an appropriate order or relief within the time limited for serving a defence.[39] Such appearance is not treated as a submission to the jurisdiction of the Singapore court.[40] However, a foreign defendant applying for a stay of proceedings on the ground of *forum non conveniens* would ordinarily be taken to have submitted to jurisdiction, as the application does not deny that the Singapore court has jurisdiction, but only asserts that such jurisdiction should not be exercised as a matter of the court's discretion.[41] Nonetheless, a foreign defendant who contests jurisdiction and, purely as a fall-back position, seeks a stay of proceedings on *forum non conveniens* grounds, would not be taken to have submitted to the Singapore court's jurisdiction.[42] It is therefore common to mount the two challenges together,

[32] *Spiliada* (n 28) 476; *Rappo* (n 22) [69]–[72].

[33] *Rappo* (n 22) [107]–[112]. See also generally Richard Fentiman, *International Commercial Litigation* (Oxford, Oxford University Press, 2015) ch 13.

[34] *Rappo* (n 22) [123], [124].

[35] ibid [122]; Chng (n 23) 654–55.

[36] ROC, Ord 110, r 8(2).

[37] cf Rules of the High Court (Cap 4A) (Hong Kong), Ord 12, rr 8(1), 8(2), 8(7).

[38] *The Jian He* [1999] 3 SLR(R) 432; *The Eternal Strength* [2006] SGHC 12.

[39] ROC, Ord 12, r 7(1). The time limit is currently 21 days after service of the writ out of the jurisdiction: ROC, Ord 12, r 4(b).

[40] ROC, Ord 12, r 7(6).

[41] ROC, Ord 12, rr 7(2), 7(6); *The Jian He* (n 38) [44]; *Zoom Communications* (n 10) [55], [56]. This is unless the appearance is withdrawn by leave of the court under ROC, Ord 21, r 1.

[42] *Zoom Communications* (n 10) [32]–[33], [42]–[47].

but this might be 'wholly unnecessary and likely counter-productive' if the two are based on the same material.[43] Similarly, it would not be appropriate to infer from steps taken in a previous suit that a party has submitted to the Singapore court's jurisdiction in a fresh suit, despite similarities in the parties and subject matter.[44] A defendant can compel a plaintiff to elect among similar proceedings in two or more forums under the *lis alibi pendens* doctrine. But this will only apply if the court finds that the alternative forum is not clearly or distinctly more appropriate. It would be more 'resource-saving [and] consonant with logic and principle' to decide first whether or not Singapore is the *forum conveniens*.[45] Once the defendant demonstrates a duplicity of actions in different jurisdictions, the plaintiff has to demonstrate 'very unusual circumstances' justifying the continuation of concurrent proceedings.[46]

iii. Interim Measures and Anti-suit Injunctions

Singapore courts have the power to grant interim measures and anti-suit injunctions under section 4(10) of the Civil Law Act (Cap 43, 1999 rev ed), which grants a wide power to grant 'a mandatory order or an injunction' in all cases when it is 'just or convenient'.[47] Interlocutory injunctions fall under this category, including *Mareva* injunctions which prevent a defendant from disposing of assets up to the claimed amount, so that a judgment in the case will not be rendered toothless. The Court of Appeal has clarified that section 4(10) gives the court the power to grant *Mareva* injunctions in support of foreign court proceedings.[48] But they cannot be free-standing: the court must have *in personam* jurisdiction over the defendant and the plaintiff must have a reasonable accrued cause of action recognisable by the court.[49] There has been substantial discussion of the principles in granting anti-suit injunctions and this chapter will not repeat those.[50] It suffices to say that the general principles in Singapore are derived from Lord Goff's speech in *Société Nationale Industrielle Aérospatiale v Lee Kui Jak*.[51] An anti-suit injunction is a discretionary equitable remedy, which should only be granted against a party amenable to the court's jurisdiction (not against a foreign court) when the 'ends of justice' require it. This means that in deciding whether to grant such an injunction the court should consider whether Singapore is the natural forum, or whether an injunction would be vexatious, oppressive, or unjust to the defendant by depriving him or her of legitimate juridical advantages in an alternative forum.[52] These principles have been repeatedly approved by the Singapore courts,[53] particularly in the succession[54] and matrimonial contexts.[55] Moreover, the breach of

[43] ibid [76]–[79].
[44] *Lakshmi Anil Salgaocar v Hadley James Chilton* [2018] 5 SLR 725.
[45] *Rappo* (n 22) [67].
[46] See eg *Australian Commercial Research and Development Ltd v ANZ McCaughan Merchant Bank Ltd* [1989] 3 All ER 65, 70; *Yusen Air & Sea Service (S) Pte Ltd v KLM Royal Dutch Airlines* [1999] 4 SLR 21 [27], [34].
[47] Civil Law Act (Cap 43, 1999 rev ed), s 4(10). A broader power is found under SCJA, s 18(2) which allows granting 'all reliefs and remedies at law and in equity' properly available to a party, whether the proceedings are *in rem* or *in personam*.
[48] *Bi Xiaoqiong v China Medical Technologies, Inc (in liq)* [2019] 2 SLR 595 [61].
[49] ibid [21c], [62]. But see Ang SJ's disagreement in *Allenger v Pelletier* (n 8) [142]–[154].
[50] Thomas Raphael, *The Anti-Suit Injunction* 2nd edn (Oxford, Oxford University Press, 2019) ch 19. See also Steven Gee, *Commercial Injunctions* 7th edn (London, Sweet and Maxwell, 2021) ch 14.
[51] *Société Nationale Industrielle Aérospatiale v Lee Kui Jak* [1987] AC 871 (PC).
[52] Some factors are provided in *Kirkham v Trane US Inc* [2009] 4 SLR(R) 428. See also *Evergreen International SA v Volkswagen Group Singapore* [2004] 2 SLR(R) 457; *Beckkett Pte Ltd v Deutsche Bank AG* [2011] 1 SLR 524.
[53] See eg *Sun Travels & Tours Pvt Ltd v Hilton International Manage (Maldives) Pvt Ltd* [2020] 2 SLR 725 [65]–[68].
[54] *Peters Roger May v Pinder Lillian Gek Lian* [2006] 2 SLR(R) 381.
[55] *VH v VI* [2008] 1 SLR(R) 742.

an exclusive forum clause is a sufficient and independent basis for an anti-suit injunction, in the absence of compelling reasons to the contrary,[56] following the English Court of Appeal's decision in *The Angelic Grace*.[57] But it will be inappropriate to bar a party from bringing any other action in the future in respect of the same subject matter before a foreign court. Such a blanket order would not be enforceable against the party (particularly if not resident in Singapore), and a later court would have every right to determine whether a claim 'is barred by laches or constitutes an abuse of process on the basis of issue estoppel, *res judicata* or analogous doctrines'.[58]

iv. Choice of Court Agreements

Singapore enacted the Choice of Court Agreements Act 2016 (No 14 of 2016) (CCAA) on 14 April 2016. The CCAA implements the 2005 Hague Convention on Choice of Court Agreements. An exclusive choice of court agreement mirrors the definition in Article 2 of the 2005 Hague Convention (CCAA section 3). Such agreement is severable from the contract and its validity is determined separately (CCAA section 5). Several matters are excluded by CCAA section 9, including choice of court agreements in cases involving family law, insolvency, succession, competition law, and intellectual property rights (other than copyright and related rights). CCAA section 11(1) provides that the court has jurisdiction to decide a dispute covered by a valid exclusive choice of court agreement. CCAA section 11(2) provides that the court cannot defer jurisdiction to another court. CCAA section 2(2) provides that 'where the High Court is designated in an exclusive choice of court agreement, the designation is to be construed as including the Singapore International Commercial Court unless a contrary intention appears in the agreement'. This will increase the flexibility of the courts in transferring appropriate cases to the SICC, hence boosting the SICC's reputation and international outlook. CCAA section 12 obliges the Singapore court to stay or dismiss a case if there is an exclusive choice of court agreement designating a court elsewhere as the forum for resolving the parties' disputes, unless the Singapore court determines that:

(a) the agreement is null and void under the law of the State of the chosen court;
(b) a party to the agreement lacked the capacity, under the law of Singapore, to enter into or conclude the agreement;
(c) giving effect to the agreement would lead to a manifest injustice or would be manifestly contrary to the public policy of Singapore;
(d) the agreement cannot reasonably be performed for exceptional reasons beyond the control of the parties to the agreement; or
(e) the chosen court has decided not to hear the case or proceeding.

The foregoing mirrors the spirit and substance of the 2005 Hague Convention and qualifies the previous common law position on exclusive jurisdiction clauses.[59] The CCAA also focuses on ensuring the reciprocal recognition and enforcement of Singapore judgments in contracting states to the 2005 Hague Convention and vice versa. Whether Singapore will become one of the first Asian states to sign the 2019 Hague Convention on the Recognition and Enforcement of Foreign Judgments in Civil or Commercial Matters remains to be seen.[60]

[56] See eg *WSG Nimbus Pte Ltd v Board of Control for Cricket in Sri Lanka* [2002] 3 SLR 629; *Sun Travels* (n 53) [67]–[68].
[57] *The Angelic Grace* [1995] 1 Lloyd's Rep 87.
[58] *Kazzaz v Standard Chartered Bank* [2020] SGHC(I) 19 [20].
[59] See eg *Donohue v Armco Inc* [2001] UKHL 64, [2002] 1 All ER 749 [24].
[60] See Chng (n 18) 161.

Under the common law, exclusive jurisdiction clauses or choice of court agreements will be enforced unless there is strong cause against such enforcement.[61] The test is possibly the same even if the parties have no control over what jurisdiction clauses they have accepted.[62] For a non-exclusive jurisdiction clause, the position is less clear and the term has to be scrutinised and interpreted.[63] A recent case has suggested that the outcome might not be much different from an exclusive jurisdiction clause if Singapore is named as the non-exclusive forum. The defendant must still show strong cause for ignoring the clause.[64]

v. *Service of Process Outside Singapore*

To invoke the jurisdiction of the Singapore High Court against a foreign defendant, a writ of summons must be personally served on the latter.[65] Therefore, unless a defendant overseas voluntarily submits to the jurisdiction, 'a plaintiff's title to sue the defendant depends upon the claim falling within the circumstances authorised by the [ROC Order 11, rule 1] as well as upon the writ being served in the manner prescribed by the Rules'.[66] The principles on service of process on a foreign party were restated in *Humpuss Sea Transport*.[67] The recognised ways of serving a writ outside of jurisdiction depends on whether the defendant resides in: (1) Malaysia and Brunei (seven methods); (2) a Civil Procedure Convention country (five methods); or (3) a non-Civil Procedure Convention country (six methods).[68] When serving an originating process on a state, the procedures in ROC Order 11, rule 7 are to be followed.

ROC Order 11, rule 1 sets out an exhaustive list of situations where service out of the jurisdiction is possible. These include if 'relief is sought against a person who is domiciled, ordinarily resident, carrying on business or who has property in Singapore',[69] if 'an injunction is sought ordering the defendant to do or refrain from doing anything in Singapore',[70] or if 'a person out of Singapore is a necessary or proper party'.[71] These are known as 'jurisdictional gateways'. A case may fall into one or multiple situations on the list. In each case, leave of the court is required. The court must also be satisfied that the case is 'a proper one for service out of Singapore'.[72] The plaintiff must show that a claim comes within one of the 'jurisdictional gateways', the claim has sufficient merit, and Singapore is the proper forum.[73] The 'proper forum' test is 'substantively

[61] See eg *Vinmar Overseas (Singapore) Pte Ltd v PTT International Trading Pte Ltd* [2018] SGCA 65.

[62] ibid [138].

[63] See eg *UBS AG v Telesto Investments Ltd* [2011] 4 SLR 503 [116]–[119].

[64] *Shanghai Turbo Enterprises Ltd v Liu Ming* [2019] 1 SLR 779 [88].

[65] SCJA, s 16(1); ROC, Ord 10, r 1(1).

[66] *Lee Hsien Loong v Review Publishing* (n 9) [21]. If a defendant submits or agrees to the jurisdiction of the Singapore court, service out is possible by ROC, Ord 11, r 1(1)(r).

[67] *Humpuss* (n 9).

[68] See summary in *Humpuss* (n 9) [58]–[62].

[69] ROC, Ord 11, r 1(1)(a). This is wider than Civil Procedure Rules Practice Direction 6B, para 3.1(1) (which only includes 'domicile') and the Rules of the High Court (Cap 4A) (Hong Kong), Ord 11, r 1(1) (which only includes 'domicile' and 'ordinary residence').

[70] ROC, Ord 11, r 1(1)(b). The injunction must be a genuine part of the substantive relief and there must be reasonable prospect of granting the injunction. An interlocutory injunction (eg a *Mareva* injunction) is not itself sufficient under this ground: *Karaha Bodas Co LLC v Pertamina Energy Trading Ltd* [2006] 1 SLR(R) 112. An application for *Norwich Pharmacal* relief also falls outside this gateway: *AB Bank Ltd v Abu Dhabi Commercial Bank PJSC* [2016] EWHC 2082 (Comm), [2017] 1 WLR 810 [17]–[18]. The power to grant a *Mareva* injunction in support of foreign proceedings is in Civil Law Act, s 4(10): see Section II.A.iii above.

[71] ROC, Ord 11, r 1(1)(c). A third party may also be a 'necessary or proper party': ROC, Ord 16, r 3(3).

[72] ROC, Ord 11, r 2(2).

[73] *Zoom Communications* (n 10) [26].

the same' as that of stay based on *forum non conveniens*, that is, the *Spiliada* test. But the burden of proof is reversed.[74] The application is made *ex parte* in the first instance with a supporting affidavit. A duty of full and frank disclosure applies, so that all material facts (whether favourable or detrimental to the application) that objectively the court will need to consider should be disclosed in the supporting affidavit.[75] Otherwise, the order granting leave to serve out of jurisdiction may be set aside for material non-disclosure,[76] although the court retains a discretion not to set aside.[77] For the SICC, ROC Order 110, rules 6 and 6A provide that in any SICC proceedings, leave is not required for the service of a writ, originating summons, summons, notice or order on a party to a written jurisdictional agreement. This seems to differ from the usual Order 11 test. Rather than the test for *forum conveniens* or 'strong cause', the test is whether the SICC is the 'appropriate' forum to hear the case.

vi. Service of Foreign Proceedings in Singapore

Singapore is not a party to the 1965 Hague Convention on the Service Abroad of Judicial and Extrajudicial Documents in Civil or Commercial Matters. Documents from foreign courts are served through diplomatic channels. There are bilateral Civil Procedure Conventions between Singapore and several foreign countries,[78] including Austria, Italy, Germany and the PRC.[79] Service in other countries will usually be effected through court process servers pursuant to a letter of request. The 1965 Hague Convention being in force in most Asian jurisdictions (including the PRC, Japan, South Korea, Vietnam, Sri Lanka, India, and the Philippines),[80] it is therefore important for Singapore to consider joining the same. Singapore is also a party to the 1970 Hague Convention on the Taking of Evidence Abroad in Civil or Commercial Matters, but it has expressly excluded the application of Chapter II of the Convention. That means consular depositions and depositions conducted pursuant to a commission are not permitted in Singapore. Instead, depositions may be taken pursuant to letters of request submitted to the Singapore High Court (the Central Authority in Singapore designated by the 1970 Convention). Further, Singapore is a party to the 1961 Hague Convention Abolishing the Legalisation of Foreign Public Documents (also known as the Apostille Convention). It came into force in Singapore on 16 September 2021. To implement the Convention, the Apostille Act 2020 (No 38 of 2020) is enacted. There is now no need to legalise ('certify') documents for use in another contracting state. Foreign public documents will be accepted in Singapore as authentic when affixed with an apostille. Singapore public documents with the apostille will similarly be recognised by other contracting states. The Singapore Academy of Law is the Competent Authority for Singapore under the Apostille Convention. The hope is that Singapore's accession to the Apostille Convention 'will streamline and modernise the process for authentication of public documents for recognition across different jurisdictions; and … save time and expense for parties'.[81]

[74] ibid [30], [77].
[75] See eg *Manharlal Trikamdas Mody v Sumikin Bussan International (HK) Ltd* [2014] 3 SLR 1161 [78].
[76] *Transniko Pte Ltd v Communication Technology Sdn Bhd* [1995] 3 SLR(R) 941 [11].
[77] *Zoom Communications* (n 10) [69].
[78] ROC, Ord 1, r 4; Ord 11, r 4(1).
[79] ROC, Appendix C.
[80] For the status table, see www.hcch.net/en/instruments/conventions/status-table/?cid=17.
[81] 'Second Reading Speech by Second Minister for Law, Mr Edwin Tong, on the Apostille Bill' (*Ministry of Law*, 2 November 2020), available online: www.mlaw.gov.sg/news/parliamentary-speeches/2020-10-05-second-reading-speech-by-2m-edwin-tong-on-apostille-bill.

B. Special Rules for Establishing Jurisdiction

i. Law of Obligations

a. Specific Contracts

ROC Order 11, rules 1(1)(d) and 1(1)(e) offer two gateways for service outside of the jurisdiction in connection with a contractual claim. The gateways apply where:

> (d) the claim is brought to enforce, rescind, dissolve, annul or otherwise affect a contract, or to recover damages or obtain other relief in respect of the breach of a contract, being (in either case) a contract which—
>
> (i) was made in Singapore, or was made as a result of an essential step being taken in Singapore;[82]
> (ii) was made by or through an agent trading or residing in Singapore on behalf of a principal trading or residing out of Singapore;
> (iii) is by its terms, or by implication, governed by the law of Singapore;[83] or
> (iv) contains a term to the effect that that Court shall have jurisdiction to hear and determine any action in respect of the contract;
>
> (e) the claim is brought in respect of a breach committed in Singapore of a contract made in or out of Singapore …

For consumer contracts, the Consumer Protection (Fair Trading) Act (Cap 52A, 2009 rev ed) offers further protection where a supplier or consumer is resident in Singapore, or where the offer or acceptance was made in or sent from Singapore. Consumers may sue the supplier in the Small Claims Tribunal if there is an 'unfair practice' (defined in section 4 as including deceptive or misleading conduct by a supplier) when entering into consumer transaction.[84]

Arbitration agreements can be enforced by any party to the agreement by applying to stay the proceedings (so far as they relate to matters which are subject to the agreement) and satisfy the court to a prima facie standard that the stay requirements have been met.[85] Sometimes, in order to achieve an efficient and fair resolution, 'case management stays' can be granted to third parties who are not privy to the arbitration agreement when issues of the court proceedings can only be properly ventilated after the resolution of the putative arbitration, although the nature and extent of any overlap has to be carefully examined.[86] Mediation settlement agreements under the Mediation Act 2017 (No 1 of 2017) and international settlement agreements under the Singapore Convention on Mediation Act (No 4 of 2020) may be recorded as orders of court for enforcement and other purposes when the relevant requirements are met.[87]

[82] This 'obviates the need to determine precisely where a contract is made': *William Jacks & Co (Singapore) Pte Ltd v Nelson Honey & Marketing (NZ) Ltd* [2015] SGHCR 21 [95].

[83] For a discussion of the proper law of contract, see *Pacific Recreation Pte Ltd v SY Technology Inc* [2008] 2 SLR(R) 491; *Shanghai Turbo Enterprises Ltd v Liu Ming* (n 64).

[84] Consumer Protection (Fair Trading) Act (Cap 52A, 2009 rev ed), ss 3–7.

[85] This applies to domestic and international arbitration: Arbitration Act (Cap 10, 2002 rev ed) (AA), s 6; International Arbitration Act (Cap 143A, 2002 rev ed) (IAA), s 6. For the required threshold, see eg *Tomolugen Holdings Ltd v Silica Investors Ltd* [2016] 1 SLR 373 [70]. For the definition of 'arbitration agreement', see AA, s 4; IAA, s 2A. For the definition of 'international arbitration', see IAA, s 5.

[86] See eg *Tomolugen Holdings* (n 85) [186]–[187]; *Rex International Holding Ltd v Gulf Hibiscus Ltd* [2019] SGCA 56 [11]. See also generally Reid Mortensen, 'The Case Management Stay in Private International Law' in Michael Douglas and others (eds), *Commercial Issues in Private International Law* (Oxford, Hart Publishing, 2019) 69–88.

[87] SCJA, ss 17(1)(g), 17(1)(h); Mediation Act 2017 (No 1 of 2017), s 12; Singapore Convention on Mediation Act (No 4 of 2020), ss 4–7.

b. Specific Torts

A gateway for service outside of the jurisdiction in respect of a tortious claim is found in ROC Order 11, rule 1(1)(f). Service is possible if:

> (f) (i) the claim is founded on a tort, wherever committed, which is constituted, at least in part, by an act or omission occurring in Singapore; or
> (ii) the claim is wholly or partly founded on, or is for the recovery of damages in respect of, damage suffered in Singapore caused by a tortious act or omission wherever occurring;

The place where a tort occurred is prima facie the natural forum for determining the claim.[88] However, Singapore applies the double actionability rule for wrongs committed abroad.[89] A plaintiff can sue in Singapore for a wrong wherever committed if: (1) the wrong would have been actionable as a tort under Singapore law if the tort had been committed Singapore; and (2) the wrong gives rise to civil liability by the law of the place where the tort was committed. The place of commission of a tort is determined by looking at the events constituting the tort and asking where in substance the tort occurred.[90] It is sufficient if significant (but not necessarily all) damage has been suffered in Singapore.[91]

c. Unjust Enrichment and Restitution

Following the recognition of unjust enrichment in England,[92] the Singapore Court of Appeal allowed unjust enrichment claims to proceed.[93] To succeed in a claim of restitution, the following elements have to be made out: (1) the defendant has been enriched; (2) the enrichment was at the plaintiff's expense; (3) the enrichment was unjust; and (4) there were no relevant defences to the claim.[94] There is a gateway in ROC Order 11, rule 1(1)(o) for service outside the jurisdiction where:

> (o) the claim is a restitutionary one (including a claim for *quantum meruit* or *quantum valebat*) or for an account or other relief against the defendant as trustee or fiduciary, and the defendant's alleged liability arises out of any act done, whether by him or otherwise, in Singapore;

Although the act giving rise to liability must take place in Singapore, such act need not to be necessarily committed by the defendant. If a series of acts are involved, there is no need for all those acts (but only an act) to have occurred in Singapore.

d. Trusts and Charitable Foundations

In addition to the 'trustee' gateway in ROC Order 11, rule 1(1)(o) above, another gateway is found in rule 1(1)(j) where:

> (j) the claim is brought to execute the trusts of a written instrument, being trusts that ought to be executed according to the law of Singapore and of which the person to be served with the originating process is a trustee, or for any relief or remedy which might be obtained in any such action;

[88] *Rickshaw Investments* (n 30) [37].

[89] *Boys v Chaplin* [1971] AC 356 (HL); *Rickshaw Investments* (n 30). This is unless either or both limbs would result in injustice and unfairness: *Rickshaw Investments* (n 30) [56]–[58].

[90] *JIO Minerals* (n 29) [90].

[91] *Metall und Rohstoff AG v Donaldson Lufkin & Jenrette Inc* [1990] 1 QB 391, 437, applied in *Nippon Catalyst Pte Ltd v PT Trans-Pacific Petrochemical Indotama* [2018] SGHC 126 [50]–[53].

[92] *Lipkin Gorman v Karpnale Ltd* [1991] 2 AC 548 (HL).

[93] *Seagate Technology Pte Ltd v Goh Han Kim* [1994] 3 SLR(R) 836.

[94] See eg *Skandinaviska Enskilda Banken AB (Publ) Singapore Branch v Asia Pacific Breweries (Singapore) Pte Ltd* [2011] 3 SLR 540 [110]. For judicial clarification on the terms 'restitution' and 'unjust enrichment', see *Alwie Handoyo v Tjong Very Sumito* [2013] 4 SLR 308 [122]–[126]. See also Rachel Leow and Timothy Liau, 'Unjust Enrichment and Restitution in Singapore: Where Now and Where Next?' [2013] *Singapore Journal of Legal Studies* 331–60.

Singapore is not a party to the 1985 Hague Convention on the Law Applicable to Trusts and on Their Recognition. A charity is defined as 'any institution, corporate or not, which is established for charitable purposes and is subject to the control of [the High Court] in exercise of the jurisdiction of [the court] with respect to charities'.[95]

ii. Law of Property

a. Immovable Property

Two gateways are available in ROC Order 11, rules 1(1)(g) and 1(1)(h):

> (g) the whole subject-matter is immovable property situate in Singapore (with or without rents or profits) or the perpetuation of testimony relating to immovable property so situate;
>
> (h) the claim is brought to construe, rectify, set aside or enforce an act, deed, will, contract, obligation or liability affecting immovable property situate in Singapore;

A writ or originating summons for the possession of immovable property can be served by affixing a copy of the document to a conspicuous part of the immovable property, if the court is satisfied on an *ex parte* application that no person appears to be in possession of the immovable property.[96] However, for foreign immovable property, the Singapore courts have no subject matter jurisdiction to determine title or possession or whether there has been trespass. This rule derives from the *Moçambique* case.[97] Nonetheless, the *Moçambique* rule is subject to exceptions. For example, the Singapore court has jurisdiction to determine issues of personal obligations in respect of foreign land founded on contract or equity.[98] The court also has jurisdiction to administer a trust or estate which may include foreign immovable property. Further, the *Moçambique* rule is inapplicable to an action *in rem* to enforce a maritime lien for tortious damage to foreign immovable property.

b. Intangible Property

There are no specific rules for intangible property. It is interesting to note that the SICC has ruled that cryptocurrencies are property and thus may be held on trust. At first instance, Simon Thorley IJ held: 'Cryptocurrencies are not legal tender in the sense of being a regulated currency issued by a government but do have the fundamental characteristic of intangible property as being an identifiable thing of value.'[99] The Court of Appeal agreed: 'There may be much to commend the view that cryptocurrencies should be capable of assimilation into the general concepts of property.'[100] However, both courts noted the difficulty in ascertaining the precise nature of the property involved. For intellectual property rights, see Section II.B.iii below.

c. Succession to Property

The civil jurisdiction of the High Court includes the grant of probate of wills and testaments, the grant of letters of administration over the estates of deceased persons, and the

[95] Charities Act (Cap 37, 2007 rev ed), s 2(1).

[96] ROC, Ord 10, rr 4, 5. For debts secured on immovable property and rights over movable property, see ROC, Ord 11, r 1(1)(i).

[97] *British South Africa Co v Companhia de Moçambique* [1893] AC 602 (HL). See also *Hesperides Hotels Ltd v Muftizade* [1979] AC 508 (HL).

[98] *Murakami Takako v Wiryadi Louise Maria* [2009] 1 SLR 508.

[99] *B2C2 Ltd v Quoine Pte Ltd* [2019] SGHC(I) 03 [142].

[100] *B2C2 Ltd v Quoine Pte Ltd* [2020] SGCA(I) 02 [144].

alteration or revocation of such grants.[101] The Syariah Court may, in proceedings relating to the administration or distribution of the estate of a deceased person according to Muslim law, certify its opinion as to the persons who can share (and to what extent) a deceased's estate upon a set of facts (whether actually found by a court or authority or hypothetically assumed).[102] Substantive succession law is governed by the Intestate Succession Act (Cap 146, 2013 rev ed), the Probate and Administration Act (Cap 251, 2000 rev ed) and the Wills Act (Cap 352, 1996 rev ed).[103] The applicable law governing succession depends on whether the property is moveable or immovable.[104] There is a need to distinguish between the law of administration of estates and the law of succession. Only if the deceased had property in Singapore will a grant of probate or letters of administration be needed. The State Courts can grant probate and letters of administration in respect of the estates of deceased persons, unless the gross value of the estate in Singapore exceeds S$3 million, in which case only the Supreme Court will have jurisdiction.[105] A claim for the administration of the estate of a person who died domiciled in Singapore can be served outside of the jurisdiction under Order 11, rule 1(1)(k). The Singapore court has no jurisdiction to determine succession to the property of a deceased person if there is no properly constituted representative of the estate before the Singapore court. Only a grant of probate or letters of administration issued in Singapore will be recognised.[106]

iii. Intellectual Property Law

Singapore announced a 10-year master plan to transform itself into a Global IP Hub in Asia.[107] One of its strategic outcomes focuses on Singapore's potential to attract international IP disputes for resolution by the courts, arbitral tribunals or mediators.[108] Singapore has domestic legislation for patents, trademarks, registered designs, plant varieties protection, copyright, geographical indications, and layout-designs of integrated circuits.[109] The Intellectual Property Office of Singapore (IPOS) is set up to administer these systems, as well as other IP matters. Singapore also joined the World Intellectual Property Organisation (WIPO) in 1990 and currently is party to 15 multilateral treaties, conventions, agreements and protocols.[110]

Previously, the intellectual property jurisdiction was divided up among the IPOS, the High Court and the state courts, depending on the nature of the IP right (IPR) in dispute, the remedy sought, and the value of the claim. For instance, the High Court only had exclusive jurisdiction

[101] SCJA, s 17(1)(f).

[102] Administration of Muslim Law Act (Cap 3, 2009 rev ed), s 115(1).

[103] For details, see eg Harish Kumar, Jonathan Toh and Jonathan Cheong, 'Singapore' in Louis Garb and John Wood (eds), *International Succession* 4th edn (Oxford, Oxford University Press, 2015) 739–56.

[104] Classification between movable and immovable property is governed by the *lex situs* (the law of the place where the property is situated). Succession to immovable property is governed by the *lex situs.* But succession to movable property is governed by the *lex domicilii* (the law of the deceased's domicile).

[105] State Courts Act, ss 3, 27. See also ROC, Ord 11, r 1(1)(l); ROC, Ord 72.

[106] Kumar, Toh and Cheong (n 103) 749, 751.

[107] Government of Singapore and Intellectual Property Office of Singapore, 'Update to the Intellectual Property Hub Master Plan' (*Intellectual Property Office of Singapore*, May 2017), available online: www.ipos.gov.sg/docs/default-source/about-ipos-doc/full-report_update-to-ip-hub-master-plan_final.pdf.

[108] ibid, paras 1.4.1–1.4.2. This includes the WIPO first and only overseas Arbitration and Mediation Centre in Singapore, set up in 2010.

[109] 'IP Legislation' (*Intellectual Property Office of Singapore*), available online: www.ipos.gov.sg/media-resources/ip-legislation.

[110] See 'Singapore' (*World Intellectual Property Organisation*), available online: www.wipo.int/directory/en/details.jsp?country_code=SG.

over disputes relating to registrable IPRs. The enforcement of IPRs has since been rationalised in the Intellectual Property (Dispute Resolution) Act 2019 (No 23 of 2019) which came into force on 21 November 2019. The High Court now has jurisdiction to hear all IPR infringement matters, including infringements of non-registrable IPRs, all declarations of non-infringement of patents and registered designs, all civil copyright disputes, and all passing off actions. The High Court has concurrent jurisdiction with the IPOS on patents, trade mark and registered design revocations, trade mark invalidations and rectifications, and plant variety cancellations. Trade secrets and breach of confidence cases in more general disputes (such as disputes over alleged breaches of employment agreements) involving damages up to S$250,000 can still be heard by the state courts.[111]

The courts in Singapore will assume jurisdiction if the alleged infringing act took place in Singapore and where *in personam* or *in rem* jurisdiction can be invoked, subject to service, appearance, and stay based on *forum non conveniens*. The leave of the court is required for service of process outside Singapore (for example, where relief is sought against an intended defendant who is domiciled or ordinarily resident, carries on business, or has property in Singapore). Leave may also be granted where an injunction is sought to compel a person to do or refrain from doing some act in Singapore. For patent disputes, the usual bases for jurisdiction are: (1) the claim is founded on a tort that has resulted in damage sustained in Singapore; or (2) the claim is founded on a tort that was constituted in whole or part by an act or omission in Singapore. For patent infringement actions where a foreign party is involved (for example, as the manufacturer or supplier of an allegedly infringing product), the latter can be included as a defendant as a joint tortfeasor or as part of a conspiracy.

In the High Court, there is a special IP docket which is subject to special case management procedures set out in the IP Court Guide published in September 2013.[112] For example, specific judges and judicial commissioners with expertise in IP law are appointed to hear interlocutory applications and relevant appeals, pre-trial conferences, and trials.[113] There are also extensive directions on issues of discovery and expert evidence, as well as milestone pre-trial conferences. These ensure that clear procedures and timelines are followed and no undue delay transpires. IP specialist judges and judicial commissioners assume an active case management role by distilling the real issues in a dispute and facilitating the timely and cost-effective disposal of a case. A specialised fast-track option is forthcoming for less complex IP disputes, thereby catering for litigants who do not have sufficient resources for a full-blown High Court suit. The 2019 Act further clarified that disputes over IPRs can be settled by arbitration, even if any law gives jurisdiction to an entity or the possibility of arbitration is not mentioned. The Arbitration Act (Cap 10, 2002 rev ed) (AA) and the International Arbitration Act (Cap 143A, 2002 rev ed) (IAA) were amended accordingly. Judgments to enforce arbitral awards only affect the parties in the arbitration.[114]

[111] Jason Chan and Liza Lam, 'Patent Litigation in Singapore: Overview' (*Practical Law*, 1 June 2020), available online: https://uk.practicallaw.thomsonreuters.com/w-014-9923.

[112] 'The Intellectual Property Court Guide' (*Supreme Court of Singapore*, 6 September 2013), available online: www.supremecourt.gov.sg/docs/default-source/default-document-library/about-us/ip-court-guide.pdf.

[113] Currently, there are nine justices and two judicial commissioners on the 'Intellectual Property/Information Technology' list: 'Structure of the Courts' (*Supreme Court of Singapore*, 19 April 2021), available online: www.supremecourt.gov.sg/who-we-are/the-supreme-court/structure-of-the-courts.

[114] AA, Part IXA; IAA, Part IIA.

iv. Family Law[115]

The High Court exercises civil jurisdiction in respect of any law relating to divorce and matrimonial causes.[116] It does not have jurisdiction over matters which fall within the jurisdiction of the Syariah Court under the Administration of Muslim Law Act (Cap 3, 2009 rev ed) (AMLA).[117] However, the High Court has jurisdiction to hear civil proceedings involving matters relating to (among others) maintenance for a wife or child, custody of a child, and the disposition of property on divorce, even if the Syariah Court also has jurisdiction.[118] There is a Family Division in the High Court. There are also the Family Courts and the Youth Courts. These courts enjoy similar jurisdiction and powers, and are regulated by the Family Justice Rules 2014.[119] The Syariah Court has jurisdiction over cases in which all the parties are Muslim or where the parties were married pursuant to Islamic law and which involve disputes relating to: (1) marriage; (2) various types of divorce;[120] (3) betrothal, nullity of marriage or judicial separation; (4) the disposition or division of property on divorce or nullification of marriage; or (5) the payment of dowry (*emas kahwin*), marriage expenses (*hantaran belanja*), maintenance, and consolatory gifts (*mutaah*).[121] The jurisdiction of the Syariah Court is governed by the AMLA, the Muslim Marriage and Divorce Rules, and the Syariah Court Practice Directions 2018 (as amended in 2021).

a. Marriage

The validity of marriage in Singapore is solely determined by statute through the Women's Charter (Cap 353, 2009 rev ed),[122] unless it is a marriage between two Muslim parties, which would then be governed by Islamic law.[123] The validity of a marriage depends on two aspects: formal and essential validity. The former concerns the formal requirements of a marriage, while the latter concerns the parties' capacity to marry. Different choice of law rules govern these aspects.[124] The formal requirements are contained in sections 17 and 22 of the Women's Charter. The Registrar will refuse to register a marriage between two persons of the same sex under the 'no lawful impediment' limb in section 17(2)(d), even if both persons are domiciled in a foreign country which allows same-sex marriages.[125] Marriages solemnised in Singapore, but

[115] This Section benefits from the comprehensive discussion in Debbie Ong, *International Issues in Family Law in Singapore* (Singapore, Academy Publishing, 2015).

[116] SCJA, s 17(1)(a).

[117] AMLA, ss 35(2)(a), 35(2)(b), 35(2)(c); SCJA, s 17A(1).

[118] SCJA, s 17A(2).

[119] Supreme Court of Judicature (Transfer of Matrimonial, Divorce and Guardianship of Infants Proceedings to District Court) Order 2007 (S 672/2007); Family Justice Rules 2014 (S 813/2014).

[120] Known in the Muslim law as *fasakh, cerai taklik, khuluk* and *talak.*

[121] AMLA, s 35(2).

[122] *Tan Ah Thee v Lim Soo Foong* [2009] 3 SLR(R) 957 [19].

[123] Women's Charter (Cap 353, 2009 rev ed), s 3(4). A marriage between two Muslims solemnised under the Women's Charter was held void: *Valberg Kevin Christopher v Heran bte Abdul Rahman* Originating Summons No 1274 of 1990 (unreported).

[124] The formalities of a marriage contract are regulated by the *lex loci contractus* or *celebrationis* (the law of the place in which the marriage is contracted or celebrated), while the essential validity of a marriage is regulated by the *lex domicilii* (the law of the parties' respective domiciles at the time of their marriage). See eg *Re Maria Huberdina Hertogh* [1951] MLJ 164; *Arpinya Rongchotiawattana v Wee Oh Ken* [1997] 3 SLR(R) 378.

[125] The prohibition is in Women's Charter, s 12. Where it was discovered after marriage that the two persons were of the same sex (one being a transsexual), the court granted a decree of nullity declaring the marriage void *ab initio*: *Lim Ying v Hiok Kian Ming Eric* [1991] 2 SLR(R) 525. The case relied on an implicit reading of the statutory definition of 'monogamous marriage', as s 12 was not introduced until the Women's Charter (Amendment) Act 1996 (Act 30 of 1996).

not solemnised by the Registrar, have to be registered within one month. The failure to do so is a criminal offence.[126]

The validity of foreign marriages is determined by applying the common law and the rules of private international law. These provide that a marriage celebrated outside Singapore will be valid if both parties had the capacity to marry under the laws of their respective domiciles and their marriage was in accordance with the formalities prescribed by the law of the place in which the marriage was celebrated (*lex loci celebrationis*).[127] If anyone (usually Singaporeans or foreigners who intend to reside in Singapore) wishes, foreign marriages solemnised under the marriage law of any place in the world may be registered in Singapore under section 182 of the Women's Charter, although registration has no effect on the validity or invalidity of the foreign marriage.[128]

b. Divorce, Nullity and Separation

The court's jurisdiction to grant decrees of divorce, nullity or separation in respect of marriages is contained in Women's Charter section 93. Section 93(1) provides that jurisdiction is exercised only if either party is domiciled in Singapore[129] or has been habitually resident in Singapore for more than three *continuous* years immediately before the commencement of the proceedings.[130] However, section 93(2) provides that for nullity of marriage, the court may grant the relief if both parties to the marriage reside in Singapore at the time of the commencement of the proceedings. The difference in wording means the latter requires less of a substantial connection with Singapore. There need not be habitual residence. Merely living in Singapore with a settled purpose will suffice.[131] The personal connection required to establish jurisdiction is necessary to 'meet the interests of the state and of those who genuinely "belong here", without allowing access to our courts to transients, "forum-shoppers", and others with no real connection with the country'.[132] There is only one ground of divorce, namely, that the marriage has 'irretrievably broken down'. This must be shown by reference to one or more of the five scenarios in section 95(3).[133] These scenarios include adultery, desertion, no reasonable expectation to live as a married couple, or (without alleging fault) separation (three years for uncontested cases, four years for contested cases). Parents with children below 21 must complete a mandatory parenting programme before any divorce is possible.[134] No divorce is possible within three years of marriage, unless exceptional hardship or depravity is proved.[135] A writ of judicial separation is based on the same grounds and circumstances as a writ of divorce. A decree of judicial separation means that the plaintiff is no longer obligatory to cohabit with the defendant, even though the parties remain legally married.[136] Judicial separation is no bar to the filing of a subsequent writ for divorce.[137]

[126] Women's Charter, ss 29, 34.

[127] Women's Charter, ss 105, 108; Ong (n 115) paras 3.91–3.98.

[128] Wai Kum Leong, *Elements of Family Law in Singapore* 2nd edn (Singapore, LexisNexis, 2013) 16.

[129] 'The domicile of a person is determined by the intention of the person's choice, not of the place where he chooses to live, but the place where he chooses to die.': *TQ v TR* [2007] 3 SLR(R) 719. See also Ong (n 115) paras 2.05–2.40.

[130] 'Habitual residence' is the same as 'ordinary residence', both of which require voluntarily adopted and continuous residence for a settled purpose: eg *Helen Diane Womersley v Nigel Maurice Womersley* [2003] SGDC 186; *Lee Mei-Chih v Chang Kuo Yuan* [2012] 4 SLR 1115. See also Ong (n 115) paras 2.41–2.48.

[131] Ong (n 115) paras 2.49–2.50.

[132] *Lee Mei-Chih* (n 130) [4], citing *Ikimi v Ikimi* [2001] EWCA Civ 873 [21].

[133] Women's Charter, s 95.

[134] ibid, s 94A.

[135] ibid, s 94.

[136] Women's Charter, s 101; *Lau Ca Cheng v Ho Kee Wai Tony* [2014] SGDC 470.

[137] Women's Charter, s 102.

Any party to a marriage may file a writ for a decree of nullity of marriage.[138] A marriage is void *ab initio* if one of the grounds in section 105 is met. These grounds are exhaustive. A marriage is voidable if one of the grounds in section 106 is met. An example of such grounds is the lack of valid consent from either party. The distinction between void and voidable marriages is important, as a voidable marriage remains valid until a decree of nullity is rendered, of which is subject to various bars of knowledge and limitation periods in section 107.[139] The legitimacy of children born to void or voidable marriages will generally not be affected.[140]

Singapore recognises decrees of divorce, nullity and separation issued by foreign courts of competent jurisdiction. Such recognition is governed by common law principles and the rules of private international law.[141] There are various bases of recognition as follows:[142]

(1) where the judgment was granted by a court of the domicile of one of the parties;
(2) where the judgment was granted by a court which exercised jurisdiction on the same basis that a Singapore court would have exercised jurisdiction; and,
(3) where there is a real and sufficient connection between the court which granted the judgment and either party to the marriage.

c. Matters Relating to the Well-being of the Child

The court is bound in every case (including cases of custody, care and control, abduction, relocation, or administration of property belonging to or held in trust for an infant) to treat the welfare of the child as the paramount consideration.[143] The court's jurisdiction in relation to guardianship and custody is provided by SCJA section 17(1)(d) and the Guardianship of Infants Act (Cap 122, 1985 rev ed) section 5. The court's jurisdiction over children is ancillary to its matrimonial jurisdiction under Women's Charter sections 124 and 125(1). This is so regardless of whether the child is a Singaporean citizen, a resident of Singapore,[144] or is outside of the jurisdiction.[145] Jurisdiction over adoption is regulated by the Adoption of Children Act (Cap 4, 2012 rev ed). The applicant and the child must be resident in Singapore with further requirements on the infant's quality of residence.[146] A child subject to a custody or care and control order cannot be taken out of Singapore except with the written consent of both parents or the leave of the court. To take the child away from Singapore would be a criminal offence. But the person having custody or care and control of the child may take the child out of Singapore for up to a month without such consent or leave.[147]

Singapore has been a party to the 1980 Hague Convention on Civil Aspects of International Child Abduction since 2010. The substantive provisions of the 1980 Hague Convention were enacted into Singapore law by the International Child Abduction Act (Cap 143C, 2011 rev ed). The Ministry of Social and Family Development has been designated as the Central Authority

[138] ibid, s 104.
[139] See eg *Tan Ah Thee* (n 122) [51].
[140] Women's Charter, s 111.
[141] ibid, s 108.
[142] *Yap Chai Ling v Hou Wa Yi* [2016] 1 SLR 660 [64], citing Ong (n 115) para 5.59.
[143] See eg Guardianship of Infants Act (Cap 122, 1985 rev ed), s 3; Women's Charter, s 125; *Re J (A Child) (Custody Rights: Jurisdiction)* [2006] 1 AC 80 (HL); *BNS v BNT* [2015] 3 SLR 973.
[144] *Re P (GE) (An Infant)* [1965] Ch 568.
[145] *Hope v Hope* (1854) 43 ER 534, 541; *Sim Hong Boon v Sim Lois Joan* [1971–1973] SLR(R) 597 [6]–[7].
[146] Adoption of Children Act, ss 4(6), 4(7); *In the matter of ABC* [1992] SGHC 9; *Re An Infant* [1995] 3 SLR 613.
[147] Women's Charter, ss 126(3), 126(4), 126(5). See also *CX v CY* [2005] 3 SLR(R) 690 for 'custody' and 'care and control'.

for the 1980 Hague Convention. The 1980 Hague Convention establishes a regime for 'the prompt return of children who have been wrongfully removed from, or retained outside, their country of habitual residence'. It 'aims to secure the dual effects of firstly, serving the child's best interests and secondly, ensuring that rights of custody and access under the law of a contracting state are respected in another contracting state'.[148] To date, there are 84 states (including the US and UK) and 1 REIO (the EU) that have mutual reciprocal enforcement arrangements with Singapore for children pursuant to the 1980 Hague Convention.[149] The decisive factors that a Singapore court will consider in an abduction case are the child's habitual residence[150] and best interests. The defences under Article 13(b) of the 1980 Hague Convention to an order for the return of an abducted child will not be invoked lightly.[151] Evidence relating to COVID-19 might be relevant but its weight is subject to the fast-evolving situation.[152] Where the child is wrongfully abducted from a non-Convention state, the courts will apply the welfare principle (that is, the individual child's welfare will be the paramount consideration).[153] The 1980 Hague Convention is applied in the same manner, even where a Muslim child is involved. The welfare principle under Muslim law is regarded by the court as no different from that at common law.[154] The details of the operation of the Convention are explored elsewhere.[155]

v. *Law of Corporations, Insolvency and Bankruptcy*

The High Court has civil jurisdiction over companies and bankruptcy.[156] Foreign companies are regulated under Part XI, Division 2 of the Companies Act (Cap 50, 2005 rev ed) and their liquidation or dissolution are regulated by Part 10, Division 2 of the Insolvency, Restructuring and Dissolution Act 2018 (No 40 of 2018) (IRDA). Foreign companies that have established a place of business, carry on business, or intend to carry on business in Singapore are subject to the High Court's jurisdiction (section 365 of the Companies Act). Claims can be served on foreign companies under one or more of the gateways in ROC Order 11. Companies Act section 376 states:

> Any document required to be served on a foreign company shall be sufficiently served —
> (a) if addressed to the foreign company and left at or sent by post to its registered office in Singapore;
> (b) if addressed to an authorised representative of the company and left at or sent by post to his registered address; or
> (c) in the case of a foreign company which has ceased to maintain a place of business in Singapore, if addressed to the foreign company and left at or sent by post to its registered office in the place of its incorporation.

The omnibus IRDA came into force on 30 July 2020, governing corporate and personal insolvency, winding up and bankruptcy. The Act's coverage includes schemes of arrangements (Part 5), receiverships (Part 6), judicial management (Parts 7 and 9) and winding up (Parts 8 and 9). It is the General Division of the High Court that has jurisdiction in these matters.[157]

[148] 1980 Hague Convention, Preamble, Art 1; *BDU v BDT* [2013] 3 SLR 535 [2].
[149] Randolph Koo and Shu Mei Hoon, 'Family Law in Singapore: Overview' (*Thomson Reuters Practical Law*), available online: https://uk.practicallaw.thomsonreuters.com/4-568-0826.
[150] 1980 Hague Convention, Art 3; *TUC v TUD* [2017] SGHCF 12.
[151] *BDU v BDT* (n 148) (HC); *BDU v BDT* [2014] 2 SLR 725 (CA).
[152] *UYK v UYJ* [2020] SGHCF 9. See also *Re PT (A Child)* [2020] EWHC 834 (Fam) [46]–[47].
[153] *Re J* (n 143); *TSF v TSE* [2018] 2 SLR 833.
[154] *Zaini bin Ibrahim v Rafidah binte Abdul Rahman* [2007] 3 SSAR 135 [29].
[155] Ong (n 115) paras 8.35–8.96; Koo and Hoon (n 149).
[156] SCJA, s 17(1)(c).
[157] Insolvency, Restructuring and Dissolution Act 2018 (No 40 of 2018), s 3.

Singapore adopted the UNCITRAL Model Law on Cross-Border Insolvency by IRDA Part 11, and the adopted text is reproduced in IRDA Schedule 3 (the 'Singapore Model Law'). The Singapore Model Law takes precedence over any Singapore insolvency law (including the IRDA, the Companies Act, subsidiary legislation, and the common law).[158] The adoption of the Singapore Model Law thus resolves the previously criticised piecemeal approach of the common law to foreign insolvency proceedings.[159] Various judicial developments have since taken place in respect of applying the Singapore Model Law to the local context. These include an analysis on determining the 'centre of main interest' (COMI) in a cross-border insolvency.[160] In contrast to Article 6 of the UNCITRAL Model Law which provides that a court may refuse assistance in relation to foreign insolvency proceedings where assistance would be 'manifestly contrary to the public policy' of the local state, the requirement in Singapore is merely that the grant of assistance would be 'contrary to the public policy'. The omission has been held to be deliberate, such that the threshold for refusing assistance on public policy grounds under the Singapore Model Law is lower than that under the UNCITRAL Model Law.[161]

IRDA Part 16 deals with bankruptcy proceedings. Section 310 states that no bankruptcy application may be made to the court against an individual debtor or a firm unless the debtor or one of the partners of the firm is: (1) domiciled in Singapore; (2) has property in Singapore; (3) has, at any time within the period of one year before the date of the making of the application, been ordinarily resident or has had a place of residence in Singapore; or (4) the debtor has, during that one-year period, carried on business in Singapore (for a debtor, this includes business by a firm in which the debtor is a partner). The debt has to be a liquidated sum, payable immediately, of not less than S$15,000. If the debt was incurred outside Singapore, the debt must be payable by virtue of a judgment or an award which is enforceable by execution in Singapore (section 311). A statutory demand has to be served on the debtor and at least 21 days must elapse without there being any compliance or an application to set aside. Alternatively, it can be shown that 'the debtor has departed from or remained outside Singapore with the intention of defeating, delaying or obstructing a creditor in the recovery of the debt' (section 312). An expedited bankruptcy application can be made within the grace period of 21 days just mentioned, if 'there is a serious possibility that the debtor's property, or the value of all or any of the debtor's property, will be significantly diminished during that period' (section 314). The court may dismiss the bankruptcy application if, for instance, it is not satisfied with the proof of the debt or proof of service (section 316(3)).

vi. Competition Law

Competition law has been important in maintaining a balance among market freedom, economic efficiency, and the protection of consumers from unfair practices. This is vital for Singapore as an open economy adhering to free trade and liberal market policies. Singapore's Competition Act (Cap 50B, 2006 rev ed) was passed in 2004 to prohibit various categories of anti-competitive behaviour. These include: (1) agreements or conduct that have the object or effect of preventing,

[158] ibid, s 253; Singapore Model Law, Art 2(k). The Model Law supplements, rather than extinguishes the common law: Singapore Model Law, Art 7; *Re Stanford International Bank* [2009] EWHC 1441 [100].

[159] See eg *Beluga Chartering GmBH (in liq) v Beluga Projects (Singapore) Pte Ltd (in liq)* [2014] 2 SLR 815; *Re Taikoo Suk* [2016] 5 SLR 787.

[160] *Re Zetta Jet Pte Ltd* [2018] SGHC 16.

[161] ibid.

restricting or distorting competition (such as price-fixing, market-sharing, and output limitation) (also known as the section 34 prohibition); (2) conduct that amounts to the abuse of a dominant market position (the section 47 prohibition); and (3) mergers that have resulted or may be expected to result in a substantial lessening of competition within any market in Singapore for goods or services (the section 54 prohibition). Section 33(1) of the Competition Act further provides that these prohibitions apply to such party, agreement, abuse of dominant position, anticipated merger or merger notwithstanding that:

(a) an agreement referred to in section 34 has been entered into outside Singapore;
(b) any party to such agreement is outside Singapore;
(c) any undertaking abusing the dominant position referred to in section 47 is outside Singapore;
(d) an anticipated merger will be carried into effect outside Singapore;
(e) a merger referred to in section 54 has taken place outside Singapore;
(f) any party to an anticipated merger or any party involved in a merger is outside Singapore; or
(g) any other matter, practice or action arising out of such agreement, such dominant position, an anticipated merger or a merger is outside Singapore[.]

However, these prohibitions do not apply to activities, agreements or conduct on the part of the Government or any statutory body.[162]

The Competition Act established the Competition Commission of Singapore on 1 January 2005. The body was re-named as the Competition and Consumer Commission of Singapore (CCCS) on 1 April 2018 when it was also tasked with administering the Consumer Protection (Fair Trading) Act. The CCCS is thus vested with powers to be 'the investigator, the adjudicator and the enforcer of competition law in Singapore'.[163] It conducts extensive investigations on reasonable grounds of suspicion. It has the right to adjudicate on activities (whether in Singapore or elsewhere) that have infringed the Competition Act. It can take enforcement actions by, for instance, giving directions (or interim directions pending the conclusion of an investigation) to businesses or imposing financial penalties.[164] If there is non-compliance, the CCCS can register the directions or penalty as a District Court order.[165] A dissatisfied party (but not third parties) may appeal to the Competition Appeals Board (CAB) against certain decisions of the CCCS (for example, in respect of infringements, interim measures, and enforcement actions).[166] The CAB has broad powers akin to those available to the District Court and can exercise active case management.[167] It can confirm, vary or set aside decisions and penalties of the CCCS. It can remit matters to the CCCS, make its own interim orders, and award costs and interest. The Singapore court only takes jurisdiction in competition law matters in two situations. First, the High Court has jurisdiction to hear appeals from the CAB.[168] Such appeal is limited to points of law or the

[162] Competition Act, s 33(4); *Re Abuse of a Dominant Position by SISTIC.com Pte Ltd* [2012] SGCAB 1 [66]–[73].

[163] Cavinder Bull, Chong Kin Lim and Ee Kia Ng, 'Competition Policy and Law' in Chong Kin Lim and Cavinder Bull (eds), 'Competition Law and Policy in Singapore' 2nd edn (Singapore, Academy Publishing, 2015) para 01.054. See also Competition Act, s 6(1) for the statutory functions and duties of CCCS, and generally Jwee Nguan Lee and Cheow Han Lee, 'Competition Law' (*Singapore Law Watch*, 15 September 2019), available online: www.singaporelawwatch.sg/About-Singapore-Law/Commercial-Law/ch-27-competition-law.

[164] For an example of interim directions, see *CCCS Notice of Interim Measures Directions on the Acquisition of Uber's Southeast Asian business by Grab and Uber's acquisition of a 27.5 per cent stake in Grab* CCCS 500/001/18, available online: www.cccs.gov.sg/public-register-and-consultation/public-consultation-items/uber-grab-merger. For the approach in the calculation of financial penalties, see eg *CCS Infringement Decision on the Section 34 Prohibition in relation to the Supply of Ball and Roller Bearings* CCS 700/002/11 [395]–[469].

[165] Competition Act, s 85.

[166] ibid, s 71. For the right to appeal of third parties, see *Calvin Cheng Ern Lee v Competition Commission of Singapore* (Competition Appeal Board Appeal No 1/2012).

[167] Competition Act, s 73; Competition (Appeals) Regulation (Cap 50B, Rg 5, 2006 rev ed), reg 19.

[168] ROC, Ord 55.

amount of a financial penalty.[169] A broader interpretation is likely to be taken as to what constitutes a 'point of law', such that the expression will be treated as including errors on the face of a relevant decision.[170] There is a further right to appeal to the Court of Appeal.[171] Second, the High Court can hear private actions in respect of anti-competitive conduct. Where parties have suffered direct (as opposed to indirect)[172] loss and damage as a result of an infringement of the Competition Act, they can commence civil actions for relief against the infringing party.[173] This ensures financial redress to victims, serving compensatory and deterrent purposes. However, private actions may only be brought on a 'follow-through' basis, subsequent to a concluded investigation and finding of infringement by the CCCS. This right of action is subject to a two-year limitation period from the time of a final decision by the CCCS (taking into account any appeals).[174]

III. Jurisdiction *in rem*

A. Jurisdiction *in rem* in Admiralty

The High Court has jurisdiction over Admiralty matters.[175] The *in rem* jurisdiction of the Singapore High Court is provided by the High Court (Admiralty Jurisdiction) Act (Cap 123, 2001 rev ed) (HCAJA).[176] An action *in rem* (or an Admiralty action *in personam*) must be begun by writ,[177] although a writ *in rem* cannot be served until the *res* comes within the jurisdiction.[178] A warrant of arrest can be obtained in an action *in rem* against a *res*: a ship, an aircraft, or cargo on board a ship or aircraft.[179] Admiralty jurisdiction is invoked whenever the vessel is either arrested or served with the writ *in rem*.[180] An action *in rem* can be commenced against a ship and its sister ships, but admiralty jurisdiction can only be invoked against one ship in respect of one claim.[181] If an action *in rem* is commenced against a ship, but the owner does not enter an appearance and judgment is obtained, 'the judgment is enforceable only against the ship and to the extent of the value of the ship'. It is 'an action against the ship itself and continues as such even though it may also be an action *in personam* against the owner'.[182] However, if the owner of the ship enters an appearance in an action *in rem*,[183] 'the action will continue as an action *in rem* against the ship

[169] Competition Act, s 74.

[170] *Ng Eng Ghee v Mamata Kapildev* [2009] 3 SLR(R) 109 [99]–[101]; Cavinder Bull and Voon Jiet Chia, 'Investigations, Enforcement and Rights of Private Action' in Lim and Bull (n 163) paras 06.210–06.215.

[171] ROC, Ord 57.

[172] cf Competition Act 1998 (UK), s 47A(1).

[173] Competition Act, s 86(1).

[174] Competition Act, s 86(6). It is unclear whether time only runs after an appeal on a discrete point (for example, the quantum of financial penalty, rather than a finding of infringement). The UK position is that time will run once the infringement decision is final: *BCL Old Co Ltd v BASF SE* [2009] EWCA Civ 434.

[175] SCJA, s 17(1)(b).

[176] For expositions of Admiralty law in Singapore, see Damien J Cremean, *Admiralty Jurisdiction: Law and Practice in Australia, New Zealand, Singapore and Hong Kong* 3rd edn (Sydney, The Federation Press, 2008); Kian Sing Toh, *Admiralty Law and Practice* 3rd edn (Singapore, LexisNexis, 2017).

[177] ROC, Ord 70, rr 2(1), 2(2).

[178] See eg *The Espanoleto* [1920] P 223, 225; *The Talabot* (1974) 132 CLR 449 (HCA).

[179] ROC, Ord 70, r 4(1). See Section III.B below.

[180] *The Fierbinti* [1994] 3 SLR 864.

[181] HCAJA, s 4(4); *The Damavand* [1993] 2 SLR 717; *The Fierbinti* (n 180) 874–75.

[182] *The Fierbinti* (n 180) 870.

[183] *Comandate Marine Corp v Pan Australian Shipping Pty Ltd* (2006) 157 FCR 45 (FCA) 77.

and an action *in personam* against the owner, and if judgment is obtained it is enforceable against the ship and also against the owner to the full extent of the judgment'.[184] The combination of an action *in rem* and an action *in personam* in the same writ is not allowed in the ROC and was expressly disapproved by the Singapore court.[185] Failure to invoke the court's *in rem* jurisdiction does not defeat the *in personam* jurisdiction.[186]

HCAJA section 3 contains a list of situations giving rise to *in rem* claims, including (for example) any claim in relation to the possession, ownership or security of a ship, damage done or received by a ship, and loss of or damage to goods carried on board a ship.[187] The Admiralty jurisdiction may be invoked by an action *in personam* in all situations,[188] or by an action *in rem* against the ship or property in question in situations concerning (for example) the possession or ownership of a ship, a mortgage or charge on a ship, or the forfeiture, condemnation, or restoration of a ship.[189] In the absence of the defendant's agreement to submit to the High Court's jurisdiction,[190] the relevant action *in personam* must satisfy any one of these requirements: (1) the defendant has a habitual residence or place of business in Singapore; (2) the cause of action arose within inland waters of Singapore[191] or within the limits of the port of Singapore; or (3) an action arising out of the same incident or series of incidents is proceeding in the High Court or has been heard and determined there.[192] There should be no foreign concurrent proceedings. The latter (if ongoing) must be either discontinued or terminated.[193] An application challenging whether the court has jurisdiction in an Admiralty action *in rem* under HCAJA section 4(4) falls within ROC Order 12, rule 7(1) and not rule 7(2).[194] The 1989 International Convention on Salvage came into force in Singapore on 24 July 2021. The Admiralty jurisdiction of the High Court is extended to any claim that arises under the 1989 Convention and any contractual claim relating to salvage services by amending HCAJA section 3(1)(i).

B. The Process of Ship Arrest

A warrant of arrest is required to arrest a *res*. The arresting party has the duty to make full and frank disclosure of all material facts.[195] The various steps and standards of proof applicable in the arrest of a ship were summarised in *The Bunga Melati 5*:[196]

> (a) prove, on the balance of probabilities, that the jurisdictional facts under the limb [the plaintiff] is relying on in [HCAJA] ss 3(1)(d) to (q) exist; and show an arguable case that [the plaintiff's] claim is of the type or nature required by the relevant statutory provision ("step 1");
> (b) prove, on the balance of probabilities, that the claim arises in connection with a ship ("step 2");

184 *The Fierbinti* (n 180) 870.
185 *The Nagasaki Spirit (No 2)* [1994] 1 SLR 445, 447.
186 *The Trade Resolve* [1999] 2 SLR(R) 107 [47]–[48] (both service of the writ *in rem* and arrest outside jurisdiction, action proceeded as *in personam*); *The Global 1* (n 3) [32] (*in rem* action initiated in error, court amended writ as *in personam* claim by ROC, Ord 2, r 1).
187 HCAJA, ss 3(1)(a)–3(1)(r).
188 ibid, s 4(1).
189 ibid, s 4(2).
190 ibid, s 5(4). The natural consequence of an agreement is that the High Court's Admiralty jurisdiction can be invoked.
191 For the definition of 'inland waters of Singapore', see ibid, s 5(8).
192 ibid, ss 5(1), 5(5).
193 ibid, s 5(2).
194 *The Eternal Strength* (n 38) [16].
195 *The Vasiliy Golovin* [2008] 4 SLR 994 [83]–[94]; *The Xin Chang Shu* [2016] 1 SLR 1096 [43]–[55].
196 *The Bunga Melati 5* [2012] 4 SLR 546 [112].

(c) identify, without having to show in argument, the person who would be liable on the claim in an action *in personam* ("step 3");
(d) prove on the balance of probabilities, that the relevant person was, when the cause of action arose, the owner or charterer of, or in possession or in control of, the ship ("step 4"); and
(e) prove on the balance of probabilities, that the relevant person was, at the time when the action was brought: (i) the beneficial owner of the offending ship as respects all the shares in it or the charterer of that ship under a demise charter; or (ii) the beneficial owner of the sister ship as respects all the shares in it ("step 5").

A plaintiff may only arrest a ship after the court issues a warrant of arrest,[197] and arrest may only take place within the port limits of Singapore.[198] A warrant of arrest is valid for 12 months from the date of issue and should be served on the property against which it is issued.[199] An arrest is carried out by the sheriff of the Supreme Court of Singapore, although a solicitor may be authorised to perform the sheriff's duty to arrest a vessel.[200] A report of the arrest is then made.[201] The owner of the ship can provide security (bail) for the release of the ship[202] or apply to the Court to set aside a defective or irregular warrant of arrest or service.[203] A shipowner may be entitled to damages if the ship arrest is proved to have been wrongful. An arrest is wrongful if 'the action and the arrest were so unwarrantably brought, or brought with so little colour, or so little foundation, as to imply malice or gross negligence on the plaintiff's part'.[204]

The current arrest process dispenses with the need to attend physically at the Maritime and Port Authority's One-Stop Document Centre. Since 1 November 2019, after a warrant of arrest has been executed, the arresting law firm is to send an email to the Authority and the Sheriff's Office, attaching the Report of Arrest and the Notification Letter. An email acknowledging receipt will be provided within an hour. The email acknowledgment and the completed Report of Arrest are then filed via e-Litigation (Singapore's integrated electronic litigation system) within one working day after the service of the warrant of arrest.[205] Any urgent request for the arrest or release of a vessel outside office hours is dealt with by the Duty Registrar. The lawyers must satisfy the Duty Registrar of the urgency of the situation. If necessary, the matter may be determined by a hearing.[206]

IV. Immunities from Jurisdiction

The main statute on immunities is the State Immunity Act (Cap 313, 2014 rev ed) (SIA), which takes a negative or restrictive approach to state immunity.[207] It provides immunity to any foreign

[197] ROC, Ord 70, rr 4(2), 4(3), 4(6), 4(7). A person who desires to prevent the arrest of any property may file a caveat against arrest, but the caveat against arrest does not automatically prevent the issue of a warrant to arrest: Ord 70, rr 5(1), 5(2).
[198] *The Trade Resolve* (n 186).
[199] ROC, Ord 70, rr 9(1), 9(6). For freight, the warrant may also be served on the cargo or on the ship of the respective freight: Ord 70, r 9(5).
[200] SCJA, s 65A; ROC, Ord 70, r 9(2).
[201] ROC, Ord 70, r 9(7).
[202] ROC, Ord 70, r 12; *The Arktis Fighter* [2001] 2 SLR(R) 157.
[203] Through eg ROC, Ord 2, r 2.
[204] *The Xin Chang Shu* (n 195) [27]–[42], approving *The Vasiliy Golovin* (n 195) [137].
[205] For details, see 'New Process at MPA for Admiralty Arrest' (*Supreme Court of Singapore*, 25 October 2019), available online: www.supremecourt.gov.sg/docs/default-source/default-document-library/services/enforcement-section/sheriff-letter-on-new-process-at-mpa-for-admiralty-arrest-(the-law-society-of-singapore).pdf.
[206] 'Sheriff's Services' (*Supreme Court of Singapore*), available online: www.supremecourt.gov.sg/services/court-services/sheriff's-services.
[207] This seems to be the general approach in recent years: Malcolm N Shaw, *International Law* 8th edn (Cambridge, Cambridge University Press, 2018) 531.

or Commonwealth states, including the sovereign and the head of that state, the government of the state and any department, but not to any 'separate entity' distinct from the government of the state (see Section IV.B below).

A. Sovereign and Diplomatic Immunity

A state (including the sovereign, government, and government department of a state)[208] is generally immune from the jurisdiction of the Singapore courts, even if the state does not appear in the proceedings in question.[209] The exceptions are specified in the SIA. These include the situation where the state voluntarily submits to the jurisdiction by a written agreement made before the dispute or by instituting, intervening, or taking any steps in proceedings (except to claim immunity or assert an interest in property for which immunity is claimed).[210] Similarly, a state is not immune in arbitrations where there is a written agreement to arbitrate.[211] A waiver of immunity can be severed from the rest of an agreement which is said to be void *ab initio*.[212] However, an agreement to Singapore law as the law governing a contract will not by itself be regarded as a submission to jurisdiction.[213] A state is also not immune in respect to commercial transactions entered into by the state or a contractual obligation to be performed wholly or partly in Singapore.[214] There are various other exceptions including, contracts of employment, claims for personal injury and damage to property, customs duties, certain IPRs, an action *in rem* against a ship belonging to a state, and an action *in personam* for enforcing a claim in connection with such ship.[215] Immunity from execution against a state's property is provided in SIA section 15(2). No injunction or order can be granted for specific performance or the recovery of land or property (unless the state gave written consent to the same in addition to submitting to the jurisdiction of the courts).[216] No enforcement against a state's property is possible unless it is 'for the time being in use or intended for use for commercial purposes'.[217] The doctrine of sovereign immunity is not absolute and should not be extended unnecessarily.[218] In particular, it should not be extended to a case involving debts or choses in action in the possession or control of a third party, in which a state claims, but has yet to prove, ownership.[219] Diplomatic immunity (immunity from *in personam* jurisdiction) is conferred under the Diplomatic and Consular Relations Act (Cap 82A, 2006 rev ed) and the International Organisations (Immunities and Privileges) Act (Cap 145, 1985 rev ed). The former gives effect to the 1961 Vienna Convention on Diplomatic Relations and the 1963 Vienna Convention on Consular Relations.

[208] SIA, s 16(1).
[209] ibid, s 3.
[210] ibid, ss 4(2), 4(3), 4(4). For the SICC, see ROC, Ord 110, r 9(1)(b).
[211] SIA, s 11.
[212] *Maldives Airports Co Ltd v GMR Malé International Airport Pte Ltd* [2013] 2 SLR 44.
[213] SIA, s 4(2).
[214] ibid, s 5. See also *WestLB AG v Philippine National Bank* [2007] 1 SLR(R) 967, where the 'whole context in which the claim against the state is made' should be considered, approving *The I Congreso del Partido* [1983] 1 AC 244 (HL) 267 (Lord Wilberforce).
[215] See SIA, ss 4–13.
[216] ibid, ss 15(2)(a), 15(3); *Maldives Airports* (n 212).
[217] SIA, ss 15(2)(b), 15(4). For the meaning of 'commercial purposes', see SIA, ss 2(1), 5(3).
[218] *Republic of the Philippines v Maler Foundation* [2008] 2 SLR(R) 857 [37], [46].
[219] ibid [53].

B. State-Owned Enterprises (SOEs)

The SIA uses the term 'separate entity' to refer to SOEs, defined as being 'distinct from the executive organs of the government of the State and capable of suing or being sued' (section 16(1)). Such an entity enjoys immunity if and only if:[220]

(a) the proceedings relate to anything done by it in the exercise of sovereign authority; and
(b) the circumstances are such that a State would have been so immune.

What exactly is meant by the 'exercise of sovereign authority' is unclear. The Australian Law Reform Commission suggested that the expression 'has no precise meaning and may indeed by impossible to define'.[221] However, in the words of Lord Mance, there is:[222]

> need for full and appropriate recognition of the existence of separate juridical entities established by states, particularly for trading purposes. … A similar recognition of their existence and separateness would be expected for purposes of liability and enforcement.

Consequently, '[t]he assets [of an SOE] which are (subject to waiver and to the commercial use exception …) protected by state immunity should be the same as those against which the state's liabilities can be enforced'.[223] When determining whether an SOE is a separate entity, the strong presumption is that 'separate corporate status should be respected, and that it and the state forming it should not have to bear each other's liabilities'. It takes 'extreme circumstances' to displace this presumption. One needs to examine 'the relevant constitutional arrangements [of the SOE], as applied in practice, as well as of the state's control exercised over the entity and of the entity's activities and functions' with a view to demonstrating that 'the affairs of the entity and the state were so closely intertwined and confused that the entity could not properly be regarded for any significant purpose as distinct from the state and vice versa'.[224] While a state's conduct may render it appropriate to lift the corporate veil to enable a creditor of an SOE to look to the state for payment, this does not automatically entitle a creditor of the state to look to an SOE for payment.[225] Recent UK cases which may be of persuasive value in Singapore have considered whether an SOE is governed by a board of directors or whether the state has control over the SOE's day-to-day operations.[226]

V. Conclusion

The Singapore court exercises jurisdiction in a wide variety of matters, but such jurisdiction is balanced by reference to established principles. This principled approach towards direct jurisidiction facilitates and consolidates Singapore's role as an international dispute resolution hub. In this light, in the post-COVID-19 era where the only constant is change, Singapore's prospects as a vibrant international business and commercial hub accordingly remain optimistic.

[220] SIA, s 16(2).
[221] 'Foreign State Immunity' [1984] ALRC 24 (*AustLII*, 10 October 1984) available online: www8.austlii.edu.au/cgi-bin/download.cgi/cgi-bin/download.cgi/download/au/other/lawreform/ALRC/1984/24.pdf. See also Woo Bih Li, 'Speech at the 5th Judicial Seminar on Commercial Litigation, Hong Kong: State Immunity in Commercial Disputes – An Overview of Singapore Law & A Re-visit to the Absolute Doctrine of State Immunity' (*Supreme Court of Singapore*, 20 October 2016), available online: www.supremecourt.gov.sg/news/speeches/year/2016/.
[222] *La Générale des Carrières et des Mines v FG Hemisphere Associates LLC* [2012] UKPC 27, [2013] 1 All ER 409 [28].
[223] ibid [29].
[224] ibid [29], [30].
[225] ibid [30].
[226] *Taurus Petroleum Ltd v State Oil Co of the Ministry of Oil, Republic of Iraq* [2015] EWCA Civ 835, [2016] 1 Lloyd's Rep 42 [42]–[45]; not pursued on appeal: [2017] UKSC 64, [2018] AC 690 [28].

8

Malaysia

NITIN V NADKARNI AND WAI FUNG TEH

I. Introduction

As a Commonwealth nation, Malaysia has retained the common law system. Much legislation mirrors or even adopts current or past English legislation. Where Malaysian law is silent on an issue, the Civil Law Act 1956 section 3(1) requires the Malaysian courts to apply the common law and rules of equity of England as they were before Malaysia gained independence.[1] Malaysian law has been judicially described as entailing three types of jurisdiction *in personam*, namely, jurisdiction over parties, subject matter, or cause of action.[2] Any foreign plaintiff may in peacetime commence an action in the High Court.[3] As the plaintiff thus submits to the jurisdiction, the defendant sued may counterclaim without leave.[4] Likewise, a defendant who appears without disputing the High Court's jurisdiction within the time limited for serving his defence is taken to submit to the jurisdiction.[5] More questions arise in relation to the law on foreign defendants who dispute jurisdiction.

II. Jurisdiction *in personam* – General Principles

Two pieces of legislation primarily govern the High Court's jurisdiction over foreign defendants: the Courts of Judicature Act 1964 (CJA 1964) section 23(1) and the Rules of Court 2012 (ROC 2012) Order 11, rule 1(1). Despite some overlap, they are independent. Where they differ is that whereas (absent consent) CJA 1964 section 23(1) applies to cases treated as being '*within* the local jurisdiction', ROC 2012 Order 11, rule 1(1) governs '*service* of [a] notice of writ *out* of the

[1] Specifically, as of 7 April 1956 for Peninsular Malaysia, 1 December 1951 for Sabah, and 12 December 1949 for Sarawak. For a brief history of the beginnings of the law on jurisdiction in Malaysia (then Malaya), see RH Hickling and Min Aun Wu, *Conflict of Laws in Malaysia* (Singapore, Butterworths Asia, 1995) 1–16.

[2] ibid 5–9.

[3] ibid 6.

[4] *Derby & Co Ltd v Larsson* [1976] 1 WLR 202 (UKHL) 205F–H (Lord Russell). That case concerned the former Rules of the Supreme Court 1965 (RSC 1965) in England and Wales. ROC 2012, Ord 11, r 1(1) of Malaysia is *in pari materia* with the relevant part of the former English RSC 1965. ROC 2012 was previously the Rules of the High Court 1980 and Rules of the Subordinate Courts 1980. ROC 2012 was enacted in exercise of the powers conferred by CJA 1964, s 17 (not s 23(1)) and Subordinate Courts Rules Act 1955, s 4. In ROC 2012, 'Order' is usually abbreviated to 'O' (or 'Ord' in this work) and 'rule' to 'r'. Thus, 'Order 11 rule 1(1)' is normally abbreviated as 'O 11 r 1(1)'.

[5] ROC 2012, Ord 12, rr 10(1), 10(2), 10(6).

jurisdiction'.[6] Thus, where CJA 1964 section 23(1) applies, ROC 2012 Order 11 is a 'mere procedural formality … to effect service abroad'.[7] Where CJA 1964 section 23(1) does not apply, ROC 2012 Order 11, rule 1(1) supplies both jurisdiction and procedure.[8] CJA 1964 section 23(1) is mandatory in effect, whereas ROC 2012 Order 11, rule 1(1) is discretionary.

A. Jurisdiction of Courts within the Territory (CJA 1964 Section 23(1))

CJA 1964 section 23(1) is general to all civil proceedings '*within* the local jurisdiction':[9]

> Civil jurisdiction – general
>
> 23. (1) Subject to the limitations contained in Article 128 of the Constitution the High Court shall have jurisdiction to try all civil proceedings where –
>
> (a) the cause of action arose;
> (b) the defendant or one of several defendants resides or has his place of business;
> (c) the facts on which the proceedings are based exist or are alleged to have occurred; or
> (d) any land the ownership of which is disputed is situated,
>
> within the local jurisdiction of the Court and notwithstanding anything contained in this section in any case where all parties consent in writing within the local jurisdiction of the other High Court.

CJA 1964 section 23(2) preserves the High Court's pre-Malaysia Day (16 September 1963)[10] jurisdiction and enshrines its inherent jurisdiction more generally. Because the Schedule to the CJA 1964 is extensive, it is not often necessary to delve into Malaysian legal history pre-Malaysia Day.[11] Two provisions should be highlighted: CJA 1964 section 23(1)(b) and 'consent' under CJA 1964 section 23(1). First, section 23(1)(b), particularly the words 'one of several defendants', have no direct English law equivalent.[12] Second, 'consent' under section 23(1) does not allow parties to consent to the jurisdiction of the courts of Malaysia as opposed to the courts of another country, but rather to elect between the High Court of Malaya or the High Court of Sabah and Sarawak,[13] which are of 'co-ordinate jurisdiction and status'.[14]

B. ROC 2012 Order 11, Rule 1(1): Service of Process Outside of the Territory

The High Court has a discretion to permit service of a notice of writ out of the jurisdiction in 13 scenarios, rules 1(1)(A) to (M), provided that the writ does not make, in broad terms, any claim for damages, loss of life or personal injury related to shipping collisions or accidents.[15]

[6] CJA 1964, s 23(1); ROC 2012, Ord 11, r 1(1) (emphasis added).
[7] *Malayan Banking Bhd v International Tin Council* [1989] 3 MLJ 286 (SC) 288C–H; *Matchplan (M) Sdn Bhd v William D Sinrich* [2004] 2 MLJ 424 (CA) [10]–[12].
[8] *American Express Bank Ltd v Mohamed Toufic Al-Ozeir* [1995] 1 MLJ 160 (SC) 166C–E.
[9] Emphasis added.
[10] Not to be confused with Malaysia's Independence Day, 31 August 1957.
[11] CJA 1964, Schedule; Hickling and Wu (n 1) 63.
[12] *Malayan Banking* (n 7) 288I.
[13] Courts of Judicature Act 1964, s 3.
[14] Federal Constitution, Art 121(1). Note, however, the difficulties with the wording of s 23(1): Hickling and Wu (n 1) 66; Arunachalam Kasi, 'Anti-Suit Injunction in Enforcement of Arbitration Agreement and Exclusive Jurisdiction Agreement' [2013] 6 *Malayan Law Journal* i, fn 62.
[15] ROC 2012, Ord 11, rr 1(1)(a), 1(1)(b), 1(1)(c).

Order 11, rule 2 adds a 14th scenario for contractual actions where a term of the contract gives jurisdiction to the Malaysian courts. Similar provisions (with modifications) govern originating summonses.[16]

i. Jurisprudential Basis of ROC 2012 Order 11

ROC 2012 Order 11 is the successor to Rules of the High Court 1980 (RHC 1980) Order 11. RHC 1980 Order 11 was modelled on the English Common Law Procedure Act 1852 (CLPA 1852).[17] Upholding territorial sovereignty and jurisdiction, ROC 2012 Order 11, rule 1(1) permits service not of a writ itself, but of a notice of a writ.[18]

ii. Court's Discretion under ROC 2012 Order 11, Rule 1(1)

Unlike CJA 1964 section 23(1), the grant of permission under ROC 2012 Order 11, rule 1(1) is discretionary. This involves three stages: (1) falling within the rule, (2) meeting the standard of proof, and (3) the High Court's exercise of discretion.

a. Falling within the Rule

As a minimum, the plaintiff must show that the case falls within one of the paragraphs of ROC 2012 Order 11, rule 11(1) in spirit and in letter.[19] The High Court will look only at the cause of action expressly pleaded by the plaintiff, even if the facts might have allowed an alternative.[20]

b. Meeting the Standard of Proof

By ROC 2012 Order 11, rule 4, the High Court will not grant leave to serve a notice of a writ out of the jurisdiction under ROC 2012 Order 11, rule 1 or rule 2 unless it is 'made sufficiently to appear' that the case is a proper one. A plaintiff must first show a 'good arguable case' so that, assuming the facts pleaded in the statement of claim and affidavit in support to be true, those facts would fit the terms of at least one subparagraph of ROC 2012 Order 11, rule 1(1).[21] Additionally, there must also be a 'serious issue to be tried' on the merits.[22]

c. Court's Discretion

At the third stage, the High Court retains a discretion to refuse leave. Generally, the High Court exercises its discretion 'with caution and biased against invading the sovereignty of

[16] ibid, Ord 11, r 9; *Gabung Trading Sdn Bhd v Borneo Pulp & Paper Sdn Bhd* [2008] 7 MLJ 67 (HC) [15]–[19].

[17] Via the English Judicature Acts 1873–75: Hickling and Wu (n 1) 68–69.

[18] Hickling and Wu (n 1) 69.

[19] *Johnson v Taylor Bros & Co Ltd* [1920] AC 144 (UKHL) 153, cited in *Malayan Banking* (n 7) 288A–D; *Bank Bumiputra Malaysia Bhd v International Tin Council* [1987] 2 MLJ 732 (OCJ) 734E–I.

[20] *Metall und Rohstoff AG v Donaldson Lufkin & Jenrette Inc* [1990] 1 QB 391 (EWCA) 449B–F, cited with approval in *Q2 Engineering Sdn Bhd v PJI-LFGC (Vietnam) Ltd* [2012] 8 CLJ 1005 (HC) [57]–[58].

[21] ROC 2012, Ord 11, r 4(2); *Oliver Tim Axmann v Celcom (M) Bhd (No 1)* [2014] 5 MLJ 695 (CA) [21]; *Joseph bin Paulus Lantip v Unilever Plc* [2018] MLJ Supp 151 (FC) [42]. However, note that the citation in *Joseph bin Paulus Lantip* of 'Lord Davey's speech' apparently in *Seaconsar Far East Ltd v Bank Markazi Jomhouri Islami Iran* [1994] 1 AC 438 (UKHL) was really a reference to Lord Davey's speech in *Chemische Fabrik vormals Sandoz v Badische Anilin und Soda Fabriks* (1904) 90 LT 733 (UKHL). See also *Vitkovice Horni a Hutni Tezirstvo v Korner* [1951] AC 869 (UKHL).

[22] ROC 2012, Ord 11, r 4(1); *Oliver Tim Axmann* (n 21) [21].

another state'.[23] The High Court also considers specific discretionary factors, such as *forum conveniens* (explored in detail below). As regards ROC 2012 Order 11, rule 1(1), jurisdiction and *forum conveniens* must be evaluated as 'separate and distinct' elements, each of which must be individually established.[24] Whereas a defendant seeking a stay bears the burden of proving *forum non conveniens*, the plaintiff seeking permission to serve must establish that Malaysia is 'clearly' the *forum conveniens*.[25]

iii. Service under ROC 2012 Order 11

Service of a notice of a writ outside of the jurisdiction is governed by ROC 2012 Order 11, rules 5–8. In line with international comity, service of a notice of a writ in a foreign country is effective if effected in accordance with that country's law[26] and nothing in ROC 2012 Order 11, rule 5 or any court order or direction can authorise or require anything contrary to that country's law.[27] This does not require a method of service to be expressly and specifically permitted by the foreign country's laws.[28] The usual procedure for substituted service applies,[29] as does the overriding consideration of how the notice can best be communicated to the defendant.[30] Service may also be effected through foreign governments, judicial authorities and Malaysian consuls, or by the plaintiff itself.[31] The procedure depends on, amongst others, whether there subsists a Civil Procedure Convention in the foreign country.[32] Although ROC 2012 Order 11, rules 5(5)–5(6) refer to the 1965 Hague Service Abroad Convention,[33] Malaysia is not a signatory. Peculiarly to Singapore and Brunei, notice of a writ can be sent to an officer of a civil court if a defendant is located there.[34]

C. *Forum conveniens, lis alibi pendens*, Anti-suit Injunctions, Interim Measures, and Choice of Court Agreements

The principles in this section will often arise in a given case, not as discrete, isolated considerations, but as different facets of a single decision. For example, in considering whether to grant an anti-suit injunction, a court will ascertain where the *forum conveniens* lies, which in turn involves consideration of *lis alibi pendens*, choice of court agreements and the availability or otherwise of interim measures.

[23] *Joseph bin Paulus Lantip* (n 21) [35], presumably quoting *Vitkovice* (n 21) 877.
[24] *Seaconsar* (n 21) 456B–457B.
[25] *Spiliada Maritime Corp v Cansulex Ltd (The Spiliada)* [1987] AC 460 (UKHL) 481D–E; *American Express* (n 8) 167F–H.
[26] ROC 2012, Ord 11, r 5(3).
[27] ibid, Ord 11, r 5(2).
[28] *Able Food Sdn Bhd v Open Country Dairy Ltd* [2021] 4 CLJ 614 (HC) [83].
[29] ibid, Ord 11, r 5(1); Ord 62, r 5.
[30] *Aw Chen v Johannes Koplan* [1969] 2 MLJ 190 (OCJ) 191H–I.
[31] ROC 2012, Ord 11, r 6.
[32] ibid, Ord 11, r 6(1)(a).
[33] ibid, Ord 11, rr 5(5)–5(6); 1965 Hague Convention on the Service Abroad of Judicial and Extrajudicial Documents in Civil or Commercial Matters.
[34] ROC 2012, Ord 11, r 5(8).

i. Forum conveniens

Malaysian law has adopted the English definition of *forum non conveniens* as:

> … where the court is satisfied that there is some other available forum, having competent jurisdiction, which is the appropriate forum for the trial of the action, i.e. in which the case may be tried more suitably for the interests of all the parties and the ends of justice.[35]

Relevant considerations have historically included logistics, cost, political climate, geographical constraints, and the locations of parties, witnesses, relevant monies or documents.[36] The Malaysian courts will also consider whether 'it would be unjust to the plaintiff to confine him to remedies elsewhere'.[37] Particular to a defendant seeking a stay on this ground, the defendant must also establish that the other forum alleged to be more appropriate is 'one with which the action has the most real and substantial connection'.[38]

ii. Lis alibi pendens *and Anti-suit Injunctions*

Lis alibi pendens has been statutorily encapsulated in differing terms in the CJA 1964 and, to an extent, the ROC 2012. Both provisions apply generally to all proceedings before the High Court, whether the parties are 'local' or 'foreign'. CJA 1964 Schedule, para 11 allows the High Court to dismiss or stay proceedings on the ground of *res judicata* or multiplicity of proceedings.[39] Meanwhile, ROC 2012 Order 18, rule 19(1)(d) gives the High Court the wider power, inter alia, to strike out the endorsement of a writ and stay or dismiss an action that is an abuse of court process. With regard to anti-suit injunctions, the Privy Council judgment in *Societe Nationale Industrielle Aerospatiale v Lee Kui Jak*,[40] a Brunei case, has received both judicial and academic acceptance in Malaysia.[41] In short, an injunction restraining foreign proceedings will be granted only where the 'ends of justice' require it.[42] The party enjoined must be amenable to the Malaysian courts' jurisdiction.[43] Injunctions will be granted with caution.[44] *SNIA v Lee Kui Jak* has been applied and discussed extensively across the Commonwealth.[45]

[35] *The Spiliada* (n 25) 476C; *American Express* (n 8) 167D–F; *Petrodar Operating Co Ltd v Nam Fatt Corp Bhd (in liq)* [2014] 6 MLJ 189 (FC) [21]; *Goodness for Import and Export v Phillip Morris Brands Sarl* [2016] 5 MLJ 171 (FC) [55].

[36] *American Express* (n 8) 165B–E; *Petrodar* (n 35) [23]; *Goodness for Import and Export* (n 35) [58]; *Punjab National Bank v Malayan Banking Bhd* [2017] 6 CLJ 180 (CA) [31]–[36]. On whether these should remain influential in light of technological advances, see Nur Syakirah Binti Mohd Adnan, 'Analysis on the Doctrine of Non-Convenience and the Malaysian Position' [2020] 1 *Legal Network Series (Article)* xcviii.

[37] *The Spiliada* (n 25) 465A; *American Express* (n 8) 167H–I.

[38] *The Abidin Daver* [1984] AC 398 (UKHL) 415F; *The Spiliada* (n 25) 478D–E; *American Express* (n 8) 168A.

[39] Given effect by CJA 1964, s 25(2).

[40] *Société Nationale Industrielle Aérospatiale v Lee Kui Jak* [1987] AC 871, [1987] 2 MLJ 397 (UKPC).

[41] For example, *BSNC Leasing Sdn Bhd v Sabah Shipyard Sdn Bhd* [2000] 2 MLJ 70 (CA) 88H–92D; RH Hickling and Min Aun Wu, 'Stay of Actions and Forum Non Conveniens' [1994] 3 *Malayan Law Journal* xcvii, cvii–cviii.

[42] *SNIA v Lee Kui Jak* (n 40) 403C.

[43] ibid 403G.

[44] ibid 403H.

[45] For example, *Salgaocar v Jitendra* [2019] SGCA 42 [49]; *Gray v Hurley* [2019] EWCA Civ 2222, [2020] 1 FLR 864 [50].

iii. Interim Measures

The question whether the grant by the High Court of interim measures against a foreign defendant, absent other relevant factors, would amount to an exercise of extra-territorial jurisdiction has not come before the Malaysian courts. The likely position seems to be that it would not.[46]

iv. Choice of Court Agreements

In considering the enforceability of parties' agreements designating the courts of a particular country as the forum in which disputes arising out of a contract are to be determined, ROC 2012 Order 11, rules 1(1)(F)(iii) and 1(2) are relevant:

> *Principal cases in which service of notice of writ out of the jurisdiction is permissible (O. 11, r. 1)*
>
> 1. (1) … service of a notice of a writ out of the jurisdiction is permissible with the leave of the Court in the following cases:
>
> (F) if the action begun by the writ is brought against a defendant to enforce, rescind, dissolve, annul or otherwise affect a contract, or to recover damages or obtain other relief in respect of the breach of a contract, being (in either case) a contract which:
>
> …
>
> (iii) is by its terms, or by implication, governed by the law of Malaysia;
>
> …
>
> *Service out of the jurisdiction in certain actions of contract (O. 11, r. 2)*
>
> 2. Where it appears to the Court that a contract contains a term to the effect that the Court shall have jurisdiction to hear and determine any action in respect of the contract, the Court may grant leave for service out of the jurisdiction of the notice of the writ by which an action in respect of the contract is begun.

The jurisdiction of the High Court cannot be ousted by private stipulation.[47] If there is an express agreement to refer disputes to a foreign court, the High Court ought usually, but is not bound, to stay the Malaysian proceedings unless there is a strong case or cause not to do so.[48] The plaintiff bears the burden of showing strong cause.[49] Ultimately, it remains a matter of discretion for the High Court, having regard to all the circumstances of the case.[50] All of this is separate from the question of the proper (or governing) law of an agreement.[51]

[46] *Siskina (Owners of Cargo Lately Laden On Board) v Distos Compania Naviera SA* [1979] AC 210 (UKHL) 256C–H. That judgment has been cited with approval in, amongst others, *Aspatra Sdn Bhd v Bank Bumiputra Malaysia Bhd* [1988] 1 MLJ 97 (SC) and *Khoo Soo Teong v Khoo Siew Ghim* [1991] 3 MLJ 158 (SC), although those cases concerned *Mareva* injunctions without cross-border elements. See also *Lee Lee Cheng (F) v Seow Peng Kwang* [1960] 1 MLJ 1 (CA) 3H–4A; *Mercedes-Benz AG v Leiduck* [1996] 1 AC 284 (UKPC); *Hap Seng Plantations (River Estates) Sdn Bhd v Excess Interpoint Sdn Bhd* [2016] 3 MLJ 553 (FC) [20]; Tan Yock Lin, 'Supreme Court of Judicature (Amendment) Act 1993' [1993] *Singapore Journal of Legal Studies* 557, 567–68; Hickling and Wu (n 1) 74.

[47] *Owners of Cargo Lately Laden on Board the Fehmarn v Owners of the Fehmarn (The Fehmarn)* [1958] 1 WLR 159 (EWCA) 162; *Globus Shipping & Trading Co (Pte) Ltd v Taiping Textiles Bhd* [1976] 2 MLJ 154 (FC) 155C.

[48] *Globus* (n 47) 155A–156C, citing *Owners of Cargo Lately Laden on Board the Fehmarn v Owners of the Fehmarn (The Fehmarn)* [1957] 1 WLR 815 (PD) 710; *Owners Of Cargo Lately Laden on Board Ship or Vessel Eleftheria v Owners of the Eleftheria (The Eleftheria)* [1969] 2 WLR 1073 (PD) 1077A. See also *American Express* (n 8) 168B.

[49] *Globus* (n 47) 155H, citing *The Eleftheria* (n 48) 1077B.

[50] *Globus* (n 47) 155D–156C, citing *Azimullah v Master of SS 'Halldor'* [1965] 1 MLJ 248 (OCJ); *The Eleftheria* (n 48) 1077B–D.

[51] *Globus* (n 47) 156B. See also *American Express* (n 8) 168E.

D. Service of Foreign Process within the Territory

This section summarises service of foreign process within Malaysia, the obtaining of evidence for foreign courts, and the reciprocal enforcement of judgments, governed by ROC 2012 Order 65, Order 66 and Order 67 respectively. Notably, all translations specifically required by these three rules are to English, not Malay (whether in addition to or instead of English).[52] This is despite the requirement that all court proceedings in Malaysia, at least in Peninsular Malaysia,[53] must be in Malay as the national language.[54]

i. ROC 2012 Order 65: Service of Foreign Process

'Foreign process' is not specifically defined in ROC 2012 Order 65, but would appear to mean any process required in connection with civil proceedings pending before a court or other tribunal of a foreign country, including a citation.[55] ROC 2012 Order 65 permits three methods of service of foreign process: a request to the Minister, service under a Civil Procedure Convention, or service by analogy under the ROC 2012's standard rules for service. At the time of writing, however, Malaysia is not party to any Civil Procedure Conventions.

ii. ROC 2012 Order 66: Obtaining Evidence for Foreign Court

The High Court may give an order for the examination of witnesses and for attendance and for production of documents, and give directions in relation to foreign proceedings, where there is 'a matter pending before a Court or tribunal in a place outside the jurisdiction'.[56] However, it seems likely that the Malaysian courts will, if the question comes before them, follow the English position[57] that this does not extend to a foreign-seated arbitration.[58] For foreign court proceedings, the application must be made by a person duly authorised by the foreign court or tribunal[59] or, in certain cases, the Attorney General, not by a foreign plaintiff personally.[60]

[52] ROC 2012, Ord 65, rr 2(2)–2(3), 3(2)–3(3); Ord, 66 r 2(2); Ord 67, r 3(1)(a).

[53] ROC 2012, Ord 92, r 1(2) requires all documents for court proceedings in Sabah and Sarawak to be in English. The Federal Constitution, Art 161 also preserves the use of English for 'proceedings' in Sabah and Sarawak. Despite the mandatory language of ROC 2012, Ord 92, r 1(2), it is uncertain to what extent this remains a strict requirement in practice. In *Wong Leh Yin v Public Prosecutor* [2013] 5 MLJ 820 (CA) [21], the Court of Appeal dismissed an objection founded on the ROC 2012, Ord 92, r 1(2) as 'purely a technicality' which had not 'occasioned a substantial miscarriage of justice'.

[54] National Language Acts 1963, s 8, as amended by the National Language (Amendment) Act 1994, s 2.

[55] ROC 2012, Ord 65, rr 1, 2(1), 2A(1), 3(1).

[56] ibid, Ord 66, r 1(1). See also *Dato Mohamed Hashim Shamsuddin v Attorney-General, Hong Kong* [1986] 2 MLJ 112 (SC) 113B–116B.

[57] *Commerce and Industry Insurance Co of Canada v Certain Underwriters at Lloyd's of London* [2002] 1 WLR 1323 (EWHC) 1326H–1327D.

[58] See *Aras Jalinan Sdn Bhd v Tipco Asphalt Public Company Ltd* [2008] 5 CLJ 654 (HC) [20]–[22], [36]–[39], [49]–[50], [56], where the High Court dealt with the courts' powers in respect of foreign-seated arbitrations. See also the Arbitration Act 2005, ss 3, 8, 11(3), 29. s 8 makes the Act the exclusive source of the courts' jurisdiction in respect of arbitrations. Unlike s 11(3), s 29 contains no words to extend its application to foreign-seated arbitrations. s 29 should, therefore, apply only to the extent stipulated in s 3, ie Malaysian-seated arbitrations. See also *Danieli & C Officine Mecchaniche SPA v Southern HRC Sdn Bhd* [2021] 1 LNS 45 (HC) [26]–[37].

[59] ROC 2012, Ord 66, r 2(1).

[60] ibid, Ord 66, r 3.

iii. ROC 2012 Order 67: Reciprocal Enforcement of Judgments

Where a foreign civil judgment is delivered by a 'superior court' of a reciprocating foreign country,[61] registration under the Reciprocal Enforcement of Judgments Act 1958 (REJA 1958), in compliance with the ROC 2012 Order 67, is the exclusive means of enforcement.[62] Once registered (and if not set aside), a judgment becomes of the same force and effect as a judgment of the registering Malaysian court.[63] For other foreign judgments, enforcement is through filing an action on the judgment at common law. The applicable rules are nevertheless similar with differences primarily in procedure.[64] Even where the REJA 1958 does not apply, the Malaysian courts will prima facie respect foreign judgments of competent jurisdiction.[65] Once a foreign judgment has been registered under the REJA 1958, an application to set aside registration may be made within the time specified in the order for registration itself.[66] Upon such an application, setting aside can be either mandatory or discretionary, depending on which set of rebuttable presumptions or discretions may apply.[67] To uphold comity, the Malaysian courts will not entertain attempts to challenge the regularity, validity or certainty of foreign judgments. Any such challenges should be made in the original jurisdiction before the foreign court.[68]

III. Jurisdiction *in personam* – Specific Cases

The sections below address specific scenarios under CJA 1964 section 23(1) and ROC 2012 Order 11, rule 1(1) in which the High Court may come to exercise jurisdiction over a foreign defendant. They are presented not in the order in which they appear in the legislation, but by topic, to aid the comparative purpose of this book.

A. Cause of Action and Alleged Facts within Jurisdiction

CJA 1964 sections 23(1)(a) and 23(1)(c) confer on the High Court jurisdiction over a foreign defendant where:

> (a) the cause of action arose;
>
> …
>
> (c) the facts on which the proceedings are based exist or are alleged to have occurred … within the local jurisdiction of the Court …

[61] Reciprocating countries (the UK, Hong Kong, Singapore, New Zealand, Sri Lanka, Brunei and parts of India) and their superior courts are set out in REJA 1958, First Schedule.

[62] REJA 1958, ss 7, 11; *The Bank of East Asia Ltd Singapore Branch v Axis Incorporation Bhd (No 2)* [2009] 6 MLJ 564 (HC) [18], [23].

[63] REJA 1958, s 4(2).

[64] *See Hua Daily News Bhd v Tan Thien Chin* [1986] 2 MLJ 107 (SC) 108I–109E. Brunei was not at a reciprocating country when this judgment was delivered.

[65] *Sakuragawa Pump (S) Pte Ltd v Perkapalan Mesra Sdn Bhd* [2007] 7 MLJ 555 (HC) [6].

[66] ROC 2012, Ord 67, r 5(2).

[67] REJA 1958, s 5(1).

[68] *Banque Nationale De Paris v Ting Kai Hoon* [2002] 7 MLJ 703 (HC) 709D–712B; *Mann Holdings Pte Ltd & Anor v Ung Yoke Hong* [2019] 6 CLJ 475 (CA) [54].

Where (c) applies, (a) will almost certainly apply, because Malaysian law regards a 'cause of action' as 'a factual situation the existence of which entitles one person to obtain from the court a remedy against another person.'[69]

B. Domicile, Residence or Business

CJA 1964 section 23(1)(b) applies where the defendant or one of several defendants resides or has a place of business within the local jurisdiction of the court. Section 23(1)(b), particularly the words 'one of several defendants', has no direct English law equivalent.[70] ROC 2012 Order 11, rule 1(1)(C) applies if, in the action begun by the writ, relief is sought against a person domiciled or ordinarily resident or carrying on business within the jurisdiction. Although both provisions deal with concepts of 'residence' and 'business' (terms judicially acknowledged to be incapable of technical definition[71]), they may arguably be in conflict.[72] In dealing with domicile, residence and business, the Malaysian courts have drawn heavily on English authorities. Carrying on business under ROC 2012 Order 11, rule 1(1)(C) should not be confused with 'carrying on business' under the Companies Act 2016 (CA 2016) sections 561(2) and 561(3).[73]

C. Necessary or Proper Party

ROC 2012 Order 11, rule 1(1)(J) applies where a foreign defendant is a 'necessary or proper party' to the action. The writ must first have been served within the jurisdiction on an existing defendant. The overriding test is whether the foreign defendant would have been a proper party to the action, if both the plaintiff and the foreign defendant had been within the jurisdiction.[74] This is influenced by whether the cause of action is 'plausible' or 'genuine',[75] whether it would be incomplete without the foreign defendant,[76] and whether there may be a relationship of agency between an existing defendant and the desired foreign defendant.[77]

D. Law of Obligations

i. Contract

a. Jurisdiction

The High Court's jurisdiction in relation to contracts can arise under CJA 1964 section 23(1) and ROC 2012 Order 11, rules 1(1)(F) and 1(1)(G). Beginning with CJA 1964 section 23(1)(a),

[69] *Letang v Cooper* [1965] 1 QB 232 (EWCA) 242G–243A, cited with approval in, amongst others, *Government of Malaysia v Lim Kit Siang* [1988] 2 MLJ 12 (SC) 19G–I and *Tenaga Nasional Bhd v Kamarstone Sdn Bhd* [2014] 2 MLJ 749 (FC) [12].

[70] *Malayan Banking* (n 7) 288I.

[71] *TPC v Abu* [1983] 2 MLJ 79 (ACJ) 82C, citing *Re Bowie* (1880) 16 Ch D 484 (EWCA) 486–87.

[72] Hickling and Wu (n 1) 70–71.

[73] And that in its predecessor, the Companies Act 1965, ss 330(1), 330(2).

[74] *Bank Bumiputra* (n 19) 734F–I, citing *Massey v Heynes & Co* (1888) 21 QBD 330 (EWCA) 338 (Lord Esher MR).

[75] *Nam Fatt Corporation Bhd v Petrodar Operating Co Ltd* [2010] 9 CLJ 732 (HC) [53], affirmed first by the Court of Appeal in *Petrodar Operating Co Ltd v Nam Fatt Corp Bhd (in liq)* [2012] 5 MLJ 445 (CA) and further affirmed by the Federal Court in *Petrodar* (n 35); *Oliver Tim Axmann* (n 21) [22].

[76] *PT Gunung Madu Plantations v Muhammad Jimmy Goh Mashun* [2018] 3 MLJ 53 (CA) [13].

[77] *Sunkyong International Inc v Malaysian Rubber Development Corporation Bhd* [1992] 2 MLJ 146 (SC) 150D.

the cause of action in an action for breach of contract is deemed to occur where the breach took place.[78] ROC 2012 Order 11, rules 1(1)(F) and 1(1)(G) are more detailed. They give the High Court the discretion to allow service of a notice of a writ to be served out of the jurisdiction:

> (F) … to enforce, rescind, dissolve, annul or otherwise affect a contract, or to recover damages or obtain other relief in respect of the breach of a contract, being (in either case) a contract which –
>
> (i) was made within the jurisdiction;
> (ii) was made by or through an agent trading or residing within the jurisdiction on behalf of a principal trading or residing out of the jurisdiction; or
> (iii) is by its terms, or by implication, governed by the law of Malaysia;
>
> (G) … in respect of a breach committed within the jurisdiction of a contract made within or out of the jurisdiction, and irrespective of the fact, if such be the case, that the breach was preceded or accompanied by a breach committed out of the jurisdiction that rendered impossible the performance of so much of the contract as ought to have been performed within the jurisdiction …

b. Substantive Issues

If (as is likely) the English position is followed,[79] then presumably the Malaysian courts will give effect to express contractual provisions on choice of governing law in determining liability.[80] Where there is no express choice, Malaysian case law would appear scarce. A single-page judgment of the High Court in 1939 suggests that the outcome will turn on both the law of the place of contracting (*lex loci contractus*) and the law where the contract is to be performed (*lex loci solutionis*).[81] But the world of international commerce is much changed some 80 years on. Irrespective of the law applicable to liability, quantum is determined applying Malaysian law as the *lex fori*.[82]

ii. Tort

a. Jurisdiction

ROC 2012 Order 11, rule 1(1)(H) gives the High Court the discretion to allow service of a notice of a writ out of the jurisdiction for torts committed within the jurisdiction. Because the cause of action arises where a tort is committed, ROC 2012 Order 11, rule 1(1)(H) may practically be considered to be equivalent in substance to CJA 1964 section 23(1)(a). CJA 1964 section 23(1)(c) is marginally wider, in that only *some* facts must be within the local jurisdiction.

b. Substantive Issues

If jurisdiction is established under ROC 2012 Order 11, rule 1(1)(H) or CJA 1964 section 23(1)(a) on the basis that the tort was committed within the jurisdiction, liability falls straightforwardly to be determined by Malaysian law alone. If, however, jurisdiction is established solely through CJA 1964 section 23(1)(b) (that is, at least one co-defendant resides in Malaysia) and the tort has

[78] *Malacca Securities Sdn Bhd v Loke Yu* [1999] 6 MLJ 112 (HC) 127A–D.
[79] Civil Law Act 1956, ss 3, 5.
[80] *Vita Food Products Inc v Unus Shipping Co Ltd* [1939] AC 277 (UKPC) 290.
[81] *Otamchand Kanji v Yassin bin Said* [1940] 1 MLJ 42 (HC) 43.
[82] *Scandinavian Bunkering (Singapore) Pte Ltd v MISC Bhd* [2015] 3 MLJ 753 (FC) [37].

been committed outside the jurisdiction, then the tort must be actionable both under the law of the country where committed (*lex loci delicti*) and under Malaysian law had it been committed in Malaysia (*lex fori*).[83]

iii. Unjust Enrichment

There are no provisions specifically on cross-border unjust enrichment. The submission has been made before the High Court that an alleged instance of unjust enrichment took place outside the jurisdiction,[84] so as to render that other place the *forum conveniens*. However, despite implicitly finding that the alleged tort took place within the jurisdiction, the Court did not (and perhaps did not have to) discuss jurisdiction in detail.

E. Trusts and Charitable Foundations

Different laws apply depending on whether a trust or charitable foundation is for the benefit of Muslims or for some other benefit.

i. Other Benefit

Under ROC 2012 Order 11, rule 1(1)(E), the decisive consideration is whether at least part of the property that is the subject of the trust or charity is situated within the jurisdiction, even if the trust is to be executed and administered outside the jurisdiction.[85] Apart from this rule, any question of jurisdiction would presumably fall to be determined according to other jurisdictional provisions of more general scope.[86]

ii. Benefit of Muslims

The Islamic law relating to non-charitable trusts, *wakaf*, charitable and religious trusts, the appointment of trustees and the incorporation of persons in respect of Islamic religious and charitable endowments, institutions, trusts, charities and charitable institutions operating wholly within a state, other than in the Federal Territories of Kuala Lumpur, Putrajaya and Labuan, is within the exclusive remit of state legislatures, rather than the Parliament.[87] It is unclear on what jurisdictional basis, if at all, a state's Syariah High Court could adjudicate over property in another state, or even outside Malaysia, especially as regards immovable property.

[83] *Attorney General of Hong Kong v Zauyah Wan Chik* [1995] 2 MLJ 620 (CA) 633E, 635I; *Jupiters Ltd v Lim Kin Tong* [2006] 5 CLJ 277 (HC) [32]–[36]; *Scandinavian Bunkering (Singapore) Pte Ltd v MISC Bhd* [2012] 4 MLJ 105 (HC) [22]; *Scandinavian Bunkering (Singapore) Pte Ltd v MISC Bhd* (n 82) (FC) [36]; TAG Beazley, 'Jurisdiction and Choice of Law in Tort Conflicts: Chan Kwon Fong & Anor. v. Chan Wah' (1977) 19 *Malaya Law Review* 391, 391, 394–400; Hickling and Wu (n 1) 183–84.

[84] *Yong Songhua v Basic Venture International Ltd* [2017] 8 MLJ 681 (HC) [9].

[85] *Re Valibhoy, decd* [1961] 1 MLJ 187 (HC) 190D–F.

[86] CJA 1964, s 23(1); ROC 2012, Ord 11, rr 1(1)(I), 1(1)(J).

[87] Federal Constitution, Ninth Schedule, List II, Item 1.

F. Law of Property

In general, immovable property is governed by the *lex situs*, and movable property by the *lex domicilii* of its proprietor.[88]

i. Immovable Property

Under CJA 1964 section 23(1)(d), the High Court has jurisdiction to try all civil proceedings where any land the ownership of which is disputed is situated within the local jurisdiction of the Court. ROC 2012 Order 11, rules 1(1)(A) and 1(1)(B) grant the High Court the discretion to allow service of a writ out of the jurisdiction:

> (A) if the whole subject matter of the action begun by the writ is immovable property situated within the jurisdiction (with or without rents or profits), or the perpetuation of testimony relating to immovable property so situated;
>
> (B) if an act, deed, will, contract, obligation or liability affecting immovable property situated within the jurisdiction is sought to be construed, rectified, set aside or enforced in the action begun by the writ …

The decisive factor, once again, is whether there is immovable property situated within the jurisdiction, even if the trust or contract, for example, is to be executed and administered abroad.[89] One exception is the High Court's power under the Probate and Administration Act 1959 (PAA 1959), discussed below. To be precise, the land itself must be affected. It seems slander of title and recovery of rent would not suffice,[90] whereas enforcement of a covenant to repair would.[91]

ii. Movable Property

ROC 2012 Order 11, rule 1(1)(K) grants the High Court the discretion to allow service of a writ out of the jurisdiction:

> (K) if the action begun by the writ is either by a charge of property situated within the jurisdiction, other than immovable property, and seeks the sale of the property, the foreclosure of the charge or delivery by the chargor of possession of the property but not an order for payment of any moneys due under the charge or by a chargor of property so situated, other than immovable property, and seeks redemption of the charge, reconveyance of the property or delivery by the chargee of possession of the property but not a personal judgment …

iii. Intangible Property

In a wider context, the Malaysian courts have recognised 'intangible property' to include intellectual property rights (which are considered below), confidential information, bank accounts

[88] *In Re Abdul Salam, decd* [1938] 1 MLJ 83 (HC) 85.

[89] *Re Valibhoy* (n 85) 190D–F. See also *British South Africa Co v Companhia de Moçambique* [1893] AC 602 (UKHL) 625, restated in *Hesperides Hotels Ltd v Muftizade* [1979] AC 508 (UKHL) 534B and approved in *Sun Holding (Sun Park Hotel) Co Ltd v Export-Import Bank of Malaysia Bhd* [2016] 1 MLJ 115 (CA) [48].

[90] *Casey v Arnott* (1876) 2 CPD 24 (EWDC) 25; *Agnew v Usher* (1884) 14 QBD 78 (EWDC) 80 (obiter), cited with approval in *The National Union of Plantation Workers v K Annamalai* [1959] 1 MLJ 9 (CA) 13D (obiter).

[91] *Tassell v Hallen* [1892] 1 QB 321 (EWCA) 323, cited with approval in *Annamalai* (n 90) 13I–A.

and choses in action.[92] However, other than in relation to intellectual property, there appear to be no reported judgments on jurisdictional issues affecting intangible property.

G. Succession to Property

As with several areas involving elements of personal law, the law surrounding succession to property differs depending on whether it concerns non-Muslims or Muslims, Peninsular Malaysia or Sabah and Sarawak, or natives of Sabah and Sarawak. Under the Federal Constitution, 'probate and letters of administration' are a matter solely for Federal legislation and for the secular civil courts, regardless of location or religion.[93] However, 'succession' and 'testate and intestate' for Muslims is the preserve of state legislatures, and for natives in Sabah and Sarawak of the state legislatures there.[94] The law exclusively for Muslims does not seem extensively developed as regards questions of jurisdiction and conflict of laws.[95] In East Malaysia, similar remarks might be made, for example, on the Administration of Estates Ordinance (Sarawak) 1933. The focus here is thus on the position of non-Muslims in Peninsular Malaysia.

i. Wills

The wills of non-Muslims in Peninsular Malaysia are governed primarily by the Wills Act 1959, as well as by the PAA 1959.[96] By the Wills Act section 27, Malaysian law will recognise a will if it has been executed in the manner required by the law of any one of up to four countries:

> 27. A will executed outside Malaysia in the manner required by –
> (a) this Act;
> (b) the law of the place where it was executed;
> (c) the law of the testator's domicile at the time of its execution; or
> (d) the law of the testator's domicile at the time of his death,
> shall be deemed to be will executed for the purpose of being admitted to probate in Malaysia, provided that such will is in writing or is a privileged will made under section 26.[97]

Section 29 provides that a subsequent change of domicile will not invalidate an otherwise valid will. Specifically for Malaysian citizens,[98] section 28 provides that a will executed in Malaysia, regardless of the testator's domicile, will be effective in respect of property in Malaysia, whether immovable or movable, so long as executed in accordance with the Act.

[92] *Tengku Abdullah Ibni Sultan Abu Bakar v Mohd Latiff Bin Shah Mohd* [1996] 2 MLJ 265 (CA) 297B; *Yukilon Manufacturing Sdn Bhd v Dato Wong Gek Meng (No 4)* [1998] 7 MLJ 551 (HC) 573B; *Mesuma Sports Sdn Bhd v Majlis Sukan Negara* [2015] 2 MLJ 176 (CA) [16].

[93] Federal Constitution, Ninth Schedule, List I, Item 4(e)(i); *In the Estate of Tunku Abdul Rahman Putra Ibni Almarhum Sultan Abdul Hamid* [1998] 4 MLJ 623 (HC) 626D–F; *Jumaaton v Raja Hizaruddin* [1998] 6 MLJ 556 (Syariah HC, Kuala Lumpur) 563.

[94] Federal Constitution, Ninth Schedule, List II, Item 1; List IIA, Item 13. See also Civil Law Act, s 25.

[95] For example, the Muslim Wills (Selangor) Enactment is expressly in its application to only 'the State of Selangor' and 'person [sic] professing the religion of Islam' (s 1(2)). Otherwise, there is no mention of what is to happen to the estate of a Muslim of Selangor that includes property situated outside Selangor. Although s 28(2) provides that '[i]n the event of a lacuna or in the absence of any matter not expressly provided for by his Enactment, the Court shall apply Islamic Law', 'Islamic Law' is defined merely as 'the Islamic laws in any of the lawful sects' (s 2(1), referring to the Selangor Administration of Islamic Law Enactment 1989, which reference appears to remain despite the repeal of 1989 Enactment).

[96] Wills Act 1959, ss 1(2), 2(2).

[97] Wills Act 1959, s 26 allows certain members of the Malaysian armed forces to make certain dispositions or exercise a power of appointment exercisable by will by a privileged will.

[98] Interpretation Acts 1948 and 1967, s 3.

ii. Probate and Letters of Administration

Probate and letters of administration for Peninsular Malaysia, regardless of religion, are governed by the PAA 1959[99] and within the jurisdiction of the secular civil courts. Accordingly, CJA 1964 section 24(f) gives the High Court jurisdiction:

> … to grant probates of wills and testaments and letters of administration of the estates of deceased persons leaving property within the territorial jurisdiction of the Court and to alter or revoke such grants.

By PAA 1959 section 27, probate or letters of administration of a will proved and deposited in a foreign court may be granted where a properly authenticated copy of the will is produced. PAA 1959 section 52 gives the High Court the power to reseal probate or letters of administration granted by a 'Court of Probate in any part of the Commonwealth' where the deceased was domiciled there upon death,[100] but only in respect of Peninsular Malaysia.[101] Where a deceased has died domiciled outside Malaysia, an application may be made under ROC 2012 Order 71, rule 25 to a Registrar of the High Court for a grant of probate or letters of administration to the person entrusted or entitled to administer the estate by the courts or the law of the foreign domicile. No application is needed where the executor is named or sufficiently described in an admissible will in the English language, and/or,[102] to the extent that the estate in Malaysia consists of immovable property, the person seeking the grant would have been entitled had the deceased died domiciled in Malaysia.[103] On service out of the jurisdiction, ROC 2012 Order 72, rule 3 incorporates ROC 2012 Order 11, rules 3 and 4. ROC 2012 Order 11, rule 1(1)(D) also gives the High Court the discretion to permit service out of the jurisdiction of a writ for the administration of the estate of a person who died domiciled in Malaysia. There appear to be no reported judgments on either provision or their equivalents, in Malaysia and across the Commonwealth, save for one by the Court of Appeal of Guyana.[104]

iii. Intestacy

Distribution of the intestate estates of non-Muslims in Peninsular Malaysia is governed by the Distribution Act 1958 (DA 1958) and the PAA 1959.[105] On conflict of laws, movable property is regulated by the *lex domicilii* upon death, and immovable property by the *lex situs.*[106] PAA 1959 sections 52, 53 and 63 (amongst others) apply also in the case of intestacy, regardless of a deceased's religion.

H. Intellectual Property

Intellectual property in Malaysia is governed by a mixture of legislation and common law. If causes of action such as trademark infringement and passing off, or the facts which found them,

[99] PAA 1959, s 1(1); Federal Constitution, Ninth Schedule, List I, Item 4(e)(i); *In the Estate of Tunku Abdul Rahman* (n 93) 626D–F; *Jumaaton v Raja Hizaruddin* (n 93) 563.
[100] See also PAA 1959, Parts IV and V more generally.
[101] ibid, s 1(1).
[102] ROC 2012, Ord 71, rr 25(A) and 25(B) are not explicit on whether they are cumulative or disjunctive.
[103] ROC 2012, Ord 71, rr 25(A), 25(B).
[104] *Nazreen Rahaman Hanoman v Kathleen Hanomon* (1971) 18 WIR 34 (CA, Guyana).
[105] Distribution Act 1958, s 1(2), 2; PAA 1959, s 1(1).
[106] Distribution Act, s 4; *Re Berchtold* [1923] 1 Ch 192 (Ch) 199; *Re Ex Parte Application of Ridzwan Ibrahim (Presumption of Death)* [2002] 4 CLJ 502 (HC) 506E.

are alleged to have occurred within the jurisdiction, that will suffice to confer jurisdiction on the High Court under CJA 1964 section 23(1)(a) or (b).[107] In an action under the previous Trade Marks Act 1976 (TMA 1976),[108] service on a foreign defendant through its Malaysian address appearing on the Register was held to be effective.[109] The ROC 2012 do not apply where some other written law (such as the TMA 1976) specifically applies.[110] It remains to be seen whether this will remain under the new Trademarks Act 2019.

I. Family Law

Because of Malaysia's diverse cultural, ethnic, religious and even geographical heritage, there are several sources of family law in Malaysia.[111] Different rules apply depending on religion, ethnicity, and geography.[112] The Islamic family laws of each state are not uniform.[113] For brevity, and because judicial pronouncements on issues of direct jurisdiction (that is, with some foreign element) in family law have historically come predominantly in relation to non-Muslims, this section will primarily discuss such issues as they relate to non-Muslims or natives.[114] Nevertheless, readers should bear in mind that the majority of the Malaysian population is Muslim, and that constitutionally, 'Islam is the religion of the Federation'.[115] The discussion which follows accordingly applies only to a minority of the population. Amongst Muslims (or rather, as between Muslims and non-Muslims), the jurisdictional conundrum is more often whether civil (secular) law or (state) Islamic or 'Syariah' law applies.[116] That tension is not discussed here.

i. Marriage

Non-Muslim marriage is governed by the Law Reform (Marriage and Divorce) Act 1976 (LRMDA 1976). Loosely, the LRMDA 1976 will recognise a 'foreign' marriage in four scenarios: (1) marriages contracted abroad from 1 March 1982; (2) marriages in foreign embassies in Malaysia from 1 March 1982; (3) marriages solemnised in Malaysian embassies abroad; and (4) marriages solemnised under any law, religion, custom or usage prior to 1 March 1982. (1) and (2) are addressed together, followed by (3) and (4) in turn.

[107] *Goodness for Import and Export* (n 35) [33].

[108] Now the Trademarks Act 2019.

[109] *Louis Vuitton Malletier v Renown Incorporated* [2017] 9 MLJ 281 (HC) [15]–[19].

[110] ROC 2012, Ord 1, r 2(2); Ord 62, r 4(2).

[111] Rita Reddy, 'Marriage and Divorce Regulation and Recognition in Malaysia' (1995) 29 *Family Law Quarterly* 613, 613.

[112] Federal Constitution, Ninth Schedule. See eg Guardianship of Infants Act 1961, s 1(2); Law Reform (Marriage and Divorce) Act 1976, ss 3(1), 3(4); Islamic Family Law (Federal Territories) Act 1984.

[113] Reddy (n 111) 619; Maznah Mohamad, 'The Islamic Divorce Contract and a Flawed Axiom of Masculine Protectionism' (2011) 39 *Asian Journal of Social Science* 821, 828.

[114] As an example of a case involving only Muslims, see *Muhammad Faizz Amin bin Roslee v Maidatul Sarah bt Mior Rosli* [2013] 2 SHLR 98 (Shariah Subordinate Court, Terengganu).

[115] Federal Constitution, Art 3(1). Art 11(1) also guarantees the right to freedom of religion with certain qualifications.

[116] For example, *Indira Gandhi a/p Mutho v Pengarah Jabatan Agama Islam Perak* [2018] 1 MLJ 545 (FC), a long-running case in which the courts grappled with the controversial issue of unilateral conversion by one spouse of a child to Islam. For a detailed discussion of that question, see Tamir Moustafa, 'Liberal Rights versus Islamic Law? The Construction of a Binary in Malaysian Politics' (2013) 47 *Law & Society Review* 771.

a. Marriages Contracted Abroad or In Embassies in Malaysia

Marriages contracted abroad from 1 March 1982 can be recognised under LRMDA 1976 section 104:

> 104. A marriage contracted outside Malaysia other than a marriage solemnized in a Malaysian Embassy, High Commission or Consulate under section 26, shall be recognised as valid for all purposes of the law of Malaysia if –
>
> *(a)* it was contracted in a form required or permitted by the law of the country where it was contracted;
>
> *(b)* each of the parties had, at the time of the marriage, capacity to marry under the law of the country of his or her domicile; and
>
> *(c)* where either of the parties is a citizen of or is domiciled in Malaysia, both parties had capacity to marry according to this Act.

Section 105 on marriages in foreign embassies is similar.

b. Marriages Solemnised in Malaysian Embassies Abroad

By LRMDA 1976 sections 26(1) and 28(4), a marriage involving at least one Malaysian citizen may be solemnised in a Malaysian Embassy, High Commission, or Consulate in any country which has not objected to such solemnisation to the Malaysian Government. Provided that the requirements of capacity and formal validity under each party's *lex domicilii* are fulfilled, these marriages are deemed to be solemnised in Malaysia.[117]

c. Marriages Solemnised under any Law, Religion, Custom or Usage Prior to 1 March 1982

This last category is governed by LRMDA 1976 sections 4(1) and 4(2):

> 4. (1) Nothing in this Act shall affect the validity of any marriage solemnized under any law, religion, custom or usage prior to the appointed date.
>
> (2) Such marriage, if valid under the law, religion, custom or usage under which it was solemnized, shall be deemed to be registered under this Act.

Section 4(1) preserves the validity of marriages validly solemnised *prior to* 1 March 1982 under, for instance, Chinese or Hindu custom, subject to adequate proof if their validity is questioned before the courts.[118] Section 4(2) deems such marriages to be registered under the LRMDA 1976 without the need for formal registration.[119]

ii. Nullity, Divorce and Separation

a. Nullity

For a declaration of nullity under the LRMDA 1976 to be granted, both parties must reside in Malaysia when the proceedings are commenced. In addition, the marriage must have been registered (or deemed to be registered) under the LRMDA 1976 or contracted under a law which

[117] LRMDA 1976, s 26(3).

[118] *Kausalya a/p M Pathmanathan v Jamuna a/p Narayanan, decd* [2014] 2 MLJ 836 (CA) [32]–[36]; *Tan Siew Sen v Nick Abu Dusuki bin Hj Abu Hassan* [2016] 4 MLJ 602 (CA) [14]–[15].

[119] This has been criticised as introducing an inconsistency: Balwant Singh Sidhu, 'Married or Not Married? – That Is the Question' [2002] 3 *Malayan Law Journal* cxxix.

observes monogamy.[120] Sections 69 and 70 stipulate the grounds on which a marriage on or after 1 March 1982 may be decreed void or voidable respectively. Of relevance to direct jurisdiction, section 72 provides that:

> 72. Where, apart from this Act, any matter affecting the validity of a marriage would fall to be determined (in accordance with the rules of Private International Law) by reference to the law of a country outside Malaysia neither section 69 nor section 70 shall –
>
> *(a)* preclude the determination of that matter as aforesaid; or
>
> *(b)* require the application to the marriage of the grounds there mentioned except so far as applicable in accordance with those rules.

b. Divorce

The LRMDA 1976 is the principal statute on non-Muslim divorce in Malaysia. Peculiarly to Part VI of LRMDA 1976 which governs divorce between non-Muslims in Malaysia, section 47 expressly retains English principles of divorce law. Two routes to divorce under LRMDA 1976 require consideration of domicile. Under the first, section 48(1), both parties must be domiciled in Malaysia when the divorce petition is presented. As such, no divorce proceedings may be brought in Malaysia in respect of a marriage contracted abroad in accordance with section 104, unless the marriage is registered or deemed registered. Under the second, section 49(1), only the wife must be and have been ordinarily resident in Malaysia for two years immediately before the proceedings, if the husband has deserted the wife or been deported and was immediately before then domiciled in Malaysia.

c. Separation

The minimum requirements for a decree of judicial separation under the LRMDA 1976 are set out in section 48(2). They are the same as those for divorce under section 48(1), save that the requirement of domicile is instead one of residence. The same additional exception under section 49(1), discussed above, applies also to judicial separation.

d. Recognition of Foreign Decrees

The LRMDA 1976 does not expressly provide for recognition of foreign decrees. Nevertheless, because of the importation of English principles by section 47, the English Family Law Act 1986, English common law, or some combination of them would likely apply *mutatis mutandis*.[121]

e. Matters Relating to the Wellbeing of the Child

Previously, the Civil Law Act 1956 section 27 expressly imported English legal principles into the adjudication of cases relating to the custody and control of infants. Subsequently, the GIA 1961 was enacted with application to non-Muslims in Peninsular Malaysia.[122] As the GIA 1961 has merely 'augmented' the inherent jurisdiction of the High Court,[123] it has been suggested

[120] LRMDA 1976, s 67.
[121] Hickling and Wu (n 1) 130–37.
[122] Guardianship of Infants Act 1961, ss 1(2), 1(3).
[123] *W v H* [1987] 2 MLJ 235 (HC) 237.

that the High Court still retains its general original jurisdiction under CJA 1964 section 24(d) to appoint and control guardians of infants and generally over the person and property of infants.[124] Foreign judgments relating to child custody will be considered but are not binding, for the welfare of the child is paramount, both under the common law[125] and GIA 1961 section 11. The Malaysian courts will normally be reluctant to allow children to be removed to another jurisdiction (perhaps because enforcement abroad of court orders issued domestically would become complicated)[126] but have done so before.[127] At the time of writing, Malaysia remains a non-signatory to the 1980 Hague Child Abduction Convention.[128] The Child Act 2001 section 52 makes it an offence for a parent or guardian without lawful custody to take a child without the consent of the person who does have lawful custody. Nevertheless, acceding to the 1980 Convention would bring Malaysia in step with other developed countries.[129]

J. Law of Corporations and Insolvency

Historically, under the former Malayan Union Companies Ordinance 1946 Part XIII, a winding up order made in Malaysia had effect in Singapore and vice versa, without the need for separate formal winding-up proceedings.[130] Today, unlike the Bankruptcy Act 1967 (BA 1967) (on which see below), the CA 2016[131] has not retained this reciprocity.[132] Neither has Malaysia adopted the UNCITRAL Model Law on Cross-Border Insolvency.[133] Instead, CJA 1964 section 24(c) confers on the High Court 'jurisdiction under any written law relating to bankruptcy or to companies'. In turn, CA 2016 section 545 (read with section 544) allows a 'foreign company'[134] to be wound up in four specified circumstances with certain modifications to the usual procedure.[135] Otherwise, the standard winding-up procedure applies.[136] Section 545(1)(c) imposes stricter criteria for the winding up of a foreign company, compared to section 465(1) for domestic winding up. More methods of service of the required notice of demand on a foreign company are allowed, including on that company's principal place of business in Malaysia.[137] Members have more exposure

[124] Hickling and Wu (n 1) 151–52.

[125] *Mahabir Prasad v Mahabir Prasad* [1981] 2 MLJ 326 (FC) 326H–327C (emphasis added). See also *Mahabir Prasad v Mahabir Prasad* [1982] 1 MLJ 189 (FC).

[126] Wai Kum Wang, 'Custody – Welfare of Infants: Teh Eng Kim v. Yew Peng Siong' (1977) 19 *Malaya Law Review* 388, 389.

[127] *Teh Eng Kim v Yew Peng Siong* [1977] 1 MLJ 234 (FC) 236G (Arulanandom J) in the High Court, whose judgment the Federal Court affirmed.

[128] The 1980 Hague Convention on the Civil Aspects of International Child Abduction.

[129] Hickling and Wu (n 1) 161; Min Aun Wu, 'Guardianship, Custody and Abduction of Children Across National Boundaries' [1995] 1 *Malayan Law Journal* i, xix–xx. For an in-depth discussion of how the Convention might fit into the Malaysian context, see *In the Marriage of Y and K Raja Bahrin* (1986) 11 Fam LR 233 (Fam Aus); Abdul Ghafur Hamid and Zaleha Kamaruddin, 'International Parental Child Abduction in the Malaysian Legal Context: Addressing Issues and the Way Forward' (2018) 26(2) *IIUM Law Journal* 275; Yiswaree Palansamy, 'Indira Gandhi Says Suing IGP for RM100m over Failure to Retrieve Daughter, to Launch Justice Trek' *Malay Mail* (Kuala Lumpur, 27 October 2020), available online: www.malaymail.com/news/malaysia/2020/10/27/indira-gandhi-says-suing-igp-for-rm100m-over-failure-to-retrieve-daughter-t/1916671.

[130] *Tong Aik (Far East) Ltd v Eastern Minerals & Trading (1959) Ltd* [1965] 2 MLJ 149 (FC) 150D–F.

[131] Like its predecessor, Companies Act 1965.

[132] Paul J Omar, 'Cross-Border Jurisdiction and Assistance in Insolvency: The Position in Malaysia and Singapore' (2008) 11(1) *Potchefstroom Electronic Law Journal* 39.

[133] 1997 UNCITRAL Model Law on Cross-Border Insolvency.

[134] Defined in Companies Act 2016, s 2(1).

[135] ibid, s 545(1)(c).

[136] ibid, s 543.

[137] ibid, s 545(2)(a); cf ibid, s 466(1)(a).

where they owe debts *qua* member.[138] It appears that the High Court will not be required to consider contingent and prospective liabilities in evaluating inability to pay debts.[139] Because the Companies (Winding-Up) Rules 1972 (Winding-Up Rules 1972) regulate the procedure for winding up, the parallel provisions in the ROC 2012 do not apply except where the Winding-Up Rules 1972 are silent.[140]

K. Law of Bankruptcy

As with corporate insolvency, the High Court's 'subject matter' jurisdiction in bankruptcy matters flows in the first place from CJA 1964 section 24(c).[141] The precise extent of that jurisdiction is in turn governed exclusively by the Insolvency Act 1967 (IA 1967)[142] and the Insolvency Rules 2017 (IR 2017).[143]

i. Territorial Aspects of Bankruptcy Jurisdiction

The IA 1967 contains numerous provisions which territorially shape the High Court's bankruptcy jurisdiction. Very broadly, the common thread is that the debtor must in some way have been present or carrying on business in Malaysia, at or close enough to the time of the act of bankruptcy. A clearer idea may be obtained by considering three non-exhaustive examples. First, one of the mandatory conditions for a creditor to present a bankruptcy petition under IA 1967 section 5(1) is that:

> ... the debtor is domiciled in Malaysia or in any State or within one year before the date of the presentation of the petition has ordinarily resided or had a dwelling house or place of business in Malaysia or has carried on business in Malaysia personally or by means of an agent or is or has been within the same period a member of a firm or partnership which has carried on business in Malaysia by means of a partner or partners or an agent or manager.[144]

As a second example, a bankruptcy petition may be presented only by or against a 'debtor',[145] which includes any person who, at the time of the act of bankruptcy, was personally present, ordinarily resided or had a place of residence, was carrying on business either personally or through an agent, or was a member of a firm or partnership which carried on business[146] in Malaysia when the act of bankruptcy took place.[147] Third, under IR 2017 rule 112, where a debtor is not in Malaysia, the High Court has a discretion to order 'service' (not merely substituted service) to be made within such time and in such manner and form as it thinks fit. It is mandatory to invoke this rule where a debtor is out of the jurisdiction.[148]

[138] ibid, ss 545(2)(b), 545(2)(c); cf ibid, s 466(1)(a).
[139] ibid, s 466(1)(c), which expressly requires this for 'standard' winding up; cf ibid, s 545(2)(d).
[140] *Fairview Schools Bhd v Indrani a/p Rajaratnam (No 1)* [1998] 1 MLJ 99 (CA) 106H–I; *Gabung Trading* (n 16) [18]–[19].
[141] *Malaysia Building Society Bhd v Tan Sri General Ungku Nazaruddin bin Ungku Mohamed* [1998] 2 MLJ 425 (CA) 432C.
[142] Formerly the Bankruptcy Act 1967.
[143] *Malaysia Building Society* (n 141) 432I.
[144] Insolvency Act 1967, s 5(1)(d); 'State' means a State of Malaysia: see Interpretation Acts 1948 and 1967 (IA 1948 and 1967), s 3.
[145] IA 1948 and 1967, ss 5(1), 7.
[146] ibid, s 3(3).
[147] *Re Leong Nyuk Weng, ex p Public Bank Bhd* [2003] 4 CLJ 260 (HC) 265F–H.
[148] *Re Peh Kong Wan, ex p United Malayan Banking Corp Bhd* [1992] 2 MLJ 292 (HC) 295H–I.

ii. Impact of Foreign Bankruptcy Proceedings

a. Acting in Aid of and Being Auxiliary to Singaporean Proceedings

IA 1967 section 104 (unlike the CA 2016) contains '[r]eciprocal provisions relating to Singapore and designated countries'. At the date of publication, the designated countries are the UK and Australia.[149] The High Court of Malaysia is required, in all matters of bankruptcy and insolvency, to 'act in aid of and be auxiliary' to the courts of those countries, so long as such treatment remains reciprocal.[150] Malaysian case law on what exactly that means is sparse, perhaps because section 104 is not widely known.[151] Section 104(3) and 104(4) in fact contemplate even greater reciprocity between Malaysia and Singapore, but the Yang di-Pertuan Agong[152] has yet to gazette any notification to that effect.[153]

b. Annulment of Bankruptcy Order

IA 1967 section 105(1) gives the High Court a discretion to annul a Malaysian bankruptcy order in certain disjunctive cases. One of these is where proceedings are pending in Singapore for the distribution of the bankrupt's estate, and the distribution 'ought to take place' there. In brief, annulment validates all sales, dispositions and payments duly made pursuant to the Malaysian bankruptcy order before annulment.[154] Property remaining vests in the person appointed by the High Court or the debtor himself.

iii. Impact of Malaysian Bankruptcy Proceedings on Assets Overseas

Consistent with the reciprocal nature of the provisions in Malaysia's IA 1967 detailed above, Singapore's Insolvency, Restructuring and Dissolution Act 2018 (SIRDA 2018) contains several provisions referring to Malaysian bankruptcy proceedings, which mirror their counterparts in the Malaysian IA 1967.

L. Competition Law

The principal piece of legislation on competition in Malaysia is the relatively recent Competition Act 2010. The main agency is the Malaysian Competition Commission (MyCC),[155] which is empowered inter alia to make findings of infringement.[156] Appeals from findings by the MyCC are exclusively to the Competition Appeal Tribunal (CAT).[157] Directions or decisions of the MyCC or the CAT may be enforced through the High Court.[158]

[149] PU(B) 2/1989.
[150] IA 1948 and 1967, s 104.
[151] Omar (n 132) 37.
[152] The Supreme Head of the Federation of Malaysia: see Federal Constitution, Art 32(1).
[153] *The Official Assignee of the Property of Tan Check Soon @ Soon Tan, A Bankrupt Under the Law of The Republic of Singapore v Yip Siew Han* [2001] 1 LNS 244 (HC); *Paksi Omega Sdn Bhd v Ku Sang @ Khoo Ah Too & Yang Lain* [2016] 1 LNS 1002 (HC) [36]–[38].
[154] IA 1948 and 1967, s 105(2).
[155] Established under the Competition Commission Act 2010.
[156] Competition Act 2010, ss 39, 40.
[157] ibid, ss 44, 51.
[158] ibid, ss 42, 59.

The Competition Act 2010 is stated to apply 'to any commercial activity transacted outside Malaysia which has an effect on competition in any market in Malaysia'.[159] The basis of this purported extraterritorial jurisdiction is unclear, for Malaysia is not a party to any binding agreement for cross-border enforcement.[160]

M. Carriage by Air

ROC 2012 Order 11, rule 1(1)(L) gives the High Court the discretion to allow service of a notice of a writ to be served out of the jurisdiction where the action is brought under any written law relating to carriage by air.

N. Arbitral Awards

Arbitration in Malaysia is governed by the Arbitration Act 2005 (AA 2005). ROC 2012 Order 11, rule 1(1)(M) gives the High Court the discretion to allow service of a notice of a writ to be served out of the jurisdiction for enforcement of, or challenges to, an arbitral award. Malaysia is a signatory to the New York Convention,[161] the relevant provisions of which have been codified in the AA 2005 section 38. Under ROC 2012 Order 69, rule 12(1), the High Court has the discretion to permit the service of an arbitration claim *originating summons* out of the jurisdiction where it involves a question of law arising out of an award made within the jurisdiction, or a question affecting an arbitration agreement, irrespective of status or seat of arbitration.

IV. Jurisdiction *in rem* with Special Focus on Shipping Claims

In Malaysia, the High Court's civil jurisdiction over admiralty claims flows from CJA 1964 section 24(b), which gives the High Court 'the same jurisdiction and authority in relation to matters of admiralty as is had by the High Court of Justice in England under the United Kingdom Supreme Court Act 1981'. Before it was amended in 1987, section 24(b) imported in 'sweeping' terms the jurisdiction and authority 'for the time being exercisable by the High Court of Justice in England'.[162] Those words were replaced by the current reference to the UK's Supreme Court Act 1981, now the Senior Courts Act 1981 (SCA 1981), when Malaysia's Courts of Judicature (Amendment) Act 1987 came into force.[163] Section 24(b) imports only SCA 1981 sections 20–24.

[159] ibid, ss 3(1), 3(2).

[160] cf Memorandum of Understanding on Implementation of Competition Law between the Competition and Consumer Commission of Singapore (CCCS) of the Republic of Singapore and the Commission for the Supervision of Business Competition (KPPU) of the Republic of Indonesia 2018, para 7.

[161] The 1958 United Nations Convention on the Recognition and Enforcement of Foreign Arbitral Awards (or the New York Convention); AA 2005, s 38; ROC 2012, Ord 69, rr 8, 9.

[162] *Asia Pacific Parcel Tankers Pte Ltd v The Owners of the Ship or Vessel 'Normar Splendour'* [1999] 6 MLJ 652 (HC) 692D.

[163] Courts of Judicature (Amendment) Act 1987, s 2. The continued wholesale adoption of another country's legislation has been criticised: Sitpah Selvaratnam, 'Maritime Reform: Arrest for Arbitration' (*Tommy Thomas*, 18 November 2005) paras 15, 33, available online: www.tommythomas.net/upload/staticpage/download/Maritime%20Reform%20-%20Arrest%20for%20Arbitration.pdf; Sitpah Selvaratnam, 'The Right of Arrest – Are We Making It Too Difficult ? A Common Law Perspective' (*Asian International Arbitration Centre*, 14 July 2017), available online: www.aiac.world/news/209/Sitpah-Selvaratnam:-The-Right-of-Arrest-%E2%80%93-Are-we-making-it-too-difficult-?-A-Common-Law-Perspective.

It does not import other English statutes even if related to Admiralty.[164] The paragraphs below highlight the features of Admiralty jurisdiction *in rem* distinctive to Malaysian law. The English position, on which existing literature abounds,[165] will be set out only insofar as it is central to this objective.

A. Jurisdiction *in rem* of the Courts within the Territory

For the purposes of the CJA 1964 section 23(1), Malaysia has two High Courts: the High Court of Malaya and the High Court of Sabah and Sarawak.[166] No territorial distinction applies to the High Court's Admiralty jurisdiction under CJA 1964 section 24(b).[167] Similarly, foreign elements do not deprive the High Court of its Admiralty jurisdiction *in rem*,[168] so long as the writ is served on the *res* within the jurisdiction.[169]

B. Types of Admiralty Actions *in rem*

The situations in which CJA 1964 section 24(b) permits the High Court's Admiralty jurisdiction *in rem* to be invoked can be compartmentalised into four categories.[170]

i. 'Proprietary' Maritime Claims under SCA 1981 Section 21(2)

This applies as it does under English law. Consideration of the owner of the *res* at the time the writ *in rem* is issued, or of who would be liable in an action *in personam*, is not necessary.[171]

ii. Maritime Liens under SCA 1981 Section 21(3)

Where there is a maritime lien or other charge on any ship, aircraft or other property for the amount claimed, an action *in rem* may be brought against that ship, aircraft or property. The attachment of a maritime lien to a ship cannot give rise to an action *in rem* against cargo laden on board that ship.[172] The Malaysian courts have adopted the classic definition of a maritime lien laid down by the Privy Council in *The Bold Buccleugh*.[173] The classes of maritime liens Malaysian

[164] *Normar Splendour* (n 162) 692F–693C.
[165] See eg Sarah C Derrington and James M Turner, *The Law and Practice of Admiralty Matters* (Oxford, Oxford University Press, 2007).
[166] CJA 1964, s 3; *Syarikat Nip Kui Cheong Timber Contractor v Safety Life and General Insurance Co Sdn Bhd* [1975] 2 MLJ 115 (OCJ) 116 (Hashim Yeop A Sani J).
[167] *Nassau Maritime Holdings Designated Activity Co v The Owners of the Ship or Vessel 'Cape Lambert' of the Port of Marshall Islands* [2020] 11 MLJ 561 (HC) [28]–[34].
[168] Senior Courts Act 1981, s 20(7); *Cape Lambert* (n 167) [14].
[169] ROC 2012, Ord 70, r 3(3).
[170] Derrington and Turner (n 165) paras 2.10–2.14.
[171] *Cape Lambert* (n 167) [13].
[172] *Tamina Navigation Ltd v The Owner of the Cargo Laden On Board the Ship or Vessel MT 'Swallow'* [2003] 8 CLJ 762 (HC) 782B–G.
[173] *Harmer v Bell, The Bold Buccleugh* 13 ER 884 (UKPC) 128, cited with approval in, amongst others, *Pemunya Kapal MV Brihope v Emmanuel E Okwuosa* [1997] 1 MLJ 453 (CA) 487C–F and *Lee Wong Yu v The Owners of The Ship or Vessel 'MV Hua Hong Satu'* [1999] 6 CLJ 197 (HC) 203A–D.

law recognises largely reflect those identified by the Privy Council in *The Halcyon Isle*,[174] namely salvage,[175] collision damage, seamen's wages,[176] bottomry and respondentia bonds (though now obsolete),[177] and masters' wages and disbursements.[178]

iii. General Maritime Claims under SCA 1981 Section 21(4)

This encompasses any claim in SCA 1981 sections 20(2)(e)–(r). Section 21(4)(a) – which requires that the claim arises in connection with a ship – does not include, for instance, cargo.[179] The identity of the 'relevant person', not the merits of the underlying claim, is material, unless unreasonableness, frivolity or vexation arise.[180] The ship register is prima facie, but not conclusive, evidence that the registered owner is the beneficial owner. A party who asserts otherwise then bears the burden of proving so.[181] Actions under section 21(4) give rise to rights of arrest of the particular ship, a 'sister ship', or a particular ship 'spirited away' into different legal ownership.[182]

iv. Certain Aircraft Claims under SCA 1981 Section 21(5)

This applies to claims in the nature of towage or pilotage in respect of an aircraft if, when the action is brought, that aircraft is beneficially owned by the person who would be liable on the claim in an action *in personam*. An action *in rem* may be brought against that aircraft.

v. *Restrictions on Admiralty Jurisdiction* in rem

There are three bars to the High Court's Admiralty jurisdiction *in rem*: (1) where the defendant is the Federal Government or a State Government of Malaysia;[183] (2) where foreign sovereign immunity applies;[184] and (3) where the general restrictions on proceedings against insolvent companies apply.[185]

[174] *Bankers Trust International Ltd v Todd Shipyards Corp (The 'Halcyon Isle')* [1981] AC 221, [1980] 2 MLJ 217 (UKPC) 219A–D, cited with approval in *The Owners of The Ship or Vessel MT 'Rowan' v The Owners of The Ship or Vessel or Property 'Singapura Timur'* [2003] 2 MLJ 441 (HC) 449C.

[175] Merchant Shipping Ordinance 1952 (MSO 1952), ss 389, 390.

[176] ibid, ss 95, 100.

[177] *The 'Halcyon Isle'* (n 174) 219B; Derrington and Turner (n 165) para 4.47.

[178] MSO 1952, ss 2, 95, 100; *MV Brihope* (n 173) 491G.

[179] *MT 'Swallow'* (n 172) 783B–I.

[180] *Middle East Tankers and Freighters v Owner of The Vessel and other Interested Party in The Vessel of MV 'Ira'* [1996] 4 MLJ 109 (HC) 117C–118H; ROC 2012, Ord 18, r 19.

[181] *Dan-Bunkering (Singapore) Pte Ltd v The Owners of The Ship or Vessel 'Pdz Mewah' (IMO No: 9064009) of Port Klang* [2020] MLJU 1574 (HC) [38]–[40], citing *Kawasaki Kisen Kaisha Ltd v Owners of the Ship or Vessel 'Able Lieutenant'* [2002] 6 MLJ 433 (HC) 452. However, note, with respect, that the Court's remark in *Able Lieutenant* that the 'prima facie' rule does not apply in Singaporean law appears to misrepresent the Singaporean judgment cited to support that suggestion: see *The 'Opal 3' Ex 'Kuchino'; Atlantis Engineering & Construction Pte Ltd v Owners of the Ship or Vessel 'Opal 3' Ex 'Kuchino'* [1992] 2 SLR 585 (SGHC) [8]–[11] in full.

[182] *Able Lieutenant* (n 181) 448E–G, citing *The Evpo Agnic* [1988] 1 WLR 1090 (EWCA) 1097E–F.

[183] Government Proceedings Act 1956, ss 2(2), 37(1), 37(2), read with IA 1948 and 1967, s 3.

[184] *United States of America v Yang Soon Ee* [1950] 1 MLJ 102b (OCJ) 104, but note that following *Commonwealth of Australia v Midford (Malaysia) Sdn Bhd* [1990] 1 MLJ 475 (SC), the position is likely to be more nuanced.

[185] CA 2016, Part 4, Division 1.

C. Issue and Service of Writ in Action *in rem*

The *res* must exist when the writ *in rem* is issued,[186] which is how such actions begin.[187] Subject to specified exceptions,[188] the writ must then be served on the *res* whilst the *res* is within the jurisdiction[189] and, forthwith upon the plaintiff or his solicitors becoming aware of any caveat against arrest, on the caveating party.[190] A defendant who then files a memorandum of appearance is, or seems to be,[191] taken to submit personally to the jurisdiction. The action then proceeds also *in personam*, but the defendant may still dispute jurisdiction.[192]

D. Available Relief

Summary judgment and default judgment may be granted in an Admiralty action *in rem*.[193] Where the High Court orders the sale of a ship, any party who has obtained judgment against the ship or proceeds of sale may apply for an order determining the order of priority of claims against the proceeds.[194] If *The Halcyon Isle*[195] applies in Malaysia on the point (and there have been no reported judgments to that effect), the order of priorities will be determined according to Malaysian law as if the events giving rise to each claim had occurred in Malaysia, starting with a prima facie order.[196]

E. Process of Ship Arrest in the Territory

In *The Able Lieutenant*,[197] the High Court acknowledged the purpose of arresting a ship in an Admiralty action *in rem* as being only to obtain security to satisfy any judgment which may be obtained.[198]

F. Availability of Arrest

After the writ is issued, a warrant of arrest is available as of right,[199] except in three situations. The first two require leave of the High Court: (1) an action *in rem* for possession or wages in relation

[186] *MT 'Swallow'* (n 172) 794G–795C.

[187] ROC 2012, Ord 70, r 2.

[188] ibid, Ord 70, rr 7(1)(a) (for freight, the writ must be served on the cargo in respect of which the freight is payable, or the ship carrying that cargo), 7(1)(b) (where the property has been sold and the proceeds paid into Court, the writ must be served on the Registrar).

[189] ibid, Ord 70, rr 3(3), 7.

[190] ibid, Ord 70, r 7(4).

[191] *The 'August 8th'; Owners of The 'August 8th' v Costas Bachas* [1983] 2 AC 450, [1983] 1 MLJ 281 (UKPC) 285B–G is a judgment of the Privy Council on appeal from the Singapore Court of Appeal. It was cited seemingly with approval in *MV Brihope* (n 173) 481C, albeit not for this specific principle.

[192] ROC 2012, Ord 70, r 2(5).

[193] Except where the claim involves allegations of libel, slander, malicious prosecution, false imprisonment, seduction, breach of promise of marriage, or fraud: ibid, Ord 14, r 1(2); *Emmanuel E Okwuosa v Owners of the Ship and other Persons Interested in the Ship MV Brihope* [1995] 1 MLJ 676 (HC) 686E–688C (affirmed on appeal), citing *The 'August 8th'* (n 191) 283F–285A; ROC 2012, Ord 70 r 2.

[194] ROC 2012, Ord 70, r 21(1).

[195] *The 'Halcyon Isle'* (n 174) 220H.

[196] *Den Norske Bank ASA v The Owners of The Ship or Vessel 'Forum Akasaka'* [1998] 3 CLJ Supp 10 (HC) 26–27.

[197] *Able Lieutenant* (n 181).

[198] ibid 441A–D.

[199] ROC 2012, Ord 70, r 4, Form 148.

to a foreign ship belonging to a state;[200] and (2) where the claim arises out of bottomry.[201] The third is where the beneficial ownership of the property has changed since issuance of the writ through a sale or disposal by any High Court exercising Admiralty jurisdiction; this seems to be an absolute bar.[202] A registered caveat against arrest[203] does not preclude the issue of a warrant of arrest,[204] but arrest without good and sufficient reason may result in the setting aside of the warrant, and an order to pay damages for wrongful arrest.[205] Similarly, failure to comply with an undertaking given through (presumably)[206] a caveat leaves a party's solicitor liable to committal.[207]

G. Procedure for Arrest

A warrant of arrest is valid for 12 months from issuance and may be executed only by the Sheriff or his officer.[208] Service is similar to or the same as service of a writ,[209] including the permitted physical methods of service.[210] Any person who has filed a memorandum of appearance, where security is sought,[211] may apply for an order specifying the amount and form of security to be provided,[212] to prevent, or obtain release from, arrest.[213]

H. Release from Arrest

Where the High Court has stayed or dismissed Malaysian *in rem* proceedings on the ground that the dispute in question should be determined by a foreign court,[214] the High Court retains a discretion to order that the property be retained as security to satisfy any foreign judgment in those specific foreign proceedings that is enforceable in Malaysia, or to impose a condition that equivalent security be provided.[215]

I. Arbitration Act 2005

After amendments in 2011 and 2018,[216] the High Court now has at its disposal a wider range of powers under the AA 2005 to support, and strengthen the efficacy of, arbitration as a method of

[200] ibid, Ord 70, r 4(4).
[201] ibid, Ord 70, r 4(5).
[202] ibid, Ord 70, r 4(11).
[203] ibid, Ord 70, r 5(1).
[204] ibid, Ord 70, r 5(2).
[205] ibid, Ord 70, r 6.
[206] 'Presumably' because ROC 2012, Ord 70, r 8 refers simply to 'a written undertaking … to enter an appearance in the action, give bail or pay money into Court in lieu of bail', but does not specify that this is the undertaking given in a caveat against arrest under Ord 70, r 5.
[207] ROC 2012, Ord 70, r 8.
[208] ibid, Ord 70, rr 9(1), 9(2).
[209] ibid, Ord 70, rr 9(5), 9(6).
[210] ibid, Ord 70, r 10.
[211] Given that the purpose of an action *in rem* is to obtain security (as recognised in *Able Lieutenant* (n 181) 441A–D), it is questionable whether the words 'and security sought' in ROC 2012, Ord 70, r 9(9) serve any purpose.
[212] ROC 2012, Ord 70, r 9(9).
[213] ibid, Ord 70, rr 9(10), 9(11), 9(12).
[214] ibid, Ord 12, r 10.
[215] ibid, Ord 70, r 12(11).
[216] Arbitration (Amendment) Act 2011, s 4; Arbitration (Amendment) (No 2) Act 2018, s 6.

resolving Admiralty disputes. Sections 10(2A), 10(2B), 10(2C), 10(4), and 11(1)(c) are *in pari materia* with the UK's Civil Jurisdiction and Judgments Act 1982 section 26. Broadly, to support arbitrations, they give the High Court a similar discretion to that discussed in relation to the release of a ship from arrest. Although as yet untested domestically, these amendments should improve Malaysia's appeal both as an arbitration hub and as a successful maritime nation.[217]

V. Immunities from Jurisdiction

Malaysian law confers a range of immunities through primary legislation (including the adoption of international treaties and conventions by such legislation), subsidiary legislation, and the common law. Presently, the basics of immunity are firmly established through legislation and judgments such as *Commonwealth of Australia v Midford (Malaysia) Sdn Bhd*.[218] However, the sophisticated intricacies of, for instance, 'reverse piercing' have yet to grace Malaysian shores.

A. Sovereign and Diplomatic Immunity

i. Foreign Sovereigns Generally

Malaysia now subscribes to the restrictive doctrine of foreign sovereign immunity,[219] which protects acts of foreign states *de jure imperii* but not *de jure gestionis*.[220] Recently, the High Court found the dismissal of a security guard at an embassy to be *acta jure imperii*, because the guard's duties were integral and not ancillary to the embassy's sovereign activity.[221] The Court of Appeal has since set aside that decision, apparently on the ground that the High Court (as opposed to the Industrial Court) was not the proper court to hear the matter.[222] Nevertheless, the doctrine itself, as endorsed by the then Supreme Court as the former apex court in *Midford*, will remain good law until the Federal Court holds otherwise. The doctrine applies similarly to public taxation officers.[223] Whether a defendant is a foreign sovereign state is conclusively determined by a certificate issued by the Yang di-Pertuan Agong or the Ministry of Foreign Affairs.[224]

ii. Foreign Diplomats and International Organisations

As well as the common law, the Diplomatic Privileges (Vienna Convention) Act 1966 and the Consular Relations (Vienna Convention) Act 1999 clothe the 1961 Vienna Convention on Diplomatic Relations (Vienna Convention) with legal force, subject to the powers of the Yang di-Pertuan Agong under section 4(1) of the former Act and section 6(1) of the latter to withdraw

[217] Nurul Huda Padulli, 'A Welcomed Change: Section 10(2a) of the Arbitration Act 2005 – Retention of Arrest of Ships for Arbitration' [2012] 4 *Malayan Law Journal* i.

[218] *Midford* (n 184).

[219] ibid; *Trendtex Trading Corp v Central Bank of Nigeria* [1977] QB 529 (EWCA); *The 'I Congreso del Partido'* [1983] 1 AC 244 (UKHL).

[220] *Midford* (n 184) 480H–B.

[221] *The United States of America v Menteri Sumber Manusia Malaysia* [2020] 11 MLJ 670 (HC) [28]–[32].

[222] Based on oral grounds delivered in Civil Appeals Nos W-01(A)-59-01/2020 and W-01(A)-66-01/2020 (CA). Written grounds of judgment have yet to be released. An appeal to the Federal Court appears to be likely, the outcome of which remains to be seen.

[223] *Hii Yii Ann v Deputy Commissioner of Taxation of The Commonwealth of Australia* [2018] 7 MLJ 393 (HC) [56]–[77].

[224] *Village Holdings Sdn Bhd v Her Majesty The Queen in Right of Canada* [1988] 2 MLJ 656 (HC) 661B–F; *Midford* (n 184) 476C–G.

those protections for reciprocity. Reciprocity is also embodied in the Foreign Representatives (Privileges and Immunities) Act 1967. Separately, by the International Organizations (Privileges and Immunities) Act 1992 (IOPIA 1992), Malaysia has given legal force to the Convention on the Privileges and Immunities of the United Nations, and the Convention on the Privileges and Immunities of the Specialized Agencies.[225]

iii. Asian International Arbitration Centre

One organisation to which the Minister of Foreign Affairs has granted protections or immunities under IOPIA 1992, sections 3(1) and 4(1) is the Asian International Arbitration Centre (AIAC), formerly known as the Kuala Lumpur Regional Centre for Arbitration (KLRCA).[226] As well as the AIAC itself, the Director for the time being and former Directors are also clothed with differing degrees of immunity, depending, for current Directors, on whether they are Malaysian citizens.[227] Non-Malaysian professional staff of the AIAC also enjoy certain immunities.[228] This (claimed) immunity (or alleged lack thereof) recently came before the Court of Appeal;[229] the Federal Court has since confirmed in oral grounds that a former Director's immunity includes immunity from criminal proceedings.[230]

iv. Malaysian Rulers

Before 1993, Federal Constitution Article 181(2) conferred absolute immunity on the Rulers of Malaysia, that is, 'Their Royal Highnesses the Rulers and the Yang di-Pertua-Yang di-Pertua Negeri of States not having a Ruler'.[231] Post-amendment, proceedings may now be brought against a Ruler in his personal capacity in the Special Court, a shift from absolute sovereign immunity for Malaysia's Rulers at one end, to no sovereign immunity for acts in a personal capacity at the other.[232] The Special Court's criminal jurisdiction encompasses only territorial offences, whereas civil jurisdiction is extraterritorial.[233]

v. State-Owned Enterprises (SOEs)

Malaysian courts have yet to confront the question of whether state-owned enterprises enjoy foreign sovereign immunity.[234] How they would rule is difficult to predict. Simply characterising a state-owned enterprise's acts as either *de jure imperii* or *de jure gestionis*, in line with the restrictive doctrine of sovereign immunity,[235] would ignore many weighty, more sophisticated questions that may arise.[236]

[225] International Organizations (Privileges and Immunities) Act 1992, ss 1A, 1B.

[226] Kuala Lumpur Regional Centre for Arbitration (Privileges and Immunities) Regulations (1996) PU(A) 120/1996.

[227] ibid, reg 3; IOPIA 1992, s 4.

[228] KLRCA Regulations (n 226), reg 4.

[229] *Menteri Hal Ehwal Luar Negeri, Malaysia v Sundra Rajoo a/l Nadarajah* [2021] 2 MLJ 787 (CA).

[230] Timothy Achariam, 'Federal Court Rules ex-AIAC Director has Immunity from Criminal Charges' *The Edge Markets* (Putrajaya, 30 April 2021), available online: www.theedgemarkets.com/article/federal-court-rules-exaiac-director-has-immunity-criminal-charges. At the time of writing, written grounds have yet to be published.

[231] Federal Constitution, Art 38, Fifth Schedule.

[232] Hickling and Wu (n 1) 94.

[233] Federal Constitution, Art 182; ibid.

[234] As opposed to in the English courts: see eg *Kensington International Ltd v Republic of Congo* [2005] EWHC 2684 (Comm); *Walker International Holdings Ltd v Republique Populaire du Congo* [2005] EWHC 2813 (Comm); *La Générale des Carrières et des Mines v FG Hemisphere Associates LLC* [2012] UKPC 27, [2013] 1 All ER 409 (UKPC).

[235] *Midford* (n 184).

[236] See eg Mevelyn Ong, 'The Interplay of Sovereignty and Consent in the Execution of Arbitral Award Debts Against Non-Party State-Owned Enterprises' (2017–18) 4 *McGill Journal of Dispute Resolution* 22, 25, 33.

B. Government and Public Officers

i. Government Generally

The Government Proceedings Act 1956 (GPA 1956) applies to proceedings against the 'Government' of Malaysia generally, defined as 'the Federal Government and the Government of the States'.[237] No proceedings other than for breach of contract may lie against the Government on account of any acts or omissions 'by the Government or any public officer in exercise of the public duties of the Government'.[238] '[E]xercise of the public duties' is stated (presumably not exhaustively) to include certain specified construction, maintenance and abandonment works.[239] Suits for damages or compensation for negligence or trespass in construction or maintenance works by the Government are not prohibited.[240] No proceedings *in rem* may be brought in respect of any claim against the Government.[241]

ii. Judicial Officers

CJA 1964 section 14 and the Subordinate Courts Act 1948 (SCA 1948) section 107 protect judges, magistrates, and other judicial officers of the courts of Malaysia.[242] No judge, magistrate or any 'other person acting judicially' may be sued in any civil court for any act done or ordered to be done in the discharge of judicial duty, whether or not within the limits of the relevant officer's jurisdiction. Nor shall any order for costs be made against the judicial officer, provided that at the time, the judicial officer believed 'in good faith' that he had jurisdiction so to act.[243] Where a judicial officer acts in bad faith, or overreaches his powers such that his act is *ultra vires* and thus of no effect, that judicial officer is not protected.[244] Court officers executing court warrants or orders, and sheriffs, bailiffs or other officers acting under duty, are also protected.[245] As well as *personal* protection of judicial officers, no proceedings may lie against the *Government* for acts or omissions of a person discharging judicial or related responsibilities vested in him.[246]

iii. Public Prosecutor and Attorney General

The Attorney General and the Public Prosecutor do not enjoy absolute prosecutorial immunity. It can be pierced where prosecutorial powers are exercised unconstitutionally, in bad faith for an extraneous purpose, or in an abuse of power.[247]

[237] GPA 1956, s 2(2).
[238] ibid, s 7(1).
[239] ibid, s 7(2).
[240] ibid, s 7(3).
[241] ibid, s 37.
[242] CJA 1964, s 14 applies to the Federal Court, the Court of Appeal and the High Court; SCA 1948, s 107 applies to the Sessions Court and the Magistrates' Court.
[243] CJA 1964, s 14(1); SCA 1948, s 107(1).
[244] *Penolong Kanan Pendaftar Mahkamah Tinggi Johor Bahru v Tan Beng Sooi* [1997] 2 MLJ 118 (CA) 129I–130B; *Rosli bin Dahlan v Tan Sri Abdul Gani bin Patail* [2014] 11 MLJ 481 (HC) [103]. In *Rosli bin Dahlan*, although the High Court included acting 'without jurisdiction' also as a ground for piercing judicial immunity, with respect, that would appear to contradict the words 'whether or not within the limits of his jurisdiction' in CJA 1964, s 14(1) and SCA 1948, s 107(1).
[245] CJA 1964, ss 14(2), 14(3); SCA 1948, ss 107(1), 107(2).
[246] GPA 1956, s 5(3).
[247] Federal Constitution, Art 146; Criminal Procedure Code, s 376; *Rosli bin Dahlan* (n 244) [86]. See also Ashgar Ali Ali Mohamed, 'Prosecutorial Immunity: A Review of Rosli Bin Dahlan v Tan Sri Abdul Gani Bin Patail & Ors' [2015] 1 *Malayan Law Journal* xcvii.

iv. Election Commission

Members of the Election Commission have the same protection as that given to a magistrate for acts or omissions when executing their office.[248] Although Malaysian law was once clear that the Election Commission could still be sued in suitable cases,[249] that position seems, questionably,[250] to have been watered down in favour of (greater) immunity by a later decision.[251]

v. Other Public Officers

Other protected parties, subject to varying degrees of conditionality, include land administrators,[252] members of Parliament[253] (except for offences under Sedition Act 1948),[254] the police,[255] the Malaysian Anti-Corruption Commission,[256] and state authorities in relation to Street, Drainage and Building Act 1974.[257] The common thread is that malice or bad faith will vitiate immunity.[258]

C. Other Immunities

Witnesses in court proceedings enjoy immunity from any form of civil action in respect of evidence given during those proceedings, as a principle of common law.[259] Under the Whistleblower Protection Act 2010 section 7, a whistleblower who discloses improper conduct by any enforcement agency pursuant to that Act is conferred with three types of protection: protection of confidential information, immunity from civil and criminal action, and protection against detrimental action.[260]

[248] Election Commission Act 1957, s 6.

[249] Cyrus V Das, 'Election Laws: The Compelling Areas for Reform from a Legal Perspective' [2002] 2 *Malayan Law Journal* cxc, cxcv, citing *Re Pengkalan Kota Bye-Election Teoh Teik Huat v Lim Kean Siew* [1981] 1 MLJ 265 (HC) and *Dewan Undangan Negeri Kelantan v Nordin Bin Salleh* [1992] 1 MLJ 697 (SC).

[250] Das (n 249) cxcvi.

[251] *Dr Lee Chong Meng v Abdul Rahman Bin Hj Abdullah, Returning Officer* [2000] 6 MLJ 98 (HC) 110D–F.

[252] National Land Code 1965, s 22.

[253] Federal Constitution, Art 63; Houses of Parliament (Privileges and Powers) Act 1952.

[254] Which has been criticised as unconducive to true parliamentary democracy: Ahmad Masum, 'Parliamentary Privilege and Its Practice in Malaysia: An Overview' [2012] 2 *Malayan Law Journal* c, cii.

[255] Police Act 1967, s 32.

[256] Malaysian Anti-Corruption Commission Act 2009, s 72.

[257] Street, Drainage and Building Act 1974, s 95(2).

[258] Ali Mohamed (n 247) iv.

[259] *Alias bin Othman v Clement Kua Hock Beng* [2018] 7 MLJ 109 (HC) [24]–[25], although note that the Court there cited *Palmer v Durnford Ford (a firm)* [1992] QB 483 (QBD), from which English law seems now to have moved on considerably: *Jones v Kaney* [2011] UKSC 13, [2011] 2 AC 398 (UKSC).

[260] Whistleblower Protection Act 2010, s 7(1).

9

Vietnam

NGUYEN THI HONG TRINH, HO MINH THANH AND HOANG THAO ANH

I. Introduction

Since the implementation of the policy of *doi moi*[1] in the late 1980s, Vietnam has developed its economy and opened up to the outside world. As a result, international civil relations and litigation have also increased.

International civil litigation is known in Vietnam as 'civil cases involving foreign elements'. In general, such cases are civil lawsuits which are between plaintiffs and defendants with different nationalities or residing in different countries, which have as their subject matter property located abroad, or which involve conduct (such as the signing of a contract or the instigation of a tort) outside Vietnam.[2] 'Civil' is understood to include matters relating to marriage, family, business, trade and labour.[3] A case may be an action arising out of a dispute or a request on a matter of personal status. Foreign elements are defined in Article 464(2) of the Civil Procedure Code 2015 (CPC) to mean the presence in a case of one or more of the following: (1) a foreign party; (2) a material connection with a foreign country (for example, a contract concluded abroad); or (3) a foreign subject matter (for example, property located abroad). Jurisdiction concerns the competence of a judicial body to adjudicate upon civil cases involving foreign elements.[4] The establishment of jurisdiction over a civil matter requires an assessment of questions such as: (1) whether the state has sufficient connection with the defendant to deliver a civil judgment affecting him or her; (2) whether the state has empowered the court to hear the matter; and (3) whether the court seised is an appropriate or convenient forum in which to deal with the matter. In answering those questions, national laws and international conventions provide rules upon which the court's determination of international jurisdiction or the lack of it may be based.[5]

In Vietnam, the sources of private international law have traditionally included international conventions, national law and international custom. Since international custom cannot be used to ascertain the international civil jurisdiction of the court of a state, the jurisdiction of Vietnamese

[1] *Đổi Mới* ('renovation') refers to the policy of economic reform (*Chính sách Đổi Mới*) initiated in Vietnam in 1986 with the goal of transforming the country from a command economy into a 'socialist-oriented market economy'.

[2] Thi Mai Hanh Do (ed), *Giáo trình Tư pháp quốc tế* [*Ho Chi Minh Law School Textbook on Private International Law*] (Hanoi, Nhà xuất bản Hồng Đức [Hong Duc Publishing House], 2019) 251.

[3] Civil Procedure Code 2015 (Law No 92/2015/QH13), Art 1.

[4] Do (n 2) 260.

[5] ibid 261.

courts in international civil cases derives from national law and international conventions to which Vietnam is a party.[6] Priority is given to international conventions, if there is a conflict with national law. Where there is no convention to which Vietnam is a party that contains relevant provisions, the court will apply Vietnamese law.[7] As of mid-2021, Vietnam has not entered into any multilateral convention regulating international civil jurisdiction.[8] However, the country is party to 17 bilateral judicial assistance treaties or agreements in civil matters,[9] of which 12 contain provisions on international civil jurisdiction.[10] For national laws, provisions on the jurisdiction of the courts with regard to international civil cases can primarily be found in the CPC with scattered provisions in laws such as the Law on Marriage and Family 2014, the Maritime Code 2015, the Law on Commercial Arbitration 2010 and their bylaws.

Vietnamese law recognises two modes of international civil jurisdiction: general and exclusive jurisdiction. General jurisdiction is jurisdiction in an international case that is not exclusive to Vietnamese courts. Forums elsewhere can accept the same case. Vietnamese laws provide principles and rules allowing a court to identify general jurisdiction. For example, where the permanent residence; place of work; headquarters, branch or representative office; or relevant property of a defendant is in Vietnam, the courts in Vietnam will typically have jurisdiction.[11] Exclusive jurisdiction arises in the situation where Vietnamese laws or applicable international treaties provide for the Vietnamese court alone to hear a case to the exclusion of all other forums elsewhere. Lawsuits involving rights to immovable property in Vietnam fall within the exclusive jurisdiction of the Vietnamese court.[12] Where general jurisdiction is concerned, parties can initiate lawsuits in the courts of other countries. Judgments of the latter in the given matter can be recognised and enforced in Vietnam. Where exclusive jurisdiction is concerned, Vietnamese law does not allow parties to sue elsewhere. The judgments of other courts in the matter will not be recognised in Vietnam.[13] Special jurisdiction has not been defined to date in codifications or textbooks. But it is manifest in certain rules granting jurisdiction to Vietnamese courts, such as in divorces cases where one spouse is a Vietnamese citizen or the parties are foreigners who have resided or worked for a long time in Vietnam.

The process of ascertaining international civil jurisdiction has changed between the 2004 and 2015 versions of the CPC. The former provided two methods for determining jurisdiction. It listed bases of international civil jurisdiction for the courts to apply,[14] but it also permitted reference to the bases of jurisdiction in domestic cases.[15] The latter distinguishes between the rules for international and domestic jurisdiction. It is no longer possible for a court to refer to the rules for direct jurisdiction as a basis for assuming international jurisdiction. The court must now first consider whether it has international jurisdiction. Only after having established that it has international jurisdiction, will the court proceed to assess whether it is a competent

[6] CPC, Art 2(3).

[7] ibid.

[8] Vietnam is party to the 1965 Hague Convention on the Service Abroad of Judicial and Extrajudicial Documents in Civil or Commercial Matters, the 1970 Hague Convention on the Taking of Evidence Abroad in Civil or Commercial Matters, and the 1993 Hague Convention on the Protection of Children and Co-operation in Respect of Intercountry Adoption.

[9] The instruments are those with Algeria, Kazakhstan, France, Cambodia, Taiwan, Belarus, Cuba, Russia, North Korea, China, Ukraine, Poland, Hungary, Laos, Mongolia, the Czech Republic, and Bulgaria.

[10] The instruments are those with Belarus, Cuba, Russia, North Korea, China, Ukraine, Poland, Hungary, Laos, Mongolia, Czech Republic, and Bulgaria.

[11] CPC, Art 469(1).

[12] ibid, Arts 470(1)(a), 470(1)(b).

[13] Do (n 2) 267.

[14] Civil Procedure Code 2004 (Law No 24/2004/QH11), Arts 410(2), 411.

[15] ibid, Art 410(1).

domestic court (provincial or district) to hear a case. Nonetheless, even at present, Vietnamese judges usually still refer directly to domestic rules of jurisdiction and omit to consider those rules dealing with international jurisdiction.

II. Jurisdiction – General Principles

A. Jurisdiction Based on the Defendant's Residence

The doctrine that a plaintiff has to attend the defendant's place of residence to sue, is applied by CPC Articles 469(1)(a) and 469(1)(b). Article 469(1)(a) confers general jurisdiction where an individual has resided, worked or lived in Vietnam for a long time. The Supreme People's Court has explained what is entailed in residing, working, and living in Vietnam in the Draft Resolution 2019.[16] If a defendant is a Vietnamese citizen in Vietnam, the criterion is satisfied,[17] but the defendant must be in Vietnam at the time the lawsuit is filed. Vietnamese nationality alone will not be enough to constitute a basis for jurisdiction. Where a defendant is non-Vietnamese,[18] the connection with Vietnam must be stronger. The Draft Resolution 2019 requires that a permanent residence card,[19] a temporary residence card,[20] or a visa exemption paper valid for no less than five years is obtained.[21] The foregoing includes those being considered for re-issue of such cards or papers pursuant to the Law on Exit, Transit and Residence of Foreigners in Vietnam.[22] Mere presence of a foreign defendant in Vietnam would not constitute a basis for a court to exercise jurisdiction against such person. Unlike domicile or habitual residence which are flexible and fact-based criteria in many countries' laws, Vietnam applies its national law on residence to determine whether the residence of a foreign defendant in Vietnam has been sufficient. The notion of residing, working or living in Vietnam therefore does not have an autonomous meaning. The court cannot interpret the criteria when faced with different situations and can only adjudicate if an intended defendant has one of the three mentioned cards. Judgment No 28/2019/KDTM-ST dated 24 July 2019 of the People's Court of Hanoi City is a practical example.[23] A company in Germany brought a tort claim against a Vietnamese citizen in Vietnam. The court assumed international jurisdiction.[24] As for an example of an action against a foreign defendant residing, working or living in Vietnam, there were certainly such cases under the CPC 2004.[25] But none have been found under

[16] The Draft Resolution 2019 is entitled 'Guiding the Implementation of the Civil Procedure Code Regarding Competence and Procedures for Settlement of Civil Cases Involving Foreign Elements'. The Vietnamese version is available online: https://vbpq.toaan.gov.vn/webcenter/portal/htvb/chi-tiet-vbdt?dDocName=TAND081751. The Draft Resolution 2019 is expected to be approved in the near future.

[17] Draft Resolution 2019, Art 2(1)(a).

[18] This includes foreign citizens and stateless persons: Law on Nationality 2008 (Law No 24/2008/QH12), Art 5(3).

[19] Law on Entry, Exit, Transit and Residence of Foreigners in Vietnam 2014 (Law No 47/2014/QH13), Art 13(4).

[20] ibid, Art 3(13).

[21] ibid, Art 12.

[22] Draft Resolution 2019, Art 2(1)(b).

[23] The case concerned intellectual property rights in a domain name, available online: https://congbobanan.toaan.gov.vn/2ta340454t1cvn/chi-tiet-ban-an.

[24] In its judgment, the court neither addressed the international character of the case, nor cited CPC, Art 469, nor explained the basis for assuming international jurisdiction. It is therefore uncertain whether the court relied on the fact that the defendant was a Vietnamese living in Vietnam as the basis for jurisdiction or whether the court treated the matter as a tort action in Vietnam and founded its jurisdiction accordingly.

[25] See the cases mentioned in Van Dai Do and Hong Quy Mai, *Tư pháp quốc tế Việt Nam* [*Vietnamese Private International Law*] (Hanoi, Nhà xuất bản chính trị quốc gia [National Political Publishing House], 2010) 85.

the current CPC 2015.[26] Where the defendant is a legal entity such as a company, CPC Article 469(1)(b) provides that the court shall have jurisdiction if the latter is headquartered or has a branch or a representative office in Vietnam. The organisation's nationality is not determinative. Judgment No 792/2018/HNGĐ-ST dated 20 June 2018 of the People's Court of Ho Chi Minh City is an example.[27] The plaintiff had its headquarters in Hong Kong and sued the defendant headquartered in Vietnam.[28] Another example is Judgment No 02/2019/KDTM-ST dated 22 March 2019 of the People's Court of Hai Phong City.[29] The plaintiff was a Vietnamese company headquartered in Vietnam and the defendant a Taiwanese Company headquartered in Taiwan but with a representative office in Vietnam.[30] In the case of a foreign company which has a branch or a representative office in Vietnam, it should be noted that the court will only have jurisdiction to hear a dispute over a case relating to the operation of the branch or representative office in Vietnam. The defendant would, however, be the foreign company, not the branch or the representative. The purpose of the legislation was to fix foreign agencies and organisations having branches or representative offices in Vietnam with civil obligations arising out of their operations.[31]

The CPC provides for only one case of special jurisdiction, that is over divorce cases. Article 469(1)(d) confers general jurisdiction over divorce cases in which one of the parties is a Vietnamese citizen or both spouses are foreigners who have been residing, working, or living for a long term in Vietnam.[32] Vietnamese courts have frequently assumed jurisdiction in divorce cases based on the first ground. See, for example, Judgment No 38/2017/HNGĐ-ST dated 22 May 2017 of the People's Court of Kien Giang Province (Korean and Vietnamese spouses),[33] Judgment No 22/2020/HNGĐ-ST dated 10 February 2020 of the People's Court of Hai Phong City (Vietnamese and Korean),[34] and Judgment No 220/2019/HNGĐ-ST dated 31 December 2019 of the People's Court of Hai Phong City (Vietnamese and German).[35] Cases in which the courts have assumed jurisdiction based on the fact that a foreign couple resides, works, or lives in Vietnam are rare. A divorce case can fall within the exclusive jurisdiction of the Vietnamese court if it is one between a Vietnamese and a foreign citizen or stateless person and both spouses reside, work, or live permanently in Vietnam. The Draft Resolution 2019 notes that there have in fact been divorce cases between Vietnamese citizens in Vietnam and foreigners residing, working, or living permanently in Vietnam.[36]

[26] The authors have made some effort to look into the judgments published online on the portal of the Supreme People's Court.

[27] The dispute involved an international sale contract, available online: https://congbobanan.toaan.gov.vn/2ta427559t1cvn/chi-tiet-ban-an.

[28] The court cited CPC, Art 469, although did not specify which clause of the article it was applying. It is likely that it had CPC, Art 469(1)(b) in mind.

[29] The dispute involved a contract for the transfer of company share capital, available online: https://congbobanan.toaan.gov.vn/2ta264281t1cvn/chi-tiet-ban-an.

[30] Again, the court cited CPC, Art 469 but did not specify the clause.

[31] Anh Tuan Tran (ed), *Bình luận khoa học Bộ luật Tố tụng dân sự* [*Commentary on the Civil Procedure Code*] (Hanoi, Nhà xuất bản Tư pháp [Judicial Publishing House], 2018) 1005.

[32] Draft Resolution 2019, Art 2(3).

[33] Available online: https://congbobanan.toaan.gov.vn/2ta6327t1cvn/chi-tiet-ban-an. The judgment does not identify the spouses' nationalities. But, from their names, in all likelihood they were Korean and Vietnamese. The court cited CPC, Art 469(1)(d).

[34] Available online: https://congbobanan.toaan.gov.vn/2ta459400t1cvn/chi-tiet-ban-an.

[35] Available online: https://congbobanan.toaan.gov.vn/2ta461711t1cvn/chi-tiet-ban-an.

[36] Draft Resolution 2019, Art 3(1)(b).

B. Jurisdiction Based on the Location of Property

CPC Article 469(1)(c) confers general jurisdiction over international civil cases where the defendant's property is in Vietnam. Property is defined in CPC Article 105 as referring to movable and immovable property and including objects, money, valuable papers, and rights or interests in property. Property may be existing or to be formed in the future. There is no minimum requirement or maximum limit to the value of the property concerned. Nor does the property have to relate to the case before the court. The property need not be the object of the dispute between the parties. There is not much case law on this ground of jurisdiction, but scholars see its ambit as being far-reaching.[37] Vietnamese courts also have general jurisdiction when the object of a civil relationship from which a dispute has arisen is property in Vietnam.[38] In such a situation, the property must be the object of the dispute in order for the court to hear the claim. An example is a dispute over the right to inherit property in Vietnam.

When civil suits involve rights to immovable property in Vietnam, CPC Article 470(1)(a) gives the Vietnamese court exclusive jurisdiction. Draft Resolution 2019 discusses this in its Article 3(1)(a), noting that the article applies to disputes where one party is a foreigner or foreign organisation. There is an exception. Where a bilateral or multilateral treaty is applicable, an agreement between the Vietnamese Government and a foreign investor providing for arbitration as the means for resolving disputes relating to immovable property will be enforceable, so that the Vietnamese court will not have exclusive jurisdiction over such matter.[39]

C. Other Bases of Jurisdiction

i. Legal Event Occurring or Acts Performed in Vietnam

CPC Article 469(1)(dd) provides that the court has general jurisdiction over cases arising from civil relations which are established, changed or terminated in Vietnam or from acts performed in Vietnam. Three situations are covered. The first is where the cause of action arose in Vietnam. An example is a tort committed in Vietnam. The second is where the subject matter is where work is done in Vietnam. The court may use this as the basis for hearing a labour dispute. The third is where a declaration is sought to the effect that some legal event happened in Vietnam. The Vietnamese court will have exclusive jurisdiction under CPC Article 470(2)(b). Instances are applications for: (1) a declaration that a Vietnamese citizen or a foreigner residing in Vietnam is missing or dead, where such declaration is related to establishing the relevant person's rights and obligations in Vietnam; and (2) a declaration that a foreigner residing in Vietnam has limited civil capacity or lacks legal capacity.[40]

ii. Contracts

CPC 2004 provided for special jurisdiction in contract disputes where the place of performance of the contract was Vietnam. The current CPC 2015 has not maintained this provision.

[37] Do (n 2) 281.
[38] CPC, Art 469(1)(dd).
[39] Supreme People's Court, 'Report on 10 Years Implementation Review of the Civil Procedure Code 2004' 29, available online: https://tinyurl.com/pdu1sjxe.
[40] CPC, Arts 470(2)(c), 470(2)(d).

Today, the court may have general or exclusive jurisdiction over contract pursuant to CPC Articles 469(1) and 470.

iii. State Interest

CPC Article 469(1)(e) stipulates a new basis of general jurisdiction arising from civil relations which are established, changed, or terminated outside Vietnam, but which additionally involve the rights and obligations of Vietnamese agencies, organisations, and individuals that are headquartered or reside in Vietnam. This ground of jurisdiction appears to be far-reaching. But in fact, its purpose is to give jurisdiction over cases concerning civil relations which are established, changed, or terminated in Vietnam's contiguous areas, exclusive economic zones, and continental shelf, including maritime disputes. Examples are claims for damages caused by ship and fishing vessel collision, salvage or rescue of ships. This provision is intended to protect the country's sovereignty in the aforesaid areas, as well as provide Vietnam with a basis for taking part in cases relating to sovereignty over the relevant areas before international tribunals.[41] There has so far been no illustrative case.

iv. Choice of Vietnamese Court by Parties

Where the Vietnamese court is designated by the parties' agreement as the forum to resolve any disputes arising out of their contract, the court will regard itself as having exclusive jurisdiction to determine such disputes, provided that Vietnamese law or an operative international treaty allows such a choice.[42] Draft Resolution 2019 comments that there are two requirements for the court to exercise exclusive jurisdiction in such a situation: (1) there is a law or treaty giving the parties the right to choose the Vietnamese court to settle their dispute; and (2) the agreement designating the Vietnamese court is in writing and identifies the court as the exclusive forum to determine the parties' dispute.[43] See also Section II.D.v below.

D. Declining Jurisdiction

i. Forum non conveniens

Vietnamese law has so far rejected the doctrine of *forum non conveniens* as far as domestic and international jurisdiction in civil cases is concerned. As a civil law system country, Vietnam strictly applies formal rules. If a basis for assuming jurisdiction exists, the court is under a duty to hear a case. However, it has been argued that the courts should adopt *forum non conveniens* to allow a measure of flexibility and discretion in the application of jurisdictional rules. For example, *forum non conveniens* would enable the court to decline to hear a case over which it would have jurisdiction, but on a basis which is unconnected with the parties' dispute.[44]

[41] Tran (n 31) 1007.
[42] CPC, Art 470(1)(c).
[43] Draft Resolution 2019, Art 3(2)(b).
[44] Hoai Nam Phan, 'Học thuyết Forum non conveniens trong Tư pháp quốc tế Hoa Kỳ – Một số kinh nghiệm tham khảo cho Việt Nam' ['The Doctrine of Forum Non Conveniens in Private International Law in the US – Some References for Vietnam'] (2017) 06(109) *Tạp chí Khoa học pháp lý* [*Vietnamese Journal of Legal Sciences*] 59–66.

ii. Lis alibi pendens

Vietnam espouses *lis alibi pendens*. This doctrine gives priority to the court of the country first seised of a case. CPC Article 472 encapsulates the principle. For *lis alibi pendens* to apply, two cases (one being heard in Vietnam, the other by a foreign court) must have the same parties and concern the same dispute.[45] Nor must the resolution of the dispute fall within the exclusive jurisdiction of the Vietnamese court, insofar as it is sought to stay proceedings in Vietnam. One of the following must also be present: (1) The parties have chosen arbitration or a foreign court to settle a case or matter; (2) The case falls within the exclusive jurisdiction of the foreign court;[46] (3) The civil case has been accepted for substantive determination by an arbitral tribunal or foreign court or have actually been decided by the judgment or award of a foreign court or tribunal;[47] (4) The defendant is eligible for legal exemption.[48]

iii. Anti-suit Injunctions

These are not available under Vietnamese law.

iv. Interim Measures

Vietnamese law does not contain any provisions on international jurisdiction in connection with provisional measures. As a matter of principle, a court seised of the substance of a dispute has jurisdiction to issue related provisional measures.[49] If a creditor applies for a provisional measure before a Vietnamese court which is not the court seized of the substance of a matter, that court will not have jurisdiction to order provisional measures.

v. Choice of Court Agreements

The CPC 2004 did not have provisions providing for choice of court agreements. It was therefore uncertain whether such choice would be respected by a Vietnamese court. But specialised statutes (such as the Maritime Code 2005,[50] the Law on Civil Aviation 2006,[51] the Law on Technology Transfer 2006,[52] and the Law on Investment 2005[53]) have provisions allowing parties to choose a dispute settlement method such as arbitration or litigation before a designated Vietnamese or foreign court. Vietnamese law provides for the application of specialised laws in priority over general laws (*lex specialis derogat legi generali*).[54] Accordingly, parties can choose a Vietnamese or foreign court to settle their disputes if so provided in specialised laws. In practice, Vietnamese courts usually accept jurisdiction when parties chose to settle their disputes before them.[55] There have also been cases of acquiescence where plaintiffs have brought

[45] Tran (n 31) 1013.
[46] CPC, Art 472(1)(b).
[47] ibid, Arts 472(1)(c), 472(1)(d).
[48] ibid, Art 472(1)(dd).
[49] CPC, Art 111 provides that a plaintiff is entitled to request the court to order provisional measures. In emergency cases, a plaintiff can request the court to issue provisional measures when submitting a claim.
[50] Law No 40/2005/QH11, Art 260(1).
[51] Law No 08/2006/L-CTN, Art 172(1).
[52] Law No 08/2006/QH11, Art 56(2).
[53] Law No 59/2005/QH11, Art 12(3).
[54] See eg Civil Code 2015 (Law No 91/2015/QH13), Art 4; Law on Enterprises 2014 (Law No 68/2014/QH13), Art 5.
[55] Supreme People's Court, 'Explanatory Report of Civil Procedure Code Project' (10 April 2015) 24, file with author.

actions before the Vietnamese courts and defendants did not oppose the exercise of jurisdiction. The courts simply assumed that the defendants were amenable to the exercise of that jurisdiction.[56] There have also been cases where courts have respected the parties' choice of a foreign court, even though at that time the CPC 2004 did not specifically allow for such choice.[57] The CPC 2015 took account of such court practice and provided for choice of court agreements. But there are slight differences depending on whether a Vietnamese or foreign court is designated. According to Draft Resolution 2019 Article 3(2)(a), the choice of a Vietnamese court is only allowed in cases falling within the general jurisdiction of the Vietnamese court as prescribed in the CPC. Draft Resolution 2019 Article 3(2)(b) notes that there must be a Vietnamese law or operative international convention authorising the parties to choose the Vietnamese court. Draft Resolution 2019 Article 3(2)(c) adds that the choice of a Vietnamese court must be in writing and specify that the court is to have exclusive jurisdiction to settle disputes between the parties.[58] In any event, provided the choice of a Vietnamese court is valid, the court will have exclusive jurisdiction over the case in accordance with CPC Article 470(1)(c). This was the result of Vietnam's efforts to align its law with the 2005 Hague Convention on Choice of Court Agreements.[59] In contrast, the choice of a foreign court is only recognised when the law applicable to the dispute allows the parties to choose how the dispute is to be resolved. If the applicable law is Vietnamese, then it will only be when relevant Vietnamese laws allow the parties to choose a dispute settlement method (for example, in maritime or investment disputes) that the parties' choice will be recognised. This would be consonant with the strict application of CPC Article 472(1)(a). But in practice, Vietnamese judges may not be in a position to determine whether an applicable foreign law permits the parties to choose a dispute settlement method.

E. Service of Process Outside Vietnam

The rules on service of process in civil matters are mainly found in the CPC, the Law on Legal Assistance 2007, Decree No 92/2008/ND-CP on Detailing and Guiding the Implementation of a Number of Articles of the Law on Legal Assistance 2007 dated 22 August 2008 (Decree 92), and Joint Circular No 12/2016/TTLT-BTP-BNG on Procedures for Mutual Legal Assistance in Civil Matters dated 19 October 2016 issued by the Ministry of Justice, the Ministry of Foreign Affairs and the Supreme People's Court (Joint Circular No 12). Beside these domestic rules, service of process must comply with procedures in applicable international conventions, specifically the 17 bilateral conventions and agreements on legal assistance between Vietnam and other states and the 1965 Hague Convention on Service Abroad of Judicial and Extrajudicial Documents in Civil or Commercial Matters.[60] The Hague Service Convention came into effect in Vietnam on 1 October 2016. CPC Article 474(1)(c) enacts the rules in Article 10(a) of the Hague Service Convention. It provides that a Vietnamese court can deliver or notify its proceedings by post to the address of a party in a foreign country if such method is accepted by the laws of that

[56] ibid.

[57] Decision No 1810/2007/QĐST-KDTM dated 26 September 2007 of the People's Court of Ho Chi Minh City; Decision No 2065/2008/QĐĐC-KDTM-ST dated 19 December 2008 of the People's Court of Ho Chi Minh City. These two cases are discussed in Van Dai Do and Viet Dung Tran, 'Về Thỏa Thuận Chọn Tòa án nước ngoài' ['Regarding Choice of Foreign Court Agreements'] (2012) 6 *Tạp chí Khoa học Pháp lý* [*Vietnamese Journal of Legal Science*] 60.

[58] Draft Resolution 2019, Art 3(3).

[59] Supreme People's Court (n 55) 24.

[60] Apart from the Hague Service Convention, Vietnam is also a party to the 1970 Hague Convention on the Taking of Evidence Abroad in Civil or Commercial Matters, which came into effect in Vietnam on 3 May 2020.

country. On the implementation of the Hague Service Convention, the Supreme Court has issued Dispatch No 33/TANDTC-HTQT dated 21 February 2017 to inform lower courts about the Central Authorities of contracting states to the Hague Service Convention, including a list of member states objecting to service in the manner prescribed by Article 10(a). The information has been updated in Dispatch No 101/TANDTC-HTQT dated 25 June 2020. Dispatch No 33 requires that a court be responsible for sending relevant documents to overseas parties by international post guaranteed service. Dispatch No 101 adds that Vietnamese courts should accept digital signatures and receipts as evidence of successful service. For service on Vietnamese citizens overseas, the court will post the documents to Vietnam representative missions abroad for delivery to the specified party.[61] Detailed procedure can be found in Joint Circular No 01/2019/TTLT-TANDTC-BNG dated 5 December 2019. CPC Article 474(3) provides for alternative methods of service if the modes of delivery just mentioned are unsuccessful. Since Vietnam signed the Hague Service Convention in 2016, there has been an increase in the number of cases of successful service of process outside Vietnam. This has contributed to the resolution of cases.[62] However, the percentage of responses to the service of process is still around 50 per cent of the total number served. In 2019, 709 out of 1245 (56.7 per cent) of processes delivered through the Hague Service Convention channel received answers.[63]

F. Service of Process of Foreign Proceedings in Vietnam

According to Joint Circular No 12,[64] the following are competent to serve process of foreign proceedings in Vietnam: provincial courts, provincial enforcement agencies (in relation to the execution of foreign judgments), and distributive agencies performing delivery of documents in accordance with the law. There are two channels for the service of foreign process in Vietnam: (1) documents sent through diplomatic channels (in which case service must comply with Vietnamese rules and the principle of reciprocity); and (2) documents sent pursuant to international conventions to which Vietnam is a signatory. With regard to service of foreign process in accordance with Hague Service Convention, the Central Authority for Vietnam is the Ministry of Justice. Vietnam has declared that: (1) the modes of service of process specified in Article 8 of the Convention shall not apply unless the documents are being served on a citizen of the sending state; (2) the modes of service in Articles 10(b) and 10(c) of the Convention shall not apply; (3) postal service under Article 10 of the Convention shall apply provided that papers are sent by guaranteed mail; (4) Article 15(2) of the Convention shall apply; and (5) the translation of documents is required together with a certification from the translator.[65] According to the Ministry of Justice, in 2019, the percentage of successful service of foreign proceedings in Vietnam under the Hague Service Convention was 54.5 per cent (149 out of 273).[66] The major reasons for delayed service of process of foreign proceedings

[61] CPC, Art 474(1)(d).

[62] See 'Kiểm tra công tác tương trợ tư pháp tại Tòa án nhân dân thành phố Hà Nội và Tòa án nhân dân thành phố Đà Nẵng' [Examination of Judicial Assistance Activities at the Hanoi City People's Court and the Da Nang City People' Court] (*Ministry of Justice*, 5 November 2018), available online: https://tinyurl.com/18gsbkq0.

[63] 'Báo Cáo Hoạt Động Tương Trợ Tư Pháp Năm 2019' [2019 Report of the Result of the Judicial Mandate of the Ministry of Justice] (*Ministry of Justice*, 12 October 2019), available online: https://moj.gov.vn/tttp/tintuc/Pages/tuong-tro-tu-phap.aspx?ItemID=13.

[64] Joint Circular No 12, Art 17(1).

[65] Announcement No 62/2016/TB-LPQT of the Ministry of International Relations dated 10 October 2016 regarding the Hague Service Convention taking effect in Vietnam.

[66] '2019 Report' (n 63).

have been: (1) incomplete addresses; and (2) the importance of the timely service of process has not been appreciated by local agencies.[67]

III. Jurisdiction *in personam* – Specific Cases

A. Obligations

i. Contracts

The court's jurisdiction over contracts involving foreign elements arises in the following three cases:

(1) contracts relating to real estate in Vietnam as provided by CPC Article 470(1)(c) which confers exclusive jurisdiction;
(2) contracts in which the parties have selected the Vietnamese court as the forum for the resolution of their disputes, thereby conferring exclusive jurisdiction on the Vietnamese court;
(3) contractual disputes meeting the *in personam* jurisdictional rules for general jurisdiction discussed above.

ii. Torts

A plaintiff may sue for tortious damages under provisions of liability for non-contractual damages in the Civil Code 2015.[68] While there is a clear distinction between contractual and non-contractual claims, determining the jurisdiction of the court in either situation is largely a matter of applying the *in personam* jurisdictional rules discussed above.

iii. Property

a. Immovable Property

The court where the property is located will have jurisdiction. According to CPC Article 470(1)(a), the Vietnamese court has exclusive jurisdiction over civil cases involving real estate in Vietnam. The court can hear a contractual or equitable claim concerning foreign immovable property against a defendant subject to the court's personal jurisdiction. This type of situation raises the question of whether the court should assume jurisdiction in relation to foreign land. the CPC does not expressly deal with this matter. However, Vietnamese courts may apply the doctrine of *lis alibi pendens* mentioned earlier.

b. Succession to Property

By CPC Article 26(5), disputes over an inheritance fall within the jurisdiction of the People's Court. If the dispute is over the right to immovable property in Vietnam, the court has exclusive

[67] ibid.
[68] Civil Code 2015, Art 584.

jurisdiction.[69] Otherwise, inheritance disputes fall under the court's general jurisdiction as stipulated in CPC Article 469.

c. Intangible Property

For disputes over rights to intangible property, the proceedings are considered to be *in personam* and the rules discussed above in respect of *in personam* jurisdiction will apply.

d. Intellectual Property

Vietnamese procedural law has no special rules for establishing jurisdiction in disputes over intellectual property rights (IPRs) involving foreign elements. In theory, jurisdiction should be determined by applying the rules of general jurisdiction in CPC Article 469. However, in Judgment No 01/2018/KDTM-ST dated 29 January 2018 by the Provincial People's Court of Hung Yen[70] on 'the use of electric scooters and its designs which are similar to those that have been protected', the court classified the dispute as one involving IPRs and thus a commercial matter under CPC Article 30(2). It then excluded the jurisdiction of the district court, given the presence of a foreign element dispute, applying CPC Article 35(2). Finally, it based its jurisdiction on CPC Article 39(1)(a). The same method was used by the People's Court of Hanoi City[71] in Judgment No 36/2018/KDTM-ST dated 19 October 2018[72] and Judgment No 28/2019/KDTM-ST dated 24 July 2019,[73] both concerning disputes over domain names.

B. Family

i. Marriage

In marriage cases involving foreign elements, jurisdiction hinges on an identification of the competent authority for marriage registration. Marriage issues involving foreign elements should in principle be handled according to judicial assistance treaties or agreements with other countries. However, the 17 treaties or agreements into which Vietnam has so far entered do not deal with marriage registration. Consequently, the competent authority is determined by reference to the Law on Marriage and Family 2014,[74] the Law on Civil Status 2014, and their bylaws. Marriage registration is usually within the competence of district level People's Committees.[75] Whether the latter can register a marriage (whether concluded in Vietnam or abroad)[76] will depend on the rules of *in personam* jurisdiction, with the dominant focus being on residence and nationality. Thus, registration will be possible where at least one spouse has Vietnamese nationality and resides in Vietnam.[77] Registration will also be possible where a marriage is between

[69] CPC, Art 470(1)(a).
[70] Available online: https://tinyurl.com/y5mogq83.
[71] Hanoi is a municipality at the same level as Vietnam's provinces, so the People's Court of Hanoi City is on par with a provincial court.
[72] Available online: https://tinyurl.com/y6s5st62.
[73] Available online: https://tinyurl.com/y456sxsy.
[74] Law No 52/2014/QH13.
[75] Law on Civil Status 2014 (Law No 60/2014/QH13), Art 17(1).
[76] ibid, Art 37(1).
[77] ibid, Art 7(2).

foreigners residing in Vietnam.[78] A marriage between a foreigner and a Vietnamese citizen contracted outside Vietnam may be registered by the Vietnamese consul in the country where the Vietnamese party resides.[79]

ii. Divorce, Nullity and Separation

Most bilateral agreements on legal assistance that Vietnam have signed consist of specific provisions on jurisdiction over divorces cases. Normally, *in personam* jurisdiction rules based on nationality and residence are applied. If the spouses have the same nationality, the court or other authority in the country of their citizenship has jurisdiction. If they reside in another state, the authority in the place of residence will have jurisdiction. Where spouses have different nationalities, the authority where they reside has jurisdiction in the first instance. If one person resides in one signatory state and the other resides in another signatory state, the authorities in both states will have jurisdiction over the case. The national law recognised the same principle to determine the jurisdiction of Vietnamese court.[80] For cases of nullity of marriage, jurisdiction should be determined according to the similar principle as in divorce cases.[81] But the CPC has no specific provision on nullity of marriages. Nonetheless, it classifies the revocation of illegal marriages as a marriage-and family-related matter falling under the Vietnamese courts' jurisdiction. In the case of 'unrecognised spousal relations', there is ongoing debate on the nature of the relevant matters.[82] There is no special rule used for determining jurisdiction in such cases. Vietnam does not have a legal regime of separation. Therefore, separation will not be recognised in Vietnam.

iii. Well-being of the Child

Matters related to the well-being of child are in principle under the jurisdiction of the competent authority where the child lives. In 2016, Vietnam promulgated the Law on Children 2016[83] and followed that with a Decree in 2017.[84] Where there are violations of children's rights and well-being, competence mainly rests with the state management agency and often results in administrative decisions. The national court will have jurisdiction if criminal offences are involved. In relation to claims for alimony, the authority at the place where the claimant resides has jurisdiction to handle the case according to Article 129(2) of the Law on Marriage and

[78] ibid, Art 37.

[79] Art 7(1) of Joint Circular No 02/2016/TTLT-BNG-BTP on Guiding the Registration and Management of Civil Status by Overseas Vietnamese Diplomatic Missions and Consular Offices dated 30 June 2016.

[80] Typically, a Vietnamese people's court (normally of the provincial level) obtains *general jurisdiction* over a divorce case according to (1) the Vietnamese nationality of the parties: the plaintiffs or the defendants being Vietnamese citizens; or (2) the domiciled-based of foreign spouses, if the case involves parties being foreigners who reside, work or live for a long term in Vietnam (CPC Art 469(1)(d)). The *exclusive jurisdiction* of Vietnamese court is limited to divorce cases between spouses consisting of a Vietnamese citizen and a foreign citizen or a stateless person if both spouses reside, work or live permanently in Vietnam (CPC Art 470(1)(b)).

[81] This is mentioned in most of Vietnam's mutual judicial assistance treaties. See eg Art 26(2) of the treaty with Cuba, Art 33(3) of the treaty with Hungary, Art 23(3) of the treaty with Bulgaria, Art 28(2) of the treaty with Laos, Art 27(2) of the treaty with Mongolia, Art 27(2) of the treaty with the Czech Republic, Art 27 of the treaty with Russia, and Art 27 of the treaty with Poland.

[82] Quang Thuan Huynh, 'Giải quyết yêu cầu không công nhận quan hệ vợ chồng là vụ án dân sự hay việc dân sự?' ['Handling a Claim of Unrecognised Spousal Relations is a Civil Dispute or a Civil Matter?'] (*Tạp chí Tòa án nhân dân điện tử* [*People's Court Electronic Journal*], 18 May 2020), available online: https://tinyurl.com/y56ybp6z.

[83] Law No 102/2016/QH13 dated 5 April 2016.

[84] Decree No 56/2017/ND-CP on Detailing a Number of Articles of the Law on Children 2016 dated 9 May 2017.

Family 2014. In practice, claims over alimony usually follow a divorce case. When existing separately, it is classified as a 'marriage and family'-related dispute falling within the court's jurisdiction under CPC Article 28(5).

C. Corporations, Insolvency and Bankruptcy

i. Jurisdiction Over Corporations-related Matters

In Vietnam, corporations are characterised as the subjects of commercial-business activities, that is, 'enterprises' having the status of a commercial legal person.[85] Vietnamese private international law normally applies the principle of nationality (essentially, for a company, the application of the law of the state of incorporation)[86] in choice of law questions relating to legal persons, including corporations from creation to dissolution.[87] However, when it comes to disputes, there is no specific rule to determine the jurisdiction of the court. Procedural law only furnishes the rules of general jurisdiction already discussed, albeit with restrictions on the subject-matter that the court will entertain. Thus, a corporation-related case involving foreign elements may fall within the jurisdiction of the Vietnamese court if it meets at least one of the criteria in CPC Article 469 on general jurisdiction. However, the Vietnamese court will only handle corporation-related cases if the dispute falls into certain specified categories:[88] (1) disputes between persons who are not members of a company but who were involved in the transfer of share capital among the company and its members; (2) disputes between a company and its shareholders; (3) disputes between a limited liability company and its manager, director, or board, regarding the company's operation, dissolution, merger, consolidation, division, organisation, or transfer of property; and (4) petitions for the revocation of shareholder and other resolutions. Normally, the provincial courts have jurisdiction to handle the foregoing disputes,[89] and district courts can deal with the petitions just mentioned.[90] Nonetheless, petitions involving foreign parties or property, or which must be judicially entrusted to representative agencies of the Vietnamese Government overseas, or foreign courts or agencies, will be heard by the provincial court.[91]

ii. Insolvency Proceedings and Bankruptcy-related Matters

The Law on Bankruptcy 2014[92] is the principal legislation governing insolvency proceedings and bankruptcy-related matters in corporations and other organisations, except for credit institutions.[93] The Law on Bankruptcy is applied to reorganisations, financial restructurings, and liquidations which are carried out as part of insolvency proceedings. Generally, the Law on Bankruptcy is applied to enterprises and cooperatives established in the territory of Vietnam, unless an operative international treaty prescribes differently.[94] Normally, an enterprise

[85] Civil Code 2015, Art 75.
[86] PM North and JJ Fawcett, *Cheshire and North's Private International Law* 12th edn (London, Butterworths, 1992) 897.
[87] Civil Code 2015, Art 676.
[88] CPC, Arts 30, 31.
[89] ibid, Arts 37(1)(a), 37(1)(b).
[90] ibid, Art 35(2)(a).
[91] ibid, Art 37(2).
[92] Law No 51/2014/QH13, which came into effect on 1 January 2015.
[93] Defined by Article 4 of the Law on Credit Institutions 2010 (Law No 47/2010/QH12) to include commercial banks, financial companies, finance leasing companies, micro-finance institutions and people's credit funds.
[94] Law on Bankruptcy 2014, Arts 2, 3.

or a cooperative registered in Vietnam, even if by foreign investors, will have the status of a Vietnamese legal person and be considered as having Vietnamese nationality.[95] However, a private enterprise has no status as a legal person. The owner of the private enterprise will be held responsible for all its operations. That means that it is impossible for a foreign enterprise to file for bankruptcy before the Vietnamese court because the domestic law has no regulation covering such a situation. But a foreign bankruptcy order may be recognised in Vietnam as a foreign judgment and based on reciprocity. A provincial court has competence in bankruptcy cases, if the business entity was established in that province or municipality and has assets[96] overseas or participants in the bankruptcy procedures are abroad.[97] The People's Court of a district has competence in the remaining cases on condition that a business entity has its headquarters in that district.[98]

iii. Competition Law

Competition Law is new to Vietnam. It is governed by the Competition Law 2004[99] and its amended version of 2018.[100] The Competition Law 2004 is the first statute codifying and synthesising substantive and procedural law in the field of competition law. As a result, competition proceedings exist independently alongside civil, criminal and administrative proceedings.[101] For competition cases involving foreign elements, the determination of jurisdiction depends on their 'scope of anti-competitive practices'. The Competition Law 2004 provided for competition-restricting acts, unfair competition acts, order and procedures for settling competition cases, measures to handle violations of competition legislation.[102] This law, with no mention of foreign markets, could be interpreted as only governing anti-competitive practices in Vietnam. Therefore, the jurisdiction of domestic authorities was set up based on the place where the delict was committed. If the anti-competitive practice was committed in Vietnam, the domestic agency would have the competence to handle the case. This jurisdiction was applied to all business individuals and organisations in Vietnam, including foreign enterprises.[103] Thus, 'the scope of anti-competitive practices' was the territory of the Vietnamese market. The Competition Law 2018 widened the scope of regulation which as now governs any activities whether by Vietnamese

[95] Civil Code 2015, Arts 80, 676.

[96] According to Art 2(1) of Resolution No 03/2016/NQ-HĐTP Guiding the Implementation of a Number of Articles of the Law on Bankruptcy 2014, issued by the Council of Justices of the Supreme People's Court, 'assets in foreign countries' means property determined in accordance with the provisions of the Civil Code which is outside Vietnam's territorial borders at the time the Court is seised with a bankruptcy application. The Resolution is available online: https://tinyurl.com/87z5cqkn.

[97] Law on Bankruptcy 2014, Art 8(1)(a). According to Resolution No 03/2016/NQ-HĐTP (n 96), 'participants in bankruptcy procedures abroad' include: (1) foreigners or stateless persons who are not settled, do not engage in business, study or work in Vietnam; or are not present in Vietnam at the time of presentation of a bankruptcy petition; (2) Vietnamese residing, working, studying or working in a foreign country at the time of presentation of a bankruptcy petition; and (3) agencies and organisations which do not have their head office, branches or representative offices in Vietnam at the time of presentation of a bankruptcy petition.

[98] Law on Bankruptcy 2014, Art 8(2).

[99] Law No 27/2004/QH11, which came into effect on 1 July 2005.

[100] Law No 23/2018/QH14, which came into effect on 1 July 2019.

[101] Danh Vinh Le (ed), *Giáo trình Luật Cạnh tranh* [*Textbook on Competition Law*] (Ho Chi Minh City, University of Economics and Law, Vietnam National University Ho Chi Minh City, 2010) 6.

[102] Competition Law 2004, Art 1.

[103] ibid, Art 2.

or foreign entities or individuals which have or may potentially have an anti-competitive impact on the Vietnamese domestic market.[104] Such an impact would be caused by restrictive practices or economic concentration.[105] Under the Competition Law 2018, the Competition Authority of Vietnam has competence to deal with offshore activities and transactions which have or may potentially have an impact on the Vietnamese market. The law will apply if an entity does not have a subsidiary or other presence in Vietnam.

Under the Competition Law 2004, the Competition Authority's jurisdiction was subject-matter based. Two types of conduct were proscribed: acts that restrict competition and acts of unfair competition acts. Complains about the former activities fell under the jurisdiction of the Competition Authority (*Cục quản lý cạnh tranh*)[106] and the Competition Council (*Hội đồng cạnh tranh*).[107] Complaints about the latter activities fell within the jurisdiction of the Competition Authority and the Minister of Industry and Trade with a different scope of competence compared to the first one mentioned above.[108] The Competition Authority had the power to investigate and prosecute cases, including imposing administrative penalties.[109] The Minister of Industry and Trade had the power to resolve complaints about the handling by the Competition Authority of cases relating to unfair competition.[110] In both situations, the People's Court had jurisdiction to settle administrative lawsuits against the relevant competition case settlement agency.[111] The Competition Law 2018 consolidated the various competences and entrusts them to a single authority, the National Competition Committee (NCC)[112] a unit under the Ministry of Industry and Trade. The NCC runs a Competition Investigation Agency as a sub-unit.[113] In the case of a disagreement with the decision of the NCC, the relevant party may initiate an administrative lawsuit before the competent court as prescribed by the Law on Administrative Proceedings. The only case when litigation relating to competition law can be classified as a civil dispute and handled through normal civil proceedings would be a dispute on compensation for wrongful application of administrative measures in a competition matter. The would be a tortious claim and the principles for determining jurisdiction over a tort case will apply. However, compensation claims settled in administrative lawsuits would be excluded from this class of case.[114]

[104] Competition Law 2018, Art 1.

[105] Minh Thuy Le, 'Vietnam's New Competition Law 2018' (*Vietnam Business Law*, 30 July 2018), available online: https://tinyurl.com/y266jq49.

[106] Established as a department under the Vietnamese Ministry of Industry and Trade with the power to investigate cases of anti-competitive conduct, but not to settle or prosecute the same. The results of an investigation were submitted to the Competition Council for handling. See Competition Law 2004, Arts 49(1)(c), 86.

[107] Competition Law 2004, Art 53(2).

[108] The People's Court had jurisdiction to resolve complaints against decisions of the Minister of Industry and Trade on matters relating to unfair competition. See Competition Law 2004, Art 115.

[109] Competition Law 2004, Arts 49(1)(c), 49(1)(d).

[110] ibid, Art 111.

[111] For complaints in relation to restrictive practices, the court (normally at provincial level) has jurisdiction to resolve administrative suits against the decisions of the Competition Council. The Court of Appeal and Council of Judges of the Supreme People's Court are competent to settle competition cases in accordance with normal appellate and cassation procedures. For complaints about unfair competition, the court has jurisdiction to resolve complaints against the decisions of the Minister of Industry and Trade in accordance with the normal procedures in administrative cases. See Competition Law 2004, Art 115.

[112] Koushan Das, 'Vietnam's Competition Law and Its Impact on Foreign Companies' (*Vietnam Briefing*, 4 July 2019), available online: www.vietnam-briefing.com/news/vietnam-competition-law-impact-foreign-companies.html.

[113] See Competition Law 2018, Arts 45–53.

[114] CPC, Art 26(7).

IV. Jurisdiction *in rem* with Special Focus on Shipping Claims

A. Jurisdiction *in rem* in Maritime Claims

Actions *in rem*, being proceedings directly against property, are a manifestation of the principle that a state has the power to determine the title, status, or condition of property within its borders. This principle is recognised by Vietnamese law on civil procedure. Under Maritime Code 2015 Article 339(2), in the case of a maritime dispute resolution where all parties involved are foreign entities and enter into a written agreement on the settlement of such dispute by the Vietnamese court, the court will have jurisdiction provided that the grounds for establishment, change or termination of the parties' relationship is governed by Vietnamese law or the asset involved is in Vietnam. This would then be a case falling under the exclusive jurisdiction of the Vietnamese court according to CPC 2015 Article 470(1)(c). A maritime claim that the parties may bring to court in the above situation would be a request by one party that the other perform an obligation in connection with maritime shipping.[115] Under Article 40(4) of the Maritime Code 2015, a claimant is vested with a maritime lien against a ship to secure rights prescribed in Article 41 of the Maritime Code 2015.[116] Where there is no choice of court agreement designating the Vietnamese court, a plaintiff can apply to the court to exercise its general jurisdiction if the defendant's property is located in Vietnam.[117]

B. Ship Arrest

The arrest of ships is considered a provisional emergency measure applied in the process of settling civil lawsuits as prescribed in CPC Article 114(16). More detailed regulations on the arrest of ships are found in the Maritime Code 2015. Accordingly, the arrest of ships refers to the detention or restriction on removal of a ship by order of a court to secure a maritime claim, apply interim injunctions, enforce civil judgments and perform mutual legal assistance.[118] The authority to arrest or release a ship is vested in the People's Court of the province where the seaport at which the ship is located. In addition, the People's Court of the province where the Arbitration Council is resolving a dispute can order the arrest of a ship as an interim measure.[119] When a ship is subject to detention or a temporary impounding order issued by a court, it will not be allowed to leave the seaport.[120] Consequently, the arrest of a ship commences when the person with the right to arrest applies to the court. The latter will then assign a judge to review the petition. Within 48 hours after the petition is received, the judge will consider whether to accept the request for the arrest of the ship or not.[121] If the application satisfies

[115] Maritime Code 2015 (Law No 95/2015/QH13), Art 40(1).

[116] ibid, Art 41. Claims giving rise to a maritime lien would include: (1) claims for salary, repatriation cost, social insurance contribution, and other monetary amounts payable to the master, officers or crew of a ship; (2) claims for compensation for loss of life, incurring a disability, or suffering personal injury in the course of a ship's operation; (3) claims in respect of deadweight, marine safety, and seaport fees or charges; (4) claims for salvage; and (5) claims for non-contractual property loss and damage relating to the operation of a ship.

[117] CPC, Art 469(1)(c).

[118] Maritime Code 2015, Art 129.

[119] ibid, Art 130. See also CPC, Arts 420, 421.

[120] Maritime Code 2015, Art 98(2)(d).

[121] CPC, Art 133(3).

all requirements, as soon as the person requesting the arrest of the ship presents receipts and documents proving that they have fulfilled their obligations in respect of the payment of fees and the provision of financial security, the judge will issue a decision to arrest the ship to secure a maritime claim.[122] The director of the port authority will thereafter issue a notice of the decision to arrest the ship. When implementing the decision, the director may designate its mooring position and limit its movement. Despite stringent regulations, there remain deficiencies in the law on ship arrest. Article 5 of the Ordinance on Procedures for the Ship Arrest of Seagoing Ships 2008 prescribes rules for the provision of financial security for the arrest of ships. But, in practice, the provision of security for the arrest of ships may be difficult for many domestic enterprises, especially small and medium enterprises (SMEs).

V. Immunities from Jurisdiction

A. Sovereign Immunity

Vietnamese scholars classify a state as a special subject when it takes part in a civil legal relationship. This classification follows the theory of state immunity in which a state when entering into certain international civil relationships may be entitled to judicial and property immunity as special privileges. Judicial immunity gives a state the right not to be subject to the court proceedings of another state, immunity from measures of constraint in connection with such proceedings, and immunity from judgment execution measures.[123] That also means, that a state has immunity from jurisdiction, unless the state submits to the jurisdiction of the other state by agreement. The ability to execute a judgment on a foreign state and to seize property or assets of a foreign country is limited. In actions against states, Vietnam will likely follow the doctrine of restrictive state immunity, whereby immunity only covers governmental acts (*acta iure imperii*) and does not attach to commercial acts (*acta iure gestionis*). Banh Quoc Tuan,[124] Nguyen Thai Mai and Vu Duc Long,[125] Le Thi Nam Giang, Do Van Dai and Mai Hong Quy[126] are notable experts who support this doctrine. Nonetheless, Vietnam does not have any special law or legal norm regulating state immunity. Previously, Article 84 of the Ordinance on Procedures for Settlement of Civil Cases dated 29 November 1989 (which came into effect on 1 January 1990) stipulated that civil cases involving foreign states or diplomats should be settled through diplomatic channels, except where the foreign state or diplomat agree to the jurisdiction of the Vietnamese court. But that ordinance had been repealed. The current CPC does not mention state immunity.[127] Scholars[128]

[122] This decision can be appealed against by the master, owner, demise charterer, or operator of the ship.

[123] Thai Mai Nguyen and Duc Long Vu, 'Chủ thể trong Tư pháp quốc tế' ['Subjects of International Private Law'] in Minh Ngoc Tran and Thi Phuong Lan Vu (eds), *Giáo trình Tư pháp quốc tế* [*Textbook on International Private Law*] (Hanoi Law University, Judicial Publisher, Hanoi, 2017) 142–43.

[124] Of the Faculty of Law, Hanoi National University.

[125] Of the Hanoi Law University.

[126] Of the Ho Chi Minh City University of Law.

[127] A similar provision is now found in the current CPC 2015, Art 2(4): 'For foreign individuals, agencies and organizations that enjoy diplomatic privileges and immunities or consular privileges and immunities under Vietnamese laws, international treaties to which the Socialist Republic of Vietnam is a signatory, the civil cases related to such individuals, agencies and/or organizations shall be settled through the diplomatic channel.' This Article no longer mentions 'state' and therefore excludes a state as a special subject having immunity.

[128] Thi Nam Giang Le, 'Chủ thể trong Tư pháp quốc tế' ['Subjects of International Private Law'] in Hong Quy Mai (ed), *Giáo trình Tư pháp quốc tế* [*Textbook on International Private Law*] (Hanoi, Hong Duc Publisher, 2016) 90.

argue that if a state's representative is entitled to immunity, it must follow as a matter of logic that the state should be entitled to the same privilege.[129] Conversely, when listing persons amenable to the court's civil jurisdiction, CPC Article 464 only mentions individuals, legal entities, and organisations, but does not mention states. Thus, the CPC has indirectly confirmed (as the argument runs) that the Vietnamese court will not exercise jurisdiction over cases against a foreign state. Civil Code 2015 Article 100 specifies that the Vietnamese Government will be liable in a civil suit, where it has given up its right to immunity by: (1) international treaty; (2) contract; or (3) waiver. In practice, most cases where Vietnam has taken part as a defendant have been based on international treaties. Examples are *Shin Dong Baig v Vietnam*[130] and *Trinh Vinh Binh v Vietnam*.[131] Both cases derive from bilateral investment treaties (BITs), one between Vietnam and Korea, the other between Vietnam and the Netherlands.

B. Diplomatic Immunity

State immunity generally extends to diplomats and senior state representatives. The relevant principles are spelled out in the 1961 Vienna Convention on Diplomatic Relations to which Vietnam is a party. In civil disputes, diplomatic persons can claim immunity from suit, except in relation to: (1) private property transactions; (2) questions of succession or inheritance; and (3) professional or commercial activities carried on outside of their official function. Diplomatic immunity is clearly recognised in CPC Article 2(4). So, in civil cases where a diplomat is involved, the court will not exercise its jurisdiction and the dispute should be settled through diplomatic channels.

C. State-Owned Enterprises

State-owned enterprises (SOEs) are not entitled to immunity from jurisdiction. More specifically, a SOE is responsible for the civil transactions that it enters into, unless the same have been guaranteed by the Vietnamese Government or a central or local regulatory agency.[132] This means that a Vietnamese SOE, when engaging in an international civil relation, will bear civil liability. This principle based on the restrictive theory of state immunity is not a new concept to Vietnam. From Vietnam's opening to the world trade market after *doi moi*, its SOEs have participated in international civil and commercial transactions like any other company or legal person and have incurred civil liability in such capacity. The Italian case of *Vietnam Airlines v Maurizio Liberati* since 1994 is well known in Vietnam. An Italian lawyer sued Falcomar, an Italian company having an agency contract with Vietnam Airlines, for unpaid wages.[133] Until 1993 Vietnam Airlines had been an airline under the Department of Civil Aviation which meant that it was a unit of the Vietnamese Government. From April 1993, it became a SOE. It was not entitled to claim immunity from the Italian court's jurisdiction in the name of the Socialist Republic of Vietnam. As a result, it had to pay compensation.

[129] Nguyen and Vu (n 123) 149.
[130] ICSID Case No ARB(AF)/18/2, available online: https://tinyurl.com/y64cnl24.
[131] See www.italaw.com/cases/155.
[132] Civil Code 2015, Art 99(3).
[133] 'Vietnam Airlines Yet to Lose 5.2 Mln-Euro Lawsuit' (*VietnamNet*, 31 March 2011), available online: https://english.vietnamnet.vn/fms/business/6204/vietnam-airlines-yet-to-lose-5-2-mln-euro-lawsuit.html.

10

Cambodia

NOBUMICHI TERAMURA*

I. Introduction

The Kingdom of Cambodia (Cambodia) is a civil law country whose private law, including rules of direct jurisdiction, is under the strong influence of Japanese law. Since 1996, the Japanese Government has been helping the development of the Cambodian legal system through, for example, offering training opportunities for young lawyers to study law in Japan.[1] Then, in 1999, the Cambodian and Japanese Governments reached an agreement on the provision of legal development aid supports to Cambodia within the scheme of 'Japanese Cooperation to Support the Formulation of Key Government Policies' that requested the Japan International Cooperation Agency (JICA) to work with the Cambodian judiciary and Ministry of Justice for the development of the Cambodian legal system on a long-term and pro bono basis.[2] Through the scheme, the Japanese Government agreed to expand the support to assist Cambodia in drafting legislation on civil matters.[3] The range of the support was comprehensive in that the Japanese Government agreed to provide – via the JICA – knowledge support through sending Japanese legal experts to Cambodia for both short-term and long-term, offering materials and equipment that are necessary for the project, training Cambodian lawyers, etc.[4] The cooperation of diligent Cambodian and Japanese lawyers brought about the promulgation of the Code of Civil Procedure of Cambodia (CCP) in 2006[5] and the Civil Code of Cambodia (CC) in 2007.[6] They have since then been working on other reform projects to maximise the effects and impacts of the new legislation.[7]

* The author is grateful to Mr Issei Sakano, Advisor of the Ministry of Justice of Kingdom of Cambodia, and other legal practitioners working in Phnom Penh for their insightful comments that helped completing the manuscript. Note that responsibility for any errors that remain is solely my own.

[1] www.moj.go.jp/housouken/houso_houkoku_cambo.html. See also the author's interview with Mr Sakano.

[2] ibid.

[3] www.jica.go.jp/project/cambodia/0701047/04/pdf/materials/02a.pdf.

[4] ibid.

[5] Unofficial English translation prepared by the JICA as part of the project is available online: www.trc.gov.kh/wp-content/uploads/2015/05/code-of-civil-procedure-en.pdf.

[6] Unofficial English translation prepared by the JICA as part of the project is available online: www.trc.gov.kh/wp-content/uploads/2015/05/civil-code-en.pdf.

[7] Including but not limited to: Japanese Technical Cooperation for the Legal and Judicial Development Project (Phase II) (April 2004–April 2007, extension period: April 2007 to April 2008), available online: www.jica.go.jp/project/cambodia/0701047/04/pdf/materials/02_02_rd.pdf; www.jica.go.jp/project/cambodia/0701047/04/pdf/materials/02_02_rdex.pdf; Legal and Judicial Development Project (Phase III) (April 2008–March 2012), available online: www.jica.go.jp/project/cambodia/0701047/04/pdf/materials/02_03_rd.pdf; Legal and Judicial Development Project (Phase IV) (April 2012–March 2017), available online: www.jica.go.jp/project/english/cambodia/014/index.html; and Legal and Judicial Development Project (Phase V) (April 2017–March 2022), available online: www.jica.go.jp/project/english/

Though colonised by France from 1863 to 1953, the influence of French law in the current Cambodian civil law is not as prevalent as it used to be. This is not because the Cambodian Government and the JICA have been attempting to sweep out the remains of French colonialism, but primarily because the old French-style Cambodian legal system was almost entirely demolished by the Communist Party of Kampuchea (CPK) during the Khmer Rouge period from 1975 to 1979.[8] The CPK's persistent persecution and execution of legal professions in ruling Cambodia without even a pretence of legality turned the country into a legal vacuum where only a handful of lawyers were able to survive with the near-total loss of legal documents and institutions.[9]

As a consequence, even when the Kingdom of Cambodia was established in 1993 as a constitutional monarchy and the new government asked Japan to assist in re-building their legal infrastructures, only a limited amount of literature was available for Cambodian lawyers and the JICA to investigate the old Civil Code and the Code of Civil Procedure.[10] Given such circumstance and the French Government's lack of adequate resources for helping Cambodia draft new legislation, the new Cambodian Government requested the JICA to work with the Ministry of Justice (MOJ) of Cambodia to draft the CC and the CCP,[11] aiming to establish private laws that not only respect Cambodian traditions and customs but also conform with market-oriented economic reforms.[12]

Because of the history, one may need to have some knowledge of Japanese law when learning about Cambodian private law. For example, Japanese experts have been responsible for building capacities of Cambodian lawyers for using the Codes (CC and CCP) and other relevant legislation, and some of their notes and reports are written only in Japanese.[13] Many other vital documents such as commentaries and textbooks are written only in Khmer and Japanese.[14] Since Cambodian lawyers have not perceived the doctrine of precedent as binding or convincing,

cambodia/025/index.html. See also generally Yuka Kaneko, 'Japan's Civil Code Drafting Support for Socialist Reform Countries: Diversity of Normative Choice' in Yuka Kaneko (ed), *Civil Law Reforms in Post-Colonial Asia: Beyond Western Capitalism* (Singapore, Springer, 2019).

[8] Kong Phallack, 'Overview of the Cambodian Legal and Judicial System and Recent Efforts at Legal and Judicial Reform' in Hor Peng, Kong Phallack and Jörg Menzel (eds), *Introduction to Cambodian Law* (Cambodia, Konrad-Adenauer-Stiftung, 2012) 7.

[9] Michael Vickery, *Kampuchea: Politics, Economy and Society* (Frances Pinter 1986) 120; Phallack (n 8) 8 (suggesting in fn 6 that only ten law graduates including five judges remained in the country as of January 1979). See also Jennifer Holligan and others, 'UPDATE: Overview of the Cambodian History, Governance and Legal Sources' (*GlobaLex*, July/August 2019) Section 2, available online: www.nyulawglobal.org/globalex/Cambodia1.html#_CPK/DK_period:_1975.

[10] Issei Sakano, 'Reflection of My Experience in Legal and Judicial Development Project for Drafting Civil and Civil Procedure Codes' [in Japanese] (*ICD NEWS*, July 2003) 97, available online: www.moj.go.jp/content/000010269.pdf.

[11] Akio Morishima, 'Reflection of My Experience in Legal and Judicial Development Project for Drafting Civil Code' [in Japanese] (*ICD NEWS*, September 2003) 5, available online: www.moj.go.jp/content/000010277.pdf (noting that the French Government initially agreed to offer support for drafting new legislation and therefore tasked French scholars to draft the Criminal Code, Criminal Procedure Code and Civil Procedure Code for Cambodia, but the scholars paid less attention to the status quo of the Cambodian society and communication with Cambodian lawyers).

[12] Hiroshi Kiyohara, 'Civil Code' in Peng, Phallack and Menzel (n 8) 99. See also generally Kong Phallack, 'Overview of Contemporary Civil Procedures of Cambodia' in Peng, Phallack and Menzel (n 8) 153–80; Anirudh Bhati, 'Japanese Law And Cambodian Justice: Beyond Legal Transplants In Contemporary Legal Reform' (*Greater Mekong Research Center*, 25 July 2017), available online: www.mekongresearch.org/blog/2017/7/25/japanese-law-and-cambodian-justice-beyond-legal-transplants-in-contemporary-legal-reform.

[13] See generally www.jica.go.jp/project/english/cambodia/014/outline/index.html and www.jica.go.jp/project/english/cambodia/025/index.html.

[14] For example, the Commentaries on the CCP of the Kingdom of Cambodia, the Textbook on Judgment Proceedings and the Textbook on Compulsory Execution and Preservative Relief, available online: www.jica.go.jp/project/english/cambodia/0701047/materials/index.html. Also, the record of the discussion by the legislative committees (working groups) for drafting the CCP and CC was written in Japanese and has been stored in the Ministry of Justice of Cambodia: Svay Leng, 'Problems in Translating Cambodian Civil Code and Civil Procedure Code and Future Prospects' [in Japanese] (*ICD NEWS*, September 2016), available online: www.moj.go.jp/content/001298242.pdf.

the value and impact of those authoritative documents may not be underestimated.[15] Therefore, this chapter provides concise guidance of direct jurisdiction in Cambodia, taking into account relevant documents written not only in English, but also in Japanese.

This chapter assumes that rules on domestic jurisdiction may apply to decide the international jurisdiction of Cambodian courts. This idea derives from previous legal practice in Japan on international jurisdiction surrounding the old version of the Japanese Code of Civil Procedure – the foundation of the current CCP. The theory behind the practice is summarised by Nishitani as follows:

> Prior to [2011], there were no written rules on international jurisdiction except for limited special rules in international instruments. Hence, jurisdiction rules have been principally established by case law …, referring to *naturalis ratio* (*jôri*) *based on the ideas of fairness between the parties and an equitable and expeditious administration of justice*. … In the concrete application of *jôri*, courts granted international jurisdiction insofar as a specific court in Japan … had local jurisdiction pursuant to the domestic jurisdiction rules provided in the [Japanese] CCP. The local jurisdiction of a particular court in Japan was considered to presuppose the existence of international jurisdiction.[16]

The doctrine of *jôri* is unlikely to exist in Cambodia as it is a Japanese legal concept proclaimed by *Daijokan* (Grand Council of State) during the *Meiji* period. No discernible evidence suggests that the doctrine has been imported into the Cambodian legal system. However, Article 4 of the CCP requires Cambodian courts to make efforts to proceed with civil actions fairly and speedily, while obliging parties to pursue civil actions honestly and in good faith.[17] In other words, the Article may play a similar role with *jôri*, and, therefore, there seem to be no outstanding problems in presupposing the existence of international jurisdiction from the local jurisdiction of a particular court in Cambodia.

II. Jurisdiction *in personam*

A. General Principles

Article 8 of the CCP sets out general rules of jurisdiction *in personam*, under which the Court of First Instance having territorial jurisdiction over 'the address of the defendant' shall hear the case. The address of the defendant is defined according to the type of the defendant as follows:

(a) **Natural person**: (1) his/her domicile; (2) the location of residence, where such a natural person does not have a domicile within Cambodia, or where his/her domicile is unknown; or (3) his/her last known domicile, where such natural person does not have a location of residence within Cambodia, or where the location of his/her residence is unknown.

[15] This is because judgments are not published in Cambodia and are not regarded as sources of law: Robin Gardner, 'Southeast Asian Legal Research Guide: Courts & Cases' (*The University of Melbourne*, 2020), available online: https://unimelb.libguides.com/c.php?g=402982&p=4816214; Phallack (n 8) 10–11 (noting that primary sources of law in the country are the Constitution, Laws (Chbab), Royal Decrees (Preah Reach Kret), Sub-Decrees (Anu-Kret), Proclamations (Prakas), Decision (Sech Kdei Samrach) (executive regulations issued by ministers), Circular (Sarachor), Bylaw (Deika), and international law). Note that the JICA and the MOJ of Cambodia aim to start publishing judgments by 2022: www.jica.go.jp/project/english/cambodia/025/outline/index.html.

[16] Yuko Nishitani, 'International Jurisdiction of Japanese Courts in a Comparative Perspective' (2013) 60 *Netherlands International Law Review* 251, 252–53 (emphasis added).

[17] CCP, Art 4.

(b) **Cambodian juridical person (corporation)**: (1) the location of its administrative headquarters or business office; or (2) the location of the domicile of the entity's representative or another principal person in charge of the operations of the entity, where there is no administrative headquarters or business office.

(c) **Foreign juridical person (corporation)**: (1) the location of the entity's administrative headquarters or business office in Cambodia; or (2) the location of the domicile of the entity's representative or another principal person in charge of the operations of the entity in Cambodia, where there is no administrative headquarters or business office within Cambodia.

Under Cambodian law, juridical persons (corporations) mean either (profit and non-profit) associations (companies) or foundations (including public and charitable foundations).[18]

i. Jurisdiction of Courts within the Territory

Cambodia has a unified judicial system. According to the Law on the Organization of the Courts (LOC),[19] Cambodian courts are classified as the Court of First Instance (first level courts), the Court of Appeal (second level courts) and the Supreme Court.[20] Cambodia consists of 25 provinces (including the autonomous municipality of capital Phnom Penh), and the capital of each province, other than Kep Province, has one Court of First Instance.[21] A Court of First Instance may exercise jurisdiction over the case if the defendant has an address in the province.[22] Moreover, the Court of Appeal in Phnom Penh had been the only second-level court in the country and handled all appeal cases until March 2020, and, since the establishment of new regional appeal courts on 1 April 2020, the four second-level courts have been dealing with appeal cases from their respective regions.[23] Finally, the Supreme Court is in Phnom Penh.

Those courts have general judicial jurisdiction over all cases, including administrative ones,[24] though courts of each level are divided into special courts and chambers. The Court of First Instance consists of the Civil Court, Criminal Court, Commercial Court, and Labour Court.[25] How these special courts share jurisdiction seems to be unclear as the LOC merely provides

[18] CC, Art 46.

[19] An unofficial translation prepared by Cambodian Center for Human Rights is available online: www.sithi.org/admin/upload/law/02_CCHR_Draft_of_Law_of_the_Organization_the_Courts_English.pdf. Although it is a translation of the draft version, the document seems to be the only available English translation of the Law on the Organization of the Courts revised in 2014.

[20] LOC, Art 3 (referring the Military Court that is in the same hierarchical level as the Court of First Instance and has special jurisdiction over military matters).

[21] Atsushi Uchiyama, 'Cambodian Judiciary: The Court of First Instance' [in Japanese] (*ICD NEWS*, December 2017) 48, available online: www.moj.go.jp/content/001246676.pdf. Cases arising in Kep Province fall under the jurisdiction of Kampot Provincial Court: https://cacj-ajp.org/web/cambodia/description-of-cambodian-courts.

[22] CCP, Art 8.

[23] Taing Vida, 'Regional Appeal Courts Open on April 1' (*Khmer Times*, 25 March 2020), available online: www.khmertimeskh.com/50705314/regional-appeal-courts-open-on-april-1/. Respectively: (1) the Tboung Khmum Appeal Court (covering Kampong Cham, Kampong Thom, Preah Vihear, Kratie, Stung Treng, Ratanakiri, Mondulkiri, and Tboung Khmum); (2) the Battambang Appeal Court (covering Pursat, Battambang, Pailin, Banteay Meanchey, Oddar Meanchey, and Siem Reap); and (3) Preah Sihanouk Appeal Court (covering Kampot, Kep, Koh Kong, and Preah Sihanouk). The Phnom Penh Appeal Court is now responsible for appeals from cases in the provincial courts of Phnom Penh, Kandal, Kampong Chhnang, Kampong Speu, Takeo, Prey Veng, and Svay Rieng.

[24] LOC, Art 4.

[25] Note that local practitioners call them 'Chambers' since no organised independent Special Courts have been established yet. Typically, in practice, each Court of First Instance consists of a Civil Law Division (Chamber) and a Criminal Law Division (Chamber) only.

that the Civil, Criminal, Commercial, and Labour Courts are competent to hear civil, criminal, commercial, and labour cases respectively.[26] To deal with the potential conflict of jurisdiction among specialised courts, Article 19 of the LOC requires the President of the Court of First Instance to hold a meeting with the Presidents of the concerned specialised courts and to decide issues of competing jurisdiction, at the President's discretion or upon request by the President of any relevant specialised court(s). It seems that the lack of standards has not caused any jurisdictional issues – at least in practice – as neither the Commercial Courts nor the Labour Courts have been established yet.[27] The LOC also requires the Court of Appeal to have Civil, Criminal, Investigating, Commercial, and Labour Chambers,[28] but only the Criminal and Civil Chambers seem to have been accepting new cases.[29]

ii. Forum non conveniens, Lis alibi pendens, *Anti-suit Injunctions, Interim Measures and Choice of Court Agreements*

There are several legal principles with similar effects to certain common law doctrines of direct jurisdiction. For example, a variation of *forum non conveniens* is stipulated in Article 19(1) of the CCP, allowing a Court of First Instance, upon a party's motion or on its own authority, to transfer all or part of an action under its jurisdiction to another court, if such a transfer is necessary to avoid significant delay or to ensure procedural fairness. The Article is unlikely to be applied to transnational transfers as it is based on Article 17 of the Japanese Civil Code that does not apply to cross-border cases.[30] In addition, *lis alibi pendens* is expressly prohibited by Article 83 of the CCP ('A party may not file suit regarding a case that is already before the court.') for purely domestic cases, but the Article may not apply to a domestic case that is already before a foreign court and a foreign case that is already before the Cambodian court. The reason is that the Article does not take cross-border cases into consideration,[31] and foreign courts do not always pay attention to whether their cases have been referred to Cambodian courts already.

As for procedural orders, courts do not issue anti-suit injunctions that are prevalent in common law countries. However, they have authority to issue interim measures (preservative reliefs) such as provisional attachment, provisional disposition of the subject matter of the dispute and, provisional disposition establishing a provisional legal status.[32] These preservative measures belong to the exclusive jurisdiction of the court having jurisdiction over merits of the case, or the Court of First Instance having jurisdiction over the objects to be attached or the subject matter of the dispute.[33]

[26] LOC, Arts 20–22, 25.

[27] See eg Uchiyama (n 21) 50, fn 4; Japan External Trade Organisation, 'Enforcement of Intellectual Property Rights in Cambodia' [in Japanese] (*JETRO*, October 2018) 15, available online: www.jetro.go.jp/ext_images/world/asia/kh/ip/pdf/survey_201810_kh.pdf. See also the author's interview with local practitioners. In January 2021, the MOJ of Cambodia set up a commission to investigate the formation of Commercial Courts, to attract more foreign investments in Cambodia. See Buth Reaksmey Kongkea, 'Commercial Courts in the Pipeline to Attract More Investors' (*Khmer Times*, 25 January 2021), available online: www.khmertimeskh.com/50806501/commercial-courts-in-the-pipeline-to-attract-more-investors.

[28] LOC, Art 42.

[29] The author's interview with local practitioners.

[30] See the note on Art 19 in the Japanese language edition of the CCP of Cambodia, available online: www.jica.go.jp/project/cambodia/0701047/04/pdf/clause/clause01_j.pdf. An English translation of Code of Civil Procedure of Japan is available online: www.japaneselawtranslation.go.jp/law/detail/?id=2834&vm=2&re=02.

[31] See the note on Art 83 in the Japanese language edition of the CCP of Cambodia.

[32] CCP, Art 531.

[33] CCP, Arts 533, 540(1).

Finally, parties may have a valid choice of court agreement upon satisfying certain conditions. According to Article 13 of the CCP, such a jurisdictional agreement is valid only where: (1) 'it is made between merchant(s) and/or juristic person(s) with regard to the court of first instance'; (2) it pertains to an action on a specific legal relationship; and (3) it is made in writing.

iii. Service of Process

As of May 2021, Cambodia has not ratified any service conventions such as the 1965 Hague Convention on the Service Abroad of Judicial and Extrajudicial Documents in Civil or Commercial Matters[34] and the 1954 Hague Convention on Civil Procedure.[35] Therefore, the service of process is to be conducted following domestic norms. For instance, the basic rules of service of process outside the territory of Cambodia are provided in Article 253 of the CCP, according to which such service shall be made by the court through entrusting a service document to a competent governmental authority of the country, or the Cambodian ambassador, envoy, or consul to that foreign country. Where the service cannot be made in this way, or where the competent authority has not delivered the proof of service within six months, the court clerk may opt for service by a publication upon a party's motion and with permission by the court.[36] The publication can be made by posting on the court's notice board an announcement stating that the service document is kept by the clerk and is ready for delivery at any time.[37] To maximise the impact, the clerk may send the defendant abroad with a notice about the publication.[38] In any event, service by publication for a defendant abroad shall take effect after six weeks have passed since the posting of the announcement on the court's notice board.[39]

B. Special Rules for Establishing Jurisdiction

i. Law of Obligations

a. Contracts

Article 9 of the CCP provides additional grounds of jurisdiction to determine obligations.[40] Parties may bring actions demanding: (1) performance of obligations, to the court having the territorial jurisdiction over the location where the obligations are to be performed;[41] (2) payment of money on bills or checks, to the court having the territorial jurisdiction over the location where payment on the bill or check is to be made;[42] (3) performance of obligations against a person whose domicile is not in Cambodia or is unknown, to the court having the territorial jurisdiction over the location of the defendant's property which is the subject of the claim or security interest, or which may be seized;[43] and (4) performance of obligations against juridical persons whose administrative headquarters or business office are not in Cambodia or are

[34] The status table is available online: www.hcch.net/en/instruments/conventions/status-table/?cid=17.
[35] The status table is available online: www.hcch.net/en/instruments/conventions/status-table/?cid=33.
[36] CCP, Arts 255(1)(c), 255(1)(d).
[37] ibid, Art 256(1).
[38] ibid, Art 256(3).
[39] ibid, Art 257.
[40] According to CC, Art 309, causes of obligation are: contracts, unilateral legal acts, management of affairs without the mandate, unjust enrichment, tortious act, and legal provisions.
[41] CCP, Art 9(a).
[42] ibid, Art 9(b).
[43] ibid, Art 9(c).

unknown, to the court having the territorial jurisdiction over the location of the defendant's property which is the subject of the claim or security interest, or which may be seized.[44] Those grounds are additional to the jurisdictional bases in Article 8 of the CCP, so that parties involved in contract disputes may rely on either Article 8 or 9 to bring their claims of obligations before the court.

Since the CCP does not provide jurisdictional standards for any specific types of contracts, the default rule is that disputes concerning consumer or labour contracts may be referred to the court designated by grounds of jurisdiction over contractual disputes under Article 9 of the CCP. However, there are other options for consumers and employees to decide where to seek remedies.

For instance, according to the Law on Consumer Protection,[45] consumers and consumer associations are expected to bring the National Consumer Protection Committee (NCPC) their complaints about an alleged infringement of consumer rights.[46] The ombudsperson in the institution first investigates the alleged infringement, and then the NCPC issues decisions that are, if necessary, accompanied by administrative sanctions against the infringement.[47] State courts are unlikely to be involved in the complaints procedures.

Moreover, alternative dispute resolution (ADR) is recommended as a means to resolve labour disputes in Cambodia. For example, the Labour Code[48] recommends parties to refer an individual labour dispute to a preliminary conciliation by the Labour Inspector of their province, capital, or municipality.[49] If the preliminary conciliation fails, the parties can file a complaint in a court of competent jurisdiction.[50] Accordingly, should parties not opt for conciliation to resolve an individual labour dispute, they can refer the case to a competent court, although such a choice has been perceived as impractical in Cambodia.[51] The Code also requires parties to have a conciliation as per the instructions from the Labour Inspector and the Labour Minister in order to solve a collective labour dispute.[52] If the conciliation fails, the parties are required to settle the dispute through arbitration by the Council of Arbitration or any other dispute resolution proceedings as they have agreed.[53] Litigation then may be a choice but not appealing to many employees and employers.

b. Torts

Article 9 of the CCP also stipulates the jurisdictional rules of tort claims, stating that parties may bring a tort action to the court having jurisdiction over the place where the alleged tort occurred.[54] The plaintiff is not required to prove the tort but prima facie showing the occurrence of the tort may be encouraged.[55] In addition, the CCP is silent as to the definition of the place of

[44] ibid, Art 9(d).

[45] Unofficial English translation is available online: https://ibccambodia.com/wp-content/uploads/2020/01/Law-on-Consumer-Protection_EN.pdf.

[46] Law on Consumer Protection, Art 28.

[47] ibid, Arts 29–32.

[48] Unofficial English translation is available online: www.ilo.org/dyn/travail/docs/701/labour.

[49] Labour Code, Art 300. See also Kong Phallack, 'Cambodian Labour and Employment Law' in Peng, Phallack and Menzel (n 8) 290–91.

[50] Labour Code, Art 301. The complaint must be submitted within two months.

[51] Shoichiro Tamagaki, 'The Arbitration Council in Cambodia: Impacts of the 2016 Law on Trade Unions and Prakas No 303 by the Ministry of Labour and Vocational Training' [in Japanese] (*ICD NEWS*, September 2019) 60, available online: www.moj.go.jp/content/001306610.pdf.

[52] Labour Code, Arts 303–06.

[53] Labour Code, Art 309. For the details of the Council of Arbitration, see generally Kong Phallack, 'Labour Arbitration in Cambodia: Law and Practice' (2010) 1 *Cambodian Yearbook of Comparative Legal Studies* 163; the Arbitration Council's website, available online: www.arbitrationcouncil.org/.

[54] CCP, Art 9(f).

[55] See the note on Art 9 in the Japanese language edition of the CCP of Cambodia.

a tort, probably following the Japanese Code of Civil Procedure before the 2011 law reforms in Japan.[56] Therefore, it is unclear whether the place of tort under Cambodian law means the place where the alleged tort was committed, the place where the alleged damage occurred, or both. Moreover, the place of the alleged damage has to be defined as it is sometimes difficult for the defendant to predict the place where the alleged damage occurred, especially in the context of product liability cases, but that is left to the discretion of the court in each individual case.[57]

c. Trusts

There are no special rules of jurisdiction for trust disputes. Accordingly, the court having jurisdiction over a trust case is the Court of First Instance of the place where the trust contract concluded between a merchant/corporation and a merchant/corporation has been designated,[58] or otherwise where: (1) the defendant maintains an address; (2) the (real) property subject to the trust agreement is located; or (3) the tort related to the trust was allegedly committed.[59] However, this may change over time. The Trust Law was newly promulgated in early 2019, and trusts are now subject to registration and supervision with the Ministry of Economy and Finance.[60] The scope of supervision is not defined, and therefore, it is still unclear how the government body is willing to intervene in trust disputes.

ii. Law of Property

a. Immovable Property

In Cambodia, real or immovable properties are classified into two categories, namely, registered lands that are with any types of titles issued by cadastral administration and non-registered lands that are without such titles.[61] As for the former, Article 9(g) of the CCP allows parties to bring claims to the court that has territorial jurisdiction over the disputed real property.[62] As for the latter, the Joint Prakas on Determination of Competence of the Court and Cadastral Commission Regarding Land Disputes (Joint Prakas)[63] provides that disputes over unregistered land shall be subject to the competence of the Cadastral Commission in the Ministry of

[56] Koji Takahashi, 'Japan's Newly Enacted Rules on International Jurisdiction: with a Reflection on Some Issues of Interpretation' (2011) 13 *Japanese Yearbook of Private International Law* 146; Koji Takahashi, 'The Jurisdiction of Japanese Courts in a Comparative Context' (2015) 11 *Journal of Private International Law* 103.

[57] The current Japanese Code of Civil Procedure states that the Japanese courts have jurisdiction over an action for a tort 'if the place where the tort occurred is within Japan (excluding if the consequences of a wrongful act committed in a foreign country have arisen within Japan but it would not ordinarily have been possible to foresee those consequences arising within Japan)' (Art 3-3(viii)). It is unclear whether the Cambodian courts will follow suit.

[58] CCP, Art 13.

[59] CCP, Arts 8, 9, 13.

[60] Patrick Jonh Smith and Tok Tavsothaly, 'Cambodian Trust Law' (*BNG Legal*, December 2019), available online: http://bnglegal.com/wp-content/uploads/2019/12/191219-BNG-Newsletter-December-Trust-law.pdf.

[61] Joint Prakas, Praka 1.

[62] According to CC, Art 120, immovable properties are land and any other objects that are immovably fixed to the land such as buildings, constructions, crops, timber, and other similar objects, which means that buildings are generally treated as part of the land to which they are attached. Note that CC, Art 123 provides that '[s]hould the right holder bear a right in relation to another person's land enforces his/her right upon any constructed buildings or structures, grown timber, crops or other such objects on the land, those objects shall not be deemed to be components of said land'.

[63] Unofficial English translation is available online: www.huskyandpartners.com/images///Law%20Library/Real%20Property%20and%20Construction/20190604-Joint%20Prakas%20on%20Determination%20of%20Competence%20of%20the%20Court%20and%20Cadastral%20Commission%20Regarding%20Land%20Disputes_2003_En.pdf.pdf.

Land Management,[64] while conferring the court the authority to hear contractual disputes over unregistered land.[65] During the Khmer Rouge period, all property rights were abolished, and most of the land registries was destroyed.[66] As a consequence, around 22 per cent of lands in the country (assuming there were seven million lands) was still unregistered as of November 2019,[67] which means that there is still potential for foreign companies to be involved in disputes over non-registered immovable properties, even though foreign individuals and companies are prohibited from owning land in Cambodia.[68]

b. Intangible Property: Intellectual Property

In Cambodia, the following intellectual property (IP) rights are legally protected: copyrights and neighbouring rights, patents, trademarks, utility models, industrial designs and new plant varieties.[69] IP rights other than copyrights and neighbouring rights shall be registered at the respective government bodies. Patents, utility models, industrial designs and new plant varieties must be registered at the Department of Industrial Property of the Ministry of Industry and Handicraft (MIH).[70] Trademarks must be registered at the IP Department of the Ministry of Commerce (MOC).[71] Parties may seek remedy from a competent court for the disputes and infringements of their IP rights, but no special rules of jurisdiction are provided.[72] Accordingly, the competent court is designated in accordance with rules for establishing the courts' jurisdiction in Articles 8 and 9 of the CCP.

c. Succession to Property

In terms of actions over succession to property, it is important to examine where the deceased was living at the point of death. Article 9(i) of the CCP provides that such actions may be brought in the court having jurisdiction over 'the location of the domicile of the deceased at the time the inheritance commences, or if such person does not have a domicile in Cambodia or his/her domicile is unknown, the location of his/her residence, or if such person does not have

[64] Joint Prakas, Praka 1. For the function of the Cadastral Commission, see generally GTZ-Cambodia Land Management Project and the World Bank Justice for the Poor Program, 'Towards Institutional Justice? A Review of the Work of Cambodia's Cadastral Commission in Relation to Land Dispute Resolution' (*The World Bank*, October 2006), available online: http://documents.worldbank.org/curated/en/309161468222269820/pdf/408230Towards01nal0Justice01PUBLIC1.pdf.

[65] Joint Prakas, Praka 4. The contracts include succession, sale/purchase contract, lease agreement, and mortgage.

[66] Miha Isoi, 'Real Property Registration in Cambodia' [in Japanese] (*ICD NEWS*, September 2014), available online: www.moj.go.jp/content/001142822.pdf.

[67] Ministry of Land Management, Urban Planning and Construction, 'Cambodia Urban Forum Report: Smart, Sustainable and Inclusive Urban Development' (*Open Development Thailand*, 27 November 2019) 4, available online: https://data.thailand.opendevelopmentmekong.net/dataset/report-on-cambodia-urban-forum/resource/39d81c29-df51-41c9-8d3e-a3c110b01152.

[68] Law on Investment, Art 16. Unofficial English translation is available online: www.wto.org/english/thewto_e/acc_e/khm_e/WTACCKHM3A3_LEG_45.pdf.

[69] Phin Sovath, 'Economic Law: Intellectual Property Rights' in Peng, Phallack and Menzel (n 8) 271.

[70] Previously called Ministry of Industry, Mines and Energy (MIME). For the structure of the Department of Industrial Property, see www.cambodiaip.gov.kh/TemplateTwo.aspx?parentId=2&menuid=235&childMasterMenuId=234. Precisely, if one claims for protection of utility models, s/he shall obtain a 'protectable utility certificate' from the Industrial Design Office in the Department of Industrial Property: Law on Patents, Utility Model Certificates and Industrial Designs (Patent Law), Arts 69, 117. For the registration of industrial designs, see Patent Law, Art 95. As for a Grant of Protection for a Plant Variety, see www.cambodiaip.gov.kh/TemplateTwo.aspx?parentId=45&menuid=291&childMasterMenuId=291&lang=en.

[71] www.cambodiaip.gov.kh/TemplateTwo.aspx?parentId=34&menuid=204&childMasterMenuId=35.

[72] See the note on Art 9 in the Japanese language edition of the CCP of Cambodia.

a location of residence in Cambodia or his/her location of residence is unknown, the location of his/her last known domicile'.[73] Though not expressly stated in the CCP, it is reasonable to assume that the 'the last known domicile' shall be in Cambodia as the CCP is not supposed to deal with succession actions in foreign courts.

Also, the Annex of the Non-Suit Civil Case Procedural Law (Annex) contains special rules for courts to establish jurisdiction for non-contentious succession cases.[74] The Annex determines the jurisdiction of courts, which depends on the matters of succession that are listed in Chapter 8 of the CC. Most of those matters are to be determined by the court of the place where the succession commenced, while other courts have jurisdiction only in exceptional cases. For example, the court having territorial jurisdiction over the deceased's address or the place where the succession commenced shall decide who will succeed the ownership of ceremonial implements, graves and movable ancestral heirlooms, if the deceased did not designate such a successor, and if there is no custom for making the decision.[75] Such a court also has the competence to hear matters related to the disqualification of presumptive successors under Articles 1151, 1152, and 1154 of the CC.[76] Moreover, the court having jurisdiction over the successor's address shall determine whether the person may renounce his or her legally reserved portion of inherited wealth.[77]

iii. Family Law

Certain proceedings are required for couples to have a valid marriage in Cambodia, as stipulated generally in Article 955 of the CC and more specifically in the Ministry of Interior Sub-Decree 103 on Civil Status (Civil Registration) (2002) (Sub-Decree 103).[78] For example, a marriage between Cambodian citizens comes into effect when the following conditions are satisfied: (1) the couple has applied for permission to marry to the Commune/Sangkat registrar at the prospective wife's residence;[79] (2) the registrar has made an announcement to the public of the scheduled marriage ceremony;[80] (3) the couple has entered into a marriage contract before the registrar at the prospective wife's residence;[81] and (4) the registrar has registered the marriage in the Marriage Book.[82] Satisfying these conditions, a couple being a Cambodian citizen and a foreigner, or an immigrant living lawfully in the country, may also have a legally binding marriage.[83] In addition, a marriage that took place abroad between Khmer citizens, or a Khmer citizen and a foreigner, is also to be deemed valid in Cambodia, provided that the marriage observed the law of the place

[73] Note that neither 'domicile' nor 'residence' is defined by the CCP.

[74] The Annex of the Non-Suit Civil Case Procedural Law (in Japanese) is available online: www.jica.go.jp/activities/issues/governance/portal/cambodia/ku57pq00002khh0b-att/non_suit_civil_case_procedural_law_ja.pdf. See also Non-Suit Civil Case Procedural Law, Art 1. Unofficial English translation is available online: www.jica.go.jp/project///cambodia/0701047/04/ku57pq00001spnva-att/non-suit_civil_case_procedural_law_03_en.pdf.

[75] Annex, Art 5.1; CC, Art 1147(2).

[76] Annex, Art 5.2; CC, Arts 1151, 1152, 1154.

[77] Annex, Art 5.10; CC, Art 1246.

[78] Unofficial English translation of Sub-Decree 103 is available online: www.skpcambodia.com/storage/uploads/files/Nationality_Immegration_Civil%20Registration/Sub-dree%20No103%20on%20Civil%20Registration-Eng.pdf. See also CC, Arts 948–68; Dorine van der Keur, 'Legal and Gender Issues of Marriage and Divorce in Cambodia' (2014) 3 *Cambodia Law and Policy Journal* 1, 4 (explaining basic rules of marriage registration in Cambodia); see generally Sar Serena, 'Cambodian Family Law: Development and Challenges Ahead' in Peng, Phallack and Menzel (n 8) 135–52.

[79] Sub-Decree 103, Art 28.

[80] ibid, Art 29.

[81] ibid, Art 30.

[82] ibid, Arts 30, 31.

[83] ibid, Art 33.

of marriage and had been registered in the Marriage Book maintained in a Cambodian diplomatic office attached to the respective jurisdiction.[84]

According to the Law on Procedures in Actions Relating to Personal Status (Personal Status Law),[85] actions relating to other aspects of marriage – divorce, nullity and separation – are to be heard by the Court of First Instance of the place where the parties reside.[86] A potential theoretical problem is how to determine jurisdiction if the respective couple has already started living separately in different addresses. Since it is difficult for such parties to invoke their residence as a basis of jurisdiction,[87] the Court of First Instance of Phnom Penh is presumed to have exclusive jurisdiction to hear the matter.[88] In any event, if the couple has agreed to divorce, they may file a petition to the court that has territorial jurisdiction over the address of the husband or wife.[89] The couple may do the same in the situation where they are unable to reach a consensus on the distribution of property.[90]

The Personal Status Law also covers matters relating to the well-being of the child, including the confirmation of paternity, confirmation of maternity, confirmation of the absence of parenthood, and dissolution of adoption.[91] These matters may be referred to the Court of First Instance having territorial jurisdiction over the place where the parties reside; if the parties are living separately, the Court of First Instance of Phnom Penh will have exclusive jurisdiction.[92] The jurisdiction is not exclusive in *sensu stricto* since the court is allowed to transfer the case to another court upon a party's motion or on its own authority, in order to avoid significant delays and ensure fairness, taking into account the circumstance of the case.[93] The court is probably encouraged to determine the transfer in light of the best interests of the child since Cambodia is a party to the 1989 United Nations Convention on the Rights of the Child,[94] albeit its limited interest in ratifying private international law treaties for child protection.[95] Such interpretation also conforms with specifications in the Non-Suit Civil Case Procedural Law that designates the court having territorial jurisdiction over the address of the child as the appropriate court to hear child-related cases.[96]

[84] ibid, Art 32.

[85] Unofficial English translation is available online: www.jica.go.jp/project/cambodia/0701047/04/ku57pq00001spnva-att/action_relating_to_personal_status_02_en.pdf.

[86] Personal Status Law, Art 5; CCP, Art 10(1). Note that the jurisdiction is not absolutely exclusive as the court may invoke the doctrine of *forum non conveniens* under Art 6 of the Personal Status Law, depending on the circumstances of the case.

[87] Personal Status Law, Art 5(2).

[88] ibid, Art 5(4).

[89] Annex, Art 4.5.

[90] Annex, Art 4.6.

[91] Personal Status Law, Art 3.

[92] ibid, Art 5.

[93] ibid, Art 6.

[94] The status of ratification is available online: https://indicators.ohchr.org/.

[95] Cambodia has not yet ratified the 1996 Hague Convention on Jurisdiction, Applicable Law, Recognition, Enforcement and Co-operation in Respect of Parental Responsibility and Measures for the Protection of Children (the Hague Children's Convention) and 1980 Hague Convention on the Civil Aspects of International Child Abduction (the Hague Abduction Convention). The status tables of the Conventions are available online, respectively: www.hcch.net/en/instruments/conventions/status-table/?cid=69; www.hcch.net/en/instruments/conventions/status-table/?cid=24. Note that Cambodia has ratified the 1993 Hague Convention on Protection of Children and Co-operation in Respect of Intercountry Adoption. The status table is available online: www.hcch.net/en/instruments/conventions/status-table/?cid=69.

[96] According to Annex, Art 4, the following matters shall be applied to the court having jurisdiction over the address of the child: petitions for simple adoption, dissolution of simple adoption by agreement, designation of the person parental authority, change of the person with parental authority, petitions for rights and obligations of the parent who does not live with the minor child, determination of the manager of a child's property provided by a third person, and appointment of a special representative for the minor whose interests conflict with the parental authority holder.

iv. Law of Corporations, Insolvency and Bankruptcy

In contrast to the revised Japanese Code of Civil Procedure,[97] the CCP does not provide any special rules for establishing jurisdiction to hear corporate matters. Therefore, Cambodian courts may decide their jurisdiction over corporate cases in light of the rules of personal jurisdiction in Article 8 of the CCP or the jurisdictional rules of contracts and torts in Article 9 of the CCP.[98] Note, however, that the Non-Suit Civil Case Procedural Law confers the court having territorial jurisdiction over the address of the company to exclusive jurisdiction for: (1) appointment of a special director;[99] (2) appointment of a special representative;[100] (3) appointment of an inspector for the inspection of capital contribution;[101] (4) the amendment of the Articles of Incorporation;[102] and (5) permission for the stakeholders to convene an extraordinary general stakeholders meeting.[103] It should also be noted that the Law on Commercial Enterprises has provisions allowing parties to refer to the arbitral tribunal matters including, but not limited to, appraisal disputes and controversies over the duty of care.[104]

Moreover, neither the CCP nor the Insolvency Law contains specific rules of jurisdiction for insolvency cases.[105] However, the Annex mandates the court of the address of the company to handle matters concerning the dissolution and liquidation of companies, including: (1) a petition for the dissolution of a legal person that is undermining the public interest;[106] (2) appointment of a liquidator upon a petition by an interested person or the Ministry of Justice;[107] (3) removal of a liquidator for grave reasons upon a petition by an interested person;[108] (4) permission for a liquidator to settle claims by creditors within the presentation period;[109] (5) appointment of a valuator to determine the sum of uncertain claims;[110] and (6) appointment of a custodian of the legal person's documents.[111]

[97] Code of Civil Procedure (Japan), Arts 3-3(vii) and 3-5(1).

[98] Foreign businesses operating in Cambodia in any form are subject to the laws and jurisdictions of Cambodia. See Law on Commercial Enterprises, Arts 270–73.

[99] Annex, Art 1.11; CC, Art 60.

[100] Annex, Art 1.12; CC, Art 61.

[101] Annex, Art 1.19; CC, Art 85(2).

[102] Annex, Art 1.20; CC, Art 85(4).

[103] Annex, Art 1.21; CC, Art 93(3). CC, Art 93(2) provides that the stakeholders who hold no less than 10 per cent of total voting rights (or other percentage as provided in the Articles of Incorporations) may request the directors to convene an extraordinary general stakeholders meeting, and the directors must follow the request without delay. CC, Art 93(2) is for the stakeholders to seek permission for the court to hold the stakeholders meeting, in case the directors cannot make it on time.

[104] Law on Commercial Enterprises, Arts 250, 289. Unofficial English translation is available online: www.wipo.int/edocs/lexdocs/laws/en/kh/kh011en.pdf.

[105] Unofficial English translation of the Insolvency Law is available online: www.cambodiainvestment.gov.kh/wp-content/uploads/2012/03/Law-on-Insolvency_full-text_071016.pdf. Note that Cambodia has not adopted the 1997 UNCITRAL Model Law on Cross-Border Insolvency: see https://uncitral.un.org/en/texts/insolvency/modellaw/cross-border_insolvency/status.

[106] Annex, Art 1.13; CC, Art 65(3).

[107] Annex, Art 1.14; CC, Arts 68(2)–68(3).

[108] Annex, Art 1.15; CC, Art 69(1).

[109] Annex, Art 1.16; CC, Art 74(2).

[110] Annex, Art 1.17; CC, Art 76(2).

[111] Annex, Art 1.18; CC, Art 81.

v. Competition Law

As of May 2021, there is no competition (antitrust) law effective in Cambodia, although the Draft Law on Competition of Cambodia (Draft Law),[112] which was prepared by the MOC, was scheduled for approval by the National Assembly by the end of 2020.[113] An innovative aspect of the Draft Law is that it intends to establish the first Competition Commission of Cambodia (CCC) – an inter-ministerial body led by the MOC to ensure fair competition.[114] This may be a great step for the Cambodian economy and consumers, although many other Southeast Asian nations have such a commission already.[115] The CCC is expected to issue various orders and decisions to restore and promote competition in the Cambodian market, upon the request of its Directorate or on its initiative.[116] The Directorate has a broad authority to file such a request based on his/her investigation and evaluation.

Further, the CCC may issue an order to any person allegedly violating the Draft Law, seeking support from a competent court – typically the Phnom Penh Municipal Court – for enforcement.[117] There are two means for the person to challenge the order. The person may file a complaint to a competent court within 15 working days from the date of receiving the order.[118] Alternatively, the person may file a petition to the CCC to reconsider, modify or revoke the order, although the CCC may refuse the petition based on reasonable grounds of which the Draft Law does not clarify the implications.[119]

III. Jurisdiction *in rem* with Special Focus on Shipping Claims

A. Jurisdiction *in rem* of the Courts within the Territory

The jurisdiction *in rem* was once understood as the competence of a court over a thing or property based on its presence in the country's territory and was therefore distinguished from the jurisdiction *in personam*.[120] However, Michaels suggests that *in rem* jurisdiction should ultimately be construed as part of *in personam* jurisdiction, and the presence of a thing or property merely constitutes the basis of jurisdiction over a person.[121] This chapter respectfully follows his argument.

[112] Unofficial English translation (version 5.7) is available online: www.asean-competition.org/file/pdf_file/Draft%20Law%20on%20Competition%202018.pdf (based on the Draft Khmer Version as of 13 February 2018). The draft has slightly changed since then, according to local Cambodia practitioners.

[113] Thou Vireak, 'Government Set to Finalise Antitrust, Competition Draft Law' (*The Phnom Penh Post*, 15 April 2020), available online: www.phnompenhpost.com/business/govt-set-finalise-antitrust-competition-draft-law. However, there are some delays due to the COVID-19 pandemic.

[114] Draft Law, Arts 5, 6. Other ministries involved are the Ministry of Economy and Finance, the Ministry of Justice, the Ministry of Interior, the Ministry of Industry and Handicraft (now called the Ministry of Industry, Science, Technology and Innovation), the Ministry of Post and Telecommunications, and the National Bank of Cambodia.

[115] See The ASEAN Secretariat, *Handbook on ASEAN Consumer Protection Laws and Regulation* (2018) 17ff, available online: https://asean.org/storage/Handbook-on-ASEAN-Consumer-Protection-Laws-and-Regulations-FINAL1.pdf.

[116] Draft Law, Arts 8, 34.

[117] ibid, Arts 34, 38.

[118] ibid, Art 36.

[119] ibid, Art 39.

[120] Ralf Michaels, 'Jurisdiction, Foundations' in Jürgen Basedow and others (eds), *Encyclopedia of Private International Law* (Cheltenham, Edward Elgar, 2017) 1043.

[121] ibid.

The CCP contains several provisions setting out explicit rules of jurisdiction *in rem*. Article 9(c) concerns actions for specific performance against persons who have no known domicile in Cambodia. It specifies the location of the person's property that is subject to the claim, security or seizure as a basis of jurisdiction. Similarly, Article 9(d) covers actions for specific performance against juridical persons that have no known administrative headquarter or business office in Cambodia. It designates the location of the legal person's property that is subject to the claim, security, or seizure as a basis of jurisdiction. Moreover, Article 9(g) deals with actions involving immovables, stating that the location of the real property determines which court has the competence to handle the case.

Note, however, that Article 9(i) concerning actions over a deceased's estate may not be regarded as a rule for *in rem* jurisdiction, as it does not decide jurisdiction based on the location of the deceased's estate, but on the address of the deceased. Moreover, the CCP does not have special jurisdictional rules for claims relating to ships, in contrast to the Japanese Civil Procedure Code containing rules of jurisdiction *in rem* for an action based on a ship claim or any other claim secured by a ship.[122] The reason for omission is unclear, even though the Cambodian CCP was inspired by that of Japan, as mentioned elsewhere in this chapter.

B. Process of Ship Arrest in the Territory

In Cambodia, ship arrest as a measure to secure a maritime claim is governed by the 1952 International Convention Relating to the Arrest of Seagoing Ships (the Arrest Convention) and the CCP.[123] Ship arrest may take place as part of the enforcement of an adjudicatory decision (that is, a court judgment or an arbitral award) or a provisional remedy.

i. Ship Arrest for Judgment Enforcement

The process of ship arrest for judgment and award enforcement is specified in Book Six (Compulsory Execution) of the CCP. The Arrest Convention is then not applicable as it does not cover the seizure of a ship in execution or satisfaction of a judgment.[124] Under the CCP, such ship arrest may take place over any ships (or vessels, including hovercrafts and hydrofoils) of any nationality that are heavier than 20 gross tonnages and within Cambodian territorial waters.[125]

Ship arrest for judgment enforcement proceeds as follows. First, the judgment creditor must file a request (motion) of compulsory execution against a vessel to the Court of First Instance having territorial jurisdiction over the ship.[126] The request, which must be in writing, shall contain: (1) the name and address of the creditor and his/her representative; (2) description of the title of obligation; (3) type of judgment execution to be requested (that is, direct compulsory execution, indirect compulsory execution, or execution by a substitute); (4) detail of the property subject to

[122] Code of Civil Procedure (Japan), Art 5(vii).

[123] Hem Darwin and Chey Rithy, 'Ship Arrest in Cambodia' (*BNG Legal*, June 2016), available online: http://bnglegal.com/cn/wp-content/uploads/2016/08/160729-Ship-Arrest-In-Cambodia-June-2016.pdf. The 1952 Arrest Convention came into force in Cambodia on 12 May 1957: https://treaties.un.org/pages/showDetails.aspx?objid=08000002801338ba. However, Cambodia is not a member of the 1999 United Nations International Convention on Arrest of Ships: https://treaties.un.org/Pages/ViewDetails.aspx?src=TREATY&mtdsg_no=XII-8&chapter=12&clang=_en.

[124] Arrest Convention, Art 1(2).

[125] CCP, Art 454; Japan International Cooperation Agency, 'Commentary on Cambodian Code of Civil Procedure: Compulsory Execution and Provisional Remedies' [in Japanese] (*Ministry of Justice*) 80, available online: www.moj.go.jp/content/000122393.pdf.

[126] CCP, Arts 455, 456.

direct compulsory execution; (5) detail of the requested decision on indirect compulsory execution or execution by a substitute; (6) location of the vessel; (7) and name and current location of the captain.[127] The request shall also be accompanied by an authenticated copy of the title of obligation and an authenticated copy of the certificate of ship registration issued by the Cambodian authority, or documents showing that the ship is more than 20 gross tonnage and is in the judgment debtor's possession.[128]

After receiving the request, the competent court issues an order for commencement of compulsory auction of the ship, ordering a bailiff (enforcement agent) to confiscate the certificate of ship registration for submission to the competent court.[129] In the order, the court shall declare its intention to attach the ship on behalf of the judgment creditor and its willingness to prohibit the judgment debtor from letting the ship leave the current location (port).[130] The order shall be served to the judgment debtor and come into effect as soon as the service process has been completed.[131] However, if the registration of the attachment has been made prior to the issuance of the order for commencement of ship auction, the ship arrest becomes effective at the time of such registration.[132] Somewhat similarly, if the bailiff confiscates the certificate of ship registration and other relevant documents prior to the service of the order for commencement of ship auction, or prior to the registration of the attachment by the registrar, the ship arrest becomes effective at the time of such confiscation.[133] Moreover, if the ship was registered in Cambodia, the court clerk would immediately have to direct the registrar to record the attachment.[134] Further, should the ship move outside the jurisdiction of the competent court, the court may transfer the case to the Court of First Instance that has territorial jurisdiction over the new location of the ship.[135]

ii. Ship Arrest as a Provisional Measure

Ship arrest as a provisional measure is to be governed by the Arrest Convention and Book Seven (Preservative Disposition) of the CCP. The Convention, however, plays a limited role in defining the process of provisional ship arrest as it provides in Article 6 that:

> The rules of procedure relating to the arrest of a ship, to the application for obtaining the authority of [a Court or of the appropriate judicial authority of the contracting State in which the arrest is made], and to all matters of procedure which the arrest may entail, shall be governed by the law of the Contracting State in which the arrest was made or applied for.

Accordingly, the process shall observe the procedural steps defined in the CCP and proceed as follows.

First, the claimant shall file a request of provisional (preservative) relief to the court having jurisdiction over the merits of the case, or the Court of First Instance having jurisdiction over the object to be attached or the subject matter of the dispute.[136] The request of provisional relief must contain: (1) names and addresses of the parties and their representatives; (2) details of the

[127] ibid, Art 455(2). See also ibid, Art 349(2).
[128] ibid, Art 455(3).
[129] ibid, Art 457(1).
[130] ibid, Art 457(2).
[131] ibid, Arts 457(3), 457(5).
[132] ibid, Art 457(5).
[133] ibid, Art 457(6).
[134] ibid, Art 457(4).
[135] ibid, Art 463.
[136] ibid, Art 540.

preservative relief to be sought; (3) details of the rights or legal relationship that are requested to be protected; and (4) the necessity of such preservative relief.[137]

Second, the court decides whether to issue a ruling for such provisional relief that can be either provisional disposition or provisional attachment.[138] To proceed with ship arrest, the claimant needs to obtain a ruling for provisional attachment, convincing the court that the subject matter of the claim is money, and compulsory execution at a later stage is likely to become impossible or extremely difficult without such provisional attachment.[139] In issuing the ruling, the court shall specify the object of the provisional attachment.[140]

Third, the claimant has to decide how s/he proceeds with enforcing the ruling for the provisional attachment, and two options are available under Article 568 of the CCP.

If the claimant opts for enforcement by way of registration of the provisional attachment, s/he shall submit the request to the court that issued the order for provisional attachment of the ship.[141] The request must contain: (1) the name and address of the claimant and his/her representative; (2) description of the title of obligation; (3) type of judgment execution to be requested at the final stage of proceedings (that is, direct compulsory execution, indirect compulsory execution or execution by a substitute); (4) detail of the property subject to direct compulsory execution; (5) detail of the requested decision on indirect compulsory execution or execution by a substitute; (6) location of the vessel; and (7) name and current location of the captain.[142] The request then shall be accompanied by an authenticated copy of the title of obligation and an authenticated copy of the certificate of ship registration issued by Cambodian authority, or documents showing that the ship is more than 20 gross tonnage and is possessed by the respondent. If the request is accepted, the tribunal will proceed with ship arrest.[143]

If the claimant opts for enforcement by way of ordering the bailiff to confiscate the certificate of ship registration and other relevant documents, s/he shall file the request to the Court of First Instance having territorial jurisdiction over the location of the ship.[144] The claimant then shall submit an authenticated copy of the title of obligation attached by an authenticated copy of the certificate of ship registration issued by Cambodian authority, or documents showing that the ship is heavier than 20 gross tonnages and is possessed by the respondent.[145] After receiving the request, the court will order the bailiff to proceed with confiscating the ship registration certificate and other relevant documentation.

IV. Immunities from Jurisdiction

A. Sovereign Immunity

There are two traditional models of state immunity: the absolute doctrine and the restrictive doctrine.[146] The absolute doctrine provides foreign states with absolute immunities from judicial

[137] ibid, Art 541.
[138] ibid, Arts 545, 548.
[139] ibid, Art 545.
[140] ibid, Art 546.
[141] ibid, Art 568(2).
[142] ibid, Arts 568(4), 455(2).
[143] ibid, Arts 568(4), 455(3).
[144] ibid, Art 568(2).
[145] ibid, Arts 568(4), 455(3).
[146] Hazel Fox and Philippa Webb, *The Law of State Immunity* revised and updated 3rd edn (Oxford, Oxford University Press, 2015) 4.

proceedings, excluding a state from addressing, deciding, or enforcing a claim brought in its municipal courts against another state unless otherwise agreed by that state.[147] The restrictive doctrine provides foreign states with limited immunities from judicial proceedings, making 'a distinction between acts performed in [the] exercise of sovereign authority which remain immune and acts of a private or commercial nature in respect of which proceedings in national courts may be brought'.[148] The Cambodian stance on this dichotomy is unclear as it has not yet signed the 2004 United Nations Convention on Jurisdictional Immunities of States and Their Property[149] that embrace the restrictive theory of sovereign immunity,[150] and no noticeable domestic legislation or regulations exist to deal with this issue. Moreover, there is no discernible discussion of sovereign immunity initiated among legal academics and practitioners in Cambodia.

B. Diplomatic Immunity

Cambodia ratified the 1961 Vienna Convention on Diplomatic Relations in 1965 with a reservation to Article 37(2).[151] Accordingly, in Cambodia, a diplomatic agent shall enjoy immunity from its civil jurisdiction, except in the case of (in Article 31(1)):

> (a) a real action relating to private immovable property situated in the territory of the receiving State, unless he holds it on behalf of the sending State for the purposes of the mission;
> (b) an action relating to succession in which the diplomatic agent is involved as executor, administrator, heir or legatee as a private person and not on behalf of the sending State;
> (c) an action relating to any professional or commercial activity exercised by the diplomatic agent in the receiving State outside his official functions.

Due to the Article 37(2) reservation, the civil immunity does not extend to members of the administrative and technical staff of the mission and their family.

C. Other Immunities

There are several other immunities in Cambodia to varying degrees. Parliamentary immunity is conferred by the Constitution to members of the National Assembly (Parliament) and the Senate, though civil cases are excluded from the scope.[152] Members of the Constitutional Council – the supreme body having the authority to decide constitutional issues – are not subject to any penal or civil sanction for the decisions made while fulfilling their duties.[153] There are no discernible laws or regulations that stipulate immunities of royal family members and state-owned enterprises, but the general practice is that they are liable for any civil liabilities.

[147] ibid.
[148] ibid.
[149] https://treaties.un.org/Pages/ViewDetails.aspx?src=TREATY&mtdsg_no=III-13&chapter=3&clang=_en.
[150] David P Stewart, 'The UN Convention on Jurisdictional Immunities of States and Their Property' (2005) 99 *American Journal of International Law* 194.
[151] https://treaties.un.org/pages/ViewDetails.aspx?src=TREATY&mtdsg_no=III-3&chapter=3&lang=en.
[152] Constitution, Arts 80, 104.
[153] Law on the Organization and the Functioning of the Constitutional Council and Law on the Amendment of the Law on the Organization and the Functioning of the Constitutional Council, Art 11. Unofficial English translation is available online: http://ngocedaw.org/wp-content/uploads/2014/10/Law-on-CC.-Eng.pdf.

V. Conclusion

The lesson learnt from the research for this chapter is clear. Laws and rules on direct jurisdiction in Cambodia are under the strong influence of Japanese law and may, therefore, be regarded as modern choice-of-court systems. However, ambiguities still persist in the laws and rules, and they might have been preventing Cambodian courts from dealing with transnational cases effectively. This chapter concludes by making three proposals for Cambodia to tackle the persistent problem of uncertainties.

First, further transparency is necessary. In Cambodia, legal research is often understood as a synonym of networking. Lawyers are expected to communicate with contact persons – judges, court clerks, government officials and politicians – to obtain 'allegedly' reliable and updated legal information.[154] While judicial proceedings are basically conducted in open courts,[155] almost no judicial judgments are made public in the most convenient manner.[156] Such private nature of legal information is unlikely to help legal professionals, especially those outside the special circle, to understand what the law is in Cambodia, not just related to the area of law on direct jurisdiction. Therefore, the Cambodian judicial system should be more open to the public. Improving judicial transparency is the key to sustainable development.[157] It may also assist Cambodian judiciary to rebut the persistent criticisms of corruption (that are often unwarranted) by addressing them with substance.[158]

Second, the doctrine of precedent needs to be further developed. Since judgments are not published and often lack adequate judicial reasoning,[159] Cambodian legal practitioners have rarely paid attention to past judgments. This should be changed since precedence and legal certainty play vital roles in the development of civil law systems even though they have no binding force.[160] In relation to direct jurisdiction, the CCP is based on an old version of the Japanese Code of Civil Procedure whose provisions of direct jurisdiction were supplemented by case law for Japanese courts to apply them to cross-border cases.[161] Unfortunately, however, this fact did not gain attention in the drafting process of the CCP, so that the vague provisions were imported into the CCP without any outstanding efforts by the drafting committee to ensure clarity. As a result, rules of direct jurisdiction in the CCP are still ambiguous. Further development of case law may be useful for the Cambodian judiciary to deal with the obscurities in the CCP.

Third, there should be increased responsiveness to foreign law reforms. For example, the Japanese Code of Civil Procedure was reformed in 2011, incorporating new rules on international

[154] The author's interview with local practitioners.

[155] For example, CCP, Arts 115, 136, 188.

[156] Shinoda Yoichiro, 'Report on Cambodian Court Judgments (1)' [in Japanese] (*ICD NEWS*, June 2019), available online: www.moj.go.jp/content/001300680.pdf; Atsushi Kamiki, 'Report on Cambodian Court Judgements' [in Japanese] (*Ministry of Justice*, 8 March 2011), available online: www.moj.go.jp/content/000073282.pdf.

[157] United Nations Development Programme, 'A Transparent and Accountable Judiciary to Deliver Justice for All' (*Transparency International Cambodia*, 2016) 10ff, available online: http://ticambodia.org/library/wp-content/files_mf/1460351755RBAPDG2016TransparentnAccountableJudiciary.pdf.

[158] Abby Seiff, 'Cambodia: Corruption in the Judiciary "Endemic"' (*International Bar Association*, 21 September 2015), available online: www.ibanet.org/Article/NewDetail.aspx?ArticleUid=63af01f5-7bf3-4433-8edb-bbeb512395d7; Alessandro Marazzi Sassoon and Mech Dara, 'Kingdom's Judiciary Perceived as Most Corrupt: UNDP' (*The Phnom Penh Post*, 11 April 2016), available online: www.phnompenhpost.com/national/kingdoms-judiciary-perceived-most-corrupt-undp.

[159] Yoichiro (n 156); Kamiki (n 156).

[160] Caslav Pejovic, 'Civil Law and Common Law: Two Different Paths Leading to the Same Goal' (2001) 32 *Victorian University of Wellington Law Review* 817, 820–21.

[161] Nishitani (n 16) 252–53.

direct jurisdiction.[162] However, the CCP has never been reformed since its promulgation in 2006, and there is no explicit ongoing debate among Cambodian lawyers as to whether Cambodia should revise the somewhat outdated rules on direct jurisdiction in the CCP. A practical option for Cambodia is to enact new international jurisdiction rules based on the current version of the Japanese Code of Civil Procedure.

A welcoming development, in relation to the first and second proposals, is that the JICA, the MOJ of Cambodia and Cambodian judiciary are now working together to establish the official process of disclosure of the court decisions, through their Legal and Judicial Development Project (Phase V).[163] Some influential private legal practitioners have made public statements reinforcing the project.[164] As for the third proposal, it may still require some time for Cambodia to undertake the reform of rules on direct jurisdiction. Hopefully, the reform will take place sooner rather than later, since many international enterprises are now operating in Cambodia to work on various types of projects and businesses, and the number of cross-border cases are expected to keep increasing.

[162] Takahashi, 'Japan's Newly Enacted Rules' (n 56).

[163] See www.jica.go.jp/project/english/cambodia/025/outline/index.html.

[164] Ly Tayseng, 'Importance of Publicity of Judicial Process and Publication of Judicial Decisions' (*The Phnom Penh Post*, 5 November 2020), available online: www.phnompenhpost.com/opinion/importance-publicity-judicial-process-and-publication-judicial-decisions.

11

Myanmar

ZAW THURA

I. Introduction

This chapter will focus on Myanmar's general rules of direct jurisdiction in cases with foreign elements. It will also briefly look at aspects of jurisdiction in specific areas of Myanmar law: competition law, arbitration law, cross-border insolvency, matrimonial causes, and *in rem* shipping claims. When going through the account of Myanmar law here, the reader should bear in mind that, having only emerged from a long period of military rule and initiated a process of opening up to the rest of the world about a decade ago, Myanmar's law inevitably remains in a state of development. More recently, on 1 February 2021, the military again took over Myanmar's Government, declaring a year-long state of emergency. According to the military, the state of emergency is to be followed by fresh elections. In the circumstances, the extent to which the laws described in this chapter will continue to apply in Myanmar during the state of emergency and beyond is unknown at this stage. Even if the laws summarised here will remain generally applicable, it may be difficult to say with certainty whether and (if so) under what conditions a Myanmar court will accept or decline jurisdiction in a given case involving foreign elements.[1]

By way of overview of the judicial system, in terms of governance the Union of Myanmar is divided into seven states,[2] seven regions,[3] five self-administered zones,[4] one self-administered division[5] and the Naypyidaw Union Territory.[6] The states and regions are divided into districts. The districts, self-administered zones and the self-administered division are sub-divided into townships. The apex court is the Supreme Court of the Union in the capital Naypyidaw. Section 63 of the Union Judiciary Act empowers the Supreme Court of the Union to prescribe the jurisdictions of district courts, courts of self-administered Divisions, courts of self-administered zones, township courts and other courts in civil and criminal cases. Regions or states have a High Court with unlimited jurisdiction in original civil cases. There are 14 High Courts.[7] District courts and the courts of the self-administered zones and self-administered division have jurisdiction to hear

[1] On general rules of jurisdiction, see Adrian Briggs, *Private International Law in Myanmar* (Oxford, Oxford University Press, 2015) 18–44.

[2] Chin, Kachin, Kayah, Kayin, Mon, Rakhine and Shan States.

[3] Ayeyarwady, Bago, Magway, Mandalay, Sagaing, Tanintharyi and Yangon Regions.

[4] Danu, Kokang, Naga, Pa'O and Pa Laung Self-Administered Zones.

[5] Wa Self-Administered Division.

[6] Where Myanmar's capital, Naypyidaw, is situated.

[7] For the purpose of judicial administration, the High Court of Mandalay Region serves as the High Court of Naypyidaw Union Territory.

original civil suits involving values of up to three billion kyats.[8] There are a total of 75 district courts and courts of the self-administered zones and self-administered division. Township courts have jurisdiction to hear original civil suits involving values of up to 10 million kyats.[9] There are 330 township courts.

II. General Rules of Jurisdiction

The general rules of jurisdiction are conveniently gathered together in Myanmar's Civil Procedure Code (CPC).[10] In principle, the courts have jurisdiction to try all civil suits, unless their authority is expressly or impliedly circumscribed by some law (CPC section 9). One such limitation to jurisdiction is *res judicata*. Where a matter is being or has been substantially heard by another court in Myanmar, then the same matter may not be litigated or re-litigated in another Myanmar court by the parties to the original suit or by parties claiming rights deriving from the parties to the original suit (CPC sections 10 and 11).[11] It should be noted, however, that (as the Explanation to CPC section 10 points out) the fact that a suit is pending before a foreign court will not preclude the Myanmar court from hearing the same matter.[12] Nonetheless, on the basis of CPC sections 9 and 10, it is submitted that Myanmar has a principle of *lis alibi pendens*, such that where a suit is pending before a foreign court, then upon the application of a party, the Myanmar court has a discretion to decline jurisdiction in favour of the foreign proceedings in appropriate circumstances. What would constitute 'appropriate circumstances' will depend on the facts of each case, but ultimately should involve a determination of where the relevant case can best be

[8] About US$2,250,000. See Notification No 1030/2020 (28 December 2020) by the Union Supreme Court.

[9] About US$7,500. See Notification No 101/2011 (19 May 2011) by the Union Supreme Court.

[10] Originally enacted as India Act V of 1908 during the British colonial period. Act V came into effect for the Union of Myanmar on 1 January 1909. The CPC has been amended on a number of occasions, the most recent amendment being on 4 July 2014.

[11] On the principles underlying *res judicata*, see *Ma Khin v Ma Pu* [1948] BLR 343 (HC) 348–349. Explanation IV to CPC section 11 states: 'Any matter which might and *ought to have been made* [a] ground of defence or attack in such former suit shall be deemed to have been a matter directly and substantially in issue in such suit' (emphasis added). Thus, Myanmar law follows the principle of issue estoppel articulated in *Henderson v Henderson* (1843) 3 Hare 100 (at 115):

> [W]here a given matter becomes the subject of litigation in, and of adjudication by, a Court of competent jurisdiction, the Court requires the parties to that litigation to bring forward their whole case, and will not (except under special circumstances) permit the same parties to open the same subject of litigation in respect of matter which might have been brought forward as part of the subject in contest, but which was not brought forward, only because they have, from negligence, inadvertence, or even accident, omitted part of their case. The plea of *res judicata* applies, except in special cases, not only to points upon which the Court was actually required by the parties to form an opinion and pronounce a judgment, but to every point which properly belonged to the subject of litigation, and which the parties, exercising reasonable diligence, might have brought forward at the time.

But see *Daw Mya v Ko Maung Than* [1963] BLR 554 (CC) where the court found that, the fact that the plaintiff had previously unsuccessfully sued the defendant under s 12(1)(f) of the Urban Rent Control Act did not preclude him for subsequently suing the defendant for ejectment under s 12(1)(e) of the same Act. Under s 12(1)(f), the plaintiff had to prove that he was the owner of the premises and reasonably required the same for occupation by himself for residential purposes. Under s 12(1)(e), he had to show that the premises were reasonably required by him for the effecting of essential and major structural repairs. The court held that Explanation IV did not operate, because 'it would be difficult to say that the plaintiff ought to aver in the same suit such contradictory statements to the effect: (1) the house in question is reasonably and *bona fide* required by him for his own occupation, and (2) that it should be pulled down for the purpose of erecting a new building in its place'.

[12] This was made clear in *Ma Hla Myint v Ma Sein Myaing* [1953] BLR 59 (HC), where the court observed (at 64): '[T]he institution of a second suit is not barred by section 10 of the [CPC] and all that it says is the trial of the second suit cannot be proceeded with. Furthermore, as the rule is one of procedure pure and simple, in civil cases the rule can be waived with the consent of the parties and when the parties expressly ask the Court to proceed along with a subsequent suit, neither side can afterwards turn round and challenge the validity of these proceedings because of section 10.'

heard in the interests of justice and of saving time and cost. Where a matter has been decided by a foreign court, the judgment of the latter court 'shall be conclusive as to any matter thereby directly adjudicated upon between the same parties, or between parties under whom they or any of them claim, litigating under the same title' (section 13).[13]

CPC sections 15 to 24 identify the court before which a particular action can be brought. Where a suit involves immovable property, it should be brought in the court of the place where the property is located (section 16, paragraph 1). But, exceptionally, where a plaintiff is seeking purely personal relief against a defendant (as opposed to making a claim of title or interest in immovable property), the action may also be brought before the court in the place where the defendant resides or carries on business (section 16, paragraph 2).[14] On the other hand, where an action is a claim for a wrong done to the person or to movable property, the action may be brought at the plaintiffs' option before the court in the place where the wrong was done or in the place where the defendant resides or carries on business (section 19). Otherwise, an action may be brought before the court where a defendant resides or carries on business (section 20(a)). Where there is more than one defendant, suit is to be brought: (1) where each defendant resides or carries on business; or, alternatively, (2) where one of the defendants resides, provided that such court gives leave to do so or the other defendants agree to the suit being brought in such court (section 20). Suit may also be instituted before the court in the place where 'the cause of action, wholly or in part, arises' (section 20(c)).[15]

There is a principle of waiver, so that on appeal a party may not object to the place where an action was brought, unless the party raised the objection at first instance (section 21).[16] There is also effectively a principle of *forum non conveniens*. A party may apply to have a case transferred to another court (section 23).[17] But such application ought to be made 'at the earliest possible opportunity'. Again, although the CPC does not identify the criteria for determining whether a case is more appropriately heard by one Myanmar court as opposed to another, in practical

[13] Section 13 is subject to exceptions, namely: '(a) where it [the judgment] has not been pronounced by a Court of competent jurisdiction; (b) where it has not been given on the merits of the case; (c) where it appears on the face of proceedings to be founded on an incorrect view of international law or a refusal to recognise the law of the Union of Myanmar in cases in which such law is applicable; (d) where the proceedings in which the judgment was obtained are opposed to natural justice; (e) where it has been obtained by fraud; (f) where it sustains a claim founded on a breach of any law in force in the Union of Myanmar'. For a detailed account of the law on the recognition and enforcement of foreign judgments in Myanmar, see Zaw Thura, 'Myanmar' in Anselmo Reyes (ed), *Recognition and Enforcement of Judgments in Civil and Commercial Matters* (Oxford, Hart Publishing, 2019) 209–21.

[14] Compare the *Moçambique* rule as stated in *British South Africa Co v Companhia de Moçambique* [1893] AC 602 (HL).

[15] In *U Saung v U Khin Maung* [1959] BLR 314 (HC), the expression 'cause of action' in CPC section 20(c) was defined (at 315) as meaning 'every fact which if traversed, it would be necessary for the plaintiff to prove in order to support his right to the judgment' or '[i]n other words, it is a bundle of facts which it is necessary for the plaintiff to prove before he can succeed in the suit'. In *Shantilal Surajmal Mehta v Marajm Bibi* [1960] BLR 359 (HC) the court held (at 370–72) that in ascertaining what the expression 'cause of action' means, reference must be made to the substance, rather than form, of the claim being made. Thus, where breach of contract is alleged, the cause of action arises in any of the following: '(1) The place where the contract was made. (2) The place where the contract was to be performed. (3) The place where in the performance of the contract any money to which the suit relates was expressly or impliedly payable.' The relevant contract of pledge having been made in Rangoon with redemption impliedly to be made in Rangoon, the fact that the defendant had repudiated the contract while in Bombay, did not mean that the cause of action arose partly in Rangoon and partly in Bombay.

[16] However, where leave to bring a case before a court is needed and has not been obtained, the requirement of leave cannot be waived and an objection to the court's jurisdiction can be taken even on appeal. See *Shantilal Surajmal Mehta* (n 15) 370.

[17] Where the court from which a case is to be transferred is subordinate to the same appellate court as the court to which the case is to be transferred, application is made to the appellate court. Where the two courts are subordinate to different appellate courts, the application is made to the High Court. Where the two courts are different High Courts, the application is made to the Union Supreme Court.

terms such determination will require the court seised to evaluate whether a case should more conveniently be heard by another Myanmar court in the interests of justice and of saving time and cost. Such doctrine of *forum conveniens* may be generalised so as to apply where the Myanmar court and a foreign court have jurisdiction over a given matter. In such a situation, it is submitted that the Myanmar court has a discretion to stay proceedings to the foreign court, if it would be more appropriate in the interests of justice and of saving time and cost for the foreign court to hear the matter.[18] Further, where the parties have designated a foreign court as the exclusive forum to decide disputes arising from their contract, the Myanmar court should decline jurisdiction, in the absence of compelling reasons to the contrary, so as to ensure that the parties adhere to their choice of court agreement.[19] It will be for case law to develop what might constitute compelling reasons for disregarding an exclusive jurisdiction clause. A corollary to this principle would be applicable to the situation where, in breach of a clause in the parties' contract conferring exclusive jurisdiction on the Myanmar court, a party commences an action before a foreign court. In those circumstances, it is submitted that the Myanmar court would be entitled where the party in breach is amenable to its jurisdiction (for example, by being resident, carrying on business, or having assets in Myanmar) to issue a temporary or perpetual anti-suit injunction ordering the party in breach not to pursue its action before the foreign court. Such measure would be consistent with section 54 of the Specific Relief Act[20] which provides:

> Subject to the other provisions contained in, or referred to by, this Chapter, a perpetual injunction may be granted to prevent the breach of an obligation existing in favour of the applicant, whether expressly or by implication.
>
> ...
>
> When the defendant invades or threatens to invade the plaintiff's right to, or enjoyment of, property, the Court may grant a perpetual injunction in the following cases:
>
> ...
>
> (e) where the injunction is necessary to prevent a multiplicity of judicial proceedings.

CPC section 26 provides that '[e]very suit shall be instituted by the presentation of a plaint or in such manner as may be prescribed'. The general rules for the institution of a suit are found in the Rules of Procedure (the Rules) annexed to the CPC in its First Schedule. The Rules comprise a set of Orders which deal with the specific procedures to be followed in given matters.

By Order I Rule 1, any person may be a plaintiff; by Order I Rule 3, any person may be a defendant. Thus, non-Myanmar nationals may sue and be sued before the Myanmar court. Neither the CPC nor the Rules expressly define who is a 'person' for the purposes of bringing an action. Clearly, natural persons would qualify. But it may be inferred that 'person' includes legal persons, such as corporations. For example, Explanation II to CPC section 20 states insofar as suing defendants where they carry on business is concerned: 'A corporation shall be deemed to carry on business at its sole or principal office in the Union of Myanmar or, in respect of any cause of action arising at any place where it has also a subordinate office, in such place.' This suggests that corporations may be sued in their place of business. Consequently, where Order I Rule 3 states that '[a]ll persons may be joined as defendants', the word 'persons' must be taken to include legal persons such as corporations. If that is so, it would be odd if the reference to 'persons' in

[18] See eg by way of guidance on the generalised application of *forum non conveniens*, the well-known case of *Spiliada Maritime Corp v Cansulex Ltd (The Spiliada)* [1987] AC 460 (HL).

[19] The agreement designating the foreign court as the forum to resolve their disputes would amount to a submission by the parties to the foreign court's jurisdiction. See *VAS Arogya Odeyar v VRRMNS Sathappa Chettiar* [1951] BLR 211 (HC), citing with approval a dictum of Bankes LJ in *Harris v Taylor* [1915] 2 KB 580, 592.

[20] Originally enacted as India Act I of 1877.

Order I Rule 1 ('[a]ll persons may be joined in one suit as plaintiffs') did not similarly refer to natural and legal persons.[21]

Order IV of the Rules requires that every action be instituted by presenting a plaint to the relevant court. The plaint will contain the particulars of the plaintiffs' case. The court before which the plaint is presented will record such particulars in a register of civil suits.[22] Once an action has been commenced, a summons is issued whereby the defendant is instructed to appear before the court and answer the plaintiff's claim on a specified date (Order V). On the hearing date appointed by the summons, the defendant may appear in person or by a legal representative. Order V Rule 4 provides that no party is to be summonsed to appear before it, unless such party resides within the limits of the court's jurisdiction or a certain distance from such limits. Order V Rule 6 goes on to say that the date on which the defendant is to appear before the court is to be fixed by reference to the defendant's place of residence, the time that it would take to serve the defendant at such place of residence, and the time that it would take to enable the defendant to appear before the court on the appointed day. Unless the court directs otherwise, service is effected on a defendant by a process-server delivering the relevant summons to the defendant's place of residence within the jurisdiction (Order V Rule 9). The CPC stipulates that '[w]herever it is practicable' service *shall* be made on the defendant in person (Order V Rule 12).[23] But, if the defendant has an agent within the jurisdiction who is authorised to accept service on the defendant's behalf, the process-server may in the alternative deliver the summons to that agent (Order V Rule 12).[24] If an action concerns immovable property and service cannot be effected on the defendant or an authorised agent of the defendant within the geographical limits of the court's jurisdiction, service may be made on the person who is in charge of the relevant piece of land on behalf of the defendant (Order V Rule 14). When a defendant is avoiding service, the court may order substituted service by posting the summons in a conspicuous place within the court building and (if the defendant has a place of residence within the court's territorial limits) by affixing the summons to a prominent spot in that residence (Order V Rule 20). A summons may be transmitted by an issuing court to any other court which has jurisdiction in the place where the defendant resides (Order V Rule 21). Where the latter court is outside Myanmar, then the summons should be in English or be accompanied by an English translation (Order V rule 21A). If a defendant resides outside of Myanmar and has no agent in Myanmar to accept service, the summons may be served by post addressed to the defendant at the place where the defendant resides (Order V Rule 25). Presumably, where such defendant is a company, its place of 'residence' outside of Myanmar would be the place where it carries on its business.

In respect of suits brought against a foreign state, CPC section 84(1) provides that:

> A foreign State may sue in any Court of the Union of Myanmar:
>
> Provided that such State has been recognized by the President of the Union:

[21] This view is supported by reference to the Interpretation of Expressions Law (Law No 22/73) (IEL), enacted by the Revolutionary Council of the Union of Myanmar on 12 May 1973 which functions as a modern revision of the Burma General Clauses Act 1898. IEL, s 2 provides for the IEL to apply to acts, laws, ordinances, rules, regulations, and proclamations made by any legislative authority prior to or subsequent to the IEL's commencement. IEL, s 5(a)(24) defines 'person' as including 'any company or association or corporation, or body of persons'.

[22] Order IV Rule 2.

[23] If there is more than one defendant, then each one needs to be served (Order V Rule 11). If the defendant is absent, service may be made on a family member residing within the defendant's place of residence (Order V Rule 15).

[24] In the situation of an action relating to the work or business of a person who does not reside within the geographical limits of a court's jurisdiction, service may be effected on a manager or agent carrying out the work or business within the court's geographical limits (Order V Rule 13). For these purposes, the master of a ship is deemed to be the agent of the owner or charterer of the vessel.

> Provided also, that the object of the suit is to enforce a private right vested in the head of such State or in any officer of such State in his public capacity.

Section 86 in turn enables suits to be brought against an ambassador or envoy of a foreign state with the consent of the President of the Union of Myanmar. The President's consent will not be given unless the relevant ambassador or envoy:

> (a) has instituted a suit in the Court against the person desiring to sue him, or
> (b) by himself or another trades within the local limits of the jurisdiction of the Court, or
> (c) is in possession of immoveable property situate within those limits and is to be sued with reference to such property or for money charged thereon.

Further, no ambassador or envoy so sued shall be arrested under the CPC and no decree shall be executed against the property of such ambassador or envoy without the consent of the Union President.

In *U Kyaw Din v His Britannic Majesty's Government of the United Kingdom*,[25] U Bo Gyi J noted that:

> [S]ection 86 provides that in certain circumstances and subject to consent of the authorities concerned suits may be instituted against a Sovereign Prince …, or against an ambassador or envoy of a foreign state, but makes no mention of a foreign state as being amenable to the jurisdiction of the Burmese Courts. It is significant that while under section 84 of the [CPC] a foreign State may sue in any Court in the Union of Burma, there is no provision in the [CPC] which permits the institution of a suit against a foreign State.
>
> It would seem therefore that the authors of the [CPC] followed the general law. There is a considerable body of weighty and unanimous authority for the view that 'although the States can sue in foreign courts, they cannot as a rule be sued there, unless they voluntarily submit to the jurisdiction of the court concerned'.[26] This, as the learned author observes, flows from the fact that all member-States of the Family of Nations are equal before International Law and consequently no State can claim jurisdiction over another.

The judge referred with approval to the following dictum of Kay LJ in *Mighell v Sultan of Johore*:[27]

> It is said that an independent sovereign may waive his right to immunity, and may treat himself as subject to the jurisdiction. I agree; but how is that to be done? This seems to me, in the first place, quite clear. Supporting, by way of illustration, that some well-known potentate, such as one of the great European emperors, were to be sued in a Court of this country, and took no kind of notice of the proceeding; it would be the duty of the Court to recognize his position and to say at once that the person cited was an independent foreign sovereign over whom it had no jurisdiction. Therefore it is not right to say that such a sovereign must come froward and assert his right. I do not think that he need. I think the Court itself would be bound to take notice of the fact that it had no jurisdiction.

As the UK steadfastly refused to submit the court's jurisdiction, the judge dismissed the suit. It would accordingly appear from the decision that, where foreign states are concerned, the Myanmar court generally adopts a doctrine of absolute immunity. Where a foreign state is sued, the court will decline jurisdiction, unless the state submits to the court's jurisdiction.

[25] *U Kyaw Din v His Britannic Majesty's Government of the United Kingdom* [1948] BLR 524 (HC). See to similar effect *U Zeya v Secretary of State of His Britannic Majesty for War Represented by Headquarters, Burma Command* [1949] BLR 402 (HC).

[26] Citing Oppenheim's *International Law*: Hersch Lauterpacht (ed), *International Law* 6th edn, vol 1 (London, Longmans, Green & Co, 1947) 239.

[27] *Mighell v Sultan of Johore* [1894] 1 QB 149, 162.

The foregoing general rules of jurisdiction may be summarised thus:

(1) Non-Myanmar nationals may sue or be sued in the Myanmar court.
(2) Foreign companies may sue and be sued in the Myanmar court.
(3) The Myanmar court in a geographical location can exercise jurisdiction where:
    (a) the defendant is resident or carries on business in that location;
    (b) at least one of several defendants is resident or carries on business in that location and either the court is of the view that it is an appropriate forum for the trial of the action or the other defendants agree to the court exercising jurisdiction in the matter;
    (c) the dispute between the parties relates to title or an interest in land and the land is situate in that location;
    (d) the dispute between the parties relates to a wrong done to the plaintiff or to the plaintiff's moveable property and such wrong was done in that location;
    (e) the cause of action 'wholly or partly arises' in such location.
(4) There is a doctrine of waiver, so that if objection to a procedural mis-step has not been taken at first instance to the court's exercise of jurisdiction, a defendant will be precluded from raising the objection on appeal.
(5) There is a doctrine of *lis alibi pendens*, so that the Myanmar court:
    (a) will refuse jurisdiction where a suit is pending before another Myanmar court; and,
    (b) may as a matter of discretion decline jurisdiction where a suit is pending before a foreign court.
(6) There is a doctrine of *res judicata*, so that the Myanmar court:
    (a) will refuse jurisdiction where a suit has been heard by another Myanmar court; and,
    (b) subject to limited exceptions, will recognise the judgment of a foreign court as conclusive on any matter decided by it and decline to re-hear such matter.
(7) There is scope for developing a general doctrine of *forum non conveniens* on the basis of CPC section 23.
(8) It is submitted that, in the absence compelling reasons to the contrary, the Myanmar court will enforce choice of court agreements. This would include, where appropriate, by issuing anti-suit injunctions.
(9) Where a defendant is resident outside of Myanmar, the defendant may be served by post at the place where the defendant resides.
(10) The Myanmar court will generally decline jurisdiction where a foreign state is sued and does not submit to the Myanmar court's jurisdiction.

III. Specific Cases

A. Competition Law and the Effects Doctrine

Myanmar enacted a Competition Law (CL) on 24 February 2015.[28] The CL prohibits conduct which restricts free and fair market competition, such as price-fixing, cartel agreements, abuse of

[28] *Pyidaungsu Hluttaw* Law No 9 of 2015.

market dominance, and collusion in tenders or auctions (CL section 13). CL section 5 establishes a Competition Commission with the duty (among others) of enforcing the prohibitions in the CL and taking administrative action against offenders. The possibility of administrative action by the Competition Commissions does not preclude the taking of criminal or civil action against wrongdoers and a victim may bring a civil action against any person convicted of breaching the CL for loss suffered as a result of anti-competitive conduct (CL sections 38 and 51).

The CL, however, says nothing about what happens when conduct carried on entirely abroad gives rise to anti-competitive effects in Myanmar. An instance of this would be where the members of a cartel of companies agree outside of Myanmar artificially to fix the prices at which goods are sold to (say) buyers in Myanmar, thereby distorting the market for the relevant goods in Myanmar. In such a case, would the Myanmar court have jurisdiction to hear civil actions against the members of the cartel, even when the latter are situated abroad and have never set foot in Myanmar? It is submitted that, applying the general principles set out above, there would be jurisdiction. The CL 'concretises' certain conduct as anti-competitive and thus wrongful. The wrong would have been inflicted on the financial well-being of a victim or class of victims (for example, consumers) or on the assets (property) of a victim or class of victims residing within the geographical limits of a particular Myanmar court (CPC section 19). In other words, the 'effects' of the wrongful conduct would be felt in Myanmar. That should be sufficient to found jurisdiction in the Myanmar court. Alternatively, the wrong would partly arise from the cartel's collusive conduct abroad and partly from the damage suffered by the victim or victims residing within the geographical limits of a given Myanmar court (CPC section 20(c)). On either analysis, subject only to *forum non conveniens*, the court in the victim's geographical location would have jurisdiction to hear the victim's grievance, because the effects of the anti-competitive conduct had an impact on the market in Myanmar.[29]

B. Enforcement of Arbitration Agreements

Myanmar acceded to the 1958 United Nations Convention on the Recognition and Enforcement of Foreign Arbitral Awards (the New York Convention, NYC) on 16 April 2013. As a result, by NYC Article II, Myanmar is obliged to recognise and give effect to arbitration agreements in writing. Where a party commences an action in the Myanmar court in breach of such arbitration agreement, the Myanmar court must decline jurisdiction unless it finds that the agreement is null and void, inoperative or incapable of being performed. In keeping with its obligations under the NYC, Myanmar passed an Arbitration Law (AL) on 5 January 2016.[30] AL section 10 requires the Myanmar court, when faced with a suit brought in breach of an arbitration agreement, to refer the parties to arbitration unless the agreement is null and void, inoperative or incapable of being performed. The court may grant interim measures in support of arbitration proceedings under AL section 11. But the Myanmar court may only deal with matters that the parties or the tribunal or relevant arbitral institution is unable to deal with (AL section 11(d)). An interim

[29] The effects doctrine can be applied to similar effect where environmental damage has been inflicted on a particular community in Myanmar as a result of a negligent accident outside of Myanmar (eg an oil spill in the high seas). Where the effects or damage from the environmental wrong are suffered in Myanmar, it is submitted that the Myanmar court would likewise have jurisdiction to hear claims against the wrongdoer even if resident or carrying on business abroad.

[30] *Pyidaungsu Hluttaw* Law No 5 of 2016.

measure ordered by the court ceases to have effect if the arbitral tribunal countermands the same (AL section 11(e)).

C. Cross-border Insolvency

Myanmar enacted an Insolvency Law (IL) on 14 February 2020.[31] With the exception of Part X, the IL came into effect on 25 March 2020.[32] Part X (sections 368 to 400) of the IL deals with cross-border insolvency. It will come into effect on a future date, as determined by the President of the Union of Myanmar. Under IL section 372 the recognition and support of foreign insolvency proceedings pursuant to the terms of the statute fall within the jurisdiction of the Supreme Court or such other court as it might designate. Representatives of foreign insolvency proceedings may apply to the Myanmar court for recognition of those foreign proceedings (IL section 383). Upon the application of the foreign representative, the Myanmar court may grant interim measures to preserve a debtor's assets within Myanmar (IL section 387). Once foreign proceedings are recognised, ongoing or fresh proceedings and execution in relation to the debtor's assets and liabilities in Myanmar are stayed (IL section 388). The Myanmar court may also make further orders to protect the debtor's assets, including permitting the foreign representative to examine witnesses and obtain information about those assets or causing the debtor's assets to be administered by a person designated by the foreign representative (IL section 389).

D. Matrimonial Causes

An account of Myanmar family law would be complex and beyond the scope of this chapter. As a matter of general principle, where proceedings for divorce or other matrimonial causes are concerned, it is unlikely that the Myanmar court will accept jurisdiction where a foreign spouse is concerned. Thus, for instance, the Myanmar Divorce Act[33] stipulates in section 2 that:

> Nothing herein contained shall authorize any Court to grant any relief under this Act except where the petitioner or respondent professes the Christian religion,[34] or to make decrees of nullity of marriage except where the marriage has been solemnised in the Union of Myanmar and the petitioner is resident in the Union of Burma at the time of presenting the petition. or to grant any relief under this Act, other than a decree of dissolution of marriage or of nullity of marriage, except where the petitioner resides in the Union of Burma at the time of presenting the petition.

[31] *Pyidaungsu Hluttaw* Law No 1 of 2020.

[32] Notification Order No 50/2020 by the President of the Union of Myanmar.

[33] Originally enacted as India Act IV of 1869, amended in June 1989 and August 2017.

[34] In relation to non-Christian marriages, s 13(1) of the Myanmar Laws Act (originally enacted as India Act XIII of 1898, amended in September 1959 and June 1989) provides:

> Where in any suit or other proceeding in the Union of Myanmar, it is necessary for the Court to decide any question regarding succession, inheritance, marriage or caste, or any religious usage or institution:
>
> (a) the Buddhist law in cases where the parties are Buddhists,
> (b) the Muhammadan law in cases where the parties are Mohammedans, and
> (c) the Hindu law in cases where the parties are Hindus,
>
> shall form the rule of decision, except in so far as such law has by enactment been altered or abolished, or is opposed to any custom having the force of law.

Otherwise, in the ordinary course of events, a petition under the Act is to be presented to the District Court or, alternatively, the High Court within the place where the couple resides or last resided together in Myanmar. The petition cannot be presented to any other Myanmar court.

E. Admiralty Claims *in rem*

On 30 June 2014, the Union Judiciary Act was amended to confer jurisdiction in Admiralty cases on the High Court.[35] What constitutes an 'Admiralty case' does not seem to be defined in any law. The precise ambit of the expression will have to be determined by future decisions of the High Court. Presumably, claims against ships (which would constitute movables) should be brought before the High Court with jurisdiction over the area in which the ship is to be found.[36]

CPC section 112 provides that 'nothing herein contained shall apply to any matter of … admiralty jurisdiction, or to appeals from orders and decrees of Prize Courts'. Despite this, section 140 in Part XI (Miscellaneous) of the CPC provides that the Myanmar court sitting in 'any Admiralty or Vice-Admiralty cause of salvage, towage or collision … may, if it thinks fit, and shall upon request of either party to such cause, summon to its assistance … two competent assessors' to sit with it.

IV. Conclusion

At best, this chapter can only serve to introduce Myanmar law on direct jurisdiction. That is inevitable, as much of the law on direct jurisdiction is in a state of development and remains to be clarified by case law and future legislation. Notwithstanding those difficulties, the general principles of jurisdiction are reasonably clear and settled. On the premise that normal life will more or less resume in 2022 after a one-year state of emergency, courts can build on those general principles as a guide to jurisdiction in specialised areas of the law. Where necessary and appropriate, details can be filled in by reference to common law cases decided elsewhere. Some possible ways of developing the law have been suggested here. The extent to which those suggestions will be taken up by the Myanmar courts remains to be seen.

See generally Maung Maung, *Law and Custom in Burma and the Burmese Family* (The Hague, Martinus Nijhoff, 1963).

[35] *Pyidaungsu Hluttaw* Law No 35 of 2014 (also known as the Law Amending the Union Judiciary Act 2014) s 2. It is unclear whether the jurisdiction conferred is meant to be exclusive.

[36] Note, however, that Myanmar is not a party to any international conventions on the arrest of ships.

12

Philippines

ARVIN KRISTOPHER A RAZON, JOCELYN P CRUZ AND JUSTIN DJ SUCGANG

I. Introduction

The earliest rules on conflict of laws in the Philippines were founded upon the civil law. In codifying various laws from general obligations and contracts to property relations and succession, Republic Act (RA) No 386 or the Civil Code of the Philippines devotes many provisions to conflict of laws. It is substantially a restatement of the Civil Code of Spain of 1888, owing to Spanish colonial rule in the Philippines that lasted for 333 years.[1] Nonetheless, the common law has also been influential in shaping conflict-of-laws rules in the Philippines. While American colonial rule lasted for only five decades, Anglo-American private international law concepts have found their way into Philippine statutes and case law.[2] Several Philippine Supreme Court decisions, which form part of the Philippine legal system under the common law regime,[3] refer to American decisions in analysing cases with a foreign element. It is important to keep in mind this hybrid legal system when understanding Philippine private international rules, as their development can be attributed to the particularities of the civil and common law traditions. Even the typically codified private international law rules introduced by the Spanish civil law system can be fully understood only in the light of the Philippine Supreme Court's judicial decisions, which are considered doctrinal precedents – characteristic of the common law tradition.

II. Jurisdiction *in personam*

A. General Principles

When a Philippine court is faced with a dispute involving cross-border elements, it may dismiss the case on the ground of lack of jurisdiction or, despite a finding that it has jurisdiction, for *forum non conveniens*. If it exercises jurisdiction and tries the case, it may apply either Philippine or foreign law. The focus in this section will be on actions *in personam*, that is, actions that have as their objective the imposition of a personal liability on the defendant by means of a court

[1] Jovito R Salonga, *Private International Law* (Pasig, Regina Publishing, 1995).
[2] ibid.
[3] Civil Code, Art 8.

judgment that will be binding on the latter and his or her successors-in-interest. Examples include contractual disputes or an action for the recovery of debt. This section will discuss how jurisdiction against a person (*in personam*) is established and when the doctrine of *forum non conveniens* may be applied in such cases.

i. Establishing Jurisdiction

In the Philippines, a conflict-of-laws problem begins with an issue of whether local courts have jurisdiction. For a Philippine court to try a case, it must have jurisdiction over one or more of the following: (1) a property or *res*; (2) the person of the plaintiff and the defendant; or (3) the subject matter.[4] Jurisdiction against property (that is, jurisdiction *in rem*) will be considered in the next section. Jurisdiction *in personam* is established over a plaintiff, including a non-resident, as a result of the latter filing a suit before the Philippine court. In so doing, the plaintiff is deemed to consent to the court's exercise of jurisdiction over him/her in connection with the suit filed and with subsequent or related proceedings arising out of that suit, including counterclaims filed by the defendant.[5] Jurisdiction over a defendant is established by the latter's voluntary entry of appearance to defend a suit before the court (generally, by the filing of a responsive pleading) or by the proper service of legal process on the defendant within the Philippines.[6] Where a defendant is unwilling to appear before the court voluntarily, the coercive process of the law, via proper service of a summons upon the defendant, may be invoked. In actions *in personam*, service of a summons may only be effected by personal or substituted service. The rules are laid down in Rule 14 of the recently amended Rules of Civil Procedure:[7]

> *Section 5. Service in person on defendant*
>
> Whenever practicable, the summons shall be served by handing a copy thereof to the defendant in person and informing the defendant that he or she is being served, or, if he or she refuses to receive and sign for it, by leaving the summons within the view and in the presence of the defendant.
>
> *Section 6. Substituted service*
>
> If, for justifiable causes, the defendant cannot be served personally after at least three (3) attempts on two (2) different dates, service may be effected:
>
> (a) By leaving copies of the summons at the defendant's residence to a person at least eighteen (18) years of age and of sufficient discretion residing therein;
> (b) By leaving copies of the summons at the defendant's office or regular place of business with some competent person in charge thereof. A competent person includes, but is not limited to, one who customarily receives correspondences for the defendant;
> (c) By leaving copies of the summons, if refused entry upon making his or her authority and purpose known, with any of the officers of the homeowners' association or condominium corporation, or its chief security officer in charge of the community or the building where the defendant may be found; and
> (d) By sending an electronic mail to the defendant's electronic mail address, if allowed by the court.

[4] Jorge R Coquia and Elizabeth Aguiling-Pangalangan, *Conflict of Laws: Cases, Materials and Comments* (Quezon, Central Book Supply, 2000) 20.

[5] ibid.

[6] *Banco Espanol Filipino v Palanca* GR No 11390 (1918).

[7] Rules of Civil Procedure (AM No 19-10-20-SC), available online: https://sc.judiciary.gov.ph/12761/. The amendments to the Rules of Civil Procedure came into effect on 1 May 2020.

The recent amendment to Rule 14 expands the modes of substituted service, which previously only allowed for service at the defendant's residence, office or regular place of business. Following the amendment, summonses may now be served by email on a defendant, thereby addressing the difficulty of expending judicial resources to serve summonses on defendants which was a common impediment to the speedy administration of justice. Finally, jurisdiction over subject matter or subject matter competence is the general power for courts to hear and determine cases of a general class to which the proceedings in question belong.[8] Jurisdiction over subject matter is conferred only by specific laws and cannot be voluntarily consented to by parties. The primary bases of this jurisdiction are the Philippine Constitution and the Judiciary Reorganization Act of 1980,[9] which specifies when various courts in the judicial system – from the lowest level (the municipal trial courts) to the highest appellate level (the Court of Appeals) – can accept certain types of cases.

ii. *Applying* forum non conveniens

Apart from the jurisdictional bases just explained, under the doctrine of *forum non conveniens*, a Philippine court may assume jurisdiction if the following requirements are met: (1) It would be more convenient in terms of saving time and cost and the interests of justice if a matter were litigated before the Philippine (as opposed to a foreign) court; (2) The Philippine court is in a position to make a meaningful decision on the law (applying the proper law, whether local or foreign, of the matter) and the facts; (3) The Philippine court's decision on the matter would be enforceable.[10] Conversely, even if the Philippine court could properly assume jurisdiction over a case, it may nonetheless decline to do so as a matter of discretion by invoking this same principle of *forum non conveniens*. In other words, the Philippine court may conclude that there is some other forum before which a matter might more conveniently be heard, insofar as saving time and cost and the interests of justice are concerned. The application of *forum non conveniens* in this second sense is often based on practical reasons, applying factors propounded in American case law such as: (1) the non-availability of witnesses or evidence in the Philippines; (2) the risk that the speedy administration of justice will not be achieved because of the court's clogged docket; (3) the prevention of forum shopping by a foreign plaintiff; and (4) the non-enforceability of a Philippine judgment in a relevant jurisdiction.[11] Such reasons for declining to try a case will not be resorted to lightly, following judicial policy to respect a plaintiff's choice of forum:

> It is well-established practice in the application of the principle of *forum non conveniens* that unless the balance is strongly in favor of the defendant, the plaintiff's choice of forum should rarely be disturbed, and that, furthermore, the consideration of inadequacy to enforce the judgment, which is one of the important factors to be considered in the application of said principle, would precisely constitute a problem to the plaintiffs if the local courts decline to assume jurisdiction on the basis of said principle, considering that the defendant is a resident of the Philippines.[12]

Ultimately, the question of whether to assume or decline jurisdiction on the ground of *forum non conveniens* will be based on the facts of the case and the court's discretion.[13] In determining

[8] *Caluag v Pecson* GR No 1403 (1948).
[9] RA No 7691.
[10] *Continental Micronesia Inc v Basso* GR Nos 178382–83 (2015).
[11] Alicia V Sempio-Diy, *Handbook on Conflict of Laws* (Quezon, Joer Printing Services, 2004) 14–15, citing *Canada Malting Co Ltd v Patterson Steamships Ltd* 285 US 413 (1932) and *Heine v New York Life Insurance Co* 45 F 2d 426 (D Or 1930).
[12] *Wing On Co v SYYAP* GR No 28130 (1967).
[13] *Raytheon International Inc v Rouzie* GR No 162894 (2008).

whether to dismiss a case on the ground of *forum non conveniens*, public and private interests will be weighed. In addition to the considerations already mentioned, other relevant factors in assessing the private interests involved would be: (1) the court's ability to access and assess evidence; (2) the possibility of securing the compulsory attendance of otherwise unwilling witnesses through existing court processes; (3) the ease by which any property in question can be accessed should the need to do so arise; and (4) all issues that would make litigation expeditious and inexpensive. On the other hand, evaluating the public interest would involve looking at: (1) the state of the court's dockets; and (2) the court's familiarity and confidence in correctly applying any governing foreign law.[14]

iii. Service of Process Outside of the Philippines

The general rule in *in personam* actions is that summonses may only be effected by personal or substituted service, with recent amendments to the law making this easier. Service of process outside of the territory, including through summonses by publication, is not sufficient for an action *in personam*, whether or not the defendant is in the Philippines.[15] An exception is where the defendant ordinarily resides within, but is temporarily out of, the Philippines. In this case, the court may permit extraterritorial service.[16] Otherwise, the rules on extraterritorial service of a summons is limited to actions *in rem* and *quasi in rem* (discussed below) and actions that affect the personal status of the plaintiff. Extraterritorial service, or service of process out of the Philippines, may be done only in the following ways:

(1) by following the same rule on service in person on defendant, outside the Philippine territory;
(2) as provided for in international conventions to which the Philippines is a party;
(3) by publication in a newspaper of general circulation in such places and for such time as the court may order, in which case a copy of the summons and order of the court shall be sent by registered mail to the last known address of the defendant; and,
(4) in any other manner as the court may deem sufficient.[17]

iv. Service of Foreign Proceedings within the Philippines

A judgment or order issued by a foreign court upon a specific thing or against a person located in the Philippines is a foreign judgment.[18] Its enforcement in the Philippines requires the filing of a specific petition for that purpose. In the case of a judgment or final order upon a specific thing, the judgment or order will be conclusive upon the title to the thing. In the case of a judgment or final order against a person, the judgment or order will be presumptive evidence of the rights between the parties and their successors-in-interest. In both cases, a retrial or re-examination of the merits of the case is generally not required, except if there is evidence that: (1) the

[14] *Gulf Oil Corp v Gilbert* 330 US 501 (1947).
[15] *Pantaleon v Asuncion* GR No 13141 (1959).
[16] Rules of Civil Procedure, r 14, s 18.
[17] ibid, r 14, s 17.
[18] Foreign arbitral awards will also be recognised, pursuant to the 1958 United Nations Convention on the Recognition and Enforcement of Foreign Arbitral Awards (the New York Convention, to which the Philippines is a Contracting State) and the Alternative Dispute Resolution Act of 2004 (RA No 9285).

foreign court lacked jurisdiction; (2) the defendant did not receive proper notice of the foreign proceedings; (3) there was collusion or fraud; or (4) there was a clear mistake of law or fact by the foreign court.[19]

B. Special Rules for Establishing Jurisdiction

This sub-section discusses specific rules over certain subject matters. When a Philippine court assumes jurisdiction over a case that presents a conflict-of-laws problem, it has the choice of either applying Philippine or foreign law, but naturally gravitates towards the former. Courts may be bound to apply Philippine law as the *lex fori* in three specific cases: (1) when Philippine law as the *lex fori* specifically requires that it should apply Philippine law; (2) foreign law was improperly proved; and (3) the case falls under any of the exceptions to the application of foreign law. On case (2), whether foreign law may be properly applied by the Philippine court ultimately depends on whether it was adequately proven by the relevant party. Since foreign law, even if found to be the proper governing law, is not a matter of judicial notice, it must be pleaded and proven as a fact by evidence.[20] Otherwise, foreign law is presumed to be the same as the *lex fori*. This is known as the doctrine of processual presumption.[21]

Of foremost consideration when Philippine courts establish jurisdiction over a subject matter is an individual's personal law – the law that follows an individual everywhere and governs many of his or her transactions, such as capacity to contract, marriage, and divorce.[22] As part of its civil law tradition, Philippine law largely follows the national law theory as the basis for a person's personal law. According to the Philippine Supreme Court, the nationality theory in conflict of laws means that the person's nationality determines jurisdiction over certain subject matters, especially matters relating to personal status such as capacity to act and family relations.[23] This principle is codified in Article 15 of the Civil Code: 'Laws relating to family rights and duties, or to status, condition and capacity of persons are binding upon citizens of the Philippines, even though living abroad.' While the provision only expressly recognises the personal law applicable to Philippine citizens, by parity of reasoning it has been used by domestic courts as the basis for applying the national law of foreign citizens in conflict-of-law cases requiring a determination of status or capacity.[24] As such, unlike common law jurisdictions that typically use domicile as the basis for a person's personal law, the determination of one's nationality is important in conflict-of-laws cases before Philippine courts.

i. Contracts

A guiding principle of Philippine contract law, which also finds expression in private international law, is party autonomy. In this connection, Article 1306 of the Civil Code provides: 'Contracting parties may establish such stipulations, clauses, terms and conditions as they may deem convenient, provided that they are not contrary to Philippine laws, morals, good customs, public

[19] Rules of Civil Procedure, r 39, s 48.
[20] *In re Testate Estate of Suntay* GR No 3087 (1954).
[21] *Arreza v Toyo* GR No 213198 (2019).
[22] Coquia and Aguiling-Pangalangan (n 4) 36.
[23] *Ellis v Republic* GR No 16922 (1963).
[24] *Gibbs v Government of the Philippines* GR No 35963 (1933).

order or public policy.'[25] Thus, if contracting parties (which may include a Philippine national) agree that their agreement will be governed by a law other than Philippine law, such choice is valid and binding. Subject to certain exceptions, the validity of the terms and conditions of that agreement will be governed by the law of the chosen jurisdiction. The underlying rationale of Article 1306 is to respect and protect the parties' expectations and secure stability in commercial transactions.

When a Philippine court construes the law applicable to a contract having foreign elements, it must necessarily assess the extrinsic and intrinsic validity of a contract, as well as the parties' capacity to enter into the contract. Extrinsic validity refers to the formal validity of the contract. A contract is extrinsically valid if it is in the form required by the law of the place where the contract was executed (*lex loci contractus*).[26] For a contract made in the Philippines, the general rule is that it will be binding whatever the form used by the parties. Article 1356 provides for the exceptions where a contract must be in writing to be valid,[27] enforceable,[28] or simply efficacious.[29] Intrinsic validity pertains to the nature, content, and effects of an agreement. There is no specifically applicable conflict-of-laws provision in respect of intrinsic validity. Since the policy is to give effect to the intention of the parties, the proper law of the contract is regarded as law expressly (*lex loci voluntatis*) or impliedly (*lex loci intentionis*) agreed by the parties. In inferring what the parties may have intended to be the governing law of an agreement, the law with the most substantial connection with the parties' transaction and the law presumed to have been intended by the parties to apply to their transaction are taken into account. An essential element is the indication of a 'test', 'connecting factor', or 'point of contact'.[30] Parties cannot choose a governing law that has no connection to any part of the agreement. Some 'connecting factors' that have been found to be relevant are:[31] (1) the place of contracting; (2) the place of negotiation; (3) the place of performance;, (4) the situs of the subject matter of the contract; (5) the domicile, residence, nationality, place of incorporation, or place of business of the parties; and (6) the place under whose law the contract will be most effective. Although the *lex loci voluntatis* or *lex loci intentionis* may have been properly determined, a Philippine court may nonetheless set it aside, if considered to be contrary to a sound and established public policy of the forum. An example would be when the application of such law would cause serious injustice to the citizens or residents of the forum.[32] Further, while the governing law may be expressly stated or implied, such choice of law agreement cannot oust any jurisdiction vested upon Philippine agencies and courts by Philippine law.[33] The Philippine Supreme Court highlighted the distinction between jurisdiction and choice of law:

> That the subject contract included a stipulation that the same shall be governed by the laws of the State of Connecticut does not suggest that the Philippine courts, or any other foreign tribunal for that matter, are precluded from hearing the civil action. Jurisdiction and choice of law are two distinct concepts. Jurisdiction considers whether it is fair to cause a defendant to travel to this state; choice of law asks the further question whether the application of a substantive law which will determine the merits of the

[25] Civil Code, Art 1306.
[26] ibid, Art 17.
[27] ibid, Art 1356. Certain documents which are intended to serve as records in a public registry, such as contracts that create, transmit, modify or extinguish real rights over immovable property, need to be executed or acknowledged before a notary. Otherwise, they are void: ibid, Arts 1771, 1773.
[28] An example of this are those documents required to be in writing, even if not notarised, pursuant to Art 1403(2) of the Civil Code (also known as the Statute of Frauds).
[29] Civil Code, Art 1358; *Tapec v Court of Appeals* GR No 111952 (1994).
[30] *Saudi Arabian Airlines v Court of Appeals* GR No 122191 (1998).
[31] *Hasegawav Kitamura* GR No 149177 (2007).
[32] *Bank of America NT & SA v American Realty Corp* GR No 133876 (1999).
[33] *Pakistan International Airlines Corp v Ople* GR No 61594 (1990).

> case is fair to both parties. The choice of law stipulation will become relevant only when the substantive issues of the instant case develop, that is, after hearing on the merits proceeds before the trial court.[34]

Philippine courts will not be divested of jurisdiction if the law provides that they are vested with jurisdiction over a case, as discussed in Section II.A.i above and Section III.A below.[35] Thus, even if a foreign choice of court or forum is stipulated in a contract, Philippine courts can decide to try a case, subject to the doctrine of *forum non conveniens*. However, an arbitration clause will be considered contractually binding and must be respected by the parties as a matter of condition precedent to court action, even if it provides for arbitration to be done in a foreign location. In a case decided by the Supreme Court, the arbitration clause provides for settlement by arbitration in London in accordance with the Arbitration Act 1950.[36]

Extrinsic and intrinsic validity remain the primary issues that Philippine courts must consider in special types of contracts with cross-border elements. Certain rules may apply in specific instances. For example, in a simple loan extended by financial institutions, the governing law is that of the financial institution's permanent place of business. If the loan is extended by an individual, the governing law is the place where the loan was obtained. For barter, sale, donation, security interests,[37] and antichresis (pledges of interests in immovable property), it is the *lex situs* or the law of the place where the property is situated. Labour-related or employment contracts may be considered a lease of service. Their extrinsic validity is governed by *lex loci contractus*, while intrinsic validity is based on the *lex loci voluntatis or lex loci intentionis*. As such contracts involve the public interest, Philippine courts, often wish to ensure that an aggrieved employee obtains social justice. Accordingly, connecting factors that are considered by the Philippine Supreme Court in determining the applicable law in an employment contract are the nationality, domicile or residence of the employee; the seat of the employer; the place where the employment contract was made; the place of performance of the employee's duties; the parties' intention as to the governing law of their contract; and the place where relevant judicial or administrative proceedings have been instituted.[38] Another specific contract worth discussing is a contract for the transportation of goods. Article 1753 of the Civil Code provides that the law of the country to which the goods are to be transported governs the liability of the common carrier in cases of loss, destruction or deterioration.[39] If Philippine law governs, the obligation of extraordinary responsibility of the common carrier from the time that the goods are unconditionally placed in the possession of the carrier until they are delivered to the consignee applies.[40]

ii. Torts

An understanding of Philippine tort law requires an appreciation of its counterpart in American common law and the concept of quasi-delict under Spanish civil law. Article 2176 of the Civil Code articulates the Spanish concept of quasi-delict or *culpa aquiliana*:

> Whoever by act or omission causes damage to another, there being fault or negligence, is obliged to pay for the damage done. Such fault or negligence, if there is no pre-existing contractual relation between the parties, is called a quasi-delict and is governed by the provisions of [the Civil Code on quasi-delicts].

[34] *Raytheon International* (n 13).
[35] *Hong Kong and Shanghai Banking Corp v Sherman* GR No 72494 (1980).
[36] *Puromines Inc v Court of Appeals* GR No 91228 (1993).
[37] The Personal Property Security Act (RA No 11057) repealed the Civil Code provisions on chattel mortgage and pledge.
[38] ibid.
[39] Civil Code, Art 1753.
[40] ibid, Arts 1367–68. See also *American President Lines Ltd v Klepper* GR No 15671 (1960).

Quasi-delicts, which must be independent of contract, may only be committed by fault or negligence. Tort is broader in that it covers not only legal wrongs committed by negligence but also those committed with malice or wilful intent. This principle is likewise codified in the Civil Code: 'Every person who, contrary to law, wilfully or negligently causes damage to another, shall indemnify the latter for the same'.[41] Generally, as in many civil law countries, liability for torts is governed by the *lex loci delicti commissii* or the law of the place where the wrong was committed. This is based on the principle that the state, where the social disturbance transpired, has the duty to redress the wrong committed, approximate the effects of the injury, and determine the proper compensation suffered by the victim. Difficulty may be encountered in deciding the situs of tortious acts, especially in cases where the later originate in one state, but the resulting injuries are sustained in another. As in the analysis of the intrinsic validity of contracts, the place where the substantive tortious conduct occurred is the connecting factor that Philippine courts will likely apply. In particular, the Supreme Court has recognised the 'state of the most significant relationship' rule, taking into account the following factors according to their pertinence to a particular issue: (1) the place where the injury occurred; (2) the place where the conduct causing the injury occurred; (3) the domicile, residence, nationality, place of incorporation, or place of business of the parties; and (4) the place where the relationship, if any, between the parties was centred. As can be observed, the connecting factors that are relevant in determining the governing law of a contract are substantially similar in determining the place 'having the most interest' insofar as tortious conduct is concerned.[42]

iii. Property

a. Real and Personal Property

For real and personal property, Philippine law follows the *lex situs* or *lex rei situs* – the law of the place where the property is situated. The conflict-of-laws provision relating to property is essentially based on Article 16 of the Civil Code:

> Real property as well as personal property is subject to the law of the country where it is situated.
>
> However, intestate and testamentary successions, both with respect to the order of succession and to the amount of successional rights and to the intrinsic validity of testamentary provisions, shall be regulated by the national law of the person whose succession is under consideration, whatever may be the nature of the property and regardless of the country wherein said property may be found.

It will be seen that Article 16 provides for an exception in the case of testate and intestate succession – the national law of the testator, not the *lex rei situs*, governs. This includes matters relating to the determination of the national law of the deceased, the order of succession, the amount of succession rights, and the intrinsic validity of a testamentary disposition. The capacity of the beneficiaries to succeed is likewise based on the national law of the testator.[43] Also, where real property is a security for a principal obligation (such as a loan or other contract), the security obligation is governed by the *lex situs*, but the principal obligation remains to be governed by the same rules as ordinary contacts. Nonetheless, if the contract does not relate to title or other

[41] Civil Code, Art 20.
[42] *Saudi Arabian Airlines* (n 30).
[43] Civil Code, Art 1039.

rights over real property, but simply concerns contractual obligations, the rights and liabilities of the parties and the proper law of the contract will either be the *lex loci voluntatis* or the *lex loci intentionis.*

Many intangible properties (such as *choses in action*) do not have a material or tangible situs. Therefore, Philippine law propounds a constructive situs for them, depending on the type of intangible property. Shares of stock are considered intangible property[44] and the governing law relating to their sale is the law of the place of incorporation of the relevant corporation. Under the Philippine Corporation Code, to be valid, a sale of shares to the public must be recorded in the books of that corporation.[45] As between the parties to the share sale contract though, the governing law is the proper law of the contract, either the *lex loci voluntatis* or the *lex loci intentionis.* The situs of debts remains unresolved under Philippine law, although it has been suggested, applying American law, that the law of the contract from which the debt arises should govern the voluntary transfer of the debt.[46] On the other hand, for an involuntary transfer of debt, such as a garnishment, the situs is where the debtor may be served with a summons. Legislative franchises, which are exclusive rights granted by the government for the operation of certain businesses, are required in certain industries. For example, public utilities (particularly the provision of electricity, water, public transportation, and courier and mail services) require legislative franchises. Many questions arise with regard to the grant of such franchises. For instance, will foreign ownership restrictions apply to a corporation incorporated outside the Philippines, but operating a public utility requiring legislative franchise (as in the case of telecommunications (which is subject to a 40 per cent foreign ownership cap)?[47] One answer might be that Philippine law as the law of the state granting the legislative franchise (and where the legislative franchise is meant to be operated) should govern.

b. Intellectual Property

Philippine conflict-of-laws rules on intellectual property are primarily based on the Intellectual Property Code and treaties such as the 1883 Paris Convention for the Protection of Industrial Property and the 1886 Berne Convention for the Protection of Literary and Artistic Works. The Paris Convention requires Contracting States to protect a trade name without an obligation of filing of registration.[48] This has been expressly adopted in the Intellectual Property Code, where trade or business names are protected, even prior to or without registration, against unlawful acts committed by third parties.[49] Thus, a corporation not engaged in business in the Philippines may, in order to protect its trade name or mark, bring an action to recover damages for infringement of its trademark, and unfair competition.[50] As a party to the Berne Convention, the Philippines expressly recognises the rights guaranteed to foreign copyright holders. Article 5 of the Berne Convention states that, in respect of protected works, authors shall enjoy in Contracting States the rights which their respective laws grant to nationals at the point of publication or thereafter, as well as the rights specifically granted by the Convention. The enjoyment and exercise of such

[44] *Collector of Internal Revenue v Anglo California National Bank* GR No 12476 (1960).
[45] Revised Corporation Code (RA No 11232), s 62.
[46] Coquia and Aguiling-Pangalangan (n 4) 314.
[47] Constitution, Art XII, s 11.
[48] Paris Convention, Art 8.
[49] Intellectual Property Code (RA No 8293), s 165.2.
[50] ibid, ss 156, 160.

rights shall not be subject to any formality. The Intellectual Property Code expressly recognises the mutual protection and reciprocity accorded to foreign corporations and persons:

> *Section 3. International Conventions and Reciprocity*
>
> Any person who is a national or who is domiciled or has a real and effective industrial establishment in a country which is a party to any convention, treaty or agreement relating to intellectual property rights or the repression of unfair competition, to which the Philippines is also a party, or extends reciprocal rights to nationals of the Philippines by law, shall be entitled to benefits to the extent necessary to give effect to any provision of such convention, treaty or reciprocal law, in addition to the rights to which any owner of an intellectual property right is otherwise entitled by this Act.

The protection has been available to corporations not engaged in business in the Philippines from as early as 1927. In *Western Equipment and Supply Co v Reyes*, on the application of Western Electric Co, a foreign corporation organised under the laws of New York and not licensed in or engaged in business in the Philippines, the Philippine Supreme Court restrained the incorporation of defendants who attempted to incorporate a domestic corporation named Western Electric Company Inc.[51] The Philippine Supreme Court has characterised a corporation's right to use its corporate and trade name as a right *in rem*, which is entitled to protection as such and which cannot be impaired or defeated through subsequent appropriation by another corporation.[52]

iv. Family

a. Marriage

Although many marriages celebrated in other countries (including same-sex marriages) do not conform to the requirements for marriage under Philippine domestic law, Philippine private international law lays down ground rules for recognising the validity of such marriages. Generally, the rules on validity of marriages are codified in the Civil Code and the later Family Code.[53] The essential and formal requirements of marriage must be met.[54] As a general rule, to contract a valid marriage the parties must have capacity to marry under the law of their nationality or domicile and the marriage ceremony must comply with the formal requirements imposed by the law of the place of celebration (*lex loci celebrationis*). Foreigners marrying in the Philippines must therefore comply with these essential and formal requirements, including by submitting a certificate of legal capacity to contract marriage issued by the diplomatic or consular officials of their home country. Stateless persons or refugees need to submit only an affidavit stating circumstances showing the capacity to contract marriage.[55] As for the validity of marriages between Filipinos celebrated abroad, the Family Code expressly states that 'all marriages outside the Philippines in accordance with the laws in force in the country where they were solemnised and valid there as such, shall also be valid in this country'.[56] The statutory exceptions to this general rule are specified in the same provision:[57]

(1) Either or both parties did not have legal capacity to marry under Philippine law.[58]
(2) The marriage is bigamous or polygamous.[59]

[51] *Western Equipment and Supply Co v Reyes* GR No 27897 (1927).
[52] *Philips Export BV v Court of Appeals* GR No 96161 (1992).
[53] Family Code (Executive Order No 209).
[54] ibid, Arts 2–3.
[55] ibid, Art 21.
[56] ibid, Art 26.
[57] ibid.
[58] ibid, Art 35(1).
[59] ibid, Art 34(4).

(3) The consent of one party was vitiated by a mistake as to the identity of the other party.[60]
(4) At the time of the marriage, a party was psychologically incapable of complying with essential marital obligations.[61]
(5) The marriage is incestuous.[62]
(6) The marriage is void by reason of public policy.[63]

Aside from the validity of the marriage contracted out of the Philippines, marriage carries implications affecting the spouses' mutual rights and obligations and their property relations. Marital relations are purely personal in nature and courts do not ordinarily interfere with them. Nonetheless, the Family Code sets out some general principles for them (if only as a matter of guidance rather than as creating enforceable rights and obligations), including (among others) mutual fidelity, respect, cohabitation, support, the right of the wife to use the husband's family name, and the establishment of a family.[64] If the spouses are of different nationalities, Philippine law governs their personal relations, regardless of whether the husband or wife is the one having Filipino nationality.[65] In a similar manner, Philippine law governs the property relations of spouses of different nationalities in the absence of a pre-nuptial agreement.[66] The rules on personal and property relations tilt the balance in favour of the application of the personal law of a Filipino citizen over that of a foreign spouse in a mixed-nationality marriage. This reflects the legislative framers' intent to protect the Filipino citizen from what may be the unfamiliar personal law of the foreign spouse.[67]

b. Nullity, Annulment and Divorce

Philippine conflict-of-laws rules on marriage are complicated by the fact that the Philippines is one of the few countries in the world where divorce is generally unavailable.[68] The modes of severing marital ties under domestic law are limited to a declaration of nullity of marriage and annulment. Legal separation, on the other hand, only frees spouses from their marital duties and dissolves their property relation, but does not sever the marriage bonds.[69] Thus the marital relationship between Filipino spouses cannot be dissolved even by a decree of divorce obtained abroad.[70] Following the nationality theory, Philippine courts have jurisdiction over nullity and annulment suits involving Filipinos. As such suits affect the personal status, their judgments would be binding on the parties as far as Philippine law is concerned, even if the defendant was a non-resident and did not participate in the proceedings. The grounds for a declaration of nullity or annulment of marriage are limited to those permitted by the *lex loci celebrationis*. However,

[60] ibid, Art 35(5).
[61] ibid, Art 36.
[62] ibid, Art 37.
[63] ibid, Art 38.
[64] ibid, Arts 68, 70–71.
[65] Sempio-Diy (n 11) 105, citing the 15, 22 and 24 November minutes of the Civil Code Revision and Family Law Committee Meetings.
[66] Family Code, Art 80.
[67] Sempio-Diy (n 11) 102.
[68] 'Why the Philippines is the Only Country where Divorce is Illegal' *The Economist* (London, 15 February 2020), available online: www.economist.com/asia/2020/02/13/why-the-philippines-is-the-only-country-where-divorce-is-illegal. However, divorce is allowed in the Philippines insofar as Muslim marriages are concerned: Code of Muslim Personal Laws (Presidential Decree No 1083) Title II.
[69] Family Code, Art 63.
[70] *Techaves v Escano* GR No 19671 (1965).

under the Family Code, a foreign decree of divorce between a Filipino and a foreign spouse may be recognised in the Philippines and thus enable the Filipino spouse to remarry. This would be possible in the specific scenario where: (1) a marriage between a Filipino and a non-Filipino was validly celebrated; and (2) a divorce was validly obtained abroad by the non-Filipino spouse.[71]

This rule has had a long history in Philippine jurisprudence, the law and the jurisprudence supporting it having initially been limited to the strict conditions. It originally had the consequence that a Filipino spouse who obtained a divorce abroad and then took on a foreign nationality, did not get the benefit of the rule. The Philippine Supreme Court held that the rule could not be applied to a foreign decree of divorce between Filipino spouses. The reasoning was that, at the time of divorce, the parties would have been Filipino and thus governed by Philippine law which did not recognise divorce.[72] But recent years have seen a relaxation in the way that the rule is applied. While the reasoning has not been specifically articulated, the rule has now been interpreted to allow a Filipino national to remarry following divorce from a Filipino spouse who later acquired foreign nationality and entered into another marriage.[73] In *Republic of the Philippines v Manalo* (2018), the second requirement was completely nullified, so that a foreign decree of divorce in a mixed marriage was recognised, despite the Filipino spouse having initiated the divorce proceedings abroad.[74] For the foreign divorce decree to be recognised, a petition for recognition must be filed. Philippine courts will then look into whether there has been a decree of divorce issued abroad and, if such decree was obtained in accordance with applicable foreign law.[75]

v. Corporations and Insolvency

Previously, summonses could be served on foreign corporations registered to transact business in the Philippines through their resident agent, officer or agent in the Philippines. A summons could also be served through a supervising regulatory agency.[76] This left a gap in the case of foreign corporations transacting business in the Philippines but neither registered nor having a resident agent in the Philippines. This lacuna led the Philippine Supreme Court to amend the rule for service in 2011. The operative rule is now found in the 2020 amendment to the Rules of Civil Procedure. Subject to prior court approval, non-registered foreign corporations may be served by the following modes:

(1) personal service through the appropriate foreign country with the assistance of the Philippine Department of Foreign Affairs;
(2) publication in a newspaper of general circulation in the country where the defendant may be found and serving a copy of the summons by registered mail to the defendant's last known address;
(3) facsimile transmission or any recognised electronic means that can generate proof of service; or
(4) such other means as the court may direct.[77]

[71] Family Code, Art 26.
[72] *Republic of the Philippines v Iyoy* GR No 152577 (2005).
[73] *Republic of the Philippines v Orbecido* GR No 154380 (2005).
[74] *Republic of the Philippines v Manalo* GR No 221029 (2018).
[75] *Garcia v Recio* GR No 138322 (2001).
[76] Rules of Civil Procedure, r 14, s 12.
[77] Amendment of Section 12, Rule 14 of the Rules of Court on Service upon Foreign Private Juridical Entity (AM No 11-3-6-SC).

III. Jurisdiction *in rem*

A. General Principles

In actions *in rem* the courts assert jurisdiction over a *res* or property. Unlike actions *in personam* that are meant to impose liability on a person who is subject to the court's jurisdiction, actions in *rem* means that courts exercise jurisdiction over the subject matter in controversy, regardless of the persons who may be interested in such property. The basis of the exercise of *in rem* jurisdiction is the presence of the relevant property within the territorial jurisdiction of the domestic courts and the purpose of the suit is to bind all persons holding an interest in the *res*. The judgment is considered to be binding on the whole world, insofar as the property is concerned, even though the court may not have acquired personal jurisdiction over the persons whose interests in the property are affected. Examples of *in rem* proceedings are land registration and Admiralty cases, where the court's judgment affects the subject land or vessel and those having interests in the same. In contrast, *quasi in rem* actions are based on a state's jurisdiction over property within its territory, but only insofar as a court's judgment will affects the interests of particular persons in the *res*. The court's judgment will only affect those persons holding interests in the property who are parties before the court. Examples of actions *quasi in rem* are a proceeding for quiet title to property, foreclosure of a mortgage, and partition of land.

The rules on service of summonses depend on whether an action is *in personam*, *in rem*, or *quasi in rem*. Extraterritorial service, including through a summons by publication, is permitted only in actions *in rem* and *quasi in rem* and the limited cases where the personal status of the plaintiff is involved.[78] Where an action: (1) affects the plaintiff's personal status; (2) relates to property in the Philippines in which the defendant claims a lien or other interest; (3) seeks the exclusion of the defendant from an interest in property situate in the Philippines; or (4) relates to property of the defendant which has been attached in the Philippines, a summons may be served extraterritorially.[79] In proceedings *in rem* and *quasi in rem*, due process requires that the defendant be given adequate notice and opportunity to be heard. These requirements may be satisfied by service in person and substituted service (both options for actions *in personam*) and extraterritorial service.

B. Ship Arrest

The jurisdiction of Philippine courts in shipping disputes is provided by the Judiciary Reorganization Act of 1980,[80] which specifies that Philippine Regional Trial Courts (RTCs) have exclusive original jurisdiction over Admiralty and maritime matters. The Ship Mortgage Decree stipulates that maritime liens may be enforced by actions *in rem* or otherwise in any foreign country in which a vessel may be found, pursuant to the relevant country's procedures and laws for the enforcement of ship mortgages constituting maritime liens.[81] The process of ship arrest in the Philippines commences with the filing of a petition for judicial foreclosure on a Preferred Ship Mortgage. The mortgagee may then apply *ex parte* for an order of arrest of the

[78] Rules of Civil Procedure, r 14, s 17.
[79] *Gomez v Court of Appeals* GR No 127692 (2004).
[80] Judiciary Reorganization Act of 1980 (Batas Pambansa Blg 129).
[81] Ship Mortgage Decree (Presidential Decree No 1521), s 10.

vessel by submitting a sworn statement that a default in the mortgage has occurred and filing a bond executed in favour of the mortgagor in an amount to be fixed by the judge. The bond is conditioned on the payment of all costs that may be adjudged to the mortgagee, including all damages that may be sustained by reason of the arrest, if the court should thereafter rule that the mortgagee was not entitled to the arrest. The *in rem* nature of a ship arrest empowers the court, during the pendency of the action, to order the sale of an arrested vessel by public auction, upon proof that 'the property attached is perishable, or that the interests of all the parties to the action will be served by the sale thereof'.[82] *Negros Navigation Co v Court of Appeals*[83] and *Tsuneishi Heavy Industries (Cebu) Inc v Negros Navigation Co*[84] are intertwined cases that illustrate how the process of ship arrest in the context of rehabilitation proceedings can lead to potential problems, if a shipping claim is made against a company undergoing rehabilitation proceedings. Tsuneishi filed a claim with the Cebu RTC to enforce a maritime lien said to arise from repairs done to a vessel. Negros commenced rehabilitation proceedings before the Manila RTC, seeking a suspension of payments and a stay of all claims filed against it. Despite the stay order of the Manila RTC, the Cebu RTC proceeded to arrest Negros' vessels. Negros sought to suspend the proceedings before the Cebu RTC. In its final review, the Supreme Court affirmed the maritime lien issued by the Cebu RTC, holding that only the Admiralty proceedings there had merely been suspended. The order of the Manila RTC had not divested the Cebu RTC of its jurisdiction over Tsuneishi's maritime claim. A maritime lien in Tsuneishi's favour could therefore be enforced upon termination of the rehabilitation proceedings or Negros' dissolution.

IV. Immunities from Jurisdiction

A. Establishing Immunity

Diplomatic and sovereign immunity are based on the generally accepted principle of international law and treaties to which the Philippines is a signatory. They have been further developed in case law. To benefit from one or other immunity, the Philippine courts must initially be informed of their existence. The practice is for a foreign government or international organisation to secure an executive endorsement of its claim to sovereign or diplomatic immunity. There is no fixed rule as to how the Philippine Department of Foreign Affairs (DFA) is expected to convey its executive endorsement to the domestic courts. It may be by virtue of a letter sent by the Secretary of Foreign Affairs or even by telegram.[85] Regardless of the means of notification, courts may not look beyond the determination of the executive branch of the government and are duty-bound to accept the claim of immunity so endorsed.[86]

B. Diplomatic Immunity

Under the doctrine of incorporation, the Philippine Constitution expressly recognises generally accepted principles of international law as part of Philippine law.[87] Customary international law

[82] ibid, s 11.
[83] *Negros Navigation Co v Court of Appeals* GR No 163156 (2008).
[84] *Tsuneishi Heavy Industries (Cebu) Inc v Negros Navigation Co* GR No 166845 (2008).
[85] *The Holy See v Rosario* GR No 101949 (1994).
[86] *World Health Organization v Aquino* GR No 35131 (1972).
[87] Constitution, Art II, s 2.

on the personal inviolability or immunity of diplomatic representatives is thus wholly incorporated into Philippine law. Additionally, the immunities prescribed by the 1961 Vienna Convention on Diplomatic Relations are applicable, the Philippines being a signatory to the same. Diplomatic representatives are therefore exempt from the criminal jurisdiction of Philippine courts and cannot be subject to arrest, prosecution and punishment for violation of the criminal law.[88] Instead, recall or expulsion of the diplomatic representative typically follows. Diplomatic representatives are also free from the civil jurisdiction of domestic courts, which will have no authority to try a case in which they are defendants or to attach or seize their property for local processes.[89] The following exceptions to diplomatic immunity under the 1961 Vienna Convention apply within the Philippines:

(1) actions relating to private immovable property situated in the Philippines, unless the diplomatic agent holds the property on behalf of his or her state for the purposes of a mission;
(2) actions relating to succession in which the diplomatic agent is involved as executor, administrator, heir or legatee as a private person and not on behalf of his or her state; and
(3) actions relating to any professional or commercial activity exercised by the diplomatic agent in the Philippines outside his or her official duties.[90]

In *Liang v People*,[91] the Philippine Supreme Court clarified that the immunity enjoyed by agents of certain international organisations does not apply to acts outside their official functions. Here, the diplomatic agent, an economist employed at the Asian Development Bank (ADB), allegedly uttered defamatory words against a colleague. He was charged with slander. The trial court received from the DFA an 'office of protocol' certifying that the accused was covered by immunity because of an agreement between the ADB and the Philippine Government relating to the headquarters of the ADB. The Supreme Court held that the defendant was not protected by immunity and the DFA communication had no binding effect on the court. It emphasised that the agreement with the ADB qualified the coverage of immunity to acts done in an official capacity. Representatives of international organisations only enjoy functional immunity, that is, immunity limited to acts necessary for the exercise of their functions within the relevant organisation and the fulfillment of the latter's purposes. The nature of immunities varies depending on the recipient. Immunities enjoyed by diplomats differ from those enjoyed by officials of international organisations.

C. Sovereign Immunity

As in diplomatic immunity, the principle of sovereign immunity is enshrined in the Philippine Constitution.[92] This doctrine has been extended to cover actions against foreign states being sued without their consent.[93] In one case, the Philippine Supreme Court concluded that the real defendant in a case for the recovery of payment of property rentals or damages was the US Government. Since the property was used for US Government purposes, it affirmed the dismissal of the case on the ground of lack of jurisdiction:

It is clear that the courts of the Philippines including the Municipal Court of Manila have no jurisdiction over the present case for unlawful detainer. The question of lack of jurisdiction was

[88] 1961 Vienna Convention on Diplomatic Relations, Arts 29, 31.
[89] ibid, Art 31.
[90] ibid, Art 31(1).
[91] *Liang v People of the Philippines* GR No 125865 (2000).
[92] Constitution, Art XVI, s 3.
[93] *Syquia v Lopez* GR No 1648 (1949).

raised and interposed at the very beginning of the action. The US Government has not given its consent to the filing of this suit which is essentially against her, though not in name. Moreover, this is not only a case of a citizen filing a suit against his own government without the latter's consent but it is of a citizen filing an action against a foreign government without said government's consent, which renders more obvious the lack of jurisdiction of the courts of his country. The principles of the law behind this rule are so elementary and of such general acceptance that we deem it unnecessary to cite authorities in support thereof.[94]

Nonetheless, international law has been evolving. As state activities have multiplied, the US, UK and other western European countries have adopted a restrictive view of state immunity. That view distinguishes between governmental acts (*jure imperii*) of a state and private, commercial and proprietary acts (*jus gestionis*). The former acts attract immunity, while the latter do not. This distinction has been followed in the Philippines:

The restrictive application of state immunity is proper only when the proceedings arise out of commercial transactions of the foreign sovereign, its commercial activities or economic affairs. Stated differently, a state may be said to have descended to the level of an individual and can thus be deemed to have tacitly given its consent to be sued only when it enters into business contracts. It does not apply where the contract relates to the exercise of its sovereign functions. In this case the projects are an integral part of the naval base which is devoted to the defence of both the US and the Philippines, indisputably a function of the government of the highest order; they are not utilised for nor dedicated to commercial or business purposes.[95]

The test that Philippine courts apply is to determine whether a foreign state is engaged in the regular conduct of a business. If the foreign state is engaged in a regular business or commercial activity, the particular act or transaction must be further tested by its purpose. If the act is in pursuit of a sovereign activity, or an incident thereof, then it would be an act *jure imperii*.[96] The existence of a clause in a contract stating that any action arising out of the agreement shall be settled according to Philippine law is by itself not necessarily a waiver of sovereign immunity.[97]

State immunity extends to officers and agents of foreign states. A foreign agent operating within the Philippine territory will likewise benefit from state immunity if it can be established that the agent was acting within the directives of the sending state and the consent of the host state (that is, the Philippines) was given. It also applies to complaints filed against state officials for acts performed by them in the discharge of their official duties. As they have acted on behalf of their principal their acts are directly imputable to their principal. Effectively, it is their government that is ultimately responsible for such officially sanctioned acts.[98] State immunity may thus be invoked by an agent of the United States Drug Enforcement Agency (USDEA) which has been allowed by the Philippine Government to conduct surveillance and other operations to contain drug trafficking within the Philippines.[99] Further distinction has to be made between a suit filed against a foreign government or its agents and one filed against entities of such foreign states (for instance, state-owned enterprises (SOEs). The test in such a situation is to determine whether the state agency is incorporated or unincorporated:

An incorporated agency has a charter of its own that invests it with a separate juridical personality, like the Social Security System, the University of the Philippines, and the City of

[94] ibid.
[95] *United States of America v Ruiz* GR No 35645 (1985).
[96] *Republic of Indonesia v Vinzon* GR No 154705 (2003).
[97] ibid.
[98] *United States of America v Guinto* GR No 76607 (1990).
[99] *Minucher v Court of Appeals* GR No 142396 (2003).

Manila. By contrast, the unincorporated agency is so called because it has no separate juridical personality but is merged in the general machinery of the government, like the Department of Justice, the Bureau of Mines and the Government Printing Office.

If the agency is incorporated, the test of its suability is found in its charter. The simple rule is that it is suable if its charter says so, and this is true regardless of the functions it is performing. Municipal corporations, for example, like provinces and cities, are agencies of the state when they are engaged in governmental functions and therefore should enjoy the sovereign immunity from suit. Nevertheless, they are subject to suit even in the performance of such functions because their charter provides that they can sue and be sued.[100]

[100] *Deutsche Gesellschaft für Technische Zusammenarbeit v Court of Appeals* GR No 152318 (2009).

13

Indonesia

AFIFAH KUSUMADARA

This chapter will explain Indonesia's rules and judicial practices with regard to the jurisdiction of Indonesian courts that involve foreign elements. It begins with presenting the general principles that establish the jurisdiction *in personam* of Indonesian courts over the parties in disputes involving foreign elements. It is followed by more detailed rules, judicial practices, and doctrines concerning the jurisdiction *in personam* of Indonesian courts in the fields of law of obligations, family law, law of corporations and insolvency, law of bankruptcy, and competition law. This chapter also discusses the rules and principles to determine the courts that have jurisdiction *in rem* over disputes concerning the right to property that involves foreign elements. The discussion also touches the issue of shipping claims and ship arrest. The last section of this chapter addresses the rules and judicial practices related to the immunities of foreign States and state-owned enterprises from the jurisdiction of Indonesian courts.

I. Jurisdiction *in personam*

A. General Principles

i. *Jurisdiction of Courts within the Territory*

Generally, the principle of *actor sequitur forum rei*, which means that the plaintiff must follow the forum of the thing, is applied by Indonesian civil procedure law to determine the jurisdiction of the court. Article 118(1) of the 1941 *Het Herziene Indonesisch Reglement* (HIR) (Renewed Indonesian Code) and in Article 99(2) of the 1847 *Reglement op de Burgerlijke Rechtsvordering* (Rv) (Civil Procedure Code) requires the plaintiff to bring the civil lawsuit in the defendant's forum. In a case of multiple defendants, the court that exercises jurisdiction over the defendants is the court in the district chosen by the plaintiff and in which one of the defendants has its residence (HIR Article 118(2) and Rv Article 99(6)).

There are other additional principles to establish the court's jurisdiction *in personam*, as explained in the following paragraphs. If the residence of the defendant cannot be identified, the court that has jurisdiction *in personam* is the court in the district of the plaintiff's residence (HIR Article 118(3) and Rv Article 99(3)). These provisions are also applicable for cases of which the residence of foreign defendants cannot be identified.

In a case of mixed actions (combination of action in *personam* and action *in rem*), a court can also have jurisdiction *in personam* if the plaintiff prefers bringing the case to the district court in the defendant's residence (Rv Article 99(10)). For example, in a shipping claim that can be characterised as a mixed action against both the ship owner and the vessel, the plaintiff could elect to bring his shipping claim to the court in the district in which the ship is situated (jurisdiction *in rem*) or to the court in the district where the ship owner resides (jurisdiction *in personam*). In several shipping claims in Indonesia,[1] the plaintiffs took their shipping claims to the district courts in the residence of ship owners (court of jurisdiction *in personam*), although the underlying actions were mixed between action *in personam* and action *in rem*.

Based on Rv Article 100, an Indonesian court has jurisdiction *in personam* over a foreigner (either a natural or legal person) that does not live or have a residence in Indonesia, if the foreigner has a legal obligation to an Indonesian plaintiff that arises in Indonesia or anywhere else. As the foreigner has no residence in Indonesia, the Indonesian court that has jurisdiction *in personam* is the court in the district of the plaintiff's residence (HIR Article 118(3) and Rv Article 99(3)). However, this jurisdiction *in personam* will not be always exercised if the parties have a choice of court agreement that appoints a court or a forum other than the Indonesian court and the defendants in the agreement reside or have their legal seat outside Indonesia. Indonesian courts usually respect the choice of court made by parties in agreements, especially if the agreement refers to an arbitration. Choice of court agreements will be discussed further in Section I.A.ii.e below.

The provisions and principles above on the court's jurisdiction *in personam* also apply to legal entities or corporations. Based on the prevailing judicial practice adopted in Indonesia, the courts that have jurisdiction *in personam* over legal entities are the courts in the district in which the statutory seat of the entities are situated, or in which the central management of the entities are located. This principle is also accepted by Article 56(1) of Act No 16 of 2001, as amended by Act No 28 of 2004, on Foundations.

In the case that a foreign legal entity does not have its legal seat or central management, or any branch or representative in Indonesia, an Indonesian court may still have jurisdiction *in personam* over the foreign entity when it has a legal obligation to an Indonesian plaintiff that arises in Indonesia or elsewhere (Rv Article 100). In this case, the Indonesian court that has jurisdiction *in personam* over the foreign entity will be the court in the district of the plaintiff's residence (HIR Article 118(3) and Rv Article 99(3)).

ii. Forum non conveniens, lis alibi pendens, *Anti-suit Injunctions, Interim Measures, and Choice of Court Agreements*

a. *Forum non conveniens*

Indonesian legal scholars and judicial practice recognise the doctrine of *forum non conveniens*,[2] although it is not part of written Indonesian law. In the case of *Richard Bruce Ness v New York Times*,[3] the Central Jakarta District Court dismissed the claim on the ground of *forum non conveniens*. The Court recognised that all parties were not Indonesian nationals, although Mr Ness domiciled in Indonesia and Ms Perlez had used to live in Indonesia. Mr Ness brought a defamation lawsuit against Ms Perlez on her article and the New York Times Company as the

[1] District Court of Jambi Decision 10/PDT.G/2013/PN.JBI (31 July 2013); District Court of Central Jakarta Decision 23/PDT.G/2011/PN.JKT.PST (1 December 2011).

[2] M Yahya Harahap, *Hukum Acara Perdata Tentang Gugatan, Persidangan, Penyitaan, Pembuktian, dan Putusan Pengadilan* 16th edn (Jakarta, Sinar Grafika, 2016) 206.

[3] District Court of Central Jakarta Decision 181/PDT.G/2007/PN.JKT.PST (8 October 2007).

article's publisher in the Central Jakarta District Court, because Ms Perlez had previously resided in Central Jakarta. The defendants raised the motion of *forum non conveniens* against the jurisdiction of the Indonesian court as Ms Perlez moved to Islamabad in Pakistan before Mr Ness brought his lawsuit. The New York Times Company did not have any representative in Indonesia. The defendants also contended that the judgment made by the Central Jakarta District Court would not be enforceable in the territories of the defendants, as there are no treaties on the recognition and enforcement of judgments between Indonesia and their countries of residence.

The Central Jakarta District Court acknowledged the defendant's motion of *forum non conveniens*. The judgment quoted M Yahya Harahap, an Indonesian legal scholar and former Supreme Court Justice, who wrote about the doctrine of *forum non conveniens* in the English courts.[4] Based on the defendants' countries of residence and nationalities, and the location where the articles were published (New York), the Central Jakarta District Court determined that it was not an appropriate forum for the parties or for the subject matter. The Court also accepted the defendants' argument that the judgment might not be enforceable in the defendants' countries of residence. The District Court declined to exercise its jurisdiction over this case.

b. *Lis alibi pendens*

Indonesian civil procedure law has a provision governing *lis alibi pendens*. Rv Article 134(1) provides that a court may be asked for a stay of action in a lawsuit that is already pending in another court or arbitration, and the lawsuit is between the same parties arising out of the same dispute. However, Rv Article 134 is only applicable to domestic proceedings and does not extend to foreign proceedings. Therefore, an Indonesian court may exercise its jurisdiction over the same lawsuit that is already pending in a foreign court, even though it can produce judgments inconsistent with the foreign court's decisions on the same case with the same parties.

For example, in the case of *PT Indah Kiat Pulp & Paper Tbk v Bank America National Trust Co*, the Bengkalis District Court in Indonesia exercised its jurisdiction over the dispute, although the same dispute with the same parties was under adjudication in a New York court. The parties in this case agreed to the laws of the State of New York as the applicable law of their contracts and agreed to the non-exclusive jurisdiction of any New York State or United States Federal court sitting in New York. Despite the parties' choice of court and choice of law, the Bengkalis District Court exercised its jurisdiction over the case and applied Indonesian law to adjudicate it. The Court held in favour of PT Indah Kiat Pulp, which was upheld by the Riau High Court and Indonesian Supreme Court.[5] On extraordinary appeal to the Indonesian Supreme Court, the justices annulled the decisions made by previous courts because the lower courts failed to apply New York law as the choice of law of the parties.[6] However, the justices affirmed the jurisdiction of the Bengkalis District Court because the choice of court was not exclusive. Thus, in their opinion, the Bengkalis District Court could exercise its jurisdiction on the case, although the same case was still pending in a New York court.[7]

This case indicates that Rv Article 134 concerning *lis alibi pendens* does not apply to foreign proceedings in general. That is because Rv Article 436(1) does not recognise and enforce foreign

[4] ibid; Harahap (n 2) 205.

[5] District Court of Bengkalis Decision 05/PDT.G./2003/PN-BKS (21 September 2004); affd High Court of Riau Decision 40/PDT/2004/PTR (16 June 2005); affd Supreme Court Decision 381 K/Pdt/2006 (24 May 2006).

[6] Supreme Court Extraordinary Appeal 445 PK/Pdt/2007 (19 August 2008).

[7] ibid 193.

judgments in Indonesia. It provides that '[a]ll judgments delivered by foreign courts are unenforceable in Indonesian territory, except in the matters mentioned in Article 724 of Commercial Code and in other regulations'.[8]

The principle of *lis alibi pendens* might be applicable if the foreign judgment can be enforced in Indonesia. Otherwise, it is understandable that an Indonesian court will exercise its jurisdiction over the dispute, even though it is still pending in another foreign court.

c. Anti-suit Injunctions

Indonesian law is silent on issues related to anti-suit injunction, but they can be found in judicial practice. In the *PT Indah Kiat* case above, the parties agreed to the non-exclusive jurisdiction of any New York State or United States Federal court sitting in New York City. The bond holders (Bank America National Trust Co and other companies) brought a lawsuit to a New York court in April 2003 when PT Indah Kiat, an Indonesian company, did not pay its overdue bonds. PT Indah Kiat joined the proceedings in the New York court. However, on 14 November 2003, PT Indah Kiat brought another lawsuit to the Bengkalis District Court in Indonesia to annul all agreements related to the bonds made by PT Indah Kiat with other parties. On 25 November 2003, the New York Supreme Court issued a temporary injunction against PT Indah Kiat and its parent company, Asia Pulp & Paper Co (APP), restraining them from pursuing the Indonesian proceedings. However, PT Indah Kiat continued with their lawsuit in the Bengkalis District Court and applied for a wide-ranging injunction order, including an anti-suit injunction against its opponents (in effect, an anti-anti-suit injunction). On 5 February 2004, APP argued in the New York Supreme Court that the Indonesian courts would not enforce any judgment from a US court because of Rv Article 436. The New York Supreme Court accepted APP's argument and lifted the injunction order against APP and PT Indah Kiat, but continued the trial. In its ruling, the New York Supreme Court stated that '[l]itigation was a predisclosed risk of investment that the plaintiffs had voluntarily accepted'.[9]

On 4 May 2004, the Bengkalis District Court issued a provisional judgment to enjoin the bond holders from taking any legal actions, inside and outside Indonesia, with the penalty of US$100,000 per day for any incompliance. Further, on 19 May 2004, the Court ruled that it had jurisdiction over the case. Finally, the Bengkalis District Court made its final judgment that annulled all agreements related to the bonds, citing that the agreements were made in bad faith and in violation of Indonesian law. The final judgment was upheld by the Riau High Court and Indonesian Supreme Court.[10] At the extraordinary appeal level, a panel of Supreme Court Justices annulled the decisions as New York law as the choice of law of the parties was not applied.[11] They also annulled the Bengkalis Court's provisional judgment that enjoined PT Indah Kiat's opponents from taking legal action inside and outside Indonesia, because it did not comply with Indonesian civil procedure law, namely Article 191 of the 1927 *Rechtsreglement Buitengewesten* (RBg) (Civil Procedure Code for Courts Outside Java and Madura), Rv Article 54, and Supreme Court Circular Letter No 3 of 2000.

[8] See Afifah Kusumadara, 'Indonesia' in Anselmo Reyes (ed), *Recognition and Enforcement of Judgments in Civil and Commercial Matters* (Oxford, Hart Publishing, 2019) 243–45.

[9] Leony Aurora, 'New York Court Rules in Favor of Asia Pulp and Paper' (*Jawawa Indonesian Business & Finance News*, 16 February 2004), available online: https://jawawa.id/newsitem/new-york-court-rules-in-favor-of-asia-pulp-and-paper-1447893297.

[10] See n 5.

[11] Supreme Court Extraordinary Appeal 445 PK/Pdt/2007 (19 August 2008) (n 6) 193.

This case indicates that there was no clear standard or reason given by the Bengkalis District Court when granting the anti-suit injunction, except that it claimed to have jurisdiction over the case. It was different from the anti-suit injunction granted by the New York Supreme Court, which was based on the fact that all parties, including PT Indah Kiat, had agreed to New York law and the jurisdiction of a New York court.[12] Moreover, while the annulment of the Bengkalis District Court's anti-suit injunction by the extraordinary appeal panel was based simply on procedural reasons, the New York Supreme Court provided grounds beyond procedural reasons when it ruled not to extend the injunction order against PT Indah Kiat. It reasoned that the New York judgment would not be enforceable in Indonesia and, therefore, that the judgment from an Indonesian court (Bengkalis District Court) was necessary to enforce the bond holders' rights to the Indonesian collateral.[13]

Another case with a foreign anti-suit injunction issue is *Perusahaan Pertambangan Minyak dan Gas Bumi Negara* (Pertamina) *v Karaha Bodas Company LLC* (KBC).[14] In this case, the Switzerland arbitral tribunal held that Pertamina breached their contracts with KBC. Accordingly, the tribunal awarded KBC US$111.1 million as compensation, and US$150 million in lost profits.[15] In March 2002, Pertamina applied for the annulment of the Switzerland arbitral award in the Central Jakarta District Court. Pertamina also sought an injunction in its petition against KBC from taking any legal actions, including enforcing the Swiss arbitral award in the US District Court for the Sothern District of Texas. The injunction was granted. *Pertamina v KBC* once again demonstrates that the reasoning behind the Indonesian courts' decision to grant an anti-suit injunction was simply that the courts claim to have jurisdiction over the case and to protect the assets of the Indonesian party from being seized by its foreign opponents.

Since there are no anti-suit injunction provisions in Indonesian civil procedure codes, the judicial practice as explained above becomes the only legal source to understand the principles of granting an anti-suit injunction in Indonesia. Based on the current judicial practice, Indonesian courts do not seem to follow the standard tests or parameters commonly applied by courts in the UK or the US when granting injunctions against foreign suits, such as potentially vexatious or oppressive litigation in foreign courts, possible injustice done to the parties, or breaches of choice of court agreement by the parties.

d. Interim Measures

Indonesian civil procedure law does not use the term 'interim measures'. Instead, it uses the terms 'provisional measures' and 'conservatory seizure' (*conservatoir beslag*). Provisional measures are mentioned in HIR Article 180. Based on current practice, an application for provisional measures shall not be filed separately from the principal claim in a lawsuit.[16] Accordingly, Indonesian courts will not have jurisdiction over provisional measures applied by parties whose disputes are being adjudicated by foreign courts, because an application for provisional measures shall

[12] Timothy Mapes, 'New York Judge Orders APP to End Efforts to Nullify Bonds' (*Wall Street Journal*, 28 November 2003), available online: www.wsj.com/articles/SB106995908981230100.

[13] Aurora (n 9).

[14] District Court of Central Jakarta Decision 86/PDT.G/2002/PN/JKT/PST (27 August 2002); Supreme Court Decision 01/BANDING/WASIT.INT/2002 (8 March 2004); Supreme Court Extraordinary Appeal 444 PK/Pdt/2007 (9 September 2008).

[15] See *Karaha Bodas Co LLC v Perusahaan Pertambangan Minyak Dan Gas Bumi Negara* 364 F 3d 274, 284–85 (5th Cir 2004).

[16] Harahap (n 2) 885.

be filed together with the principal claims in Indonesian courts (HIR Articles 180, 185, and Supreme Court Circular Letter No 3 of 2000).

Conservatory seizure employs different procedures from provisional measures. Conservatory seizure is governed under HIR Articles 226 and 227. An application for conservatory seizure can be filed in a court separately from the applicant's principal claim, and consequently, can be appealed separately by the affected party. Therefore, an Indonesian court theoretically may have jurisdiction over conservatory seizure applied by a party whose dispute is being processed outside Indonesia, as long as the Indonesian court has jurisdiction *in personam* or *in rem* over the merits of the case. However, it shall be noted that a conservatory seizure application separate from the principal claim could be unworthy, because the foreign judgment on the parties' principal claims is unenforceable in Indonesia, as governed by Rv Article 436.

In *PT Bayan Resources TBK v BCBC Singapore Pte Ltd* there was a dispute related to a joint venture agreement arose between BCBC Singapore Pte Ltd (BCBC) and PT Bayan Resources TBK (Bayan). BCBC was incorporated in Singapore and Bayan was incorporated in Indonesia. In December 2011, BCBC took Bayan to the Singapore International Commercial Court (SICC) claiming, among other things, damages for breach of the joint venture agreement, in which Bayan and BCBC had agreed to the SICC as the forum to resolve their dispute.[17] Before the SICC entered their judgment, in April 2012, BCBC applied to the Supreme Court of Western Australia (WA) for freezing orders against Bayan's assets in Australia. Besides having assets in Indonesia, Bayan also held shares in an Australian company named Kangaroo Resources Limited (KRL). The Supreme Court of WA granted freezing orders against Bayan and KRL in respect of Bayan's shares in KRL.[18] In 2013, when the case was remitted by the High Court of Australia to the Supreme Court of WA, it revoked its freezing order against KRL which was regarded as a third party, but kept its freezing order against Bayan.[19] The High Court of Australia upheld the freezing order against Bayan.[20]

In this case, BCBC never filed for freezing orders or conservatory seizure in an Indonesian court against Bayan's assets in Indonesia. That was because Indonesian courts would refuse to exercise jurisdiction on BCBC's application for conservatory seizure, as the Singapore judgment on the merits of the case could not be recognised and enforced in Indonesia based on Rv Article 436.

Regarding provisional measures and conservatory seizure against a defendant's properties and his/her actions outside Indonesia, theoretically, an Indonesian court has jurisdiction to order those interim measures, as long as the court has jurisdiction over the merits of the case. However, it is unclear how the interim measures imposed by Indonesian courts can have extraterritorial effect given that there is no order of civil contempt in the Indonesian legal system against parties who are violating the court orders outside Indonesia.

e. Choice of Court Agreements

Indonesian civil code (BW, *Burgerlijk Wetboek voor Nederlandsch-Indie*) and civil procedure codes contain provisions concerning choice of court agreements. BW Article 24 stipulates that choice of court by parties shall be made in written agreements. HIR Article 118(4) and

[17] Debby Lim, 'SICC Releases Its First Decision' (*Financier Worldwide*, August 2016), available online: www.financierworldwide.com/sicc-releases-its-first-decision#.Xbs2ROgzaUk.
[18] *BCBC Singapore Pte Ltd v PT Bayan Resources TBK* [2012] WASC 170.
[19] *BCBC Singapore Pte Ltd v PT Bayan Resources TBK (No 3)* [2013] WASC 239.
[20] *PT Bayan Resources TBK v BCBC Singapore Pte Ltd* [2015] HCA 36.

Rv Article 99(16) provide that while parties in a dispute may have made a choice of court agreement, it depends on the plaintiff to decide where he files his claim. The plaintiff is allowed to file his claim in the court chosen by the parties, or to file his claim in the court in the district of the defendant's residence in accordance with the principle of *actor sequitur forum rei*. Mr Harahap wrote that the principle of *actor sequitur forum rei* stated in HIR Article 118(1) may prevail over choice of court agreements, depending on the plaintiff's choice.[21]

Indonesian civil procedure codes are silent on the choice of court agreements that involve a foreign court. That is understandable because judgments made by foreign courts cannot be enforced in Indonesia pursuant to Rv Article 436. Nevertheless, there is no prohibition for parties in Indonesia to choose foreign courts. Article 18(4) of Act No 11 of 2008, as amended by Act No 19 of 2016, on Electronic Information and Transactions, allows the parties to make choice of court agreements. Article 74 of Government Regulation No 80 of 2019 on Electronic Commerce also contains the same provision. However, because of the absence of procedural law concerning choice of foreign court agreements, Indonesian courts still apply HIR Article 118(4) and Rv Article 99(16) to the parties who make choice of foreign court agreements. Hence, an Indonesian court may exercise jurisdiction over parties who have chosen a foreign court, if the plaintiff prefers filing his lawsuit in an Indonesian district court instead of the foreign court.

The case of *Bali Energi Ltd v Mitomo Shoji KK* demonstrates the principles above. Bali Energi Ltd was a Bermuda company with its legal seat in Central Jakarta, Indonesia; Mitomo Shoji KK was a Japanese company with its legal seat in Japan. In this case, Bali Energi Ltd objected to the jurisdiction of the Central Jakarta District Court because in their investor financing agreement, the parties had a choice of court agreement which designated the Tokyo District Court. Mitomo Shoji KK brought its lawsuit to the Central Jakarta District Court because Bali Energi Ltd had residence in Central Jakarta. In their preliminary decision, the Central Jakarta District Court dismissed the objection and decided that it had jurisdiction over the parties' dispute.[22] The Jakarta High Court affirmed the Central Jakarta District Court's preliminary decision.[23] This case indicates that HIR Article 118 prevails over the parties' choice of court.

iii. Service of Process Outside of the Territory

An Indonesian court shall deliver a proper service of process to a party outside Indonesia when it exercises jurisdiction over the party. There are only a few provisions concerning service of process outside Indonesia in Indonesian civil procedure codes.

HIR Article 118(3) and Rv Article 99(3) provide that a lawsuit against a defendant whose presence and residence in Indonesia are unknown, shall be brought to the court in the district of the plaintiff's residence. Government Regulation No 9 of 1975 concerning Implementation of the Marriage Act 1974 (the Marriage Regulation 1975) also has a similar provision. Article 20(3) of the Marriage Regulation 1975 states that a divorce petition served on a defendant living abroad shall be filed in a court in the district of the petitioner's residence. Accordingly, the court that has jurisdiction over a defendant or respondent outside Indonesia is the court in the district of the plaintiff's residence.

In serving the process on defendants outside Indonesia, the courts in the plaintiff's districts shall comply with Rv Article 6(8), which provides that the court shall serve process on the defendant

[21] Harahap (n 2) 200–02.
[22] District Court of Central Jakarta Decision 359/Pdt.G/2011/PN.Jkt.Pst (31 July 2012).
[23] High Court of Jakarta Decision 186/PDT/2014/PT.DKI (23 July 2014).

through the public prosecutor at the court. The service of process on the defendant or respondent abroad will be effected by the Indonesian Government through its diplomatic or consular office in the defendant's or respondent's country (Article 20(3) of the Marriage Regulation 1975, and Act No 1 of 1982 on the Ratification of the Vienna Convention on Diplomatic Relations and the Optional Protocol concerning Acquisition of Nationality of 1961 and the Vienna Convention on Consular Relations and the Optional Protocol concerning Acquisition of Nationality of 1963).

The provisions above are applicable in cases in which the foreign location of the defendant or respondent can be identified. If the whereabouts are unknown, HIR Article 390(3) and Rv Article 6(7) provide that the process will be served by general convocation attached to the court's main door in the plaintiff's district and by publication in a newspaper available in the district.

Based on the provisions above, service of process outside Indonesia only covers service of judicial documents that emanate from legal proceedings and are directly connected with lawsuits, such as court summons, court verdicts, notices of appeal, and so on. The Indonesian legal system does not recognise service abroad of extrajudicial documents. To date, Indonesia is not a party to the 1965 Hague Convention on the Service Abroad of Judicial and Extrajudicial Documents in Civil or Commercial Matters.

Although the provisions in the civil procedure codes are never revoked, in practice, they are not fully implemented anymore. For example, public prosecutors are no longer involved in the service of process outside Indonesia.[24] Several new regulations have also been issued by the Ministry of Foreign Affairs and the Supreme Court to govern the procedure of service abroad.[25] In addition, the Republic of Indonesia and the Kingdom of Thailand entered into an Agreement on Judicial Cooperation in 1978. This agreement was ratified by Presidential Decree No 6 of 1978.

iv. Service of Foreign Proceedings within the Territory

Indonesian civil procedure codes are silent on service of foreign proceedings in Indonesia. However, a plaintiff or a court outside Indonesia is allowed to serve process on a person in Indonesia. The 1978 Agreement on Judicial Cooperation between the Republic of Indonesia and the Kingdom of Thailand ('the 1978 Agreement') allows a plaintiff in a Thai court to serve judicial documents on a respondent in Indonesia (Article 3).

For other parties outside the Thai jurisdiction, the Indonesian Ministry of Foreign Affairs and Supreme Court issued the procedure outlined in the 2018 Memorandum of Understanding Between the Indonesian Ministry of Foreign Affairs and the Supreme Court (No PRJ/HI/102/02/2018/01, No 01/NK/MA/2/2018). Based on the procedure, service of foreign proceedings in Indonesia only covers service of judicial documents that emanate from legal proceedings and are directly connected with lawsuits in foreign courts. It does not cover service of foreign extrajudicial documents.

In accordance with Act No 24 of 2009 on Flag, Language, State Emblem, and National Anthem which requires the use of Indonesian language in official documents, the Indonesian Ministry of Foreign Affairs requires the foreign judicial documents served in Indonesia be translated into Indonesian, unless agreed otherwise in an agreement between Indonesia and another state.[26]

[24] Harahap (n 2) 224.

[25] See eg No PRJ/HI/102/02/2018/01, No 01/NK/MA/2/2018; No PRJ/HI/103/02/2018/01, No 03/PK/MA/2/2018; No PRJ/HI/104/02/2018/01, No 04/PK/MA/2018.

[26] 'Ketentuan Nasional' (*Rogatory Online Monitoring*), available online: https://rogatori.kemlu.go.id/ketentuan-nasional-dan-internasional.

However, the ministry does not require that the translation be certified by a sworn translator like the requirement in the 1978 Agreement.

Unlike Article 13 of the 1965 Hague Service Convention and Article 8 of the 1978 Agreement that provide the grounds for refusal to comply with a request for service due to the infringement of the requested state's sovereignty and security, the procedure of service of foreign proceedings in the cooperative agreements between the Ministry of Foreign Affairs and the Supreme Court does not have such provisions. The lack of such provision may allow Indonesian authorities to arbitrarily refuse to comply with a request for service of foreign proceedings. This could trigger reciprocal treatment from other states that receive a request for service of process from Indonesia.

Despite Article 8(3) of the 1978 Agreement that requires the Parties to execute a request for service of judicial documents expeditiously in the manner prescribed by the law of requested state, the procedure of service of foreign proceedings written in the cooperative agreements between the Ministry of Foreign Affairs and the Supreme Court does not stipulate the length of time that must be met by Indonesian authorities to execute the request for service. The lack of time limit provision could cause the request for service to be processed for an unnecessarily extended period of time by Indonesian authorities. If that were to happen, it could trigger reciprocal treatment from other states not to process the Indonesian request for service of process expeditiously.

B. Special Rules

i. Law of Obligations

a. Specific Contracts

Based on the freedom of contract principle, parties to specific contracts are generally allowed to make choice of court agreements, with the exception of contracts related to land and employment, due to public policy reasons. Therefore, courts that have jurisdiction over specific contracts are generally the courts expressly chosen by parties in their written contracts. However, it shall be noted that in practice, Indonesian courts often exercise jurisdiction over contracts even though the parties have made choice of court agreements. The reason for this is HIR Article 118(4) and Rv Article 99(16).[27]

In the absence of choice of court agreements, the courts that have jurisdiction over the contracts are established by Indonesian civil procedure codes and by the specific law that governs the specific contracts, as explained in the following paragraphs.

In contracts related to movable goods, for example, contracts for sale of goods, the hire of goods, the carriage of goods, the principle of *actor sequitur forum rei* stipulated in HIR Article 118 and Rv Article 99 apply to establish the courts that have jurisdiction over the contracts. This principle also applies to contracts with foreign elements.

In electronic commerce that involves Indonesian nationals and foreigners, the principles of private international law, namely the basis of presence and effectiveness, are applied to establish the jurisdiction of a forum to settle the dispute (Elucidation of Article 74(2) of Government Regulation No 80 of 2019 on Electronic Commerce).

In contracts related to movable goods that involve end users or consumers whose rights need to be protected, Act No 8 of 1999 on Consumer Protection (Consumer Protection Act 1999) has

[27] See Section I.A.ii.e above.

special provisions dealing with jurisdiction in relation to consumer contracts, including electronic consumer contracts. To protect consumers, these jurisdiction provisions in the Consumer Protection Act 1999 supersede the choice of court agreements made by the parties. They also supersede jurisdiction provisions stipulated in the Indonesian civil procedure codes.

Article 23 of the Consumer Protection Act 1999 provides that consumers can take merchants to the Consumer Dispute Resolution Body or to the court in the district of consumer's residence. Based on Article 23, it is the consumer who determines the jurisdiction of the forum in a consumer contract dispute. Pursuant to Supreme Court Regulation No 1 of 2006 on Procedure to File Objection to the Decision of the Consumer Dispute Resolution Body, consumers or merchants can file an objection to the court in the district of consumer's residence (Article 3(1)). A consumer who has no domicile in Indonesia shall file his/her objection to the court in the district in which the Consumer Dispute Resolution Body issued its decision (Article 3(2)). In the case of *PT Garuda Indonesia (Persero) v Mahsin SH*, the principle of the consumer's place of residence was applied. Mahsin, an Indonesian passenger, filed a lawsuit against PT Garuda Indonesia (Persero) (Garuda) in the Consumer Dispute Resolution Body in the district of Medan, where Mahsin lived. Garuda objected to, among other things, the jurisdiction of the Medan Consumer Dispute Resolution Body over the dispute. The Medan District Court dismissed Garuda's objection. The Supreme Court affirmed the Medan District Court's judgment.[28]

In contracts related to immovable property, especially land and building, the courts that have jurisdiction over the contracts shall be the Indonesian courts. Based on HIR Article 118(3) and Rv Article 99(8), if the main dispute in the contracts relates to the ownership or title of the immovables, the court that exercises jurisdiction is the court in the district of the immovable property. But, if the dispute in the contract is the combination of action *in rem* and action *in personam*, the court that exercises jurisdiction is the court in the district where the immovable property is located, or where the defendant resides, depending on the plaintiff's choice of jurisdiction (Rv Article 99(10)). Those provisions also apply to contracts with foreign elements.

Regarding employment contracts, Act No 13 of 2003 on Manpower recognises several types of employment contracts, including employment contracts between foreign workers and Indonesian companies (Chapter VIII). Since employees are in general considered to be the weaker party, choice of court agreements are not allowed in their employment contracts. To protect the employees or workers, the Indonesian Industrial Relations Court shall have jurisdiction over employment contracts. The Industrial Relations Court is a specialist court that hears cases of industrial employment disputes and is established within the district court in the capital cities of provinces in Indonesia.

b. Specific Torts

To establish the court that has jurisdiction over torts, including those involving foreign elements, one must apply the rules and principles provided in the Indonesian civil procedure codes, as well as the *forum non conveniens* doctrine.[29]

In the Extraordinary Appeal of *Time Inc Asia* (Time) *v HM Soeharto* (Soeharto), the Indonesian Supreme Court affirmed the interlocutory judgment made by the Central Jakarta District Court

[28] Consumer Dispute Resolution Body of Medan Decision 145/ARB/XII/2016/BPSK-Mdn (9 February 2017); affd District Court of Medan Decision 125/Pdt.Sus-BPSK/2017/PN Mdn (21 April 2017); affd Supreme Court Decision 1317 K/Pdt.Sus-BPSK/2017 (19 December 2017).

[29] See Section I.A above for the discussion of rules and principles to determine jurisdiction.

on its jurisdiction over the case. In this case, Soeharto filed a defamation lawsuit against Time over the article published in *TIME Magazine* and its cover page. In the article, the journalists reported the corruption committed by Soeharto and his families. Soeharto based his lawsuit on BW Article 1372 that specifically governed defamation. In response, Time filed its objection to the jurisdiction of the Central Jakarta District Court, contending that all responsible parties did not have seat or domicile in Indonesia. The Central Jakarta District Court dismissed Time's objection.[30] Although the Court did not refer to specific provisions to justify its jurisdiction in its interlocutory judgment, pursuant to Rv Article 100, an Indonesian court shall have jurisdiction *in personam* over a foreigner if the foreigner has a legal obligation arising in Indonesia or elsewhere to the Indonesian plaintiff. As such, the Central Jakarta District Court had jurisdiction over the case because it was the district court of the plaintiff's residence. The Jakarta High Court and the Supreme Court in extraordinary appeal affirmed the judgment made by the Central Jakarta District Court.[31]

In the defamation case above, the Central Jakarta District Court exercised its jurisdiction based on the rules and principles stipulated in the Indonesian civil procedure codes. However, in the other defamation case *Richard Bruce Ness v New York Times*,[32] the Central Jakarta District Court refused to exercise its jurisdiction on the ground of *forum non conveniens*, as explained in Section I.A.ii.a above.

c. Unjust Enrichment

Unlike the New Civil Code of the Netherlands (*Nieuw Burgerlijk Wetboek*) that introduced a specific Article 6:212 on unjust enrichment in 1992, the Indonesian Civil Code or BW only has provisions concerning undue performance or undue payment to govern *condictio indebiti*. Since Indonesian law only governs undue performance and not unjust enrichment, this section will only discuss undue performance.

HIR Article 118 and Rv Article 99 govern the jurisdiction of Indonesian courts over personal obligations, including undue performance. Besides that, Rv Article 100 governs the court jurisdiction over undue performance involving foreign elements. The application of the provisions can be explained by the following illustrative example. In an export-import agreement with a Japanese party, the Indonesian party thought that it had to pay the purchase price of the products sold by the Japanese party. Later, however, because Japanese law prohibits the exportation of the items, the parties' agreement becomes voidable. Consequently, the payment made by the Indonesian party in this voidable agreement is deemed as undue performance. The Japanese party has an obligation to return the received payment to the Indonesian party. The Indonesian court in the district of the Indonesian party's residence has jurisdiction *in personam* over the Japanese party.

d. Trusts and Charitable Foundations

The concept of ownership in a trust that gives a trustee only a legal ownership – because the beneficial ownership is given to a third party (beneficiary) – is unknown to the Indonesian legal system. It contradicts Article 570 in Book II of the BW that defines ownership as the right to have

[30] District Court of Central Jakarta Interlocutory Decision 338/PDT.G/1999/PN.JKT.PST (9 September 1999).

[31] High Court of Jakarta Decision 551/PDT/2000/PT.DKI (16 March 2001); affd Supreme Court Extraordinary Appeal 273 PK/Pdt/2008 (16 April 2009).

[32] See n 3.

full enjoyment of property and to freely use the property. As a result, the court will not exercise its jurisdiction over a trust agreement.

Unlike trusts, charitable foundations are recognised in the Indonesian legal system through Act No 16 of 2001, as amended by Act No 28 of 2004, on Foundations. Article 1(2) of the Act stipulates that the competent court is the court in the district in which the foundation has its legal seat. In principle, this court has jurisdiction over foundations and their organs (Articles 34 and 46). The court also has jurisdiction to dissolve a foundation due to public policy and morality, insolvency, or bankruptcy (Article 62).

Foreigners alone, or foreigners in cooperation with Indonesians, are allowed to establish foundations in Indonesia by complying with the requirements of Government Regulation No 63 of 2008, as amended by Government Regulation No 2 of 2013, on the Implementation of the Act on Foundations. In the case of a dispute between foreigners and their Indonesian partners concerning their foundation established in Indonesia, the court that has jurisdiction *in personam* is the court in the district of the foundation's legal seat. The same jurisdiction principle applies to a dispute between foreigners who establish a foundation in Indonesia without any Indonesian partners.

However, different rules of court jurisdiction apply in the case that a dispute is arisen from the transaction made by a foundation and third parties. These include situations in which a foundation invests in another company, or one of the foundation's businesses gives a loan to another party. The rules and principles in HIR Article 118 and Rv Articles 99 and 100 apply to establish which court has jurisdiction over the dispute.

ii. Law of Property

a. Immovable Property

The court that has jurisdiction to establish the title or the right to immovable property is the court in the district in which the immovable property is situated (HIR Article 118(3), Rv Article 99(8), and the *forum rei sitae* principle).[33]

In mixed cases that combine the action *in rem* and action *in personam* over immovable property, such as a lawsuit for the division of marital property that is immovable, the court that has jurisdiction is the court in the district where the immovable property is situated, or where the defendant resides, depending on the plaintiff's choice of jurisdiction (Rv Article 102). These provisions also determine the jurisdiction of Indonesian courts over immovable property with foreign elements.

b. Intangible Property

Indonesian civil procedure codes do not have specific provisions governing court jurisdiction over intangible property. As such, the rules to establish the jurisdiction of court over intangible property are based on the principles of court jurisdiction over movable and immovable properties. In the case that the intangible property is related to immovable property, for instance land mortgage and hypothec,[34] the court that exercises jurisdiction over the intangible property

[33] Harahap (n 2) 199.

[34] Security interests over immovable properties in Indonesia are divided into land (real property) mortgage and hypothec. Land mortgage is related to land, buildings, and crops affixed to the land (real property). Hypothec is related to other types of immovable properties, including Indonesian-flagged vessels with the minimum gross weight of 20 cubic meters, which is classified as immovable property under Art 314 of the Commercial Code. Land mortgage is governed under Act No 4 of 1996 on Mortgage, and hypothec is governed under BW Arts 1162–1232.

is the court in the district in which the immovable property is situated (HIR Article 118(3), Rv Article 99(8), and Act No 4 of 1996 on Mortgage).

In the case the intangible property is not related to immovable property, for instance, security interests on movable properties; shares; commercial papers, the principle of *actor sequitur forum rei* applies (HIR Article 118(1) and Rv Articles 99(1) and 99(2)).

c. Succession to Property

The court that has jurisdiction over succession to property is the court in the district in which the deceased had his last residence (Rv Article 99(12) and BW Article 23). The court jurisdiction covers succession to property, whether it is immovable or movable, tangible or intangible property.

After the enactment of Act No 3 of 2006 on Amendment of Act No 7 of 1989 on Religious Court, the court that has jurisdiction in succession to property of a deceased Muslim is the religious court in the district where the deceased last resided. If the deceased was a non-Muslim, the court that has jurisdiction is the district court in the district where the deceased last resided.[35]

There are no provisions in the Indonesian civil procedure codes that govern the court jurisdiction over succession to property of a deceased whose last residence and deathplace are outside Indonesia. There are no published court judgments found in this matter. However, based on Rv Article 7 and BW Article 467, the court that has jurisdiction shall be the court in the district of the last residence of the deceased in Indonesia before he left for another country. Rv Article 7 provides that any notice and claims to the deceased shall be brought to the last residence of the deceased. BW Article 467 grants jurisdiction over the succession to property of a missing person to the court in the district of his last residence before he was presumed dead in Indonesia or somewhere else.

iii. Intellectual Property

Indonesian intellectual property law is silent on the court's jurisdiction over intellectual property (IP) matters involving foreign elements. Consequently, the *actor sequitur forum rei* principle (HIR Article 118(1) and Rv Articles 99(1) and 99(2)) applies to determine the jurisdiction of the court. Indonesian courts also have jurisdiction over legal persons when they have places of business in Indonesia.

A foreigner who does not stay or have a residence in Indonesia and has contractual or non-contractual obligations to an Indonesian citizen, such as intellectual property infringement, breach of IP agreement, or transfer of IP rights, whether it occurs in Indonesia or elsewhere, can be brought to an Indonesian court, based on Rv Article 100. This principle does not apply to an intellectual property contract in which the parties have made a choice of court agreement that appoints a court or a forum other than an Indonesian court.

iv. Family Law

a. Marriage

Act No 1 of 1974 on Marriage (the Marriage Act 1974), the Marriage Regulation 1975, and Act No 7 of 1989, as amended by Act No 3 of 2006 and as amended by Act No 50 of 2009, on Religious

[35] District Court is also known as *Pengadilan Negeri* (literally means State Court) that exercises general subject matter jurisdiction in civil and criminal cases: Act No 2 of 1986 on Courts of General Jurisdiction, Art 50.

Court (the Religious Court Act) provide rules to establish the jurisdiction of court over matters of marriage.

Basically, the courts that have jurisdiction *in personam* over marriages in Indonesia are the district courts and religious courts and their respective appellate courts. District Courts, High Courts, and the Supreme Court have jurisdiction over the parties who perform their marriages based on religions other than Islam. Religious Courts, Religious High Courts, and the Supreme Court have jurisdiction over the parties who perform their marriages based on Islamic law.

Those courts exercise jurisdiction over matters related to permissions or preventions to perform marriages. For example, a written parental consent, or if such is not available, a written consent from a guardian, is required for a marriage of an adult under 21 years old (Article 6 of the Marriage Act 1974). If the person fails to obtain parental or guardian consent, the person may file an application for marriage to the court in the person's district of residence. The court may issue a ruling of marriage permission after hearing all the parties involved (Article 6(5) of the Marriage Act 1974). The district courts have jurisdiction over the matter if the applicants are not Muslims. The religious courts have jurisdiction if the applicants are Muslims (Article 49 of the Religious Court Act). A written parental or familial consent is also required by a foreigner under 21 years old who intends to perform a mixed marriage with an Indonesian national in Indonesia (Article 59 of the Marriage Act 1974). If the foreigner fails to obtain the consent, the foreigner may file an application for marriage permission in the court in the district in which the applicant resides in Indonesia.

For Islamic marriages, Indonesian marriage law requires a Muslim bride to obtain the consent of her father, or if he is not available, of her male relatives of her patrilineal side (Part 3 of Chapter IV of the Compilation of Islamic Law). If the bride cannot obtain the consent of her father or her male relatives (*wali* or guardian), she can request a religious court to issue a ruling that appoints a *qadi* to give consent to her marriage and to marry her to the groom in her wedding ceremony (Article 23(2) of the Compilation of Islamic Law). A *qadi* is an official appointed by the government to function as a *wali* (guardian) for a Muslim bride, in addition to other functions as prescribed by the Compilation of Islamic Law (also known as *Kompilasi Hukum Islam* or KHI). Although not expressly stipulated in Indonesian marriage law, a religious court in Indonesia should have jurisdiction over a foreign bride performing an Islamic marriage in Indonesia who cannot obtain the consent of her father or her male relatives. The religious court can appoint a *qadi* to act as a *wali* for her marriage. The competent religious court should be the court in the district where she stays in Indonesia.

The Indonesian courts also have jurisdiction over polygamous marriages (General Elucidation of the Marriage Act 1974) to issue rulings in allowing or not allowing polygamous marriages in Indonesia after examining all the legal requirements for polygamous marriages. The district courts have jurisdiction over polygamous marriages if the applicants are not Muslims. The religious courts have jurisdiction if the applicants are Muslims.

The courts also have jurisdiction over polygamous marriages performed by foreigners in Indonesia. Pursuant to the principle of *locus regit actum* of AB Article 18, a foreigner who has capacity to perform a polygamous marriage in Indonesia must comply with all formal requirements of a polygamous marriage in Indonesia, including obtaining a court ruling that allows him to marry more than one wife in Indonesia (Article 4 of the Marriage Act 1974 and Article 41 of the Marriage Regulation 1975). The court ruling is mandatory for polygamous marriages in Indonesia. It cannot be substituted by the Certificate of No Impediment to Marriage issued by the foreigner's embassy in Indonesia. The courts that have jurisdiction over this matter are the courts in the districts where the foreigners reside in Indonesia.

The Indonesian district courts also have jurisdiction over inter-faith marriages, either performed by Indonesian couples or mixed marriage couples in Indonesia. Since some religions in Indonesia, for example, Islam, do not allow their followers to marry those who do not embrace the same religions, the followers of those religions who will perform inter-faith marriages shall first obtain court rulings that allow them to perform marriages with people of a different faith. The courts that have jurisdictions over this matter are the district courts of the places of the marriages (Elucidation of Article 35(a) of Act No 23 of 2006, as amended by Act No 24 of 2013, on Population Administration ('the Population Administration Act')).

b. Divorce, Nullity and Separation

The courts that have jurisdiction over marital disputes, including divorce, are district courts and religious courts (Articles 39(1) and 40(1) of the Marriage Act 1974, and Article 65 of the Religious Court Act). District courts have jurisdiction over the parties who performed their marriages based on religions other than Islam. Religious courts have jurisdiction over the parties who performed their marriages based on Islamic law.

The parties that can file divorce petitions in Indonesian districts and religious courts – besides Indonesian couples – are mixed-marriage couples living in Indonesia and foreign couples having domicile in Indonesia. It has been an established practice after Indonesia's independence that Indonesian courts exercise their jurisdiction over the divorce of foreign couples having domicile in Indonesia and apply the *renvoi* doctrine to adjudicate the divorce. In the case No 2640 K/Pdt/2009, the Supreme Court affirmed the jurisdiction of the South Jakarta District Court over the divorce of an American couple because they had residence in the South Jakarta district. This principle was adopted by the District Court of Bali in the case No 172/Pdt.G/2014/PN.Dps in which the court exercised its jurisdiction over the divorce of a South African couple because the spouses had residence in Bali.

The parties, either Indonesians or foreigners, filing a petition for divorce in Indonesian courts shall observe the rules concerning court jurisdiction as explained in the following paragraphs.

A Muslim husband, either an Indonesian or a foreigner, who intends to utter *talaq* divorce to his wife in Indonesia, must file his petition in a religious court in the district of his wife's residence, along with the reason for the *talaq*. Accordingly, the court that has jurisdiction over the *talaq* divorce is always the court in the district of the wife's residence (Article 129 of the Compilation of Islamic Law).

With regard to a Muslim wife, either an Indonesian or a foreigner, who intends to divorce her husband in Indonesia, she must file her petition for divorce in a religious court in the district of her residence, unless she has moved out from the couple's shared residence without her husband's consent (Article 73(1) of the Religious Court Act and Article 132(1) of the Compilation of Islamic Law). This provision means that when a wife has moved out from the residence she shared with her husband, without his consent, the principle of *actor sequitur forum rei* will apply.

With regard to divorce of couples that were married under religions other than Islam, Article 20 and its Elucidation of the Marriage Regulation 1975 provide that the petitioners, either husbands or wives, shall file their divorce petitions in the district courts located in the residences of the respondents. This provision applies to both Indonesian couples and foreign couples having domicile in Indonesia. In general, the rules in the Marriage Regulation 1975 concerning the jurisdiction of district courts over divorce are the same as the rules set in the Indonesian civil procedure codes (HIR Article 118 and Rv Article 99). In the case that the residence of the respondent in Indonesia cannot be identified, or the respondent's residence is outside Indonesia, the court that has jurisdiction over the divorce is the court in the district of the petitioner's residence (Articles 20(2) and 20(3) of the Marriage Regulation 1975 and Article 66(3) of the Religious Court Act). These provisions can be applied to both Indonesian and foreign respondents.

In the case an Indonesian couple or mixed marriage couple who domicile outside Indonesia intends to divorce, there are different rules to establish the courts that have jurisdiction over their divorce. Article 41 of the Population Administration Act recognises the divorce decrees obtained by Indonesian citizens from foreign courts and requires the divorce decrees from foreign courts to be registered in the civil registry offices in the cities of their residence in Indonesia within 30 days of their return to Indonesia. Based on this provision, an Indonesian couple or mixed marriage couple who domicile outside Indonesia are allowed to file their divorce in a court of their domicile abroad, as long as both spouses agree with the jurisdiction of the foreign court over their divorce. It is a prevailing doctrine in Indonesia that a foreign decree of divorce is recognised in Indonesia, because a decree of divorce is categorised as a constitutive judgment. The couple shall file their divorce petition in an Indonesian court only if one of the divorcing spouses refuses to submit the divorce to the jurisdiction of the foreign court.

Regarding an Indonesian Muslim couple or Muslim mixed marriage couple who domicile outside Indonesia and intends to divorce, they can file their divorce petition only in an Indonesian religious court, although both husband and wife agree to the jurisdiction of foreign courts. This is based on Articles 66(4) and 73(3) of the Religious Court Act. The Articles provide that in the case the petitioner and respondent domicile outside Indonesia, the petition for divorce shall be filed in the religious court in the district where the couple registered their marriage or in the Central Jakarta Religious Court. Despite the provision, there are judges of religious courts who suggest divorce decrees obtained by Muslim spouses from foreign courts be recognised and registered in Indonesia. The couples do not need to bring the same cause of action to Indonesian religious courts.[36] This assertion applies in the case that both the husband and wife have agreed with the jurisdiction of foreign courts over their divorce, and the grounds for their divorce abroad are legal under Indonesian law. This argument is based on the doctrine of *lex posterior derogat legi priori* (a later law repeals an earlier law) and the doctrine that categorises a divorce decree as a constitutive judgment. Those that adopt these doctrines assert that Article 41 of the Population Administration Act supersedes the earlier provisions of Religious Court Act.[37]

In Indonesian law, there is no distinction between nullity and annulment of marriages. For a marriage that was performed under Islamic law, the petition for its nullity shall be filed in the religious court of the place of the marriage or of the residence of either spouse (Article 74 of the Compilation of Islamic Law). For a marriage that was performed under religions other than Islam, nullity of marriage should be filed in the district courts of the place of the marriage or in the district courts of the residence of the couple, or of the residence of either spouse (Article 25 of the Marriage Act 1974 and Article 38 of the Marriage Regulation 1975).

The claimants in nullity of marriage are not only the husband and the wife, but also their families of direct parental lineage and other parties who have interests in the nullity (Article 23 of the Marriage Act 1974 and Article 73 of the Compilation of Islamic Law). In theory, like in the

[36] This opinion was provided by Justice Tamah, a judge at the South Jakarta Religious Court during an interview with Astrid Pratiwi for her thesis: Astrid Pratiwi, 'Aspek-aspek Hukum Acara Perdata Internasional dalam Perceraian di Indonesia' (Undergraduate thesis, Universitas Indonesia, 2011) 118, 119. The same opinion was also presented by Justice Mohamad Thoha, a judge at the Ponorogo Religious Court in his writing titled 'Hukum Perceraian di luar negeri'. His writing was published on 12 September 2008, but the original link is no longer available. An archived version is available online: https://materikuliahfhunibraw.files.wordpress.com/2014/09/perceraian-pasutri-indo-jepang-clear.pdf.

[37] Mariam Yasmin, 'Akibat Perkawinan Campuran Terhadap Anak dan Harta Benda yang Diperoleh Sebelum dan Sesudah Perkawinan (Studi Banding Indonesia-Malaysia)' (Undergraduate thesis, Universitas Indonesia, 2011) 21, 23.

case of divorce, an Indonesian court could exercise jurisdiction over marriage nullity in which both spouses are foreigners having domicile in Indonesia, insofar as the grounds for their nullity are known in Indonesian law. Although there are no court judgments on the nullity of foreign couples in Indonesia, there are court judgments on the nullity of mixed marriages, which are marriages between Indonesians and foreigners. For example, in the case of *Ludwig Franz Willibald Maria Josepf Leonhard Erbgraf von Waldburg-Wolfegg-Waldsee v Yesisca Iskandar.* Ludwig, Hereditary Prince of Waldburg-Wolfegg and Waldsee (mediatised), filed a petition for nullity of his marriage to Ms Iskandar, an Indonesian, in the South Jakarta District Court in October 2014. Prince Ludwig is a German and lived in Germany when filing his petition for marriage nullity. Ms Iskandar lived in South Jakarta. Pursuant to Article 25 of the Marriage Act 1974, the South Jakarta District Court exercised its jurisdiction over the petition for nullity because the wife's residence was in the South Jakarta district, their alleged marriage was solemnised in a church located in South Jakarta, and it was registered in a civil registry office in South Jakarta. The South Jakarta District Court decided in favour of Prince Ludwig.[38]

Indonesian law is silent on the nullity of marriage outside Indonesia. There are no provisions concerning the registration of foreign nullity decrees in the Population Administration Act. The Act only governs the registration of nullity decrees issued by Indonesian courts (Article 39). Accordingly, only Indonesian courts have jurisdiction over the marriage nullity of Indonesian or mixed marriage couple that domicile outside Indonesia.

Regarding legal separation, the concept does not exist in Indonesia after the enactment of the Marriage Act 1974. The Indonesian Civil Code (BW) that recognised legal separation has been superseded by the Marriage Act 1974.

c. Matters Relating to the Well-being of the Child

Maintenance (child support) and custody of children are important matters related to the well-being of children in cases of marital disputes or dissolution of marriages in Indonesia. Since the issue of children maintenance is part of a divorce proceeding, the court that has jurisdiction over the maintenance of children is the same court that exercises its jurisdiction over the divorce. In the case that a father does not comply with a court order of child support, the mother or the family of his children may file a civil lawsuit against him in the court that issued the divorce decree (HIR Articles 196 and 197). This principle of court jurisdiction also applies to the matter of custody as a result of divorce.

Indonesian courts also exercise jurisdiction over the matters of maintenance and custody of children of mixed marriage couples and foreign couples having domicile in Indonesia. The basis of the court jurisdiction is the habitual residence of the children in Indonesia in order to protect the best interest of the children. The 2015 Academic Paper of Indonesian Private International Law Bill suggests the principle of habitual residence of the child to determine the law applicable to matters pertaining to the welfare of the child.[39] In the author's opinion, although the Academic Paper is silent on the court's jurisdiction over matters relating to the well-being of the child, the principle of habitual residence of the child can be applied to determine the court jurisdiction over the matters.

[38] District Court of South Jakarta Decision 586/Pdt.G/2014/PN.Jkt.Sel (15 October 2015).

[39] IBR Supancana, *Naskah Akademik Rancangan Undang-Undang tentang Hukum Perdata Internasional (lanjutan)* [*Academic Paper of Indonesian Private International Law Bill*] (Jakarta, Badan Pembinaan Hukum Nasional Kementerian Hukum dan Hak Asasi Manusia RI [National Law Development Agency, the Ministry of Law and Human Rights of the Republic of Indonesia], 2015) 213.

In the case of *Purnima Ralhan v Jonathan I Kine*, which involved matters relating to the well-being of the child, the court exercised its jurisdiction based on the principle of habitual residence of the parties, including that of the child. The couple were American citizens married in Philadelphia, and had lived in Jakarta since 2000. Their daughter, Lara Rose, was born in Jakarta in 2001 and had American citizenship. In September 2007, Ms Ralhan reported her husband to the Jakarta Police Office for domestic violence. Based on Act No 23 of 2004 on the Elimination of Domestic Violence, the court temporarily revoked Mr Kine's parental authority over Lara Rose and granted the parental authority to Ms Ralhan.[40] Based on the court ruling, Ms Ralhan filed a petition for divorce in the South Jakarta District Court in 2008. In her divorce petition, she also asked the court to order her husband to pay Lara Rose's maintenance. Mr Kine objected to the jurisdiction of the South Jakarta District Court, as the parties were all foreigners and their marriage was performed in Philadelphia. The Court rejected Mr Kine's objection and exercised its jurisdiction over Ms Ralhan's petition for divorce along with her application for child support and custody. In the Court's opinion, it would take longer for the parties to settle their dispute if they had to return to Philadelphia which required them to obtain bona fide residence in Philadelphia to file a lawsuit in a Philadelphia court.[41] Although the Court's provisional judgment did not expressly mention the child's habitual residence as the reason of its jurisdiction, it was evident that the Court considered the family's habitual residence in the South Jakarta district to establish its jurisdiction over the case.

v. Law of Corporations and Insolvency

Based on Act No 37 of 2004 on Bankruptcy and Suspension of Debt Payment Obligations, corporate insolvency takes place after a commercial court declares a corporation bankrupt. The corporation is declared bankrupt when it has two or more creditors and does not repay in full at least one debt which is due and payable (Article 2(1)). The bankrupt corporate debtor shall offer a composition plan to its creditors. If the composition plan is rejected by its creditors, the corporate debtor will enter insolvency. Insolvency means the condition of being unable to pay debts (Elucidation of Article 57(1)). After the corporate debtor enters insolvency, the receiver starts the liquidation process under the supervision of a supervisory judge (Article 178).

The corporate debtor, or at least one of its creditors, or one of third parties mentioned in Article 2, can file a bankruptcy petition that could lead to corporate insolvency. Foreign creditors can also file a bankruptcy petition under the Act. For instance, in the case of *Oxedon Enterprises Ltd v PT Beruangmas Perkasa*,[42] the creditor (Oxedon Enterprises Limited) was a British Virgin Island corporation, and the debtor was an Indonesian corporation.

The commercial court is the court that has jurisdiction *in personam* over corporate insolvency in Indonesia (Article 1(7)). Based on Article 3, the commercial court that has jurisdiction is the one whose jurisdiction includes the province in which the corporate debtor has its legal seat. The corporate debtor's legal seat is the seat of the corporate stated in its Memorandum of Association. If the corporate debtor does not have its legal seat in Indonesia but runs its business in Indonesia, the commercial court that has jurisdiction is the one whose jurisdiction includes the province

[40] District Court of South Jakarta Decision 394/Pdt.P/2007/PN.Jak.Sel (21 January 2008); affd Supreme Court Extraordinary Appeal 76PK/PDT/2009 (26 November 2009).
[41] District Court of South Jakarta Decision 47/Pdt.G/2008/PN.Jak.Sel (not published); affd High Court of Jakarta Decision 141/PDT/2009/PT.DKI (not published); affd Supreme Court Decision 2640 K/Pdt/2009 (not published).
[42] Commercial Court of Jakarta Decision 16/Pailit/2006/PN.JKT.PST (13 June 2006).

where the corporate debtor runs its business or where its Indonesian office is situated. The relevant commercial court can also exercise its jurisdiction over a corporate debtor whose assets are located outside Indonesia. The court may declare bankruptcy on all assets of a corporate debtor, including the assets that are located outside Indonesia (Articles 21, 212, 213, 214).

Article 303 governs that a commercial court also has jurisdiction over corporate insolvency, although it is related to a situation in which a contract involving the corporation contains an arbitration clause.

vi. Law of Bankruptcy

The Bankruptcy and Suspension of Debt Payment Act 2004 applies to all types of debtors, be they individuals, non-legal entities, or corporations. The court that has jurisdiction over personal bankruptcy and corporate bankruptcy is the commercial court (Article 3). In the case the debtor has left Indonesia, the commercial court that has jurisdiction is the one whose jurisdiction includes the province in which the debtor had its last domicile in Indonesia. In the case the debtor is a partner in a firm, the commercial court that has jurisdiction is the one whose jurisdiction includes the province in which the firm has its legal seat.

The commercial court also has jurisdiction to declare bankruptcy on the assets of a deceased person, provided that there are two or more creditors who file a petition for bankruptcy and can prove that the deceased had debt that was not paid in full during his lifetime, or when he died, his assets was not sufficient to pay his debt (Article 207). The court that has jurisdiction over the bankruptcy of a deceased's estate is the commercial court whose jurisdiction includes the province of the deceased's last residence (Article 208). The petition for bankruptcy on a deceased's estate shall be filed in the relevant commercial court within 90 days after the death of the deceased (Article 210). The creditors who can file the petition can be Indonesian as well as foreign nationals, like in the case of *Michael Kong Kenneth Kitson v William Bong Kon Ho*,[43] where Mr Kitson, a Singaporean, filed a petition for bankruptcy in the Jakarta Commercial Court on the estate of Mr Ho, an Indonesian.

The Act does not have provisions governing the estate of a deceased person who no longer live in Indonesia before his death, but left his assets in Indonesia. In the author's opinion, the commercial court that has jurisdiction over this matter should be the one whose jurisdiction includes the province of the last residence of the deceased before he left.

Another alternative of bankruptcy procedure is the suspension of debt payment obligation. The suspension is intended as a mechanism to restructure a debtor's debts. This procedure could be filed by a debtor, a creditor, or one of the government agencies listed in Article 2 of the Act. The commercial court that has jurisdiction over the suspension of debt payment obligation is the relevant commercial court mentioned in Article 3 of the Act.

vii. Competition Law

Under Act No 5 of 1999 on the Prohibition of Monopolistic Practices and Unfair Business Competition, institutions that are responsible for enforcing the competition law in Indonesia are the Commission for the Supervision of Business Competition (the Indonesia Competition Commission) and the courts. The decision of the Indonesia Competition Commission (the

[43] Jakarta Commercial Court Decision 18/Pailit/2008/PN.NIAGA.JKT.PST (16 June 2008) (not published).

Commission) could be an imposition of administrative measures, a ruling of compensation for damages, and/or imposition of a fine (Article 47). The Commission's decision can be appealed to the District Court, with a final appeal to the Supreme Court.

In cases of unfair competition involving foreign elements, the Commission has jurisdiction *in personam* over the Indonesian business actors and their foreign partners – irrespective of the foreigners' presence in Indonesia – as long as they have made business agreements in any form with Indonesians (Article 16; for the definition of 'agreement', see Article 1(7)). Additionally, the Commission has jurisdiction *in personam* over foreign parties that neither establish any business agreements with Indonesian business actors nor have any presence in Indonesia, if they meet the requirements of the single economic entity doctrine. The doctrine was applied by the Commission to determine whether separate foreign legal entities can constitute a single economic entity for competition law purposes. For example, a foreign holding company that neither operates nor establishes any agreement with business actors in Indonesia will still be under the jurisdiction of the Commission if it has subsidiary companies that make agreements with business actors in Indonesia which create anti-competitive effects in Indonesia, and those subsidiary companies are under its control and do not have economic independence from the holding company.

In the case of *Temasek Holdings*, the Commission exercised its jurisdiction over Temasek Holdings, even though it was a Singaporean-holding company, was not present in Indonesia, and did not make any agreement with Indonesian business actors. In this case, the Commission found that Temasek Holdings' subsidiaries, STT Communications Ltd and Singapore Telecommunications Ltd, had shares in PT Telekomunikasi Selular and in PT Indosat, Indonesia's first and second biggest mobile operators. This business structure generated a price leadership in Indonesia's telecommunications industry. The Commission found that these subsidiaries were under Temasek Holdings' control and did not have economic independence. Hence, for competition law purposes, the Commission found that Temasek Holdings along with its subsidiaries operated as a single economic entity in Indonesia.[44] Therefore, the Commission had jurisdiction over Temasek Holdings.

Article 44(2) provides that the parties can appeal the Commission's judgment to a district court. The district court that has jurisdiction over a competition case is the court in the district of the business actor's legal seat (Article 1(19)). Since the appellants were foreign companies that did not have legal seats in Indonesia, the Central Jakarta District Court exercised its jurisdiction over the appeal. When the Central Jakarta District Court dismissed their appeal, they brought their case to the court of cassation under the Supreme Court, and finally to the extraordinary appellate court that was also under the Supreme Court.[45]

In another case that also involved foreign business actors, the Commission exercised its jurisdiction over Goldman Sachs (Singapore) Pte, a Singaporean company, because Goldman Sachs (Singapore) Pte made an agreement to provide the service as financial advisor for PT Pertamina, an Indonesian state-owned company, when PT Pertamina sold its crude carriers to Frontline Ltd. The Commission also exercised its jurisdiction over Frontline Ltd, a Bermuda company, because it made a Sales and Purchase Agreement with PT Pertamina regarding the crude carriers. Although Goldman Sachs (Singapore) Pte and Frontline Ltd were not

[44] Commission for the Supervision of Business Competition Decision 07/KPPU-L/2007 (19 November 2007) 607–12.

[45] District Court of Central Jakarta Decision 02/KPPU/2007/PN.JKT.PST (9 May 2008); affd Supreme Court Decision 496 K/Pdt.Sus/2008 (10 September 2008); affd Supreme Court Extraordinary Appeal 128 PK/PDT.SUS/2009 (5 May 2010).

incorporated and did not have operations in Indonesia, the Commission had jurisdiction over them because of their business agreements with PT Pertamina, in which the conditions of the agreements potentially violated Article 16.[46]

II. Jurisdiction *in rem* with Special Focus on Shipping Claims

A. Jurisdiction *in rem* of the Courts within the Territory

The Elucidation of Article 223(1) of Act No 17 of 2008 on Shipping (Shipping Act 2008) lists 22 maritime claims that can result in ship arrest. The Shipping Act 2008 itself does not have specific provisions concerning shipping claims involving foreign elements. The Act also does not have provisions concerning the court's jurisdiction in shipping claims. Some law practitioners argue that the court that has the jurisdiction shall be the district court in the residence of the defendant or in the location of the ship.[47] Since there is no specific Maritime Court in Indonesia that deals with shipping claims,[48] shipping claims are litigated in the district courts.

Article 223 of the Shipping Act 2008 is the only provision that mentions shipping claims resulting in ship arrest. Article 223(2) requires the government to issue a ministerial regulation that governs the procedure of ship arrest in relation to shipping claims. To date, the government has not issued the required ministerial regulation.

Due to the absence of a specific regulation on the jurisdiction of Indonesian courts over shipping claims, parties refer to Indonesian Civil Procedure Law. Pursuant to Rv Article 100, the ship owner's presence in Indonesia is not required for an Indonesian court to exercise jurisdiction over shipping claims, as long as the ship owner owes an obligation to an Indonesian claimant. Because a shipping claim that leads to ship arrest can be characterised as a mixed action against both the defendant (ship owner) and the property (the ship), the court that exercises jurisdiction in the shipping claim is the court chosen by the claimant either in the district in which the ship is situated or in the district in which the ship owner resides (Rv Article 99(10)). The jurisdiction of the Indonesian court over shipping claims that leads to the arrest of the ship is determined by the existence of the ship within Indonesian territory. Because of Rv Article 431, if the ship is located outside Indonesian territory, the Indonesian court will not have jurisdiction in those shipping claims, even if both the claimant and the defendant are in Indonesia.

B. The Process of Ship Arrest in the Territory

Ships involved in either criminal or civil cases are subject to arrest by the harbourmaster under a court order (Article 222). Article 223(1) provides that the ship arrest in civil cases shall be

[46] Commission for the Supervision of Business Competition Decision 07/KPPU-L/2004 (3 March 2005).

[47] James Gosling and Tessaj Huzarski (eds), *The Shipping Law Review* 3rd edn (London, Law Business Research Ltd, 2016) 267.

[48] The Maritime Court in Indonesia (*Mahkamah Pelayaran*) does not litigate shipping disputes, but merely examines indications or allegations of error or negligence in the event of a ship accident. It is not a tribunal, but a panel of experts under the Ministry of Transportation: see the Shipping Act 2008.

based on maritime claims, and a party may request an order from the court for the arrestation without filing a civil lawsuit. However, because of the lack of implementing regulations, Articles 222 and 223 are deemed ineffective. As mentioned above, the required ministerial regulation in Article 223(2) to be issued by the government is absent. In addition, Indonesia is not a party to the 1952 International Convention Relating to the Arrest of Seagoing Ships, and although it is a signatory to the 1999 International Convention on Arrest of Ships, that Convention is yet to be ratified in Indonesia. As such, there is no specific procedure for ship arrest under Indonesian law.

As there is no implementing regulation governing the process of ship arrest, no court order for ship arrest can be found in Indonesian case law. As such, claimants usually combine the request of arrest and conservatory seizure of the ships in one civil lawsuit against the ship owners.[49] A claimant can also request that the harbourmaster postpones the issuance of Port Clearance (*Surat Persetujuan Izin Berlayar*, SPIB) of the ship; thus, the ship will not be able to sail. The postponement of the SPIB issuance will be lifted by the harbourmaster when the claimant and the ship owner settle their dispute as mediated by the harbourmaster.[50] These are the main practices of ship arrest that are currently carried out as a result of the absence of specific ship arrest procedures.

III. Immunities from Jurisdiction

A. Sovereign and Diplomatic Immunity

There is no specific law concerning the jurisdictional immunity of states in Indonesia. In spite of this, the ratification of the 1965 Convention on the Settlement of Investment Disputes between States and Nationals of Other States (the ICSID Convention) by Indonesia under Act No 5 of 1968 on Investment Disputes Settlement Between States and Foreign Nationals may indicate that Indonesia accepts the doctrine of restrictive immunity. With the ratification of the ICSID Convention, Indonesia waives its immunity in front of the ICSID arbitration for matters of investment disputes between Indonesia and foreign investors.

Another provision in Indonesian law that mentions the court's jurisdiction over a state without addressing jurisdictional immunity is Rv Article 99(18), which stipulates that '[i]n the case that the Indonesian Government represents the State, either as a plaintiff or a defendant, Jakarta is assumed as their residence'. This provision indicates that, in civil cases, the Indonesian state is not immune from the court's jurisdiction. M Yahya Harahap, a former Indonesian Supreme Court Justice, suggests that it is not only the Jakarta District Court, but also other courts in other districts in which the Indonesian Government has its representatives, that have jurisdiction over the Indonesian state.[51] The district courts all over Indonesia have exercised jurisdiction over the Indonesian Government and its representatives in many civil lawsuits that are brought by private

[49] District Court of Jambi Decision 10/PDT.G/2013/PN.JBI. (31 July 2013) (n 1); District Court of Central Jakarta Decision 23/PDT.G/2011/PN.JKT.PST (1 December 2011) (n 1).

[50] District Court of Central Jakarta Decision 451/PDT.G/2010/PN.JKT.PST (8 December 2011); Indra Firman, 'Ship Arrest Process in Indonesia' (*Indra Firman & Associates*, 14 September 2016), available online: http://indrafirman.com/en/2016/09/14/ship-arrest-process-in-indonesia.

[51] That is to implement the principle of simple, quick and economical judiciary stated in Art 2(4) of Act No 48 of 2009 on Judicial Power: Harahap (n 2) 136.

entities or individuals.[52] However, Rv Article 99(18) only governs the court's jurisdiction over the Indonesian state. It does not govern the jurisdiction of Indonesian courts over foreign states.

To know whether foreign states are immune from court jurisdiction in Indonesia, one must look at the doctrines, law reports, and judicial practice. The report on the Third Session of the Asian-African Legal Consultative Committee, held in Colombo in 1960, mentioned that Indonesia adopted the doctrine of absolute immunity.[53] That was indeed the case when private entities or individuals in civil cases brought the Republic of Indonesia to foreign courts. For instance, in the case of *The Republic of Indonesia, His Excellency Ambassador Soeratmin, Minister Counsellor Azhari Kasim v James Vinzon*,[54] the Republic of Indonesia, as the defendant, maintained its sovereign immunity defence, although it was involved in a commercial activity by entering into a maintenance agreement with James Vinzon, who was required to maintain some facilities in the embassy area and in the ambassador residence. The Makati Trial Court held that the Republic of Indonesia waived its immunity when it entered into the maintenance agreement with James Vinzon. However, the Philippine Supreme Court overruled the Makati Trial Court's judgment and agreed with the Indonesia's defence on the ground that the Republic of Indonesia acted in a sovereign activity when entering into a contract with James Vinzon.

The Republic of Indonesia also asserted its sovereign immunity defence when a claim was brought in other commercial cases in the foreign courts, such as *Juan Ysmael & Co Inc v Government of the Republic of Indonesia*,[55] *Velasco v Government of Indonesia*,[56] and *Phaneuf v Republic of Indonesia*.[57]

Unlike the Indonesian Government, which adheres to the doctrine of absolute sovereign immunity, the Indonesian courts apply the doctrine of restrictive immunity to foreign states in their disputes of employment contracts with Indonesian nationals. The application of the doctrine by Indonesian courts was the result of the issuance of the Supreme Court Circular Letter No 4 of 2016 that was addressed to all Indonesian courts. In the Circular Letter, the Supreme Court wrote that the Industrial Relations Court has jurisdiction over labour disputes between the representatives of foreign states in Indonesia (such as embassies) and Indonesian employees. It also wrote that the employment contracts made in Indonesia between the foreign states' representatives and Indonesian employees shall be governed by Act No 13 of 2003 on Manpower. The Circular Letter No 4 of 2016 was followed by a stable jurisprudence established by the Supreme Court in 2017. In its 2017 Yearly Report, the Supreme Court categorised its judgment on the case of *The Brazilian Embassy in Jakarta v Luis FSS Pereira* as a stable jurisprudence.[58] In this case, Mr Pereira, an Indonesian local staff, brought the Brazilian Embassy to the Industrial Relations Court in Central Jakarta for a labour dispute concerning breach of the employment contract. The Brazilian Embassy as the defendant maintained the diplomatic immunity defence and argued that it was not subject to Indonesian law and, consequently, was not under the jurisdiction of an Indonesian court. The Central Jakarta Industrial Relations Court dismissed the Brazilian Embassy's defence and

[52] Decisions of the courts that exercised their jurisdiction over the Indonesian Government or its representatives can be found in the directory of court decisions compiled by the Indonesian Supreme Court, available online: https://putusan.mahkamahagung.go.id/.

[53] Sompong Sucharitkul, 'Fourth Report on Jurisdictional Immunities of States and Their Property' UN Doc A/CN.4/357 and Corr.1 (31 March 1982) 226; Ernest K Bankas, *The State Immunity Controversy in International Law: Private Suits Against Sovereign States in Domestic Courts* (Berlin, Springer, 2005) 103, 202, 330.

[54] *Republic of Indonesia v Vinzon* GR No 154705 (26 June 2003) (Supreme Court of the Philippines).

[55] *Juan Ysmael & Co Inc v Government of the Republic of Indonesia* [1955] AC 72 (PC, on appeal from Hong Kong).

[56] *Velasco v Government of Indonesia* 370 F 3d 392 (4th Cir 2004).

[57] *Phaneuf v Republic of Indonesia* 106 F 3d 302 (9th Cir 1997).

[58] Supreme Court Decision 376 K/Pdt.Sus-PHI/2013 (29 October 2013).

ordered the embassy to pay compensation to Mr Pereira, because in the employment contract, the parties agreed that they were governed by Indonesian labour law and that any dispute arising out of the agreement would be settled by the ruling of a labour dispute settlement body in Indonesia. The Indonesian Supreme Court affirmed the decision and stated in its judgment that employment contracts between the representatives of foreign states in Indonesia and Indonesian employees was governed by Act No 13 of 2003 on Manpower. The Supreme Court also stated that the diplomatic immunity under the 1963 Vienna Convention on Consular Relations and Optional Protocol to the Vienna Convention on Consular Relations concerning Acquisition of Nationality was waived when the representatives of foreign states entered into employment contracts with Indonesian employees. As a consequence of the Supreme Court Circular Letter and the jurisprudence, the representatives of foreign states in Indonesia are deemed to waive their sovereign and diplomatic immunity when entering into employment contracts with Indonesian nationals and the Indonesian Relations Court has jurisdiction over the representatives of foreign states.

In spite of several court judgments that dismissed the sovereign and diplomatic immunity defences raised by foreign embassies, there was uncertainty regarding the enforcement of those judgments, because the Indonesian nationals who won their cases did not receive the compensation from the foreign embassies after the courts delivered their judgments. This uncertainty occurs because the Supreme Court Circular Letter No 4 of 2016 and the jurisprudence only waive the immunity of representatives of foreign states from the jurisdiction of Industrial Relations Court. They are silent on the waiver of foreign state immunity from execution in Indonesia. As a result, the judgments of the Industrial Relations Court cannot be enforced against the representatives of foreign states in Indonesia on the ground of foreign state's immunity from execution.

In conclusion, foreign states are in principle immune from the jurisdiction of Indonesian courts, except when they entered into employment contracts with Indonesian employees. The Industrial Relations Court will have jurisdiction over the foreign states on labour disputes arising out of the employment contracts. However, the judgments of the court cannot be enforced against the foreign states because they remain immune from execution in Indonesia. This situation might change if Indonesia passes a law that governs the immunities of states or when Indonesia joins the 2004 United Nations Convention on Jurisdictional Immunities of States and Their Property.

B. State-Owned Enterprises (SOEs)

The issue of jurisdictional immunity of state-owned enterprises (SOEs) is not expressly governed in Indonesian law. However, the judicial practice shows that SOEs do not enjoy immunity from the jurisdiction of Indonesian courts, for example, in *PT Globex Indonesia v PT Djakarta Lloyd* in which PT Djakarta Lloyd is 100 per cent owned by the Indonesian Government.[59] This judicial practice resulted from the decision taken at the 2010 National Work Meeting of the Indonesian Supreme Court. The decision states that courts have jurisdiction to seize the assets of Indonesian SOEs in civil and commercial claims. Even though Article 50 of Act No 1 of 2004 on State Treasury prohibits the seizure or execution against state assets in whatever form, the Supreme

[59] District Court of Central Jakarta Decision 288/PDT.G/2008/PN.JKT.PST (25 March 2009); affd High Court of Jakarta Decision 323/PDT.2009/PT.DKI (19 November 2009).

Court concludes that Article 50 does not include the state assets that have been invested in and become the capital of SOEs.[60]

The decision taken at the 2010 Supreme Court meeting has not been adopted in any regulation yet, but it provides Indonesian courts with the authority to exercise its jurisdiction over SOEs and execute the SOEs' assets. Despite the fact that the decision does not mention foreign SOEs, the judicial practice indicates that foreign SOEs are similarly not immune from the jurisdiction of Indonesian courts, for example, in *Temasek Holdings (Pte) Ltd v Komisi Pengawas Persaingan Usaha Republik Indonesia (KPPU)* in which Temasek Holding is 100 per cent owned by the Government of Singapore.[61]

[60] Decision taken at the 2010 National Work Meeting of the Indonesian Supreme Court in Balikpapan, 11–14 October 2020, as summarised in Ali Ali, 'Pengadilan Boleh Sita Harta BUMN' (*hukumonline.com*, 18 October 2010), available online: www.hukumonline.com/berita/baca/lt4cbc1bcd43fa9/pengadilan-boleh-sita-harta-bumn?page=all.

[61] See n 45.

14

Thailand

AKAWAT LAOWONSIRI

I. Introduction

Thailand is essentially a civil law jurisdiction. Over the last century or so, its legal system has undergone a process of westernisation, notably through the inclusion into its Civil and Commercial Code of rules drawn from continental European sources. But, for the procedural aspects of its civil and commercial law, English common law has significantly inspired the Thai Civil Procedure Code (CPC). This is true, at least to the extent that the general rules of the CPC are based on an adversarial (rather than inquisitorial) model.[1] As a result, the judicial process in Thailand envisages less collaboration between lawyers and judges. Thai judges play a comparatively less active role than their counterparts in the continental European legal tradition that has influenced the development of Thai substantive private law.[2] On the other hand, it would not be accurate either to label Thailand as having entirely adopted a common law approach to procedural matters. Thailand has sorted out its substantive law into distinct areas much as has been done in Europe and the laws of each area are enforced by different judicial authorities and through special procedures. In cases subject to particular judicial authorities and special procedures, courts can be more active and collaborative than normal. Thus, to fully understand Thailand's legal system from a comparative perspective, one has to examine relevant jurisdictional and procedural rules in each area of substantive law. It will then be found that these jurisdictional and procedural rules have been drawn from different sources, both common and civil law, to be assembled together by the Thai legislature and judiciary.

The development of Thai rules, norms and practices in relation to direct jurisdiction involves historical complexity, dating back to when Thailand's neighbours were colonised while Siam (as Thailand was then known) attempted to shield itself from intrusion. Although Siam was never colonised by a European state, pressure was exerted upon it by the colonial powers to modernise its substantive and procedural law within a limited timeframe. In the course of restructuring its legal system, Siam did not cede judicial authority to any European power. However, in light of their political and economic superiority, those powers were able to force through the establishment in Siam of extraterritorial courts with European judges to resolve disputes in which at least

[1] See eg Udom Ratamarit, *Law of Evidence* (Bangkok, Thammasat University Faculty of Law, 2012) 25–34.

[2] Contrast the position in Germany where judges proactively work with the parties' legal representatives to ascertain relevant facts and law. See John Bell, *Judiciaries within Europe: A Comparative Review* (Cambridge, Cambridge University Press, 2006) 134–35.

one party was European. Such courts applied foreign law. This exercise by the European colonial powers of extraterritorial jurisdiction within Thai territory has shaped the collective consciousness of Thai elites, especially policy-makers and judges.[3] Thai aversion to extraterritoriality continues to resonate today. One consequence has been manifest in Thailand's attitude towards treaties or convention which might be characterised as enabling the exercise in Thailand of extraterritorial jurisdiction by another country. Thailand has consistently taken the position that it will not accede to such instruments.[4] A second repercussion has been in the development of the legal framework for the exercise of direct jurisdiction by the Thai courts. The relevant provisions of domestic law, especially in the CPC, recognise the exercise of exorbitant jurisdiction by the Thai courts. This is despite the heavy caseload[5] and clogged dockets of many Thai courts. Nonetheless, provisions enabling the extraterritorial jurisdiction of the Thai courts have been promulgated in the past as a means of protecting Thailand's national interests. Such provisions empower the Thai courts to assert jurisdiction as a matter of public policy whenever Thai national interests may be at stake, regardless of whether Thailand is a natural or convenient forum for the resolution of the relevant dispute. But this public policy-oriented approach has become less widely accepted over time and a functional approach focusing on the best interests of the contentious parties is gradually superseding it. At the time of writing, an ongoing discussion within the Thai judiciary indicates a likely paradigmatic shift in viewpoint at some point in the future. The fact that the debate between a purely public policy and a more functional approach may mean Thai positive law on direct jurisdiction will be uncertain for some time. But, instead of merely describing current black letter law and practices, it is also important to bear in mind the likely trajectories that the Thai courts may take in the future when resolving questions of direct jurisdiction.

II. Sources of Direct Jurisdiction Rules, Norms and Practices

The fact that a case involves international elements will not necessarily lead to the application by the Thai court of private international law rules for establishing or declining jurisdiction. Thailand does not have a systematic structure of dealing with legal problems concerning the court's competence in cross-border matters. In practice, international cases are often subjected to domestic law and the provisions of the CPC.[6] A possible explanation may be the absence of specific provisions in Thai law covering situations having international elements. Typically, the Thai court relies on the provisions of some written law and, there being none covering the international elements of a case, will generally end up applying provisions designed for use in purely domestic cases. In actuality, whether the court references private international law rules as a

[3] See Akawat Laowonsiri, 'Thailand' in Anselmo Reyes (ed), *Recognition and Enforcement of Foreign Judgments in Civil and Commercial Matters* (Oxford, Hart Publishing, 2019) 259–60.

[4] For example, the 2005 Hague Convention on Choice of Court Agreements has been the subject of internal scrutiny by the Thai judiciary. There has, however, been resistance to accession within the government sector. The resistance has been cognizant to those working in the area normally in informal settings.

[5] For caseload statistics, see eg Office of the Judiciary, 'Annual Judicial Statistics, Thailand 2018 (BE 2561)' (*Office of Planning and Budget*, 2019) https://oppb.coj.go.th/th/content/category/detail/id/8/cid/2086/iid/143806. For a comparison with other countries, see Organisation for Economic Cooperation and Development (OECD), 'Judicial Performance and Its Determinants: A Cross-Country Perspective', (*OECD*, OECD Economic Policy Papers No 5, 2013) www.oecd.org/economy/growth/FINAL%20Civil%20Justice%20Policy%20Paper.pdf.

[6] See Pitikul Cheeramongkolpanich, *Civil Procedure Law: Books 1-2-3* (Bangkok, October Publishing House, 2019) 76–98.

basis for assuming or declining jurisdiction will frequently depend upon whether a party's legal representatives highlight the existence of international elements in a matter[7] and submit that the court should therefore apply widely accepted conflict of laws principles. If a party's lawyer failed to do so at the outset, the court will simply default to applying domestic law without any consideration (much less analysis) of cross-border jurisdictional issues. Occasionally, where a judge has had some legal education or training abroad, the court itself may of its own motion initiate an investigation into whether any private international law principles are applicable without initiation by the parties. At this point, one may ask: what is actually the pattern of judicial functioning in Thailand? Unfortunately, there is no critical or consistent mass of Thai jurisprudence on direct jurisdiction establishing any clear judicial pattern for the application or non-application of private international law principles in international civil litigation. Ideally, the operative principles of direct jurisdiction should be codified or legislated. But there are no initiatives along these lines at present.

The uncertainty just mentioned has significantly affected the way that legal professionals search for applicable law on direct jurisdiction. There is a divergence of views. Some assume that it is for the court as opposed to their responsibility to raise questions of direct jurisdiction. Others pro-actively seek to influence Thai jurisprudence by advocating for the court to adopt the approach of some foreign country with whose laws they are familiar. This would be an exercise in persuading a court to say what the law should be, instead of what it actually is.

In private international law cases, section 3 of the Conflict of Laws Act BE 2481 (1938) (CLA) stipulates that '[w]henever there is no provision in this Act or in any other laws of Thailand to govern a case of conflict of laws, the general principles of private international law shall apply'.[8] On its face, CLA section 3 seemingly mandates reference to generally accepted principles of international jurisdiction in a determination of the Thai court's jurisdiction in a case having foreign elements. However, the CLA drafting record suggests that its drafters intended to exclude procedural rules from the ambit of section 3 and envisaged the CLA as narrowly applying a choice of law issue.[9] It is possibly for this reason that the Thai Court has never relied on CLA section 3 to support the application of general private international law principles to matters of direct jurisdiction. Nonetheless, it is submitted that there is no reason to read down the clear wording of CLA section 3. The provision can and should instead be read as not merely permitting reference to general principles but requiring the same ('shall apply') where no provision of Thai law deals with an issue of direct jurisdiction.

If that is correct, upon what sources might a judge or lawyer draw for general principles of private international law relating to direct jurisdiction?

General principles of international civil litigation may be found in written materials (for example, well-established textbooks) and unwritten rules and norms (for example, custom and practice). There are four principal sources of domestic law that might provide guidance on jurisdictional and procedural rules: (1) the CPC; (2) jurisprudence (case law); (3) instruments issued by judicial authorities; and (4) special legislation.[10] Enough has already been said about the CPC

[7] See Phunthip Saisoonthorn, *Lecture on Private International Law: General Concepts of Private Relations with International Character* (Bangkok, Winyuchon, 2005) 35–45.

[8] Compare with the Thai Civil and Commercial Code BE 2468 (1925), s 4: 'Where no provision is applicable, the case shall be decided by analogy to the provision most nearly applicable and, in default of such provision, by the general principles of law.'

[9] See Prasit Piwawatanapanich, *Lecture on Private International Law* (Bangkok, Thammasat University Press, 2018) 321.

[10] State contracts between Thailand and a foreign company can contain clauses dealing with jurisdiction in the event of disputes. Whether and to what extent the court is bound by such clauses is open to discussion. See Akawat Laowonsiri,

and its limitations in international cases. Jurisprudence can supplement the provisions of the CPC. Pertinently, in the absence of specific rules, the judiciary retains a high degree of discretion in the articulation of jurisdictional and procedural principles applicable in international cases. The court may borrow not just from the rules applicable to domestic cases, but it can also consider rules from foreign jurisdictions, adapting them as necessary to the Thai context. Within bounds, the Thai courts may even ascertain or create new rules. Principles, norms and practices may also be contained in instruments enacted by judicial authorities. These can have direct and indirect effects on how the Thai court functions in international civil and commercial litigation and include Regulations of the President of the Supreme Court (ข้อบังคับประธานศาลฎีกา) and the Judges' Code of Ethics (ประมวลจริยธรรมข้าราชการตุลาการ)[11] among others. Reference might further be made to special legislation. Examples are the Act on the Establishment and Procedure of the Intellectual Property and International Trade Court BE 2539 (1996), the Act on the Establishment and Procedure of the Labour Court BE 2522 (1979), and the Juvenile and Family Court and Juvenile and Family Case Procedure Act BE 2553 (2010). Where it makes sense to do so, the Thai court can discern, and then apply by analogy to private international law questions, the principles underlying procedural rules established by special legislation. This should especially be the case when in due course the specialised courts established by such legislation have generated sufficient case law dealing with the jurisdictional and procedural aspects of cases containing foreign elements.

As for non-domestic sources, Thailand has not entered into any binding regional or international instrument. There is no treaty having binding effect on the country. The Association of Southeast Asian Nations (ASEAN) (of which Thailand is a party) may take part in developing regional rules on civil and commercial matters (including procedural matters) to facilitate trade and investment flows within the region, but ASEAN has so far not done so.[12] Nevertheless, there is a regional soft law project, the 'Asian Principles of Private International Law' (APPIL),[13] in which Thai delegates are involved and which has as its goal the identification of general principles of private international law that are or should be common to major countries in Asia.[14] Nothing in the CPC, Thai jurisprudence, or special legislation[15] prevents judges from applying procedural rules identified in APPIL to jurisdictional questions before them. Further, it is true that multilateral treaties dealing with the establishment of direct jurisdiction (for instance, the 2005 Hague Convention on Choice of Court Agreements) are not a formal source of jurisdictional or procedural rules in Thailand. This is because the country has not acceded to any multilateral treaty touching on the competence of the Thai court in civil and commercial matters. But an informal means of solving jurisdictional and procedural problems could involve an examination of the norms and practices in relevant multilateral instruments. Conventions would then function as soft law instruments, evidencing a consensus of states on best practice in relation to private international law issues, including questions of direct jurisdiction.

Diagonal Contract between Foreign Tech Company and Sovereign State: Extending the Spectrum of Party Autonomy (Bangkok, Thammasat University Faculty of Law, 2021).

[11] The Judges' Code of Ethics was issued by the Judicial Commission. The Code does not have direct, as opposed to indirect, effects on judicial functioning in the international civil and commercial cases. It does not provide guidelines for exercising jurisdiction in international cases, but instead identifies best practices expected from judges. This can concern direct jurisdiction, for example, the judicial role in respecting choice of court agreements or declining jurisdiction on grounds of *forum non conveniens* in cases containing foreign elements.

[12] See https://agreement.asean.org/.

[13] Weizuo Chen and Gerald Goldstein, 'The Asian Principles of Private International Law: Objectives, Contents, Structure and Selected Topics on Choice of Law' (2017) 13 *Journal of Private International Law* 411–34.

[14] The Thai delegates to the APPIL Project include Prof Dr Kanapon Chanhom and the author.

[15] Intellectual Property and International Trade Court Act BE 2539 (1996), s 7 confers a discretion on the court to accept or decline jurisdiction.

III. Grounds for Assuming and Declining Jurisdiction

There are general grounds of jurisdiction in sections 2 to 5 of the CPC. These refer to domestic civil and commercial cases, but they have been applied to cases having an international element. Since the CPC's enactment in BE 2477 (1934), amendments in BE 2543 (2000) and BE 2558 (2015) have expanded, rather than reduced the general grounds of jurisdiction. The relevant sections read (in translation):[16]

Section 2

No plaint may be submitted to a Court unless:

(1) having regard to the nature of the plaint and the grade of the Court, it appears that such Court is competent to try and adjudicate the case under the provisions of law governing the organization of Courts of Justice, and

(2) having regard to the plaint, it appears that the case is within the territorial jurisdiction of such Court under the provisions of this Code governing venue and also under the provisions of law fixing the territorial jurisdiction of Courts.

Section 3

For the purpose in the submission of the plaint:

(1) in the case where the cause of action occurs in the Thai vessel or aeroplane outside the Kingdom, the Civil Court shall be the Court of the territorial jurisdiction,

(2) in the case where the defendant is not domiciled within the Kingdom,

 (a) if the defendant is ever domiciled at any place of the Kingdom within the prescription of two years before the date of submitting the plaint, it shall be deemed that such place is domicile of the defendant,

 (b) if the defendant carries on or ever carried on the whole or some part of transaction within the Kingdom, irrespective of himself or agent or by having any person for being in continuance with such transaction within the Kingdom, it shall be deemed that the place used or ever used to carry on such transaction or continuance, or the place which is residence of the agent or continuous person in the date of submitting the plaint or before such prescription of two years, is domicile of the defendant.

Section 4

Unless otherwise provided by law,

(1) the plaints shall be submitted to the Court within the territorial jurisdiction of which the defendant is domiciled or to the Court within the territorial jurisdiction of which the cause of action arose, whether the defendant shall have domicile within the Kingdom or not.

(2) the request shall be submitted to the Court within the territorial jurisdiction of which the cause of action arose or to the Court within the territorial jurisdiction of which the applicant is domiciled.

Section 4 bis

The plaint concerning immovable property, or any right or interest concerning immovable property shall be submitted to the Court within the territorial jurisdiction of which the immovable property is situated, whether the defendant shall have domicile within the Kingdom or not, or to the Court within the territorial jurisdiction of which the defendant is domiciled.

[16] The excerpt is from a widely cited English translation of the CPC, available online: www.imolin.org/doc/amlid/Thailand_The%20Civil%20Procedure%20Code.pdf.

Section 4 ter

The other plaint as provided other than the Section 4 bis, which the defendant is not domiciled within the Kingdom and the cause of action is not arose within the Kingdom, if the plaintiff has Thai nation[ality] or domicile within the Kingdom, it shall be submitted to the Civil Court or to the Court within the territorial jurisdiction of which the plaintiff is domiciled.

In the case of the plaint according to the first paragraph, if the defendant has the property liable to execution within the Kingdom, irrespective of temporization or permanence, the plaintiff shall submit the plaint to the Court within the territorial jurisdiction of which such property is situated.

Section 4 quarter

The request appointing an administrator of the estate shall be submitted to the Court within the territorial jurisdiction of which the *de cujus*[17] is domiciled at the time of the *de cujus* to be dead.

In the case of the *de cujus* is not domiciled within the Kingdom, it shall be submitted to the Court within the territorial jurisdiction of which such estate is situated.

Section 4 quinque

The request of cancelling the resolution of meeting or general meeting of the juristic person, the request of dissolving the juristic person, the request of appointing or removing the liquidator of the juristic person, or other request concerning to the juristic person, shall be submitted to the Court within the territorial jurisdiction of which the principal office is situated.

Section 4 sex

The request concerning the property situated within the Kingdom, or the request, provided that the Court shall issue order according to such request, it will result [a] procurance or [a] dismissal of procurance of the property to be situated within the Kingdom, which the cause of action does not arise within the Kingdom, shall be submitted to the Court within the territorial jurisdiction of which the aforesaid property is situated.

Section 5

In the case of the plaint or request may be submitted to the two or more Courts, irrespective of being by reason of the domicile of the person, the situation of property, the place to arise the cause of action or having the several claims, and if the subject matter of the case are connected, the plaintiff or applicant may submit the plaint or request to any one of such Courts.

Section 4(1) provides for the situs of a cause of action or the defendant's domicile[18] as grounds for a Thai court to assume jurisdiction. Section 4 *bis* adopts the situs of immovable property as a basis for jurisdiction. The provision covers cases involving any question concerning land in Thailand, including questions of rights and interests over such land. Section 4 *ter* is extremely wide in ambit. It enables a Thai national to sue a non-resident defendant (whether a Thai national or not) before the Thai court, despite the cause of action having arisen outside Thailand. On their terms, sections 4 *bis* and 4 *ter* would appear to be mutually exclusive. If a plaintiff has a claim relating to land in Thailand, then it would follow that the plaintiff's cause of action arises within (and not outside) Thailand, so that section 4 *ter* would be inapplicable. Sections 4 *quarter*, 4 *quinque* and 4 *sex* are typically used in non-contentious litigation. Section 5 stipulates that, where a party is able to file a suit in more than one court, that party may commence an action in any of the relevant courts.

Mention has been made of specialised courts. These are bound by the jurisdictional rules of the special legislation establishing them.[19] Some special jurisdictional rules are applied by the

[17] That is, the deceased.

[18] Under Thai law, a person's nationality is usually treated as that person's domicile.

[19] See eg Act on the Establishment and Procedure of the Labour Court BE 2522 (1979), s 8; Act on the Establishment and Procedure of the Intellectual Property and International Trade Court BE 2539 (1996), ss 7, 9; Act on the Establishment

courts of general jurisdiction to specific types of cases, for example, cases concerning consumer protection. Most of the legislation setting up specialised courts or special procedures for specific cases do not contain jurisdictional rules for the resolution of conflicting claims to jurisdiction. The legislation simply contains broad provisions. For instance, section 7 of the Act on the Establishment and Procedure of the Intellectual Property and International Trade Court BE 2539 (1996) merely provides that 'the … Court shall have jurisdiction over …'[20] without specifying criteria for establishing or declining jurisdiction. It has instead been common practice for specialised courts to refer by analogy to sections 2 to 5 of the CPC for assuming or declining jurisdiction.[21] It is submitted that this would be a valid means of determining jurisdiction in domestic and international cases.

On choice of court agreements whereby the parties designate the Thai court as the forum to resolve their disputes, there are instances of the Thai court assessing whether Thailand is the *forum conveniens*.[22] In such instances, Thailand has been held to be the *forum conveniens* because the evidence (including witnesses) was located there and dismissal of the claim would lead to unfair consequences. As for *lis alibi pendens*, it is submitted that guidance may be obtained from section 173(1) of the CPC.[23] The court could broadly interpret this section as a long-arm provision, empowering it to stop a party from commencing (or proceeding with) a claim in a foreign jurisdiction when the same matter is already before the Thai court or enabling the court to decline jurisdiction where a similar action is already being litigated before a foreign court. On when precisely a court might grant an anti-suit injunction restraining the bringing or continuation of proceedings in another country, there has so far been no case in Thailand. The author submits that the operative principle should be that a party enjoys the freedom to initiate a claim in a jurisdiction of his or her choice as long as the exercise of such right is not abusive in the sense that there are cogent (as opposed to purely tactical) reasons for so doing.

IV. Immunities from Jurisdiction

Certain categories of complaint are generally dismissed by the Thai court. These complaints are those brought against entities and persons enjoying immunity from suit under international law. Such entities are foreign states, international organisations (IOs), diplomats and IO officers. The claims brought against an IO, a diplomat and/or foreign state representative can be dismissed if the Thai court is satisfied that the requirements in relevant legislation have been met. Such statutes include the Privileges and Immunity Act BE 2527 (1984), and the Privileges and Immunity for International Organizations and International Conferences in Thailand Act BE 2561 (2017). It should be noted that the immunity from domestic jurisdiction provided by these laws is basically accorded to diplomats and officers of IOs in relation to the performance of their duties as representatives of sovereign states or IOs. Immunity from criminal prosecution is generally accorded

and Procedure of the Bankruptcy Court BE 2542 (1999), ss 7, 9; Act on the Establishment of Administrative Courts and Administrative Court Procedure BE 2542 (1999), ss 8, 9; Juvenile and Family Court and Juvenile and Family Case Procedure Act BE 2553 (2010), ss 10, 11.

[20] In cases of doubt, the President of the Supreme Court can resolve problems of conflicting jurisdiction pursuant to s 9 of the same Act. This actually leaves the President with considerable discretion in the subject matter.

[21] SCJ 9524/2544 is an example of a specialised court relying on CPC, ss 2–5.

[22] See Supreme Court Judgments (SCJ) 9524/2544, 3537/2546 and 3882/2549.

[23] CPC, s 173 provides: 'From the time of the entry of the plaint, the case is pending and, in consequence thereof, (1) the plaintiff is not allowed to enter the same plaint in the same Court or in another Court …'

even though the wrongdoer has committed the crime outside of his or her official capacity. In contrast, immunity from civil suit is only available when a person has acted in his or her official capacity. In other words, immunity from civil suit is not accorded to a diplomat or IO officer for acts done in a purely private capacity. Similarly, state immunity in civil and commercial matters is by nature more restrictive than in criminal ones where it tends to be more absolute. There is though some uncertainty about the correctness of the last proposition as a matter of Thai law, because Thailand does not have specific legislation on sovereign immunity and the court simply applies general rules of international law. This leaves the court with considerable latitude when delineating the extent of state immunity. Although many jurisdictions do not hold state immunity to be absolute, as opposed to restrictive, in civil and commercial matters,[24] some countries had adopted the position that immunity is absolute. In a recent case a Thai businessman sued the US before the Chiang Mai court for damage resulting from COVID-19.[25] The court dismissed the case on the principle of absolute immunity, although the claim was characterised at the outset as a civil dispute. In civil suits against state-owned enterprises, it is unclear how whether the courts will construe Thai law as conferring absolute or restrictive immunity.

[24] Alfred Verdross and Bruno Simma, *Universelles Völkerrecht: Theorie und Praxis* (Berlin, Duncker & Humblot, 1984) 762–74.

[25] See the press release of the Chiang Mai Provincial Court (in Thai), available online: https://cmic.coj.go.th/th/content/category/detail/id/22/iid/200582.

15

Sri Lanka

RAMESH FERNANDO

I. Introduction

A. Historical Background

The legal system of Sri Lanka is a by-product of its rich and diverse cultures, religions and its colonisation. The population consists of Sinhalese, Tamils, Muslims and other ethnic groups, professing different faiths, mainly Buddhism, Hinduism, Islam and Christianity. Officially, Sri Lanka has a mixed legal system, similar to that of South Africa. The system comprises civil and common law traditions, as Sri Lanka was initially a colony of the Dutch and subsequently of the British. Prior to colonisation, the population abided by their respective cultural and religious laws. Some customary laws continue to be in force, although significantly diminished in usage. These include the Kandyan, Thesavalamai, Islamic and Mukkuvar[1] personal laws, as well as Buddhist and Hindu ecclesiastical laws. The Portuguese were the first European power to arrive in Sri Lanka in 1505–6, but they did not aim at territorial conquest and did not establish dominance over the politics of South Asia.[2] Accordingly, they did not introduce their own system of law into Sri Lanka.[3] In contrast, the Dutch, who by 1658 had completely expelled the Portuguese from the island, introduced an elaborate court structure and applied Roman-Dutch law as a residuary law, where local customary laws were silent on an issue at hand or were considered unsuitable.[4] The English East India Company took control of the island from the Dutch in 1796. Although the British established their own system of civil and judicial administration, they pledged to continue applying local customary laws and the residual Roman-Dutch law. Lord Mansfield in *Campbell v Hall*,[5] referring to the Articles of Capitulation pertaining to Grenada, considered that 'the laws of a conquered country continue to be in force, until they are altered by the conqueror'. The judgment considered the Articles of Capitulation to be 'sacred and inviolable according to their true intent and meaning.' This principle was given

[1] Mukkuvar law was arguably abrogated by the Matrimonial Rights and Inheritance Ordinance No 15 of 1876, which was made applicable to all Sri Lankans.

[2] Kingsley Muthumuni de Silva, *A History of Sri Lanka* (Colombo, Vijitha Yapa Publications, 2005) 147.

[3] LJ Mark Cooray, *An Introduction to the Legal System of Sri Lanka* 2nd edn (Pannipitiya, Stamford Lake Publications, 2003) 4.

[4] ibid 5.

[5] *Campbell v Hall* (1774) 1 Cowp 204, 209–10; 98 ER 1045, 1047.

effect in Sri Lanka through the Proclamation of 23 September 1799 by Governor Sir Francis North[6] and the Proclamation of 2 March 1815.[7] However, local laws were applied by judges trained in English law who were unfamiliar with Roman-Dutch law or the customary laws which they were supposed to apply. It has been suggested that it was due to this unfamiliarity or due to dissatisfaction with the state of customary, that the British administration introduced English law to areas of law previously governed by Roman-Dutch law.[8] Eventually, English law occupied a greater presence in Sri Lanka through legislation and judicial law-making which modified or repealed previous Roman-Dutch law.[9]

During the British occupation, Sri Lanka was the beneficiary of modern legislation through: (1) the copying of statutory enactments passed in the UK; (2) the codification of principles established by English case law; (3) the incorporation of English law in particular areas by reference; (4) the incorporation of English law in the event of a *casus omissus*; and (5) the extension before 1948 of Acts of the UK Parliament to Sri Lanka as a consequence of its colonial status.[10] Examples of relevant enactments include the Sale of Goods Ordinance No 11 of 1896, the Bills of Exchange Ordinance No 25 of 1927, the Penal Code Ordinance No 2 of 1883, and the Evidence Ordinance No 14 of 1895. Significantly, in the absence of specific enactments, the Civil Law Ordinance introduced English law with respect to the law of partnerships, corporations, banks and banking, principals and agents, carriers by land, and life and fire insurance.[11] The Reciprocal Enforcement of Judgments Ordinance,[12] the only enactment relating to the enforcement of foreign judgments currently in force in Sri Lanka, is another example of important legislation received in Sri Lankan law during the British occupation. Following independence in 1948 and especially since it emerged free from dominion status in 1972, Sri Lanka has been lagging behind in updating its laws to match evolving global trends. For instance, it was only in 2016 that a Right to Information Act[13] was passed in Sri Lanka, 15 years after the Freedom of Information Act 2000 came into force in the UK. A Data Protection Bill was only finalised in 2019 and is yet to come into force, although the UK enacted its first Data Protection Act in 1984. This lag in adapting the existing legal infrastructure to cater to modern day demands is also evident in the sphere of private international law. Furthermore, the judiciary has been slow to depart from established legal principles, even where these principles have long since been repositioned in other jurisdictions to address contemporary issues brought before the court by modern day well-informed, well-advised and resourceful litigants.

[6] The Proclamation of 23 September 1799 stated that 'the temporary Administration of Justice and Police in the Settlements of the Island […] should, as nearly as the circumstances will permit, be exercised by us, in conformity to the laws and Institutions that subsisted under the ancient Government of the United Provinces, subject to such deviations in consequence of sudden and unforeseen emergencies, or to such expedients and useful alterations as may render a departure therefrom, either absolutely necessary and unavoidable, or evidently beneficial and desirable'.

[7] The Proclamation of 2 March 1815 which followed the annexation of the Kandy, the last Kingdom of Sri Lanka, guaranteed 'to all classes of people the safety of their persons and property with their civil rights and immunities according to the laws, institutions and customs established and in force amongst them'.

[8] Anton Cooray, 'Oriental and Occidental Laws in Harmonious Co-existence: The Case of Trusts in Sri Lanka' (2008) 12(1) *Electronic Journal of Comparative Law* 2, available online: www.ejcl.org/121/art121-5.pdf.

[9] ibid 3.

[10] See de Silva (n 2) 31–37.

[11] Ordinance No 5 of 1852, s 3.

[12] Ordinance No 41 of 1921.

[13] Act No 12 of 2016.

B. Court Structure

Sri Lanka's courts system, largely modelled after the British system, consists of various tribunals, including the Labour Tribunal, the Magistrate's Courts, District Courts, High Courts (including the Commercial High Court and the Civil Appellate High Courts), the Court of Appeal and the Supreme Court. The Labour Tribunal has jurisdiction to hear applications pertaining to the termination of employment contracts, issues on payment or forfeiture of gratuity and matters relating to the terms or conditions of employment.[14] The Magistrates' Courts exercise original jurisdiction over criminal offences,[15] but this jurisdiction is restricted to minor offences as a Magistrate's Court is only empowered to impose a maximum prison sentence which does not exceed two years or a fine that does not exceed 1,500 rupees.[16] The District Court, within its judicial district, has unlimited original jurisdiction in all civil, revenue, trust, insolvency and testamentary matters[17] and also functions as the Family Court. The High Court, exercises original criminal jurisdiction and has power to impose any sentence or other penalty as prescribed by law.[18] The High Court has jurisdiction to hear, try and determine all prosecutions in respect of any offence committed by any person wholly or partly in Sri Lanka, in its territorial waters or air space, offences of piracy committed on the high seas, offences committed on board or in relation to any ship or aircraft registered in Sri Lanka, or, any offence, committed by a citizen of Sri Lanka in any place outside Sri Lanka.[19] The High Court also has appellate and revisionary jurisdiction in respect of convictions, sentences and orders entered or imposed by Magistrates' Courts.[20] Currently, the High Court acts as an appellate body to hear appeals on questions of law arising out of Orders handed down by the Labour Tribunal,[21] although there have been calls for a specialised Labour Appeals High Court to be established to hear appeals from the Labour Tribunals.

The High Court of the Provinces (Special Provisions) Act No 10 of 1996 section 5A, added by the High Court (Special Provisions) (Amendment) Act No 54 of 2006, granted appellate and revisionary jurisdiction to provincial Civil Appellate High Courts for the correction of all errors in fact or law pertaining to any judgment, decree or order delivered by the District Court. Appeals lie directly to the Supreme Court.[22] The 1996 Act established a specialised High Court (referred to as the Commercial High Court) with full jurisdiction to hear and determine all actions referred to in the First Schedule to the Act. These include causes of action arising out of commercial transactions in which the debt, damage or demand is for a sum exceeding 20 million rupees[23] and proceedings brought under the Code of Intellectual Property Act No 52 of 1979. Applications made under the Admiralty Jurisdiction Act No 40 of 1983 are now heard by the Commercial High Court. Applications for enforcement,[24] setting aside of an arbitral award,[25] or the recognition and enforcement of foreign arbitral awards[26] must also be made to the Commercial High Court.

[14] Industrial Disputes Act No 43 of 1950, s 31B (1).
[15] Judicature Act No 2 of 1978, s 30.
[16] Code of Criminal Procedure Act No 15 of 1979, s 14.
[17] Judicature Act, s 19.
[18] ibid, s 13.
[19] See Judicature Act, s 9; High Court of the Provinces (Special Provisions) Act No 19 of 1990 (as amended), s 3.
[20] Constitution, Art 154P(3).
[21] High Court of the Provinces (Special Provisions) Act, s 31C(2).
[22] High Court of the Provinces (Special Provisions) (Amendment) Act No 54 of 2006, s 2, adding s 5C to the Act (n 21).
[23] Gazette Extraordinary No 2112/33 (28 February 2019).
[24] Arbitration Act No 11 of 1995, s 31.
[25] ibid, s 32.
[26] ibid, s 33.

The only Commercial High Court so far established is in the Western Province, where Sri Jayawardenapura Kotte (the administrative capital) and Colombo (the commercial capital) are situated. Appeals against judgments of the Commercial High Court are referred to the Supreme Court.[27] The Court of Appeal has appellate jurisdiction for the correction of all errors in fact or in law committed by the High Court in the exercise of its appellate or original jurisdiction or by any Court of First Instance, tribunal or other institution.[28] The Court of Appeal has power to affirm, reverse, correct or modify any order, decree or sentence according to law; to give directions to a Court of First Instance, tribunal or other institution; or to order a new trial.[29] Significantly, the Court of Appeal has jurisdiction to issue writs of *certiorari*, *prohibition*, *procedendo*, *mandamus* and *quo warranto* against a judge of any Court of First Instance or tribunal or other institution or any other person[30] and to issue writs of *habeas corpus*.[31] The Supreme Court is the highest and final superior court. It has final appellate jurisdiction[32] and jurisdiction on matters such as the constitutionality of Bills of Parliament,[33] the protection of fundamental rights,[34] and election petitions.[35] It has consultative jurisdiction in relation to opinions sought by the President of Sri Lanka[36] and jurisdiction in respect of breaches of Parliamentary privilege.[37]

II. Jurisdiction *in personam*

A. General Principles

The general guiding principles of jurisdiction are set out in the Civil Procedure Code (CPC). It provides that:

> subject to the pecuniary or other limitations prescribed by any law, action shall be instituted in the court within the local limits of whose jurisdiction –
>
> (a) a party defendant resides; or
> (b) the land in respect of which the action is brought lies or is situated in whole or in part; or
> (c) the cause of action arises; or
> (d) the contract sought to be enforced was made.[38]

As the provision indicates, the above must be read with and subject to other law which specifically lay down the limits of jurisdiction of each organ within the court structure of Sri Lanka. However, it provides the basis for a Sri Lankan court hearing a matter where there is some clear connection with Sri Lanka. This is in contrast to the position under English common law rules on jurisdiction, whereby a party may fall within the jurisdiction of the English courts provided they have been properly served with a claim form within the jurisdiction, where the defendant has submitted to the English court's jurisdiction, or where there has been service of a claim form

[27] High Court of the Provinces (Special Provisions) Act, s 5.
[28] Constitution, Art 137.
[29] ibid, Art 139.
[30] ibid, Art 140.
[31] ibid, Art 141.
[32] ibid, Art 118.
[33] ibid, Art 120.
[34] ibid, Art 126.
[35] ibid, Art 130.
[36] ibid, Art 129.
[37] ibid, Art 131.
[38] Civil Procedure Code Ordinance No 2 of 1889 (as amended), s 9.

out of the jurisdiction under rule 6.36 of the English Civil Procedure Rules.[39] The English courts have traditionally been unconcerned whether the parties or their dispute have a connection with England, but simply focused on have whether the defendant can be served.[40] As the House of Lords has held, at common law 'whoever is served with the King's writ and can be compelled consequently to submit to the decree made is a person over whom the courts have jurisdiction'.[41] A Sri Lankan court, on the other hand, is unlikely to exercise jurisdiction beyond national borders in a situation where none of the abovementioned factors in the CPC connect a dispute to Sri Lanka. This is regardless of the law governing the action, whether a claim in tort, property, contract, labour or commercial law. The only exception to this is in divorce cases as discussed below.

B. *Forum non conveniens*

In England, courts allow service of a claim form on a defendant abroad based on the doctrine of *forum conveniens*. As recognised by the House of Lords in *Spiliada Maritime Corp v Cansulex Ltd*,[42] this is a discretionary power to stay actions where the defendant is able to establish that there is some other available forum, having jurisdiction, which is the more appropriate forum for the trial of an action. The appropriate forum is determined by identifying the country with which the action has the most real and substantial connection. This is subject to the requirements of justice. These may dictate that a stay should not be granted even though there is a more appropriate forum elsewhere. Sri Lankan courts have not adopted a doctrine of *forum non conveniens* and it is questionable whether the Sri Lankan court would issue a stay of proceedings in a situation where a plaintiff has properly invoked jurisdiction in accordance with the CPC and other applicable statutes.[43]

C. *Lis alibi pendens*

Lis alibi pendens refers to the situation where there is simultaneous litigation involving the same parties on the same issues in two different countries. Such simultaneous litigation is undesirable for several reasons, especially due to the possibility of having two irreconcilable judgments.[44] Although *lis pendens* is recognised under Article 29 of Brussels I Regulation (recast)[45] where concurrent proceedings subsist in two EU member states, English common law does not have its own doctrine of *lis alibi pendens*. Instead, the possibility of parallel proceedings is a relevant consideration when the English courts consider whether to grant a stay of proceedings under the doctrine of *forum non conveniens*.[46] Although the doctrine of *lis pendens*

[39] Paul Torremans and others (eds), *Cheshire, North & Fawcett Private International Law* 15th edn (Oxford, Oxford University Press, 2017) 324.

[40] ibid 323.

[41] *John Russell and Co Ltd v Cayzer, Irvine and Co Ltd* [1916] 2 AC 298 (HL) 302.

[42] *Spiliada Maritime Corp v Cansulex Ltd* [1987] AC 460 (HL).

[43] See *Murugappan Chettiar v Nadarajan Chettiar* (1952) 55 NLR 104 (SC) 106, where Gratiaen J considered staying (but ultimately did not stay) local proceedings where there were parallel proceedings in India.

[44] *The Abidin Daver* [1984] AC 398 (HL).

[45] Regulation (EU) No 1215/2012 of the European Parliament and of the Council of 12 December 2012 on jurisdiction and the recognition and enforcement of judgments in civil and commercial matters [2012] OJ L351/1.

[46] *Cleveland Museum of Art v Capricorn Art International SA* [1990] 2 Lloyd's Rep 166 (QB).

under Roman-Dutch law prevails in Sri Lanka, it must be distinguished from the doctrine of *lis alibi pendens* as referred to above. *Lis pendens* under Sri Lankan law is a registrable document that serves as a notice to the public (interested parties) that there is an ongoing suit in relation to particular land.[47] The CPC does not make express provision for the stay of proceedings in general, irrespective of whether concurrent proceedings are concerned within or outside Sri Lanka. However, the courts have worked around this lacuna by granting stays by reference to the courts' inherent powers under the CPC,[48] where there are concurrent local proceedings between the same parties on identical issues.[49] Similarly, there have been older cases where the courts have considered the possibility of granting stays pending the decision of a foreign court in a parallel action. This, too, has been in reliance on the inherent power granted to courts to 'make such orders as may be necessary for the ends of justice to prevent abuse of the process of the court'. In *Raman Chettiar v Vyraven Chettiar*,[50] Wijewardene J opined (at [375]):

> I have no doubt that this Court has the power to make an order staying an action in a Court in Ceylon pending the final decision in another action between the parties where the matters in dispute in the first case are directly and substantially in issue in the second case *(vide* Civil Procedure Code, section 839). But as these inherent powers are very wide and indefinable a Court has to guard against an arbitrary exercise of such powers.

Referring to English law, the court laid down guiding principles on granting a stay (which were cited with approval by Gratiaen J in *Murugappan Chettiar v Nadarajan Chettiar*):[51]

(1) The burden is on the party asking for the interference of court to prove that he is doubly vexed by reason of two actions being brought against him.
(2) Where the two actions are brought in the same country, there is a *prima facie* presumption of an intent to cause vexation.
(3) Where the party is sued in one country and also in a foreign country, a court will not presume an intent to cause vexation –
    (a) in the absence of evidence that the plaintiff cannot obtain an additional advantage in continuing both his actions; or
    (b) from the mere fact of inconvenience or additional expenditure caused to a party; or
    (c) from the fact that by staying one action less evidence would have to be ultimately led in the first action.

In *Murugappan Chettiar*, Gratiaen J additionally approved Scott LJ's dictum in *St Pierre v South American Stores (Gath and Chaves) Ltd*:[52]

(1) A mere balance of convenience is not a sufficient ground for depriving a plaintiff of the advantages of prosecuting his action in an English court if it is otherwise properly brought. The right of access to the King's Court must not be lightly refused.
(2) In order to justify a stay, two conditions must be satisfied:
    (a) the defendant must satisfy the court that the continuance of the action would work an injustice to him because it would be oppressive or vexatious to him or would be an abuse of the process of the court in some other way; and
    (b) the stay must not cause an injustice to the plaintiff.

[47] Registration of Documents Ordinance No 23 of 1927 (as amended), s 11.
[48] CPC, s 839.
[49] *Selvadurai v Raja* (1940) 41 NLR 423 (SC).
[50] *Raman Chettiar v Vyraven Chettiar* (1940) 41 NLR 371 (SC).
[51] *Murugappan Chettiar* (n 43) 105.
[52] *St Pierre v South American Stores (Gath and Chaves) Ltd* [1936] 1 KB 382, 398.

In both *Raman Chettiar* and *Murugappan Chettiar*, the courts refused to grant stays of the local proceedings and exhibited a high degree of caution in taking cognisance of the fact that a stay would have the effect of denying a litigant the 'privilege of obtaining legal redress in proceedings over which our courts are vested with jurisdiction'.[53] Although there have not been more recent reported cases where the courts have considered *lis alibi pendens*, given the authorities cited above, Sri Lankan courts would in principle consider staying local proceedings pending the decision of a foreign court. But they would require proof of oppressive or vexatious conduct to a standard that is higher than a balance of convenience, the standard applicable in applications for injunctions.[54]

D. Anti-suit Injunctions

Anti-suit injunctions, commonly granted by the English courts, operate *in personam*, and are aimed at restraining a person from proceeding with an action in a foreign court at the same time as pending substantive proceedings in England to which the person is a party.[55] The English Court of Appeal[56] has interpreted the judgment of the House of Lords in *Turner v Grovit*[57] as laying down two categories of cases where an anti-suit injunction would be granted, namely: (1) to prevent unconscionable conduct by the party to be restrained; or (2) where the foreign proceedings breach a jurisdiction agreement. There is no express provision in the CPC for the granting of such anti-suit injunctions by the Sri Lankan courts and there are no reported cases where such injunctions have been granted in the exercise of the courts' inherent powers.

Although the courts in Sri Lanka have not adopted the *Spiliada* principles or the doctrine of *forum non conveniens*, and although there are no known cases of anti-suit injunctions being granted, it cannot be said that this is because the courts' hands are tied due to the lack of statutory empowerment. The courts in Sri Lanka are not prevented from creatively and innovatively adopting such private international law principles, merely because the CPC or other statute does not make express provision for this. As seen in the cases discussed previously, the Sri Lankan courts have consistently relied on their inherent powers where there have been no express provision covering the issue. Sri Lankan courts have followed the principle laid down by the High Court of Allahabad (India) in *Narsingh Das v Mangal Dubey*:[58]

> I may therefore at the outset state that according to my view of the rules of construction applicable to statutes like the Civil Procedure Code, the Courts are not to act upon the principle that every procedure is to be taken as prohibited unless it is expressly provided for by the Code, but on the converse principle that every procedure is to be understood as permissible till is shown to be prohibited by the law. As a matter of general principle, prohibitions cannot be presumed …[59]

Therefore, in principle, should the need arise, the courts of Sri Lanka are equipped to meet the modern demands of private international law with their existing means.

[53] See *Murugappan Chettiar* (n 43) 106.
[54] *Felix Dias Bandaranayake v The State Film Corporation* [1981] 2 Sri LR 287 (CA) 303 (Soza J).
[55] *Masri v Consolidated Contractors International Company SAL* [2008] EWCA Civ 625, [2009] QB 503.
[56] *Sabah Shipyard (Pakistan) Ltd v The Islamic Republic of Pakistan* [2002] EWCA Civ 1643 [39]–[40].
[57] *Turner v Grovit* [2001] UKHL 65, [2002] 1 WLR 107.
[58] *Narsingh Das v Mangal Dubey* (1883) ILR 5 All 163.
[59] See *Hevavitharana v Themis de Silva* (1961) 63 NLR 68 (SC); *Atapattu v People's Bank* [1997] 1 Sri LR 208 (SC); *Forbes & Walker Tea Brokers v Maligaspe* [1998] 2 Sri LR 378 (CA); *Aryaratne v Laksiri Fernando* [2004] 1 Sri LR 184 (CA).

E. Interim Remedies

A plaintiff is able to seek an interlocutory injunction from the court where the defendant, during the pendency of an action and prior to judgment, commits an act in violation of the plaintiff's rights in respect of the subject matter which may render the judgment ineffectual or where the defendant threatens[60] (or is about) to remove or dispose of property with intent to defraud the plaintiff.[61] Injunctions can take the form of orders restraining a person from committing an act or a nuisance. Exceptionally, they may be mandatory injunctions which compel the performance of a positive act. There has been some controversy as to whether section 54(1)(c) of the Judicature Act allows the courts to grant mandatory injunctions compelling the performance of an act, as the provision merely refers to 'restraining' defendants. However, as Weeramantry comments,[62] Indian courts have exercised the power, albeit rarely, to grant mandatory injunctions even though the Indian Civil Procedure Code only uses the word 'refrain'. Further, the Sri Lankan Civil Procedure Code[63] provides that courts are able to grant orders commanding a person to do any act. This is reflected in the decision of the Court of Appeal in *Peiris v Perera*.[64] Mandatory injunctions are usually granted only where the injury done to the plaintiff cannot be estimated and can only be sufficiently compensated for by damages.[65] A defendant in an action, who has set up a claim in reconvention (essentially, a related counterclaim) in his answer is also able to apply for injunctions.[66] The procedure for applying for an injunction is provided in CPC Chapter XLVIII.[67] When considering the grant of an injunction the court applies a sequential test and inquires: (1) whether the plaintiff has made out a strong prima facie case of infringement or imminent infringement of a legal right;[68] (2) where the balance of convenience lies;[69] and (3) whether equitable considerations favour the grant of an injunction.[70] An important bar on the District Court's power to grant injunctions is contained in the Interpretation Ordinance.[71] As re-affirmed by the courts,[72] no injunctions may be granted against the state or a public officer in any circumstances whatsoever. However, this does not prevent the Court of Appeal from issuing writs to restrain administrative authorities from proceeding with a particular course of action.[73]

F. Choice of Court Agreements

There are only a few reported judgments where the Sri Lankan courts have considered jurisdiction clauses which operate to oust the jurisdiction of the courts of Sri Lanka. Most of the judgments relate to arbitration, and not jurisdiction, clauses. The Arbitration Act provides

[60] Judicature Act, s 54(1)(b).
[61] ibid, s 54(1)(c).
[62] Christopher Gregory Weeramantry, *The Law of Contracts* (Pannipitiya, Stamford Lake Publications, 1967) 1004.
[63] CPC, s 217(e).
[64] *Peiris v Perera* [2002] 2 Sri LR 128 (CA) 130.
[65] See Weeramantry (n 62) 1005.
[66] See Judicature Act, s 54(2).
[67] CPC, ss 662–67.
[68] *Jinadasa v Weerasinghe* (1929) 31 NLR 33; *Felix Dias Bandaranayake* (n 54); *Amerasekera v Mitsui Co Ltd* [1993] 1 Sri LR 22 (SC); *Free Lanka Trading Co v Bank of Ceylon* [1996] 2 Sri LR 231 (CA).
[69] *Felix Dias Bandaranayake* (n 54).
[70] CA LA No 16/2006 (13 January 2010) (Chitrasiri J).
[71] Act No 18 of 1972 (as amended by Act No 29 of 1974), s 24.
[72] *Harsha P de Silva v Attorney General* CA Application 79/93 (19 July 1993).
[73] *Environmental Foundation Ltd v The Land Commissioner* [1993] 1 Sri LR 41 (CA).

that where a party to an arbitration agreement institutes proceedings, the court shall have no jurisdiction to hear and determine such matter if the other party objects to the court exercising jurisdiction in respect of such matter.[74] In relation to such arbitration agreements, the courts have expressed willingness to uphold clauses which oust the jurisdiction of the courts, if such clauses are agreements which make an arbitrator's award a condition precedent to any right of action under the contract and not bare arbitration agreements which provide for arbitration as a mere matter of procedure not excluding a party's right of action before a court.[75] However, in another case, which also involved an arbitration clause contained in a bill of lading, the Supreme Court made reference to exclusive jurisdiction clauses which oust the jurisdiction of local courts, and stated that:[76]

> Usually stay of local proceedings is sought in favour of a foreign jurisdiction where the dispute arises out of a contract which contains an exclusive jurisdiction clause and Courts generally uphold such clause on the basis that such clauses represent the agreement of the parties.

In the same case, the court concluded that the arbitration clause in a bill of lading cannot constitute a valid arbitration agreement which has the effect of ousting the jurisdiction of the courts, because such a clause could not be considered a clause which was negotiated and one where contractual obligations were undertaken between parties of equal bargaining power. In the case, the court also considered that the bill of lading contained an English governing law clause and, since English law and the law of Sri Lanka were similar in areas such as commercial law, banking and international law, there would be no prejudice to the defendant by the High Court of Colombo exercising jurisdiction. Further, it is important to note the Court of Appeal's decision in *Colombo Commercial Fertilizer v Motor Vessel 'SCI Mumbai'*,[77] in relation to arbitration clauses that exclude the jurisdiction of courts. In the case, a jurisdictional objection was raised based on an arbitration clause incorporated in the bill of lading. The High Court judge upheld the objection on the basis that, although the Admiralty Jurisdiction Act[78] confers Admiralty jurisdiction on the High Court 'notwithstanding anything to the contrary in any other law,' when there is an arbitration agreement, it is best practice to respect party autonomy. The High Court relied on the judgment of the Court of Appeal in *Scarlet Shipping Co Ltd v Mettalloyd Ltd*.[79] However, in *SCI Mumbai*, the Court of Appeal disagreed with the High Court. It considered that the Admiralty Jurisdiction Act, which came into existence prior to the Arbitration Act, was a special provision relating to Admiralty matters, unlike the Arbitration Act which was of a general nature. The Court of Appeal, applying the maxim *generalia specialibus non derogant* (general words do not derogate from special provisions),[80] held that:

> Section 5 of the Arbitration Act cannot have any adverse effects on the provisions of Section 2(1) of the Admiralty Jurisdiction Act which confers jurisdiction on the Admiralty Court to hear and determine claims 'notwithstanding anything to the contrary in any other law'.

[74] Arbitration Act, s 5.

[75] *Hotel Galaxy (Pvt) Ltd v Mercantile Hotels Management Ltd* [1987] 1 Sri LR 5 (SC) (Sharavananda CJ); *Ramachandran v Commercial Leasing Co Ltd* [2003] 2 Sri LR 182 (CA).

[76] *Murughasan Chandrika v Romav Ltd* SC/CHC/Appeal 04/2006 (3 April 2018) (HNJ Perera J) 9, available online: www.supremecourt.lk/images/documents/sc_chc_04_06.pdf.

[77] *Colombo Commercial Fertilizer v Motor Vessel 'SCI Mumbai'* CA PHC APN 47/2013 (CA Minute, 5 May 2014) (AWA Salam J), available online: www.slideshare.net/awasalam/47-2013-rem-impact-of-arbitaration-act-on-admiralty-jurisdiction-act-1.

[78] No 40 of 1983.

[79] *Scarlet Shipping Co Ltd v Mettalloyd Ltd* CA LA 69/2007, Action in Rem No 8/2007 (CA Minute, 28 May 2008).

[80] Narotam Singh Bindra, *Interpretation of Statutes* 12th edn (Gurgaon, LexisNexis, 2017).

The Court of Appeal also considered that section 2 of the Admiralty Jurisdiction Act 'cries out for the application of the presumption against ousting an established jurisdiction'. It therefore appears that the courts in Sri Lanka are generally wary of jurisdiction clauses which exclude the courts' jurisdiction. Nevertheless, the cases do indicate that, in matters falling outside the scope of the Admiralty Jurisdiction Act, the courts would be willing to uphold exclusive jurisdiction agreements and grant stays of local proceedings, provided that such agreements: (1) clearly evince an intention on the part of the parties to exclude the jurisdiction of the courts of Sri Lanka; and (2) have been entered into following negotiation between parties of equal bargaining power.

G. Service of Process Outside Sri Lanka

The provisions governing the issue and service of summonses is contained in CPC Chapter VIII. Sections 69–71 therein relate to service out of Sri Lanka. Similar to the UK, the plaintiff is required to make an application to the court to obtain leave to serve a summons outside Sri Lanka.[81] Such application must be made by motion supported by evidence (in the form of an affidavit or otherwise) and must indicate the place or country in which the defendant is or may probably be found. The grounds on which the application is made should also be specified. The order of a court granting leave to effect service out of the jurisdiction must direct the mode by which service is to be effected and will also direct that the defendant shall file an answer before a specified date, such date being no later than six months from the date of the order for service outside Sri Lanka.[82]

H. Service of Foreign Proceedings in Sri Lanka

Sri Lanka is a signatory to the 1965 Hague Service Abroad Convention[83] which was implemented into local law by the Mutual Assistance in Civil and Commercial Matters Act.[84] The Act covers all countries which are parties to the Convention and any country which has entered into an agreement with Sri Lanka extending the application of the Act to that country, as published by the Minister of Justice in the *Gazette*.[85] In order for foreign civil or commercial proceedings to be served within Sri Lanka, a request for assistance must be made to the Central Authority, which is the Ministry of Justice, through the embassy of the foreign country in the manner prescribed by the Act and must be accompanied by the summons or other document required to be served.[86] Thereafter, the Ministry of Justice sends the summons or other document to the District Court in the place where the party to be served resides and the District judge causes such summons or other document to be served on the party.[87] However, the Act contains a provision to the effect that the Ministry of Justice shall refuse to execute a request for service if

[81] CPC, s 69.
[82] CPC, s 70.
[83] 1965 Hague Convention on the Service Abroad of Judicial and Extrajudicial Documents in Civil or Commercial Matters.
[84] Act No 39 of 2000.
[85] ibid, s 4.
[86] ibid, s 5(1).
[87] ibid, ss 6(1), 6(2).

it considers that the execution of the request will be prejudicial to the sovereignty or security of Sri Lanka.[88] Sri Lanka has also enacted the Mutual Assistance in Criminal Matters Act,[89] which facilitates the provision of assistance in criminal matters by Sri Lanka, including the service of process or documents.[90]

III. Special Rules for Establishing Jurisdiction

A. Obligations

Under the CPC, actions pertaining to contracts must be instituted in the court within the local limits of whose jurisdiction a defendant resides, the cause of action arises, or the contract sought to be enforced was made. Where there are several defendants, an action can be brought in the court within whose jurisdiction one of several defendants reside.[91] An action may even be instituted in Sri Lanka against a defendant who is resident abroad and is not domiciled in Sri Lanka.[92] Courts have considered that jurisdiction depends upon local municipal law and is unaffected by whether a judgment once obtained is enforceable in the courts of a foreign state.[93] In respect of commercial agreements, courts have applied the English principle that, where a debt is due but the loan agreement does not specify the place of payment, the debtor must seek out the creditor at the latter's residence or place of business. Accordingly, in such situations, an action for non-payment of the debt may be filed where the plaintiff resides or maintains a place of business as that would be the place where the cause of action arose.[94] At present, in relation to commercial transactions over a threshold of 20 million rupees, if: (1) the defendant resides within the Western Province; (2) the cause of action has arisen within the Western Province; (3) the agreement sought to be enforced was made within the Western Province; or (4) the action involves a company with its registered office within the Western Province, suit must be filed in the Commercial High Court in Colombo. The respective District Courts have jurisdiction to hear matters that do not fall within the criteria just mentioned. It is important to have regard to the time bars under the Prescription Ordinance.[95] For actions based on a written promise, bargain or agreement (including a promissory note or bill of exchange), the Ordinance imposes a prescriptive period of six years from the date of breach or the date when a bill became due.[96] In respect of unwritten contracts, the prescriptive period is three years.[97]

B. Property

Roman-Dutch law is the foundation of the law of property in Sri Lanka, but it has been amended by legislation and customary law. According to CPC section 9(b), an action in respect of land

[88] ibid, s 13.
[89] Mutual Assistance in Criminal Matters Act No 25 of 2002.
[90] ibid, s 8.
[91] *Fernando v Waas* (1891) 9 SCC 189.
[92] *Miller v Murray* (1952) 54 NLR 25 (SC).
[93] ibid 27 (Rose CJ).
[94] *Ponnaiah v Kanagasabai* (1932) 35 NLR 128, 129 (Macdonell CJ).
[95] No 22 of 1971 (as amended).
[96] ibid, s 6.
[97] ibid, s 7.

must be instituted in the court within the local limits of whose jurisdiction the land is situated in whole or in part. An action for specific performance on an agreement to sell land is not considered an action in respect of land within the meaning of section 9.[98]

Intellectual property rights (IPRs) are governed by the Intellectual Property Act,[99] which is based on the WIPO Model Law. In general, jurisdiction for civil actions based on the Act rest with the Commercial High Court (presently only in Colombo).[100] Actions may be instituted for infringement or imminent infringement of IPRs[101] or to seek protection against unfair competition.[102] Further, the Act makes counterfeiting a criminal offence[103] punishable with a fine not exceeding 500,000 rupees and imprisonment for a term not exceeding two years, with double the sentence for each subsequent conviction.[104] Criminal proceedings can be instituted before the Magistrates Court directly by the rights holder through a private plaint or filing a complaint with the police. Upon investigation, the latter may institute proceedings before the Magistrate.

C. Divorce

Under the Marriage Registration Ordinance,[105] Sri Lanka only recognises three grounds for divorce: (1) adultery after marriage; (2) malicious desertion; and (3) incurable impotency at the time of marriage.[106] According to the CPC, all actions for divorce must be by way of plaint and answer.[107] However, diverging from the rules governing jurisdiction in relation to other types of actions, the CPC provides that either spouse may present a plaint to the District Court within the local limits of the jurisdiction in which he or she resides.[108] Accordingly, a spouse is able to file an action in the District Court that exercises jurisdiction over the place in which he is resident. In *Asokan nee Kandasamy v Asokan*, it was held that the divorce jurisdiction of the District Court is exercisable irrespective of where the marriage was contracted, thus including marriages contracted outside Sri Lanka.[109]

D. Corporations and Insolvency

The primary legislation dealing with private corporations and insolvency is the Companies Act 2007. The Act makes provision for the registration of offshore[110] and overseas companies. An offshore company is not entitled to carry on business within Sri Lanka.[111] Under the Act, companies may be wound up voluntarily or subject to the supervision of the court. When a

[98] *Pelis v Silva* (1958) 60 NLR 289.
[99] No 36 of 2003.
[100] ibid, s 30.
[101] ibid, s 170.
[102] ibid, s 160(7).
[103] ibid, s 186(2).
[104] ibid, s 186(4).
[105] No 19 of 1907.
[106] ibid, s 19(1).
[107] CPC, s 596.
[108] ibid, s 597.
[109] *Asokan nee Kandasamy v Asokan* [1994] 1 Sri LR 413.
[110] Companies Act No 7 of 2007, ss 261, 262.
[111] ibid, s 264.

company passes a resolution for voluntary winding up, the court, upon being petitioned, may make an order that the winding up shall continue but subject to such supervision of the court, and with the possibility for creditors or others to apply to the court.[112]

IV. Jurisdiction *in rem*

A. Admiralty Jurisdiction Generally

The High Court[113] is conferred with Admiralty jurisdiction under the Judicature Act[114] and the Admiralty Jurisdiction Act.[115] Section 2(1) of the latter specifies the types of claims that may be made:

(a) any claim to the possession or ownership of a ship or to the ownership of any share therein;
(b) any question arising between the co-owners of a ship as to possession, employment or earnings of that ship;
(c) any claim in respect of a mortgage of or charge on a ship or any share therein;
(d) any claim for damage received by a ship;
(e) any claim for damage done by a ship;
(f) any claim for loss of life or personal injury sustained in consequence of:
    (i) any defect in a ship or in her apparel or equipment; or
    (ii) the wrongful act, neglect or default of the owners, charterers or persons in possession or control of a ship or of the master or crew thereof or of any other person for whose wrongful acts, neglect or defaults the owners, charterers or persons in possession or control of a ship are responsible, being an act, neglect or default in the navigation or management of the ship, in the loading, carriage or discharge of good on, in or from the ship or in the embarkation, carriage or disembarkation of persons on, in or from the ship;
(g) any claim for loss of or damage to goods carried in a ship;
(h) any claim arising out of any agreement relating to the carriage of goods in a ship or to the use or, hire of a ship;
    (i) any claim in the nature of salvage;
(j) any claim in the nature of towage in respect of a ship;
(k) any claim in the nature of pilotage in respect of a ship;
(l) any claim in respect of:
    (i) goods or materials supplied, or
    (ii) services rendered, to a ship for her operation or maintenance;
(m) any claim in respect of the construction, repair or equipment of a ship or dock charges or dues;
(n) any claim by a master or member of the crew of a ship for wages and any claim by or in respect of a master or member of the crew of a ship for any money or property which under any law in force for the time being is recoverable as wages;
(o) any claim by a master, shipper, charterer or agent in respect of disbursements made on account of a ship;
(p) any claim arising out of an act which is or is claimed to be a general average act;

[112] ibid, ss 351, 352.
[113] Admiralty cases are heard before the Commercial High Court in Colombo. See Ismail J's judgment in *The Shantha Rohan* [1994] 3 Sri LR 54 (CA) for an account of the historical development of the Admiralty jurisdiction in Sri Lanka.
[114] Act No 2 of 1978, s 13.
[115] Act No 40 of 1983.

(q) any claim arising out of bottomry;
(r) any claim for the forfeiture or condemnation of a ship or of goods which are being or have been carried or have been attempted to be carried, in a ship, or for the restoration of a ship or any such goods after seizure, or for jetsam, flotsam, lagan and derelict found in or on the sea, the shores of the sea or any tidal water or for property found in the possession of convicted pirates.

The jurisdiction of the court in these types of claims is applicable in relation to all ships whether registered in any port in Sri Lanka or outside, wherever the residence and domicile of their owners may be, and in relation to claims wheresoever arising.[116] Additionally, in the event of a *casus omissus*, the High Court exercising Admiralty jurisdiction is required to have regard to the practice of the Admiralty courts in England, as long as it is not inconsistent with any provisions under the Admiralty Jurisdiction Act of Sri Lanka.[117] This was affirmed by the Court of Appeal in *MV Ocean Envoy v Al-Linshirah Bulk Carriers Ltd.*[118]

B. Admiralty Jurisdiction *in rem* and Ship Arrest

Sri Lanka is a party to the 1952 Arrest Convention,[119] but not the International Convention on Arrest of Ships of 1999. This is despite the fact that it was one of the states that participated in the UN/International Maritime Organisation Diplomatic Conference on the Arrest of Ships.[120] Under the Admiralty Jurisdiction Act, a ship can be served with a writ of arrest in respect of the claims set out in sections 2(1)(e) to 2(1)(q). Where an action *in rem* has been instituted under this Act and the judge is satisfied that the relevant vessel will be removed from the jurisdiction before the plaintiff's claim is satisfied, the judge may issue a warrant for the arrest and detention of that vessel.[121] An application for a writ of arrest is made *ex parte* through the filing of an affidavit setting out the claim with all supporting documentary evidence annexed and a draft of the warrant of arrest to be issued by the judge. The application is heard by way of motion before the Commercial High Court in Colombo. Where a vessel has been arrested pursuant to a warrant, the defendant is able to apply for the vessel's release, by paying into court the amount claimed in the action or an amount equal to the appraised value of the vessel or by furnishing a bank guarantee or other security to the satisfaction of the plaintiff in the action.[122]

V. Immunities from Jurisdiction

A. Sovereign and Diplomatic Immunity

As with a host of other international treaties, Sri Lanka is also a state party to the 1961 Vienna Convention on Diplomatic Relations. Although ratified on 2 June 1978, it was only incorporated into domestic law when the Diplomatic Privileges Act was enacted in 1996.[123]

[116] ibid, s 2(6).
[117] ibid, s 12.
[118] *MV Ocean Envoy v Al-Linshirah Bulk Carriers Ltd* [2002] 2 Sri LR 337 (CA) (Kulatilake J).
[119] The 1952 International Convention Relating to the Arrest of Seagoing Ships.
[120] 'Report of the United Nations/International Maritime Organisation Diplomatic Conference on Arrest of Ships' UN Doc A/CONF.188/5 (19 July 1999).
[121] Admiralty Jurisdiction Act, s 7.
[122] ibid, s 7(2).
[123] No 9 of 1996, s 2.

Accordingly, diplomats and diplomatic organisations are exempted from the civil and criminal jurisdiction of the Sri Lankan courts. However, the Ministry of Foreign Affairs in its website specifically mentions that exemption from jurisdiction will not be provided if any diplomatic or non-diplomatic staff member of a foreign mission are involved in violations of traffic rules. The website also states that Sri Lanka's laws on employees' provident fund and employees' trust fund contributions apply to all missions in relation to locally recruited staff members. In *British High Commission v Jansen*[124] the Supreme Court recognised that the world has shifted from absolute immunity towards restrictive immunity, making a distinction between *jure imperii* (a state acting in a public or sovereign capacity) and *jure gestionis* (a state acting in a private capacity. The purpose of the distinction, according to the court, is to treat a state as a normal litigant when it behaves like one, and as a sovereign when it exercises sovereign power.[125] Despite the forgoing, the court found that there was no waiver of immunity or submission to jurisdiction by the British High Commission by the mere fact that an employment contract stipulated that Sri Lankan labour law would apply to the terms and conditions of the contract. The Supreme Court concluded that the High Court had erred in holding that the Labour Tribunal had jurisdiction to hear and determine the former High Commission employee's application. In an unreported judgment concerning the Norwegian ambassador and other Norwegian state officials, the District Court of Colombo took a different approach.[126] The District Judge found that a condition in a document to which some of the Norwegian officials were party and which stipulated that any dispute be referred to a competent Sri Lankan court and settled in accordance with Sri Lankan law, was tantamount to a waiver of immunity. There have been no reported cases in Sri Lanka where sovereign immunity was disputed. However, going by the decisions of the courts on diplomatic immunity, it is likely that Sri Lankan courts would be reluctant to disregard sovereign immunity.

B. State-Owned Enterprises (SOEs)

Although Article 35(1) of the Constitution grants the President immunity from civil or criminal legal proceedings, this immunity does not extend to SOEs or public corporations. SOEs and public corporations may sue or be sued just like any other incorporated body.

VI. Proposed Colombo International Financial City

Colombo Port City is a project of the China Harbour Engineering Company (CHEC), a wholly-owned subsidiary of the China Communications Construction Company Ltd. The design of the project is to reclaim 269 hectares of land from the sea and to develop a planned city with five precincts, including a Financial District, a Central Park Living area, a Marina and an International Island.[127] Colombo Port City will also function as an International Financial City and Special Economic Zone (SEZ) with separate commercial and financial laws based on English law (with reference to similar international commercial hubs in Singapore, Dubai.

[124] *British High Commission v Jansen* [2014] 1 Sri LR 234 (SC) (Mohan Pieris CJ).
[125] ibid 248.
[126] Case No 03438/2011 DMR (30 April 2013) (Amali Ranaweera J).
[127] 'About' (*Port City Colombo*), available online: www.portcitycolombo.lk/about.

Abu Dhabi and Malaysia) in order to attract foreign investment.[128] The Colombo Port City Economic Commission Bill, which inter alia provides for the establishment of a Special Economic Zone within the Port City, was approved by the Cabinet of Ministers, gazetted and issued on 24 March 2021.[129] The Bill envisages setting up a Colombo Port City Economic Commission being tasked with creating a safe, easy and efficient business environment, instilling investor confidence and making the Colombo Port City an attractive investment destination.[130] To this end, the Commission is to function as a Single Window Investment Facilitator for any investors into the Port City.[131] Furthermore, the Bill provides for offshore companies and banks to operate in and from the Port City.[132] Quite significantly, the Bill also provides for the establishment of an International Commercial Dispute Resolution Centre to resolve, by way of arbitration, any disputes that may arise within the Colombo Port City between the Commission and any authorised person as defined under the Bill, or between the Commission and any resident, provided that there is an arbitration agreement in relation to this.[133] It can also make or adopt rules of procedure for conciliation, mediation, adjudication, arbitration and any other alternative dispute resolution services. Moreover, although foreign lawyers who are not enrolled in Sri Lanka as attorneys-at-law are not allowed to practise law in the country, the Bill provides for an 'internationally reputed professional' to be 'involved' in the arbitration process in the International Commercial Dispute Resolution Centre,[134] but the provision is vague on the extent and capacity of such involvement.

The constitutionality of the Bill was challenged before the Supreme Court by several petitioners. After several days of hearings, the Court's determination was tabled in Parliament on 18 May 2021. In its 62-page Determination, the Supreme Court opined that several clauses of the Bill required a two-third majority vote in Parliament, and that some required a two-third majority and a referendum.[135] Among other things, the Supreme Court has considered that the clauses which stipulate that the Regulatory Authorities could be compelled by the Port City Economic Commission to grant requisite approvals violate the equality provision of the Constitution, thereby allowing the Regulatory Authorities to retain their discretion. The Court has also concluded that the power granted to the Commission to make rules with penal sanctions, and the clauses which sought to grant taxation powers to the Commission, were inconsistent with provisions in the Constitution. Furthermore, whilst the Bill permits an 'Authorised Person' to engage in business outside the area of the Port City in partnership with a citizen, the Supreme Court has stipulated that the exemptions granted under the Bill cannot apply to business carried on outside the Port City zone.

During the hearings, the Attorney General, representing the Government, indicated to the Court that the Government was agreeable to making any necessary amendments to the Bill in order to avoid inconsistencies with Constitutional provisions. Following the Determination of

[128] Ravi Laduwahetty, 'New Laws for Port City – Malik Samarawickrama' (*Port City Colombo*, 12 February 2017), available online: www.portcitycolombo.lk/2017/02/12/new-laws-for-port-city.html.

[129] The Colombo Port City Economic Commission Bill is available online: www.documents.gov.lk/files/bill/2021/3/43-2021_E.pdf.

[130] Colombo Port City Economic Commission Bill, s 5.

[131] ibid, Pt VI.

[132] ibid, Pts VII and VIII.

[133] ibid, Pt XIII.

[134] ibid, s 62(6).

[135] *Colombo Port City Economic Commission Bill* SCSD Nos 04/2021, 05/2021, 07/2021 to 23/2021 (SC). The determination is available online: www.parliament.lk/uploads/bills/gbills/scdet/6218.pdf.

the Court, members of the Government have indicated that they are in acceptance of the decision of the Court. Therefore, although there is no post-enactment judicial review in Sri Lanka, it is likely that final version of the Bill will have incorporated the changes suggested by the Court whilst still retaining the pith and substance of its original form.

At present, due to the failure of the national arbitration system in Sri Lanka, particularly in relation to delays in proceedings and delays in the enforcement of arbitral awards, parties prefer to resolve commercial disputes through the Commercial High Court. Moreover, the bulk of international arbitrations involving Sri Lankan parties are conducted in Singapore which involves significant costs. The Minister of Justice in 2020 appointed a sub-committee to propose reforms to Sri Lanka's commercial and procedural laws. This includes possible reforms to the arbitration regime and the introduction of measures to ensure efficacious resolution of investor disputes. Allowing an international commercial arbitration centre with qualified professionals to operate within the Colombo Port City will go a long way towards establishing investor confidence to attract investment.

VII. Conclusion

There are two main issues in relation to private international law in Sri Lanka. There is a lethargy on the part of the legislature in expeditiously enacting laws that would facilitate the development of private international law in Sri Lanka. This includes revising the CPC and making express provision for the granting of stays in keeping with the doctrine of *forum non conveniens*, recognising the doctrine of *lis alibi pendens*, enabling the grant of anti-suit and worldwide freezing injunctions, and importantly the recognition and enforcement of foreign judgments. In order for the government to realise its vision of making Sri Lanka an international financial capital, its commercial, financial, procedural and alternate dispute resolution laws need to be modernised and brought in-line with legal systems such as those in the UK, Singapore and Hong Kong. It is vital to have the necessary robust legal infrastructure in place to make Sri Lanka an attractive destination for foreign direct investment. The government has recently taken an important step towards addressing the issue of law's delays, by increasing the number of judges in the Supreme Court from 11 to 17[136] and the number of judges in the Court of Appeal from 12 to 20.[137] This increase may aide in clearing the large backlog of cases in the appellate courts. Furthermore, judicial decisions need to reflect the significant developments and changes in the core principles of private international law that have come about in the last 40 years. For instance, foreign courts take cognisance of the fact that modern-day litigants, especially in cross-border commercial disputes, tend to be resourceful, well-informed and well-advised on the implications of their commercial agreements. Therefore, at-least in those types of cases, the courts should give precedence to party autonomy, such as where there are exclusive jurisdiction or arbitration clauses. Upholding such clauses is crucial, as commercial parties need to be able to make calculated assessments of their litigation risk. Engaging in international commercial litigation is an investment decision for parties and legal uncertainty discourages them from engaging with jurisdictions where uncertainty exists and from undertaking the risk of being

[136] Twentieth Amendment to the Constitution, s 25.
[137] ibid, s 31.

sued in such countries. Even if the legislature delays passing the necessary laws, the courts need not be hampered by the lack of express statutory provision enabling the granting of stays, anti-suit injunctions, worldwide freezing orders and the like, since they have inherent power to order the same in the interests of doing justice in a given case. This inherent power may be resorted to, as the legislature has acknowledged that it cannot envisage and legislate for every circumstance that can conceivably arise.

16

India

SAI RAMANI GARIMELLA

I. Introduction

India's introduction to English law dates to the Charter of George I of 1726, when Mayors' Courts were established in the three Presidency towns of Madras, Calcutta, and Bombay.[1] The Charter of 1753 expressly provided that the Mayors' Courts were not to try actions between Indians, such actions being left to be determined among themselves, unless both parties by consent submitted to this jurisdiction. The Regulation of 1781 provided that, in all cases where no specific directions were given, the judges of the East India Company's Court should act 'according to justice, equity and good conscience'. In the same year, the British Parliament bestowed civil jurisdiction on the Supreme Court in Calcutta (which was the successor of the Mayor's Court and was a court of the British King and not of the East India Company) over Indian inhabitants in the city. But it was directed that 'inheritance and succession to lands, rents and goods, and all matters of contract and dealing between party and party' should be determined in the case of Muslims and Hindus by their respective laws and, where only one of the parties was a Muslim or Hindu, 'by the laws and usage of the defendant'. The parliamentary Order was later extended to the other Presidency towns of Madras and Bombay.[2] By the early nineteenth century, British rule covered most of India and law was administered through two sets of courts – the Queen's courts in the Presidency towns and the East India Company's courts in the *mofussil* (as the territories held by the Company as feudatory of the Mughal Emperor came to be known). Both within the Presidency towns and outside, Hindus and Muslims were allowed to be governed by their own laws. However, within the three towns, apart from these personal laws, there was a general territorial law or *lex loci* applicable to all persons, namely, English common law as introduced by the Charter of 1726. Outside the towns, there was no *lex loci* at all.[3] The vacuum was to some extent filled by the courts by reference to 'justice, equity and good conscience' in accordance with the Regulation of 1781. While the Indian High Courts Act 1861 abolished the dichotomy between the royal courts and the Company's courts, it preserved provisions relating to the jurisdiction of the courts.

[1] TS Rama Rao, 'Conflict of Laws in India' (1958) 23 *Rabels Zeitschrift Für Ausländisches und Internationales Privatrecht* 259, 260–62. For a detailed discussion on the introduction of English law – common law and statute law – and a set of legal institutions for administration of justice in the presidency towns of Madras, Bombay and Calcutta, see John Shaw, *Charters Relating to the East India Company from 1600 to 1761* (Madras, Madras Government Press, 1887); Atul Chandra Patra, 'Historical Background of the Indian Contract Act, 1872' (1962) 4(3) *Journal of the Indian Law Institute* 373.

[2] ibid 260.

[3] George Claus Rankin, *Background to Indian Law* (Cambridge, Cambridge University Press, 1946) 1, 30. Rankin was of the view that English law became *ipso jure* the *lex loci* in India as soon as the country became a possession of the British Crown.

Thus, *mofussil* courts retained the residual power (conferred by the Regulation of 1781) to act 'according to justice, equity and good conscience'.

Commercial dispute resolution in independent India, a federal state, is largely handled by the civil courts established in India's 719 districts. The jurisdiction of these courts is founded upon territorial and pecuniary grounds. India's legal system is based on English common law, codified laws, and non-codified religious and customary laws. The judiciary, at the apex, has the Supreme Court exercising appellate jurisdiction for final appeals in civil, criminal and administrative matters, as well as original jurisdiction in constitutional matters.[4] The state judiciary consists of a High Court and lower courts. The High Courts exercise appellate jurisdiction from the lower courts in each state or assigned union territory.[5]

Modern rules of private international law in India are derived from statutes and decisions of courts. The influence of the English common law is much visible and often perceived as all pervading. Sir George Rankin wrote:

> the influence of the common law in India is due not so much to a reception, though that has played no inconsiderable part, as to a process of codification carried out on the grand scale, not merely with a view to putting into form a system of law which was already in force, but to lay down a rule of decision where there seemed to be none.[6]

However, there have been deviations from English law, especially when the latter was found unsuited to Indian conditions. For example, the Indian Contract Act 1872 provides that every person is competent to contract who is of the age of majority according to the law to which he or she is subject and the Indian Majority Act 1875 regulates the age of majority for all persons domiciled in India in a uniform manner. By virtue of these provisions, capacity to contract is governed in all cases by the *lex domicilii*. Thus, the modern view that capacity in cases of mercantile contracts is governed by the *lex loci contractus* and not the *lex domicilii* is not followed in India.

The gateway question of jurisdiction may be addressed, when a foreign element is present, through the lens of extra-territoriality. But the basic rule of jurisdiction (*quidquid est in territorio est etiam de territorio*)[7] is not forsaken. Jurisdiction is normally co-extensive with territory, with such jurisdiction being unavailable only in the context of foreign sovereigns and members of diplomatic missions and international organisations. Nonetheless, India's constitution recognised a concept of extra-territoriality,[8] specifying that extra-territorial laws are valid and operational if they have a nexus with India.[9] Penal and revenue laws of foreign states though will not be given extra-territorial effect by domestic courts. As a counterbalance, the principle of allegiance provides a basis for domestic courts exercising jurisdiction even over non-citizens. Under this principle of allegiance, it is assumed that all persons present within the jurisdiction owe allegiance to India. Accordingly, Indian law recognises the applicability of the *lex fori* in matters relating to procedure.[10]

[4] The original jurisdiction of the Supreme Court extends to any dispute between the Union and the states or between the states.

[5] Only six High Courts (Madras, Delhi, Himachal Pradesh, Jammu and Kashmir, Calcutta, and Bombay) exercise original civil jurisdiction.

[6] Rankin (n 3) 19.

[7] 'Whatever is in the territory is also of the territory.'

[8] Art 245(2) of the Constitution states: 'No law made by Parliament shall be deemed to be invalid on the ground that it would have extraterritorial operation.'

[9] *GVK Industries Ltd v Income Tax Officer* [2011] 4 SCC 36.

[10] *Ramanathan Chettiar v Somasundram Chettiar* AIR [1964] Mad 527.

II. Jurisdiction *in personam*

A. General Principles

i. Overview

Jurisdiction-related questions in private international law attempt to identify the competence of courts to decide on matters. In a matter having a foreign element, the preliminary question arises: does the domestic court possess jurisdiction to try such suit? Following affirmation of the preliminary question, further questions arise: (1) who and against whom can the action be brought; and (2) what types of actions may be filed. Disputes before the court on questions of jurisdiction are classified under three heads: (1) actions *in personam* or personal actions; (2) actions *in rem* relating to interests in property; and (3) actions relating to status. The following section will specify the general rules of jurisdiction in the Indian law applicable to *in personam* actions involving a foreign element.

India, like other common law countries, uses domicile as a basis for the jurisdiction of courts to establish a primary connection between an individual and a place. Habitual residence, prevalent in many legal systems and given normative status in many international conventions,[11] is also known in Indian law, especially with regard to disputes related to property and inheritance involving immovable property. Habitual residence is a question of fact[12] and refers to 'a quality of residence'[13] not a certain period of residence. In India, the jurisdiction of the court will often depend on factors linking a claim to a locality, such as a party's domicile, the place of solemnisation of a couple's marriage (*lex loci celebrationis*), or a party's residence.

The Supreme Court of India in *Central Bank of India Ltd v Ram Narain* acknowledged the concept of domicile as established under English law.[14] It held that the two constituent elements that are necessary for the existence of domicile are: (1) residence of a particular kind, which need not be continuous but which must be indefinite and not merely fleeting; and (2) an intention of a particular kind, that is, a present intention permanently to reside in the country where residence has been taken up. Several judgments have followed the foregoing ratio.[15] An intention to hold a permanent residence at a different place could be proof of a change of domicile.[16] The test for establishing change of domicile is that a person acquires a new domicile when settling in a new country with the intention of making it one's permanent place of residence.[17]

[11] See eg the 1980 Rome Convention on the Law Applicable to Contractual Obligations and the 1980 Hague Convention on the Civil Aspects of International Child Abduction.

[12] Elisa Pérez-Vera, *Explanatory Report to the Hague Convention on Intercountry Child Abduction* (*Hague Conference on Private International Law*, April 1981), available online: www.hcch.net/upload/expl28.pdf, commenting (at para 66) that the 1980 Hague Convention regards 'habitual residence' as 'a question of pure fact'.

[13] *Cruse v Chittum* [1974] 2 All ER 940, 942–43. See also Clifford Hall, '*Cruse* v. *Chittum*: Habitual Residence Judicially Explored' (1975) 24(1) *International and Comparative Law Quarterly* 1.

[14] *Central Bank of India Ltd v Ram Narain* AIR [1955] SC 36, [1955] 1 SCR 697. The court referred to the opinion of Chitty J in *Craignish v Craignish* (1892) 3 Ch 180: 'That place is properly the domicile of a person in which his habitation is fixed without any present intention of removing therefrom.'

[15] See eg *Sankaran Govindan v Lakshmi Bharati* AIR [1974] SC 1764, [1975] 1 SCR 57; *Poosarilar Ekambaram Pillai v Visalakshmi* AIR [1991] Mad 203.

[16] *Kedar Pandey v Narain Bikram Sah* AIR [1966] SC 160, [1965] 3 SCR 793, where the *Central Bank* ratio was reiterated by the Supreme Court.

[17] *Louis De Raedt v Union of India* [1991] 3 SCC 554.

Jurisdiction of the court exists, if a foreign defendant makes an unconditional and unequivocal appearance and pleads the case on merits.[18] But, having consented to have a controversy resolved by arbitration, a party loses the right to question the authority of the court to refer the matter to arbitration.[19] Waiver of objections[20] to jurisdiction also amounts to submission to jurisdiction.[21] A reaffirmation of the above view can be seen in *Bahrain Petroleum Co Ltd v PJ Pappu*[22] wherein Justice Bachawat observed that long and continued participation by the defendant in proceedings without protest may, in an appropriate case, amount to a waiver of objection to jurisdiction. The absence of submission to jurisdiction by a foreign sovereign or state renders a judgment null and void.[23]

Sections 15 to 20 of the Code of Civil Procedure 1908 (CPC) regulate the forum for the institution of suits. Section 15 refers to the pecuniary jurisdiction of the courts and provides that every suit shall be instituted in the court of the lowest grade competent to try it. Subject matter jurisdiction is further divided into three classes: (1) suits in respect of movable property; (2) suits in respect of immovable property; and (3) suits for other kinds of property (such as intangible property). CPC sections 16 to 18 relate to immovable property. However, the Explanation to those provisions makes it clear that they were not designed to deal with cases involving foreign land. The Explanation instead says that the property in those provisions refers to property in India, that is, the *lex situs* rule.

Rules concerning actions *in personam* are specified in CPC sections 19 and 20. Section 19 is confined to suits for compensation for wrongs to person or movables. Actions *in personam* involving a foreign element are covered under section 20. The jurisdiction of an Indian court can be invoked if the defendant resides or engages in business or is employed within the court's jurisdiction or, if the cause of action in whole or part arises within that jurisdiction. In *Gurdial Singh v Rajah of Faridkot*,[24] the Privy Council explained that jurisdiction must remain with the courts of the territory where the defendant resides. A plaintiff ought not be allowed to raise claims in the courts of the place of the cause of action or (in cases of contract) the place of performance (*locus solutionis*). Thus, as a general rule, personal actions can be brought before the appropriate court in the territory where the defendant resides.[25] A similar regime exists with regard to the original jurisdiction of the higher courts. For instance, clause 12 of the Letters Patent[26] conferred jurisdiction on the High Courts on the basis of the residence of a defendant within their jurisdiction. The High Courts have gone so far as to hold that 'residence' includes temporary residence or even mere presence of a defendant.[27] In *Suresh Narayan Sinha v Akhauri Balbhadra Prasad*,[28] the Patna High Court held that a court has no jurisdiction to entertain a suit against a foreigner who

[18] See eg *Anant Narayan v Massey Ferguson Ltd* [1965] 1 MLJ 550.

[19] *Hiralal Patni v Kali Nath* AIR [1962] SC 199, [1962] 2 SCR 747.

[20] CPC, s 21 states that objections to jurisdiction shall not be entertained in the appellate or revisional court unless such objections were taken in the court of first instance at the earliest possible opportunity.

[21] *Hiralal Patni* (n 19).

[22] *Bahrein Petroleum Co Ltd v PJ Pappu* AIR [1966] SC 634, [1966] 1 SCR 461.

[23] *Royal Nepal Airlines Corp v Monorama Mehar Singh Legha* AIR [1966] Cal 319.

[24] *Sirdar Gurdyal Singh v The Rajah of Faridkot* [1894] AC 670, (1895) ILR 22 Cal 222.

[25] ibid. See also *Kashinath v Anant* (1899) ILR 24 Bom 407; *Srinivasa Moorthy v Venkata Varada Ayyangar* (1906) ILR 29 Mad 239; *Seth Chand Mull Dudha CIE v Purushothamdoss* (1926) 50 MLJ 348.

[26] The Letters Patent are a form of legal instrument issued by a monarch, president, or other head of state, generally granting an office, right, monopoly, title, or status to a person or corporation. Following the transfer of power over the Indian territories from the East India Company to the Crown, the British Parliament enacted the Indian High Courts Act 1861. Consequently, by Letters Patent dated 26 June 1862, the earlier Letters Patent setting up the Supreme Courts were revoked. New High Courts were established in Bombay on 14 August 1862, Calcutta on 2 July 1862, and Madras on 15 August 1862.

[27] See eg *THP De Silva v S Soosai Pillai Morais* [1954] TC 141.

[28] *Suresh Narain Sinha v Akhauri Balbhadra Prasad* AIR [1957] Pat 256.

does not permanently or temporarily reside within its jurisdiction or who has not submitted to its jurisdiction. By extension, the place of a cause of action being immaterial, Indian courts have consistently exercised jurisdiction where a defendant has been engaged in business personally or through an agent within their territory, regardless of where a cause of action arose.[29]

CPC section 10 states:

> **Stay of suit**
>
> No Court shall proceed with the trial of any suit in which the matter in issue is also directly and substantially in issue in a previously instituted suit between the same parties, or between parties under whom they or any of them claim litigating under the same title where such suit is pending in the same or any other Court in 6 [India] have jurisdiction to grant the relief claimed, or in any Court beyond the limits of 6 [India] established or continued by the Central Government and having like jurisdiction, or before the Supreme Court.
>
> Explanation. – The pendency of a suit in a foreign Court does not preclude the Courts in India from trying a suit founded on the same cause of action.

Two or more courts are thereby prevented from exercising concurrent jurisdiction in parallel litigation on the same cause of action, obviating the possibility of contradictory decisions.[30] However, section 10 does not concern itself with the power of the courts to stay a domestic suit pending foreign court proceedings. Neither does the section say anything about the power of the courts in India to restrain proceedings in a foreign court. Nevertheless, Indian courts have ordered the stay of a domestic suit[31] when there have been pending proceedings in a foreign court, through their inherent powers under CPC section 151.[32] Interestingly, Indian courts have founded their jurisdiction on an equity to restrain a party from continuing with a suit in a foreign court.[33] The Punjab High Court allowed a subsequent action filed before it to continue, despite knowledge of pending proceedings in a foreign court. It held that, while the court where the prior application was pending had jurisdiction over the matter, it was allowing the subsequent application to ensure that the applicant was not denied the relief sought.[34] Differently, in *Jethabhai v Amar Chand*,[35] the court stayed a suit, as evidence relating to the dispute was located in Rangoon (now Yangon, Myanmar). Quoting with approval from *Logan v Bank of Scotland (No 2)*,[36] the court explained that the continuance of the suit would cause injustice to the defendant by subjecting it to vexatious litigation and a stay would not cause any injustice to the plaintiff.

ii. Choice of Court Agreements

Courts in India have indulged in a detailed examination of jurisdiction clauses – exclusive and non-exclusive. They have applied the law of contract to identify the applicable law and

[29] See eg *Haveli Shah v Khan Sahib Sheikh Painda Khan* AIR [1926] PC 88; *Chunnilal Kasturchand v Dundappa Damappa* AIR [1951] Bom 190. The precedent set by the Privy Council was followed by the Punjab High Court in *Frontier Bank Ltd v Shiromani Prakash Wati Bahl* AIR [1950] Punjab 635.

[30] *Balkishan v Kishan Lal* (1889) ILR 11 All 148; *Naurati v Mehma Singh* AIR [1972] P & H 421.

[31] *Jethabhai Versey and Co v Amarchand Madhavji and Co* AIR [1924] Bom 90; *Bhagat Singh Bugga v Dewan Jagbir Sawhney* AIR [1941] Cal 670.

[32] Section 151 states: 'Nothing in this Code shall be deemed to limit or otherwise affect the inherent power of the Court to make such orders as may be necessary for the ends of justice or to prevent abuse of the process of the Court.'

[33] *Nath Bank Ltd v Andhar Manick Tea Co Ltd* AIR [1960] Cal 779.

[34] *Ladli Prasad Jaiswal v Karnal Distillery Co Ltd* AIR [1954] Punjab 94.

[35] *Jethabhai* (n 31).

[36] *Logan v Bank of Scotland (No 2)* [1906] 1 KB 141.

examined the validity of jurisdiction clauses in light of that applicable law. But they have also based their assessment of jurisdiction clauses on Indian law.[37] In one of the earliest decisions on jurisdiction clauses, the Madras High Court found expediency as a reason to rule against the enforcement of a jurisdiction clause that explicitly identified a foreign jurisdiction for dispute resolution. In *Black Sea State Steamship Line v Minerals and Metals Trading Corp of India Ltd*,[38] the court heard a dispute over an international shipment under a bill of lading containing the following clauses:

> 26. All claims and disputes arising under and in connection with this bill of lading shall be judged in the USSR.
> 27. All questions and disputes not mentioned in this bill of lading shall be determined according to the Merchant Shipping Code of the USSR.[39]

The court, applying common law principles,[40] held that with foreign jurisdiction clauses the question was not so much of freedom of contract but of expediency, in light of the balance of convenience and the ends of justice in the case at hand.[41] Dismissing the plaintiff's application, the court held that the balance of convenience as well as the ends of justice tended toward sustaining the jurisdiction of the Court of Small Causes to dispose of the suit and not the chosen forum.[42] In contrast, in *Hakam Singh v Gammon (India) Ltd*,[43] the Supreme Court adopted a conjoint reading of the Indian Contract Act 1872 and the CPC to determine the validity of the jurisdiction clause. The Supreme Court stated that when two courts had jurisdiction to entertain a dispute, the choice of one by agreement would not amount to a restraint of legal proceedings, nor violate public policy, under sections 23 and 28 of the Indian Contract Act 1872.[44] Nonetheless, the parties could not by agreement confer jurisdiction on a court that would not otherwise have had jurisdiction to adjudicate upon a dispute. In *British India Steam Navigation Co v Shanmughavilas Cashew Industries*,[45] the Supreme Court noted the jurisdiction clause in the relevant bills of lading[46] and held that the respondent as consignee and holder of the bills was prima facie bound by that clause. But the Supreme Court went on to hold that on the facts the appellant carrier had submitted to the jurisdiction of the court in Cochin (Kochi), and therefore rejected arguments of a lack of jurisdiction.[47]

[37] See also Poomintr Sooksripaisarnkit and Sai Ramani Garimella, 'Choice of Court Agreements: Selected Common-Law Jurisdictions and Indian Laws Compared: Time for the Convention of 30 June 2005 on Choice of Court Agreements?' (2021) 30 *Journal of Transnational Law and Policy* (forthcoming).

[38] *Black Sea State Steamship Line v Minerals and Metals Trading Corp of India Ltd* [1970] 1 MLJ 548.

[39] ibid [2].

[40] ibid, referring to *The Fehrman* [1958] 1 WLR 159.

[41] ibid [6].

[42] ibid [11].

[43] *Hakam Singh v Gammon (India) Ltd* AIR [1971] SC 740, [1971] 1 SCC 286. See also *Globe Transport Corp v Triveni Engineering Works* [1983] 4 SCC 707.

[44] *Hakam* (n 43) 287.

[45] *British India Steam Navigation Co v Shanmughavilas Cashew Industries* [1990] 1 SCR 884, [1990] 3 SCC 481.

[46] The appellant's submission that the courts at Cochin had no jurisdiction was based on clause 3 of the bills of lading, which reads: 'JURISDICTION: The contract evidence by this bill of lading shall be governed by English law and disputes determined in England or, at the option of the Carrier, at the port of destination according to English law to the exclusion of the jurisdiction of the Courts of any other country.'

[47] ibid 27. The Supreme Court went on to hold, however, that the court below ought to have determined liability in accordance with English law (not Indian law), as agreed by the parties under the bills of lading. The Supreme Court therefore remitted the case to the court below for determination in accordance with English law.

In *Modi Entertainment Network v WSG Cricket Pte Ltd*[48] the Supreme Court offered guidelines on enforcing foreign jurisdiction clauses through the grant of anti-suit injunctions. The Court drew on the House of Lords' decision in *Spiliada Maritime Corp v Cansulex Ltd*:[49]

> In *Spiliada Maritime*'s case …, the House of Lords laid down the following principle: 'The fundamental principle applicable to both the stay of English proceedings on the ground that some other forum was the appropriate forum and also the grant of leave to serve proceedings out of the jurisdiction was that the court would choose that forum in which the case could be tried more suitably for the interests of all the parties and for the ends of justice.[50]

Referring further to Rules 31(5) and 32(4) in *Dicey and Morris on the Conflict of Laws* 13th edn (2000), the Court concluded:[51]

> (2) in a case where more forums than one are available, the Court in exercise of its discretion to grant anti-suit injunction will examine as to which is the appropriate forum (*forum conveniens*) having regard to the convenience of the parties and may grant anti-suit injunction in regard to proceedings which are oppressive or vexatious or in a *forum non-conveniens*;
>
> …
>
> (7) the burden of establishing that the forum of choice is a *forum non-conveniens* or the proceedings therein are oppressive or vexatious would be on the party so contending to aver and prove the same.

In *Kumarina Investment Ltd v Digital Media Convergence Ltd*,[52] the court identified situations when a non-chosen court could exercise jurisdiction despite the presence of a clause designating some other court as the forum to resolve disputes:

> the contracting parties being subject to the municipal law of the country with which the case has the connection or where the cause of action may have arisen; the governing law clause of the contract is violative of the public policy of the country and such clause does not confer exclusive jurisdiction on the forum chosen, or it is possible according to the chosen applicable law to override the chosen forum.[53]

In *Rhodia Ltd v Neon Laboratories Ltd*,[54] the Bombay High Court heard an application relating to the enforcement of a foreign jurisdiction clause. The court ordered that evidence about the governing foreign law ought to be adduced to enable it to decide whether the jurisdiction clause should be over-ridden.

Indian law allows presumptive validity to be attributed to exclusive jurisdiction clauses if such exclusivity was expressly agreed by the parties. Such clauses remain valid unless it is proven that they are not founded upon a *consensus ad idem*. In *ABC Laminart Pvt Ltd v AP Agencies*,[55] the court held:

> From the foregoing decisions it can be reasonably deduced that where such an ouster clause occurs, it is pertinent to see whether there is ouster of jurisdiction of other courts. When the clause is clear, unambiguous and specific accepted notions of contract would bind the parties and unless the absence of ad

[48] *Modi Entertainment Network v WSG Cricket Pte Ltd* AIR [2003] SC 1177, [2003] 4 SCC 341.

[49] *Spiliada Maritime Corp v Cansulex Ltd* [1987] AC 460 (HL).

[50] *Modi Entertainment Network* (n 48) [19].

[51] ibid [12], [24]; Lawrence Collins and others (eds), *Dicey and Morris on the Conflict of Laws* 13th edn (London, Sweet & Maxwell, 2000).

[52] *Kumarina Investment Ltd v Digital Media Convergence Ltd* Petition No 221(C) of 2010.

[53] ibid 20.

[54] *Rhodia Ltd v Neon Laboratories Ltd* AIR [2002] Bom 502.

[55] *ABC Laminart Pvt Ltd v AP Agencies* AIR [1989] SC 1239, [1989] 2 SCR 1. See also *Swastik Gases Pvt Ltd v Indian Oil Corp Ltd* [2013] 9 SCC 32.

> idem can be shown, the other Courts should avoid exercising jurisdiction. As regards construction of the ouster clause when words like 'alone', 'only', 'exclusive' and the like have been used there may be no difficulty.[56]

iii. Forum non conveniens

An important doctrine impacting on the existence and exercise of jurisdiction by the courts is *forum non conveniens*. It concerns the power to decline to exercise jurisdiction in certain exceptional circumstances.[57] Known to have its origins in the law of Scotland, the development of the doctrine has been influenced by the deference accorded to the interests of the parties and the requirements of justice.[58] *Forum non conveniens* has been explained by the Indian courts as the discretionary power of the court to decline jurisdiction because there exists a more appropriate forum to try a matter.[59] In *Glaxosmithkline Consumer Healthcare Ltd v Heinz Pvt Ltd*,[60] the court explained that the doctrine will apply in a dispute where the other more appropriate forum is primarily a court of competent jurisdiction. Judicial scrutiny related to *forum non conveniens* decisions in India addresses two questions:

(1) Is there an alternative competent forum that is more appropriate?
(2) Is it in the interest of justice and equity to relegate the parties to that forum?[61]

Such approach was adopted in *Independent News Services Pvt Ltd v India Broadcast Live LLC*[62] which held that, in determining whether a more appropriate forum exists, factors such as the convenience of the parties, the expenses involved, and the law governing the relevant transaction need to be considered. The burden to prove that the chosen forum is *non conveniens* or that proceedings there would be oppressive or vexatious is on the party so contending.[63] The ratio in *Modi Entertainment Network* with regard to *forum non conveniens* was applied in matrimonial proceedings in *Krishna Veni Nagam v Harish Nigam*.[64] The court held that a decision related to the appropriateness of the forum is founded upon the exercise of the inherent jurisdiction to stay proceedings in the interests of all parties and the ends of justice.

iv. Injunctions

In *Modi Entertainment Network* the court examined the principles governing the grant of an anti-suit injunction by a court of natural jurisdiction to restrain one party from instituting or

[56] *ABC Laminart* (n 55) 21.

[57] *Gulf Oil Corp v Gilbert* 330 US 501, 504 (1947). See also Charles T Plambeck, 'The Razor's Edge: The Doctrine of Forum non Conveniens and the Union Carbide Methyl Isocyanate Gas Disaster at Bhopal, India' (1985) 10 *North Carolina Journal of International Law and Commercial Regulation* 743, available online: http://scholarship.law.unc.edu/ncilj/vol10/iss3/11.

[58] Robert Braucher, 'The Inconvenient Federal Forum' (1947) 60 *Harvard Law Review* 908, 909, 950, available online: www.jstor.org/stable/pdf/1335558.pdf.

[59] *Modi Entertainment Network* (n 48). The court discussed the appropriate forum for injunctive relief in a contractual dispute where there was a jurisdiction clause as well. See also *Moser Baer India Ltd v Koninklijke Philips Electronics NV* [2008] 1 CTLJ 421 (Del), (2008) 102 DRJ 713.

[60] *Glaxosmithkline Consumer Healthcare Ltd v Heinz Pvt Ltd* MANU/DE/0011/2009 (India).

[61] *Modi Entertainment Network* (n 48).

[62] *Independent News Services Pvt Ltd v India Broadcast Live LLC* [2007] SCC Online Del 960.

[63] *Modi Entertainment Network* (n 48) [24].

[64] *Krishna Veni Nagam v Harish Nigam* [2017] 4 SCC 150.

prosecuting a suit in a foreign court contractually agreed upon by both parties.[65] The court referred to *Oil and Natural Gas Commission v Western Company of North America*[66] which held that the jurisdiction to grant an anti-suit injunction exists: (1) when necessary and expedient or when the ends of justice so require; and (2) when it would be unfair to issue a restraint order because the action in the foreign court would be oppressive in the facts and circumstances of a case. An injunction may be granted if the court is satisfied that: (1) the defendant against whom the injunction is sought is amenable to the personal jurisdiction of the court; (2) refusal of relief will cause injustice; and (3) comity (that is, respect for the foreign court in which the commencement or continuance of an action is sought to be restrained) will not be affected. However, no anti-suit injunction will be granted in cases where the parties have agreed to submit to the exclusive or non-exclusive jurisdiction of a court, as it may be presumed that the parties have taken account of their convenience and the other court cannot be regarded as an alternative forum. Neither can a party to a contract containing a jurisdiction clause be prevented from approaching the court designated by the parties, as otherwise there would a breach of the contract. Nor can proceedings instituted in a court which has exclusive or non-exclusive jurisdiction by the party's agreement, be treated as vexatious or oppressive. In such situations, the designated court cannot be characterised as a *forum non conveniens*.[67] The foregoing ratio was applied in *Anuradha v Divyanshu Gautam*[68] where the court held that, in decisions related to the appropriateness of a forum, it is necessary to see where justice can be done at substantially less inconvenience and expense and where an action has the most real and substantial connection (that is, taking account of factors such as the availability of witnesses, the law governing the relevant transaction, and the places where the parties respectively reside or carry on business).

v. *Service of Process*

a. Service of Indian Proceedings Outside of India

India acceded to the 1965 Hague Convention on the Service Abroad of Judicial and Extrajudicial Documents in Civil or Commercial Matters on 23 November 2006. The 1965 Convention entered into force in India on 1 August 2007. The 1965 Convention envisages the establishment of channels of transmission for judicial or extra-judicial documents between one state party to the Convention and another for service within their respective jurisdictions. The substantive rules relating to the service of process are addressed through the legal framework of a contracting state, as seen in CPC Order V, Rules 25 and 26. Order V Rule 25 specifies that where a defendant resides abroad and has no agent in India, the summons shall be addressed to the defendant at the latter's residence through a postal communication marked 'to be acknowledged'. Were such service impossible to be effectuated, Order V Rule 26 provides an alternative mechanism for service abroad.[69]

b. Substituted Service

When the court is satisfied that the defendant is purposefully avoiding receipt of summons, it may attempt substituted service. A summons can be sent through a political agent, appointed

[65] *Modi Entertainment Network* (n 48).
[66] *Oil and Natural Gas Commission v Western Company of North America* AIR [1987] SC 674, [1987] 1 SCR 1024.
[67] *Modi Entertainment Network* (n 48). See also *Moser Baer* (n 59).
[68] *Anuradha v Divyanshu Gautam* [2016] SDC 564.
[69] Ord V, r 26(a).

for the purpose of conveying the same to the defendant. When the political agent returns the summons with an endorsement that the summons has been served, such endorsement shall be deemed as evidence of service.

c. Service of Foreign Proceedings in India

In accordance with the 1965 Convention, India has designated the Department of Legal Affairs within the Ministry of Law and Justice as its Central Authority. The service of summonses in India has to be effected pursuant to the steps contemplated under the Convention. The Central Authority of the foreign state is to effect service through the Ministry of Law and Justice in the prescribed format.[70] Such request and the document to be served shall be submitted in duplicate.[71] The Ministry shall, upon receipt of such process, serve the document or arrange to have it served by an appropriate agency, either by a method prescribed by internal law or by a particular method requested by the applicant unless the latter is incompatible with the Indian domestic law.[72] Upon completion of service by the Ministry, a certificate will be forwarded to the applicant certifying that the document has been served and specifying the method, place and date of service and the person to whom the document was delivered.[73] If service could not be effected, the certificate would set out the reasons preventing service.[74] In *Anupama Sharma v Union of India*,[75] the summons issued by the New York court was privately delivered to the petitioner in the pending foreign court proceedings. The petitioner contended that the service was contrary to Articles 3 and 5 of the 1965 Hague Convention since the summons was not served through the Indian Government, but instead delivered privately. The petitioner submitted that India had specifically opposed Article 10 of the Convention, permitting service by postal channels to persons abroad. The Bombay High Court observed that the service and operation of the summons could not be stayed by reason of Article 226 of the Constitution of India. The petitioner could instead apply to the New York court with the relevant objection and that court would decide whether to order a fresh service of the summons in accordance with Articles 3 and 5 of the Convention.

B. Specific Cases

i. Obligations

The law of obligations, including contract and tort, derives from the act of a person or persons resulting in a legal obligation. While the contractual legal obligation is retrospective, the obligation founded upon a tort-based action is 'prospective and pathological', as Professor Morris characterised it.[76]

[70] Prescribed model forms are available online at the website of the Hague Convention: https://assets.hcch.net/docs/18774c6c-2c85-41a7-8fe6-55c23acd498b.pdf.

[71] 1965 Hague Convention, Art 3.

[72] ibid, Art 5(1).

[73] ibid, Art 6.

[74] ibid.

[75] *Anupama Sharma v Union of India* WP(L) No 119 of 2014.

[76] VC Govindaraj, *The Conflict of Laws in India: Inter-Territorial and Inter-Personal Conflict* (Oxford, Oxford University Press, 2019) 1, 53.

a. Contracts

In conformity with the proper law doctrine,[77] Indian private international law of contract recognises the principle of party autonomy. Parties are normally entitled to choose the law applicable to their contract.[78] Where there has been no express choice of law, the governing law is determined by reference to the inferred intention of the parties.[79] Such intention can be discovered by applying 'sound ideas of business, convenience and sense to the language of the contract itself'.[80] For example, the 'selection of courts of a particular country as having jurisdiction in matters arising under the contract is usually, but not invariably, the indication of the intention of the parties that the system of law followed by those courts is the proper law by which they intend their contract to be governed'. In *British India Steam Navigation Co Ltd v Shanmughavilas Cashew Industries*,[81] the court ruled on the 'fixed' nature of the proper law of the contract and explained that there cannot be a 'floating' proper law.[82] Choice of law, founded upon the freedom of the parties, ought to be bona fide, legal, and not impinge upon public policy.[83] In the absence of an express or implied choice of law, Indian courts have dallied with the notion of an objective choice of law. In *Rabindra N Maitra v Life Insurance Corp of India*,[84] the Supreme Court listed the factors to be considered when imputing an objective choice of law – the place where the contract was made; the place of performance; the place of domicile, residence or business of the parties; the national character of a corporation; the subject matter of the contract, and any other facts that localise the contract.

b. Torts

The law of torts in India, largely modelled on English common law, exists through a few judicial pronouncements, most recently in the space of the tort of defamation. Civil wrongs involving a foreign element, are decided as at common law, based upon the 'double actionability' rule. This is evident in a recent pronouncement[85] on cross-border defamation. This rule

[77] Professor Morris combined the 'rule selection' rule of Professor Cavers and the issue-based approach to resolving conflicts of Professor WW Cook into a philosophic doctrine of the 'proper law' – a concept for the resolution of disputes relating to the law of obligations in order to achieve results which are 'commercially convenient and sound' in respect of contracts and 'socially convenient and sound' in respect of torts. See eg *R v International Trustee for the Protection of Bondholders AG* [1937] AC 500; FA Mann, 'The Proper Law in the Conflict of Laws' (1987) 36(4) *International and Comparative Law Quarterly* 437, 445.

[78] Jan L Neels, 'Choice of Forum and Tacit Choice of Law: The Supreme Court of India and the Hague Principles on Choice of Law in International Commercial Contracts (An Appeal for an Inclusive Comparative Approach to Private International Law)' in UNIDROIT (ed), *Eppur si Muove: The Age of Uniform Law – Essays in Honour of Michael Joachim Bonell to Celebrate His 70th Birthday* vol 1 (Rome, UNIDROIT, 2016) 358, 366. See also eg *Dhanrajamal Gobindram v Shamji Kalidas and Co* AIR [1961] SC 1285, [1961] 3 SCR 1020; *Taprogge Gesellschaft MBH v IAEC India Ltd* AIR [1988] Bom 157, [20]; *British India Steam Navigation* (n 45) [29]–[30]; *National Thermal Power Corp v Singer Co* [1992] 3 SCC 551 [25], [28]; *Shreejee Traco (I) Pvt Ltd v Paperline International Inc* [2003] 9 SCC 79 [7]; *Sara International Ltd v Arab Shipping Co (P) Ltd* OMP No 325/2005 (Delhi) [25]; *Kumarina Investment* (n 52); *Sakuma Exports Ltd v Louis Dreyfus Commodities and Uisse SA* Appeal No 337 of 2013 [10].

[79] *National Thermal Power* (n 78) [15], where the court quoted with approval *Dicey*'s Rule 180(2): 'When the intention of the parties to a contract with regard to the law governing the contract is not expressed in words, their intention is to be inferred from the terms and nature of the contract, and from the general circumstances of the case, and such inferred intention determines the proper law of the contract.'

[80] ibid [15]. The court referred with approval to the ratio in *Jacobs Marcus & Co v Credit Lyonnais* (1884) 12 QBD 589, 601.

[81] *British India Steam Navigation* (n 45).

[82] ibid [29].

[83] ibid [31].

[84] *Rabindra N Maitra v Life Insurance Corp of India* AIR [1964] Cal 141.

[85] *Sarine Technologies Ltd v Diyora and Bhanderi Corp* [2020] SCC Online Guj 140, where the court applied s 20 of the CPC.

requires that: (1) the act must be actionable as a tort in India; and (2) the act must be non-justifiable by the law of the place where it was committed.[86] In India, the CPC does not contain any specific rule for the resolution of conflicts related to foreign torts. Nevertheless, a statutory provision exists specifying the jurisdiction of the local court in the case of a wrong occurring within its territorial limits or the defendant being present there:

> Where a suit is for compensation for a wrong done to a person or to movable property, if the wrong was done within the local limits of the jurisdiction of one court and the defendant was resident, or carried on business, or personally worked for gain, within the local limits of the jurisdiction of another court, the suit may be instituted at the option of the plaintiff in either of the courts.[87]

In *Haveli Shah v Painda Khan*,[88] the court held that, in the case of torts committed abroad, courts in India may be approached for compensation if the residence of the defendant is located in India or the defendant engages in business, or personally works for gain in India. Regarding applicable law, there is no legislative directive. The solitary guidance has been the case of *Kotah Transport Ltd, Kotah v Jhalawar Transport Service Ltd*,[89] where the English law principle of double actionability was applied. Ironically, this is no longer the position in England where double actionability has been abolished by the Private International Law (Miscellaneous Provisions) Act 1995.[90]

The tort of defamation witnessed judicial delineation in *Govindan Nair v Achuta Menon*.[91] In this case, defamatory statements were made and published outside British India whereas the defendant was a resident of British India. The court observed:

> The omission in the Code to provide specifically for a case where the defendant resides in British India but is alleged to have committed a personal tort beyond the limits of British India, does not however take away the general jurisdiction of the Courts in British India under section 9. To assume jurisdiction where a person residing within the local limits of the jurisdiction of the Court is alleged to have committed a tort beyond such limits, is in accordance with the principles of Private International Law recognized in England: *The Halley* … The Code of Civil Procedure indicates that the same rule is to be followed by the Courts in British India.[92]

Contemporary jurisprudence provides insights into India's efforts at developing a mature normative regime for foreign torts. In *YouTube LLC v Geeta Shroff*,[93] the Delhi High Court affirmed a temporary injunction directing YouTube to take down defamatory materials uploaded on its platform worldwide. The High Court rejected YouTube's argument that the post had not been uploaded in India and therefore was outside of the court's jurisdiction. The ratio specifies: (1) if content was uploaded in India or from an IP addresses in India, the content can be taken down, blocked or restricted on a global basis; and (2) if uploaded from outside India, the court may refrain from exercising its jurisdiction. Any exercise of jurisdiction must ensure that the court gives due regard to extraterritorial jurisdictional issues. The international jurisprudence on global takedown orders has been instrumental in establishing India's position with respect to personal jurisdiction in cyber-transactions. But it remains to be seen whether

[86] *Phillips v Eyre* (1870) LR 6 QB 1, 28.
[87] CPC, s 9.
[88] *Haveli Shah* (n 29).
[89] *Kotah Transport Ltd, Kotah v Jhalawar Transport Service Ltd* AIR [1960] Raj 224.
[90] By s 10 of the Act.
[91] *Govindan Nair v Achuta Menon* (1915) ILR 39 Mad 433.
[92] ibid 439–40.
[93] *YouTube LLC v Geeta Shroff* [2018] SCC Online Del 9439 (17 May 2018).

concrete principles governing extraterritorial injunctions will emerge in the coming years. In *Swami Ramdev v Facebook Inc*,[94] the Delhi High Court held that it could order internet intermediaries like Facebook, Google, and Twitter globally to refrain from publishing defamatory content by users on their platforms. The court further held that it possessed jurisdiction even when such content or material was disseminated outside the territorial jurisdiction of an Indian court. The jurisdiction of the Indian court hinges on content being uploaded from India. The court reinforced its stand on worldwide take-downs by referring to jurisprudence from Canada and the EU. Thus, in *Equustek Solutions Inc v Jack*,[95] the Supreme Court of Canada ruled in favour of a global take-down and asked Google to de-index listings for the protection of trade secret rights of a subject. In *Eva Glawischnig-Piesczek v Facebook Ireland Ltd*,[96] the Court of Justice of the EU asked Facebook to take down defamatory content against Ms Piesczek from its global service.

c. Negotiable Instruments

Chapter XVI section 134 of the Negotiable Instruments Act 1881[97] specifies the law governing the liability of the maker, acceptor or indorser of a foreign instrument:

> In the absence of a contract to the contrary, the liability of the maker or drawer of a foreign promissory note, bill of exchange or cheque is regulated in all essential matters by the law of the place where he made the instrument, and the respective liabilities of the acceptor and indorser by the law of the place where the instrument is made payable.

In the absence of any other provision regarding transferability, it appears that this rule also governs the acceptability or the indorsement by the law of the place where the bill is made payable.[98] Noting that such rule may cause restrictions on negotiability, especially of instruments governed according to a foreign law but made payable in India, the section has been drafted with a *non-obstante* clause 'in the absence of a contract to the contrary …'. That allows the off-setting of this concern, through party autonomy in choice of law.

d. Unjust Enrichment

Unlike jurisdictions that make separate provisions related to remedial rights in conflict of laws scenarios, in India all remedial measures for enforcing a right (such as an injunction, an order for specific performance, or an order for the rendition of accounts of profits), being matters of procedure, are governed by the *lex fori*. The concept of unjust enrichment presupposes three elements: (1) the defendant has been enriched by the receipt of a benefit; (2) the defendant must have been so enriched at the plaintiffs expense; and (3) it would be unjust to allow the defendant to keep the benefit. Normative content impacting remedies against unjust enrichment or restitution are located within the Indian Contract Act 1872 (sections 68–72) and the Central Excise and Customs Law (Amendment) Act 1991.

[94] *Swami Ramdev v Facebook Inc* CS(OS) 27/2019 (23 October 2019).

[95] *Equustek Solutions Inc v Jack* [2018] BCSC 610 (Canada).

[96] Case C–18/18 *Eva Glawischnig-Piesczek v Facebook Ireland Ltd* (3 October 2019).

[97] Indian law does not specify the governing law for matters related to form and substance of, or the formalities related to issuing, negotiable instruments. It regulates the liabilities of the maker, indorser, and acceptor of instruments. See Govindaraj (n 76) 70.

[98] See Govindaraj (n 76) 71–72.

ii. Family Law

a. Marriage and Matrimonial Causes

Marriage and matrimonial causes are governed by personal laws, there has not been much legislation in this regard: the Hindu Marriage Act 1955, the Parsi Marriage and Divorce Act 1936, the Indian Christian Marriage Act 1872, and the Foreign Marriage Act 1969. The Foreign Marriage Act 1969 recognises the marriage of an Indian national in the following circumstances: (1) marriage to another Indian national abroad; (2) marriage to a national of another country; or (3) marriage to a person domiciled in another country.[99] The marriage itself must be valid under the *lex loci celebrationis*.[100] The Special Marriage Act 1954 governs matrimonial causes arising from relationships solemnised under that law.

b. Jurisdiction of Courts in Matrimonial Causes

The Marriage Laws Amendment Act 1976 specified that a marriage which is void under the Hindu Marriage Act and the Special Marriage Act shall be null and void and may, on the petition of either party to the marriage be declared to be so.[101] Any marriage solemnised before or after the commencement of the 1976 Act is voidable and may be annulled by a decree of nullity for reasons of non-consummation due to impotency of the respondent or if the marriage contravenes the condition in clause (ii) of section 5. A marriage may also be declared voidable and annulled if the consent of the petitioner or (where applicable) the guardian (prior to the commencement of the Child Marriage Restraint Amendment Act 1978) was obtained by coercion or fraud as to the nature of the ceremony or as to any material fact or circumstance concerning the respondent. The petitioner may apply for annulment within one year of the discovery of such fraud. Courts need to assure themselves that the petitioner was ignorant of the facts alleged.

The Indian Divorce Act 1869 states that the husband or wife may obtain a decree of judicial separation on grounds of adultery, cruelty, or desertion without reasonable excuse for two years or upwards. Under the Parsi Marriage and Divorce Act, either spouse may obtain a decree of judicial separation on similar grounds for obtaining a divorce. The Hindu Marriage Act 1955 has analogous provisions. Special Marriage Act section 23 is in like terms. Muslim law, as practiced in India, does not recognise judicial separation.

Much of Indian law relating to marriage and matrimonial causes is grounded in personal laws that vary with each religious community. Hence conflicts arise out of inter-marriage, when a person of one religious community marries a person of another. Though monogamy exists in the practice of most religions in India, except Islam, difficulties related to inter-marriage do arise. For example, a Hindu marriage can only take place between two Hindus according to Hindu Marriage Act 1955 section 5. When a Christian husband converts to Islam, it appears that he can unilaterally terminate his prior marriage and take up to four wives after divorcing his first wife.[102] Courts in India have rendered conflicting decisions on the legal effects of such unilateral divorces.[103] It is not an overstatement therefore to say that there is nothing like a *lex domicilii* or *lex loci* for Indian communities. In matters such as the grant of maintenance to a

[99] Foreign Marriages Act 1969, s 4.
[100] ibid, s 17.
[101] Law Commission of India, 'Fifty-Ninth Report on Hindu Marriage Act, 1955 and Special Marriage Act, 1954' (*Law Commission of India*, 1974) para 6.1A, available online: http://lawcommissionofindia.nic.in/51-100/report59.pdf.
[102] *John Jiban Chandra Dutta v Abinash Chandra Sen* [1939] ILR 2 Cal 12.
[103] Govindaraj (n 76) 118.

divorced wife, the recognition of foreign judgments of divorce rendered *ex parte* (for instance, the unilateral divorce of a Hindu wife by the husband upon embracing Islam and the unilateral pronouncement of *talaq*), the courts have been active.[104] The Supreme Court's jurisprudence[105] has reiterated that a divorced Muslim woman is entitled to maintenance from her divorced husband beyond the period prescribed by the *shari'a* and the provisions of section 125 of the Criminal Procedure Code relating to maintenance apply to India's Muslim population as well. In *Shayara Bano*,[106] the Supreme Court, hearing a batch of writ petitions, held the practice of '*talaq-e-biddat*' (triple *talaq*) as unconstitutional. The Supreme Court has been critical of the recognition of *ex parte* decrees of divorce granted by foreign courts based only on the domicile that a spouse claims to have acquired by a minimum period of residence. This was seen in *Satya v Teja Singh*[107] and *Y Narsimha Rao v Y Venkatalakshmi*.[108] Unilateral divorce, upon conversion to Islam was condemned by the Delhi High Court in *Vilayat Raj v Sunila*.[109] The Supreme Court in *Sarla Mudgal v Union of India*[110] held that a marriage solemnised between two Hindus in accordance with Hindu rites and ceremonies can only be dissolved under the Hindu Marriage Act 1955. As case to case decisions do not add up to a system of justice, statutes need to be enacted in the foregoing areas which concern secular matters. That would help raise the awareness among members of the public of their rights and duties.

c. Custody, Guardianship and Adoption, Intercountry Child Removal

Hindu law governing custody of children is closely linked with the law on guardianship. Guardianship refers to a bundle of rights and powers that an adult has in relation to the person and property of a minor, while custody is a narrower concept regarding the upbringing and day-to-day care and control of a minor.[111] The Guardians and Wards Act 1890 (GWA) defined 'guardian' as a person having the care of the person of a minor or of their property or of both their person and property. The 1890 Act is a secular law regulating questions of guardianship and custody for all children within India, irrespective of religion. While issues of substantive law can still be handled under religious law, the GWA is the applicable procedural law. The Hindu Minority and Guardianship Act 1956 (HMGA) designates the father as the natural guardian of a minor and, after him, the mother. The GWA and the HMGA, however, differ on the welfare principle. While the former places parental authority before the welfare principle, the latter upholds the primacy of the welfare principle in determining guardianship.

The concept of shared custody or residence orders is a recent occurrence in India. In *Eugenia Archetti Abdullah v State of Kerala*,[112] the court, pending custody proceedings in the foreign court, granted custody of the children to the mother with the stipulation of shared custody and visitation rights until the mother left India. In *Leeladhar Kachroo v Umang Bhat Kachroo*,[113] the court held that it was empowered to entrust the custody of a child to a parent who resides

[104] ibid 119.

[105] *Mohammad Ahmed Khan v Shah Bano Begum* AIR [1985] SC 945, [1985] 3 SCR 844; *Danial Latifi v Union of India* [2001] 7 SCC 740; *Shabana Bano v Imran Khan* [2010] 1 SCC 666.

[106] *Shayara Bano v Union of India* Writ Petition (C) No 118 of 2016 (22 August 2017).

[107] *Satya v Teja Singh* AIR [1975] SC 105, [1975] 2 SCR 97.

[108] *Y Narasimha Rao v Y Venkata Lakshmi* [1991] 2 SCR 821, [1991] 3 SCC 451.

[109] *Vilayat Raj v Sunila* AIR [1983] Del 351.

[110] *Sarla Mudgal v Union of India* AIR [1995] SC 1531, [1995] 3 SCC 635.

[111] See generally Sai Ramani Garimella, 'International Parental Child Abduction and the Fragmented Law in India – Time to Accede to the Hague Convention?' (2017) 17 *Macquarie Law Journal* 38–55.

[112] *Eugenia Archetti Abdullah v State of Kerala* [2005] 1 HLR (Ker) 34.

[113] *Leeladhar Kachroo v Umang Bhat Kachroo* [2005] 2 HLR (Del) 449.

outside its jurisdiction, if it is conducive to the welfare of the child. Owing to the absence of a statutory provision regarding shared residence orders, the courts interpret foreign courts' shared residence orders in light of the best interests of the child. The judgments just described lead to a few conclusions. First, the 'most intimate contact' and the 'closest concern' determinants derived from *Surinder Kaur Sandhu v Harbax Singh Sandhu*[114] remain the law. Second, the principle of comity of courts remains the preferred interpretation rule. Foreign court orders are disregarded only when there exist special and compelling reasons. Third, the best interests and welfare of the child, in the absence of specific criteria, is typically based on the religious law of the parents. Fourth, the habitual residence of a minor and the parents can be an important consideration, a feature that has been adopted by the courts of contracting states to the 1980 Hague Convention on the Civil Aspects of International Child Abduction. India, however, is not a signatory to the 1980 Convention.

iii. Law of Property

a. Jurisdiction Over Foreign Property

Indian private international law of contract specifies that the capacity to convey property and transfer the property is governed by the *lex situs*. An Indian court will not entertain an action for a declaration of title to or division of foreign immovables or for the possession of such immovables.[115] Claims related to partition of a property situated abroad or a right to share in the annual allowances charged on the revenue of a foreign village cannot be presented to an Indian court.[116] But Indian courts exercise jurisdiction in certain actions in *personam* arising out of foreign immovable property on grounds of equity, contract, fraud or trust.[117] In *Mahadev v Ramachandra*,[118] the court exercised jurisdiction in a suit for mesne profits against the defendant who was amenable to the jurisdiction of the court. Courts will also assume jurisdiction in suits in respect of trusts affecting property situated abroad or for the preservation or protection of a trust of property situated in a foreign country provided the trustee is in India. Even so, the courts will not interfere with the administration of foreign trusts.[119] Indian courts can order specific performance of a contract for the sale of immovable property in India against a non-resident foreigner, even if the contract was executed outside the country. However, an absentee owner is amenable to the jurisdiction of an Indian court only if the court is otherwise competent. Mere presence of property in India will not necessarily invest a court with jurisdiction.[120] CPC sections 19 and 20 apply to determinations of the requisite competence to pass a decree against an absentee owner.[121] Indian courts have also exercised jurisdiction in matters of fraud, such as the forgery of a will relating to properties situated abroad[122] or for a declaration of nullity of an adoption.[123]

[114] *Surinder Kaur Sandhu v Harbax Singh Sandhu* AIR [1984] SC 1224, [1984] 3 SCR 422.

[115] *Krishnaji Pandurang Sathe v Gajanan Balvant Kulkarni* (1909) ILR 33 Bom 373; *Nilkanth Balwant Natu v Vidya Narasingh Bharathi Swami* AIR [1930] PC 188; *Nachiappa Chettiar v Muthu Karuppan Chettiar* AIR [1946] Mad 398.

[116] *Keshav v Vinayak* (1899) ILR 23 Bom 22; *Puzhavakkath Madathil Gopala Pattar's Sons Subramanya Iyer v Puzhavakkath Madathil Gopal Pattar's Sons Lakshmana Ayyar* AIR [1951] Mad 742.

[117] See eg *Kashinath v Anant* (n 25); *Dev Samaj Council, Lahore v Amritlal Motilal* AIR [1934] Sind 123; *Chidambaram Chettiar v Subramanian Chettiar* AIR [1953] Mad 492.

[118] *Mahadeo v Ramachandra* AIR [1922] Bom 188.

[119] *Bilasrai Joharmal v Shivnarayan Sarupchand* AIR [1944] PC 39.

[120] *Muhammad Eusoof Maricar v K Subramanian Chettiar* AIR [1950] Mad 272.

[121] Govindaraj (n 76) 162.

[122] *Niyyala Achayya v Nittala Yellamma* AIR [1923] Mad 109, (1922) 43 MLJ 615.

[123] *Ramakrishnayya v Mahalakshamma* 30 MLW 691.

The Companies Act 1956 specifies that the transfer of intangible movables, made by or on behalf of a transferor is complete upon its registration in the name of the transferee. The effect of the transfer as between the company and the shareholder would be determined by the *lex situs* of the share certificate that is the place where the register for the registration of shares is kept. The proper law of the transaction governs the effect of a transfer as between the transferor and the transferee and claimants through them.

b. Succession to Property

An Indian court will give effect to the decision of the court of domicile of the deceased at the date of death on any question in respect of succession to movables.[124] In the matter of succession to immovables, an Indian court will follow the decision of the court of the country where the immovables are situated.[125] In matters related to intestate succession the Indian Succession Act 1925 applies the well-established principle that succession to movables intestate, wherever situate, is governed by the law of domicile at the date of death. Issues relating to succession to immovables of the deceased intestate are governed by the *lex situs*.[126] Regarding testamentary succession, a will related to movables is valid if it is in conformity with the formalities prescribed by the law of the testator's domicile at the date of his death. *Lex domicilii*, as interpreted and applied by courts in India, refers to substantive law to the exclusion of choice of law rules (that is, to the exclusion of *renvoi*.)[127] A beneficiary has the capacity to receive a legacy of movables under a will if the beneficiary has capacity by the law of one's own or the testator's domicile. The *lex situs* governs capacity to make a will of immovables as well as to take under the will.[128]

c. Trusts

The Indian Trusts Act 1882 does not have a provision related to disputes involving a foreign element, nor does it have a conflict of laws rule. The law of contracts is applied to trusts in such matters. Such law regulates all aspects of a trust such as its formation and validity; the capacity to create a trust; the rights, duties and liabilities of trustees; the rights and liabilities of beneficiaries and the process of extinction of a trust. To be recognised as subject to a trust, property must be characterised as a separate fund. The trustee may sue and be sued as such. The personal assets of a trustee and the rights and obligations that arise therefrom are outside the purview of the trust or the trust fund. India is not a signatory to the 1985 Hague Convention on the Law Applicable to Trusts and on Their Recognition.

d. Intellectual Property Rights (IPRs)

The legal regime related to IPRs in India is diverse and largely in consonance with India's Agreement on Trade-Related Aspects of Intellectual Property Rights (TRIPS) and other treaty obligations. India's normative regime on IPRs is mainly to be found in the Patents Act 1970, the Trade Marks Act 1999, the Copyright Act 1957, the Designs Act 2000, the Geographical

[124] Indian Succession Act 1925, s 5(2). See also eg *Sankaran Govindan* (n 15).
[125] Govindaraj (n 76) 174.
[126] Indian Succession Act 1925, s 5(10).
[127] Govindaraj (n 76) 175–76.
[128] *Ratan Shah v Bomanji* [1938] ILR Bom 238; *Keshaji v Khai Khusroo* (1939) 41 Bom LR 478.

Indication of Goods (Registration and Protection) Act 1999, the Semiconductor Integrated Circuits Layout-Design Act 2000, the Protection of Plant Varieties and Farmers' Rights Act 2001, and judicial precedent. The Indian regime on IPRs can be understood under the heads of protection and remedial jurisdiction. Protection is dependent upon the nature of international obligations to which India has acceded. In the area of patents, Indian law offers protection and requires registration. For copyright and trademarks, India allows for multiple protection and does not require a separate registration in India for a right to be enforced. Trade secrets are protected in India through contract law and the equitable doctrine of breach of confidence.[129] In cases where confidential information and trade secrets are not protected by a contract, the person seeking to enforce the confidentiality or secrecy of information can do so if certain conditions are fulfilled: (1) the information must be confidential; (2) there was an obligation of secrecy; and (3) there was an attempt to use or disclose the information. Regarding remedial jurisdiction, a foreign judgment creditor will still have to bring a domestic cause of action against the judgment debtor through a civil suit or an application for injunctive relief. The foreign judgment would be of evidentiary value, although it may not operate as *res judicata*. Jurisdiction may depend upon the relevant territory of the court, and the pecuniary value and subject matter of the dispute. Each of these determinants are independently considered for a court to assume jurisdiction.

An Indian court can exercise jurisdiction if an infringement took place (or the cause of action arose) within its territorial jurisdiction or if the defendant is resident or employed within its territorial jurisdiction (CPC section 20). The plaintiff's location is not a consideration. In *Sholay Media Entertainment Ltd v Yogesh Patel*,[130] the Division Bench of the Delhi High Court held that even an infinitesimal fraction of a cause of action being located within its territory would confer jurisdiction on the court. But, in an action for infringement of a registered copyright or trademark, the civil court within whose jurisdiction the claimant actually and voluntarily resides, or carries on business or personally works for gain, also has jurisdiction.[131] Indian courts can hear disputes related to validity or registration of an IPR only if such right is to be registered in India. Foreign entities can, however, challenge the validity or registration of IPRs granted in India. Further, even if rectification proceedings instituted by a defendant in a foreign court are pending, an Indian court can grant interlocutory relief in favour of the claimant in trademark matters. To ensure expedited dispute resolution in IPR disputes, the Commercial Courts, Commercial Division and Commercial Appellate Division of High Courts Act 2015 categorises IPR disputes as commercial disputes with a modified procedural law to expedite and manage their timeline. Additionally, to avoid a multiplicity of proceedings, the Supreme Court has held that a party who has sought revocation of a patent before the Intellectual Property Appellate Board (IPAB) is precluded from filing a counterclaim challenging the validity of the same patent in a suit for infringement of the patent.[132] Further, section 104 of the Patents Act 1970 and section 22(4) of the Designs Act provide that if the defendant has challenged the validity of the patent through a counterclaim and challenged the validity of a design by way of a defence in a patent and design infringement suit respectively, then such suits are liable be transferred to the High Court for adjudication.

[129] *Konrad Wiedemann GmbH v Standard Castings Pvt Ltd* [1985] 10 IPLR 243; *John Richard Brady v Chemical Process Equip Pvt Ltd* AIR [1987] Del 372.
[130] *Sholay Media Entertainment Ltd v Yogesh Patel* FAO (OS) No 222 of 2010 (13 March 2014).
[131] Copyright Act 1957, s 62(2); Trade Marks Act 1999, s 134(2).
[132] *Aloys Wobben v Yogesh Mehra* (2014) 15 SCC 360.

The Patents Act 1970 is silent on what qualifies as an infringement of a patent. Section 48 vests certain exclusive rights upon the patentee or his or her agent. Violation of the rights conferred on the patentee under the Act would thus constitute infringement. In a patent infringement suit, the court assesses the liability of the defendant as well as the quantum of damages. By Patents Act 1970 section 108, a court may grant infringement relief, including an injunction subject to such terms as it sees fit, damages, or an account of profits. Further, the court may order seizure, forfeiture and destruction of goods found to be infringing, including the implements used in creating the same, without payment of compensation. In suits for trademark and patent infringement, a plaintiff is entitled to seek damages or an account of profits.[133] By Copyright Act section 56, in a suit for copyright infringement, the claimant may be entitled to damages, accounts and conversion damages (unless the defendant establishes that it was unaware (and had no reasonable grounds to believe) that copyright was being violated). A trend of awarding damages has been observed in cases pertaining to software piracy.[134] Indian law on IPRs allows injunctive relief in the form of *Anton Piller* orders, *Mareva* injunctions and John Doe orders. *Ex parte* injunctions have also been granted by the courts.[135] Such relief can be sought before the Commercial Courts and Commercial Divisions of the High Courts depending upon the pecuniary value of the claim. An appellate review can be made to the High Courts and thereafter the Supreme Court.

e. Competition Law

Competition Law is a matter of public law in India requiring claims to be based upon a domestic cause of action in accordance with the provisions of the Competition Act 2002. Claims for identified violations are presented to the Competition Commission and appeals are brought before the National Company Law Appellate Tribunal. The legislation attempts to curtail market arrangements that constitute the abuse of a dominant position, predatory pricing, and unfair trade practices. The legislation additionally covers the interface between competition law with IPRs. Section 3 deals with anti-competitive agreements. The legislation states that an agreement is perceived as having an 'appreciable adverse impact' if it: (1) directly or indirectly determines sale or purchase prices; (2) limits or controls production, supply, markets, technical development, investment or provision of services; (3) shares the market or source of production or provision of services by allocation of inter alia geographical areas, nature of goods, number of customers, or similar methods; or (4) directly or indirectly results in bid rigging or collusive bidding. The legislation also regulates combination agreements that exceed statutory threshold limits.

The Competition Commission is similar to a civil court and empowered to conduct enquiries into certain agreements, the dominant position of enterprises, and combinations. It is also engaged with regulating mergers and acquisitions that will have an adverse impact on competition.

f. Insolvency Law

The Insolvency and Bankruptcy Code 2016 (IBC) contains two provisions (sections 234 and 235) on cross-border insolvency addressing jurisdiction-related issues: (1) jurisdiction of

[133] Patents Act 1970, s 198; Trade Marks Act 1999, s 135.

[134] *Microsoft Corp v Amritbir Singh* CS(OS) No 732 of 2010 (Delhi High Court).

[135] See eg *Bucyrus Europe Ltd v Vulcan Industries Engineering* [2005] (1) CHN 106 (Calcutta High Court).

the local court of the state where insolvency proceedings have been initiated over the assets of the debtor located in a foreign jurisdiction; and (2) jurisdiction in concurrent insolvency proceedings where more than one proceeding has been simultaneously going on against the same debtor in different jurisdictions. Any contemporary insolvency framework must answer these fundamental issues. IBC sections 234 and 235 collectively allow an insolvency resolution professional to apply to the adjudicatory authority to take appropriate action for preserving a corporate debtor's assets that may be outside India in a country with which India shares a bilateral cross-border insolvency agreement. To date, there has been no instance where either of the two sections have been utilised. No cross-border agreement has been signed by the Indian Government, nor has any application been made. The IBC governs insolvency, restructuring and liquidation proceedings for all classes of legal person, but not financial entities (eg, banks, non-banking financial companies and mutual funds which render financial services and offer financial products).

The recognition in India of foreign insolvency proceedings is governed by the rules applicable to foreign proceedings under the CPC. Section 44A allows Indian courts to enforce orders passed by non-Indian courts in 'reciprocating territories'. A country would be considered a reciprocating territory if it was so notified by the government in the Official Gazette. Section 13 prescribes that courts in India, when enforcing a foreign judgment or decree, shall ensure that the judgment or decree is a conclusive one, passed on the merits of the case and by a superior court having competent jurisdiction.

In *Jet Airways India Ltd v State Bank of India*,[136] the National Company Law Appellate Tribunal (NCLAT) allowed a Dutch administrator appointed by the Noord District Court in Holland to participate in meetings of the committee of creditors constituted for the corporate insolvency resolution process (CIRP) of Jet Airways. The appeal was necessitated because the order[137] of the National Company Law Tribunal (NCLT) Mumbai Bench held that the Dutch court did not have jurisdiction to initiate offshore insolvency proceedings against the debtor company Jet Airways, a company registered in India. The NCLT opined that the continuation of parallel proceedings would vitiate the insolvency process in India. According to the NCLT, a Cross-Border Insolvency Protocol had been executed between a resolution professional and the administrator and a joint CIRP would continue in accordance with the IBC.

The Report of the Insolvency Law Committee on Cross-Border Insolvency[138] constituted by the Ministry of Corporate Affairs has recommended the incorporation into Indian law of cross-border insolvency provisions in accordance with the UNICTRAL Model Law[139] to create an 'internationally aligned and comprehensive insolvency framework for corporate debtors … which is most essential in a globalised environment'.[140] It is hoped that the Indian Government will engage with law reform towards aligning the normative structure on cross-border insolvency with global best practices.

[136] *Jet Airways India Ltd v State Bank of India* Company Appeal (AT) (Insolvency) No 707 of 2019.

[137] *State Bank of India v Jet Airways India Ltd* CP (IB) 2205/MB/2019.

[138] Ministry of Corporate Affairs, 'Report of Insolvency Law Committee on Cross Border Insolvency' (*Ministry of Corporate Affairs*, October 2018), available online: www.mca.gov.in/Ministry/pdf/CrossBorderInsolvencyReport_22102018.pdf.

[139] 'UNCITRAL Model Law on Cross-Border Insolvency with Guide to Enactment and Interpretation' (*UNCITRAL*, January 2014), available online: www.uncitral.org/pdf/english/texts/insolven/1997-Model-Law-Insol-2013-Guide-Enactment-e.pdf. See also S Chandra Mohan, 'Cross-border Insolvency Problems: Is the UNCITRAL Model Law the Answer?' (2012) 21(3) *International Insolvency Review* 199.

[140] Ministry of Corporate Affairs (n 138) 7.

III. Jurisdiction *in rem*

A. General Principles

An action *in rem* is an action against a thing (*res*) (such as goods, a ship, or cargo) rather than a person. By proceeding against a *res*, a plaintiff can obtain security for a claim. The *res* may be arrested by the court and sold to satisfy a judgment. An action may be brought *in rem* provided the relevant property is within the jurisdiction. *In rem* jurisdiction is exercised exclusively over a few types of claims arising at sea or on tidal waters. In an action *in rem*, an arrested ship is personified as a defendant distinct from its owner. The foundation of an action *in rem* in such cases is a maritime lien or certain claims imposing a personal liability on the owner of a vessel.[141] Admiralty jurisdiction was first known in British India in 1890 when the High Courts of Madras, Bombay and Calcutta were vested with the same by the Colonial Court of Admiralty Act 1890. Article 372 of the Constitution of India which dealt with the status of pre-constitution laws ensured the continuity of this legislation and thereby the Admiralty jurisdiction of the High Courts. Unlike England, where there has been much legislative activity, Admiralty law in India has developed only through the jurisprudence of courts, foremost being the Supreme Court of India's decision in *MV Elisabeth v Harwan Investments and Trading Pvt Ltd*,[142] involving the jurisdiction of the courts in India for claims against a vessel owned by a foreign company. The High Court heard the matter and ordered the ship to be arrested upon reaching local ports within the Court's jurisdiction. On appeal, the Supreme Court parsed the Admiralty law in India, minimal as it is, and the normative content of international law applicable to the dispute. The 1983 United Nations Convention on the Law of the Sea (UNCLOS) specifies that all foreign merchant ships and persons fall under the civil and criminal jurisdiction of a coastal state, as they enter its waters subject to the rights of innocent passage. A coastal state is also entitled to exercise jurisdiction in respect of maritime claims, including actions for ship arrest and detention in fulfilment of maritime claims, against foreign merchant ships lying in their waters. The courts of the country in which a foreign ship had been arrested may determine the case according to merits provided they are empowered to so under domestic law or according to applicable Arrest Conventions. The *MV Elisabeth* ratio was further explained in *Videsh Sanchar Nigam Ltd v MV Kapitan Kud*,[143] where the Supreme Court upheld the exercise of the Admiralty *in rem* jurisdiction in respect of a maritime claim leading to the arrest of a ship, without regard to the place of business, domicile or residence of its owners or the place where the cause of action arose.

India has since enacted comprehensive legislation on Admiralty law, the Admiralty (Jurisdiction and Settlement of Maritime Claims) Act 2017 (Admiralty Act) came into force in India on 1 April 2018. The Admiralty Act expressly vests Admiralty jurisdiction in the High Courts of all the coastal states in India, that is, the High Courts of Calcutta, Bombay, Madras, Karnataka, Gujarat, Orissa, Kerala and Hyderabad. Each Court has jurisdiction over the waters up to the limits of its territorial sea. The Admiralty Act permits the Central Government to vest Admiralty jurisdiction in other High Courts and extend the jurisdiction of the High Courts by

[141] Shrikant Hathi and Binita Hathi, *Ship Arrest in India and Admiralty Laws of India* (Mumbai, Brus Chambers, 2019) 43, available online: http://admiraltypractice.com/Book.pdf. See also Omana George, 'Admiralty Jurisdiction and Ship Arrest in India' (2015) 7(7) *International Journal of Current Research* 18034, available online: www.journalcra.com/sites/default/files/issue-pdf/9635.pdf.

[142] *MV Elisabeth v Harwan Investments and Trading Pvt Ltd* AIR [1993] SC 1014, [1992] 1 SCR 1003.

[143] *Videsh Sanchar Nigam Ltd v MV Kapitan Kud* AIR [1996] SC 516, [1996] 7 SCC 127.

notification. Every High Court that has acquired Admiralty jurisdiction under the Admiralty Act needs to frame its rules for the exercise of that jurisdiction. The legislation provides a list of maritime claims that are subject to the Admiralty jurisdiction; the list is similar to those in the 1952 International Convention Relating to the Arrest of Seagoing Ships and the 1999 International Convention on Arrest of Ships. Further the definition of maritime claims includes claims related to port or harbour dues, canal, dock or light tolls, waterway charges and such like; particular average claims; claims by master or crew or their heirs/dependents for wages, cost of repatriation or social insurance contributions; insurance premiums, mutual insurance calls; commission/brokerage agency fees payable by vessel owners or demise charterers; environment damage claims or threat thereof; and wreck removal claims. The legislation also confers Admiralty jurisdiction *in personam* in respect of certain maritime claims arising out of a collision and related claims. An *in personam* action can be initiated against the defendant only if the cause of action, wholly or in part arises in India or if the jurisdiction over the defendant can be achieved under a provision of the CPC.

B. Ship Arrest

The Admiralty Act legislated detailed provisions on ship arrest. The law grants jurisdiction to the High Courts to order the arrest of a vessel or its sister ship within their jurisdiction where (among other situations): (1) a claim is made against the owner, demise charterer, manager or operator of a vessel relating to the carriage of goods by the vessel; (2) a claim is based on a mortgage or similar charge over a vessel; or (3) a claim relates to possession or ownership of a vessel. The owner of the vessel may settle the claim or appear before the court to challenge the same. The vessel may be allowed to sail subject to furnishing of security for the claim. Upon default of an owner, an arrested vessel may be sold and the proceeds used to settle a claim.

IV. Immunities from Jurisdiction

Indian Law on the immunity from jurisdiction of foreign sovereigns, states, state-owned enterprises (SOEs) and diplomatic representatives is found in CPC sections 84 to 87A. The provisions require the court to take judicial notice of the recognition of a foreign state by the Indian Government.[144] Section 86 confers immunity from suit on: (1) rulers or heads of foreign states; (2) ambassadors or envoys of foreign states; (3) High Commissioners of Commonwealth states; and (4) members of the staff or retinue of the heads or rulers of foreign states, ambassadors, High Commissioners, as the Central Government may by general or special order specify. Those within categories (1) to (4) may not be subject to judicial proceedings in any court in India except with the prior consent[145] of the government. The immunity extends to all civil actions as well as execution proceedings. The government may consent only in the following situations: (1) when a foreign state, etc has instituted a suit in the court against the person desiring to sue; (2) when a

[144] In *German Democratic Republic v Dynamic Industrial Undertaking Ltd* AIR [1972] Bom 27, the court opined that the judicial forum hearing the suit should obtain information about the recognition of a foreign state from the Indian Government and such information would be conclusive proof of the matter.

[145] See *Mirza Ali Akbar v United Arab Republic* AIR [1966] SC 230, [1966] 1 SCR 319. See also *Gaekwar-Baroda State Railway v Hafiz Habib-ul-Haq* AIR [1938] PC 165.

foreign state by itself or with another trades within the local limits of the court; (3) when a foreign state is in possession of immovable property within the territorial limits of the local court and the suit is with regard to such property or for money charged thereon; or (4) when the foreign state has expressly or impliedly waived the privilege accorded to it.

On the immunity of foreign SOEs, the CPC does not mention corporations in section 86. But there is much jurisprudence lending clarity on the law. For example, the Calcutta High Court in *Royal Nepal Airlines Corp v Manorama*,[146] hearing a claim for damages against a corporate entity, held that a government department of a foreign state or a foreign corporation which is a government department is entitled to immunity. In *New Central Jute Mills Co Ltd v VED Dentfracht Sureedarci Rostock*,[147] the Calcutta High Court held that immunity did not exist outside CPC section 86. Since section 86 only applied to foreign states and sovereigns, the defendant, an East German nationalised company involved in the supply and carriage of goods, did not enjoy immunity. On the immunity of diplomatic representatives and staff, Indian Law is codified in the Diplomatic Relations (Vienna Convention) Act 1972, giving effect to the 1961 Vienna Convention on Diplomatic Relations. The heads of diplomatic missions and their members are exempt from civil and criminal jurisdiction in regard to both official and private acts. No remedy is enforceable against such personnel either at the instance of the state or a private individual. Where a representative or staff member is an Indian citizen working in the diplomatic mission, immunity only extends to official acts. A foreign state may waive the immunity of a diplomat by express action. But it would still require the consent of the government under CPC section 86 to sue the diplomat.

V. Conclusion

India's private international law is an interesting amalgam of rules on jurisdiction and choice of law based on personal law requirements, India's colonial legacy, and the need to respond to the requirements of contemporary commerce. However, it would be well for India to align its laws with international best practices by increased participation in harmonised legal regimes. It would be appropriate if India were to enact systematic, consistent and comprehensive legislation on matters relating to private international law, including the exercise of direct jurisdiction.

[146] *Royal Nepal Airlines* (n 23).
[147] *New Central Jute Mills Co Ltd v VEB Deutfracht Seereederei Rostock* AIR [1983] Cal 225.

17

Conclusion

ANSELMO REYES AND WILSON LUI

I. Introduction

The first chapter identified similarities in the general rules of direct jurisdiction of the 15 states examined in this book. This final chapter discusses whether there would be any utility in a convention or soft law instrument setting out Asian general principles of direct jurisdiction. The focus will be on jurisdiction *in personam* in matters of contract, tort and movable and immovable property. The closing section of this chapter will consider what the future might hold in respect of direct jurisdiction, not just by way of beneficial initiative to improve Asian systems, but also as consequences of the COVID-19 pandemic and the political and economic tensions currently besetting the world.

II. An International Convention on Direct Jurisdiction?

In the 1990s, the Hague Conference's Judgment Project attempted to draft a convention covering direct jurisdiction and the recognition and enforcement of judgments. A double convention, however, proved a bridge too far.[1] The Judgments Project led to the 2005 Hague Convention on Choice of Court Agreements and, more recently, the 2019 Hague Convention on the Recognition and Enforcement of Foreign Judgments in Civil or Commercial Matters (the 2019 Hague Convention). But so far there has been no Hague Convention or even Hague Principles on direct jurisdiction. The Hague Conference is currently undertaking what it has called the Jurisdiction Project to look into three questions:

(1) the grounds by which the parties to a civil or commercial dispute can seise the courts of a given state;
(2) the grounds by which a state can exercise jurisdiction in civil and commercial matters; and
(3) how harmonised rules on jurisdiction can reduce the risk of parallel litigation in different states?

The Hague Conference's Experts' Group on Jurisdiction met for a fifth and final time in February 2021 to discuss what sort of instrument on direct jurisdiction (for instance, a convention,

[1] For a detailed analysis of the Judgments Project and why it failed to come up with a double convention after more than a decade, see Guangjian Tu, *A Study on a Global Jurisdiction and Judgments Convention* (Hong Kong, Sweet & Maxwell, 2009).

guidelines, principles, or model law) might usefully be produced by the Jurisdiction Project. Following the March 2021 meeting of the Hague Conference's General Council on General Affairs and Policy, the Experts' Group has been superseded by a Working Group tasked with drafting provisions on direct jurisdiction in civil or commercial matters and on parallel litigation. It is unknown at the time of writing what will result from the Jurisdiction Project.[2]

The stumbling block to a double convention was direct jurisdiction. Essentially, common law jurisdictions (especially the US) favoured an instrument with a liberal list of grounds for assuming jurisdiction (including extra-territorial jurisdiction). That would enable a plaintiff readily to establish jurisdiction before the court of a given state. But, to counter the ease with which jurisdiction could be established, it was proposed that the convention allow countries to decline jurisdiction on the basis of *forum non conveniens*. In contrast, civil law jurisdictions (especially within the EU) favoured a convention with specific grounds for establishing jurisdiction. This would mean that once a party is able to show that a claim falls within an identified ground, the court of a given state would be bound to accept jurisdiction. Insofar, as the proposed instrument might allow for *forum non conveniens*, the ambit of the latter doctrine would be circumscribed so as to apply only exceptionally.[3] The common law proposal would ensure greater fairness in a given set of circumstances. Through *forum non conveniens*, a court can ensure that a case will be heard in the jurisdiction with which it is most closely connected, such as the place where the majority of witnesses and the bulk of evidence are situated. Jurisdiction can be closely tailored to the circumstances of a case. That would be conducive, not just to saving time and cost, but also to the interests of justice. The US in particular was unable to accept a more rigid system of direct jurisdiction, because it regarded the application of *forum non conveniens* to a case as involving a question of due process and thus a matter which is constitutionally guaranteed by the Fourteenth Amendment. Civil law states, on the other hand, argued that their proposal would promote certainty. Litigants would know precisely where they stood, without having to second guess which forum was better (or even best) suited to the resolution of a dispute. Ultimately, the two views could not be reconciled and the idea of a double convention was put on hold. The Hague Conference eventually decided first to proceed with the 2005, and later the 2019, Hague Conventions.

Of the 15 states canvassed here, five belong to the common law family (Hong Kong, Singapore, Malaysia, Myanmar and India), eight to the civil law family (China, Taiwan, Japan, South Korea, Vietnam, Cambodia, Indonesia and Thailand), and two are mixed common and civil law countries (the Philippines and Sri Lanka). Here and there among the chapters of this book, the reader will have heard faint echoes of the debate that troubled the Judgments Project. However, in actuality the jurisdictions surveyed here are not so far apart from each other when it comes to exercising direct jurisdiction in a case having foreign elements. Some (but by no means all) of the common law states covered have a broad range of grounds for establishing jurisdiction (including extra-territorial jurisdiction). But those states can usually apply *forum non conveniens* as a safety valve where an action might more properly be litigated elsewhere. By and large (but by no means uniformly) the civil law states have specific lists of jurisdictional grounds, with limited scope for the application of *forum non conveniens*. Myanmar and India are interesting because their Civil Procedure Codes (where their rules of direct jurisdiction are largely to be found) derive from the same colonial statute, the India Act V of 1908. Both countries have not followed

[2] The latest information on the Jurisdiction Project is available online: www.hcch.net/en/projects/legislative-projects/jurisdiction-project.

[3] Although *forum non conveniens* is frequently characterised as a common law doctrine, in *Spiliada Maritime Corp v Cansulex Ltd* [1987] AC 460 (HL) the House of Lords noted that English law had adopted the doctrine from Scotland, a civil law jurisdiction.

Singapore, Malaysia and Hong Kong (also former British colonies) in enlarging the scope of their extraterritorial grounds of jurisdiction by adding numerous grounds to their Civil Procedure Codes for asserting jurisdiction (including extraterritorial jurisdiction), similar to the rules in place in England. Instead, both countries' rules for establishing direct jurisdiction are narrower. Both countries have scope for the application of *forum non conveniens*, although the doctrine has not been explicitly identified as such in their Civil Procedure Codes. Unsurprisingly, given the narrower range of situations in which a party can establish jurisdiction, the application of *forum non conveniens* in both countries is seemingly restricted to exceptional circumstances. In that sense, both countries are more akin to civil law states in their approach to direct jurisdiction. The Philippines and Sri Lanka are not so clear-cut. Although a common law state in the sense of having a legal system based on *stare decisis*, the Philippines having been governed by a civil law jurisdiction (Spain) for nearly 350 years before being taken over by the US in 1898, largely follows a civil law approach when it comes to direct jurisdiction. It has specific narrow criteria for establishing jurisdiction, but it also allows a court to accept jurisdiction when on the facts it would be the *forum conveniens* and to decline jurisdiction on *forum non conveniens* grounds when litigation before the court of some other country would be more apposite. Despite the strong influence of its English colonial heritage in the development of its procedural rules, Sri Lanka has narrow grounds of direct jurisdiction and eschews *forum non conveniens*.

In matters of contract, tort and property, it will be important to a plaintiff to be able to enforce a judgment in his or her favour. An unenforceable civil or commercial judgment would be a waste of time and money. Where a plaintiff brings a case in state X and obtains a favourable judgment, it should be possible to enforce the judgment against the defendant's assets in X. It would be odd if state X refused to enforce the judgment of its own court. Where a case involves cross-border elements and a defendant has assets in some other state Y, a plaintiff who obtains final judgment in state X may want to enforce the same against the defendant's assets in state Y. Consequently, the bottom line insofar as direct jurisdiction is concerned must be whether other states: (1) accept that the court of state X was entitled to accept jurisdiction in a matter; and (2) consequently enforce the resulting judgment of state X in that matter.

The Introduction chapter of this book proposes (at Section V) six grounds of direct jurisdiction in Asia, based on the certain minimal grounds of indirect or international jurisdiction under the rudimentary system for the recognition and enforcement of judgments.[4] These include:

(1) The court of a given state may assume jurisdiction if, at the start of the relevant proceedings, the defendant is habitually resident in that state.
(2) The court of a given state may assume jurisdiction if, at the start of the relevant proceedings the defendant has a principal place of business or an establishment, branch or agency in that state, provided that such place of business, establishment, branch or agency is closely connected to the plaintiff's claim,
(3) The court of a given state may assume jurisdiction if a defendant has submitted to that court's jurisdiction:
    (a) by express agreement (for example, a choice of court agreement before the dispute arose or a bespoke agreement after a dispute has arisen),
    (b) by appearing before that court without challenging jurisdiction, or
    (c) by bringing a counterclaim related to the plaintiff's claim.

[4] See Section V and Table I of ch 1; Anselmo Reyes, 'Introduction: Towards a System for the Recognition and Enforcement of Judgments' in Anselmo Reyes (ed), *Recognition and Enforcement of Judgments in Civil and Commercial Matters* (Oxford, Hart Publishing, 2019) 29–30.

(4) When a claim concerns title to immovable property located a given state, that state may assume jurisdiction.
(5) When a claim concerns a non-contractual obligation and the act that gave rise to the relevant damage occurred in a given state, that state may assume jurisdiction.
(6) When a claim involves a contractual obligation which was agreed, performed or breached in that state, that state may assume jurisdiction.

As shown in Table I of Chapter 1, in core areas such as contract, tort and movable and immovable property, the jurisdictional rules of Asian states are already more or less similar. Therefore, it would seem that there is no pressing need for a convention or other instrument setting out Asian principles of direct jurisdiction.

Provided that a court in state X assumes jurisdiction on one of the grounds listed above as situations (1) to (6), then subject only to questions of reciprocity and public policy a plaintiff will normally be able to enforce the judgment of state X's court against the defendant's assets in state Y. Therefore, given that the 15 states here apply grounds of direct jurisdiction corresponding to the grounds of indirect jurisdiction of the rudimentary system, it is not apparent that codifying grounds of direct jurisdiction into a convention or even soft law instrument will materially improve the present situation in Asia. Nations can of course decide that they will recognise and enforce judgments based on grounds of indirect jurisdiction that are additional to those of the rudimentary system. But realistically there is little prospect of states doing so in the near future. The grounds of indirect jurisdiction identified in the 2019 Hague Convention are similar to those in the rudimentary system. At the time of writing, the 2019 Hague Convention has yet to come into effect. Even if it comes into effect in the near future following ratification by three states, it will be some time yet before a sufficient number of countries (let alone Asian countries) accede to the same and achieve a critical mass making it worthwhile to join the 2019 Hague Convention. Consequently, it is doubtful that there is traction in expanding the list of grounds of indirect jurisdiction in the 2019 Hague Convention at present. By parity of reasoning, there would be little point at this stage in going beyond the grounds of direct jurisdiction which are widely accepted by Asian countries and incorporating expanded grounds in some hard or soft law instrument. There would be little interest among states generally, let alone Asian countries, in signing up to such instruments, since judgments based on any expanded grounds are unlikely to be recognised and enforced elsewhere.[5]

State X may wish to empower its courts to assume jurisdiction in a wider range of circumstances than situations (1) to (6). For instance, much as has been the case in Hong Kong, Singapore and Malaysia, state X may wish to enable its courts to exercise jurisdiction over a long list of acts done outside of state X's territory. It might wish to do this for a variety of reasons, not least of which would be the protection of its citizens' rights or entitlements in cross-border transactions. A simple example would be the situation where a defendant's habitual residence cannot be determined. In such a situation, state X may wish to enable a citizen to bring an action against the untraceable defendant in the courts of X as a means of safeguarding the citizen's rights at least to some extent. The citizen would still have to worry about how a judgment in his or her favour can be enforced against the defendant where the latter has no assets in state X. But the expanded

[5] Contrast the position in the EU, where there would be obvious utility in having a convention dealing with jurisdiction (such as the Brussels I (recast) Regulation) to ensure that courts in different member states do not claim conflicting jurisdiction over a case involving cross-border issues. But there is no equivalent regional economic integration organisation (REIO) to which individual Asian states have surrendered some of their sovereignty, so as to be bound by an REIO's directives, legislation and rulings.

ground of jurisdiction at least allows the citizen to obtain a judgment against the defendant in a jurisdiction (state X) having some connection (the plaintiff's presence in X) to the facts of the suit. Another example, one often employed in common law jurisdictions, would be empowering the state's court to exercise jurisdiction where a third party is a proper and necessary person to be joined to a pending action before that court. The logic would be that time and cost can be saved and the interests of justice thereby promoted, if all issues in an action were resolved by the same court with the resultant judgment being binding on all persons concerned. The measure would prevent limping judgments whereby the courts in different countries come to different, possibly contradictory, factual findings. The point is that it is difficult to see why a state should constrain itself, by accession to a convention or adoption of principles in a soft law instrument, from legislating on direct jurisdiction in the manner that it sees fit to protect its population and safeguard its interests from time to time. Professor Brand has observed that many countries apply a wider range of grounds for direct jurisdiction than they recognise as grounds for indirect jurisdiction.[6] To correct this, he has advocated a mirror principle in relation to indirect jurisdiction, arguing that as much as possible grounds of direct and indirect jurisdiction applied by a given country should correspond with each other. That may be a worthwhile ideal for which to aim. But it would only be an argument for broadening a country's grounds of indirect jurisdiction, not for narrowing down the country's grounds of direct jurisdiction.

It might be suggested that a convention or soft law instrument would at least highlight best international practice in relation to direct jurisdiction. An instrument could identify desirable bases for establishing direct jurisdiction and act as a curb on any propensity in a state endlessly to multiply the circumstances upon which its courts are able to claim jurisdiction. The wider the list of situations in which the courts of a state can exercise jurisdiction, the more those courts will need to resort to a doctrine like *forum non conveniens* to whittle down the number of cases coming before the court. If direct jurisdiction is too easily established, cases which should more appropriately be tried elsewhere may gravitate to a particular state and clog its judicial system. However, there would also be the danger that, with increased resort by the courts to *forum non conveniens* or something akin to it, jurisdiction will become uncertain. A plaintiff might literally fall within the terms of a jurisdictional rule and so be able to commence a case before a particular court. But that will not be the end of the story. The plaintiff would have to contend with applications by the defendant to stay or dismiss the proceedings so initiated, on the ground of *forum non conveniens*. Whatever their outcome, such interlocutory skirmishes over jurisdiction can entail considerable expense to resolve and therefore cause significant delay to the substantive determination of a dispute.

The argument just summarised is basically a restatement of the dilemma that took place in the Judgments Project. At the end of the day, it is submitted that direct jurisdiction is a balancing exercise. Countries must decide for themselves whether, as a matter of their domestic public policy, it should or should not be possible readily to establish direct jurisdiction before their courts in a given matter. One the one hand, the more easily jurisdiction can be founded in a wide range of matters, the more probable it is that the courts will have to develop or apply *forum non conveniens* to screen out cases which plainly should be heard elsewhere. A reasonable use of *forum non conveniens* will allow the courts to do justice by remitting cases to the state best suited to hear the same. But overuse of *forum non conveniens* will lead to uncertainty over whether a

[6] Ronald A Brand, 'The Circulation of Judgments under the Draft Hague Convention' University of Pittsburgh School of Law Legal Studies Research Paper Series Working Paper No 2019-02 (February 2019) 22–23, available online: https:// papers.ssrn.com/sol3/papers.cfm?abstract_id=3334647.

case will be heard by a given court and can thus lead to serious injustice. On the other hand, a compact list of specific grounds of direct jurisdiction which leaves little or no room for a discretion to decline a case that comes within a listed ground, would undoubtedly promote certainty. But that may be at the expense of justice. Nationals or habitual residents of a state may have few (if any) practical avenues for recourse against parties abroad, especially where the latter prove to be elusive or make themselves difficult to pursue in their home jurisdictions. Consequently, in actions relating to personal status, employment, consumer claims, competition claims and environmental wrongs (among others), states may wish to protect their nationals or long-term residents by enacting more expansive grounds of jurisdiction (including mandatory or exclusive jurisdiction), subject only to escape clauses or resort to *forum non conveniens* where appropriate. Given those premises, a convention or other instrument which stipulates an 'A-grade list' of grounds for assuming jurisdiction and which defines an ambit for *forum non conveniens*, will not really assist Asian legislators on how best to protect their national interests. Nor will such a list and definition effectively guide Asian judges on how best to carry out the balancing exercise involved in deciding whether to accept or refuse jurisdiction.

III. A Glimpse into the Future

The COVID-19 pandemic, with its lockdowns and travel and quarantine restrictions, has led to an acceleration in the use of remote technology (that is, computer apps such as Zoom, Cisco Webex, BlueJeans, and Microsoft Teams) for court hearings. It has also brought financial hardship on a wide scale. Businesses have suffered or have had to close down as customers have been urged or required by their governments to stay at home. Demand for many types of goods and services has witnessed a substantial downturn. The world appears to have entered into economic recession. The brunt of COVID-19's impact was felt in 2020. In the course of that year, vaccines against COVID-19 were rapidly developed and, at the moment of writing, countries in Asia and elsewhere are rolling out their programmes for the inoculation of large numbers of their populations. But it will be months at least before sufficient herd immunity or resistance to the virus builds up among populations all over the world. Consequently, in the meanwhile, there will be more of the same regime in the short to medium term – restricted business hours and periodic lockdowns in this or that geographical area accompanied by travel and quarantine restrictions imposed by this or that state to deal with an outbreak. The COVID-19 virus, itself constantly mutating, will probably be with the world for many years to come and its economic and other effects will be long-lasting despite mass vaccination.

In such a world environment, a priority for improvement would be the system for serving process abroad. Notwithstanding the availability for some time now of technologies (the internet, email, blockchain, digital signatures, etc) that have the potential significantly to speed up how service is achieved across borders, little or nothing has been done among the 15 jurisdictions examined here to enter into mutual arrangements or memorandums of understanding (MOUs) to enable service of process to take place electronically between one country and another. A shift to electronic service can be readily accomplished within the framework of the 1965 Hague Convention on the Service Abroad of Judicial and Extrajudicial Documents in Civil or Commercial Matters (the 1965 Hague Convention). As its long title implies, the 1965 Hague Convention facilitates the service of court documents across borders. It does this through a simple mechanism. A contracting state X is required to designate a Central Authority through which a person in another contracting state Y may accomplish service on a party in state X. The Central Authority in a receiving state carries out service pursuant to that state's domestic law.

Where the party in the originating state requests that service be by a particular method (say, electronically), the Central Authority in the receiving state will effect service accordingly, but only if the requested method is compatible with the receiving state's procedural law. Once service has been accomplished, the Central Authority in the receiving state certifies that to be the case. As of 1 January 2021, there are 78 parties to the 1965 Hague Convention. Of the 15 jurisdictions in this book, eight (China, Hong Kong (through China), Japan, South Korea, Vietnam, the Philippines, Sri Lanka and India) are parties to the instrument. Joining the 1965 Hague Convention would be a good start towards improving a country's systems for effecting service of its processes overseas and effecting service of foreign proceedings within its borders. But the reality is that the mechanisms of the 1965 Hague Convention currently take a long time to operate. Where a state is not a party to the instrument, the alternative involving service through diplomatic channels would take even longer. What is needed to speed up matters would be for member states of the 1965 Hague Convention, including those in Asia, to agree bilateral or multilateral arrangements for carrying out service electronically through the existing network of Central Authorities. The benefits to be reaped if service can be done through a computer in one's home or office, are obvious. Social distancing can be maintained thereby minimising the risk of contracting COVID-19; judicial proceedings can progress more efficiently; and the costs of cross-border litigation can be reduced correspondingly. Once MOUs for electronic service have been reached among two or more contracting states to the 1965 Hague Convention, there would be no need to amend the instrument to embody those arrangements. The 1965 Hague Convention is sufficiently flexible on its present terms. By simply revising its code of civil procedure to allow for electronic service in specified matters, a contracting state would be able through its Central Authority to accept requests from litigants in another contracting state for service to be carried out electronically in the specified matters.

The pandemic coincided with trade wars and tensions between various Asian countries and between Asian countries and countries elsewhere. The latter problems have not disappeared, even as the pandemic rages. There are currently tensions between China and the US, China and Australia, China and India, and Japan and South Korea, to name only a few.[7] Those tensions have led to trade embargoes and sanctions being imposed by one country against another (for example, by the US against China, by China against Australia, by Japan against South Korea). Such sanctions and embargoes provoke counter-sanctions and counter-embargoes. Nationals and businesses of one or other country to a dispute are caught in the middle. COVID-19 has exacerbated the financial difficulties that have been stoked by the persistent trade wars, sanctions and tensions which (like the pandemic) will probably not be resolved in the short to medium term.

Given the double whammy of COVID-19 and political-economic tensions, there will be pressure on Asian states to be more protective of their domestic debtors as against overseas creditors. One response to that pressure would be to expand grounds of direct jurisdiction. Consider the case of trade sanctions. State X threatens to penalise anyone in the world (not necessarily just nationals of state X) engaging in trade with specified persons in state Y. State Y retaliates by passing legislation making it an offence for anyone in the world (not necessarily just nationals of

[7] See eg 'Why the Japan-South Korea Trade War Is Worrying for the World' (*Time*, 3 October 2019), available online: https://time.com/5691631/japan-south-korea-trade-war; 'A Quick Guide to the US-China Trade War' (*BBC News*, 16 January 2020), available online: www.bbc.com/news/business-45899310; 'India-China Dispute: The Border Row Explained in 400 Words' (*BBC News*, 10 September 2020), available online: www.bbc.com/news/world-asia-53062484; 'Everything You Want to Know about Australia-China Trade War But Were Too Afraid to Ask' (*ABC News*, 10 December 2020), available online: www.abc.net.au/news/2020-12-10/china-australia-trade-war-your-questions-answered/12971434; 'China Takes Aim at Foreign Companies Swayed by US Sanctions' (*Nikkei Asia*, 10 January 2021), available online: https://asia.nikkei.com/Economy/Trade-war/China-takes-aim-at-foreign-companies-swayed-by-US-sanctions.

state Y) to refuse to do business with the specified persons from state Y on account of the sanctions imposed by state X. A recent example has been the issue by China's Ministry of Commerce (MOFCOM) of 'Rules on Counteracting Unjustified Extraterritorial Application of Foreign Legislation and Other Measures' (the Rules).[8] The Rules came into effect on 9 January 2021, the day of their issue. According to its Article 1, the Rules were issued pursuant to China's National Security Law:

> for the purpose of counteracting the impact on China caused by unjustified extra-territorial application of foreign legislation and other measures, safeguarding national sovereignty, security and development interests, and protecting the legitimate rights and interests of citizens, legal persons and other organizations of China.

Under Article 9 of the Rules, where a person causes harm to a Chinese citizen, legal person or organisation through compliance with a foreign sanction, the latter may bring legal proceedings and claim compensation against the former before the People's Court. Article 9 further provides that, if a person causes loss to a Chinese citizen, legal person or organisation by enforcing a judgment based on a foreign sanction, the latter may seek compensation against the former for the loss.[9] The future is likely to see the promulgation in different countries of similar protective measures expanding grounds of direct jurisdiction.

A second protective technique would be the more aggressive use of injunctions. The courts of a given state may, in the interests of protecting a local debtor, be more willing to issue anti-suit injunctions to prevent a foreign creditor from litigating an action in an overseas jurisdiction pursuant (say) to a dispute resolution clause. The future may thus see an increasing number of tactical battles between parties conducted through applications for anti-suit and anti-anti-suit injunctions. In conjunction with obtaining an anti-suit injunction from its home court, the debtor in the example just posited might attempt to forestall the foreign creditor's suit by pursuing an action as plaintiff in its own jurisdiction. The action would be seeking a negative declaration, that is, a declaration of non-liability to the foreign creditor for some reason (for instance, force majeure due to the pandemic). The foreign creditor might in its turn apply for an anti-anti-suit injunction from the court designated in the parties' contract. The latter injunction would prohibit the debtor from pursuing its action in the latter's home jurisdiction. The foreign creditor may also apply to the designated court for an interlocutory order that the debtor indemnify the creditor against loss and damage arising from the breach of the dispute resolution agreement. To increase pressure, the creditor may seek to enforce any indemnity in its favour by applying for a freezing order against the debtor's assets wherever the same might be found. This game of thrust and counterthrust will only ramp up costs without being very productive. It may succeed in delaying the day when the debtor has to pay the creditor. But courts should ask themselves whether they should be encouraging procedural jockeying of this nature. In deciding whether to grant an anti-suit or anti-anti-suit injunction, judges should constantly be asking themselves in which forum a

[8] MOFCOM Order No 1 of 2021, available online: http://english.mofcom.gov.cn/article/policyrelease/announcement/202101/20210103029708.shtml. See also the Law of the People's Republic of China on Countering Foreign Sanctions (10 June 2021, effective 10 June 2021).

[9] See also the Countering Foreign Sanctions Law (n 8), Art 12. As discussed above, an expansion of direct jurisdiction may necessitate the enactment of an escape clause. For instance, Art 7 of the Rules empowers the State Council to issue a prohibition order declaring that the relevant foreign sanctions are 'not [to be] accepted, executed or observed'. A difficulty is that ignoring a foreign sanction pursuant to a prohibition order may lead to a person being exposed to penalties imposed by the foreign state on the person's assets abroad. Art 8 caters for this possibility by stipulating that a person may apply to the State Council for an exemption from having to comply with a prohibition order. It is unclear whether, if a person is granted an exemption, such person must nonetheless compensate a party in China who incurs loss or damage as result of the person complying with the foreign sanction.

matter should most conveniently be litigated in the interests of justice and of saving time and cost. Where there has been a submission to a given court's jurisdiction in the form of a dispute resolution clause, other courts should be wary of ignoring such agreement in the absence of compelling reason.[10] Judges should be especially wary of entertaining claims for negative declarations as these are often artifices used to turn the person who should naturally be the defendant in an action into a plaintiff. The employment of such device would be indicative that the jurisdiction in which the negative declaration is being sought, is not an appropriate forum for the determination of the parties' dispute.

A third technique would be a re-evaluation of sovereign immunity. In the wake of COVID-19, cases in the US have been brought against China and the Chinese Communist Party seeking damages in connection with the COVID-19 virus.[11] There have been similar cases in China against the US seeking compensation in relation to COVID-19.[12] These actions are most likely all bound to fail on the ground (among others) of sovereign immunity, as many internet commentators have acknowledged.[13] Further, it is difficult to see how countries can be held liable for judgment calls on how best to handle the COVID-19 pandemic in the interests of their nationals. This would be the position whether one takes an absolute or restrictive view of sovereign immunity. A country's handling of COVID-19 (for example, whether or not to impose a lockdown and for how long) cannot be regarded as the state engaging in normal commercial activities. The outcome should be similar in common law and civil law jurisdictions. Thus, these types of suits should not lead to a re-evaluation of the law relating to sovereign immunity.

But in January 2021 the Seoul Central District Court has found Japan liable to pay damages to former Korean 'comfort women' forced to serve as prostitutes during the Second World War.[14] Japan was ordered to pay 100 million won to each of 12 plaintiffs. Japan did not defend the proceedings. Nonetheless, the Korean court of its own motion considered the defence of sovereign immunity. It concluded that, by forcing the plaintiffs to serve as 'comfort women', Japan engaged in a crime against humanity and so was not entitled to rely on sovereign immunity. It followed that the 12 plaintiffs could enforce the judgment in their favour against Japanese Government assets in South Korea and the court made an order to that effect. Japan's treatment of 'comfort women' during World War II has been a controversial topic between Korea and Japan for a long time. The tensions between the two countries arising from that subject cannot be

[10] A compelling reason might be that the agreement was entered into in bad faith as a means of avoiding domestic mandatory law.

[11] See eg 'Lawsuits Demand Compensation from China for COVID-19; UK Reconsiders Huawei's 5G Role' (*Lawfare*, 24 April 2020), available online: www.lawfareblog.com/lawsuits-demand-compensation-china-covid-19-uk-reconsiders-huaweis-5g-role; 'Holding the Chinese Communist Party Accountable for Infecting Americans Act Would Allow US Citizens to Sue China over COVID-19' (*GovTrack.us*), available online: https://govtrackinsider.com/holding-the-chinese-communist-party-accountable-for-infecting-americans-act-would-allow-u-s-e204b5fbde52.

[12] See eg 'Chinese Lawyers Sue US over "Coronavirus Cover-up"' (*Radio Free Asia*, 26 March 2020), available online: www.rfa.org/english/news/china/wuhan-lawsuit-03262020122653.html.

[13] See eg 'What You Need to Know about Missouri's Lawsuit against China over COVID-19' (*Heritage Foundation*, 23 April 2020), available online: www.heritage.org/courts/commentary/what-you-need-know-about-missouris-lawsuit-against-china-over-covid-19; 'Can the U.S. Sue China for COVID-19 Damages? Not Really' (*Washington Post*, 29 April 2020), available online: www.washingtonpost.com/politics/2020/04/29/can-us-sue-china-covid-19-damages-not-really-this-could-quickly-backfire; 'Can China Be Sued in the US and Forced to Pay for Coronavirus Losses? Legal Experts Say No' (*Los Angeles Times*, 15 May 2020), available online: www.latimes.com/politics/story/2020-05-15/can-china-be-sued-in-the-u-s-and-forced-to-pay-for-coronavirus-losses-legal-experts-say-no; 'Suing China over COVID-19 against International Law: Expert' (*Xinhua*, 27 May 2020), available online: www.xinhuanet.com/english/2020-05/27/c_139092848.htm.

[14] Judgment of the Seoul Central District Court, 8 January 2021, 2016Gahap505092; 'In a First, South Korean Court Orders Japan to Compensate Former "Comfort Women"' (*Japan Times*, 8 January 2021), available online: www.japantimes.co.jp/news/2021/01/08/national/first-south-korean-court-comfort-women. See also Section VI.A of ch 6.

attributed to COVID-19 and the correctness of the South Korean District Court's January 2021 decision is outside the scope of this book.[15] The decision is simply raised here as an example of how countries can expand direct jurisdiction by whittling down the scope of immunities, including sovereign immunity. There may be drastic political consequences in doing so. Nonetheless, the pressure on governments to be more protective of their interests and citizens in the wake of COVID-19, trade wars, sanctions and other tensions may mean that the world in general and Asia in particular will be witnessing greater resort to this stratagem in coming years.[16]

IV. Direct Jurisdiction as Balancing

What is apparent from the foregoing is that the future of direct jurisdiction in Asia and elsewhere will be a bumpy ride. There will be forces pushing countries to increase the use of remote technology in the provision of legal services, including facilitating service of process across borders. There will be forces pushing countries to be more protectionist of their business interests through the expansion of direct jurisdiction, a greater willingness to grant anti-suit injunctions, and (possibly) a whittling down of the scope of sovereign immunity. It is hoped that the latter forces will not cancel out the former. Thus, electronic service will require cooperation and mutual agreement among states. That will enable persons in one state more easily to initiate proceedings against persons in the other state. But while a state X may be happy for its nationals to be able to sue debtors in other states more easily, it may be less happy with facilitating the means whereby creditors in other states can initiate proceedings against debtors in X. The pressure to be more protective of one's nationals, may thus mean that states fail mutually to agree on electronic service across borders.

What perhaps all this brings home is that, although ostensibly boring and tedious as a subject, the regulation of direct jurisdiction at heart involves a fine balance between affording certainty and protecting a state's nationals. On the one hand, it would be desirable to have foreseeability as to precisely when a state's courts can or cannot exercise jurisdiction. On the other hand, the state must ensure that its nationals (especially the vulnerable among them) are protected in certain situations (for instance, consumer and labour disputes) and not left without remedy in others (for example, in matters involving family and personal status). At heart, direct jurisdiction involves questions of policy and cannot merely be a matter of drawing up lists of jurisdictional grounds and exceptions to them.

[15] On 21 April 2021, a differently constituted bench of the Seoul Central District Court dismissed a similar action by different plaintiffs on the ground of Japan's sovereign immunity: 2016Gahap580239. The Seoul District Court has itself therefore taken contradictory approaches to sovereign immunity. See eg 'South Korean Court Dismisses Lawsuit by Former "Comfort Women" against Japan' (*Japan Times*, 21 April 2021), available online: www.japantimes.co.jp/news/2021/04/21/national/comfort-women-lawsuit-dismissed. See also Section VI.A of ch 6.

[16] The Seoul Central District Court's January 2021 decision on sovereign immunity may be compared to the approach of the Institute of International Law (IIL). On 30 August 2015, the IIL adopted the Tallinn Resolution on Universal Civil Jurisdiction with Regard to Reparation for International Crimes, declaring that courts should be able to exercise universal jurisdiction over claims for reparation by victims of international crimes. Such universal jurisdiction is subject to two conditions: (1) that no other state has a stronger connection with the claim; and (2) where one or more states has a stronger connection, the victims do not have available remedies in the courts of those other states. The Resolution deals with sovereign immunity in Article 5: 'The immunity of States should not deprive victims of their right to reparation.' See also Andreas Bucher (rapporteur), 'Universal Civil Jurisdiction with Regard to Reparation for International Crimes' (2015) 76 *Yearbook of Institute of International Law* 107–33, available online: www.idi-iil.org/app/uploads/2017/06/01-Bucher-Competence_universel.pdf. See further the 2004 United Nations Convention on Jurisdictional Immunities of States and Their Property, Part III, Arts 10–17. The Convention is not yet in force. Of the countries covered in this book, Japan has accepted the Convention, while China and India have signed (but not ratified) the instrument.

BIBLIOGRAPHY

Chapter 1. Introduction

Brand, Ronald A, 'The Circulation of Judgments under the Draft Hague Convention' University of Pittsburgh School of Law Legal Studies Research Paper Series Working Paper No 2019-02, https://papers.ssrn.com/sol3/papers.cfm?abstract_id=3334647, February 2019.

Briggs, Adrian, *Agreements on Jurisdiction and Choice of Law* (Oxford, Oxford University Press, 2008).

—— *Civil Jurisdiction and Judgments* 7th edn (London, Informa Law, 2021).

—— *The Conflict of Laws* 4th edn (Oxford, Oxford University Press, 2019).

Carballo Leyda, Alejandro (ed), *Asian Conflict of Laws: East and South East Asia* (Alphen aan den Rijn, Kluwer Law International, 2015).

Chng, Kenny, 'A Theoretical Perspective of the Public Policy Doctrine in the Conflict of Laws' (2018) 14(1) *Journal of Private International Law* 130–59.

Chng, Wei Yao Kenny, 'Exploring a New Frontier in Singapore's Private International Law: *IM Skaugen SE v MAN Diesel & Turbo SE* [2016] SGHCR 6' (2016) 28 *Singapore Academy of Law Journal* 649–66.

Collins, Lord of Mapesbury and others (eds), *Dicey, Morris and Collins on Conflict of Laws* 15th edn, vol 1 (London, Sweet and Maxwell, 2012).

'Comparative Table on Grounds of Jurisdiction' (*Hague Conference on Private International Law*, January 2015), https://assets.hcch.net/docs/03c39e9f-878b-400d-a359-e70b7937edde.pdf.

Crawford, James, *Brownlie's Principles of Public International Law* (Oxford, Oxford University Press, 2019).

Evans, Malcolm D (ed), *International Law* 5th edn (Oxford, Oxford University Press, 2018).

Fawcett, JJ, 'General Report' in JJ Fawcett (ed), *Declining Jurisdiction in Private International Law* (New York, Oxford University Press, 1995) 1–70.

Fentiman, Richard, *International Commercial Litigation* (Oxford, Oxford University Press, 2015).

Ferrari, Franco, *Forum Shopping Despite Unification of Law* (Leiden, Brill, 2021).

Fox, Hazel, 'Approaches of Domestic Courts to the Assertion of International Jurisdiction' in Patrick Capps, Malcolm Evans and Stratos Konstadinidis (eds), *Asserting Jurisdiction: International and European Legal Perspectives* (Portland, Hart Publishing, 2003) 175–88.

Fox, Hazel, and Webb, Philippa, *The Law of State Immunity* revised and updated 3rd edn (Oxford, Oxford University Press, 2015).

Gee, Steven, *Commercial Injunctions* 7th edn (London, Sweet and Maxwell, 2021).

Hay, Peter, *Advanced Introduction to Private International Law and Procedure* (Cheltenham, Edward Elgar, 2018).

Hill, David, *Private International Law* (Edinburgh, Edinburgh University Press, 2014).

Institut de Droit International, 'The Principles for Determining When the Use of the Doctrine of Forum Non Conveniens and Anti-suit Injunctions is Appropriate', *Institut de Droit International*, www.idi-iil.org/app/uploads/2017/06/2003_bru_01_en.pdf, 2 September 2003.

Jueptner, Eva, 'The Hague Jurisdiction Project – What Options for the Hague Conference?' (2020) 16(2) *Journal of Private International Law* 247–74.

Kessedjian, Catherine, 'Synthesis of the Work of the Special Commission of March 1998 on International Jurisdiction and the Effects of Foreign Judgments in Civil and Commercial Matters', *Hague Conference on Private International Law*, https://assets.hcch.net/docs/3385edb5-6f63-4624-934c-4d4245fdcef6.pdf, July 1998.

Menon, Sundaresh, 'Taming the Unruly Horse: The Treatment of Public Policy Arguments in the Courts', *Supreme Court of Singapore*, www.supremecourt.gov.sg/Data/Editor/Documents/Public%20Policy%20Lecture%20-%2019Feb2019.pdf, 19 February 2019.

Michaels, Ralf, 'Some Fundamental Jurisdictional Concepts as Applied in Judgment Conventions' in Eckart Gottschalk and others (eds), *Conflict of Laws in a Globalized World* (Cambridge, Cambridge University Press, 2007) 29–62.

Mills, Alex, 'The Dimensions of Public Policy in Private International Law' (2008) 4(2) *Journal of Private International Law* 201–36.

North, Peter, *Essays in Private International Law* (Oxford, Oxford University Press, 1993).
Nussbaum, Arthur, 'Jurisdiction and Foreign Judgments' (1941) 41(2) *Columbia Law Review* 221–38.
Nygh, Peter, 'Declining Jurisdiction under the Brussels I Regulation and the Preliminary Draft Hague Judgments Convention: A Comparison' in James Fawcett (ed), *Reform and Development of Private International Law: Esssays in Honour of Sir Peter North* (Oxford, Oxford University Press, 2002) 303–34.
Raphael, Thomas, *The Anti-Suit Injunction* 2nd edn (Oxford, Oxford University Press, 2019).
Reyes, Anselmo, 'Conclusion: Towards an Asia of Judgments without Borders' in Anselmo Reyes (ed), *Recognition and Enforcement of Judgments in Civil and Commercial Matters* (Oxford, Hart Publishing, 2019) 309–26.
—— 'Introduction: Towards a System for the Recognition and Enforcement of Judgments' in Anselmo Reyes (ed), *Recognition and Enforcement of Judgments in Civil and Commercial Matters* (Oxford, Hart Publishing, 2019) 1–30.
Shaw, Malcolm N, *International Law* 8th edn (Cambridge, Cambridge University Press, 2018).
Szásky, István, *International Civil Procedure: A Comparative Study* (Leyden, AW Sijthoff, 1967).
Tang, Zheng Sophia, *Jurisdiction and Arbitration Agreements in International Commercial Law* (Oxon, Routledge, 2014).
Torremans, Paul and others (eds), *Cheshire, North & Fawcett Private International Law* 15th edn (Oxford, Oxford University Press, 2017).
von Mehren, Arthur Taylor, *Recognition and Enforcement of Foreign Judgments -General Theory and the Role of Jurisdictional Requirements* (Alphen aan den Rijn, Sijthoff and Noordhoff, 1981).

Chapter 2. China

Brand, Ronald A, 'Comparative Method and International Litigation' [2020] 2 *Journal of Dispute Resolution* 273–92.
Deng, Yizhou, *The Practice Essence of PRC Cross-Border Civil and Commercial Litigation* (Beijing, China Legal Publishing House, 2018).
Ding, Yilin, 'Absolute, Restrictive, or Something More: Did Beijing Choose the Right Type of Sovereign Immunity for Hong Kong?' (2012) 26 *Emory International Law Review* 997–1037.
Fawcett, JJ, 'General Report' in JJ Fawcett (ed), *Declining Jurisdiction in Private International Law* (New York, Oxford University Press, 1995) 1–70.
Guo, Yujun, and Liu, Yuanyuan, 'On the case of *FG Hemisphere Associates LLC v Democratic Republic of the Congo and Others*' [2012] 2 *Law of the Times* 3–10.
Han, Depei and Xiao, Yongping, *Private International Law* 1st edn (Beijing, People's Court Press and China Social Science Press, 2004).
He, Qisheng, *Studies on Service of Process Abroad* (Beijing, Peking University Press, 2006).
Huang, Jin (ed), *Private International Law* (Beijing, Legal Publishing House, 1999).
Li, Shuang-yuan, *Private International Law* 3rd edn (Beijing, Beijing University Publishing House, 2012).
Li, Wang, 'The Analysis on Jurisdiction of Transnational Civil Litigation: Evaluating the Provisions on Jurisdiction of Transnational Civil Litigation in Civil Procedure Law of PR China (Amended in 2012)' [2014] 1 *Chinese Review of International Law* 89–98.
Liu, Li (ed), *The Study on Legislation of International Civil Procedure Jurisdiction and Judicial Assistance* (Beijing, China University of Political Science and Law Press, 2016).
Liu, Minmin, 'Reconstruction of China's Cross-border Bankruptcy Jurisdiction Distribution System' [2016] 2 *Daqing Social Science* 39–45.
Liu, Ping, 'Study on Jurisdiction of Temporary Protection Measures in International Civil Litigation' [2004] 9 *Journal of Litigation Law* 454–93.
Liu, Xiaohong, and Zhang, Zhengyi (eds), 'Chinese Private International Law' (Oxford, Hart Publishing, 2021).
Liu, Xiaohong, and Zhou, Qi, 'The Principle of Actual Connection in the System of Agreement Jurisdiction and the Principle of Inconvenient Court' (2014) 12 *Law Science* 43–50.
Ma, Yuan (ed), *Explanation of 'Opinions on the Application of the Civil Procedure Law'* (Beijing, China Procuratorate Publishing House, 1994).
Perdue, Wendy Collins (ed), *Procedure and Private International Law* (Cheltenham, Edward Elgar Publishing, 2017).
Shi, Jianping, and Zhai, Zijun, 'Immunities from Jurisdiction' in Xiaohong Liu and Zhengyi Zhang (eds) 'Chinese Private International Law' (Oxford, Hart Publishing, 2021).
—— and —— 'Jurisdiction *in personam*' in Xiaohong Liu and Zhengyi Zhang (eds) 'Chinese Private International Law' (Oxford, Hart Publishing, 2021).
—— and —— 'Jurisdiction in Shipping Claims' in Xiaohong Liu and Zhengyi Zhang (eds) 'Chinese Private International Law' (Oxford, Hart Publishing, 2021).
Song, Jianli, 'Choice of Court Convention and its Influence to China' [2019] 4 *People's Judiciary* 103–07.

Tao, Lifeng, and Gao, Yongfu, 'Reconstruction of the Exclusive Jurisdiction Clause over Three Types of Contract Disputes Involving Foreign Element in China' [2013] 4 *International Business Research* 77–84.

Xiao, Yongping, 'The pros and cons of Ratifying the Convention on Choice of Court Agreements and China's Countermeasures' [2017] 5 *Wuhan University International Law Review* 1–16.

Xu, Guojian, 'Establishing a Uniform International System of Jurisdiction and Recognition and Enforcement of Foreign Judgments – Comments on the Hague Convention on Choice of Court Agreements' [2005] 5 *Present Day Law Science* 5–16.

—— 'To Establish an International Legal System for Global Circulation of Court Judgments' [2017] 5 *Wuhan University International Law Review* 100–30.

Zhao, Xianglin, *Private International Law* (Beijing, China University of Political Science and Law Press, 2000).

Zhou, Qi, and Zhao, Jun, 'The Origin and Development of International Civil and Commercial Agreement Jurisdiction System Theory' [2014] 6 *Nanjing Social Science* 104–112.

Chapter 3. Hong Kong

Briggs, Adrian, *The Conflict of Laws* 4th edn (London, Oxford University Press, 2019).

—— and Rees, Peter, *Civil Jurisdiction and Judgments* 5th edn (London, Informa Law, 2009).

Chen, Albert HY, 'The Concept of Justiciability and the Jurisdiction of the Hong Kong Courts' (1997) 27 *Hong Kong Law Journal* 387–90.

Hong Kong Civil Procedure 2021 (Hong Kong, Sweet and Maxwell, 2020).

Johnston, Graeme, and Harris, Paul, *The Conflict of Laws in Hong Kong* 3rd edn (Hong Kong, Sweet and Maxwell, 2017).

Ng, Hon Wah, 'Hong Kong Courts' Jurisdiction to Enforce Intellectual Property Rights Infringed by Internet Contents' (2005) 35(2) *Hong Kong Law Journal* 367–94.

Sherrin, Christopher H, *Probate Practice in Hong Kong* 3rd edn (Hong Kong, Sweet and Maxwell, 2012).

Wilkinson, Michael, Cheung, Eric TM, and Meggitt, Gary, *Civil Procedure in Hong Kong* 6th edn (Hong Kong, LexisNexis, 2017).

Wong, James YP, 'Hong Kong' in Anselmo Reyes (ed), *Recognition and Enforcement of Judgments in Civil and Commercial Matters* (Oxford, Hart Publishing, 2019) 51–84.

Chapter 4. Taiwan

Chen, Rong-chwan, 'International Civil Litigations on Patent Infringements: Focusing on the Supreme Court Decisions and the Application of the Latest Legislation' (2013) 215 *Taiwan Law Journal* 1–10 (Part 1); (2013) 216 *Taiwan Law Journal* 1–17 (Part 2).

—— 'Jurisdiction and the Law Applicable to Anti Competitive Conduct Involving Foreign Elements' (2014) 22(2) *Fair Trade Quarterly* 93–162.

—— 'Jurisdiction, Choice of Law and the Recognition of Foreign Judgments in Taiwan' in Jürgen Basedow and Knut B Pissler (eds), *Private International Law in Mainland China, Taiwan and Europe* (Tübingen, Mohr Siebeck, 2014) 17–38.

—— 'Legislation and Practice on Choice of Court Agreements in Taiwan' in Mary Keyes (ed), *Optional Choice of Court Agreements in Private International Law* (Switzerland, Springer, 2020) 387–407.

—— 'Taiwan (National Report)' in Jürgen Basedow and others (eds), *Encyclopedia of Private International Law* vol 3 (Cheltenham, Edward Elgar Publishing, 2017) 2560–69.

—— The Domestic Effects of an Insolvency Decree of Foreign Court' (2015) 154 *Taiwan Jurist* 30–32.

—— 'The Immunity of Diplomatic Personnel from Foreign Countries' (2005) 24 *Taiwan Jurist* 24–25.

Liu, Tieh-cheng, and Chen, Rong-chwan, *Liu and Chen on Private International Law* 6th edn (Taipei, San Min, 2018).

Weintraub, Russell J, *Commentary on the Conflict of Laws* 4th edn (New York, Foundation Press, 2000).

Chapter 5. Japan

Chaen, Shigeki, Kono, Toshiyuki, and Yokomizo, Dai, 'Jurisdiction in Intellectual Property Cases: The Transparency Proposal' in Jürgen Basedow, Toshiyuki Kono and Andreas Metzger (eds), *Intellectual Property in the Global Arena* (Tübingen, Mohr Siebeck, 2010) 77–145.

Counsellor's Office of the Civil Affairs Bureau of the Ministry of Justice, 'Kokusai Saibankankatsu Hosei ni kansuru Chukan Shian Hosoku Setsumei' [*Supplemental Explanatory Note on the Interim Draft on the Institution on International Jurisdiction*], *Doshisha University*, www1.doshisha.ac.jp/~tradelaw/UnpublishedWorks/ExplanatoryNoteOnBillOfJurisdictionAct.pdf, July 2009.

—— 'Jinji Sosho Jiken oyobi Kaji Jiken no Kokusai Saibankankatsu Hosei ni kansuru Chukan Shian' ['Interim Draft on the Institution on International Jurisdiction in Personal Status Litigation and Domestic Relation Cases'], *Ministry of Justice*, www.moj.go.jp/content/001141605.pdf, February 2015.

—— 'Jinji Sosho Jiken oyobi Kaji Jiken no Kokusai Saibankankatsu Hosei ni kansuru Chukan Shian no Hosoku Setsumei' ['Supplemental Explanatory Note on the Interim Draft on the Institution on International Jurisdiction in Personal Status Litigation and Domestic Relations Cases'], *Ministry of Justice*, www.moj.go.jp/content/001141607.pdf, March 2015.

Dogauchi, Masato, 'Concurrent Litigations in Japan and the United States' (1994) 37 *JAIL* 72–94.

—— 'New Japanese Rules on International Jurisdiction: General Observation' (2011) 54 *Japanese Yearbook of International Law* 260–77.

Furuta, Yoshimasa, 'Sosho Sashitome Meirei' in Akira Takakuwa and Masato Dogauchi (eds), *Shin Saiban Jitsumu Taikei (3) Kokusai Minji Sosho-ho (Zaisan-ho Kankei)* [*International Civil Litigation Law (Proprietary Matters)*] (Tokyo, Seirinshoin, 2002).

Hayashi, Takami, 'International Jurisdiction in Case Related to Succession: New Rules in Japan' (2019) 62 *Japanese Yearbook of International Law* 209–25.

Honma, Yasunori, Nakano, Shun'ichiro, and Sakai, Hajime, *Kokusai Minji Tetsuzuki Ho* [*International Civil Procedure Law*] 2nd edn (Tokyo, Yuhikaku, 2012).

Ikeda, Ayako (ed), *Shokai Kokusai Kaji Jiken no Saiban Kankatsu* [*Commentary on Jurisdictional Rules in International Family Cases*] (Tokyo, Nihon Kajo Syuppan, 2019).

Ito, Makoto, and others, *Jokai Hasan Ho* [*Commentary on Bankruptcy Act*] 2nd edn (Tokyo, Kobundo, 2014).

Japan Institute of Business Law, 'Kokusai Saibankankatsu ni kansuru Chosa Kenkyu Hokokusho' ['Research Report on International Jurisdiction'], *Ministry of Justice*, www.moj.go.jp/content/000012193.pdf, April 2008.

Kanzaki, Tadashi, 'Jurisdiction over Consumer Contracts and Individual Labour-Related Civil Disputes' (2012) 55 *Japanese Yearbook of International Law* 306–22.

Kato, Shiho, 'Recent Developments in Rules on Choice of Court Agreements in Japan: New Codification and Remaining Problems' in Alexander Bruns and Masabumi Suzuki (eds), *Preventive Instruments of Social Governance* (Tübingen, Mohr Siebeck, 2017) 173–94.

Koide, Kunio (ed), *Chikujo Kaisetsu Ho no Tekiyo ni kansuru Tsusokuho* [*Commentary on the Act on General Rules for Application of Laws*] expanded edn (Tokyo, Shojihomu, 2015).

Kono, Toshiyuki, 'Recent Judgments in Japan on Intellectual Property Rights, Conflict of Laws and International Jurisdiction' in Josef Drexl and Annette Kur (eds), *Intellectual Property and Private International Law: Heading for the Future* (Oxford, Hart Publishing, 2005) 229–40.

Murakami, Masako, 'International Jurisdiction of Child-Related Cases in Japan' (2019) 62 *Japanese Yearbook of International Law* 189–208.

Nakano, Shun'ichiro, 'Agreement on Jurisdiction' (2011) 54 *Japanese Yearbook of International Law* 278–94.

Nishioka, Kazuaki, and Nishitani, Yuko, *Japanese Private International Law* (Oxford, Hart Publishing, 2021).

Nishitani, Yuko, 'Intellectual Property in Japanese Private International Law' (2005) 48 *JAIL* 87–108.

—— 'International Adjudicatory Jurisdiction in Matrimonial Matters in Japan' (2019) 62 *Japanese Yearbook of International Law* 151–88.

—— 'International Jurisdiction of Japanese Courts in A Comparative Perspective' (2013) 60 *Netherlands International Law Review* 251–77.

—— 'Internationales Privat-und Zivilverfahrensrecht' ['International Private and Civil Procedure Law'] in Harald Baum and Moritz Bälz (eds), *Handbuch Japanisches Handels- und Wirtschaftsrecht* [*Handbook on Japanese Commercial and Business Law*] (Köln, Carl Heymanns Verlag, 2011) 1211–86.

—— 'Jinji Sosho Jiken oyobi Kaji Jiken no Kokusai Saibankankatsu tou ni kansuru Shin Hosei (2)' ['New Rules on International Jurisdiction in Personal Status Litigation and Domestic Relations Cases (2)'] (2019) 71(4) *Hoso Jiho* [*Lawyers Association Journal*] 715–62.

—— 'New International Civil Procedure Law of Japan in Status and Family Matters' (2019) 62 *Japanese Yearbook of International Law* 119–50.

—— 'Supreme Court 26 September 2002, Fujimoto v. Neuron Co. Ltd. ('Card Reader' case)' in Moritz Bälz and others (eds), *Business Law in Japan* (Alphen aan den Rijn, Kluwer Law International, 2012) 679–89.

Nomura, Yoshiaki, 'Activity-Based Jurisdiction of Japanese Courts–A Bold but Unnecessary Departure –' (2012) 55 *Japanese Yearbook of International Law* 263–86.

Saiko Saibansho Jimu Sokyoku Minjikyoku (ed), *Kokusai Minji Jiken Tetsuzuki Handbook [Handbook on International Civil Procedure Cases]* (Tokyo, Hosokai, 2013).

Saito, Akira, 'International Civil Jurisdiction Based on the Place of Performance of Obligation Relating to a Contract' (2011) 54 *Japanese Yearbook of International Law* 295–310.

Sato, Tatsufumi, and Kobayashi, Yasuhiko, *Ichimon Itto Heisei 23 Nen Minji Soshoho to Kaisei: Kokusai Saiban Kankatsu Hosei no Seibi [Explanatory Note on the 2011 Reform of the Code of Civil Procedure and Others: Improvement of the Institution on International Jurisdiction]* (Tokyo, Shojihomu, 2012).

Sawaki, Takao, and Dogauchi, Masato, *Kokusai Shiho Nyumon* 8th edn (Tokyo, Yuhikaku, 2018).

Tada, Nozomi, 'International Civil Jurisdiction Based on the Place of the Tort' (2012) 55 *Japanese Yearbook of International Law* 287–305.

Takahashi, Koji, 'Japan's Newly Enacted Rules on International Jurisdiction: with a Reflection on Some Issues of Interpretation' (2011) 13 *Japanese Yearbook of Private International Law* 146–70.

—— 'The Jurisdiction of Japanese Courts in A Comparative Context' (2015) 11(1) *Journal of Private International Law* 103–27.

Tobisawa, Tomoyuki, *Chikujo Kaisetsu Taigaikoku Minji Saibanken Ho – waga kuni no Syuken Menjo Hosei ni tsuite [Commentary on the Act on Civil Jurisdiction of Japan with respect to a Foreign State, etc]* (Tokyo, Shojihomu, 2009).

Uchino, Muneki (ed), *Ichimon Itto Heisei 30 Nen Jinji Soshoho Kaji Jiken Tetsuzukiho to Kaisei: Kokusai Saiban Kankatsu Hosei no Seibi [Explanatory Note on the 2018 Reform of the Personal Status Litigation Act, Domestic Relations Case Procedure Act: Improvement of the Institution on International Jurisdiction]* (Tokyo, Shojihomu, 2019).

Yakushiji, Kimio, 'Legislation of the Act on Civil Jurisdiction Over Foreign States, Acceptance of the UN Convention on Jurisdictional Immunity of States and their Property, and their Possible Effects upon the Jurisprudence of Japanese Domestic Courts on State Immunity' (2010) 53 *Japanese Yearbook of International Law* 202–42.

Yamamoto, Kazuhiko, 'International Jurisdiction Based on the Location of Property' (2011) 54 *Japanese Yearbook of International Law* 311–23.

Yokoyama, Jun, *Private International Law in Japan* 2nd edn (Alphen aan den Rijn, Kluwer Law International, 2020).

Chapter 6. Korea

'Act on Private International Law', *National Law Information Center*, https://law.go.kr/LSW/eng/engLsSc.do?menuId=2&section=lawNm&query=act+on+private+international+law&x=0&y=0.

Bub-mu-bu [Ministry of Justice], *Gae-jong Guk-je-sa-bob hae-sol [Commentary on the Revised Act on International Private Law]* (Gyeonggi-do, Ministry of Justice, 2001), https://academic.naver.com/openUrl.naver?doc_id=18073775&linkType=doclink.

Choi, Jong Hyun, *Hae-sang-bub-sang-ron [Notes on Maritime Law]* 2nd edn (Seoul, Pakyoungsa, 2014).

'Civil Procedure Act', *Korea Legislation Research Institute*, https://elaw.klri.re.kr/kor_service/lawView.do?hseq=45913&lang=ENG.

'Glossary: Forum non conveniens', *Thomson Reuters Practical Law*, https://uk.practicallaw.thomsonreuters.com/2-341-8952?transitionType=Default&contextData=(sc.Default)&firstPage=true.

Han, Ae Ra, 'Guk-je-jae-pan-gwan-hal-gwa gwan-ryon-deon pan-gyul-ui choo-yi mit guk-je-sa-bub-ui gae-jong-bang-an – Guk-jejae-pan-gwan-hal-ui pan-dan-gu-jo mit bub-in-e dae-han yil-bu gwa-ying-gwan-hal jaeng-jom-gwa gwan-ryon-ha-yo –' ['Trends of Court Judgments on International Jurisdiction and Amendment Proposals to the Private International Act of Korea – Focusing on the Reasoning Structure of Judgments and on Certain Exorbitant Jurisdiction Issues Regarding a Legal Entity –'] (2013) 35 *Min-sa-pan-rye-yon-gu [Studies on Civil Judgments]* 1079–1174.

'Jo-yak-jung-bo' ['Information on International Convention'], *Ministry of Foreign Affairs*, www.mofa.go.kr/www/wpge/m_3835/contents.do.

Jung, Hye Jung. 'Yi-yong-soo hal-mo-ni "We-an-bu son-bae-so gak-ha" hang-so "jung-ui in-gwon yi-gil gut"' ['Yi Yong Soo Grandmother to File an Appeal to "Dismissal of Claim for Compensation for Comfort Women" "Justice and Human Rights will Prevail"'], *Joong-ang-il-bo* [Joongang Daily], https://news.joins.com/article/24050690?cloc=joongang-section-moredigitalfirst, 5 May 2021.

Kim, Jong Ho, 'Mi-guk-bub-sang Dae-mul-so-song Je-do-e Gwan-han so-go' ('A Legal Consideration for the Action in Rem in the American Judicial System') (2012) 40 *Han-yang-bup-hak [Hanyang Law Review]* 259–93.

Lee, Chang Hyun, 'Guk-je-juk-bun-jaeng-hae-gyul-e it-oh-so so-song-gum-ji-myung-ryung-ui hwal-yong-e gwan-han yon-gu han-kuk-e-so-ui jeok-yong-ga-nung-sung-ul jung-sim-ui-ro' ('The Use of Anti-suit Injunction in Transnational Dispute Resolutions: Focusing on the Applicability in Korea'), SJD dissertation, Seoul National University, http://dcollection.snu.ac.kr/common/orgView/000000162277, 2020.

Lee, Choon-Won, and Kim, Dahee, 'Korea' in Andrew Bicknell (ed), *The International Comparative Guide to: Shipping Law 2019* (London, Global Legal Group, 2019) 158–63.
Lee, Hun Mook, 'Guk-je-jeok so-song-gyong-hap-ui cho-ri-e gwan-han bi-gyo-bup-juk yeon-gu' ['A Comparative Analysis on How to Deal with Lis Pendens in International Litigation'] [2019] *Guk-je-sa-bub-yeon-gu* [*Studies on Private International Law*] 383–416.
Lee, Yong Kyong, 'Il-bon-un we-wan-bu pi-hae-ja-e-ge- 1-oek-sik bae-sang-ha-ra' ['Japanese Government Ordered to Compensate KRW 100 Million to Victims of Comfort Women'], *Bup-ryul-sin-mun* [*Legal Times*], www.lawtimes.co.kr/Case-Curation/view?serial=167147, 8 January 2021.
Rho, Tae Ak, 'Guk-je-jae-pan-gwan-hal-e gwan-han choi-gun dae-bub-won-pan-gyul-ui bun-suk – sil-jil-jeok gwan-ryun-won-chik-gwa guk-je-sa-bub je-2-jo-ui hae-seok-ron-ul joong-sim-ui-ro –' ['Analysis of Recent Supreme Court Decisions on International Jurisdiction – With the Focus on Interpretation of Article 2 of the Private International Act and the Substantial Connection Principle –'] (2012) 22(1) *Sa-bub* [*Private Law Journal*] 197–244.
Sa-bub-jeong-chaek-yon-gu-won [Judicial Policy Research Institute], *Oi-guk-jae-pan-ui sung-in-gwa jip-haeng-e gwan-han yon-gu* [*Study on the Recognition and Enforcement of Foreign Judgments*], *Judicial Policy Research Institute*, http://jpri.scourt.go.kr/fileDownLoad.do?seq=1307, 2020.
Seoul-joong-ang-ji-bang-bup-won Je-15-Min-sa-bu [15th Civil Division of the Seoul Central District Court], 'Seoul-joong-ang-ji-bang-bup-won 2016-ga-hap-580239 pan-gyul seon-go ja-ryo' ['Press Release Materials for the Judgment of the Seoul Central District Court Case Number 2016Gahap580239'], https://womenandwar.net/kr/wp-content/uploads/2021/04/2016%EA%B0%80%ED%95%A9580239_%EC%84%A0%EA%B3%A0%EB%AC%B8_%EC%86%A1%EB%B6%80%EC%9A%A9.pdf, 21 April 2021.
Sohn, Kyung Han, 'Guk-je-sa-bub gae-jong bang-an yon-gu choi-jong-bo-go-seo' ['Final Report on the Research on the Revision of the Private International Law Act'], *National Library*, www.nl.go.kr/app/nl/search/common/download.jsp?file_id=FILE-00008504595, 30 November 2012.
Sook, Hee Han, 'Guk-je-ga-sa-sa-geon-ui guk-je-jae-pan-gwan-hal-gwa oi-guk-pan-gyul-ui sung-in mit jip-haeng – yi-hon-uil jung-sim-ui-ro –' ('Jurisdiction in an International Family Case and Execution of Foreign Judicial Decision – Focus on Divorce –') (2006) 12 *Guk-je-sa-bup-yon-gu* (*Studies on Private International Law*) 3–57.
Suk, Kwang Hyun, 'Guk-je-chin-gwon hoo-gyun-bup-ui dong-hyang-gwa woo-ri-yip-bup-gwa-je' ('Trends of International Parental Authority and Guardianship Law and Korea's Future Legislation') (2014) 55(4) *Seoul-dae-hak-kyo-bup-hak* [*Seoul Law Journal*] 473–521.
—— *Guk-je-min-so-bub* [*International Civil Procedure Law*] (Seoul, Pakyoungsa, 2012).
—— *Guk-je-sa-bob-gwa Guk-je-so-song* [*International Private Law and International Litigation*] vol 4 (Seoul, Pakyoungsa, 2007).
—— *Guk-je-sa-bob-gwa Guk-je-so-song* [*International Private Law and International Litigation*] vol 5 (Seoul, Pakyoungsa, 2012).
—— *Guk-je-sa-bub Hae-sol* [*Commentary on Private International Law*] (Seoul, Pakyoungsa, 2013).

Chapter 7. Singapore

Bull, Cavinder, and Chia, Voon Jiet, 'Investigations, Enforcement and Rights of Private Action' in Chong Kin Lim and Cavinder Bull (eds), 'Competition Law and Policy in Singapore' 2nd edn (Singapore, Academy Publishing, 2015) 227–318.
Bull, Cavinder, Lim, Chong Kin, and Ng, Ee Kia, 'Competition Policy and Law' in Chong Kin Lim and Cavinder Bull (eds), 'Competition Law and Policy in Singapore' 2nd edn (Singapore, Academy Publishing, 2015) 1–26.
Chan, Jason, and Lam, Liza, 'Patent Litigation in Singapore: Overview', *Practical Law*, https://uk.practicallaw.thomsonreuters.com/w-014-9923, 1 June 2020.
Chng, Kenny, 'Singapore' in Anselmo Reyes (ed), *Recognition and Enforcement of Judgments in Civil and Commercial Matters* (Oxford, Hart Publishing, 2019) 141–62.
Chng, Wei Yao Kenny, 'Exploring a New Frontier in Singapore's Private International Law: *IM Skaugen SE v MAN Diesel & Turbo SE* [2016] SGHCR 6' (2016) 28 *Singapore Academy of Law Journal* 649–66.
Cremean, Damien J, *Admiralty Jurisdiction: Law and Practice in Australia, New Zealand, Singapore and Hong Kong* 3rd edn (Sydney, The Federation Press, 2008).
Fentiman, Richard, *International Commercial Litigation* (Oxford, Oxford University Press, 2015).
'Foreign State Immunity' [1984] ALRC 24, *AustLII*, www8.austlii.edu.au/cgi-bin/download.cgi/cgi-bin/download.cgi/download/au/other/lawreform/ALRC/1984/24.pdf, 10 October 1984.
Gee, Steven, *Commercial Injunctions* 7th edn (London, Sweet and Maxwell, 2021).

Godwin, Andrew, Ramsay, Ian, and Webster, Miranda, 'International Commercial Courts: The Singapore Experience' (2017) 18(2) *Melbourne Journal of International Law* 219–59.
Government of Singapore and Intellectual Property Office of Singapore, 'Update to the Intellectual Property Hub Master Plan', *Intellectual Property Office of Singapore*, www.ipos.gov.sg/docs/default-source/about-ipos-doc/full-report_update-to-ip-hub-master-plan_final.pdf, May 2017.
'IP Legislation' (*Intellectual Property Office of Singapore*), www.ipos.gov.sg/media-resources/ip-legislation.
Koo, Randolph, and Hoon, Shu Mei, 'Family Law in Singapore: Overview', *Thomson Reuters Practical Law*, https://uk.practicallaw.thomsonreuters.com/4-568-0826.
Kumar, Harish, Toh, Jonathan, and Cheong, Jonathan, 'Singapore' in Louis Garb and John Wood (eds), *International Succession* 4th edn (Oxford, Oxford University Press, 2015) 739–56.
Lee, Jwee Nguan, and Lee, Cheow Han, 'Competition Law', *Singapore Law Watch*, www.singaporelawwatch.sg/About-Singapore-Law/Commercial-Law/ch-27-competition-law, 15 September 2019.
Leong, Wai Kum, *Elements of Family Law in Singapore* 2nd edn (Singapore, LexisNexis, 2013).
Leow, Rachel, and Liau, Timothy, 'Unjust Enrichment and Restitution in Singapore: Where Now and Where Next?' [2013] *Singapore Journal of Legal Studies* 331–60.
Menon, Sundaresh, 'The Somewhat Uncommon Law of Commerce' (2014) 26 *Singapore Academy of Law Journal* 23–49.
Mortensen, Reid, 'The Case Management Stay in Private International Law' in Michael Douglas and others (eds), *Commercial Issues in Private International Law* (Oxford, Hart Publishing, 2019) 69–88.
'New Process at MPA for Admiralty Arrest', *Supreme Court of Singapore*, www.supremecourt.gov.sg/docs/default-source/default-document-library/services/enforcement-section/sheriff-letter-on-new-process-at-mpa-for-admiralty-arrest-(the-law-society-of-singapore).pdf, 25 October 2019.
Ong, Debbie, *International Issues in Family Law in Singapore* (Singapore, Academy Publishing, 2015).
Raphael, Thomas, *The Anti-Suit Injunction* 2nd edn (Oxford, Oxford University Press, 2019).
'Report of the Singapore International Commercial Court Committee', www.sicc.gov.sg/docs/default-source/about-sicc/annex-a-sicc-committee-report.pdf, November 2013.
Reyes, Anselmo, 'Conclusion: Towards an Asia of Judgments without Borders' in Anselmo Reyes (ed), *Recognition and Enforcement of Judgments in Civil and Commercial Matters* (Oxford, Hart Publishing, 2019) 309–26.
—— 'Recognition and Enforcement of Interlocutory and Final Judgments of the Singapore International Commercial Court' (2015) 2 *Journal of International and Comparative Law* 337–58.
'Second Reading Speech by Second Minister for Law, Mr Edwin Tong, on the Apostille Bill' (*Ministry of Law*, 2 November 2020), www.mlaw.gov.sg/news/parliamentary-speeches/2020-10-05-second-reading-speech-by-2m-edwin-tong-on-apostille-bill.
'Second Reading Speech by Senior Minister of State for Law, Mr Edwin Tong, on the Supreme Court of Judicature (Amendment) Bill', *Ministry of Law*, www.mlaw.gov.sg/news/parliamentary-speeches/second-reading-speech-by-senior-minister-of-state-for-law-mr-edwin-tong-on-scj-amendment-bill, 6 November 2019.
Shaw, Malcolm N, *International Law* 8th edn (Cambridge, Cambridge University Press, 2018).
'Sheriff's Services', *Supreme Court of Singapore*, www.supremecourt.gov.sg/services/court-services/sheriff's-services.
'Singapore' (*World Intellectual Property Organisation*), www.wipo.int/directory/en/details.jsp?country_code=SG.
'Structure of the Courts', *Supreme Court of Singapore*, www.supremecourt.gov.sg/who-we-are/the-supreme-court/structure-of-the-courts, 19 April 2021.
'The Intellectual Property Court Guide', *Supreme Court of Singapore*, www.supremecourt.gov.sg/docs/default-source/default-document-library/about-us/ip-court-guide.pdf, 6 September 2013.
Toh, Kian Sing, *Admiralty Law and Practice* 3rd edn (Singapore, LexisNexis, 2017).
Woo, Bih Li, 'Speech at the 5th Judicial Seminar on Commercial Litigation, Hong Kong: State Immunity in Commercial Disputes – An Overview of Singapore Law & A Re-visit to the Absolute Doctrine of State Immunity', *Supreme Court of Singapore*, www.supremecourt.gov.sg/news/speeches/year/2016, 20 October 2016.
Yip, Man, 'The Resolution of Disputes Before the Singapore International Commercial Court' (2016) 65 *International and Comparative Law Quarterly* 439–73.
—— 'The Singapore International Commercial Court: The Future of Litigation?' (2019) 12(1) *Erasmus Law Review* 82–97.

Chapter 8. Malaysia

Achariam, Timothy, 'Federal Court Rules ex-AIAC Director has Immunity from Criminal Charges', *The Edge Markets*, Putrajaya, www.theedgemarkets.com/article/federal-court-rules-exaiac-director-has-immunity-criminal-charges, 30 April 2021.

Adnan, Nur Syakirah Binti Mohd, 'Analysis on the Doctrine of Non-Convenience and the Malaysian Position' [2020] 1 *Legal Network Series (Article)* xcviii.
Ali Mohamed, Ashgar Ali, 'Prosecutorial Immunity: A Review of Rosli Bin Dahlan v Tan Sri Abdul Gani Bin Patail & Ors' [2015] 1 *Malayan Law Journal* xcvii–xv.
Beazley, TAG, 'Jurisdiction and Choice of Law in Tort Conflicts: Chan Kwon Fong & Anor. v. Chan Wah' (1977) 19 *Malaya Law Review* 391–400.
Das, Cyrus V, 'Election Laws: The Compelling Areas for Reform from a Legal Perspective' [2002] 2 *Malayan Law Journal* cxc–cxcix.
Derrington, Sarah C, and Turner, James M, *The Law and Practice of Admiralty Matters* (Oxford, Oxford University Press, 2007).
Hamid, Abdul Ghafur, and Kamaruddin, Zaleha, 'International Parental Child Abduction in the Malaysian Legal Context: Addressing Issues and the Way Forward' (2018) 26(2) *IIUM Law Journal* 275–306.
Hickling, RH, and Wu, Min Aun, 'Stay of Actions and Forum Non Conveniens' [1994] 3 *Malayan Law Journal* xcvii–cxi.
—— and —— *Conflict of Laws in Malaysia* (Singapore, Butterworths Asia, 1995).
Kasi, Arunachalam, 'Anti-Suit Injunction in Enforcement of Arbitration Agreement and Exclusive Jurisdiction Agreement' [2013] 6 *Malayan Law Journal* i–xx.
Lin, Tan Yock, 'Supreme Court of Judicature (Amendment) Act 1993' [1993] *Singapore Journal of Legal Studies* 557–77.
Masum, Ahmad, 'Parliamentary Privilege and Its Practice in Malaysia: An Overview' [2012] 2 *Malayan Law Journal* c–cxvii.
Moustafa, Tamir, 'Liberal Rights versus Islamic Law? The Construction of a Binary in Malaysian Politics' (2013) 47 *Law & Society Review* 771–802.
Omar, Paul J, 'Cross-Border Jurisdiction and Assistance in Insolvency: The Position in Malaysia and Singapore' (2008) 11(1) *Potchefstroom Electronic Law Journal* 1–54.
Ong, Mevelyn, 'The Interplay of Sovereignty and Consent in the Execution of Arbitral Award Debts Against Non-Party State-Owned Enterprises' (2017–18) 4 *McGill Journal of Dispute Resolution* 22–42.
Padulli, Nurul Huda, 'A Welcomed Change: Section 10(2a) of the Arbitration Act 2005 – Retention of Arrest of Ships for Arbitration' [2012] 4 *Malayan Law Journal* i–ix.
Palansamy, Yiswaree, 'Indira Gandhi Says Suing IGP for RM100m over Failure to Retrieve Daughter, to Launch Justice Trek', *Malay Mail*, Kuala Lumpur, www.malaymail.com/news/malaysia/2020/10/27/indira-gandhi-says-suing-igp-for-rm100m-over-failure-to-retrieve-daughter-t/1916671, 27 October 2020.
Reddy, Rita, 'Marriage and Divorce Regulation and Recognition in Malaysia' (1995) 29 *Family Law Quarterly* 613–25.
Selvaratnam, Sitpah, 'Maritime Reform: Arrest for Arbitration', *Tommy Thomas*, www.tommythomas.net/upload/staticpage/download/Maritime%20Reform%20-%20Arrest%20for%20Arbitration.pdf, 18 November 2005.
—— 'The Right of Arrest – Are We Making It Too Difficult ? A Common Law Perspective', *Asian International Arbitration Centre*, www.aiac.world/news/209/Sitpah-Selvaratnam:-The-Right-of-Arrest-%E2%80%93-Are-we-making-it-too-difficult-?-A-Common-Law-Perspective, 14 July 2017.
Sidhu, Balwant Singh, 'Married or Not Married? – That Is the Question' [2002] 3 *Malayan Law Journal* cxxix–cxlii
Wang, Wai Kum, 'Custody – Welfare of Infants: Teh Eng Kim v. Yew Peng Siong' (1977) 19 *Malaya Law Review* 388–91.
Wu, Min Aun, 'Guardianship, Custody and Abduction of Children Across National Boundaries' [1995] 1 *Malayan Law Journal* i–xx.

Chapter 9. Vietnam

'Báo Cáo Hoạt Động Tương Trợ Tư Pháp Năm 2019' [2019 Report of the Result of the Judicial Mandate of the Ministry of Justice], *Ministry of Justice*, https://moj.gov.vn/tttp/tintuc/Pages/tuong-tro-tu-phap.aspx?ItemID=13, 12 October 2019.
Das, Koushan, 'Vietnam's Competition Law and Its Impact on Foreign Companies', *Vietnam Briefing*, www.vietnam-briefing.com/news/vietnam-competition-law-impact-foreign-companies.html, 4 July 2019.
Do, Thi Mai Hanh (ed), *Giáo trình Tư pháp quốc tế* [*Ho Chi Minh Law School Textbook on Private International Law*] (Hanoi, Nhà xuất bản Hồng Đức [Hong Duc Publishing House], 2019).
Do, Van Dai, and Mai, Hong Quy, *Tư pháp quốc tế Việt Nam* [*Vietnamese Private International Law*] (Hanoi, Nhà xuất bản chính trị quốc gia [National Political Publishing House], 2010).
Do, Van Dai, and Tran, Viet Dung, 'Về Thỏa Thuận Chọn Tòa án nước ngoài' ['Regarding Choice of Foreign Court Agreements'] (2012) 6 *Tạp chí Khoa học Pháp lý* [*Vietnamese Journal of Legal Science*] 58–64.
Huynh, Quang Thuan, 'Giải quyết yêu cầu không công nhận quan hệ vợ chồng là vụ án dân sự hay việc dân sự?' ['Handling a Claim of Unrecognised Spousal Relations is a Civil Dispute or a Civil Matter?'], *Tạp chí Tòa án nhân dân điện tử* [*People's Court Electronic Journal*], https://tinyurl.com/y56ybp6z, 18 May 2020.

'Kiểm tra công tác tương trợ tư pháp tại Tòa án nhân dân thành phố Hà Nội và Tòa án nhân dân thành phố Đà Nẵng' [Examination of Judicial Assistance Activities at the Hanoi City People's Court and the Da Nang City People' Court], *Ministry of Justice*, https://tinyurl.com/18gsbkq0, 5 November 2018.

Le, Danh Vinh (ed), *Giáo trình Luật Cạnh tranh* [*Textbook on Competition Law*] (Ho Chi Minh City, University of Economics and Law, Vietnam National University Ho Chi Minh City, 2010).

Le, Minh Thuy, 'Vietnam's New Competition Law 2018', *Vietnam Business Law*, https://tinyurl.com/y266jq49, 30 July 2018.

Le, Thi Nam Giang, 'Chủ thể trong Tư pháp quốc tế' ['Subjects of International Private Law'] in Hong Quy Mai (ed), *Giáo trình Tư pháp quốc tế* [*Textbook on International Private Law*] (Hanoi, Hong Duc Publisher, 2016) 86–90.

Nguyen, Thai Mai, and Vu, Duc Long, 'Chủ thể trong Tư pháp quốc tế' ['Subjects of International Private Law'] in Minh Ngoc Tran and Thi Phuong Lan Vu (eds), *Giáo trình Tư pháp quốc tế* [*Textbook on International Private Law*] (Hanoi Law University, Judicial Publisher, Hanoi, 2017) 103–52.

North, PM, and Fawcett, JJ, *Cheshire and North's Private International Law* 12th edn (London, Butterworths, 1992).

Phan, Hoai Nam, 'Học thuyết Forum non conveniens trong Tư pháp quốc tế Hoa Kỳ – Một số kinh nghiệm tham khảo cho Việt Nam' ['The Doctrine of Forum Non Conveniens in Private International Law in the US – Some References for Vietnam'] (2017) 06(109) *Tạp chí Khoa học pháp lý* [*Vietnamese Journal of Legal Sciences*] 59–66.

Supreme People's Court, 'Explanatory Report of Civil Procedure Code Project' (10 April 2015), file with author.

Tran, Anh Tuan (ed), *Bình luận khoa học Bộ luật Tố tụng dân sự* [*Commentary on the Civil Procedure Code*] (Hanoi, Nhà xuất bản Tư pháp [Judicial Publishing House], 2018).

'Vietnam Airlines Yet to Lose 5.2 Mln-Euro Lawsuit', *VietnamNet*, https://english.vietnamnet.vn/fms/business/6204/vietnam-airlines-yet-to-lose-5-2-mln-euro-lawsuit.html, 31 March 2011.

Chapter 10. Cambodia

Bhati, Anirudh, 'Japanese Law And Cambodian Justice: Beyond Legal Transplants In Contemporary Legal Reform', *Greater Mekong Research Center*, www.mekongresearch.org/blog/2017/7/25/japanese-law-and-cambodian-justice-beyond-legal-transplants-in-contemporary-legal-reform, 25 July 2017.

Darwin, Hem, and Rithy, Chey, 'Ship Arrest in Cambodia', *BNG Legal*, http://bnglegal.com/cn/wp-content/uploads/2016/08/160729-Ship-Arrest-In-Cambodia-June-2016.pdf, June 2016.

Fox, Hazel, and Webb, Philippa, *The Law of State Immunity* revised and updated 3rd edn (Oxford, Oxford University Press, 2015).

Gardner, Robin, 'Southeast Asian Legal Research Guide: Courts & Cases', *The University of Melbourne*, https://unimelb.libguides.com/c.php?g=402982&p=4816214, 2020.

GTZ-Cambodia Land Management Project, and the World Bank Justice for the Poor Program, 'Towards Institutional Justice? A Review of the Work of Cambodia's Cadastral Commission in Relation to Land Dispute Resolution', *The World Bank*, http://documents.worldbank.org/curated/en/309161468222269820/pdf/408230Towards01nal0Justice01PUBLIC1.pdf, October 2006.

Holligan, Jennifer, and others, 'UPDATE: Overview of the Cambodian History, Governance and Legal Sources', *GlobaLex*, www.nyulawglobal.org/globalex/Cambodia1.html#_CPK/DK_period:_1975, July/August 2019.

Isoi, Miha, 'Real Property Registration in Cambodia' [in Japanese], *ICD NEWS*, www.moj.go.jp/content/001142822.pdf, September 2014.

Japan External Trade Organisation, 'Enforcement of Intellectual Property Rights in Cambodia' [in Japanese], *JETRO*, www.jetro.go.jp/ext_images/world/asia/kh/ip/pdf/survey_201810_kh.pdf, October 2018.

Japan International Cooperation Agency, 'Commentary on Cambodian Code of Civil Procedure: Compulsory Execution and Provisional Remedies' [in Japanese], *Ministry of Justice*, www.moj.go.jp/content/000122393.pdf.

Kamiki, Atsushi, 'Report on Cambodian Court Judgements' [in Japanese], *Ministry of Justice*, www.moj.go.jp/content/000073282.pdf, 8 March 2011.

Kaneko, Yuka, 'Japan's Civil Code Drafting Support for Socialist Reform Countries: Diversity of Normative Choice' in Yuka Kaneko (ed), *Civil Law Reforms in Post-Colonial Asia: Beyond Western Capitalism* (Singapore, Springer, 2019) 155–76.

Kiyohara, Hiroshi, 'Civil Code' in Hor Peng, Kong Phallack and Jörg Menzel (eds), *Introduction to Cambodian Law* (Cambodia, Konrad-Adenauer-Stiftung, 2012) 97–134.

Kongkea, Buth Reaksmey, 'Commercial Courts in the Pipeline to Attract More Investors', *Khmer Times*, www.khmertimeskh.com/50806501/commercial-courts-in-the-pipeline-to-attract-more-investors, 25 January 2021.

Leng, Svay, 'Problems in Translating Cambodian Civil Code and Civil Procedure Code and Future Prospects' [in Japanese], *ICD NEWS*, www.moj.go.jp/content/001298242.pdf, September 2016.

Michaels, Ralf, 'Jurisdiction, Foundations' in Jürgen Basedow and others (eds), *Encyclopedia of Private International Law* (Cheltenham, Edward Elgar, 2017) 1043–51.

Ministry of Land Management, Urban Planning and Construction, 'Cambodia Urban Forum Report: Smart, Sustainable and Inclusive Urban Development', *Open Development Thailand*, https://data.thailand.opendevelopmentmekong.net/dataset/report-on-cambodia-urban-forum/resource/39d81c29-df51-41c9-8d3e-a3c110b01152, 27 November 2019.

Morishima, Akio, 'Reflection of My Experience in Legal and Judicial Development Project for Drafting Civil Code' [in Japanese], *ICD NEWS*, www.moj.go.jp/content/000010277.pdf, September 2003.

Nishitani, Yuko, 'International Jurisdiction of Japanese Courts in a Comparative Perspective' (2013) 60 *Netherlands International Law Review* 251–77.

Pejovic, Caslav, 'Civil Law and Common Law: Two Different Paths Leading to the Same Goal' (2001) 32 *Victorian University of Wellington Law Review* 817–42.

—— 'Cambodian Labour and Employment Law' in Hor Peng, Kong Phallack and Jörg Menzel (eds), *Introduction to Cambodian Law* (Cambodia, Konrad-Adenauer-Stiftung, 2012) 285–312.

—— 'Labour Arbitration in Cambodia: Law and Practice' (2010) 1 *Cambodian Yearbook of Comparative Legal Studies* 163–71.

—— 'Overview of Contemporary Civil Procedures of Cambodia' in Hor Peng, Kong Phallack and Jörg Menzel (eds), *Introduction to Cambodian Law* (Cambodia, Konrad-Adenauer-Stiftung, 2012) 153–80.

—— 'Overview of the Cambodian Legal and Judicial System and Recent Efforts at Legal and Judicial Reform' in Hor Peng, Kong Phallack and Jörg Menzel (eds), *Introduction to Cambodian Law* (Cambodia, Konrad-Adenauer-Stiftung, 2012) 5–22.

Sakano, Issei, 'Reflection of My Experience in Legal and Judicial Development Project for Drafting Civil and Civil Procedure Codes' [in Japanese], *ICD NEWS*, www.moj.go.jp/content/000010269.pdf, July 2003.

Sassoon, Alessandro Marazzi, and Dara, Mech, 'Kingdom's Judiciary Perceived as Most Corrupt: UNDP', *The Phnom Penh Post*, www.phnompenhpost.com/national/kingdoms-judiciary-perceived-most-corrupt-undp, 11 April 2016.

Seiff, Abby, 'Cambodia: Corruption in the Judiciary "Endemic"', *International Bar Association*, www.ibanet.org/Article/NewDetail.aspx?ArticleUid=63af01f5-7bf3-4433-8edb-bbeb512395d7, 21 September 2015.

Serena, Sar, 'Cambodian Family Law: Development and Challenges Ahead' in Hor Peng, Kong Phallack and Jörg Menzel (eds), *Introduction to Cambodian Law* (Cambodia, Konrad-Adenauer-Stiftung 2012) 135–52.

Smith, Patrick Jonh, and Tavsothaly, Tok, 'Cambodian Trust Law', *BNG Legal*, http://bnglegal.com/wp-content/uploads/2019/12/191219-BNG-Newsletter-December-Trust-law.pdf, December 2019.

Sovath, Phin, 'Economic Law: Intellectual Property Rights' in Hor Peng, Kong Phallack and Jörg Menzel (eds), *Introduction to Cambodian Law* (Cambodia, Konrad-Adenauer-Stiftung, 2012) 265–284.

Stewart, David P, 'The UN Convention on Jurisdictional Immunities of States and Their Property' (2005) 99 *American Journal of International Law* 194–211.

Takahashi, Koji, 'Japan's Newly Enacted Rules on International Jurisdiction: with a Reflection on Some Issues of Interpretation' (2011) 13 *Japanese Yearbook of Private International Law* 146–70.

—— 'The Jurisdiction of Japanese Courts in a Comparative Context' (2015) 11 *Journal of Private International Law* 103–27.

Tamagaki, Shoichiro, 'The Arbitration Council in Cambodia: Impacts of the 2016 Law on Trade Unions and Prakas No 303 by the Ministry of Labour and Vocational Training' [in Japanese], *ICD NEWS*, www.moj.go.jp/content/001306610.pdf, September 2019.

Tayseng, Ly, 'Importance of Publicity of Judicial Process and Publication of Judicial Decisions', *The Phnom Penh Post*, www.phnompenhpost.com/opinion/importance-publicity-judicial-process-and-publication-judicial-decisions, 5 November 2020.

The ASEAN Secretariat, *Handbook on ASEAN Consumer Protection Laws and Regulation* (2018), https://asean.org/storage/Handbook-on-ASEAN-Consumer-Protection-Laws-and-Regulations-FINAL1.pdf.

Uchiyama, Atsushi, 'Cambodian Judiciary: The Court of First Instance' [in Japanese], *ICD NEWS*, www.moj.go.jp/content/001246676.pdf, December 2017.

United Nations Development Programme, 'A Transparent and Accountable Judiciary to Deliver Justice for All', *Transparency International Cambodia*, http://ticambodia.org/library/wp-content/files_mf/1460351755RBAPDG2016TransparentnAccountableJudiciary.pdf, 2016.

van der Keur, Dorine, 'Legal and Gender Issues of Marriage and Divorce in Cambodia' (2014) 3 *Cambodia Law and Policy Journal* 1–22.

Vickery, Michael, *Kampuchea: Politics, Economy and Society* (Frances Pinter 1986).

Vida, Taing, 'Regional Appeal Courts Open on April 1', *Khmer Times*, www.khmertimeskh.com/50705314/regional-appeal-courts-open-on-april-1/, 25 March 2020.
Vireak, Thou, 'Government Set to Finalise Antitrust, Competition Draft Law', *The Phnom Penh Post*, www.phnompenhpost.com/business/govt-set-finalise-antitrust-competition-draft-law, 15 April 2020.
Yoichiro, Shinoda, 'Report on Cambodian Court Judgments (1)' [in Japanese], *ICD NEWS*, www.moj.go.jp/content/001300680.pdf, June 2019.

Chapter 11. Myanmar

Briggs, Adrian, *Private International Law in Myanmar* (Oxford, Oxford University Press, 2015).
Lauterpacht, Hersch (ed), *International Law* 6th edn, vol 1 (London, Longmans, Green & Co, 1947).
Maung, Maung, *Law and Custom in Burma and the Burmese Family* (The Hague, Martinus Nijhoff, 1963).
Thura, Zaw, 'Myanmar' in Anselmo Reyes (ed), *Recognition and Enforcement of Judgments in Civil and Commercial Matters* (Oxford, Hart Publishing, 2019) 209–21.

Chapter 12. Philippines

Coquia, Jorge R, and Aguiling-Pangalangan, Elizabeth, *Conflict of Laws: Cases, Materials and Comments* (Quezon, Central Book Supply, 2000).
Salonga, Jovito R, *Private International Law* (Pasig, Regina Publishing, 1995).
Sempio-Diy, Alicia V, *Handbook on Conflict of Laws* (Quezon, Joer Printing Services, 2004).
'Why the Philippines is the Only Country where Divorce is Illegal', *The Economist*, London, www.economist.com/asia/2020/02/13/why-the-philippines-is-the-only-country-where-divorce-is-illegal, 15 February 2020.

Chapter 13. Indonesia

Aurora, Leony, 'New York Court Rules in Favor of Asia Pulp and Paper', *Jawawa Indonesian Business & Finance News*, https://jawawa.id/newsitem/new-york-court-rules-in-favor-of-asia-pulp-and-paper-1447893297, 16 February 2004.
Bankas, Ernest K, *The State Immunity Controversy in International Law: Private Suits Against Sovereign States in Domestic Courts* (Berlin, Springer, 2005).
Firman, Indra, 'Ship Arrest Process in Indonesia', *Indra Firman & Associates*, http://indrafirman.com/en/2016/09/14/ship-arrest-process-in-indonesia, 14 September 2016.
Gosling, James, and Huzarski, Tessaj (eds), *The Shipping Law Review* 3rd edn (London, Law Business Research Ltd, 2016).
Harahap, M Yahya, *Hukum Acara Perdata Tentang Gugatan, Persidangan, Penyitaan, Pembuktian, dan Putusan Pengadilan* 16th edn (Jakarta, Sinar Grafika, 2016).
'Ketentuan Nasional', *Rogatory Online Monitoring*, https://rogatori.kemlu.go.id/ketentuan-nasional-dan-internasional.
Kusumadara, Afifah, 'Indonesia' in Anselmo Reyes (ed), *Recognition and Enforcement of Judgments in Civil and Commercial Matters* (Oxford, Hart Publishing, 2019) 243–57.
Lim, Debby, 'SICC Releases Its First Decision', *Financier Worldwide*, www.financierworldwide.com/sicc-releases-its-first-decision#.Xbs2ROgzaUk, August 2016.
Mapes, Timothy, 'New York Judge Orders APP to End Efforts to Nullify Bonds', *Wall Street Journal*, www.wsj.com/articles/SB106995908981230100, 28 November 2003.
Pratiwi, Astrid, 'Aspek-aspek Hukum Acara Perdata Internasional dalam Perceraian di Indonesia', Undergraduate thesis, Universitas Indonesia, 2011.
Sucharitkul, Sompong, 'Fourth Report on Jurisdictional Immunities of States and Their Property' UN Doc A/CN.4/357 and Corr.1 (31 March 1982).
Supancana, IBR, *Naskah Akademik Rancangan Undang-Undang tentang Hukum Perdata Internasional (lanjutan)* [*Academic Paper of Indonesian Private International Law Bill*] (Jakarta, Badan Pembinaan Hukum Nasional Kementerian Hukum dan Hak Asasi Manusia RI [National Law Development Agency, the Ministry of Law and Human Rights of the Republic of Indonesia], 2015).

Yasmin, Mariam, 'Akibat Perkawinan Campuran Terhadap Anak dan Harta Benda yang Diperoleh Sebelum dan Sesudah Perkawinan (Studi Banding Indonesia-Malaysia)', Undergraduate thesis, Universitas Indonesia, 2011.

Chapter 14. Thailand

Bell, John, *Judiciaries within Europe: A Comparative Review* (Cambridge, Cambridge University Press, 2006).
Cheeramongkolpanich, Pitikul, *Civil Procedure Law: Books 1-2-3* (Bangkok, October Publishing House, 2019).
Chen, Weizuo, and Goldstein, Gerald, 'The Asian Principles of Private International Law: Objectives, Contents, Structure and Selected Topics on Choice of Law' (2017) 13 *Journal of Private International Law* 411–34.
Laowonsiri, Akawat, 'Thailand' in Anselmo Reyes (ed), *Recognition and Enforcement of Foreign Judgments in Civil and commercial Matters* (Oxford, Hart Publishing, 2019) 259–69.
—— *Diagonal Contract between Foreign Tech Company and Sovereign State: Extending the Spectrum of Party Autonomy* (Bangkok, Thammasat University Faculty of Law, 2021).
Office of the Judiciary, 'Annual Judicial Statistics, Thailand 2018 (BE 2561)', *Office of Planning and Budget*, https://oppb.coj.go.th/th/content/category/detail/id/8/cid/2086/iid/143806, 2019.
Organisation for Economic Cooperation and Development (OECD), 'Judicial Performance and Its Determinants: A Cross-Country Perspective', *OECD*, OECD Economic Policy Papers No 5, www.oecd.org/economy/growth/FINAL%20Civil%20Justice%20Policy%20Paper.pdf, 2013.
Piwawatanapanich, Prasit, *Lecture on Private International Law* (Bangkok, Thammasat University Press, 2018).
Ratamarit, Udom, *Law of Evidence* (Bangkok, Thammasat University Faculty of Law, 2012).
Saisoonthorn, Phunthip, *Lecture on Private International Law: General Concepts of Private Relations with International Character* (Bangkok, Winyuchon, 2005).
Verdross, Alfred, and Simma, Bruno, *Universelles Völkerrecht: Theorie und Praxis* (Berlin, Duncker & Humblot, 1984).

Chapter 15. Sri Lanka

'About', *Port City Colombo*, www.portcitycolombo.lk/about.
Bindra, Narotam Singh, *Interpretation of Statutes* 12th edn (Gurgaon, LexisNexis, 2017).
Cooray, Anton, 'Oriental and Occidental Laws in Harmonious Co-existence: The Case of Trusts in Sri Lanka' (2008) 12(1) *Electronic Journal of Comparative Law* 1–17, www.ejcl.org/121/art121-5.pdf.
Cooray, LJ Mark, *An Introduction to the Legal System of Sri Lanka* 2nd edn (Pannipitiya, Stamford Lake Publications, 2003).
de Silva, Kingsley Muthumuni, *A History of Sri Lanka* (Colombo, Vijitha Yapa Publications, 2005).
Laduwahetty, Ravi, 'New Laws for Port City – Malik Samarawickrama', *Port City Colombo*, www.portcitycolombo.lk/2017/02/12/new-laws-for-port-city.html, 12 February 2017.
'Report of the United Nations/International Maritime Organisation Diplomatic Conference on Arrest of Ships' UN Doc A/CONF.188/5 (19 July 1999).
Torremans, Paul, and others (eds), *Cheshire, North & Fawcett Private International Law* 15th edn (Oxford, Oxford University Press, 2017).
Weeramantry, Christopher Gregory, *The Law of Contracts* (Pannipitiya, Stamford Lake Publications, 1967).

Chapter 16. India

Braucher, Robert, 'The Inconvenient Federal Forum' (1947) 60 *Harvard Law Review* 908–39.
Collins, Lawrence, and others (eds), *Dicey and Morris on the Conflict of Laws* 13th edn (London, Sweet & Maxwell, 2000).
Garimella, Sai Ramani, 'International Parental Child Abduction and the Fragmented Law in India – Time to Accede to the Hague Convention?' (2017) 17 *Macquarie Law Journal* 38–55
George, Omana, 'Admiralty Jurisdiction and Ship Arrest in India' (2015) 7(7) *International Journal of Current Research* 18034–37.
Govindaraj, VC, *The Conflict of Laws in India: Inter-Territorial and Inter-Personal Conflict* (Oxford, Oxford University Press, 2019).

Hall, Clifford, '*Cruse* v. *Chittum*: Habitual Residence Judicially Explored' (1975) 24(1) *International and Comparative Law Quarterly* 1–30.

Hathi, Shrikant, and Hathi, Binita, *Ship Arrest in India and Admiralty Laws of India* (Mumbai, Brus Chambers, 2019), http://admiraltypractice.com/Book.pdf.

Law Commission of India, 'Fifty-Ninth Report on Hindu Marriage Act, 1955 and Special Marriage Act, 1954', *Law Commission of India*, http://lawcommissionofindia.nic.in/51-100/report59.pdf, 1974.

Mann, FA, 'The Proper Law in the Conflict of Laws' (1987) 36(4) *International and Comparative Law Quarterly* 437–53.

Ministry of Corporate Affairs, 'Report of Insolvency Law Committee on Cross Border Insolvency', *Ministry of Corporate Affairs*, www.mca.gov.in/Ministry/pdf/CrossBorderInsolvencyReport_22102018.pdf, October 2018.

Mohan, S Chandra, 'Cross-border Insolvency Problems: Is the UNCITRAL Model Law the Answer?' (2012) 21(3) *International Insolvency Review* 199–223.

Neels, Jan L, 'Choice of Forum and Tacit Choice of Law: The Supreme Court of India and the Hague Principles on Choice of Law in International Commercial Contracts (An Appeal for an Inclusive Comparative Approach to Private International Law)' in UNIDROIT (ed), *Eppur si Muove: The Age of Uniform Law – Essays in Honour of Michael Joachim Bonell to Celebrate His 70th Birthday* vol 1 (Rome, UNIDROIT, 2016) 358–71.

Patra, Atul Chandra, 'Historical Background of the Indian Contract Act, 1872' (1962) 4(3) *Journal of the Indian Law Institute* 373–400.

Pérez-Vera, Elisa, *Explanatory Report to the Hague Convention on Intercountry Child Abduction, Hague Conference on Private International Law*, www.hcch.net/upload/expl28.pdf, April 1981.

Plambeck, Charles T, 'The Razor's Edge: The Doctrine of Forum non Conveniens and the Union Carbide Methyl Isocyanate Gas Disaster at Bhopal, India' (1985) 10 *North Carolina Journal of International Law and Commercial Regulation* 743–59.

Rankin, George Claus, *Background to Indian Law* (Cambridge, Cambridge University Press, 1946).

Rao, TS Rama, 'Conflict of Laws in India' (1958) 23 *Rabels Zeitschrift Für Ausländisches und Internationales Privatrecht* 259–79.

Shaw, John, *Charters Relating to the East India Company from 1600 to 1761* (Madras, Madras Government Press, 1887).

Sooksripaisarnkit, Poomintr, and Garimella, Sai Ramani, 'Choice of Court Agreements: Selected Common-Law Jurisdictions and Indian Laws Compared: Time for the Convention of 30 June 2005 on Choice of Court Agreements?' (2021) 30 *Journal of Transnational Law and Policy* (forthcoming).

'UNCITRAL Model Law on Cross-Border Insolvency with Guide to Enactment and Interpretation', *UNCITRAL*, www.uncitral.org/pdf/english/texts/insolven/1997-Model-Law-Insol-2013-Guide-Enactment-e.pdf, January 2014.

Chapter 17. Conclusion

'A Quick Guide to the US-China Trade War', *BBC News*, www.bbc.com/news/business-45899310, 16 January 2020.

Brand, Ronald A, 'The Circulation of Judgments under the Draft Hague Convention' University of Pittsburgh School of Law Legal Studies Research Paper Series Working Paper No 2019-02, https://papers.ssrn.com/sol3/papers.cfm?abstract_id=3334647, February 2019.

Bucher, Andreas (rapporteur), 'Universal Civil Jurisdiction with Regard to Reparation for International Crimes' (2015) 76 *Yearbook of Institute of International Law* 1–266.

'Can China Be Sued in the US and Forced to Pay for Coronavirus Losses? Legal Experts Say No', *Los Angeles Times*, www.latimes.com/politics/story/2020-05-15/can-china-be-sued-in-the-u-s-and-forced-to-pay-for-coronavirus-losses-legal-experts-say-no, 15 May 2020.

'Can the U.S. Sue China for COVID-19 Damages? Not Really', *Washington Post*, www.washingtonpost.com/politics/2020/04/29/can-us-sue-china-covid-19-damages-not-really-this-could-quickly-backfire, 29 April 2020.

'China Takes Aim at Foreign Companies Swayed by US Sanctions', *Nikkei Asia*, https://asia.nikkei.com/Economy/Trade-war/China-takes-aim-at-foreign-companies-swayed-by-US-sanctions, 10 January 2021.

'Chinese Lawyers Sue US over "Coronavirus Cover-up"', *Radio Free Asia*, www.rfa.org/english/news/china/wuhan-lawsuit-03262020122653.html, 26 March 2020.

'Everything You Want to Know about Australia-China Trade War But Were Too Afraid to Ask', *ABC News*, www.abc.net.au/news/2020-12-10/china-australia-trade-war-your-questions-answered/12971434, 10 December 2020.

'Holding the Chinese Communist Party Accountable for Infecting Americans Act Would Allow US Citizens to Sue China over COVID-19', *GovTrack.us*, https://govtrackinsider.com/holding-the-chinese-communist-party-accountable-for-infecting-americans-act-would-allow-u-s-e204b5fbde52.

'In a First, South Korean Court Orders Japan to Compensate Former "Comfort Women"', *Japan Times*, www.japantimes.co.jp/news/2021/01/08/national/first-south-korean-court-comfort-women, 8 January 2021.

'India-China Dispute: The Border Row Explained in 400 Words', *BBC News*, www.bbc.com/news/world-asia-53062484, 10 September 2020.

'Lawsuits Demand Compensation from China for COVID-19; UK Reconsiders Huawei's 5G Role', *Lawfare*, www.lawfareblog.com/lawsuits-demand-compensation-china-covid-19-uk-reconsiders-huaweis-5g-role, 24 April 2020.

Reyes, Anselmo, 'Introduction: Towards a System for the Recognition and Enforcement of Judgments' in Anselmo Reyes (ed), *Recognition and Enforcement of Judgments in Civil and Commercial Matters* (Oxford, Hart Publishing, 2019) 1–30.

'South Korean Court Dismisses Lawsuit by Former "Comfort Women" against Japan', *Japan Times*, www.japantimes.co.jp/news/2021/04/21/national/comfort-women-lawsuit-dismissed, 21 April 2021.

'Suing China over COVID-19 against International Law: Expert', *Xinhua*, www.xinhuanet.com/english/2020-05/27/c_139092848.htm, 27 May 2020.

Tu, Guangjian, *A Study on a Global Jurisdiction and Judgments Convention* (Hong Kong, Sweet & Maxwell, 2009).

'What You Need to Know about Missouri's Lawsuit against China over COVID-19', *Heritage Foundation*, www.heritage.org/courts/commentary/what-you-need-know-about-missouris-lawsuit-against-china-over-covid-19, 23 April 2020.

'Why the Japan-South Korea Trade War Is Worrying for the World', *Time*, https://time.com/5691631/japan-south-korea-trade-war, 3 October 2019.

INDEX

www.ingramcontent.com/pod-product-compliance
Ingram Content Group UK Ltd.
Pitfield, Milton Keynes, MK11 3LW, UK
UKHW051932150926
475560UK00005B/350

9 781509 936427